Eighth Edition

PUBLIC ADMINISTRATION

Understanding Management, Politics, and Law in the Public Sector

David H. Rosenbloom
American University

Robert S. Kravchuk
Indiana University

Richard M. Clerkin
North Carolina State University

Mc
Graw
Hill
Education

PUBLIC ADMINISTRATION: UNDERSTANDING MANAGEMENT, POLITICS, AND LAW
IN THE PUBLIC SECTOR, EIGHTH EDITION
International Edition 2015

10 09 08 07 06 05 04 03 02 01
20 15 14
CTP   MPM

When ordering this title, use ISBN 978-1-259-01084-2 or MHID 1-259-01084-8

The Internet addresses listed in the text were accurate at the time of publication. The inclusion of a
website does not indicate an endorsement by the authors or McGraw-Hill Education, and McGraw-Hill
Education does not guarantee the accuracy of the information presented at these sites.

Printed in Singapore

www.mhhe.com

ABOUT THE AUTHORS

David H. Rosenbloom is Distinguished Professor of Public Administration at American University in Washington, DC. He earned a Ph.D. in political science from the University of Chicago. Professor Rosenbloom writes extensively about public administration and democratic-constitutionalism. He is the recipient of the 1999 Dwight Waldo Award for outstanding contributions to the field of public administration, the 2001 John Gaus Award for exemplary scholarship in the joint tradition of political science and public administration, and the 2012 Leslie A. Whittington Award for excellence in teaching. He is a fellow in the U.S. National Academy of Public Administration, from which he received the 2001 Louis Brownlow Award for his book *Building a Legislative-Centered Public Administration*. Rosenbloom is editor-in-chief of the CRC/Taylor & Francis Series in Public Administration and Public Policy, serves on the editorial boards of more than a dozen professional journals, and is a Life Associate Trustee Board Member at Marietta College. He was Visiting Chair Professor of Public Management at City University of Hong Kong in 2009 and 2010 and frequently lectures at universities in China and Taiwan. In 1992 he was appointed to the Clinton-Gore Presidential Transition Team for the Office of Personnel Management.

Robert S. Kravchuk is Professor and Director of the Master of Public Affairs Program in the School of Public and Environmental Affairs at Indiana University in Bloomington, Indiana. His teaching and research focus on public budgeting and finance, administrative theory, and the political economy of formerly socialist countries in transition, with a special emphasis on Ukraine and Russia. His administrative experience includes service as Under Secretary in the Connecticut State Budget Office, U.S. Treasury Resident Budget Advisor to the Minister of Finance of Ukraine, and appointment by the U.S. Secretaries of State and the Treasury as Financial Advisor to the President of Bosnia-Herzegovina. He is a frequent writer and lecturer on public budgeting, administrative reform, and government capacity-building. Currently, he is researching the emergence of complex financial networks among U.S. Defense Department major weapons acquisition projects, and is writing a modern text on public financial management. His future projects include a canonical history of American administrative thought, and a comprehensive history of Russian public administration from Ivan the Terrible to Vladimir Putin. In addition to Indiana University, Professor Kravchuk has taught at the University of North Carolina–Charlotte, the University of Connecticut, University of Hartford, and LeMoyne College. He lives in Bloomington, Indiana, with his family.

Richard M. Clerkin is an Associate Professor in the Public Administration Department in the School of Public and International Affairs and the Interim Director of the Institute for Nonprofit Research, Education, and Engagement at North Carolina State University. He received his Ph.D. in Public Affairs from Indiana University–Bloomington, where he was a Chancellor's Fellow. The main focus of his research is on the interplay of government and nonprofit sectors. In particular, he studies motivations for public service and public benefiting activities. Recent research in this vein has examined public service motivation in sector work preferences and in the decision of active duty military to reenlist. A new stream of research, the Changing Philanthropy Project, explores the impact of geographic mobility and regional philanthropic traditions on 1) the volunteering and donating behavior of individuals and 2) the ability of nonprofit organizations to adapt to these changes in their community. His research has been published in *Public Administration Review, American Review of Public Administration, Armed Forces & Society, Nonprofit and Voluntary Sector Quarterly,* and *Nonprofit Management and Leadership.* He lives in Raleigh, North Carolina, with his wife and children.

CONTENTS IN BRIEF

CONTENTS

PART II
CORE FUNCTIONS 145

CHAPTER 4   *Organization: Structure and Process 146*

PART III

The Convergence of Management, Politics, and
Law in the Public Sector 361

PART IV

PUBLIC ADMINISTRATION AND THE PUBLIC 451

CHAPTER 10 *Public Administration and the Public* 452

PREFACE

The fourth edition of *Public Administration: Understanding Management, Politics, and Law in the Public Sector* was named the fifth most influential book in the field of public administration published from 1990 to 2010 in a study by David O. Kasdan appearing in *Administration & Society* in 2012. This was an amazing achievement for a textbook in competition with books on administrative theory and specific topics such as organization theory, human resources management, policymaking, and budget and finance. Kasdan's finding is bolstered by the book's status as a "world text." It is used in English or translation as the core text in MPA programs throughout China, and to the best of our knowledge, as a core or assigned text in Australia, Canada, Hong Kong, India, Indonesia, Iran, Israel, Kyrgyzstan, Lebanon, Malaysia, Nepal, Netherlands, Pakistan, Portugal, Republic of Georgia, Romania, Singapore, South Africa, South Korea, Taiwan, Thailand, Ukraine, as well, of course, as in the United States.

At first thought, the worldwide use of the book seems odd. After all, its framework is informed by features of the U.S. political system that are central to public administration here, but unusual singularly or in combination in developed and developing nations across the globe. These include the constitutional separation of powers, federalism based on a particular blend of dual sovereignty, and our legal system. It could be that students abroad want to learn about U.S. administrative practices, believing correctly or incorrectly that they can serve as a model for their own countries. However, on further consideration it is more likely that the book has attained its measure of success because all public administrative systems have managerial, political, and legal dimensions and, to some extent, these share common characteristics almost everywhere. Management typically values efficiency and cost-effectiveness; in democracies and even some autocracies, political accountability and responsiveness are valued; the legal dimension's concern with human rights and the rule of law is also widespread, though far from universal. In several countries, classes include student presentations analyzing local administrative issues from each of the three perspectives and discussions of strategies for incorporating elements of management, politics, and law into their potential resolution. Our effort in this eighth edition has been to retain the U.S. focus while broadening much of the discussion and themes in ways that enhance their utility elsewhere.

This comports with the original mission of the book—to ground students in the fundamentals of public administration while embracing its complexity through what has become known as the "three-perspectives" or "competing-perspectives" model. The eighth edition, like those before it, describes, explains, and analyzes public administration through the lenses of three well-established, coherent ways of conceptualizing and understanding public administration: management; politics (primarily with regard to policy implementation and the values of participation, representation, responsiveness, and accountability); and law. These perspectives are embedded in the U.S. Constitution and American political culture.

Each perspective has a distinctive set of core values, decision procedures, organizational arrangements, view of the individual, way of knowing and learning, budget making, and *modi operandi*. In the midst of President Bill Clinton's second term, when his administration's effort by the National Performance Review to "reinvent government" was in full swing, the fourth edition split the management perspective into "traditional management" and "new public management" (NPM). The NPM is no longer new—and some might say the label is *passé*. It has been augmented, but not replaced, by "collaborative governance," a topic to which this edition pays considerable attention. In turn, collaborative governance necessarily (and happily) requires greater coverage of the roles of nonprofit organizations in today's public administration. Realistically, contemporary management consists of a mix of traditional, NPM, and collaborative governance perspectives and practices. The continuing development of the management perspective, however, does not eclipse the importance of the political and legal approaches to public administration and their continuing evolution.

The book remains divided into four parts. Part I introduces the book's intellectual framework and discusses the development of public administration in the United States. Part II considers public administration's core functions: organization, personnel, budgeting and finance, and decision making. Part III shows how management, politics, and law converge in the practice of policy analysis and implementation evaluation and regulatory administration. Part IV focuses on the place of the "public" and the "public interest" in public administration. Chapters are devoted to public administration and the public, democratic constitutionalism, and accountability and ethics. The concluding chapter looks at trends that are likely to impact public administration in the near-term future.

In keeping with previous revisions, we have sought throughout the text to update, maintain relevance by incorporating vital developments in U.S. governance and administrative thought, including court decisions, and to jettison material that is no longer pertinent or useful in explaining contemporary public administrative theory, techniques, and practices to students. Few texts reach an eighth edition or the global stature this one has attained. Attribution goes to the staying power of the basic framework and appeal of a comprehensive look at the challenges of governing in the late modern era. We continue to believe that the three-perspectives approach to analyzing and understanding administrative matters in all their complexity is the key to educating future public administrators to systematically approach the ever-changing and "complexifying" environments in which they will work. (*Note*: A password-protected Web site at www.mhhe.com/rosenbloom8 contains a comprehensive Instructor's Manual and Test Bank.)

A book reaching an eighth edition generates many debts of gratitude to those reviewers and readers who have offered excellent suggestions for improvements along the way. They have become too numerous to name individually, but their contributions are now part of the book and greatly appreciated. We also want to thank our readers for their loyalty over the years. You are responsible for the book's success and we welcome your comments and suggestions for continually upgrading it.

David H. Rosenbloom
Robert S. Kravchuk
Richard M. Clerkin

PART I

Introduction: Definitions, Concepts, and Setting

CHAPTER 1

THE PRACTICE AND DISCIPLINE OF PUBLIC ADMINISTRATION

Competing Concerns

Key Learning Objectives

1. Be able to define public administration, and to identify its principal concerns.

2. Understand the differences between public administration and private management.

3. Learn the managerial, political, and legal approaches to public administration and the tensions among them.

4. Learn about six trends that are transforming government in the 21st century and management of private enterprises—changing the rules of the game; using performance measurement; providing competition, choice, and incentives; "government on demand"; engaging citizens; and using networks and partnerships.

This chapter considers what distinguishes *public* administration from the administration and management of private enterprises, focusing on the roles of the Constitution, the public interest, economic market forces, and state sovereignty. The principal focus of public administration with providing both *service* and *regulation* is explored. The chapter discusses a framework for understanding public administration that consists of three general and competing approaches to administrative theory and practice. One approach sees public administration as essentially management, another emphasizes its political nature, and the third focuses on its legalistic aspect. In the past twenty-five years, the traditional managerial approach took on a new variant, called the "new public management" (NPM), in response to calls for more responsive and efficient government. The NPM in turn has a relatively distinctive off-shoot called "collaborative governance," which relies on for-profit and non-profit organizations, often generically referred to as "third parties," to achieve public administrative program objectives. Each perspective embraces a different set of values, offers distinctive organizational approaches for maximizing those values, and considers the individual citizen in different ways.

Public administration has historically been difficult to define. Nonetheless, we all have a general sense of what it is, though we may disagree about how it should be carried out. In part, this is because public administration involves a vast amount of activity. Public sector jobs range from providing homeland security, to the exploration of outer space, to sweeping the streets. Some public administrators are highly educated professionals who may be at the forefront of their fields of special expertise (like NASA engineers and rocket scientists); others possess few skills that differentiate them from ordinary workers. Some public administrators make policies that have a nationwide impact and may benefit millions of people; others have virtually no responsibility for policy making and simply carry out mundane but necessary clerical tasks. Public administrators are doctors, lawyers, scientists, engineers, accountants, budgeters, policy analysts, personnel officers, managers, baggage screeners, clerks, keyboarders, manual laborers, and individuals engaged in a host of other occupations and functions. But knowing what public administrators *do* does not resolve the problem of defining what public administration *is*.

It was pointed out some time ago that any one-paragraph or even one-sentence definition of public administration may prove temporarily mind-paralyzing.[1] This is because "public administration" as a category is so abstract and varied that it can be described only in vague, general, and somewhat competing terms. Yet some attention to definition is important. First, it is necessary to establish the general boundaries, and to convey the major concerns of the discipline and practice of public administration. Second, defining public administration helps place the field in a broader political, economic, and social context. Third, and perhaps most importantly, consideration of the leading definitions of public administration reveals that there are at least three distinct underlying approaches to the field. For years the tendency among scholars and practitioners has been to stress one or another of these approaches. But this has promoted confusion, because each approach tends to emphasize different values, different organizational arrangements, different methods of developing knowledge, and radically distinct views of the individual citizen.

◆ SOME DEFINITIONS

One can find a wide variety of definitions of public administration, but the following are among the most serious and influential efforts to define the field. [2]

1. "Public administration . . . is the action part of government, the means by which the purposes and goals of government are realized."
2. "Public administration as a field is mainly concerned with the means for implementing political values. . . ."
3. ". . . Public administration can be best identified with the executive branch of government."
4. "The process of public administration consists of the actions involved in effecting the intent or desire of a government. It is thus the continuously active, 'business' part of government, concerned with carrying out the law, as made by legislative bodies (or other authoritative agents) and interpreted by the courts, through the processes of organization and management."
5. Public administration: (a) is a cooperative group effort in a public setting; (b) covers all three branches—executive, legislative, and judicial—and their interrelationships; (c) has an important role in the formulation of public policy, and is thus part of the political process; (d) is different in significant ways from private administration; and (e) is closely associated with numerous private groups and individuals.

What conclusions can be drawn from the variety of definitions of public administration and their myriad nuances? One is that public administration is indeed difficult to pin down. Another conclusion is that there is really no such subject as "public administration," as such, but rather that public administration means different things to different observers and lacks a significant common theoretical or applied meaning. However, this perspective has limited appeal because the problem is certainly not that there is no public administration—we not only know it exists, but also are often acutely aware of its contributions and/or its shortcomings.

Ironically, another conclusion that can be drawn from the multiplicity of definitions is that public administration is everywhere. Some have argued that there is no field or discipline of public administration per se because the study of public administration overlaps a number of other disciplines, including political science, sociology, economics, psychology, and business administration. Although this approach contains a great deal of truth, in practical terms it is unsatisfactory because it leaves us without the ability to analyze coherently a major aspect of contemporary public life—the emergence of large and powerful governmental agencies. In a word: *bureaucracy*.

This book concludes that all the previous definitions are helpful, but limited to some extent. Public administration does involve *activity,* it is concerned with *politics* and *policy making,* it tends to be concentrated in the *executive* branch of government, it does differ from private administration, and it is concerned with *implementing the law.* But we can be much more specific by offering a definition of our own: *Public administration is the use of managerial, political, and legal theories, practices, and processes to fulfill legislative, executive, and judicial mandates for the conduct of governmental regulatory and service functions.* There are several points here that require further elaboration.

◆✦ EMPHASIZING THE *PUBLIC* IN PUBLIC ADMINISTRATION

First, public administration differs from private administration in significant ways. The lines between the public and private sectors are often blurred, insofar as several aspects of management and law are generic to both sectors. However, on balance, public administration remains a separate field. The reasons for this are outlined in the pages which follow.

Constitutions

In the United States, the federal and state constitutions define the environment of public administration and place constraints on it. First, constitutions fragment power and control over public administration (see Box 1.1). The separation of powers places public administration effectively under three "masters." Americans have become accustomed to thinking of governors and presidents as being in control of public administration, but in practice legislatures possess as much or more constitutional power over administrative operations. This is clearly true at the federal level, where Congress has the constitutional authority to create agencies and departments by law; fix their size in terms of personnel and budget; determine their missions and legal authority, internal structures, and locations; and establish procedures for human resources management. Congress has also enacted a large body of **administrative law** to regulate administrative procedures, including rule making, open meetings, public participation, and the gathering and release of information.

The courts also often exercise considerable power and control over public administration. They help define the legal rights and obligations of agencies and those of the individuals and groups on which public administrators act. They define the constitutional rights of public employees and the nature of their liabilities for breaches of law or the Constitution. The judiciary has also been active in the restructuring of school systems, public mental health facilities, public housing, and prisons in an effort to make certain they comply with constitutional standards. Judicial review of agency activities is so extensive that the courts and public administrators are now widely regarded as "partners."[3] The extent of legislative and judicial authority over public administration leaves chief executives with only limited control over the executive branch,

1.1   PUBLIC ADMINISTRATION'S CONSTITUTIONAL STATUS*: WHOSE EXECUTIVE BRANCH IS IT, ANYWAY?

The Ethics in Government Act of 1978, which expired in 1992, provided for the appointment of an independent counsel much like Kenneth Starr, independent counsel in the impeachment of former President Bill Clinton in 1999. The independent counsel's job was to investigate and prosecute certain high-ranking government officials for federal crimes. The independent counsel was located in the Department of Justice and had "full power and independent authority to exercise all investigative and prosecutorial functions and powers of the Department, . . . the Attorney General, and other department [personnel]." The independent counsel was appointed by a special court, called the Special Division, and could not be removed by the attorney general except for "good cause, physical disability, mental incapacity, or any other condition that substantially impairs the performance of such independent counsel's duties." The key question before the U.S. Supreme Court in *Morrison v. Olson* was whether these arrangements violated the constitutional separation of powers. The Court, per Chief Justice William Rehnquist, held that they did not. First, the appointment of an executive officer by a court under these circumstances was not "incongruous" because it did not have "the potential to impair the constitutional functions assigned to one of the branches" of the government. Second, the Court noted that in its "present considered view . . . the determination of whether the Constitution allows Congress to impose a 'good cause'-type restriction on the President's power to remove an official cannot be made to turn on whether or not that official is 'purely executive.'" Rather, "the real question is whether the removal restrictions are of such a nature that they impede the President's ability to perform his constitutional duty" to take care that the laws be faithfully executed. The Court

concluded that although "[i]t is undeniable that the Act reduces the amount of control or supervision that the Attorney General and, through him, the President exercises over the investigation and prosecution of a certain class of criminal activity," the executive branch retained "sufficient control over the independent counsel to ensure that the President is able to perform his constitutionally assigned duties."

Justice Antonin Scalia heatedly dissented:

> There are now no lines. If the removal of a prosecutor, the virtual embodiment of the power to "take care that the laws be faithfully executed," can be restricted, what officer's removal cannot? This is an open invitation for Congress to experiment. What about a special Assistant Secretary of State, with responsibility for one very narrow area of foreign policy, who would not only have to be confirmed by the Senate, but could also be removed only pursuant to certain carefully designed restrictions? . . . Or a special Assistant Secretary of Defense for Procurement? The possibilities are endless. . . . As far as I can discern from the Court's opinion it is now open season upon the President's removal power for all executive officers. . . . The Court essentially says to the President: "Trust us. We will make sure that you are able to accomplish your constitutional role." I think the Constitution gives the President—and the people—more protection than that.

So an executive official with law enforcement duties can be appointed by a court and dismissed only for limited reasons specified by Congress. Whose executive branch is it, anyway?

**Morrison v. Olson* 487 U.S. 654 (1988).

and far less authority than is commonly found in the hands of chief executive officers of private organizations, whether profit-seeking or not. The text of the federal Constitution grants presidents only two specific powers that they can exercise over domestic federal administration on their own: the power to ask department heads for their opinions in writing on various subjects and to make temporary appointments to vacant offices when the Senate is in recess. In practice, of course, chief executives in the public sector now often exercise statutory powers given to them by legislatures—but legislative bodies almost always retain a strong interest in how public agencies are operating.

The separation of powers not only provides each branch with somewhat different authority over public administration but also may frustrate coordination among them. Chief executives, legislatures, and courts are responsive to different constituencies, political pressures, and time constraints. All three branches have legitimate interests in public administration. However, they often differ with regard to what they think agencies should do and how they ought to do it.

The federal constitutional framework also embodies a system of federalism that allows for considerable overlap in the activities of federal, state, and local administrators. Often the federal government will create a program and rely on the states to implement it. Funding and authority may be shared. In practice, state and local agencies may be responsible to federal departments to a greater extent than they are to state governors or state legislatures.

The federal courts also have a substantial impact on state and local administration. They define the constitutional or legal rights of citizens as they are affected by governmental activity. Over the years the federal courts have ordered extensive reforms in state and local administrative systems and processes.[4]

The separation of powers and federalism result in a fragmentation of authority that is generally not seen in the private sector. Legal restrictions and requirements affect private management, but they do not fragment authority over it in the same way or to the same extent, nor do they provide so many parties with a legal right to observe and participate in private firms' policy decisions and other affairs.

Constitutional concerns are important in another way as well. They embrace values in the public sector that frequently run counter to the values embodied in private management. Efficiency in government is often subordinated to political principles such as representativeness, accountability, and transparency. Efficiency is also trumped by legalistic considerations such as due process. Remember that, with the exception of the Thirteenth Amendment, which prohibits slavery and involuntary servitude, the Constitution does not directly regulate relationships between purely private parties. Rather, it applies to relationships among units of government, such as Congress and the president or the federal and state governments, and to those between the public and its governments. Further, in most of the public sector, there is no genuine equivalent to the profit motive that is so central to private enterprise.

The Public Interest

The governmental obligation to promote the public interest also distinguishes public administration from private management. In a moral and basic sense, government must serve "a higher purpose."[5] Even though reasonable people may disagree about precisely what is in the public interest, there can be no dispute about the obligation of public administrators to consider it as a general guide for their actions. When they fail to do so, public administrators may rightly be criticized. A central issue is assuring that public administrators represent and respond to the interests of the citizenry.[6] Various regulations have been enacted over the years in an effort to assure that those exercising public power will not use it for narrow partisan or purely private gain or engage in subversion. Many public personnel systems in the United States and abroad place restrictions on the political activities of civil servants, some have comprehensive conflict-of-interest regulations, and all are concerned with the political loyalty of their employees.

By contrast, private firms are thought to best serve the general interest by vigorously pursuing their own economic interests. Their task is to be highly efficient and competitive in the marketplace. Not only is profit the motivating factor in the world of business, the profit motive is viewed as a positive social and economic good. Private companies should not endanger the health and safety of their workers or that of the general community. Nor should they damage or destroy the environment. By and large, however, it is assumed to be government's role to ensure, through proper regulation, that the private sector does not harm society at large. This is partly why it is plausible to hold that "public administration is not a kind of technology but a form of moral endeavor."[7]

The Market

A closely related distinction between public and private administration concerns the market. Public agencies traditionally have not faced free, competitive markets in which their services or products are sold.[8] For the most part, the price tags attached to governmental operations are established through budgetary procedures rather than fixed in the market through free transactions between buyer and seller. Revenues are generated largely through taxation, although in some cases user fees may be a substantial source of operating budgets. Additionally, bonds may be sold to pay for capital projects. Even where user fees are important, however, a governmental agency may be operating as a legal monopoly or be under a mandate to provide service to all people at a fixed cost, no matter how difficult or expensive it may be to reach them. The U.S. Postal Service's mission regarding first-class mail is an example: The price of sending a letter from Miami to North Miami is the same as that of sending one to Honolulu or Nome.

The market is less constraining in the public sector than in the private sector. The market becomes most salient for public agencies when governments, primarily cities, are under severe fiscal constraints. In the long run, excessive taxation of the public in support of undesired or inefficient governmental operations can cause citizens (who are the consumers or customers of public administrative operations) to "opt out" of the system, by moving to another jurisdiction. Governments may also seek to contract out some services, such as trash collection. The federal, state, and local governments also face market forces when they borrow money. The less strong their financial shape is, the more expensive borrowing is likely to be. But the governments in question are not likely to go out of existence. Unlike private firms, they cannot move "off shore" and rarely dissolve through bankruptcy.

The "public choice" movement holds that government agencies will be more responsive and efficient if they can be compelled to react to market-like forces. For instance, public schools might be made to compete with one another by allowing parents the opportunity to choose which schools to send their children to within a general geographic area. Voucher systems can be used to promote competition between public and private schools.

Private firms typically face markets more directly. Under free-market conditions, if they fail to produce products or services at competitive prices, consumers take their business elsewhere, and a company's income declines. Eventually the noncompetitive private firm will go out of business. In between the typical public agency and the private firm is a gray area in which not-for-profit organizations and highly regulated industries, such as many utilities, operate. Not-for-profit organizations (NPOs) fill an important niche in the economy, providing services that may not be sustained through market pricing, either because their clients lack the funds to pay for them, or because the goods provided have merit but cannot feasibly be provided either by the market (because they are public or quasi-public goods) or through government (because the services are provided on the basis of social or religious criteria that governments must steer clear of).

A vast number of NPOs operate in the United States. In 2011 the country had around 1.08 million tax-exempt organizations, the vast majority of them charitable or religious in nature. Social welfare agencies, business leagues, labor groups, social and veterans' clubs, and fraternal societies make up the rest. NPOs received more than $298.42 billion in contributions in 2011, or around 2.0% of GDP, including $217.79 billion in the form of individual contributions (equal to 1.9% of household disposable income). In fact, some two-thirds of American households routinely donate money to NPOs, with the average gift in 2008 reaching $2,321. The remainder came from foundations ($41.67 billion), corporate donors ($14.55 billion), and bequests ($24.41 billion). NPOs also derive a substantial amount of revenue both from government sources and from their own business-type (for-profit) activities. This makes NPOs a significant partner with governments in addressing certain areas of social concern and need. It also formed the basis for the efforts of President George W. Bush to lever the activities of "faith-based and community initiatives" in the service of meeting some federal priorities.[9]

The remoteness of market forces from most public administrative operations has profound consequences. It enables government to provide services and products that could not profitably be offered by private firms. Some of these services and products are referred to as **public goods** or quasi-public goods. Broadly speaking, these are goods, such as national defense and lighthouses, that individuals cannot be excluded from enjoying, that are not exhausted or significantly diminished as more individuals use them, and for which individuals do not compete with one another to acquire. It would be impossible to provide such goods in open, competitive markets, because individuals lack the incentive to purchase the goods, no matter how desirable they are. Why would an individual ship owner pay the full cost for a lighthouse when others, including competitors, would be able to benefit from it for free? Having a lighthouse might be in the public's interest, but it would also be in everyone's self-interest to obtain it free by letting someone else build and maintain it. Under these conditions, especially if the costs are significant, everyone may seek to be a "free rider" on another's lighthouse. The net result would most likely be that no one would individually invest in lighthouses and their benefit to ships would be forgone.

Governments are not immune to the need to make economic trade-offs. Sometimes the trade-offs involve deciding how much to spend on highways versus welfare programs in the current budget. Sometimes they involve deciding whether to invest in preparation for natural disasters that may or may not occur versus spending on programs that are badly needed now. Box 1.2

1.2   TRADE-OFFS AND PUBLIC EXPECTATIONS: WHY THE U.S. WASN'T PREPARED FOR HURRICANE KATRINA, AND WHY IT PROBABLY WON'T BE PREPARED FOR THE NEXT ONE

Storms the scale of magnitude and destruction of Hurricane Katrina are appropriately called "100-year storms." This tagline implies that storms bringing such destruction are a rare occurrence. It does not mean that Katrinas happen every 100 years, like clockwork. Rather, it is a crude way of indicating that the magnitude of the storm is inversely proportional to its probability of occurrence. Thus, smaller storms occur rather frequently; more violent ones occur more infrequently. Scientists know this as "Zipf's Law," and it describes the frequency and magnitude of many natural disasters, including not only hurricanes but also tornadoes, volcanoes, and earthquakes. Obviously, an appropriate understanding of the likelihood of a disaster's occurrence is vital to government officials in providing the resources necessary for responding to them.

In the hurricane's aftermath, it was clear that the United States—at all levels of government—was unprepared for Katrina's devastating effects. A moment's reflection, however, will reveal that the situation could not have been otherwise. To be fully prepared for such disasters, governments at all levels would have to have many hundreds of millions of dollars' worth of materiel and personnel in place, poised and waiting to respond. But the infrequency of these disasters cannot justify such a standing investment, especially in the face of more immediate and acute needs for funding education, health, and welfare. Hurricane preparedness simply cannot compete effectively against demands for immediately funding big-ticket items such as Social Security, Medicare, and Medicaid—all of which the public wants and expects. Further, in some important sense it does not appear to be rational to make such an overwhelming investment in a hurricane-specific response, because the next disaster may well be a major earthquake, volcano, or terror attack. It is difficult in the extreme to prepare for these calamities. As a consequence, the United States was not prepared for Hurricane Katrina, it was not prepared for super storm Sandy, which devastated the New York City region and New Jersey in 2012, and it probably won't be adequately prepared for the next disaster either.

discusses how it may be considered rational to spend on current needs rather than prepare for another Hurricane Katrina. Such "impossible choices" are common in public administration, making government service both rewarding and inherently difficult.

The remoteness of market forces in the public sector often makes it difficult to assess or evaluate the worth and efficiency of public administrative operations. If government agencies produce a product that is not sold freely in open markets, it is hard to determine what the product or service is worth. Proxy measures such as opinion surveys that try to determine what the public is willing to pay for a good or a service are sometimes helpful, but they can be expensive to conduct and are approximations at best. This means that accurately measuring performance and efficiency can sometimes be nearly impossible in the public sector. One way governments try to get around this problem is to contract out some of their functions to private organizations. Theoretically at least, private companies will compete against one another to obtain the public sector's business.[10] But the long-term economic and political benefits and costs of contracting out some traditional governmental functions, such as prison management, remain unclear.

Sovereignty

Sovereignty is the concept that government is the ultimate repository of supreme political power and authority. It involves a monopoly over the legitimate use of force in the society. In the United States, sovereignty resides in the people, as a whole, who exercise it through their elected governments. In our constitutional framework, the people govern themselves through a representative system of governments. Public administration and public employment, in particular, are consequently considered to be a "public trust." As subordinates of the sovereign people, public administrators are also placed in a position that differs considerably from that of managers and employees in the private sector. Public administrators are agents of the sovereign, which means that the actions of public administrators have the force of law and the coercive power of the government behind them. Private firms also make policies and are engaged in activities that affect the lives of individuals in the society as a whole, but unless specifically empowered to use physical force (as in the case of privately managed prisons), their policies cannot be enforced through legitimate coercive physical power. Rather, the private sector must turn to the public sector's courts and police power for the enforcement of contracts.

Public administrators, being agents of the sovereign, are inevitably engaged in matters of public policy making and implementation. From the 1880s to the 1940s, public administrative theory in the United States held that administration and politics should be almost completely separate from one another. Perhaps this dichotomy between politics and administration was primarily concerned with eliminating partisan or electoral politics from the public service. But today it is broadly accepted that public administrators do have a legitimate role in all phases of the public policy cycle.* In other words, theory and practice now support the idea that the political system should take advantage of public administrators' expertise when it is appropriate to the identification and definition of problems to which public policy ought to be addressed as well as to the formulation, analysis, evaluation, and revision of policies. It is now also recognized that public administrators are often required to make policy choices while implementing statutes and executive orders. They exercise discretion because their mandates from legislatures are general (rather than specific) and/or because of a scarcity of resources that virtually requires the selective enforcement of the law.

Public administrators' involvement in the public policy cycle makes politics far more salient in the public sector than in private enterprise. Public administrators are perforce required to build and maintain political support for the policies and programs they implement. They must try to convince members of the legislature, chief executives, political appointees, interest groups, private individuals, and the public at large that their activities and policies are desirable and responsive.

Involvement in policy making and politics raises the question of how it can be assured that those exercising a public trust will do so properly. This brings a variety of public values, such as representation and transparency, to bear on public administrative practice. For instance, federal policy has sought to make federal administration representative by assuring that the civil service "looks like America" in terms of race, ethnicity, gender, and other social factors.[11] It also provides formal processes through which interested parties can express their views on the adoption of administrative policies and rules.

Transparency is embodied in the federal Freedom of Information Act of 1966 (FOIA) and the Government in the Sunshine Act of 1976. FOIA provides public access to a great deal of information about the operation of agencies. The Sunshine Act requires multiheaded federal boards and commissions, such as the Federal Communications Commission, to do a great deal of their decision making in open forums. Similar statutes regulate state and local governments throughout the nation.

Such values are less relevant to the private sector. Private enterprise is built around the principle of the profit motive, not that of providing representation to different groups or information about their business decisions and operations to the public. Subjecting private firms to an equivalent of the federal FOIA or Sunshine Act would make it almost impossible for many of them to operate.

In sum, any definition of public administration must lay heavy stress on the *public*. There are many similarities between public and private administration, but these are often relatively unimportant in conveying the essence

---

* The notion of the public policy cycle is a conceptual tool that views public policy as moving through the following stages: agenda setting (identification of an issue); problem definition; policy formulation; implementation; analysis/evaluation of impact or implementation process; and revision of some sort, including termination and succession.

of each. Public administration is concerned with administration of the public interest, it is constrained by constitutions and relatively unconstrained by market forces, and it is considered a public trust exercised on behalf of the sovereign. Private administration, in contrast, generally has a narrower concept of the public interest; profit-making firms are heavily constrained by market forces, not by constitutions. Moreover, private administration is not connected to the issue of sovereignty and is rarely considered to be a public trust of any kind. The lines between public and private administration may become blurred when government contracts out public functions to not-for-profit organizations or other third parties. The same is sometimes true in the case of some public agencies that are run like corporations, in the form of public enterprises, such as water and utility districts and transportation systems. But the private sector is not dominated or characterized by not-for-profit organizations or firms exclusively on government contracts, nor is the public sector largely organized in corporate form. Substantial differences between the public and private sectors remain, and, importantly, they promote reliance on different values and processes.

It is often asked, "Why can't the government be run like a business?" The short answer is that we would have to drastically reduce the importance of representation, transparency, and other public values in order for it to do so.

◆▶ REGULATION AND SERVICE

In the discussion of sovereignty, it was mentioned that the activities of public administrators have a binding quality and that, in general, they have the force of law and can rely on the coercive physical power of the government for enforcement. This raises another point that is crucial to a satisfactory definition of public administration. Although we often think of public administration in terms of providing services to the public, public administrators are also engaged in *regulation* of the public.

Political conservatives opposed to governmental administration have long charged that the public service or the civil service is not a "service," but rather an unelected regulatory force used to place constraints on the public. In truth, one person's service often turns out to be another's constraint, and it is common to find regulation and service intertwined in governmental programs, mainly to provide incentives to behave in ways that are considered economically and socially desirable. For instance, welfare programs undeniably provide a service, but at the same time they place constraints on the behavior of the recipients. Benefits have been denied to recipients who will not allow social workers to inspect their homes and to mothers who refuse to identify the fathers of their children. One could go down the list of government functions and find that service after service turns out also to be a constraint. Occupational licenses serve the public by assuring that doctors, hairdressers, and plumbers are competent, but they also regulate entry into those occupations. Driver's licensing and vehicle inspections promote highway safety, but they also regulate the use of the roads. Food and drug regulations certainly constrain producers and serve consumers. Sometimes agencies with the word "service" in their titles are the most directly engaged in regulation. The Internal Revenue *Service* and the Selective *Service* System (former military drafting agency) are examples. Similarly, public *service* commissions are involved in the regulations of utilities. The student of public administration should be continually cognizant of the fact that by exercising public power on behalf of the sovereign people, public *servants* frequently place constraints on the behavior of individuals or corporations.

◆◆ MANAGERIAL, POLITICAL, AND LEGAL APPROACHES

Public administration involves a number of complex concerns and functions. Not surprisingly, therefore, as an intellectual discipline or body or theory, public administration lacks a certain coherence. Public administration embodies at least three relatively distinct approaches that grow out of different perspectives on its functions. Some have viewed it as a managerial endeavor, similar to practices in the private sector. Others, stressing the "publicness" of public administration, have emphasized its political and policymaking aspects. Still others, noting the importance of sovereignty, constitutions, and regulation in public administration, have viewed it as a distinctly legal matter. Each of these approaches tends to stress different values and procedural and structural arrangements for the operation of public administration, each views the citizen in a remarkably different way, and each adopts a different perspective on how to develop knowledge.

A further complexity is that the managerial approach has developed a new variant: the contemporary reform-oriented new public management (NPM). Bear in mind that these approaches are embedded in our political culture. They reflect the same ideas and sentiments that have found an institutional expression in the constitutional separation of powers and assignment of functions to different branches. Thus, in the United States, political power has been divided in order to protect individual rights from the arbitrary use of governmental power. In public administration theory, this has been reflected in the managerial, political, and legal approaches. The managerial approach is associated with the executive branch's interest in faithful execution or implementation of the law. The political approach is associated with legislative policymaking concerns. The legal approach focuses on government's adjudicatory function, commitment to maintaining constitutional rights (the "blessings of liberty"), and the rule of law.

The Managerial Approach to Public Administration

Those who define public administration in managerial terms take a business-like approach to it that tends to minimize the distinctions between public and private administration. In their view, public administration is essentially the same as big business and ought to be run according to the same managerial principles and values. This outlook is frequently voiced in the media and found among elective political leaders who tend to resent the costs of "bureaucracy" and the collective policy influence exercised by civil servants.

Today, those who view public administration as management fall into two main groups. Traditionalists are being overtaken by reformers who call for "reinventing government" and developing an NPM. The NPM is supplanting the traditional approach in several federal agencies and state and local governments. It is also strong in a number of other countries, including the United Kingdom, Australia, New Zealand, and the Scandinavian nations. Nevertheless, both traditional and NPM variants thrive in some organizations and jurisdictions. The traditional approach may be better for some functions—homeland security, perhaps—whereas the NPM may be more suitable for others, such as social welfare programs.

Traditional Managerial Approach to Public Administration

The roots of the traditional managerial approach go back to the 19th-century civil service reformers who first promoted the approach as a means of organizing the public service. The reformers' chief complaints were that political patronage appointments to the public services at all levels of government led to corruption, inefficiency, and the emergence of a class of politicians— "spoilsmen," as they were frequently called—who were fundamentally unfit to lead the nation. One well-known historian of the 1850s insisted that the federal service had become staffed by the nation's "refuse" (garbage).[12] In the reformers' view, "What civil service reform demand[ed], [was] that the business part of the government shall be carried on in a sound businesslike manner."[13] For it to become businesslike, it had to become nonpolitical. Consequently, appointments were to be made on the basis of "merit" and "fitness" rather than political partisanship. Many reformers thought that public employees should be prohibited from taking an active part in electoral politics other than voting. Once politics was rejected as the basis for hiring and firing public administrators, the reformers believed that the selection and tenure of public servants could be based on their efficiency and performance.

To sustain this logic, the reformers had to insist that the vast majority of public administrators had no legitimate political or policymaking functions. Much of their thinking and the logic of the traditional managerial approach depended on the existence of a separation, or "dichotomy," between politics and administration. Woodrow Wilson (1856–1924), U.S. president from 1913 to 1921, was a strong supporter of civil service reform in the 1880s and is often considered the founder of self-conscious American public administrative thought. In his famous 1887 essay "The Study of Administration," Wilson wrote, "Administration lies outside the proper sphere of *politics*. Administrative questions are not political questions."[14] Rather, they are managerial questions because, as Wilson expressed it, public administration is "a field of business."

Wilson was also influential in his straightforward articulation of managerial values: "It is the object of administrative study to discover, first, what government can properly and successfully do, and, secondly, how it can do these proper things with the utmost possible efficiency and at the least possible cost either of money or of energy."[15] In other words, according to the traditional managerial approach, public administration is to be geared toward maximizing effectiveness, efficiency, and economy.

The advocacy of businesslike public administration eventually became the orthodox or classical view of how the public service should be run. Managers, not politicians, should be in control, and efficiency was the ultimate value, the "axiom number one in the value scale of administration."[16] Politics should be eliminated because it produced inefficiency. Moreover, despite the growing regulatory activities of the public service, law was deemphasized because, as Leonard White's influential *Introduction to the Study of Public Administration* (1926) contended, "the study of administration should start from the base of management rather than the foundation of law."[17]

From the 1910s to the 1940s, a worldwide "scientific management" movement, based on the work of Frederick Winslow Taylor (1856–1915),[18] developed and advocated the premise that effective, efficient management could be reduced to a set of scientific principles. In the view of critics of this approach, the result in terms of administrative values was that "the 'goodness' or 'badness' of a particular organizational pattern was a mathematical relationship of 'inputs' to 'outputs.' Where the latter was maximized and the former minimized, a moral 'good' resulted. Virtue or 'goodness' was therefore equated with the relationship of these two factors, that is, 'efficiency' or 'inefficiency.'"[19] Wastefulness, through inefficiency, was considered immoral.

Organizational Structure

In an effort to maximize the attainment of these values, the traditional managerial approach promotes an organizational structure universally identified as *bureaucratic*. This may strike the contemporary reader as odd, because today *bureaucratic* is often used as a synonym for *inefficient*. In Chapter 4, we will consider the complicated reasons why bureaucratic organizations often develop inefficiencies. Nevertheless, it remains true that many of their organizational principles are *intended* to maximize the amount of output per unit of input. Bureaucracies stress the need for a division of labor that enables employees to specialize in the accomplishment of a given set of tasks. Specialization enables each worker to become expert at what he or she does, although the work of any individual may be only a small part of the organization's total activity. *Specialization* requires coordination, and bureaucracy relies on *hierarchy* for this purpose. Hierarchy creates a chain of authority to manage and coordinate the work divided according to the principle of specialization. Hierarchy, in turn, requires that programs and functions be clearly assigned to specific organizational units. Otherwise there will be overlapping authorities likely to lead to conflicts. Bureaucratic organizations are also organized along *formalistic* lines, which spell out the functions and responsibilities of each employee. Positions are classified according to "scientific" principles and are organized into a rational scheme. The selection of employees is based on their ability to perform the tasks at hand, that is, on their merit. Other factors, such as political affiliation, race, and gender, should not be taken into account.

View of the Individual

The traditional managerial approach to public administration promotes an impersonal view of individuals. This is true whether the individuals in question are the employees, clients, or "victims" of public administrative agencies.[20] (The traditional approach rarely considers members of the public to be "customers.") Max Weber (1864–1920), the foremost analyst of bureaucracy, considered "dehumanization" to be the "special virtue" of bureaucracy, with the bureaucrat viewed as a "cog" in an organizational machine over which he or she has virtually no control.[21] Weber saw this as an advantage of bureaucracy because it meant that "irrational" emotions would not interfere with the bureaucrat's job performance. This perspective was promoted by the Scientific Management Movement, which tends to turn the individual worker into an appendage to a mechanized means of production. The worker has to adapt to the machine; not the other way around (see Box 1.3).

1.3   SCIENTIFIC MANAGEMENT FROM SHOVELING TO BASEBALL

Shoveling: "There is a scientific fact. A first-class shoveler ought to take twenty-one and one-half pounds on his shovel in order to work to the best possible advantage. You are not giving that man a chance unless you give him a shovel which will hold twenty-one pounds. . . .

"There is only one way to do it right. Put your forearm down onto the upper part of your leg, and when you push into the pile, throw your weight against it. That relieves your arm of work. You then have an automatic push, we will say, about eighty pounds, the weight of your body thrown on to it."

Baseball: "I think this instance represents one of the best illustrations of the application of the principles of scientific management. I refer to the management of a first-class American baseball team. In such a team you will find almost all of the elements of scientific management.

"You will see that the science of doing every little act that is done by every player on the baseball field has been developed. Every single element of the game of baseball has been the subject of the most intimate, closest study of many men, and, finally, the best way of doing each act that takes place on the baseball field has been fairly well agreed upon and established as a standard throughout the country. The players have not only been told the best way of making each important motion or play, but they have been taught, coached, and trained to it through months of drilling. And I think that every man who has watched first-class play, or who knows anything of the management of the modern baseball team, realizes fully the utter impossibility of winning with the best team of individual players that was ever gotten together unless every man on the team obeys the signals or orders of the coach and obeys them at once."

Sources: Frederick Winslow Taylor, "The Principles of Scientific Management," in Jay Shafritz and J. Steven Ott, Eds., *Classics of Organization Theory* 4th ed. (Belmont, CA, 1996), 74, 75; and *Hearings Before Special Committee of the House of Representatives to Investigate the Taylor and Other Systems of Shop Management.* Under Authority of House Resolution 90; vol. III, pp. 1377–1508. Reprinted in *Scientific Management* by Frederick Winslow Taylor (Westport, Conn.: Greenwood Press, 1972), pp. 107–111.

By 1920, this view of the employee was firmly embodied in the principles of **position classification** (that is, the description of duties and rank) in the public sector: "The individual characteristics of an employee occupying a position should have no bearing on the classification of the position."[22] The strong "position orientation" of the traditional managerial approach to public administration diminishes the importance of the individual employee to the organization. Again, this was in order to maximize efficiency and to reduce the possibility of favoritism.

Clients, too, have been depersonalized and turned into cases in an effort to promote the traditional managerial values of efficiency, economy, and effectiveness. Ralph Hummel explains:

> Bureaucracy is an efficient means for handling large numbers of people. "Efficient" in its own terms. It would be impossible to handle large numbers of people in their full depth and complexity. Bureaucracy is a tool for ferreting out what is "relevant" to the task for which bureaucracy was established. As a result, only those facts in the complex lives of individuals that are relevant to that task need to be communicated between the individual and the bureaucracy.
>
> To achieve this simplification, the modern bureaucrat has invented the "case." At the intake level of the bureaucracy, individual personalities are converted into cases. Only if a person can qualify as a case, is he or she allowed treatment by the bureaucracy. More accurately, a bureaucracy is never set up to treat or deal with persons: it "processes" only "cases."[23]

The subjects of public administrators' activities may be depersonalized to such an extent that they are treated as subhuman, especially where physical force or coercion is employed, as, historically, in public mental health facilities, prisons, and some police functions.[24]

Other approaches to organization argue that reliance on impersonality tends to be counterproductive because it generates dysfunctions. These matters will be discussed in Chapters 4 and 10. Nevertheless, the impersonal view of individuals is deeply ingrained in the traditional managerial approach and is considered essential to the maximization of efficiency, economy, and effectiveness.

Cognitive Approach

The traditional managerial approach emphasizes the scientific method in developing knowledge. The kernel of the idea that public administration could be a science was contained in Woodrow Wilson's 1887 essay.[25] By 1926, Leonard White noted that public administration was being transformed from an art into a science, and, in 1937, Luther Gulick and L. Urwick would publish, most influentially, *Papers on the Science of Administration*.[26] The commitment to developing a science of public administration remains strong—probably dominant—in contemporary American public administrative research and scholarship.

In practice, treating public administration as a science has promoted an effort to develop generalizations about administrative behavior. This involves the formulation of hypotheses that can be tested empirically. Data are gathered, aggregated, and statistically analyzed. The basic orientation is deductive; knowledge consists of statistically verifiable generalizations that can be applied, with caution, to specific cases.

Resource Allocation

The traditional managerial approach's commitment to the values of efficiency, economy, effectiveness, and science leads it to favor rational budgeting systems (see Chapter 6). Such systems emphasize the need to build cost-effectiveness considerations into the formulation of budgets.

Decision Making

The traditional managerial approach also favors rational decision making, as explored in Chapter 7. Essentially, it holds that in making decisions public administrators should consider all plausible alternatives comprehensively and choose the one that is most cost-effective. Relying on scientific expertise, including that of social scientists, this approach does not favor broad public participation.

The New Public Management (NPM)

In the early 1990s, a variant on the managerial approach to public administration began to take hold in the United States. Like the traditional managerial approach at its inception, the newer approach is reform-oriented and seeks to improve public sector performance. It starts from the premise that traditional, bureaucratically organized public administration is "broke" and "broken," and consequently the public has lost faith in government.[27] After years of antigovernment political rhetoric, "bureaucrat bashing," and negative press coverage, public administration was broadly viewed as incredibly inept and wasteful. Public opinion polls revealed that in 1993 only 20 percent of the public trusted the federal government to do the right thing most of the time—a steep drop from 76 percent in 1963.[28] In public opinion polls conducted since the early 1960s, fully half of all Americans polled expressed a belief that around one-half of all federal spending was "waste."[29]

The image of state and local governments has also fared badly. Taxpayer revolts broke out from California to Massachusetts. By 1991, nineteen states had enacted limits on taxes and expenditures—up from two in 1978, when California's tax-limiting Proposition 13 first captured a great deal of public attention. A majority of the states had also placed tax limits of one kind or another on their local governments.[30] Governments throughout the United States were viewed as needing drastic reforms, even "reinvention," as David Osborne and Ted Gaebler put it in the title of their best-selling 1992 book, *Reinventing Government.*[31]

Fortunately for the new managerial reformers, some models for improvement were already available. In the English-speaking world abroad, New Zealand,

Australia, and the United Kingdom had been undertaking drastic administrative reforms.[32] As Osborne and Gaebler reported, several cities and states in the United States had successfully done the same. Taken as a whole, these reforms appear to embrace the following premises:

1. *Focus on Results.* Public administration should focus on achieving results rather than primarily on conforming to procedures.

2. *Marketization.* To achieve results, public administration should make better use of marketlike competition in the provision of goods and services. This may be accomplished in several ways. Contracting out can enable government to buy services that it once produced itself. Agencies can be reorganized to more closely resemble private corporations (the U.S. Postal Service, for instance). Agencies can be made to compete with each other and/or nongovernmental organizations. For example, a central personnel agency can be transformed into a service center that competes with private firms.

3. *Customer-Driven.* A corollary of making public administration more marketlike is to make it customer-driven. The public and agency clients are viewed as customers to whom the government should be responsive. Where an agency sells a product or service in competition with private firms, the logic of responding to customers is obvious. But even when government provides service and regulation on a monopoly basis or without charging fees, treating the public and clients like customers can enhance public administration's service ethic and efficiency. Overall, agencies should focus their resources on creating value for their citizen-customers.

4. *"Steering, Not Rowing."* Government should "steer, not row," in Osborne and Gaebler's phrase. Government's job is to assure that public goods and services are provided, not necessarily to produce them itself. In other words, governments may appropriately rely on third parties such as other governments, not-for-profit organizations, and corporations to deliver their services, implement their policies, and enforce some of their regulations.

5. *Deregulation.* Government should be deregulated. Traditional bureaucracy's emphasis on centralized control of staffing, personnel administration, budgeting, auditing, procurement, and allocation of agency resources is inappropriate to results-oriented public administration. Agency managers will be driven by competition, customers, and accountability for results to make the best use of their employees and budgets.

6. *Employee Empowerment.* An extension of deregulation is that employees should be empowered to use their creativity in serving customers and doing their jobs. Empowerment is not only possible, it is highly desirable because today's public sector workers are well educated, and information technology makes a great deal more information available to them. Empowerment, as opposed to hierarchy, promotes teamwork.

7. *Flexibility.* Overall, public administrative culture should change to be flexible, innovative, problem solving, entrepreneurial, and enterprising as opposed to rule-bound, process-oriented, and focused on inputs rather than results.

At the national level, the NPM approach was adopted in the early 1990s by Vice President Al Gore's National Performance Review (NPR). Its 1993 report, *From Red Tape to Results: Creating a Government That Works Better & Costs Less,* explicitly sought "a new customer service contract with the American people, a new guarantee of effective, efficient, and responsive government."[33] It called for the following steps, among others: putting customers first, making service organizations compete, creating market dynamics, using market mechanisms to solve problems, empowering employees to get results, decentralizing decision making power, streamlining the budget process, decentralizing personnel policy, and streamlining procurement.

The NPR report explicitly relied on the traditional managerial approach's insistence that there can be a separation between politics and administration. In the preface, Gore admonished, "This performance review is not about politics. . . . We want to make improving the way government does business a permanent part of how government works, regardless of which party is in power."[34] The view that public administration is largely apolitical and businesslike is essential to the NPM more generally. To work in democracies and to maintain accountability, deregulated, empowered, results-oriented public administrators must stick to achieving the policy goals established by elected and politically appointed officials. Market mechanisms as construed by the NPM are not substitutes for public participation in politics and policymaking. Employees and agencies are not empowered to make public policy.

Several states and local governments have consciously adopted NPM measures. For example, Oregon began a highly innovative benchmark program in 1989. Under the direction of the Oregon Progress Board, "Oregon Benchmarks" established clear, quantified goals for improving health, family life, education, civic participation, equal opportunity, social harmony, the environment, housing, transportation, public safety, per capita income, industrial diversification, economic growth, and public sector performance.[35] Under Governor John Kitzhaber, the program has been revised with new benchmarks set in five key areas: education, jobs and innovation, healthy people, safety, and healthy environment.[36] Further, these benchmarks are built into the state budget document as resource allocation guides. The benchmark approach is explained in Box 1.4. It promotes results-oriented public administration and, as used in Oregon, encourages experimentation by local governments.

Benchmarking also facilitates setting priorities. Some benchmarks, such as reducing teen drug use and protecting wild salmon runs, are considered "urgent." They may overlap "core" benchmarks, especially good indicators of progress. Among these are increasing student achievement and the percentage of the state's population with college degrees.

1.4   WHAT ARE BENCHMARKS?

Oregon Benchmarks measure progress toward Oregon's strategic vision, *Oregon Shines*. It is a comprehensive approach to performance management and measuring the state's performance as well as societal outcomes, using a *Key Performance Measure* system (KPM). In 1997 the state broadened the vision, focusing on more holistic means, outcomes, and measures, known as *Oregon Shines II*. A current revision, known as *Oregon Shines III* is underway. A total of 31 KPMs are organized into five categories: education, jobs and innovation, healthy people, safety, and healthy environment. In 2006, responsibility for the KPM system was shared between the Legislative Fiscal Office and the governor's budget office, the Budget and Management Division. Following is a sample of goals, strategies, and metrics for education for 2013–2015.

10-Year Goals *What We Want to Accomplish*	Strategies *How We Get There*	Success Metrics *How We Measure Progress*
Every Oregonian has the knowledge, skills, and credentials to succeed in life.	*Align funding, outcomes, and education strategies across the entire continuum of a child's development — from birth to k-12 to post-secondary education and training.*	*Every child enters kindergarten ready to learn.*
	Streamline early childhood services and invest in Oregon kids from an early age so they are set up to succeed before they enter kindergarten.	*All 3rd graders are reading at grade level.*
	Use early screening to identify and help students who need it most.	*Achieve "40-40-20" by the year 2025:* - *40% of adults will have earned a bachelor's degree or higher.* - *40% of adults will have earned an associate degree or post-secondary credential.* - *20% of adults will have earned a high school diploma or the equivalent.*

Sources: Oregon Progress Board, *Oregon Benchmarks: Standards for Measuring Statewide Progress and Institutional Performance* (Salem: Oregon Progress Board); Oregon Progress Board, *Achieving the Oregon Shines Vision: The 2007 Highlights Report* (Salem: Oregon Progress Board, April 2007). 2013–2015 data are from State of Oregon, Office of the Governor, *Governor's Balanced Budget, 2013–2015.* (Salem: Oregon: State of Oregon, 2012).

The NPM has become the dominant managerial approach in the United States. Its key concepts—somewhat revolutionary two decades ago—are now the standard language of public administration. Terms such as "results oriented," "customer focused," "employee empowerment," "entrepreneurship," and "outsourcing" have entered the mainstream. President George W. Bush endorsed the NPM, though his emphasis was somewhat different from that of the Clinton-Gore administration.[37] Bush went further than the previous administration in emphasizing contracting out government activities, including to religious organizations as part of his faith-based initiatives. He was more enthusiastic about managerial flexibility than employee empowerment and favored coordinating some functions, including homeland security, through clear hierarchical controls. Much of the input orientation and procedural focus of the traditional managerial approach has been eclipsed by the NPM's overriding interest in achieving results. The fundamental characteristics of NPM can be summarized as follows.

Organizational Structure

The NPM favors organizing administrative activities to increase the extent to which administrative units can act like firms in a market serving customers. From its perspective, this should create cost-effectiveness and responsiveness. It relies on decentralization to enable individual units to act as service centers. Consequently, overall agency organizations become flatter (less hierarchical, having fewer layers) and subunits become more autonomous. Coordination is achieved through competition rather than hierarchy. Employee empowerment also diminishes the need for hierarchy because it abandons "command and control"–style management in favor of teams consisting of employees and managers. Information systems are to be used to monitor service activity and results. The boundaries between agencies and their environments become less distinct as administrators respond more directly and immediately to customers' needs, and as contracting out requires them to devote more attention to negotiating with and monitoring private service providers.

View of the Individual

The NPM views individuals as customers. Customers can also be other agencies, governments, and private organizations. Customers within the same government are called "internal" customers. For instance, a central personnel agency such as a civil service commission can recruit, test, investigate, and train employees for other agencies. Service agencies are frequently used to provide internal customers with vehicle and building maintenance, protection, and equipment. Customer relationships among different governments are also common because so much public policy involves more than one government.

The idea that public administrative agencies have customers is not new. As early as 1936, administrative theorist Marshall Dimock advised, "The customer-satisfaction criterion applies with as much force to government as to business. . . . If the administrator keeps his eyes constantly on the end result, namely customer satisfaction, then the steps which need to be taken in order to improve the internal administration are usually self-apparent."[38]

Customers in a market differ from citizens in a community, however. Customers seek to maximize their individual welfare; so do citizens, but public participation in politics is aimed at solving common problems and defining governmental (rather than personal) objectives. Public policy driven by customer demand and/or satisfaction may differ from that based on political agreement or administrative expertise. Because resources are limited, allocating them according to customer preferences is not necessarily the same as basing them on electoral outcomes. The appropriate limits to customer responsiveness is an issue that has to be worked out by governments over time.

Cognitive Approach

The NPM borrows heavily from the public choice approach to public policy. Public choice posits the individual as a consumer of government services and theorizes that both consumer choice and administrative efficiency will be enhanced if governments can be made to compete for individuals' purchases of goods and services as firms in a market do. Public choice also argues that, generally speaking, government should not supply a service or apply a regulation unless it cannot be done as well by the private sector. Markets are thus generally viewed as superior to public administrative operations in satisfying individual preferences, developing technical efficiency, and operating in cost-effective ways. Metrics such as program performance measures can be used to see whether policies and programs are effective in achieving certain social objectives, such as reduced crime, teenage pregnancy, infant mortality, and dropout rates. Even where it is not possible to use quantitative indicators of performance, surveys can be used to determine levels of customer satisfaction.

Resource Allocation

NPM budgeting focuses on the production of services and regulatory enforcement (outputs) and results (outcomes) rather than on inputs such as money, personnel, and equipment. If feasible, it prefers that agencies or administrative units generate their own revenues, or some share of them, by charging user fees. Legislative appropriations should be based on performance and the creation of value for customers, the public, and the national interest. Lack of output should be investigated to see whether greater investment in the function is warranted or if the function should be terminated, privatized, or shifted to some other level or unit of government. Agencies should have great flexibility in handling their budgets as long as they produce results. Centralized controls should be reduced, and budgetary decision making decentralized. The ideal is (1) to allow agencies to "manage to budget," that is, to spend money as they think best to achieve results, and (2) to be entrepreneurial in developing markets for services they can produce at competitive costs.

Decision Making

Decisions should be based on responsiveness to customers, performance levels, and cost-effectiveness. Generally, decision making should be decentralized. However, decisions regarding missions and entrepreneurial opportunities should be made by agency leaders, generally with input from rank and file employees. NPM decision making is cost-conscious. Box 1.5 presents an

1.5 SAMPLE DECISION TREE FOR ANALYZING AGENCY PROGRAMS

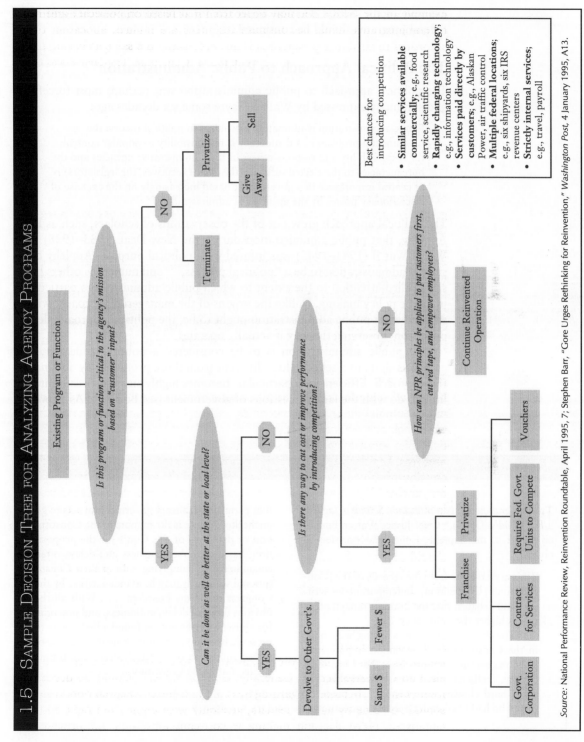

Best chances for
introducing competition

- **Similar services available
  commercially**; e.g., food
  service, scientific research
- **Rapidly changing technology**;
  e.g., information technology
- **Services paid directly by
  customers**; e.g., Alaskan
  Power, air traffic control
- **Multiple federal locations**;
  e.g., six shipyards, six IRS
  revenue centers
- **Strictly internal services**;
  e.g., travel, payroll

Existing Program or Function

Is this program or function critical to the agency's mission
based on "customer" input?

NO

Privatize

Terminate   Give   Sell
             Away

YES

Can it be done as well or better at the state or local level?

NO

Is there any way to cut cost or improve performance
by introducing competition?

YES

Devolve to Other Govt's.

Same $ Fewer $

Govt.   Contract   Require Fed. Govt.   Vouchers
Corporation for Services Units to Compete

Franchise   Privatize

How can NPR principles be applied to put customers first,
cut red tape, and empower employees?

Continue Reinvented
Operation

Source: National Performance Review, Reinvention Roundtable, April 1995, 7; Stephen Barr, "Gore Urges Rethinking for Reinvention," *Washington Post,* 4 January 1995, A13.

example of the NPR's decision approach for determining whether and how federal programs should be continued.

The Political Approach to Public Administration

The political approach to public administration was perhaps most forcefully and succinctly expressed by Wallace Sayre some six decades ago:

> Public administration is ultimately a problem in political theory: the fundamental problem in a democracy is responsibility to popular control; the responsibility and responsiveness of the administrative agencies and the bureaucracies to the elected officials (the chief executives, the legislators) is of central importance in a government based increasingly on the exercise of discretionary power by the agencies of administration.[39]

The political approach grew out of the observations of scholars, such as Paul Appleby, that public administration during the New Deal (1933–1938) and World War II (1941–1945) was infused with political purpose. Appleby considered administration to be a "political process,"[40] and numerous others have since called attention to the extent to which public administrators participate in public policy making. Unlike the origins of the managerial approach, which stressed what public administration ought to be, the political approach developed from observing the way it actually operates.

If public administration is to be considered a political endeavor, the emphasis shifts to a set of values different from those promoted by a managerial approach. Efficiency, in particular, becomes highly suspect, because it has little to do with the larger questions of government (see Box 1.6). As Supreme

---

1.6   THE SUPREME COURT ON "EFFICIENCY"

In *Immigration and Naturalization Service v. Jagdish Rai Chadha* (1983),* Chief Justice Warren Burger, on behalf of the Supreme Court, had occasion to observe:

> [I]t is crystal clear from the records of the [Constitutional] Convention, contemporaneous writings and debates, that the Framers ranked other values higher than efficiency. . . .
>
> The choices we discern as having been made in the Constitutional Convention impose burdens on governmental processes that often seem clumsy, inefficient, and even unworkable, but those hard choices were consciously made by men who had lived under a form of government

that permitted arbitrary governmental acts to go unchecked. There is no support in the Constitution or decisions of this Court for the proposition that the cumbersomeness and delays often encountered in complying with explicit Constitutional standards may be avoided, either by the Congress or by the President. . . . With all the obvious flaws of delay, untidiness, and potential for abuse, we have not yet found a better way to preserve freedom than by making the exercise of power subject to the carefully crafted restraints spelled out in the Constitution.

*462 U.S. 919, 958–959.

Court Justice Louis Brandeis pointed out in dissent in *Myers v. United States* (1926):

> The doctrine of the separation of powers was adopted by the [Constitutional] Convention in 1787, not to promote efficiency but to preclude the exercise of arbitrary power. The purpose was, not to avoid friction, but, by means of the inevitable friction incident to the distribution of governmental powers among these three departments, to save the people from autocracy.[41]

The political approach to public administration stresses the values of representativeness, political responsiveness, and accountability through elected officials to the citizenry. These are basic requirements of constitutional democracy, and incorporating them into all aspects of government, including public management, is considered necessary. These values may have little to do with being results-oriented in the NPM's sense.[42] They can even frustrate agencies' cost-effectiveness in achieving their missions. Democracy does not come cheap!

Many governmental reforms have been aimed at maximizing the political values of representativeness, responsiveness, and accountability within public administration. For instance, the Federal Civil Service Reform Act of 1978 seeks representativeness by making it "the policy of the United States . . . to provide a . . . Federal work force reflective of the Nation's diversity" by endeavoring "to achieve a work force from all segments of society." The Federal Advisory Committee Act of 1972 tries to make the committees that advise agencies on rule making and other matters more representative. It declares that such committees "are frequently a useful and beneficial means of furnishing expert advice, ideas, diverse opinions to the Federal Government" and requires that "the membership of advisory committee(s) . . . be fairly balanced in terms of the points of view represented." Earlier, the poverty and model cities programs of the 1960s sought to use citizen participation to promote political responsiveness in administrative operations.

The political approach to public administration is frequently in tension with the traditional managerial approach and its NPM variant. For instance, efficiency in the managerial sense is not necessarily served through sunshine regulations that open aspects of public administration to public scrutiny and can even dissuade public administrators from taking some actions even though they may be the most efficient. Consultation with advisory committees and "citizen participants" can be time-consuming and costly. Civil service regulations aimed at creating a socially representative workforce add complexity to public personnel systems. Public managers have long complained that their effectiveness is hampered by the large congressional role in public administration. The NPM seeks to promote effectiveness by focusing attention on results and eliminating many of the accountability mechanisms traditionally used to regulate administrative operations.

Organizational Structure

Public administration organized around the political values of representative-ness, responsiveness, and accountability tends to be at odds with the manage-rial approach to organization. The political approach stresses the extent and advantages of political **pluralism** within public administration. On this view, "[e]xecutive branch structure is in fact a microcosm of our society. Inevitably it reflects the values, conflicts, and competing forces to be found in a pluralistic society. The ideal of a neatly symmetrical, frictionless organization structure is a dangerous illusion."[43] Overlapping programs and authority, broad gen-eral missions, and multiple field offices are common when politics dominates administrative organization. Roger Davidson finds a political virtue where the managerially inclined might see disorder: "In many respects, the civil service represents the American people more comprehensively than does Congress."[44]

The basic concept behind pluralism within public administration is that because the administrative branch is, in fact, a policymaking center of gov-ernment, it must enable competing groups to interact with and to check each other by providing political representation to a comprehensive variety of the organized political, economic, and social groups. To the extent that this is achieved, the structure of public administration becomes politicized, with dif-ferent groups continually seeking representation.

Overlapping missions and programs can become common as the admin-istrative structure comes to resemble a political party platform that promises something to almost everyone without establishing clear priorities for resolv-ing conflicts among them. Agency becomes adversary of agency, and the reso-lution of conflict is shifted to the legislature, the office of the chief executive, interagency committees, and the courts. Moreover, the number of bureaus and agencies tends to grow, partly in response to the political demands of organized interests for representation. This approach to administrative orga-nization has been widely denounced as making government "unmanageable," "costly," and "inefficient," but it persists because administrative organiza-tion is frequently viewed as a political question heavily influenced by political values.

View of the Individual

The political approach to public administration tends to aggregate the individ-ual into a broad social, economic, or political group. It does not depersonalize the individual by turning her into a "case" or treat her as a customer. Rather it identifies the individual's interests as being similar or identical to those of oth-ers within the same group. Once grouped, individuals are viewed as the targets or beneficiaries of public policies.

For example, affirmative action within the government service has been aimed at specific groups, such as African Americans, Hispanics, and women, without inquiry as to the particular circumstances of any individual member of these broad and diverse groups. Similarly, farmers growing the same crops and/or located in the same national geopolitical subdivisions are considered alike, despite individual differences among them. This fits the political culture well—politicians tend to think in terms of groups, for example, the "black" vote, the "Hispanic" vote, the "labor" vote, the gender gap, and so forth. In the political approach, then, individuals are seen as members of communities of interest.

Cognitive Approach

The political approach is so concerned with representativeness and responsiveness that it looks for consensus or the development of broad coalitions in determining what is correct, rather than relying largely upon science to establish the "facts." It often bases decisions on the opinions of the public, interest groups, and the media. Elections, public opinion surveys, content analysis of constituents' letters and news coverage, and review of citizens' views expressed at hearings or in focus groups are among the political approach's prime techniques for gaining the information it finds relevant. Informed public administration reflects public preferences,[45] which may or may not coincide with generalizations that are scientifically derived.

Resource Allocation

The political perspective on public administration views budgets as political, rather than business, documents. Allocations are formal statements of how the political system ranks competing values, not necessarily of how the money will be used most effectively or best satisfy customer demand. Budgeting is a contest among a plethora of groups competing for the public's money. The outcome of the competition is likely to shift over time, roughly in conjunction with changes in the relative strength of different groups, political actors, and points of view held by the public.

Historically, this approach has contributed to **incrementalism,** a budgetary process that largely accepts agencies' current budgets as a base on which next year's allocations will be made. Financial analysis is focused on what new programs or expansions of existing programs agencies are asking for. This has the twin advantages of conserving scarce analytical resources in the government's budgeting agency and avoiding the need to raise politically difficult funding issues that were settled in years past.

Decision Making

The political approach tends to favor an incremental style of decision making often called "muddling through" (see Chapter 7). It views political pluralism, limited time, and resource pressures on public administrators as significant constraints on decision making. Consequently, administrators typically can take only small steps toward some general policy objective. This is a political fact of life: the desirability of a decision tends to be measured in terms of political support or opposition rather than cost-effectiveness or scientific analysis.

The Legal Approach to Public Administration

In the United States, the legal approach to public administration historically has been eclipsed by the other approaches, especially the orthodox managerial approach. Nevertheless, it has a venerable tradition and has emerged as a full-fledged approach to modern American public administration. It views public administration as applying and enforcing the law in concrete circumstances. As such, public administration is infused with legal and adjudicatory concerns and should be subordinated to the rule of law.

Main Sources. This approach has its primary roots in three interrelated sources. The first is **administrative law,** which can be defined as the body of law and regulations that control administrative processes in general. It consists of statutes; executive orders; the binding directives of central personnel, budget, service, and related agencies; and constitutional law decisions. Because the latter have had a great and relatively distinctive impact on American public administration, constitutional law is given separate treatment here. The federal and typical state administrative procedure statutes address the handling of information, rule making, adjudication, enforcement, and open government.

A second source of the legal approach has been the movement toward the **judicialization** of public administration. Judicialization is the tendency for administrative processes increasingly to resemble courtroom procedures designed to safeguard individual rights. Decisions are made in an adjudicatory format by hearing examiners or administrative law judges. Agencies in this mode function more like courts, and consequently legal values come to play a greater role in their activities. For example, their decisions must meet specific standards of proof, such as "substantial evidence" or a "preponderance of evidence."

Constitutional law provides a third source of the contemporary legal approach to public administration. Since the 1950s, the federal judiciary has virtually redefined the procedural, equal protection, privacy, and substantive rights and liberties of the citizenry in relation to public administrators. Public employees were recognized as possessing a wide array of new constitutional rights. There was a vast expansion in the requirement that public administrators afford constitutional procedural due process, such as trial-like hearings, to the specific individuals whose governmental benefits, including welfare, public employment, and public education, were terminated through administrative action.

New rights, including the rights to treatment and habilitation, have been articulated for those confined to public mental health facilities. The right to equal protection was vastly strengthened and applied in a variety of administrative matters ranging from public personnel recruitment systems to the operation of public schools and prisons. Individuals involved in encounters with **"street-level" administrators,** such as police and housing or health inspectors, were afforded stronger Fourth Amendment protection against unreasonable searches and seizures. Privacy rights involving matters such as marriage and family were also afforded clearer protection. (These developments are addressed throughout the book. The place of constitutional values in public administration is the subject of Chapter 11.)[46]

Increasing Relevance of the Law. The expansion of the constitutional rights of individuals in relation to public administrators has been enforced primarily in two ways, both of which enhance the relevance of the legal approach to contemporary public administration. The courts have sought to force public administrators to scrupulously avoid violating individuals' constitutional rights by reducing public officials' once "absolute immunity" from civil suits for money damages to "qualified immunity" from such lawsuits. In a remarkable development, discussed further in the next chapter, under qualified immunity many public administrators may be held liable for damages if they reasonably should have known that their actions abridged someone's constitutional rights. This is one reason why the student and practitioner of public administration must have an understanding of relevant aspects of constitutional law. Public administrators who violate someone's constitutional rights may well find themselves *personally* responsible to pay damages to the injured individual. In the Supreme Court's view, this approach, "in addition to compensating victims, serves a deterrent purpose" that "should create an incentive for officials who may harbor doubts about the lawfulness of their intended actions to err on the side of protecting citizens' constitutional rights."[47] Consequently, the concept of administrative competence is expanded to include reasonable knowledge of constitutional law. In addition, in suits challenging the constitutionality or legality of public institutions such as schools, prisons, and mental health facilities, the courts have frequently directly supervised the work of public administrators. In some instances of **remedial law,** judges have taken it upon themselves to revamp entire public school, prison, and state mental health systems. They have even established such administrative details as minimum dietary standards, the number of mental patients there should be per shower or toilet, and where prison guards should be stationed.

The constitutional law affecting public administration is continually changing as the judiciary applies the Constitution to new situations and revises its interpretations of older ones. Some rights that have not yet been recognized legally will be declared; the scope of others will be reduced. But constitutional law, and therefore the courts, will continue to define the rights of individuals in relation to public administrative activity.

Legal Values. The legal approach to public administration emphasizes the rule of law. It embodies several central values. One is **procedural due process,** which stands for the value of fundamental fairness, requiring procedures designed to protect individuals from malicious, arbitrary, erroneous, or capricious deprivation of life, liberty, or property at the hands of government.

A second value concerns individual **substantive rights** and equal protection of the laws as embodied in evolving interpretations of the Bill of Rights and the Fourteenth Amendment. In general, the judiciary views broad individual rights and liberties as a positive good and a core feature of the United States political system. Limitations of these rights may be tolerated by the courts when, on balance, some essential governmental function, such as homeland security, requires their abridgment. However, the usual presumption is against the government in such circumstances; consequently, judicial doctrines place a heavy burden on official administrative action that infringes on the constitutional rights of individuals.

Third, the judiciary values **equity,** a concept that, like due process, is subject to varying interpretation. In terms of public administration in general, equity is probably now most central in empowering judges to fashion remedies for individuals or groups whose constitutional or statutory rights have been violated by public administrators. Additionally, the legal approach values constitutional integrity and opposes efforts to take shortcuts, such as the legislative veto, to get around the strict application of constitutional procedures (see again Box 1.6).

One of the major features of the values of the legal approach to public administration is downplaying the cost-effectiveness reasoning associated with the managerial approach. The judiciary is not oblivious to the costs of its decisions, but its central focus tends to be on the protection of the individual's rights and adherence to legal–constitutional procedures. As one court said, "Inadequate resources can never be an adequate justification for the state's depriving any person of his constitutional rights."[48]

Organizational Structure

As suggested in the discussion of judicialization, the preferred structure of the legal approach to public administration is adversary procedure: the full-fledged judicial trial is the clearest model of this structure. Adversary procedure calls two opposing parties to marshal facts and arguments in support of their positions. These are brought before an impartial referee (e.g., a judge or a jury) who weighs them and ultimately decides which side is sufficiently persuasive. In public administration, however, adversary procedure is generally modified to allow greater flexibility in the presentation of "evidence" and interpretation of the facts. Juries are not used, and hearing examiners often play a more active role than traditional judges in bringing out relevant information. Although this structure is often associated with regulatory commissions, it has a broad presence in public administration. For example, it is heavily relied on in contemporary public personnel administration, especially in the areas of dismissals and disciplinary actions against employees, equal employment opportunity, and labor relations. It is also common in instances where governmental benefits, such as welfare and public school education, are being withheld or withdrawn from individuals.

The precise structure of administrative law varies from context to context, but the common element running through it is the relative independence and impartiality of the hearing examiner. To a large extent, this independence runs counter to the traditional managerial approach's reliance on hierarchy, especially in the sense of "unity of command." Hearing examiners stand outside administrative hierarchies in an important sense. Although they can be told what to do, that is, which cases to hear, they cannot be told how to rule or decide, because cases turn on matters of judgment. Moreover, their rulings may be binding on public agencies. This may introduce serious limitations on administrative coordination because the hearing examiner's interpretation of law and agency rules may differ from that of the agency's management.

To a considerable extent, therefore, this organizational structure is at odds with all the values embodied in the other approaches: it turns customer service into a legal procedure; it militates against efficiency, economy, and managerial effectiveness, but also against representativeness, responsiveness, and political accountability. It is intended, rather, to afford maximum protection of the rights of private parties against illegal, unconstitutional, or invidious administrative action. However, because it is so cumbersome and time-consuming, interest in **alternative dispute resolution** (ADR) has been growing. ADR typically involves negotiation, mediation, and/or arbitration. It is discussed further in Chapter 9.

View of the Individual

The legal approach's emphasis on procedural due process, substantive rights, and equity leads it to consider the individual as a unique person in a specific set of circumstances. The notion that every person is entitled to a "day in court" is appropriate here. Adversary procedure is designed to enable an individual to explain his or her unique or particular situation, thinking, motivation, and so forth, to the governmental decision maker. A decision may turn precisely on such state-of-mind considerations, which become part of the "merits" of the case. There are some outstanding examples of this in the realm of public administration. The Supreme Court has ruled that before a mandatory maternity leave could be imposed on a pregnant public school teacher, she was entitled to an individualized medical determination of her fitness to continue on the job.[49] In *Wyatt v. Stickney* (1971),[50] a federal district court required that an individual treatment plan be developed for each person involuntarily confined to Alabama's public mental health facilities. Whether an individual's right to equal protection has been violated may depend not only on the administrative action taken but also on the public administrators' *intent* or purpose in taking it.[51] Emphasis on the individual as an individual does not preclude the aggregation of individuals into a broader group, as in the case of class action suits. Although such a suit may be desirable to obtain widespread change, it does not diminish the legal approach's focus on the rights of specific individuals.

Cognitive Approach

The legal approach favors adjudication as the method of developing knowledge. Facts are established through adversary procedure and rules of evidence that screen the information that can be considered by the decision maker. Individuals' intentions or states of mind are treated as objective facts rather than as subjective conditions. Science is not rejected, but the legal approach is wary about applying generalizations to individual cases. The adjudicatory method is frequently inductive. It relies on the specific elements of the case at hand to develop broad, general legal principles. The whole inquiry may involve choosing between competing values. Because individual constitutional rights are intended to protect political, economic, and social minorities from a majoritarian government, the "public will," as expressed in opinion polls and elections, is not necessarily of immediate relevance in adjudicatory proceedings.

One of the most striking differences between the intellectual orientation of the legal approach and those of the others concerns the use of social classifications for the sake of analyzing and predicting individual behavior. The traditional managerial approach's reliance on social science may involve the use of such categories as race and gender in analyzing behavior. The customer and entrepreneurial emphasis on marketing may do the same. The political approach, being concerned with representation and responsiveness in the distribution of governmental benefits and burdens, is frequently intensely interested in how programs affect women, minorities, and members of other social groups. By contrast, the legal approach views some social classifications as "suspect" because—based on U.S. historical and legal experience—they are presumed to threaten the constitutional requirement of equal protection. Racial classifications are the preeminent example. Such classifications may be constitutional, depending on a number of factors (discussed in Chapter 11), but the courts review them with strict scrutiny to ensure that the government has a compelling need to use them.

Resource Allocation

The legal approach to budgeting emphasizes constitutional integrity and the need to protect constitutional rights even though those exercising them may be an unpopular minority. In a broad range of cases, the federal courts have required states either to fund activities, such as incarceration and public mental health care, at levels that ensure the protection of constitutional rights or, alternatively, to release the prisoners and mental patients. In one case, *Missouri v. Jenkins* (1990),[52] a federal district court even required increases in local taxation to pay for court-ordered public school desegregation. Eventually, however, the court's remedy was found to be too broad an exercise of equity powers.[53]

Decision Making

Judicial decision making is generally incremental. Decisions are based on precedent: the facts of each new case are evaluated in light of the applicable principles of law derived from past decisions. Even where cases present wholly new issues (cases of "first impression"), the courts are apt to reason by analogy to more familiar cases, using past decisions as a guide. Decisions are often framed in narrow terms, or as a balance between competing concerns. This enables the courts to adjust their rulings in future cases while applying the concepts and language of those of the past. It also lends stability to judicial doctrines and may generally yield better decisions. The use of precedent probably also increases the judiciary's legitimacy because it structures their decisions and, to some degree, binds them to past tradition.

The Six Trends Transforming Government

In late 2006, Mark Abramson, Jonathan Breul, and John Kamensky of the IBM Center for the Business of Government published a report titled *Six Trends Transforming Government*.[54] Impressed by the changing nature of the problems facing the nation, the great need for change in management approaches driven by these problems, and the accelerating rate of intensity in the use of information technology in society, the authors of the report identified six trends that together define an emerging paradigm of management in the public sector. These trends are consistent with much of the new public management approach, but go beyond NPM in significant respects. Not every public organization is affected by all of these changes, nor are they all affected in the same ways. These are general trends, but their importance is already apparent in the public sector. Following is a brief summary.

Changing the Rules of the Game

The traditional core administrative practices, and the culture of which they have been a part, are changing dramatically. Unprecedented flexibility in responding to shifting public needs is being given to public managers in respect to certain key functional areas, including finance, human capital development and management, and organizational structure and design. Such flexibility is increasingly accompanied by stiffer accountability requirements.

Using Performance Measurement

As government agencies become more adept at linking strategic goals and objectives to results, the traditional emphasis on process and procedure is giving way to a new emphasis on genuine performance improvement. Traditional approaches to administrative management are being infused with a focus on meeting performance goals, tying budgeting, contracting, and managers' pay to performance.

Providing Competition, Choice, and Incentives

Where appropriate, governments are employing market-based approaches to service delivery in order to economize on scarce resources. An elaborate array of new tools and approaches has been developed, including some that are by now very familiar: privatization, outsourcing, bartering, charging service users, competing directly with private firms, vouchers, tradable permits, internal "transfer" prices, and specific performance contracts among agencies that do business with one another. Despite the controversy that surrounds some of these methods, their use is increasing.

"Government on Demand"

Citizens are pressing governments to make services available "as needed," some on a 24/7 basis. This is viewed as permitting government to respond with speed and agility to demands and challenges. This trend takes the NPM to a higher level, requiring government to more fully employ information technology to meet citizens' demands. To cite the report at some length:

> On demand government has four major characteristics. The first is *responsiveness:* Whatever the legislative, organizational, or operational change, governments are able to react quickly to meet present or potential needs. The second is *focus:* As organizational processes are transformed and the roles of key players, including suppliers, are optimized, governments have greater insight into what functions should be done by the government itself or could be done by other institutions, public or private. The third is *variability:* Open, integrated technology infrastructures foster collaboration and the creation of services to meet evolving needs, enabling governments to deliver the right service, at the right place and time, to the right degree. The fourth is *resilience:* Governments can maintain their service levels no matter the impediment or threat. While technology has always supported governmental operations, in on demand it is the prime enabler of resilience.[55]

Engaging Citizens

Over the Internet, citizens are connected to one another and to government agencies as never before. The nature and course of citizen involvement in government is changing rapidly. More than a source of information about the activities and services of government, real-time consultation with citizens, decision making, and service delivery can be provided on an interactive basis. The potential exists for citizens to participate actively with public officials in customizing the services that they and their communities receive.

Using Networks and Partnerships

This trend is obviously related to the above on citizen engagement and on-demand service provision, as well as to the NPM idea of steering, not rowing. Governments increasingly find the need to reach across agency lines—and sometimes across federal–state–local lines—especially in the case of nonroutine occurrences, such as hurricanes, tornadoes, volcanoes, floods, and other natural disasters. Collaborative approaches such as networks and partnerships are viewed as the means to leverage scarce resources across agencies and levels of government in order to optimize the use of governmental assets.

Collaborative governance lacks a standard definition. Some draw a distinction between collaborative arrangements and contracting out. However, all would probably agree that the key element in collaborative governance is that it is "something less than authoritative coordination and something more than tacit cooperation" and "usually understood as a convergent arrangement among organizations that have similar and congruent goals but are not bound by authority relationships."[56] To those concerned with governmental

regulatory policy and procedure, collaboration suggests regulation by negotiation ("reg-neg," see Chapter 9). Here we follow those who include contractors in collaborative governance because although contractors are in
principal–agent relationships with government agencies, they are not part of
administrative hierarchies or chains of command per se. Like others engaged
in collaborative relationships, to some extent they also share common goals
with public administrators.

Collaborative governance has several potential advantages. They enable
government to benefit from the activities of private entities* in reaching shared
objectives such as sheltering homeless persons and providing nutritional support to those who lack food security. It can promote cost effectiveness by
coordinating public administrative efforts with those of corporations and nonprofits. It can take advantage of private organizations' specialization, expertise, capacity, flexibility, and creativity in providing services to segments of the
public. It can also rely on their ability to use processes that are constitutionally
prohibited in direct public administrative action such as "faith-based" sociotherapy in alcohol and drug rehabilitation and dealing with at risk populations.

There are also a number of potential pitfalls. Coordination can be difficult in the absence of hierarchy. The goals of entities engaged in collaborative
governance arrangements are apt to be overlapping, but not identical, with
those of government, especially in terms of resource allocation. Dependence on
collaborating organizations makes government hostage to their continued participation, which may require modifying agencies' missions. Government may
also lose the capacity to deliver services directly. In short, collaborative governance has the potential to modify government's ability to both steer and row.

It is clear to even the most casual observer that these trends are very
real, and that they hold great potential to transform public administration
in new, exciting, and socially beneficial ways. However, given the historical
development of the United States administrative state and the three dominant
approaches inherent in American administrative theory, the most important
innovation that may be necessary at this time is a fresh theory of the place of
administrative power and authority in the U.S. constitutional system.

Conclusion: Public Administration Reconsidered

Public administration is a highly complicated endeavor. It embodies at least
the major approaches just discussed. Each of these approaches emphasizes values, organizational arrangements, views of the individual, and intellectual orientations sometimes at odds with those of the others. Box 1.7 summarizes the
varying approaches to public administration. In analyzing the chart, consider
the ways in which the three approaches are sometimes in tension and sometimes in harmony with one another.

---

*Although nonprofit organizations enjoy advantages under section 501 of the federal tax code, as a matter of
law they are private, nongovernmental organizations.

1.7   PERSPECTIVES ON PUBLIC ADMINISTRATION

Characteristic	Perspectives			
	Management		Politics	Law
	Traditional	NPM Variant		
Values	Economy, efficiency, effectiveness	Cost-effectiveness, responsiveness to customers	Representation, responsiveness, accountability	Constitutional integrity, procedural due process, robust substantive rights, equal protection, equity
Organizational structure	Ideal-typical bureaucracy	Competitive, firmlike	Organizational pluralism	Adjudicatory (adversary)
View of individual	Impersonal case, rational actor	Customer	Member of group	Individual and/or member of class, reasonable person
Cognitive approach	Rational-scientific	Theory, observation, measurement, experimentation	Agreement and public opinion, debate	Inductive case analysis, deductive legal analysis, normative reasoning, adversary process
Resource allocation	Rational (cost-benefit)	Performance-based, market-driven	Incremental (distribution of benefits and burdens)	Rights funding
Decision making	Rational-comprehensive	Decentralized, cost-minimizing	Incremental muddling through	Precedential incrementalism
Governmental function characterized by	Execution	Execution	Legislation	Adjudication

Public administrators are called upon to be managers, policy makers, and constitutional lawyers. They are stuck between the proverbial "rock and a hard place" when called on to act in a fashion that will integrate administrative approaches that may defy successful integration. This is one reason why politicians and the society generally have become so critical of public administration. It is often virtually impossible to satisfy all the managerial, political, and legal/constitutional demands placed on public agencies and public administrators. Efficient management may reduce political representation and due process. Emphasizing one approach is certain to provoke criticisms from those who think the others are more important. No doubt this is discouraging in some respects, but it also makes public administration challenging and fascinating. Public administrators are called on to help solve the nation's problems and improve its quality of life. However, there is little consensus on how they should proceed. Although their jobs are sometimes impossible, public administration can be rewarding.

STUDY QUESTIONS

1. Consider public administrative operations with which you have recently dealt. List all their functions that (a) provide services, (b) enforce regulations, or (c) provide a mix of service and regulation.
2. Think of those in government with whom the public interacts on a regular basis. List as many as you can. Does your list contain teachers? post office letter carriers? park rangers? If not, then your list would be incomplete, for they are all public administrators.
3. Think about some public administrative issue that has recently been in the news. Consider whether the managerial, political, and legal perspectives emphasized in this chapter are present in the general discussion of the issue. If so, are the proponents and opponents addressing each other's concerns?
4. What do you consider to be the chief advantages and disadvantages of the NPM? Have NPM approaches been adopted in your home state or by the local jurisdiction in which you reside? By your university or college?

NOTES

1. Dwight Waldo, "What Is Public Administration?" in Jay Shafritz and Albert Hyde, Eds., *Classics of Public Administration,* 2d ed. rev. and exp. (Chicago: Dorsey Press, 1987), 230.
2. The following definitions can be found in *Public Administration: Concepts and Cases,* Richard Stillman, Ed. (Boston: Houghton Mifflin, 1978), 2–4. They are offered by John J. Corson and J. P. Harris; John Pfiffner and Robert Presthus; James W. Davis, Jr.; Nicholas Henry; Dwight Waldo; and Felix and Lloyd Nigro, respectively.
3. David Bazelon, "The Impact of the Courts on Public Administration," *Indiana Law Journal* 52 (1976): 101–110. See also David H. Rosenbloom, "Public Administrators and the Judiciary: The 'New Partnership,'" *Public Administration Review* 47 (January/February 1987): 75–83.
4. See David H. Rosenbloom, Rosemary O'Leary, and Joshua Chanin, *Public Administration and Law,* 3rd ed. (Boca Raton, FL: CRC/Taylor & Francis, 2010). See also David H. Rosenbloom, *Administrative Law for Public Managers,* 2d ed. (Boulder, CO: Westview Press, 2014).
5. David K. Hart, "The Virtuous Citizen, the Honorable Bureaucrat, and 'Public' Administration," *Public Administration Review* 44 (March 1984): 112.
6. Frederick Mosher, *Democracy and the Public Service,* 2d ed. (New York: Oxford University Press, 1981).
7. Hart, "The Virtuous Citizen," 116.
8. See Anthony Downs, *Inside Bureaucracy* (Boston: Little, Brown, 1967).

9. For these and other relevant statistics, see Indiana University Center on Philanthropy, *Giving USA 2012* (Glenview, IL: Giving USA Foundation, 2012); Foundation Center, *Foundation Growth and Giving Estimates 2012* (New York: Foundation Center, 2012); and Indiana University Center on Philanthropy, Center on Philanthropy Panel Study (COPPS) 2003 Wave (March 2006), available online at http://www.philanthropy.iupui.edu/Research/COPPS/Average%20Amounts-Household%20Giving%20&%20Volunteering-2002.pdf.

10. But private firms are not always interested in doing business with the government. See Susan A. MacManus, "Why Businesses Are Reluctant to Sell to Governments," *Public Administration Review* 51 (July/August 1991): 308–316.

11. These goals are embodied in the Civil Service Reform Act of 1978 (PL 95-454) and the Federal Advisory Committee Act of 1972 (PL 92-463). See also Katherine Naff, *To Look Like America* (Boulder, CO: Westview Press, 2001).

12. James Parton, *The Life of Andrew Jackson,* vol. 3 (Boston: Houghton Mifflin, 1887), 220.

13. Carl Schurz, *The Necessity and Progress of Civil Service Reform* (Washington, DC: Good Government, 1894), 3.

14. Woodrow Wilson, "The Study of Administration," *Political Science Quarterly* 56 (December 1941): 494 (originally published in 1887).

15. Ibid., 481.

16. See Luther Gulick and L. Urwick, Eds., *Papers on the Science of Administration* (New York: Institute of Public Administration, 1937), 10, 192. See also Alan Altshuler and Norman Thomas, Eds., *The Politics of the Federal Bureaucracy* (New York: Harper & Row, 1977), 2–17.

17. Leonard D. White, *Introduction to the Study of Public Administration* (New York: Macmillan, 1926), vii–viii. See also Herbert J. Storing, "Leonard D. White and the Study of Public Administration," *Public Administration Review* 25 (March 1965): 38–51.

18. Frederick Taylor, *The Principles of Scientific Management* (New York: Harper & Bros., 1911).

19. Robert Simmons and Eugene Dvorin, *Public Administration* (Port Washington, NY: Alfred Publishing, 1977), 217.

20. See Eugene Lewis, *American Politics in a Bureaucratic Age: Citizens, Constituents, Clients, and Victims* (Cambridge, MA: Winthrop, 1977).

21. Max Weber, *From Max Weber: Essays in Sociology,* in H. H. Gerth and C. W. Mills, Trans. and Eds. (New York: Oxford University Press, 1958), 196–244.

22. Jay Shafritz et al., *Personnel Management in Government,* 4th ed. (New York: Marcel Dekker, 1992), 137.

23. Ralph Hummel, *The Bureaucratic Experience*, 3d ed. (New York: St. Martin's, 1987), 29.

24. Rosenbloom, O'Leary, and Chanin, *Public Administration and Law,* chap. 7.

25. Wilson, "The Study of Administration," 481–482. Wilson noted that "the eminently practical science of administration is finding its way into college courses." He also maintained that "the science of administration is the latest fruit of that study of the science of politics."

26. White, *Introduction to the Study of Public Administration,* vii–viii, 4; Gulick and Urwick, *Papers on the Science of Administration.*

27. Al Gore, *From Red Tape to Results: Creating a Government That Works Better & Costs Less: The Report of the National Performance Review* (Washington, DC: Government Printing Office, 1993), 1.

28. Ibid.

29. Jeffrey M. Jones, "Americans Say Federal Gov't Wastes Over Half of Every Dollar." (Princeton, New Jersey: Gallup Polls, 2011). Available online at: http://www.gallup .com/poll/149543/americans-say-federal-gov-wastes-half-every-dollar.aspx.

30. Philip Joyce and Daniel Mullins, "The Changing Fiscal Structure of the State and Local Public Sector: The Impact of Tax and Expenditure Limitations," *Public Administration Review* 51 (May/June 1991): 240–253.

31. Reading, MA: Addison-Wesley.

32. R. C. Mascarenhas, "Building an Enterprise Culture in the Public Sector: Reform of the Public Sector in Australia, Britain, and New Zealand," *Public Administration Review* 53 (July/August 1993): 319–328. See also Kai Masser, "Public Sector Reforms," in Jay Shafritz, Ed., *International Encyclopedia of Public Policy and Administration* (Boulder, CO: Westview Press, 1998), 1851–1862; and Donald F. Kettl, *The Global Public Management Revolution* (Washington, DC: The Brookings Institution, 2000).

33. Gore, *From Red Tape to Results,* i.

34. Ibid., iv.

35. Oregon Progress Board, *Achieving the Oregon Shines Vision: The 2007 Highlights Report* (Salem: Oregon Progress Board, April 2007).

36. State of Oregon, Office of the Governor, *Governor's Balanced Budget, 2013–2015* (Salem: Oregon: State of Oregon, 2012).

37. George W. Bush, "Building a Responsive, Innovative Government," *Federal Times* (June 26, 2000), 15.

38. Quoted in Laurence Lynn, Jr., *Public Management as Art, Science, and Profession* (Chatham, NJ: Chatham House, 1996), 82, note 4.

39. Wallace Sayre, "Premises of Public Administration: Past and Emerging," in Jay Shafritz and Albert Hyde, Eds., *Classics of Public Administration* (Oak Park, IL: Moore Publishing, 1978), 201. Dwight Waldo, *The Administrative State* (New York: Ronald Press, 1948), demonstrates how the basic value choices of managerial public administration are ultimately statements of political preference.

40. Paul Appleby, *Policy and Administration* (University, AL: University of Alabama Press, 1949). See also Theodore J. Lowi, *The End of Liberalism* (New York: Norton, 1969).

41. *Myers v. United States,* 272 U.S. 52, 293 (1926).

42. Suzanne J. Piotrowski and David H. Rosenbloom, "Nonmission-Based Values in Results-Oriented Public Management: The Case of Freedom of Information," *Public Administration Review* 62 (November/December 2002): 643–657.

43. Harold Seidman, *Politics, Position, and Power* (New York: Oxford University Press, 1970), 13.

44. Roger Davidson, "Congress and the Executive: The Race for Representation," in A. DeGrazia, Ed., *Congress: The First Branch of Government* (New York: Anchor, 1967), 383.

45. See Gordon Tullock, *The Politics of Bureaucracy* (Washington, DC: Public Affairs Press, 1965); and Vincent Ostrom, *The Intellectual Crisis in American Public Administration* (University, AL: University of Alabama Press, 1973).

46. See also Rosenbloom, O'Leary, and Chanin, *Public Administration and Law.*

47. *Carlson v. Green,* 446 U.S. 14, 21 (1980); *Owen v. City of Independence,* 445 U.S. 622, 652 (1980); *Harlow v. Fitzgerald,* 457 U.S. 800, 819 (1982).

48. *Hamilton v. Love,* 328 F. Supp. 1182, 1194 (1971). See Rosenbloom and O'Leary, *Public Administration and Law,* for an extended discussion.

49. *Cleveland Board of Education v. LaFleur* and *Cohen v. Chesterfield Co. School Board,* argued and decided together, 414 U.S. 632 (1974).
50. *Wyatt v. Stickney,* 325 F. Supp. 781 (1971); 334 F. Supp. 387 (1972).
51. *Washington v. Davis,* 426 U.S. 229 (1976); *Baker v. St. Petersburg,* 400 F.2d 294 (1968).
52. *Missouri v. Jenkins,* 495 U.S. 33 (1990).
53. *Missouri v. Jenkins,* 515 U.S. 70 (1995).
54. Mark Abramson, Jonathan Breul, and John Kamensky, *Six Trends Transforming Government* (Washington, DC: IBM Center for the Business of Government, 2006). Available online at http://www.businessofgovernment.org/pdfs/SixTrends.pdf.
55. Ibid., 17.
56. Jeffrey Brudney, Chung-Lae Cho, and Deil Wright. "Understanding the Collaborative Public Manager: Exploring Contracting Patterns and Performance for Service Delivery by State Administrative Agencies in 1998 and 2004," pp. 117–135 in Rosemary O'Leary and Lisa Bingham, Eds., *The Collaborative Public Manager* (Washington, DC: Georgetown University Press, 2009), pp. 117, 127.

ADDITIONAL READING

Cohen, Steven, William Eimicke, and Tanya Heikkila. *The Effective Public Manager,* 4th ed. San Francisco: Jossey-Bass, 2008.

Kettl, Donald. *The Global Public Management Revolution: A Report on the Transference of Governance.* Washington, DC: Brookings Institution, 2005.

Knowles, Eddie Ade, and Norma Riccucci. "Drug Testing in the Public Sector: An Interpretation Grounded in Rosenbloom's Competing Perspectives Model." *Public Administration Review* 61 (July/August 2001): 424–431.

Lynn, Lawrence, Jr. *Public Management: Art, Science, and Profession.* New York: Chatham House, 1996.

Rosenbloom, David H. *Administrative Law for Public Managers* (Boulder, CO: Westview Press, 2003).

Rosenbloom, David H., Rosemary O'Leary, and Joshua Chanin. *Public Administration and Law,* 3d ed. New York: CRC Press, 2010.

Simon, Herbert. *Administrative Behavior,* 3d ed. New York: Free Press, 1976.

Waldo, Dwight. *The Enterprise of Public Administration.* Novoto, CA: Chandler & Sharp, 1980.

PUBLIC ADMINISTRATIVE THEORY WEB SITES

Interesting discussions on public administrative theory can be found on the Public Administration Theory Network's Web site http://www.patheory.org.

The American Society for Public Administration and the National Academy of Public Administration have Web sites containing information about public administration as a profession as well as news about and new developments in public administration at http://www.aspanet.org and http://www.napawash.org.

CHAPTER 2

THE AMERICAN ADMINISTRATIVE STATE

Development and Political Environment

Key Learning Objectives

1. Identify the causes and consequences of administrative growth.
2. Understand the means by which the president, Congress, and the federal courts influence federal administration.
3. Understand the general avenues of interest group participation in public administration.

The chapter begins by addressing how and why public administration became so central to U.S. government. It considers the authority and responsibilities of public administrative agencies. It addresses the ways in which various other political actors have responded to public administration: the presidency, Congress, the judiciary, interest groups (including public employees and both nonprofit and for-profit contractors), the politically involved public, and political parties. These actors are part of public administration's political environment and affect the scope and nature of public administrators' activity. Public administration in the United States has a long and checkered history. It reaches back to colonial days, yet public administration has almost always been considered problematic in some respects. Part of the difficulty has been figuring out how to organize it under the separation of powers systems that characterize the federal, state, and many local governments. Another concern is making it more reflective of the nation's democratic-constitutional political values.

THE RISE OF THE AMERICAN ADMINISTRATIVE STATE

Today, there are roughly 22 million civilian public employees in the United States (see Boxes 2.1 and 2.2). The vast majority work for state and local governments. More than 12 of every 100 workers in the nation work for state or local governments, and another 2 per 100 are civilian employees at the federal level. As substantial as these numbers are, they underestimate the "true size of government," which includes people employed by governments through contracts and grants rather than as civil servants. It is estimated that there are an additional 4.25 such workers for every nonpostal federal employee.[1] The overall ratio of government employees to those employed through contracts and grants at the state and local levels is unknown. However, much government work is clearly done by individuals who are not public employees per se. Moreover, the reach of administrative law and government regulation into the society adds a further element of complexity into measurement of the extent of the administrative state. To the extent that such trends continue, the ratio of the true size of government to those directly on government payrolls will increase.

The growth of public employment in the 20th century and the development of large administrative components in governments at all levels are generally referred to as the "rise of the administrative state." The term *administrative state* is intended to convey several realities of contemporary government: that a great deal of the society's resources flow through public agencies; that public administrators are central to contemporary government; and that the nation has decided on a course of attempting to solve its problems and achieve its aims through substantial reliance on administrative action. The growth of administrative power is a worldwide phenomenon that affects government in virtually all nations. The traditional managerial, political, and legal approaches discussed in the previous chapter have contributed to the expansion of public administration in the United States.

2.1 GROWTH OF FEDERAL EMPLOYMENT

Year	Number of Employees
1791	4,479
1821	6,914
1831	11,491
1841	18,038
1851	26,274
1861	36,672
1871	51,020
1881	100,020
1891	157,442
1901	239,476
1911	395,905
1921	561,143
1931	609,746
1941	1,437,682
1945	3,800,000*
1951	2,482,666
1961	2,435,808
1971	2,862,926
1981	2,865,000
1991	3,111,912
2001	2,710,000
2002	2,749,274
2003	2,714,727
2004	2,692,098
2005	2,700,583
2006	2,700,392
2007	2,698,989
2008	2,730,040
2009	2,803,909
2010	2,841,143

*Plus 330,000 working without compensation or for a dollar per year.

Sources: Richard Stillman, *The American Bureaucracy* (Chicago: Nelson-Hall, 1987), 13, Fig. 1.4.
Through 1951 (except 1945), U.S. Bureau of the Census and Social Science Research Council,
Statistical History of the United States from Colonial Times to the Present (Stamford, CT: Fairfield
Publishers, 1965), 10. The source for 1945 is Paul P. Van Riper, *History of the United States Civil
Service* (Evanston, IL: Row, Peterson, 1958), 373. Figures for 1961 and 1971 are from U.S. Civil Service
Commission, *Annual Report,* 78, 88, App. A. The U.S. Bureau of the Census is the source for 1981 and
1991. The source for 2001–2007 is U.S. Office of Personnel Management, *Monthly Report of Civilian
Employment* (SF113-A), various years, 2002–2007. The source for 2008–2010 is U.S. Census Bureau,
Statistical Abstract of the United States: 2012 (Washington, DC: Government Printing Office, 2012),
327, Table 499.

2.2 STATE AND LOCAL GOVERNMENT EMPLOYMENT (FULL- AND PART-TIME), 1980–2004

Type of Government	Employees (1,000)						
	1980	*1985*	*1990*	*1992*	*1997*	*2002*	*2004*
State	3,753	3,984	4,503	4,595	4,733	5,072	5,041
County	1,853	1,891	2,167	2,253	2,425	2,729	n.a.
Municipal	2,561	2,467	2,642	2,665	2,755	2,972	n.a.
School Districts	4,270	4,416	4,950	5,134	5,675	6,367	n.a.
Townships	394	392	418	424	455	488	n.a.
Special Districts	484	519	585	627	691	721	n.a.
Total	13,315	13,669	15,265	15,698	16,734	18,349	18,760

Source: Department of Commerce, *Statistical Abstract of the United States* (Washington, DC: Government Printing Office, 2005), 322, Table 450; U.S. Bureau of the Census, *Compendium of Public Employment: 2002* (Washington, DC: Government Printing Office, March 2002), Table 1.

The Political Roots of the American Administrative State

Goals of Government

The constitutional government of the United States came into existence in 1789 with some clearly stated formal goals. These are found in the Preamble to the Constitution, which reads:

> WE THE PEOPLE of the United States, in Order to form a more perfect Union, establish Justice, insure domestic Tranquility, provide for the common defence, promote the general Welfare, and secure the Blessings of Liberty to ourselves and our Posterity, do ordain and establish this CONSTITUTION for the United States of America.

In this passage can be found some of the classic purposes of almost all contemporary nations: the desire to provide for the defense of the political community, for law and order, and for the general welfare. The latter generally includes a commitment to economic development and to the provision of services by the government for the purpose of advancing the common good. The idea that the state should provide such services did not begin to develop in western Europe until the 1660s but now is a prominent feature of modern governments. In the United States, governments provide educational services, child care services, transportation services, communications services, and many other services intended to promote health, social, and economic well-being in general.

Public Policy

The decision to pursue these purposes is political. So is the choice of a means for achieving them. Several alternatives to direct governmental provision of services exist. Governments could rely heavily on private resources and incentives to serve their purposes. Education was once a private or church-related endeavor. Taking care of individuals' health and welfare needs was once left up to families and religious institutions. Private action has frequently been augmented by the provision of governmental financial assistance to those individuals whose actions promote general national goals. Governmental subsidies and grants promote a broad variety of activities, including research, health care, training, education, sound agricultural practices, and technological development. Today, some policy analysts argue that people who use government services should be allowed to make choices as to where they receive their services rather than relying on the monopoly of the state. For example, educational reformers argue that education should be supplied by private organizations through a scheme in which the parents of schoolchildren would receive tuition vouchers from the government. These could be used at any school the parents felt best suited their children's educational needs. Such an approach, it is argued, would create a greater incentive for schools to operate efficiently and effectively and would also maximize the freedom of parents to choose among competing educational services. In 2002, Cleveland, Ohio's mix of educational choices, which included vouchers for use in both secular and religious private schools, was upheld by the U.S. Supreme Court.[2] In the early 1980s, the Department of Housing and Urban Development tested a voucher system as a means of helping people obtain housing. Rather than build more housing units directly, the department's policy assumed that vouchers would make some already available housing units more affordable. It might also stimulate some growth in the number of housing units by increasing the demand for them. Similarly, various incentives can be built into the government's system of taxation to promote individual behavior deemed in the common interest. The federal tax structure has used deductions and differential rates to promote investment and home owning by private individuals.

"Third-Party Government"

The federal government pursues so many purposes through grants, direct loans, loan guarantees, tax provisions, contracts, and other indirect means that the United States has a great deal of "third-party government." In other words, "many of the newer or most rapidly growing tools of government action share a common characteristic: they are *indirect;* they rely upon a variety of non-federal 'third parties'—states, cities, banks, industrial corporations, hospitals, nonprofit organizations, etc.—for their operation."[3] But throughout much of the 20th century governments sought to achieve many of their goals through direct governmental action. For instance, in addition to encouraging home ownership through the tax code, governments sought to assure that everyone was adequately housed by building and running public housing projects. They also maintained shelters for those who remained homeless.

The essence of the 20th-century administrative state was the policy choice to rely heavily on public administration to achieve the nation's political goals. In the language of the NPM, the administrative state has rowed as well as steered. The Constitution indicates a preference for governmental action in some areas. For instance, it authorizes the federal government to establish post offices and post roads and to raise and direct an army and a navy. Even a brief review of the development of large-scale public administration in the United States during the past two centuries indicates the extent to which such direct administrative action became increasingly commonplace.

Drivers of Growth

The primary drivers of administrative growth and development have been associated with the increasing complexity of modern society, expanded public demands for public services, and the rise of the national defense establishment. In this vein, James Q. Wilson identified several roots of the development of the contemporary American administrative state.[4] One was to provide a reliable postal service. The U.S. Post Office was not viewed as an end in itself but rather as a means of promoting economic development and national cohesion and integration. It was also spurred by a desire for political patronage. Wilson observes that "from 1816 to 1861, federal civilian employment in the executive branch increased nearly eightfold (from 4,837 to 36,672), but 86 percent of this growth was the result of additions to the postal service."[5]

A second source of administrative growth has been the desire to promote economic development and social well-being through governmental action in various sectors of the economy. The Department of Agriculture was created in 1862, and the Departments of Commerce and Labor came into existence in 1913. More recently, the Department of Health, Education, and Welfare (now Health and Human Services) and the Departments of Housing and Urban Development, Transportation, Energy, and Education were created to promote governmental goals in these economic and social areas of American life. The Veterans Administration was made the Department of Veterans Affairs in the late 1980s.

Departments such as Agriculture, Labor, Veterans Affairs, and Commerce are often called **clientele departments** because they deal largely with a relatively well-defined category of people who are assumed to have common economic interests. Clientele departments are often directly engaged in supplying services. For example, the Department of Agriculture seeks to educate farmers in improved agricultural techniques and to provide direct economic assistance to them in a variety of ways. It has also undertaken projects to conserve soil, and it manages a system of national forests. Departments such as Health and Human Services, having a broader mission, also engage in direct action, such as research and disease prevention.

Another source of administrative growth has been defense. The Departments of War and Navy were created in the 18th century, but the military establishment did not emerge as the federal government's largest administrative operation until after World War II. Since that time, the Department of Defense has often employed one-third or more of civilian federal workers. The Department of Veterans Affairs, functionally related to Defense, is also large (about 304,665 civilian employees). Interestingly, this means that more than 60 percent of federal civilian employees are employed in three agencies—Defense, Veterans Affairs, and the Postal Service. The creation of a standing army, navy, and air force and a large civilian administrative component to manage the military reflects the government's view that providing for the common defense requires centralized planning for the procurement and deployment of weapons and personnel.

In sum, the political roots of the development of contemporary public administration in the United States lie primarily in two political choices made by the government and society. First was that government would exist to promote such objectives as the common defense, economic development, and the general welfare. At the national level, this was a choice first made in the late 1780s and reinforced subsequently on many occasions. Second has been the choice, beginning in the 1880s or so, of placing heavy reliance on direct provision of services and functions by government as opposed to relying solely on the manipulation of subsidies for private action. As noted earlier, today the balance between steering and rowing is changing in conjunction with the NPM.

The Legal Origins of American Public Administration

Political communities seek to promote law and order within their jurisdictions. Otherwise, political, economic, and social conditions become chaotic. It is possible to promote law and order through private means. Private religious groups, social leaders, and private schools can imbue individuals with the sense of a moral and civic obligation to obey the law and avoid violating the rights of others. Social sanctions—such as excommunication, ostracism, and shunning—can act as powerful controls on individual behavior. However, governments have typically played a large role in promoting law and order through the creation and enforcement of criminal and civil law. These bodies of law establish the obligations of individuals toward one another and toward the community.

Regulation

James Q. Wilson points to regulatory activity as another source of administrative growth in the United States.[6] He traces the emergence and development of regulatory agencies during four periods, each having a common set of political features. The first period was 1887 to 1890, when the Interstate Commerce Commission (1887) was created to regulate transportation (primarily railroads) and the Sherman Act (1890) was passed as a rudimentary means of controlling the development of economic monopolies. During the second period, from 1906 to 1915, some of these regulatory activities were strengthened and the quality of foods and drugs was regulated by the Pure Food and Drug Act (1906) and the Meat Inspection Act (1907) in the interests of protecting consumers' health and safety. Banks were regulated by the Federal Reserve Act (1913). Additional economic and trade practices were brought under regulatory administration by the Clayton and Federal Trade Commission Acts (1914). During the 1930s, the third period, numerous industries were added to the list of the federally regulated, including cosmetics, utilities, securities, airlines, and communications. Private sector labor relations also came under federal regulation at this time. Finally, during the 1960s and early 1970s, federal regulatory activities focused on environmental and workplace safety concerns (in the Environmental Protection Agency and the Occupational Safety and Health Administration, respectively) and the protection of racial and ethnic minorities and women from discrimination in employment (in the Equal Employment Opportunity Commission).

A major political problem with governmental regulatory activities is that although they do tend to promote domestic tranquility, they are also widely viewed as compromising the government's commitment to secure the "blessings of liberty." Traditionally in the United States, liberty included the freedom to pursue one's economic interests free of wide-ranging governmental control. To a large extent, early regulation was through the **common law,** if at all. However, by the 1890s, it was evident that the common law would have to be supplemented or replaced by administrative regulation. A major stimulus for change was conceptual and biological, as legal historian Lawrence Friedman explains:

> The discovery of germs, insidious, hidden in every spot of filth, had a profound effect on the legal system. To a much greater extent than before [the 1890s], goods—including food—were packaged and sent long distances, to be marketed impersonally, in bulk, rather than to be felt, handled, and squeezed at the point of purchase. This meant that a person was dependent on others, on strangers, on far-off corporations, for necessities of life, that society was more than ever a complex cellular organism; these strangers, these distant others had the capacity to inflict catastrophic irreparable harm.[7]

Society also needed protection against toxic industrial pollution, unsafe vehicles, and a host of products that could not sensibly be evaluated by the public. Harmful products and production practices, it was agreed, could best be controlled through governmental regulation.

Balancing Liberty and Equality

To some extent, the political conflict over regulation is related to a much wider historical political tension between liberty and equality. This conflict has been a characteristic political problem in the United States since its founding. Liberty to pursue one's economic interests results in differences in individual wealth. These economic disparities can be translated into inequalities in terms of political influence and economic and social power. Government intervention, often generated by populist opposition to the practices of big business, inevitably reduces economic liberty. Minimum wage and hours legislation and regulation of child labor are excellent examples of this phenomenon. Fearing the exploitation of workers by large corporations that can exercise great power over labor markets, government stepped in and limited how little a worker can be paid, how long he or she may be required to work per week, and how young or old he or she may be. Originally, such legislation was opposed by many, including the U.S. Supreme Court, on the grounds that it limited workers' liberty to contract out their labor at their discretion, but nowadays the Fair Labor Standards Act is generally viewed as an important constraint on employers. Equal employment opportunity legislation presents another example of the tension between liberty and equality found in regulatory legislation. In the absence of statutes barring discrimination against members of minority groups, individuals with disabilities, and women, private employers would be free to exclude them from their workforces. But this would, and did, promote economic, social, and political inequality. At the same time, requiring nondiscrimination interferes with an employer's liberty to hire and fire as it pleases.

Because governmental regulation of economic practices is in tension with the stated constitutional goal of securing the blessings of liberty, far-reaching efforts have been made to ensure that such governmental intervention is not arbitrary, capricious, or unduly violative of the economic liberty of individuals and businesses. These efforts generally use law and legal processes as a check on the regulatory activities of public administrators. Consequently, regulatory activities become law-bound, and the agencies engaging in regulation are structured to emphasize the values of the legal approach to public administration. Their procedures for rule making, adjudication, enforcement, and transparency are substantially regulated by administrative law. Many regulatory agencies are headed by a bipartisan board or commission.

The Administrative Procedure Act

By the mid-1940s, Congress had come to believe that the regulatory process should afford greater protection to industries, firms, and the public from encroachments by administrative agencies. It enacted the Administrative Procedure Act (1946). Although the act, as amended, contains many exceptions, it affords the following protections to private parties being regulated:

- *Publication.* An agency must publish in the *Federal Register* descriptions of its organization, general method of operation, **procedural rules,** and **substantive rules.**
- *Rule Making Procedures.* With some exceptions, proposed changes in substantive rules (also called "legislative rules") must be published in the *Federal Register,* an opportunity for response by interested parties must be granted, and such responses are to be taken into account by the agency before it adopts its final rule on the matter. Substantive rules are the equivalent of statutes, but they are made by administrative agencies rather than by an elected legislature. The final rule must be published in the *Federal Register,* and not less than 30 days must elapse between its publication and its initial application. In some cases, called "formal rule making" or "rule making on the record," a judicial-like hearing is held before an administrative law judge or agency officials to determine the desirability of a new rule or rule change. (Box 2.3 presents an example of an agency's efforts to obtain comments in connection with potential rule making for a headlamp standard.)

2.3   SEEKING COMMENTS FOR A POTENTIAL HEADLAMP STANDARD

Department of Transportation
National Highway Traffic Safety Administration
49 CFR Part 571
[Docket No. NHTSA-02-13957;
Notice 01] RIN 2127-AI97

Glare from Headlamps and Other Front-Mounted Lamps: Adaptive Frontal-lighting Systems Federal Motor Vehicle Safety Standard No. 108; Lamps, Reflective Devices, and Associated Equipment.

AGENCY: National Highway Traffic Safety Administration (NHTSA), Department of Transportation (DOT).

ACTION: Request for comments.

SUMMARY: This document requests comments on Adaptive Frontal-lighting Systems (AFS). The automotive industry is introducing Adaptive Frontal-lighting Systems that can actively change the intensity and direction of headlamp illumination in response to changes in vehicle speed or roadway geometry, such as providing more light to the left in a left-hand curve. The agency is concerned that such headlighting systems may cause additional glare to oncoming drivers, change the easily recognizable and consistent appearance of oncoming vehicles, and have failure modes that may cause glare for long periods of time. The agency is also interested in learning whether these adaptive systems can provide any demonstrated reduction in crash risk during nighttime driving. Thus, the Agency is seeking information on these systems to assess their potential for a net increase or decrease in the risk of a crash. Of special interest to us are the human factors and fleet study research that may have been completed to assure these systems do not increase the safety risk for oncoming and preceding drivers.

DATES: Comments must be received on or before April 14, 2003.

ADDRESSES: Comments must refer to the docket and notice number cited at the beginning of this notice and be submitted to: Docket Management, Room PL-401, 400 Seventh Street SW., Washington, DC 20590. It is requested, but not required, that two copies of the comments be provided. The Docket Section is open on weekdays from 10 A.M. to 5 P.M. Comments may be submitted electronically by logging onto the Dockets Management System website at http://dms.dot.gov. Click on "Help" to obtain instructions for filing the document electronically.

FOR FURTHER INFORMATION CONTACT: For technical issues, please contact Mr. Richard L. Van Iderstine, Office of Rulemaking, NHTSA, 400 Seventh Street, SW., Washington, DC 20590. Mr. Van Iderstine's telephone number is (202) 366-2720 and his facsimile number is (202) 366-4329. For legal issues please contact Mr. Taylor Vinson, Office of Chief Counsel, at the same address. Mr. Vinson's telephone number is (202) 366-5263.

SUPPLEMENTARY INFORMATION: The development of Adaptive Frontal-lighting Systems (AFS) has been ongoing for about a decade. . . .

The balance between roadway illumination and glare is something that has always concerned us. The public shares our concern, too, as evidenced by the unprecedented response to Docket 8885, NHTSA's docket on glare from headlamps. Besides the more than four thousand comments to date, that docket has the highest number of Internet visits of all dockets in the DOT Docket Management System: more than 64,000 hits. The public's concern is that glare is increasing at an alarming rate

- *Adjudication.* Adjudicatory procedures within the agency must include the opportunity for aggrieved parties to be heard, to submit information and arguments on their behalf, and to have an initial recommendation for disposition of the case made by an impartial hearing examiner (administrative law judge) or other decision maker.

whether from approaching vehicles or rear view mirrors. Thus, the agency is concerned whether the implementation of AFS will produce a volume of complaints similar to those in Docket 8885 regarding the installations of high intensity discharge, high-mounted, and supplemental headlamps.

Given this concern, we have a number of questions for drivers, and the lighting and the motor vehicle industries, relative to the safety, implementation and use of AFS, especially as it may be offered to the U.S. market. These questions are:

Questions for Drivers

Question 1: Do you have problems seeing around curves because of the limitations of the headlamps on the vehicles that you drive, or because of glare from an approaching vehicle? Please describe the problems, including road, ambient lighting, and weather conditions.

Question 2: Is the glare that you described above worse than the glare from vehicles approaching on straight roads? Is it because the light is brighter or because it is longer lasting?

Question 3: Under what nighttime driving conditions have you thought you needed extra headlight illumination to help you see the road, signs, or objects; When turning at intersections, when driving on curved roads, at intersections, driving in rain, when driving in fog, when driving on interstate highways, driving in cities, etc.? . . .

Question 7: If a headlighting rating were available for new vehicles in the same manner as crashworthiness and rollover star ratings, would you use these headlighting ratings in the decisions that lead to your purchase of a new vehicle? On a scale of 1 to 10 with 1 being of little value and 10 being extremely important, how might you rate the importance of the headlamp rating, if available, to your purchase decision for a new vehicle?

Questions for Industry

. . . Question 10: Have vehicle manufacturers evaluated prototype AFS-equipped vehicles at night as occupants of other vehicles to evaluate the potential glare from AFS? If so, please describe the evaluation and the results. . . .

Question 14: While we are aware of many studies to demonstrate and promote the efficacy of AFS, we are not aware of a single study that has been done on the effects on other drivers facing AFS-equipped vehicles or on drivers using AFS-equipped vehicles. Please identify any such studies.

Question 15: Has glare been studied specifically for younger and older drivers facing or preceding the various modes of AFS operation on vehicles? If so, please list the studies. . . .

Question 29: Should AFS be mandatory? What data exist showing safety benefits to justify amending the Standard to require AFS? If not mandatory, why not?

How Do I Prepare and Submit Comments?

Your comments must be written and in English. To ensure that your comments are correctly filed in the Docket, please include the docket number of this document in your comments.

Your comments must not be more than 15 pages long (49 CFR 553.21). We established this limit to encourage you to write your primary comments in a concise fashion. However, you may attach necessary additional documents to your comments. There is no limit on the length of the attachments.

Please submit two copies of your comments, including the attachments, to Docket Management at the address given at the beginning of this document, under ADDRESSES.

Source: Federal Register 68, no. 29 (February 12, 2003), pp. 7101–7104. From the Federal Register Online via GPO Access [www.access.gpo.gov] [DOCID:fr12fe03-19].

- *Judicial Review.* A right to judicial review is required for a person suffering legal wrong or adversely affected by agency actions. Judicial review is intended to check arbitrary or capricious abuses of discretion, actions not authorized by law, violations of constitutional rights and statutes, breaches of procedural regularity, and agency decisions unwarranted by the facts of the case.

About two-thirds of the states also have administrative procedure acts (APAs). There are three main models: a 1961 state model APA, a 1981 version, and a 2010 revision. More than half the state APAs were enacted between 1955 and 1980. The 2010 revision recognizes the growing role of electronic communications in state government. It strives to ensure fairness in administrative proceedings, to increase public access, and to promote efficiency through use of information technologies. None of the models apply directly to local governments.[8]

Clearly, governmental regulatory activities have not only promoted the growth of public administration but also infused it with a legalistic character. A great deal of administrative time and resources at all levels of government are devoted to regulatory hearings for setting utility rates, issuing licenses, controlling a host of economic endeavors, and monitoring practitioners of a wide variety of occupations. Many view regulation as going too far and becoming too expensive. During the early 1980s, there was a broad move toward *deregulation,* as in the banking, trucking, and airline industries. Telecommunications have also been substantially deregulated. Much of the deregulation was considered "procompetitive"; that is, it was intended to allow markets rather than administrative agencies to establish price and service levels. However, there has been little support for deregulation of safety, as in the case of the Federal Aviation Administration or the Food and Drug Administration. Some have even argued that the repeal of the Glass-Steagall Act played a part in the banking crisis of late 2007 and the Great Recession, which may lead to re-regulation in the future. Chapter 9 deals more comprehensively with administrative regulation.

The Managerial Origins of the Contemporary American Administrative State

Public administration has developed and expanded in pursuit of broad political goals, including the provision of defense, infrastructure, economic development and stability, education, health, and protection of the environment, workers, and consumers. The administrative activities of agencies assigned to achieve these substantive goals not only should follow a reasonably standardized and fair set of procedures, they also should comply with the standards of good management. The day-to-day organizational operations of administrative agencies should be managed well, meaning they should be efficient, effective, and economical in their operations. Perhaps surprisingly, this too has been a source of the growth of the American administrative state.

Good management may immediately suggest getting more done for less money—a government "that works better and costs less," as the federal National Performance Review (NPR) put it[9]—which in turn might mean that fewer people would be employed in the public sector. Certainly it is true that well-managed agencies may realize such savings. However, it may also be desirable to rely on **overhead agencies.** Such administrative units perform services for other agencies and/or exercise oversight over some of their operations.

The traditional managerial approach relies heavily on overhead agencies for supplying government with materials, internal services (such as vehicle maintenance), and personnel. In this view, centralization promotes expertise and economies of scale. For example, a central procurement agency may be able to buy office products in huge quantities at substantial discounts. A central personnel agency can develop highly specialized knowledge regarding selection and promotion examinations. By contrast, the NPM contends that centralization costs too much in lost flexibility. In its view, overhead agencies promote red tape, delay, rigid and sometimes bizarre requirements, and unnecessary expense. They frustrate results and customer-oriented public administration by emphasizing procedures rather than the achievement of substantive goals.

The following are examples of classic overhead agencies.

- The *Office of Management and Budget* (OMB) is part of the Executive Office of the President. It works with the president, his advisers, and federal agencies to prepare the nation's annual budget for congressional consideration. In formulating the budget, the OMB evaluates agency requests for funding and evaluates their activities. It also makes recommendations to the president when agencies seek new legislation or the issuance of presidential executive orders to aid them in fulfilling their functions. In practice, the OMB exercises a veto over such requests. It plays a major role in overseeing proposed regulatory rule making by executive branch agencies. Although these functions are less developed than its budgeting activities, the OMB also tries to advise agencies on good management practices and to evaluate their managerial operations.

- The *Office of Personnel Management* (OPM) is an executive branch agency with the mission to "Recruit, retain and honor a world-class workforce to serve the American People."[10] Established in 1979, it initially regulated the way agencies recruited, selected, trained, promoted, transferred, classified, paid, and treated federal employees. It also developed centralized merit examinations. For the most part, these functions were previously performed by a Civil Service Commission, created in 1883 and abolished in 1979. Following the NPR report in 1993, many of the OPM's responsibilities were given directly to the various agencies and departments. In 1994, the Clinton administration created a media event by having the then OPM director, James King, use a wheelbarrow to throw out the *Federal Personnel Manual*. The voluminous, 10,000-page, highly detailed compendium of often arcane federal personnel regulations symbolized much of the NPR's critique of traditional management. OPM still administers federal retirement and health programs, operates the Federal Executive Institute for training high-level career employees, and enforces some remaining government-wide regulations. A major role of OPM is to serve as a consultant to other federal agencies and to advise and assist them on strategic human resources management.

- The *General Services Administration* (GSA) traditionally supplied other agencies' needs, ranging from rubber bands to the most sophisticated office technologies. Today, agencies have more flexibility in purchasing what they need. However, the GSA is still involved in obtaining office space for agencies and acquisitions. It provides maintenance and policing functions for agency buildings and operates various food services within them. The GSA can buy products in huge quantities at significant discounts. Centralized purchasing allows agencies to rely on the GSA's expertise in obtaining supplies economically and efficiently and to focus on their substantive missions without the distraction of having to shop around for the goods and services they need.
- The *Government Accountability Office* (GAO) is part of the Congress. It was established in 1921 (as the General Accounting Office) to facilitate Congress's ability to monitor the use of governmental funds by administrative agencies. Over time, Congress has called upon the GAO to evaluate the general quality of management of specific administrative agencies and programs, and to evaluate the policies agencies are pursuing. For the most part, GAO serves core governmental functions unlikely to be privatized. It is central to Congress's constitutional role in overseeing federal administration.
- The *Merit Systems Protection Board* (MSPB), the *Federal Labor Relations Authority* (FLRA), and the *Equal Employment Opportunity Commission* (EEOC) regulate limited aspects of the federal personnel system. MSPB is charged with ensuring that the federal merit system is not violated, and it hears appeals involving employee discipline and dismissal. The FLRA oversees the federal labor-management relations program and adjudicates charges of unfair labor practices. The EEOC is primarily concerned with combating illegal discrimination in private employment, but it also has responsibilities for ensuring equal opportunity in the public sector at all governmental levels.

State and local governments typically make use of overhead agencies as well. Budget and civil service (or personnel) agencies are particularly common.

The work of several of these overhead units is augmented by a number of specialized positions charged with improving the way government-wide administrative systems operate within the agencies. For instance, at the federal level, budget analysts help prepare agencies' budgets for OMB's consideration. Inspectors general (IGs) and chief financial officers (CFOs) are other functionaries whose work complements that of some of the overhead agencies. The IGs were established on a systematic statutory basis in 1978. They are heavily involved in monitoring administrative operations and systems, generally with a view to checking waste, fraud, abuse, and other forms of maladministration. The CFOs were established in 1990. They are primarily responsible for improving agencies' accounting systems, financial management, and financial reporting. Toward the end of the 1990s, the IGs and CFOs were joined by chief information officers (CIOs), whose mission is to improve the agencies' use of information technology. The Homeland Security Act of 2002 added chief human capital officers (CHCOs) to the list of such positions. They are responsible for promoting better personnel management within the agencies. The Government Performance and Results Act Modernization Act of 2010 calls on chief operating officers (COOs) to upgrade agencies' overall performance.

In sum, the quest for good management, as well as the desire to promote various political, social, and economic goals while protecting the rights of private parties, has contributed to the growth of public administration in the United States.

◆▶   ADMINISTRATIVE AUTHORITY AND RESPONSIBILITY

The Paradox of Administrative Power

We have been discussing the rise of the administrative state in terms of the development and growth of administrative units. But the phenomenon of the administrative state and what makes public administration so interesting goes well beyond counting the number of units, employees, or money spent. Contemporary public administration is of fundamental concern not only because it is large and expensive but also because of its authority and responsibilities. It is sometimes difficult to imagine that public employees have emerged as major—in some policy areas, the major—actors in the American political system. After all, what does a postal letter carrier, a government accountant, a personnel official, a record-keeping clerk, or a typist have to do with the exercise of governmental power? What kind of impact can even high-level officials have in administrative systems that are dominated by organizations rather than individuals, that are rule-bound, and that place major constraints on individual action? These questions hint at a paradox of contemporary public administration. Cumulatively, public administrators have a great deal of authority, but individually they are often likened to cogs in a machine over which they have little control.[11] Each administrator's discretion is constrained by many rules, procedures, and checks, yet public administration has become a center for the development of policy choices for American society as a whole. The French writer Honoré de Balzac unflatteringly captured this irony by referring to bureaucracy as "giant power wielded by pygmies."[12]

One way to begin a consideration of the nature of administrative authority is to consider what public administrators do. As was discussed earlier, public administrators have become a vehicle through which society has chosen to carry out public action aimed at securing political objectives, such as economic development and regulation to promote the public's health and safety. The scope of their activities is astounding. It is difficult to find more than a few interests or concerns in the society that are not in some way addressed through administrative action (see Box 2.4). There is no denying that the contemporary administrative state is characterized by a high degree of penetration of the daily life of society. This is true whether it steers, rows, or both.

2.4   The Reach of the Federal Bureaucracy: "Touching You, Touching Me"

In 2007, the *U.S. Government Manual* indicated that administrative agencies dealt with an immense range of American life. Reforms, budget cuts, partisan shifts, and policy changes have come and gone, but few, if any of the items, are ever dropped from the list. No doubt, some other items dealing with recent technological breakthroughs and other noteworthy developments will be added. The following were indexed in the *2006–07 Manual*: Accounting; Actuaries; African American History and Culture; the Aged; Agricultural Statistics Service; Air quality; Airport development; Alcohol and alcohol abuse; Alhurra; Aliens; Amtrak; Appalachian Regional Commission; Arctic Research Commission; Arts and the Humanities; Bankruptcy; Banks and banking; Bilingual education; Blind persons; Business and industry; Cancer; Census; Children and Families; Civil rights; Colleges and universities; Communications; Community development; Conservation; Consumer protection; Copyrights; Credit; Crime; Cultural exchange programs; Dairy products; the Deaf; national Defense; Delaware River Basin Commission; Disaster assistance; Disease Control and Prevention; Drugs and drug abuse; Economic policy; Education; Electric power; Emergency preparedness; Employment; Energy; Engineering; Environmental protection; Equal Employment Opportunity Commission; Fire prevention; Fisheries; Flood control; Folklife programs; Food Safety; Foreign relations; Forests and forest products; Fossil fuels; Genetics; Government contracts; HIV/AIDS; Hazardous substances; Hazardous waste; Health and health care; Hearing impaired; Highways and roads; Historic Preservation; Homeless persons; Hydroelectric power; IMAX Theater; Immigration; Immigration and naturalization; Imports; Individuals with disabilities; Infants and children; Information technology; Insurance; Inventions and patents; Investments; Labor-management relations; Laboratories; Law enforcement; Lawyers; Libraries; Licensing; Loans; Manpower training; Maps and mapping; Marine life; Maritime activities; Marketing; Measurements and standards; Meat and meat products; Merchant marine; Migratory Bird Conservation Commission; Mining and minerals; Minorities; Mississippi River Commission; Mortgages; Motor vehicles; Museums; Native Americans; Natural gas; North American Free Trade Agreement; Nuclear energy; Nutrition; Occupational safety and health; Passports and visas; Peace Corps; Pensions; Pests and pesticides; Pipelines; Plants; Ports; Power administrations; Price controls; Price supports; Printing; Prisoners of war; Probation and parole; Public assistance programs; Public health and safety; Racketeering; Radiation protection; Railroads; Records management; Recreation and recreational areas; Refugees; Rural development; Saint Lawrence Seaway Development Corporation; Savings bonds; Scholarships and fellowships; Schools; Science and technology; Small businesses; Space shuttle; Statistics; Surface transportation; Taxes; Telecommunications; Tennessee Valley Authority; Terrorism; Textiles; Tobacco; Trademarks; Travel; Urban areas; Utilities; Veterans; Veterinary services; Volunteer programs; Wages; Waste management; Water pollution control; Water supply; Waterways; Weather; Welfare; Wetlands; Wildlife; Women; Youth.

Source: U.S. Census Bureau, *U.S. Government Manual 2006–07* (Washington, DC: U.S. Government Printing Office, 2007). Available online at http://www.gpoaccess.gov/gmanual/search .html.

Administrative Independence

The centrality of public administration does not automatically make it powerful. It is at least theoretically possible that public administrative action could be wholly directed by law and political arrangements to the extent that it simply carried out the will of the elected legislative and executive officials. But in practice administrative organizations have considerable independence, for at least two reasons.

First, public administrators develop a great deal of expertise on which the society becomes dependent. All the functional specialization, record keeping, and information gathering that go on in public administration enable public administrators to develop expertise on some matters that cannot be matched elsewhere in society. (Take a careful look at the information sought by the form reproduced in Box 2.5.) Not only do public administrators often know more about many aspects of the economy and society than does anyone else, they also know more about how to accomplish programmatic ends than do legislators or elected officials.

Second, elected officials frequently delegate decision making authority to public administrators. In part this delegation flows from deference to administrative expertise. It also stems from recognition that public administrative directives, rules, and adjudicatory decisions are more flexible than legislation in the sense that they can be modified through a far less elaborate process than enacting a statute. When the legislature believes that standards for regulation or for eligibility for various governmental benefits will have to be changed frequently, or applied in a great variety of circumstances, it may be apt to delegate power to administrative agencies. For instance, the goal of the Occupational Safety and Health Administration Act (1970) is to promote workplace safety. Among other issues, this requires that somebody determine which levels of which substances used in manufacturing and other sectors are toxic. Given the vast number of production practices and potentially toxic chemicals used (not to mention their combination), it is unlikely that Congress *could* address every such danger through specific legislation. Instead, it delegated its legislative authority to the Occupational Safety and Health Administration to make and enforce rules regarding workers' safety.

Delegations of legislative authority can contain clear and forceful legislative guidance. As a matter of constitutional law at the federal level, delegations must contain an "intelligible principle" to guide administrative action.[13] But this requirement is frequently honored in the breach. Congress may place only the vaguest of conditions on the exercise of powers it delegates to public administrators. For example, the Federal Communications Commission (FCC), which regulates radio and television broadcasting, is supposed to exercise the powers granted to it by Congress in "the public convenience, interest, or necessity." If you were chairperson of the FCC, what kind of guidance would you find in these words? Delegations with little guidance often result from the legislature's inability or unwillingness, for political reasons, to set clear standards for the use of the powers it delegates to administrative agencies. Sometimes the subject matter of the agency's jurisdiction is so complex that the legislature does not have the time or staff resources to truly master it. At other times, political expediency dictates that the legislature will not take a firm stand on an issue, which may be politically controversial, be divisive, and lead to a loss of support among segments of the electorate. The net result of reliance on the expertise of public administrators and the scope and frequency

INFORMATION FOR YOUR BABY'S BIRTH CERTIFICATE

1. FILL IN ALL UNSHADED PORTIONS OF THE FORM. THE SHADED SECTIONS WILL BE COMPLETED BY YOUR PHYSICIAN AT THE TIME YOUR BABY IS BORN.
2. PLEASE TYPE OR PRINT IN PERMANENT BLACK INK.
3. WHEN COMPLETED, RETURN THIS FORM TO YOUR PHYSICIAN OR HOSPITAL.

PARENT—
MAY NEWSPAPERS BE FURNISHED
NOTICE OF THIS BIRTH? YES ☐ NO ☐
SIGNATURE ▶

INFANT

1A. NAME: FIRST — MIDDLE — LAST | 1B. MEDICAL RECORD NO. | 2A. DATE OF BIRTH: MONTH DAY YEAR | 2B. HOUR: ___ m

3. SEX: MALE ☐1 FEMALE ☐2 | 4A. IS BIRTH: SINGLE ☐1 TWIN ☐2 OTHER ☐3 | 4B. IF NOT SINGLE BIRTH: (Specify) FIRST ☐1 SECOND ☐2 OTHER ☐3 | 5. PLACE OF BIRTH: (Check type and specify if other) HOSPITAL ☐ RESIDENCE ☐ BIRTHING CENTER ☐ CLINIC OR DR'S OFFICE ☐ OTHER ☐

6A. FACILITY NAME: (If not facility, give address) | 6B. LOCALITY: (Check one and specify) CITY OF ☐ VILLAGE OF ☐ TOWN OF ☐ | 6C. COUNTY OF BIRTH:

MOTHER

7A. MAIDEN NAME: FIRST — MIDDLE — LAST | 7B. AGE: | 7C. CITY AND STATE OF BIRTH: (Country if not U.S.A.) | 7D. SOCIAL SECURITY NUMBER:

8A. RESIDENCE, STATE: | 8B. COUNTY: | 8C. LOCALITY: (check one and specify) CITY OF ☐ VILLAGE OF ☐ TOWN OF ☐ | 8D. IF CITY OR VILLAGE, IS RESIDENCE WITHIN CITY OR VILLAGE LIMITS? ☐ YES ☐ NO IF NO, SPECIFY TOWN

8E. STREET AND NUMBER OF RESIDENCE: | 8F. ZIP CODE:

8G. MAILING ADDRESS: (If different from above) | 8H. ZIP CODE: | 8I. MEDICAL RECORD NO:

FATHER

9A. NAME: FIRST — MIDDLE — LAST | 9B. AGE: | 9C. CITY AND STATE OF BIRTH: (Country if not U.S.A.) | 9D. SOCIAL SECURITY NUMBER:

10A. NAME OF INFORMANT FIRST MIDDLE LAST | 10B RELATION TO INFANT

CONFIDENTIAL INFORMATION
SEE INSTRUCTION SHEET FOR COMPLETION SHEET OF THIS SECTION

FATHER

12. RACE: (Black, White, etc.) | 13. HISPANIC ORIGIN?: (If yes, specify) NO ☐ YES ☐ | 14. EDUCATION: (Check highest grade completed) 0-11 ☐1 12 ☐2 13-15 ☐3 16 ☐4 17+ ☐5

15A. USUAL OCCUPATION: | 15B. KIND OF BUSINESS OR INDUSTRY: | 15C. NAME AND LOCALITY OF COMPANY OR FIRM:

MOTHER

16. RACE: (Black, White, etc.) | 17. HISPANIC ORIGIN? (If yes, specify) NO ☐ YES ☐ | 18. EDUCATION: (Check highest grade completed) 0-11 ☐1 12 ☐2 13-15 ☐3 16 ☐4 17+ ☐5 | 19. DATE LAST NORMAL MENSES BEGAN: MONTH DAY YEAR

20A. MOST RECENT OCCUPATION: | 20B. KIND OF BUSINESS OR INDUSTRY: | 20C. NAME AND LOCALITY OF COMPANY OR FIRM: | 20D. EMPLOYED DURING THIS PREGNANCY? NO ☐0 YES ☐1

21A. MONTH IN WHICH PRENATAL BEGAN: NONE ☐0 1ST ☐1 2ND ☐2 3RD ☐3 4TH ☐4 5TH ☐5 6TH ☐6 7TH ☐7 8TH ☐8 9TH ☐9 | 21B. TOTAL NUMBER OF PRENATAL VISITS: NONE OR NUMBER | 21C. PROVIDER: PRVT PHYS ☐0 HOSP ☐1 MIC ☐2 OTHER ☐3 | 22. TOTAL NUMBER OF PREVIOUS PREGNANCIES: NONE OR NUMBER | 23. SEROLOGICAL TEST FOR SYPHILIS: MONTH DAY YEAR OR REASON IF NONE

24A. PREVIOUS LIVE BIRTHS: NOW LIVING: NONE NUMBER / NOW DEAD: NONE NUMBER | 24B. PREVIOUS SPONTANEOUS ABORTIONS: Less than 20 wks: NONE NUMBER / 20 wks or more: NONE NUMBER | 24C. PREVIOUS INDUCED ABORTIONS: NONE NUMBER | 24D. DATE OF FIRST LIVE BIRTH: MONTH YEAR | 24E. DATE OF LAST LIVE BIRTH: MONTH YEAR | 24F. DATE OF LAST OTHER TERMINATION: MONTH YEAR

25. PRIMARY FINANCIAL COVERAGE THIS BIRTH: MEDICAID ☐1 HMO ☐2 OTHER PRIVATE INSURANCE ☐3 SELF PAY ☐4 | 26. DID MOTHER PARTICIPATE IN ANY FOLLOWING PROGRAMS DURING THIS PREGNANCY? (Check all that apply) WIC ☐1 SNAP ☐2 PCNP ☐3 AFDC ☐4 OTHER (Specify) ☐5

27A. WAS HOSPITAL OF THIS DELIVERY A PRELABOR REFERRAL FOR HIGH RISK? NO ☐0 YES ☐1 | 27B. WAS MOTHER TRANSFERRED FROM ANOTHER FACILITY? (If yes, specify facility name, city and state)

INFANT

28. BIRTHWEIGHT: (LBS. & OUNCES) OR (GRAMS) | 29. CLINICAL ESTIMATE OF GESTATION: ___ wks | 30. APGAR SCORE: 1 MINUTE 5 MINUTES | 31. INFANT TRANSFERRED TO ANOTHER HOSPITAL? (If yes, specify hospital name, city and state) NO ☐ YES ☐

32. DID INFANT RECEIVE NEONATAL INTENSIVE CARE? NO ☐0 YES ☐1 | 33. CONGENITAL MALFORMATIONS: (Specify each type) NONE ☐ | 34. PREVENTIVE TREATMENT FOR CONJUNCTIVITIS? NO ☐0 YES ☐1

35. OTHER ABNORMAL CONDITIONS OF THE NEWBORN: (Check all that apply) NONE ☐ BIRTH INJURY ☐ ANEMIA ☐ RDS ☐ ASSISTED VENTILATION INTUBATION ☐ OTHER ☐ SEIZURES ☐ OTHER (Specify) | 36. AT THE TIME OF THIS REPORT WAS THE INFANT ALIVE ☐0 DEAD ☐1

MEDICAL

37. OBSTETRIC PROCEDURES: (Check all that apply) NONE ☐ ULTRASOUND ☐ STRESS TEST ☐ NONSTRESS TEST ☐ AMNIOCENTESIS GENETIC ☐ MATURITY ☐ ELECTRONIC MONITORING INTERNAL ☐ EXTERNAL ☐ INDUCTION ☐ STIMULATION ☐ TOCOLYSIS ☐ OTHER (Specify)

38A. MEDICAL RISK FACTORS THIS PREGNANCY: (Check all that apply) NONE ☐ ECLAMPSIA ☐ ANEMIA ☐ DIABETES ☐ RH SENSITIZED ☐ UTERINE BLEEDING ☐ VIRAL DISEASE ☐ DISEASES OF THE HEART LUNG KIDNEY ☐ CHRONIC HYPERTENSION ☐ HYPERTENSION PREGNANCY RELATED ☐ PREVIOUS LBWT INFANT ☐ OTHER (Specify)

38B. OTHER RISK FACTORS THIS PREGNANCY: SMOKING NO ☐0 YES ☐1 ALCOHOL NO ☐0 YES ☐1 DRUG USAGE NO ☐0 YES ☐1 | 38C. PREPREGNANCY WEIGHT: | 38D. WEIGHT GAIN DURING PREGNANCY: | 39A. PRIOR C-SECTION? NO ☐0 YES ☐1 | 39B. METHOD OF DELIVERY: VAGINAL ☐ VAGINAL CESAREAN ☐ VAGINAL BREECH ☐ FORCEPS MID LOW ☐ VACUUM ☐ OTHER (Specify)

39C. IF C-SECTION, SPECIFY INDICATION: | 40. ANALGESIA? NO ☐0 YES ☐1 | 41. ANESTHESIA? (If yes, specify type) NO ☐0 YES ☐1 | 42. OTHER PROCEDURES PERFORMED? (If yes, specify) NO ☐0 YES ☐1

43. COMPLICATIONS OF LABOR AND DELIVERY: (Check all that apply) NONE ☐ PREMATURE RUPTURE OF MEMBRANES ☐ ABRUPTIO PLACENTA ☐ PLACENTA PREVIA ☐ OTHER HEMORRHAGE ☐ MECONIUM STAINING ☐ PROLAPSE OF CORD ☐ CONDITIONS OF CORD ☐ NONVERTEX PRESENTATION ☐ PRECIPITOUS LABOR ☐

PROLONGED LABOR ☐ FAILURE TO PROGRESS ☐ ANESTHETIC COMPLICATIONS ☐ RETAINED PLACENTA ☐ SEIZURES ☐ FETAL DISTRESS ☐ FEBRILE ☐ OTHER (Specify) ☐

MOTHER'S RESIDENCE

Residence is the city, town, or incorporated village where the mother has set up housekeeping.
Residence information should be reported in items 8A and 8F.
Residence is not necessarily the same as mailing address.
Mailing address, if different from residence address, should be reported in items 8G and 8H.

RACE AND HISPANIC ORIGIN

Responses to the items on race and Hispanic origin should be handled separately. Do not infer one from the other. Each item should be based on self identification, i.e., what the mother and father consider themselves to be.

Source: New York State Department of Health, Albany, 1988.

of vague delegations is that public administrators, as a group, become influential in policy making. They are consulted by committees and subcommittees in Congress, by officials in the Executive Office of the President, and by the politically appointed department heads and their staffs. Moreover, despite the denunciations of "bureaucratic power" at election times, political officials often acknowledge the legitimacy of including agency administrators in the policy-making process.

Public Policy Making

Public administrators are even more influential when it comes to choosing the means through which public policies will be implemented. The choice of means and the pace and regularity of enforcement can be as much a policy-making exercise as the choice of ends. In many cases, universal enforcement is precluded by inadequate resources. Consequently, selective enforcement and nonenforcement are common. Where selective enforcement manifests a pattern—aimed at large firms rather than small ones, for example, or poorer neighborhoods rather than richer areas—administrative decisions have clear political consequences because they determine the distribution of benefits and/ or burdens created by public policies. Alleged racial profiling by police and other enforcement agencies is an example that has attracted a good deal of attention in recent years.[14]

Public administrative authority in the United States is also evidenced in the volume of rule making and adjudication by administrative agencies, which far exceeds the volume of legislation passed by the nation's legislatures and noncriminal matters decided by its courts. Public administrative agencies are also a main source of ideas for new legislation. The power of individual agencies and officials varies with a variety of factors, a topic generally called **bureaucratic politics.** But, overall, administrative influence has developed to such an extent that it has had a major impact on the nature of the other branches of government. The rise of the administrative state was perhaps the most important governmental development of the 20th century: it transformed the nature of the political system.

◆→ RESPONSES TO THE RISE OF THE ADMINISTRATIVE STATE

Over the long run, a successful public administrator must have a deep understanding of the environment in which he or she operates. That environment includes many actors and the managerial, political, and legalistic approaches and values discussed in the first chapter. Among the leading actors are elected chief executives, legislatures, courts, interest groups, and the public at large. In some jurisdictions where there are a large number of elected and/or politically appointed administrative officials, political parties are important as well. Depending on their strength, public employee unions and contractors and their associations may also be significant actors. The successful practitioner of public administration may come to develop a feel for the way these actors influence public administration, for their values and objectives. In this section we will explain how the president, Congress, the federal judiciary, interest groups, the public, and, to a lesser extent, political parties have responded to the rise of the administrative state. Related developments at the state and local levels are summarized at the end of the chapter under "State and Local Governments."

The President and Public Administration

The Mythical Presidency

The office of the president of the United States is surrounded by so much myth that it is sometimes difficult to begin to figure out what really goes on in the White House, much less in the president's mind. For some reason—a psychological need for a mythical hero figure, perhaps—Americans have built up the image of the president in a way that does not correspond to reality. It has been claimed that "the President of the United States of America is, without question, the most powerful elected executive in the world"[15] and "there is virtually no limit to what the President can do if he does it for democratic ends and by democratic means."[16] But the experience of recent presidents has often been characterized by an inability to achieve their stated goals and deliver on their promises to the public. More to the point, why have many modern presidents come into office promising that they could do something constructive to control "the bureaucracy," only to leave office with questionable accomplishments and a sense of defeat?

President Jimmy Carter managed to introduce major reforms in the federal personnel system but eventually admitted that he was unable to overcome the entrenched force of the federal bureaucracy. Carter hardly mentions civil service reform in his memoirs, *Keeping Faith*. Despite President Ronald Reagan's vows to cut the federal bureaucracy's size, toward the end of his second term the budget deficit was larger than ever and, although some agencies had been shrunk, overall levels of federal employment were higher than when he took office. Not only were no federal departments eliminated during Reagan's presidency, the Department of Veterans Affairs was created. Perhaps even more telling, government spending continued to rise as a proportion of the gross domestic product (GDP). President George H. W. Bush, a man with much Washington experience, avoided challenging federal administration head on. But he did vow to cut the budget deficit, which nevertheless continued to grow.

The Clinton administration's NPR promised major reforms and an overall culture change in federal administration. By most accounts, it had a very ambitious agenda that met with limited success, though perhaps more than many had initially predicted. By its close in 2001, the NPR had reported the following achievements: reduction of the full-time civilian federal workforce by 426,000 positions, including 78,000 managerial slots; savings of nearly $137 billion; the elimination of 16,000 pages from the government's regulatory rule book, the *Code of Federal Regulations,* as well as deletion of 640,000 pages of internal agency regulations and conversion of 31,000 pages from "legalese" to plain English; the closure of 2,000 "obsolete field offices"; termination of 250 "useless" administrative units; and a cultural shift toward "an environment where federal employees think differently about their jobs and who their customers are."[17] However, critics contend that as federal employment shrank, the number of people employed on federal contracts grew and that the claimed cost savings included activities that were only peripheral to the NPR, such as military base closings.[18]

During the 2000 election campaign, George W. Bush charged that "[t]he General Accounting Office looked into some of these claims of big savings. Of those reviewed by the GAO, two-thirds had no evidence to back them up."[19] Only 35 percent of all federal employees thought the NPR was a priority in their agencies.[20] In all probability, somewhat less than half of its several hundred action items were implemented.[21] Perhaps most telling, a survey of federal employees in 2000 found that only 36 percent rated federal government reinvention favorably, though some aspects of it, such as customer service, fared much better (71 percent favorable rating).[22] Another survey in 2001 found that more federal employees thought reinvention had made their jobs harder (49 percent) than easier (42 percent).[23] The NPR's downsizing figures excluded the Postal Service, which added about 100,000 jobs. Anecdotal information suggests that the highly celebrated formal demise of the *Federal Personnel Manual* did not prevent agency field offices from continuing to use it because they lacked the capacity or will to develop new human resources management procedures on their own.

Like so many of his recent predecessors, President George W. Bush came into office favoring administrative downsizing and the cost-effective pursuit of results. He also sought to strengthen presidential control of federal administration by asserting unilateral executive powers. However, downsizing was a casualty of the events of September 11, 2001, as the Transportation Security Administration was created and other agencies were beefed up to deal with the threat of terrorism. Ironically, the quest for homeland security also showed the very real limits of presidential authority over administration.

Initially, Bush established the Office of Homeland Security (OHS) within the White House Office. It relied on existing budget and presidential legal authority, having no independent statutory powers or congressional appropriation of its own. This arrangement gave Bush great flexibility in trying to manage homeland security but almost immediately proved untenable. Coordination presented insuperable problems because the government's budget for homeland security was scattered over 2,000 separate accounts.[24] Congressional opposition to the lack of legislative input on homeland security mounted, particularly as OHS Director Tom Ridge refused to testify before Congress on the grounds that he was "a security advisor to the president, rather than a Cabinet member" and "didn't have authority over any federal agency . . . [or] spending."[25] In 2002, Bush had little choice but to support the replacement of OHS with a Department of Homeland Security, whose powers and funding, like those of other departments, are based on statute, whose secretary is subject to senatorial approval, and which is subject to congressional oversight.

President Obama's approach to management continues the theme of adopting best practices, especially those focused on leveraging information technologies, throughout the federal government to reduce costs and improve effectiveness. The President's Management Council (PMC), initially established under President Clinton in 1993, is the tool President Obama has used to pursue reform initiatives in his administration. The PMC's purpose is to provide performance and management leadership throughout the Executive Branch and to assist the president in government reforms. There are three initiatives that the PMC is pursuing under President Obama: 1) Executive Order 13538 created the *President's Management Advisory Board*, which is a group of private sector CEOs appointed by the president to recommend strategies for implementing business practices that can improve Federal Government management and productivity. 2) *Cross-cutting improvement initiatives*, which are focused on identifying and adopting best practices to streamline policy development and cost savings initiatives that can be employed across federal agencies. 3) *Collaboration streamlining*, which is focused on developing and adopting interagency collaboration technologies (http://gsa.gov/portal/content/133811; accessed August 22, 2012).

The gap between the imaginary presidency and the real powers and influence available to the president is vast. Virtually all presidential administrations since the days of Franklin D. Roosevelt (1933–1945) have noted how difficult it is for presidents to get things done. As former Vice President Richard Cheney, who was previously chief of staff in the Ford administration and subsequently secretary of defense under George H. W. Bush, commented on the same phenomenon:

> There's a tendency before you get to the White House or when you're just observing it from outside to say, "Gee, that's a powerful position that person has." The fact of the matter is that while you're here trying to do things, you are far more aware of the constraints than you are of the power. You spend most of your time trying to overcome obstacles getting what the President wants done.[26]

President Carter, never a friend of bureaucracy, once exclaimed, "I can't even get a damn mouse out of my office," after its removal was delayed by a jurisdictional dispute between the Department of the Interior (White House grounds) and the General Services Administration (White House building)!

Limits to Presidential Authority

Clearly, the president has significant independent authority in dealing with foreign nations and as commander in chief. But in domestic affairs presidential powers over public administration are particularly limited. It is customary to view the president as the chief executive, but almost all of his powers over the executive branch are shared with Congress and the courts. The presidential appointment of principal officers is shared with the Senate. Dismissals, even of some presidential appointments such as the chair of the Federal Trade Commission, have been constrained by constitutional and statutory law.[27] Funding for agencies and salaries must be authorized by Congress. Likewise, agencies must be created by law or pursuant to a congressional delegation of power to the president. In either case, their creation requires at least the tacit approval of the legislature. Agency missions are rarely if ever established or significantly formally modified by the president alone. The federal personnel system is based on statute and consequently requires congressional involvement. Collective bargaining arrangements also place constraints on what the president can do in managing people in the executive branch. Presidential executive orders are subject to challenge in the federal courts. They may not be legally binding on the independent regulatory commissions.[28] Nor can presidents refuse to spend money allocated by Congress without congressional approval. During the Reagan, Bush I, Clinton, the first two years of the Bush II administrations, and the final two years of Obama's first term as well as his second term, the problem of presidential control of administration was complicated by "divided government"; that is, the White House and one or both houses of Congress were controlled by different political parties.

Tools of Presidential Management

What are these presidential powers of which so many have so long been in awe? Some would point to the president's duty to faithfully execute the laws. Yet this and other significant powers are shared with the legislature and the courts—and that presents the crux of the president's problem in relation to large-scale federal public administration. Stated concisely, the president is held responsible and accountable for the performance of the executive branch but in terms of domestic administration does not have the constitutional powers necessary to control its performance. This has led presidents to augment their constitutional authority with "tools" for better management.

Executive Office of the President (EOP). The **Executive Office of the President (EOP)**, created in 1939, is one of the more formidable of these managerial tools—a veritable tool kit, really. It was originally designed to be relatively small. It was intended to strengthen the president's ability to provide executive branch agencies with policy direction and to control their budgets. The EOP has since grown substantially and taken on something of a life of its own. The Fiscal Year 2013 budget is projected to be over $710 million, employing over 1,800 full-time equivalent employees—no small staff agency! Today its main units are the following:

1. The *White House Office* provides staff and managerial assistance to the president. Basically it serves to coordinate the activities of the executive branch, enable the president to exert greater influence over administration, generate ideas for solutions to pressing problems, and deal with outsiders such as Congress, interest groups, and the media. The White House Office has grown from 45 full-time employees in 1939 to over 400 under recent presidents.

2. The *Office of Management and Budget* (OMB) was discussed earlier. Created in 1970, it encompassed the old Bureau of the Budget, established in 1921, as an independent unit within the Treasury Department and moved to the EOP in 1939. OMB has been a powerful voice in dealing with executive branch agencies and has provided the presidential office with a strong tool for coordinating budgets and policy. It has sometimes been used to blunt congressional influence on agencies and administrative processes. According to its own information, OMB has housed more than 500 employees in recent years.

3. The *Office of National Drug Control Policy* (ONDCP) was established by the Anti-Drug Abuse Act of 1988. ONDCP produces the annual National Drug Control Strategy, which outlines how the Administration plans to reduce the manufacturing, trafficking, and use of illicit drugs and drug-related crime and violence.

4. The *National Security Council* (NSC) was established in 1947. The NSC advises the president on the integration of domestic, foreign, and military policies as they relate to national security. The NSC has sometimes been a competitor of the Departments of State and Defense in defining policy.

When viewed in organizational terms, these four units can be seen as "superagencies" intended to make it possible to run a great deal of the executive branch directly out of the presidential office. The OMB deals with policy coordination, budgets, economic matters, and management. The National Security Council deals with foreign affairs. Several additional units focus on housekeeping, economic, and domestic policy matters. The operations of the OMB, the NSC, and these specialized units are coordinated by the White House Office, which controls access to the president. The Executive Office of the President is intended to serve as a presidential tool for management and policy making in the executive branch.

From the administrative side, the EOP increases the number of actors to whom attention must be paid. No longer does the chain of command reach from the president to the career public administrators through the politically appointed agency heads and their assistants. Rather, the agency heads are for the most part responsible and subordinate to people in the EOP. Most lack direct access to the president, but rather must go through functionaries in the White House Office.

This arrangement *might* enable presidents to gain authority more commensurate with their responsibilities. The president has great freedom to make appointments to the White House Office, because these functionaries do not require senatorial approval. Many of the operations of the Executive Office of the President can be cloaked in the secrecy afforded by the principle of executive privilege, which limits congressional inquiry into its affairs. But in practice the EOP has not wholly solved the presidential dilemma, primarily because it has grown too large to serve, in any simple sense, as a direct arm of the president or be under the president's direct, personal control.

Political Appointments. Political executives—that is, department and agency heads, assistant secretaries, and other political appointees to executive agencies and independent regulatory commissions—are a means of bringing presidential policy direction to federal administration. The president appoints more than 700 political executives to positions in the Executive Office and executive branch agencies. These include the cabinet members and about 20 other individuals in each of the departments as well as appointees in the independent agencies, including their heads. Additionally, more than 2,100 political appointees are scattered throughout the upper and middle levels of the executive branch. About 720 of these political appointees are in the noncareer ranks of the Senior Executive Service (SES) at the top of federal service, and more than 1,400 are in **Schedule C** slots in the middle levels.[29]

Traditionally, political executives and appointees have had a dual allegiance. On the one hand, they are presidential appointments and consequently are expected to be loyal to the chief executive. On the other hand, political executives must be able to work with the top-ranking career staffs of the agencies to which they are assigned. This job is complicated by the likelihood that a typical political executive will not serve throughout the president's four-year term. Consequently, political executives often depend considerably on the expertise of the career staffs to achieve policy objectives. A politically appointed secretary not only represents the president's will to the agency but must also represent the agency to the president. That most political executives no longer enjoy direct access to the president complicates their jobs considerably.

Part of the difficulty in using political appointees to steer and coordinate the president's initiatives is that the layers of positions in the appointed hierarchy have grown over the years. In 1960, there were 17 layers, but the number had reached 32 by 1995.[30] They include not only the easily recognized titles of "secretary" and "deputy secretary" but also those of "principal associate deputy undersecretary" and "deputy associate deputy assistant secretary." According to Paul Light, who has closely studied layering, "As this sediment has thickened over the decades, presidents have grown increasingly distant from their front lines of government, and the front lines from them."[31] Light concludes that this "thickening" process "distorts front-line requests for help upward and policy clarity downward"[32]—precisely a condition that administrative managers and leaders would ordinarily hope to avoid.

Political appointees cannot automatically or easily steer federal administration for the president. However, some recent presidents have been more effective than others. The Reagan administration is generally credited with excelling in the use of political executives. The following were among Reagan's strategies.

1. "[T]he appointment to top government positions of men and women who share my economic philosophy. We will have an administration in which the word from the top isn't lost or hidden in the bureaucracy."[33]

2. Appointees who would be "the managers of the national administration—not the captives of the bureaucracy or the special interests they are supposed to direct."[34]
3. A willingness to appoint individuals opposed to the programs being managed by the agencies to which they were appointed, as in the Departments of Labor and Housing and Urban Development; the Commission on Civil Rights; the Equal Employment Opportunity Commission; and, in the early 1980s, the Environmental Protection Agency.
4. Considerable care in making appointments to political positions in the SES and to Schedule C.

The Reagan appointees' overall success may have come partly at the price of maintaining good relationships with career Senior Executive Servants. Box 2.6 indicates that former SES members were not inclined to view the appointees as having good leadership qualities or management skills. They also tended to think the appointees failed to support merit principles or bring valuable experience to the job. Noncareer executives were much more positive in their evaluations.

The Bush I administration followed the Reagan strategies but was less ideological in making appointments.[35] The Clinton administration adopted a novel approach for integrating the work of political executives with the missions of their agencies. In keeping with the results orientation of the NPM, the NPR called on the president to "craft agreements with cabinet secretaries and agency heads to focus on the administration's strategy and policy objectives. These agreements should not 'micro-manage' the work of the agency heads.

2.6   CAREER AND NONCAREER FORMER SENIOR EXECUTIVE SERVANTS' EVALUATIONS OF NONCAREER EXECUTIVES

Item	Percent Agreeing/Disagreeing	
	Career	*Noncareer*
Noncareer executives:		
• *Bring valuable experience to the job*	25/42	62/12
• *Have good leadership qualities*	18/41	54/17
• *Have good management skills*	15/44	39/17
• *View job as opportunity to make long-term improvements in government*	27/42	70/17
• *Support merit principles*	15/45	46/20

Source: U.S. Merit Systems Protection Board, *The Senior Executive Service* (Washington, DC: MSPB, 1989), 20.

They do not row the boat. They should set a course."[36] The agreements were intended to include quantitative performance measures as well as clear objectives. However, the performance agreements never received a fair test. After the 1994 elections put the Republicans in control of both houses of Congress, the administration became increasingly engulfed in struggles over budgets, policies, programs, performance, a variety of matters involving ethical questions, and ultimately Clinton's impeachment.

Formal Coordination Instruments. The George W. Bush Administration adopted a centralized approach to controlling federal administration. Policy decisions tended to be made in the White House and communicated downward to the political executives, who were expected to enforce them with unbending loyalty to the president. Bush II also used executive orders to exert presidential authority and relied on claims of **executive privilege** to block congressional oversight of the administration's top-level policy making.[37] In efforts to improve management, the Bush II administration introduced "scorecards" and a Program Assessment Rating Tool (PART).[38] Scorecard ratings are analogous to traffic lights, with green, yellow, and red "lights" being awarded to agencies based on their personnel management, financial management, pursuit of electronic government (e-gov), efforts to link budgets to performance, and outsourcing of decisions. PART specifically looks at the achievement of goals, efficiency, and managerial systems (such as finance) in an effort to link agencies' performance to their budgets. The administration also called for enactment of a Freedom to Manage Act, which would have required Congress to respond to presidential proposals for administrative reforms and innovations on a fast track basis.[39]

Several additional presidential tools bear mention. The president can often block administrative actions sought by Congress and/or agencies. The OMB and political executives can be especially adroit at getting agencies to do less—that is, initiate fewer regulations and enforcement actions. The president can also use the veto power to block legislative initiatives for administrative change or action and can try to block agencies from using funds for purposes to which the president is opposed through impoundments (see Chapter 6 on budgeting). However, these tools are crude and subject to congressional override. The line-item veto, which is available to many state governors but not to the president, offers a more finely honed instrument for vetoing legislative efforts to fund agencies and programs at levels above those desired by the chief executive. Finally, under various statutes enacted since 1939, the president has sometimes had considerable power to initiate extensive agency and departmental reorganizations, subject ultimately to congressional assent.

Many observers view these tools as inadequate. They believe the president needs more control over federal agencies and a greater ability to coordinate their activities. Beyond the adequacy of these tools and the ability of the president to coordinate activities, Phillip J. Cooper[40] argues that there is a more fundamental problem facing the Obama and future Administrations; a capacity crisis. With over 50 percent of the federal workforce eligible to retire in 2015, and inadequate plans in place to recruit new employees, federal agencies will be unable to meet their statutory obligations to faithfully execute the laws of the United States. Those imbued with a managerial perspective also tend to argue that Congress should reduce its involvement in administrative decision making. The NPR and others contended that biennial (instead of annual) budgeting and a drastic reduction in congressional reporting requirements would give the agencies more time to focus on achieving their statutory and policy objectives.

Congress and the Administrative State

The response of legislatures to the rise of the contemporary administrative state has been complex and uneven. Their problem is not a lack of adequate constitutional or legal authority to control the actions of public administrative agencies. Rather, the problem is one of technical ability to exercise oversight (review) of public administrators and the political interest or will to do so. The U.S. Congress presents an excellent and well-researched example of how the growth of public administration affects the operation of legislatures.

During the New Deal and World War II, Congress delegated a great deal of its legislative authority to federal agencies in an effort to stem the deep and prolonged economic and military crises confronting the nation. By the end of the war, the executive branch had grown so large and powerful that several legislative leaders publicly wondered whether Congress could maintain "its constitutional place in the federal scheme," if it would "survive the next twenty years," and even whether it was "necessary."[41] In 1946, after considerable thought and debate, Congress developed a multipronged institutional response to the administrative state that has served as a platform for an expansive legislative role in federal administration.[42]

First, Congress reluctantly agreed that the complexity of public policy would increasingly require it to delegate legislative authority to the agencies. In effect, administrators would legislate by making rules and adjudicating legal standards, such as what constitutes an unfair labor practice. However, unlike past practice, Congress would now specify the procedures agencies must use when exercising its legislative authority. This was initially accomplished through the Administrative Procedure Act of 1946 (APA). As mentioned, the act regulates agency rule making, adjudication, enforcement, and transparency. The key idea was that when agencies serve as extensions of Congress for performing legislative functions, they should be made to adhere to legislative values.

Second, Congress would enhance its capacity to oversee or supervise the agencies. This was one of the core purposes of the Legislative Reorganization Act of 1946, which simplified and modernized the congressional committee system. The objective was to give the standing committees in the Senate and House of Representatives coordinate jurisdictions and to organize the entire committee system so that it more or less paralleled the structure of the departments and agencies. For example, both chambers had committees on agriculture, banking and currency, international relations, labor, commerce, and public lands. Most important, the standing committees were charged with exercising "continuous watchfulness" over the agencies under their jurisdictions. In 1970, this mandate was enlarged to require the committees to "review and study" the agencies on a continuing basis.

Third, Congress took steps to professionalize and increase the committees' staff. These staffers aid in drafting legislation, assist the members of Congress during committee hearings, and engage in the oversight of administrative agencies. Although committee staff hold no formal tenure, many of them remain in office for long periods and develop strong working relationships with top-level career administrators in the agencies. Committee staff often write the reports that accompany bills, which can provide useful guidance for administrators seeking to understand the legislature's intent.

In 1946, members of Congress anticipated that the committee staff would work "in close contact with executive agencies."[43] The most comprehensive study of congressional oversight of administrative operations concludes that by the 1990s, the staff were key participants in an "impressive" system of oversight that corrects errors, involving an "often aggressively operated intelligence system" and frequent activity that probably improves public policy.[44]

Congress also sought to improve its personal staffing arrangements in 1946, though significant changes came somewhat later. Personal staff are attached to the individual members and can be organized and used at their discretion. In practice, most members of Congress organize them according to similar functions, including administrative assistance, legislative assistance, and clerical. Personal staff assist the members in developing legislation, responding to constituents, and engaging in oversight. From the standpoint of federal administration, personal staff are most important in providing "constituency service" or "casework." This often involves helping constituents who have some sort of problem with a federal agency or with filling out forms for federal grants and benefits. In 1946, there was apparently no standard term for it. One representative called it acting as a "personal representative" or "Washington Representative."[45] However, today it is treated as a legitimate institutional role by everyone involved: the public, the legislators, and the agencies.

After 1946, Congress strengthened this institutional response in a variety of ways. The APA has been amended and augmented to ensure that federal administration is more transparent, representative, and participatory, as well as sensitive to the paperwork burdens it thrusts on the society and the special concerns of small businesses. The overall number and capability of congressional staff have increased dramatically over time. Even after the substantial staff cuts of the mid-1990s, total committee staff numbered 2,492 in 2000, while the personal staffs of members of Congress stood at about 11,700. Two-thirds of all staff are housed in the House. In addition, the leadership has another approximately 275 staffers on the payroll. And Congress itself employs nearly 5,100 persons as "housekeeping," grounds keepers, and Capitol police, among other duties.[46] In 1970, the former Legislative Reference Service was transformed into a much stronger Congressional Research Service, which serves as Congress's think tank. Congress dramatically improved its capacity to deal with the federal budget by creating the Congressional Budget Office in 1974. The Government Accountability Office has been substantially upgraded over the years and is now heavily involved in evaluating administrative programs and performance. Together, the staffs of the Congressional Research Service, Congressional Budget Office, and Government Accountability Office number about 4,500.

Casework and pork barrel have emerged as major congressional activities and are widely viewed as important keys to continued incumbency. The members of Congress handle tens of thousands of cases each year. They advertise their willingness and ability to engage in this function. The proportion of personal staff assigned to the home district has grown partly in accordance with a desire to provide more and better casework. Casework is important to a member's effort to be reelected because it provides favors that may presumably be repaid with votes. For example, when a member of Congress helps someone receive Social Security benefits, he or she is likely to win at least one vote—perhaps more, depending on the recipient's family and circle of friends and acquaintances. (See Box 2.7 for examples of Congressmen and women's commitments to casework.)

There is little doubt that the main purpose of casework is to provide a valuable service to constituents. However, it also enables the members of Congress and their personal staff to learn more about how the agencies operate. Sometimes it reveals such serious maladministration that Congress feels a need to change an agency's fundamentals, including its leadership, authority, processes, and organizational structure. For instance, a good case can be made for the proposition that casework played a substantial role in prompting Congress to enact the far-reaching Internal Revenue Service Restructuring and Reform Act of 1998.[47]

Pork-barrel legislation, which involves bringing special projects to the legislator's home district, has been a staple of American politics at least since the rivers and harbors legislation of 1824. However, its scope and scale have increased dramatically, and it is now keenly perceived by members of Congress as a key to reelection. Federal funds come in a variety of shapes and sizes for infrastructure, federal office buildings, military installations, contracts, and research grants. It was no surprise that in 1993 the first choice of a majority of the 110 new members in the House was a seat on the Public Works and Transportation Committee. The desire was bipartisan—29 Democratic and 27 Republican first-termers sought a seat on the 63-member committee. When one new member was asked whether critics might label his pet projects "pork," he replied, "There ain't much beef up here."[48] Even the intense concern with budget deficits and the cost of government at the time failed to dampen the members' ardor for pork. The 1998 Transportation Equity Act for the Twenty-first Century is considered perhaps the best example "of a pork-laden bill . . . ever passed."[49] The act is more than 400 pages long and authorized projects totaling $218 billion over six years. One member said it

2.7   A CONGRESSMAN'S "DEAR POSTAL PATRON" LETTER

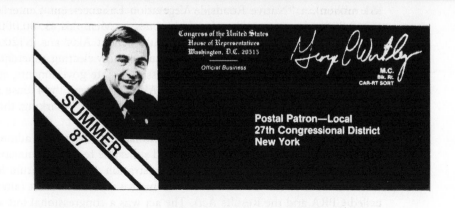

Congress of the United States
House of Representatives
Washington, D.C. 20515

Official Business

George C. Wortley
M.C.
Blk. Rt.
CAR-RT SORT

SUMMER 87

Postal Patron—Local
27th Congressional District
New York

Need Assistance? Have an Opinion? I'm Eager to Listen and Help

Besides voting in Congress, one of my most important responsibilities is to help constituents solve problems that they encounter with any federal agency. . . .

Whenever you, members of your family, or friends have an opinion on any legislative issue or federal policy or program, please express your views in a letter to me and send it to my Washington office. I'll give it my personal attention.

Send your letter to:
Congressman George C. Wortley
229 Cannon House Office Building
Washington, D.C. 20515

Because my legislative duties require my presence in Washington on most weekdays throughout the year, the quickest way to get my help when experiencing any federal problem is to telephone, visit or write my district office in Syracuse. Should you experience a problem with the Internal Revenue Service, an undue delay in receiving a benefit check, or any difficulty with a federal agency, the members of my district staff are eager to try and solve your problems as quickly as possible.

Each member of my staff, in the 27th district and in Washington, is an authority in dealing with specific agencies. My staff helps constituents who encounter bureaucratic difficulties obtaining education grants, Social Security, pension and disability benefits. They help to resolve medicare, medicaid and workers' compensation claims. They provide advice to applicants seeking federal jobs, and assist veterans who are eligible for home loans and educational benefits. They help constituents in the military services to obtain emergency leaves and reassignments under certain hardship circumstances. Planning a visit to Washington? My staff can arrange White House and FBI tours. We fulfill requests for flags that have been flown over the U.S. Capitol as well as requests for federal documents. We also assist persons who seek small business loans and federal contracts.

If you live in Onondaga County and need assistance, please telephone or write my Syracuse district office. The telephone number is 423-5657. The office address is:

1269 Federal Building
Clinton Square
Syracuse, New York 13260

If you reside in Madison County, telephone 687-5027 or toll free, 1-800-462-8080. The address of my Madison County office is:

601 Lake Port Road
Chittenango, New York 13037

has "more pork than a Memphis barbecue." Among the items were bike paths in Rhode Island ($5.85 million), traffic signs to the Rays' stadium in Tampa ($1 million), a "Native Roadside Vegetation Enhancement Center" in Iowa ($760,000), the restoration of cobblestones in Memphis ($700,000), and a highway exclusively in Canada that would benefit Alaskans ($120 million). However, with the Tea Party movement successfully electing adherents to their small government philosophy to Congress and state governments, such pork barrel spending may be on the decline. Although, given the House and Senate's inability to pass legislation to end the practice of earmarking, this may be more of a change in rhetoric than practice.

These aspects of Congress's institutional response to the administrative state enhance its capacity to regulate and supervise federal administration. In 1993, its potential involvement in administration took a quantum leap with the enactment of the Government Performance and Results Act (alternatively called GPRA and the Results Act). The act was a congressional initiative that enjoyed presidential support for its promotion of results-oriented administration. It required agencies to formulate strategic plans with concrete goals and indicators, preferably quantitative, for assessing progress toward them.[50] A key provision specifically required the agencies to "consult with the Congress" when formulating their strategic plans. What one measures is often what one gets, so Congress sometimes insisted on being involved in the selection of performance indicators as well. GPRA also required agencies to submit annual performance reports to Congress and looked toward eventually basing budget decisions on administrative performance. The 1993 act was superseded by the Government Performance and Results Act Modernization Act of 2010. The act coordinates agency strategic planning with the presidential term of office and contains several provisions requiring agencies to consult with and report to congressional committees.

When one considers Congress's constitutional authority and its institutional response to the development of federal administration as a major power center, it is not unreasonable to ask "Whose bureaucracy is this, anyway?"[51] Nor to answer that Congress has at least joint custody over the executive branch.

The Courts: A Judicial Response to Modern Public Administration

The federal and state judiciaries have also reacted to the rise of public administrative power. It is common to find judges heavily involved in public administrative matters, such as equal opportunity in personnel administration and the management of prisons, public mental health facilities, and schools. Judges sometimes question public administrators' expertise and second-guess their decisions. To a large extent, **judicial activism** of this kind has been decried as inappropriate, undemocratic, a threat to federalism, and a breach of the separation of powers.[52] Yet it arises as a direct response to the growth of authority in the hands of public agencies.

One of the chief constitutional problems of the contemporary administrative state is that the separation of powers tends to collapse as more and more legislative and judicial activity takes place in public administrative agencies in the executive branch. In the abstract, to say that these agencies make rules, enforce their rules, and adjudicate challenges to their enforcement actions may hardly sound like a matter of grave constitutional concern. But when these powers are exercised over specific individuals or corporations, a sense of unfairness and injustice may occur. For example, suppose an agency makes rules for eligibility to receive welfare benefits, enforces them by holding predawn raids on the homes of recipients, and then decides its actions are reasonable and constitutional.[53] Or suppose a personnel agency refuses to hire a member of a minority group, who then challenges its personnel rules on the grounds that they are racially discriminatory, only to be told by the agency after it holds a hearing that the rules are valid and have been properly followed.[54] These "supposals" are based on actual cases, and when public administrators act as legislature, prosecutor, judge, and jury in ways that are harmful to individuals or businesses, the judiciary, often viewed as the constitutional guardian of individuals' rights, may find it difficult to sit idly by.

Yet, from the late 1930s until the 1950s, this is largely what the courts did.[55] The federal judiciary in particular was politically weakened by its opposition to the New Deal in the 1930s. After President Franklin D. Roosevelt threatened in 1937 to "pack" the Supreme Court with justices more favorable to his approaches, the judiciary as a whole began to ignore the genuine constitutional problems posed by the vesting of legislative and judicial authority in executive branch administrative agencies. By the 1950s, however, neither the power of public administrators over individual citizens nor the injustices they perpetrated could be ignored. For example, during the "Red scare" of the late 1940s and 1950s, there were cases of federal employees losing their jobs, accused of "disloyalty" for having been readers of the *New York Times,* favoring racial integration, believing in the desirability of sex before marriage, or having intelligent or clever friends.[56] Until the 1960s and 1970s, welfare recipients were subject to all manner of harassments, and anyone seeking an occupational license could seem to be almost completely at the mercy of petty administrative tyrants.

Since the 1950s, when the federal courts rekindled their interest in the actions of public administrators, the judiciary has responded to the rise of administrative power primarily in four ways. These have a great deal to do with the contemporary legal approach and legal constraints on public administration, and they also explain how the courts have become full-fledged partners in public administration.[57]

Strengthening and Articulating Constitutional Rights

The federal judiciary has "created" or had occasion to declare new constitutional rights for individuals as they come into contact with public administrators in some contexts, and it has strengthened individuals' rights in others.

The courts have provided individuals greater constitutional protections when assuming the role of public employee or that of client or customer of public administrative agencies. In both instances, the First Amendment, equal protection, and due process constitutional rights of the individual have been strengthened considerably. Prior to the 1950s, clients' and public employees' rights were governed by the constitutional doctrine of privilege, which had the effect of denying them protection against administrative infringements on the civil rights and liberties normally held by United States citizens. If they wanted a public sector job or a benefit such as public housing, they had to accept the conditions attached to it. Individuals can no longer be denied welfare benefits because they do not meet an extended residency test, nor can they be denied unemployment compensation because their religious beliefs preclude their acceptance of work on Saturdays. They are also often entitled to due process when benefits are being withdrawn or denied. Similarly, the right of public employees to speak out as citizens in nonpartisan fashion on matters of public concern has been upheld, as has their right to belong (or not belong) to associations, including political parties and labor unions. Public employees also enjoy extensive constitutional procedural protections when facing dismissals for causes that would seriously damage their reputations or future employability or infringe on a property interest, such as tenure, that they hold in their jobs. Contractors' rights parallel those of public employees in some respects.[58] The courts have also afforded greater protection to prisoners and to people confined to public mental health facilities. The latter now have a constitutional right to treatment or training.[59] Street-level administration has also been brought under some Fourth Amendment constitutional constraints.

Stricter Scrutiny of Administrative Decisions

Although this policy is somewhat haphazardly applied, the federal judiciary often requires public administrators to explain the basis of their policy-making decisions with great precision. From the late 1930s until the 1970s, the courts tended to pay great deference to the expertise of public administrators and rarely questioned their decisions on technical or policy matters. Since the early 1970s, however, the judiciary has frequently demanded that the substance of agency decisions be logical. For instance, the United States Supreme Court followed this approach in *FTC v. Sperry & Hutchinson* (1972), when it set aside an FTC decision on the grounds that the agency's reasoning was illogical—one could not rationally proceed from its premise to its conclusion. Other important cases in this line, often called the "hard look" approach, include *Citizens to Preserve Overton Park v. Volpe* (1971), *Motor Vehicle Manufacturers Association v. State Farm* (1983), and *Industrial Union Department, AFL-CIO v. American Petroleum Institute* (1980, discussed in Chapter 9).[60] The Court's rulings have not been one-sidedly against government agencies, however. The Supreme Court has decisively told the federal judiciary to grant agencies considerable flexibility in their choice of rule-making procedures, statutory interpretation, and enforcement decisions.[61]

Public Law Litigation or Remedial Law

In a far more complex development, the federal judiciary has altered the model of the traditional lawsuit in a fashion that makes it far easier for the courts to intervene in public administration. The new model is often called *public law litigation* or *remedial law*.[62] Familiar examples include public school desegregation and prison reform cases. Three major features of the remedial law model should be emphasized. First, it was developed by the courts as a means of intervening in administrative operations.

Second, remedial law enables the judiciary to become directly involved in public management. For instance, in decreeing that public mental health facilities and prisons be brought up to constitutional standards, federal judges have used their powers to provide equitable relief to specify such matters as staffing ratios, temperatures ranges, the placement of guards, and sanitation and anticrowding requirements.

Third, judicial involvement in public administration has budgetary ramifications. Consequently, the remedial law model enables judges to have an expanded impact on budgeting. For instance, in 1980, 48 percent of Boston's budgetary appropriations were "presided" over by federal and state judges seeking to reform aspects of public education, public housing, public personnel administration, jails, and care of the mentally retarded.[63]

The remedial law model of judicial review is a powerful tool for enabling the judiciary to assume direction of many aspects of public administration, where it is deemed warranted. In 1995, a *Washington Post* editorial approvingly explained "Why the Courts Are Running D.C."[64] Today, one could write a similar piece about "Why the Courts Have Been Running California's Prisons."[65] In the 1970s and 1980s, public administrators found themselves working with the judiciary in a way that was unheard of previously. As constitutional requirements continue to permeate public administrative practice, prisons, public mental health facilities, and administrative systems, the application of remedial law should become less common. However, remedial law will remain an important check on egregiously unconstitutional administrative operations.

Liability and Immunity

A final and equally dramatic aspect of the judiciary's response to the rise of the contemporary administrative state has been to drastically reduce public administrators' immunity from civil suits for money damages for breaches of individuals' constitutional rights. Traditionally, under American common law and with some broad general support from constitutional law, public administrators were absolutely immune from such suits, called **constitutional torts.** Under the doctrine of absolute immunity, a public administrator who abridged someone's constitutional rights, through racial discrimination, for instance, could not be sued for money damages by the injured individual. Or, as happens with some frequency, police, FBI, narcotics agents, and other law enforcement personnel might act in an overzealous manner, violating an individual's Fourth

Amendment rights against unreasonable searches and seizures. Under the doctrine of absolute immunity, however, there would be no effective recourse available to the injured party.

During the 1970s, the Supreme Court abandoned the prevailing approach of *absolute* immunity and substituted a *qualified* immunity. Although some public administrative actions—primarily those involving adjudicatory functions—still enjoy absolute immunity, today most public employees are potentially *personally* liable for any actions within the scope of their official duties that abridge the constitutional or federally protected legal rights of other individuals. In other words, a public administrator who unconstitutionally or illegally injures another person can be sued for damages, and if damages are awarded, the public administrator is personally responsible for the settlement. However, he or she may be indemnified by the agency or government employing him or her.

It is important to grasp the connection between the changing presumption from immunity to liability and the creation of new constitutional rights for individuals in relation to public administration, as discussed previously. The Supreme Court has flatly stated that the greater liability of public administrators is a means of assuring that those officials will scrupulously avoid violating individuals' constitutional rights.[66] The Court has sought to assure that when in doubt, public administrators will err on the side of protecting constitutional rights. This approach is contained in the current standard for determining the scope of qualified immunity: in plain language, a public administrator is likely to be personally liable if he or she violated clearly established constitutional or federal statutory rights of which a reasonable person would have been aware.[67]

The switch from a presumption of absolute immunity to a presumption of potential liability has placed many public administrators in difficult positions. Nobody likes to be sued or to pay damages out of his or her pocket. Many seek legal insurance. Some probably quit their jobs and sought private sector employment. Others have complained bitterly that this aspect of the judicial response to the administrative state has made their jobs almost impossible. They are afraid to take action and afraid to remain inactive. The problem is compounded by the sometimes severe economic plight of many agencies and political jurisdictions, coupled with the continuing requirement under federal law that they meet their obligations to various groups, whether schoolchildren, prisoners, mental patients, the handicapped, members of disadvantaged minority groups, or others.

The Supreme Court is not oblivious to the problems involved, but it remains committed to qualified immunity. Although the Court has held that state and federal agencies cannot be sued for money damages in federal court for their constitutional torts, public employees and officials at all governmental levels remain vulnerable to such suits and local governments may even be sued for failure to train their employees to protect individuals' constitutional rights.[68] Liability does not end with compensating the injured party. It can also involve punitive or exemplary damages intended to punish the public administrator involved and deter others from committing similar offenses.

At the federal level, indemnification is at the agencies' discretion. State and local arrangements vary. In rare cases, violations of constitutional rights can result in criminal prosecution.

A public administrator is potentially liable if he or she violates someone's constitutional rights. But constitutional rights, as they now exist, are not simply engraved in the Constitution. As former Supreme Court Justice Lewis Powell pointed out, constitutional law is "what the courts say it is."[69] At any given time, individual constitutional rights are a reflection of the judiciary's values and interpretation of constitutional history. Standards of individual civil rights and liberties, equal protection, and due process are forever undergoing change. Prior to 1954, legally mandated racial segregation in public schools was permissible, pupils could be expelled without any established or fair procedure, public employees could be fired for "wrong thoughts," mental patients and prisoners could be "warehoused" under incredibly harsh and brutal conditions, and citizens had little or no legal protection against public administrative action denying them various benefits or occupational licenses. Today, the picture is radically different as a result of newer judicial views of what the Constitution requires. The courts created the present standard of public administrators' liability to force public administrators to be responsive not only to declared constitutional law but also to constitutional values.

The absence of a specific precedent in the constitutional case law does not afford protection from liability today. The facts surrounding a public administrator's actions may not have previously arisen or been litigated. Or they may have been litigated at a time when the content of the constitutional law was clearly different. This does not mean that public administrators operate in an atmosphere of complete chaos, or that there are no standards of conduct. Public employees can be held liable if they clearly violate an articulated constitutional principle, or if the thrust of the evolving law provides "fair warning" that their conduct is unconstitutional.[70] The smart public administrator will not look only to the most recent case, but rather will consider how the next one—the one he or she may be involved in—is likely to be decided. To do this effectively, public administrators must have a broad understanding of constitutional values and contemporary judicial philosophies. Public administrators must now be responsive to the judiciary's values, and therefore, the judiciary gains greater ability to exercise influence over the activities of the administrative state.

The judicial response to the rise of the contemporary administrative state considerably strengthens the role of the courts in public administration. Public administrators find themselves working as partners with judges. They are under greater pressure to explain their decisions and actions to the courts. Knowledge of constitutional values, as expressed by the judiciary, becomes a positive job requirement for many public administrators. One cannot really manage public employees today without paying considerable attention to constitutional law. The same is true with regard to managing prisons and public housing and engaging in a variety of inspections, policing, and other regulatory functions.

Interest Groups

Organized interest groups have long been an important feature of American politics.[71] These organizations typically are established to represent the economic or social interests of a relatively well-defined group of people such as cotton farmers or sugar growers. There are literally thousands of such groups, representing everything from A (American Civil Liberties Union) to Z (zinc producers). A quick check of the Washington, DC, phone book yields examples of groups representing bankers, bikers, physicians' assistants, baseball fans, corn growers, ornithologists, nonsmokers, sugarbeet growers, association executives, and many others.

Traditionally, interest groups lobbied in the legislature in order to convince its members to sponsor or vote for a bill that would be of benefit to a group's members. Conversely, they might try to persuade a legislator to oppose a policy that might be harmful to their interests. However, lobbying is no longer confined to just the legislature. As the importance of rule making has increased in executive agencies, so has lobbying during the rule making process to shape how laws are implemented. Although much criticism has been levied at lobbyists, essentially they exercise First Amendment rights to freedom of speech and association and to petition the government for a redress of grievances. As long as bribery, excessive favor seeking, or other corruption does not take place, the activities of pressure groups can be viewed as valuable in informing policy makers of where important interests stand on any given matter. Despite much criticism of interest group politics, many Americans find such groups an efficient means for representing their points of view—more efficient in some cases than seeking to promote their policy objectives through electoral politics.

Advisory Committees

Naturally, as public administrators became more involved in agenda setting and policy formulation, interest group lobbying became more common in the executive branch. Nowadays, public administrators interact with representatives of more than 1,000 interest groups. Such contacts often take place in an institutional format involving meeting with formally established advisory committees. These groups are quasi-governmental and are sometimes considered a "fifth branch" of government. Through frequent meetings, they provide agencies with advice and perspectives regarding policy development, rule making, and program implementation. Many of the federal government's approximately 900 advisory committees focus on relatively narrow concerns, such as a particular technology, geographic place, crop, disease, chemical, or food. For instance, there are advisory committees on footwear leather, exported textiles, children's educational television, medical devices, small farms, automotive parts, and Maine Acadian culture preservation.

By 1972, the role of interest groups in pressing for their policy preferences was fully legitimized by the Federal Advisory Committee Act.

This statute started from the premise that such committees are a useful source of opinion and information. The purpose of the act was to improve the quality of interest group interaction with public administrative agencies by assuring that the lobbying process was representative. An important part of this act was the requirement that as a general rule the official meetings between advisory committees and public administrators be open to the public.

Congress's recognition that public administration should promote representativeness in its dealings with interest groups and, presumably, in its policy making is of considerable significance. Traditionally, representation was the function of legislative bodies such as the House of Representatives, not of executive branch agencies. This change captures the essence of the political approach to public administration that we discussed in the previous chapter. The lines between politics and administration become hopelessly blurred because "advisory committees are connected to administrative agencies, but they are established as frequently by Congress as by the agencies involved."[72] Moreover, as Henry Steck explains, "Congress and agencies look to advisory groups to introduce representational and participatory legitimacy into the administrative process."[73] Accordingly, "Advisory committees become a technique for reducing political uncertainty vis-à-vis clientele groups, stabilizing existing political relations, deflecting group opposition, securing group cooperation, and mobilizing political support."[74]

Negotiated Rule Making

Negotiated rule making is another formal mechanism through which organized interests can influence administrative policy making. The federal Negotiated Rulemaking Act of 1990 (NRMA) supplements the APA's provisions for informal rule making. It authorizes agencies to make rules through face-to-face negotiation with interested parties. The general procedure is for agencies to establish rule making committees after notice and comment in the *Federal Register*. Typically, these will include not more than 25 members drawn from the agency, regulated entities, trade unions, associations, and the public. Facilitators or mediators can be used to try to bring the parties to agreement on a proposed rule. Meetings are open to public observation, according to the same criteria that apply under the Federal Advisory Committee Act. A negotiated rule is subject to the same notice-and-comment requirements that apply to informal rule making. An agency could rewrite a negotiated proposed rule after receiving outside comments, but this would seriously undermine its credibility with those involved in the negotiations.

The main purposes of negotiated rule making, also called "reg-neg" (i.e., regulatory negotiation), are to fashion better rules, speed up the rule making process, and reduce the amount of litigation challenging agencies' rules. The object is to develop consensus among all affected parties. Participation in rule making enhances the influence of interest groups and moderates that of the agencies. So far experience has been mixed, and it is unclear whether reg-neg will make rule making better, faster, cheaper, and less litigious.[75]

Legislative Review of Rules

Interest groups not only interact with public administrators through the use of advisory committees and in negotiated rule making, they also lobby outright and work indirectly through the legislature. In several states, rules are subject to legislative review, which can enhance the influence of organized interests.

At the federal level, a provision of the Small Business Regulatory Enforcement Fairness Act of 1996 (SBREFA) is potentially important in this regard. Also called the Congressional Review Act, with some exceptions it requires that newly enacted major rules be submitted to Congress for formal review before they can go into effect. Major rules are those that will have at least a $100 million annual impact on the economy or have a substantial impact on costs, prices, employment, competition, productivity, or other economic concerns. Congress has up to 60 days to pass a joint resolution of disapproval. The resolution is subject to presidential veto and potential congressional override by a two-thirds majority in each house. A rule that is disapproved cannot be reissued in identical or similar form unless the agency receives specific statutory authorization.

Like advisory committees and negotiated rule making, SBREFA gives organized interests an avenue of influence over rule making. Formal congressional disapproval is likely to be a last resort. Interest groups voice their concerns to congressional committees, which, if sympathetic, will try to influence the direction of agencies' rule making. Although only one rule—the Department of Labor's 2001 ergonomic rule—was successfully disapproved, the potential for such congressional action should be of considerable concern to agency rule writers, who do not want to devote limited resources to writing politically untenable rules.

Other Avenues of Influence

Interest groups can influence public policy by gaining an informal veto power over appointments to the political executive positions in administrative agencies. In practice, this means that the leadership of many agencies, especially regulatory commissions, may come directly from the industry being regulated. In some ways, this is necessary if the appointees are to be familiar with the industry in question, but it also tends to turn would-be regulation into "collusion." There has been concern that career civil servants and political appointees will be influenced in their decision making and enforcement activities by the opportunity to join private firms represented by interest groups and by the sometimes lavish hospitality and honoraria the latter provide at their annual or other general meetings. At the federal level, ethics legislation has sought to close the "revolving door" through which federal administrators or appointees and corporate executives change positions and to outlaw the acceptance of substantial job-related hospitality and honoraria.

The Government Performance and Results Act Modernization Act provides another potential avenue of influence. It requires federal agencies' strategic plans to address goals, objectives, implementation strategies, and methods for evaluating administrative performance. From interest groups' perspectives, a key provision mandates that an agency "shall solicit and consider the views and suggestions of those entities potentially affected by or interested in such a plan."[76] In other words, the act invites interest group input into agencies' strategic decisions about what they should be doing and how they should be doing it.

Contemporary research points to several models of interest group influence.[77] The "iron triangle," also known as the "cozy triangle," is perhaps the classic model. Here interest groups interact with agency bureaus and congressional (sub)committees. Relationships are mutually supportive and harmonious. The three corners of the triangle share a similar worldview. A second model contends that to the extent that iron triangles were once dominant, they are now much more permeable to competing interests and outside expertise. This is largely because public policy issues, such as environmental protection, have become increasingly complex and likely to affect a large number of interests. When participants in these more open systems of influence are relatively limited, are stable, and have relatively fixed outlooks, the pattern of interaction is called a "policy" or "issue" network. Paul Sabatier has developed the Advocacy Coalition Framework (ACF)[78] to understand policy making involving a large number of groups and individuals who are sporadically active in an issue area and only weakly linked to one another. "Hollow cores" exist where "no interest groups, individual free-lance lawyers or lobbyists, or government officials [are] providing much connective tissue across the [policy] domain."[79]

In both the iron triangle and network models, interest groups track agency activity, seek access, provide administrators with information and perspectives, and try to influence their decision making, especially in the context of regulatory rule making. A major check on interest groups' influence is that "lobbyists know that their effectiveness is only as good as their credibility."[80]

The overall system of interaction with interest groups leads to discrimination against two types of interests. One is that of weak minorities and small entities unable to organize and gain access to the system of representation through interaction with public administrators. The other is the general public interest, too diffuse and not salient enough to any particular group to gather sufficient support to be promoted actively in this fashion.[81] A number of measures are used to protect weak or small interests. Federal administrative law requires agencies to consider the impact of proposed rules on small businesses and other entities. Agencies may be required to seek the views of small entities, including local governments, when considering drafting or proposing a rule. Presidents have issued executive orders to require agencies to consider the impact their actions may have on environmental justice and sustainability, federalism, family functioning, and other concerns.

Public interest groups try to ensure that the broad public interest is taken into account in agency decision making. A public interest group has been defined as "one that seeks a collective good, the achievement of which will not selectively and materially benefit the membership or activists of the organization."[82] Yet when discussing public interest groups, it should not be forgotten that traditional interest groups often promote what they believe to be in the public interest. Therefore, the distinction is not perfect. Among the organizations considered to be public interest groups are the Consumers Union, Common Cause, the League of Women Voters, and a variety of environmental and public interest research groups.

Public Employee Unions and Contractors' Associations

Most interest groups are concerned primarily with agencies' policies and implementation strategies. Although they may care intensely about agency leadership and direction, they pay little, if any, attention to matters of internal administrative management. Public employee unions and contractors' associations are an important exception. Both seek to influence the way agencies do business. When unions secure the right to engage in collective bargaining, they can negotiate a variety of working conditions with the agencies whose employees they represent (see Chapter 5). However, they can also lobby in legislatures in an effort to obtain what they are unable to gain at the bargaining table. As the NPM's emphasis on outsourcing gained strength in the 1990s, contractors ratcheted up their lobbying efforts to have more and more work contracted out. Among other groups, a Coalition for Government Procurement and a Professional Services Council represent contractors who seek to streamline and increase the level of federal outsourcing.

Much of the contractors' effort has involved implementation of the Federal Activities Inventory Reform Act of 1998 (FAIR), which requires agencies to identify all their positions that are commercial in nature, and therefore potentially outsourced. As of October 2000, some 390,000 jobs were identified as commercial. However, the agencies made only about 53,000 of those jobs potential candidates for outsourcing.[83] In the contractors' view, much of the slowness to outsource is due to procedures specified in OMB's Circular A-76, which requires complex, expensive, and cumbersome cost comparisons between having government employees and contractors do designated commercial work. In 2003, OMB revised A-76 procedures to make them simpler, less time-consuming, and fairer from the contractors' point of view.[84] However, in 2009 Congress placed a government wide moratorium on the A-76 public-private competition process, known as "competitive sourcing," for outsourcing. The moratorium remains in effect and substantially limits the importance of A-76 and outsourcing generally.[85]

The Public

Promotion of the public interest is certainly a prime goal of contemporary public administration in the United States. But defining the public interest is often difficult. Public administrators, like all human beings, are limited in their ability to foresee all the immediate and long-term consequences of their policy choices. They are subject to a number of influences that may distort their perception and definition of the public interest. Public interest groups may come forth in an effort to correct this tendency, but they may also represent a rather select perspective. Their membership appears to be overwhelmingly composed of middle-class activists. So, the question arises: How can the public respond to the growth of administrative power?

The public's reaction to the rise of the administrative state involves elements of opposition, satisfaction, support for specific programs, and interest in reforms. Public opinion regarding public administration is complex, divided, and perhaps inconsistent. Despite political rhetoric that would suggest otherwise, public bureaucracy is by no means universally or consistently opposed. The public is aware that administrative agencies are a central component of government and recognizes that the citizenry is dependent on them. Politically, the public seems to demand candidates who can manage bureaucracy. Sometimes it favors cutting back on public administrative activities. However, there is limited support for abandoning a host of regulatory functions intended to protect the public's safety. The public also rates some public administrative operations much higher than those of private sector service providers. As a practical matter, public administrators may accurately view public opinion as both a constraint on and a stimulus for a variety of administrative actions. This is precisely a point made by Woodrow Wilson, more than a century ago, in his famous essay "The Study of Administration": "In order to make any advance at all we must instruct and persuade a multitudinous monarch called public opinion."[86]

Political Parties

Historically, there has been a strong link between political parties and public administration.[87] In many countries, including the United States, political parties promoted the growth of large-scale public administration as a means of creating and securing patronage positions for their members. During the 19th century, this **spoils system** was instrumental in the development of American political parties and in the increasing size of several public agencies. However, patronage politics led to widespread political corruption, administrative inefficiency, and mismanagement. In the effort to remove the pernicious effects of partisan politics from public administration through civil service reform, political parties were weakened in an organizational sense.

Civil service reforms mandating the use of merit systems were instituted in the federal government and a few states and cities in the 1880s. The rationale behind them was that public administration was essentially a field of business, and consequently ought to be run according to businesslike, managerial principles. There is no doubt that merit-oriented reforms vastly improved the honesty, morality, efficiency, economy, and administrative effectiveness of public agencies. But they also weakened the political parties.

The parties' first response was to turn to the rising industrial sector for support. Patronage could be replaced by large-scale financial donations—in return for various policy and other considerations, of course. Soon the Senate became known as a "millionaires' club," and the politics associated with patronage and the "common man" of President Andrew Jackson's day rapidly receded. Yet reliance on large monetary contributions also caused corruption, and from the turn of the century until the 1920s, several political reforms were inspired by the Progressive movement. Especially important among these was the institution of the primary election and the promotion of restrictions on the political activities of public employees. Further, cities were reorganized under the city management model of municipal government created during this period. Many other administrative operations were depoliticized by organizing them as "public authorities" for the management of bridges, parks, ports, and other infrastructure. Taking public works projects out of politics reduced corruption and deprived political parties of kickbacks from construction contractors. Such reforms were aimed at destroying political machines and political bossism. Although largely successful in this regard, they also further weakened the parties. When the federal government passed the Hatch Acts (1939, 1940), regulating the political activities of federal and some categories of state and local public employees, some opponents in Congress argued that limiting the participation of those employees in political conventions would lead to the destruction of political parties.

Reforms along these lines have had the effect not only of weakening the political parties but also of freeing public administration from their influence and control. Merit systems prevent partisan intrusion in the selection, assignment, promotion, dismissal, and general treatment of public employees. It is an illegal personnel practice to ask a federal civil servant or an applicant for such a position what political party he or she belongs to. Political officials have long complained that the lack of power to make civil service assignments on a partisan basis undercuts their ability to steer administrative operations. They feel that members of the opposition party are forever subverting their electoral mandates. In at least one sense, though, public administrators may be nonpartisan, as the late president Gerald R. Ford explained: "There are bureaucratic fiefdoms out in the states or in various regions [that] have been disregarding Presidents for years, both Democratic and Republican."[88] Sometimes this leads politicians to engage in illegal maneuvers or questionable practices to get around "all the civil service restrictions." On balance, however, the political community has opted for politically neutral public personnel administration as opposed to pronounced partisan intrusion in public administration. The Supreme Court has even held that unless the government can show that political affiliation is positively related to on-the-job performance, public personnel decisions based on partisanship can be unconstitutional infringements on a public employee's First and Fourteenth Amendment rights (see Box 2.8). In this area, then, we see both the conflict and the congruence of managerial, political, and legal considerations pertaining to public administration.

2.8 THE "UNCONSTITUTIONALIZING" OF POLITICAL PATRONAGE

In *Elrod v. Burns* (1976), the Supreme Court held that patronage dismissals of rank-and-file employees of the Cook County, Illinois, Sheriff's Office were unconstitutional. Justice Brennan announced the judgment of the Court. He expressed the view that "patronage dismissals severely restrict political belief and association. Though there is a vital need for government efficiency and effectiveness, such dismissals are on balance not the least restrictive means for fostering that end. There is also a need to insure that policies which the electorate has sanctioned are effectively implemented. That interest can be fully satisfied by limiting patronage dismissals to policy-making positions. . . . [A]ny contribution of patronage dismissals to the democratic process does not suffice to override their severe encroachment on First Amendment freedoms." In dissent, Justice Powell admonished that "history and long prevailing practice across the country support the view that patronage hiring practices make a sufficiently substantial contribution to the practical functioning of our democratic system to support their relatively modest intrusion on First Amendment interests. The judgment today unnecessarily constitutionalizes another element of American life." *Branti v. Finkel* (1980) went even further in making patronage dismissals unconstitutional. A majority of the Supreme Court held that because such dismissals infringe on First Amendments rights, "the ultimate inquiry is not whether the label 'policymaker' or 'confidential' fits a particular position; rather, the question is whether the hiring authority can demonstrate that party affiliation is an appropriate requirement for the effective performance of the public office involved."

Patronage was made even tougher, if not altogether impossible, in *Rutan v. Republican Party of Illinois* (1990). There the Court held that "the rule of *Elrod* and *Branti* extends to promotion, transfer, recall, and hiring decisions based on party affiliation and support." Together, these decisions essentially constitutionalize the goal of the 19th-century civil service reformers who sought to take partisan politics out of the civil service and the civil service out of partisan politics.

Sources: Elrod v. Burns, 427 U.S. 347 (1976); Branti v. Finkel, 445 U.S. 506 (1980); Rutan v. Republican Party of Illinois, 497 U.S. 62 (1990).

❖❖ STATE AND LOCAL GOVERNMENTS

It would take a large volume to discuss comprehensively the impact of administrative growth on the structure and policy making of state and local governments. Although there are clear parallels to the responses to the federal administrative state, as outlined in this chapter, there are also differences. And there is remarkable variation. In general, the following observations seem pertinent here. First, the gubernatorial office has been strengthened as a means of providing governors with greater managerial and policy direction over administrative agencies. More than 40 governors possess a line-item veto. Many also make appointments to 50 to 100 or so top administrative posts, often subject to legislative confirmation, and hundreds more appointments to citizen boards and commissions. The governorship has also become increasingly institutionalized and professionalized.[89] Second, state governments have been reorganized, largely with a view toward the consolidation of functions and reduction in the number of administrative units. However, as in the case of the federal government, a great deal of fragmentation remains. Third, the extent of legislative oversight of administration and delegation of authority to it varies widely. Only a handful of states continue to hold biennial rather than annual legislative sessions. However, in some states, sessions are relatively brief and legislatures tend to leave administrative matters to the governor and his or her appointees. In about a dozen states, however, legislative committees can veto agency rules, and this strengthens their involvement in administrative matters. Fourth, there are also considerable differences in the impact of state courts on administration. Strong state supreme courts, as in New Jersey, for example, have been deeply engaged in large-scale educational and/or prison reform. Finally, the overall context of administration differs, as noted by Bonfield and Asimow:

> Federal agencies are, in general, much larger and better financed and staffed than state agencies. On the whole, state agencies deal with less affluent, less influential, and less well educated people than federal agencies, and handle matters of smaller economic value than those handled by federal agencies. Persons dealing with state agencies are also less likely to be represented by a lawyer than persons dealing with federal agencies. State agencies are closer to the people and usually have smaller constituencies that can more easily communicate with them than federal agencies. In addition, state constitutions often differ significantly from the federal Constitution in important particulars that relate to their respective administrative processes. State and federal constitutions often differ in the way in which they create administrative units within governments, allocate authority among units, and impose procedural or substantive limits on those units. For example, some state agencies are created directly by their state constitution; and some state agency heads are directly elected by the people.[90]

Several state constitutions also recognize rights in the administrative context that do not exist at the federal level, such as a right to public education.

It is more hazardous to generalize about local governmental responses to large-scale administration because they vary extensively. For the most part, these governments are becoming more executive-centered and professional, though not necessarily in response to administrative pressures alone. It is common to rely on county executives and city managers to act as the chief administrative officers of these governments.

◆◆   Extensions to the Administrative State

The reach of government in the United States extends beyond direct contact by the arms of government agencies at the federal, state, and local level. Much like managerial, political, and legal perspectives on the direct growth of the organs of government, we can take those perspectives and apply them to better understand the indirect expansion of the administrative state through the growth of the nonprofit sector in the United States.

The Managerial Approach

Some theorists argue that nonprofit organizations come into existence because of market or government failures.[91] At their essence, the most defining distinction between nonprofit and for-profit organizations is the **non-distribution constraint**[92] faced by nonprofit organizations. While nonprofits are allowed to have revenues exceed expenses (i.e., generate a profit) they are not allowed to distribute those excess revenues to stakeholders. This lack of a profit-motive is used to explain why nonprofit organizations come into existence to provide goods and services that for-profit and government organizations fail to produce in sufficient quantities.

Market failure theories fall into two broad camps. First, lack of a profit margin in the production of some types of goods and services (for example, housing for the homeless or foster care placement services for children) will lead the private for-profit sector to underproduce (or not produce at all) these goods or services. Since the non-distribution constraint greatly reduces the incentive to maximize excess revenues (i.e., profits), nonprofit organizations are able to operate on smaller profit margins and can provide these services because their primary purpose is to maximize achieving their mission rather than shareholder value. The non-distribution constraint is also associated with nonprofits being viewed as more trustworthy than for-profits because they have less of an incentive to "cheat" customers. Therefore, for goods and services that are complex to understand (e.g., university education), whose quality can only be evaluated after consumption (e.g., hospital services), or where the beneficiaries of the service are not the same as the purchasers of the service (e.g., child care services), nonprofits have less of an incentive to withhold information from clients/customers/beneficiaries than do for-profits.

Second, government failure theory argues that since politicians need to be elected, they authorize government to only provide services that meet the preferences of the **"median voter"**; authorizing higher levels of service will cause more voters to be against rather than for a policy, thus reducing the likelihood of the politician being re-elected.[93] For example, voters have different preferences for how much safety they are willing to pay for. There are some voters who highly value safety and are willing to be taxed highly to support a large police force, while others are willing to give up some level of safety to reduce some of their tax burden. Politicians will set the size of the police force at the level that the median voter is willing to pay for. However, for 50 percent minus one of the voters, their safety preference is still not met; they are willing to pay more for more safety. At least two different types of nonprofit organizations can come into existence to meet this unmet preference for increased safety; a homeowners association or a neighborhood watch group. People who desire higher levels of safety can choose to live in a neighborhood with a homeowners association and pay a fee that can be used to maintain a fence and gate to limit access to the neighborhood and pay for private security guards to staff the gate. Residents of a neighborhood may also decide to volunteer their time as part of a neighborhood watch group to keep their neighborhood safe.

Regardless of which theory drives the creation of nonprofit organizations, nonprofits represent an instrumental choice to provide levels of public goods or services the market and government are unable or unwilling to provide directly. However, through grants and contracts, public services can be provided indirectly through nonprofit organizations.

The Political Approach

Other theorists argue that nonprofits are an important part of our pluralist society. A vibrant voluntary nonprofit sector allows for the representation of diverse views and interests in the public sphere; nonprofit organizations represent interests. Individuals freely associate to create an organization to promote an interest or to meet a social need. Nonprofits are representative of values and interest groups.

From the founding of the republic, it has been recognized that the preservation and defense of liberty necessarily entails the creation of particularistic factions that do not have the public good as their main purpose. As James Madison explained in *Federalist* No. 10:

> The latent cause of faction are thus sown in the nature of man; and we see them everywhere brought into different degrees of activity, according to different circumstances of civil society. A zeal for different opinions concerning religion, concerning government, and many other points, as well as speculation as of practice; an attachment to different leaders ambitiously contending for pre-eminence and power; or to persons of other descriptions whose fortunes have been interesting to human passions, have, in turn, divided mankind into parties, inflamed with mutual animosity, and rendered them much more disposed to vex and oppress each other than to co-operate for their common good (Publius 1787, pg. 2).[94]

Madison contended that a republican form of government is necessary to distribute the power among many factions to prevent a tyranny of the majority arising. An "improper or wicked project" that benefits the few may be promoted, but the distribution of power among other interests will prevent the public will from being co-opted. Therefore, while the development of factions is inevitable, and may pose a threat to the efficient functioning of government, they are necessary to preserve the liberty of citizens of the republic.

A socially and politically fractured American polity makes it descriptively and normatively difficult for government to provide the same services to all citizens. Since citizens have different values and desire different qualities in the services they receive, nonprofit organizations are used to increase the flexibility of government. For example, consider the case of charter schools. These are schools that are typically created to operate outside of the traditional public school bureaucracy. The rhetoric behind the charter school movement is that the bureaucracy and rules of the traditional public school systems constrain the abilities of educators to creatively meet the needs of students. The one-size-fits-all approach of public schools allows students to fall through the cracks. Nonprofit, and in some states for-profit, organizations can apply for a school charter in which they detail the segment of the student population they will serve and the pedagogical approach they will take to serve those specific needs. While these schools are private organizations, charter schools are publically funded; dollars that would follow the student to a traditional public school instead follow the student to the charter school. Through charter school policies, government not only creates the space for private organizations to provide a public good, it actively subsidizes these organizations.

Cemeteries also provide an interesting case of government subsidizing nonprofit activity to achieve a public purpose. People of different faith traditions desire different qualities in their cemeteries; Catholics may prefer to be buried in cemeteries consecrated by Catholic priests rather than Muslim imams. Rather than government being responsible for providing sectarian burial grounds, sectarian nonprofit organizations are created to provide burial services tailored to the specific needs and interests of their coreligionists.

In fact, even if a government in the United States were inclined to provide cemeteries for different religious groups, it would be prohibited from doing so by the Constitution's First and Fourteenth Amendment barrier against governmental "establishment of religion." Although government cannot contract with nonprofits to provide religious services or indoctrination, it may contract out secular services, such as those involving health, welfare, and hunger prevention, to faith-based organizations. In something of a constitutional anomaly, governments can and generally do exempt churches, synagogues, and mosques from property taxes even though this indirectly subsidizes their religious activities.[95] This is partly because governments may also give property tax exemptions to nonprofit facilities such as museums, private schools and universities, and clinics, which if denied to houses of worship could be construed as discriminating against religious organizations in violation of the Constitution's guarantee of "free exercise" of religion, also found in the First Amendment and applied to state and local governments through the Fourteenth (see Chapter 11).

Under the political approach to understanding how nonprofits extend the reach of the administrative state, we come to understand the growth of the nonprofit sector as a way to allow the government to indirectly provide services that meet the values and interests of different groups in American society.

The Legal Approach

As nonprofit legal scholar Evelyn Brody[96] argues, "Private philanthropy and the nonprofit sector rest on the fundamental constitutional guarantees of private property, liberty of contract, and freedom of worship and expression."[97] These constitutional limitations on the state have allowed the nonprofit sector in the United States to grow and flourish. Indeed, the legal history of the nonprofit sector in the United States predates the Constitution. The legal framework for Anglo-American philanthropy was developed in 1601 with the Elizabethan Statute of Charitable Uses. As Brody explains, its preamble enumerates many charitable purposes,

> ... ranging from "relief of aged, impotent and poor people" and "supportation, aid and help of young tradesmen, handicraftsmen, and persons decayed" to "maintenance of ... schools of learning" and "repair of bridges, ports, havens, causeways, churches, sea-banks, and highways."[98]

In this legal tradition, nonprofit organizations have historically provided services associated with the modern welfare state. As the scope and complexity of society have increased, the **voluntary sector failures**[99] of philanthropic insufficiency, philanthropic amateurism, philanthropic particularism, and philanthropic paternalism prevent the nonprofit sector from being able to address these social issues on its own. Government with the powers of the administrative state has stepped in to support the nonprofit sector to increase its capacity as a partner to meet its charitable purposes.

At the federal level, section 501(c) of the tax code provides income tax exemptions to nonprofits under certain circumstances and legal tests. These exemptions subsidize nonprofits and thereby contribute to their growth and the extension of the administrative state. Section 501(c)(3) applies to foundations, such as the Bill and Melinda Gates Foundation, community foundations (e.g., the Cleveland Foundation, Greater Kansas City Community Foundation), public charities (United Way, the Salvation Army, Catholic Charities USA), health care organizations (Catholic Health Initiatives, hospitals affiliated with private universities), private colleges and universities, and thousands of generally small organizations operating for a variety of purposes. You can find a list of these in your zip code at http://foundationcenter.org/findfunders/990finder/ (accessed August 17, 2012).

Section 501(c)(3) organizations are not only tax exempt, individuals who donate funds to them may deduct those donations from their federal income taxes. However, these organizations cannot engage in political activity without losing their exempt status. They nevertheless may form 501(c)(4) affiliated advocacy organizations while retaining their tax exempt status under 501(c)(3). The American Association of Retired Persons (AARP) is an example. Its nonpolitical activities are housed in the AARP Foundation, a 501(c)(3) organization, while its advocacy is undertaken by AARP, which falls under 501(c)(4). Labor unions, organizations such as the American Bar Association, local chambers of commerce, and veterans' organizations may also benefit from various provisions of section 501(c). It is important to remember that 501(c) and other nonprofits are particular types of private organizations. Although sometimes referred to as the "third sector," "civil society," and "public," they are nongovernmental and as a matter of much law treated identically to private for-profit corporations. What is different about them is that many become extensions of the administrative state through the federal tax advantages they receive.

Conclusion: The Administrative State

The American administrative state has developed in response to a host of factors, including political, managerial, and legal concerns. The growth of public administration has enabled governments, directly and indirectly through nonprofit organizations, to exercise greater influence over the society and the economy. However, contemporary public administration poses several problems. One is the question of principles according to which public administration should be organized—political, managerial, legal, or some combination of these? Another problem is whether the administrative state can be adequately controlled by elected public officials or political processes in general without becoming highly inefficient and expensive. Yet another concerns the proper role of the judiciary in public administration and whether contemporary public administrators can harmoniously incorporate the judiciary's constitutional values. The presidential, legislative, and judicial responses to the rise of the administrative state have certainly enhanced their influence over it. But they have also promoted the development of a large Executive Office of the President that is hard to manage effectively, a "thickening" among political appointees within the executive branch, a proliferation of subcommittees and staff in Congress that has fragmented the legislative process and made it difficult for the institution to act in a coordinated fashion, and a judiciary sometimes heavily involved in administrative micromanagement. Overarching these concerns is the major issue of the public's relationship to government in the contemporary administrative age. Finally, although not stressed here, the cost of running the administrative state has become increasingly problematic—hence the widespread desire to limit taxes and make government more economical.

If the political community knew how to solve all these problems simultaneously and were willing to do so, American politics would be considerably different. In truth, however, lasting solutions have been elusive and some of the problems consequently appear intractable. The constitutional separation of powers places most public administration in the United States under three sometimes competing branches with different institutional and political interests. It complicates public administration immensely and makes fundamental reforms difficult. Federalism and intergovernmental relations, the topics of the next chapter, add to the challenges public administrators face.

Study Questions

1. The reach of public administration is considered too broad by some people. Can you identify public administrative functions and programs that you think deal with matters that should be left up to private individuals, families, and/or private groups? What distinguishes these activities from those you think are appropriately dealt with through public administration?
2. Are there areas of social or economic life that you believe require more governmental involvement through public administration?

3. Think about a recent political campaign with which you are familiar. Did the candidates express concern with matters of public administration? If so, from what perspectives? How might a practicing public administrator respond to their campaign statements?

4. Does the rise of the nonprofit sector as an extension of the administrative state make the life of a public administrator easier or harder?

NOTES

1. Paul Light, *The True Size of Government* (Washington, DC: Brookings Institution, 1999), Appendix A, 198–199.
2. *Zelman v. Simmons-Harris,* 536 U.S. 639 (2002).
3. Lester Salamon, "The Rise of Third Party Government: Implications for Public Management," in Donald Kettl, Ed., *Third Party Government and the Public Manager* (Washington, DC: National Academy of Public Administration, 1987), 12.
4. James Q. Wilson, "The Rise of the Bureaucratic State," *The Public Interest* 41 (Fall 1975): 77–103.
5. Ibid., 82.
6. Ibid., 89–91, 95–96.
7. Lawrence Friedman, *A History of American Law* (New York: Simon & Schuster, 1973), 458.
8. Arthur Bonfield and Michael Asimow, *State and Federal Administrative Law* (St. Paul, MN: West, 1989), chap. 1.
9. Al Gore, *From Red Tape to Results: Creating a Government That Works Better & Costs Less: The Report of the National Performance Review* (Washington, DC: Government Printing Office, 1993).
10. United States Office of Personnel Management, *Strategic Plan 2010–2015* (Washington, DC: United States Office of Personnel Management). Document can be found at: http://www.opm.gov/about-us/budget-performance/strategic-plans/2010-2015-strategic-plan.pdf.
11. Max Weber, *From Max Weber: Essays in Sociology,* by H. H. Gerth and C. W. Mills, Trans. and Eds. (New York: Oxford University Press, 1958), 228.
12. Honoré de Balzac, *Les Employées,* 1836. Quoted in Martin Albrow, *Bureaucracy* (New York: Praeger, 1970), 18.
13. *J. W. Hampton, Jr. & Co. v. United States,* 276 U.S. 394 (1928).
14. Jennifer Larrabee, "'DWB (Driving While Black)' and Equal Protection: The Realities of an Unconstitutional Police Practice," *Journal of Law and Policy* 6, no. 1 (1997): 291–328.
15. Thomas E. Cronin, *The State of the Presidency* (Boston: Little, Brown, 1975), 27.
16. Ibid., 28.
17. Moreley Winograd, "NPR Reforms Leave Their Mark on Government," *Federal Times,* 29 January 2001, 15; Ian Littman, Ed., *The Business of Government* (Arlington, VA: PriceWaterhouseCoopers, 1999), 7.
18. Light, *The True Size of Government.*
19. George W. Bush, "Building a Responsive, Innovative Government," *Federal Times,* 26 June 2000, 15.
20. Stephen Barr, "Some Pessimism on 'Reinvention,'" *Washington Post,* 31 March 2000, A27.

21. U.S. General Accounting Office, *Management Reform: Completion Status of Agency Actions under the National Performance Review* (Washington, DC: U.S. General Accounting Office, 1996), 5; *Reinventing Government: Status of NPR Recommendations in 10 Federal Agencies* (Washington, DC: U.S. General Accounting Office, 2000), 10.

22. Tim Kauffman, "Poor Performers, Recruiting Top Workers' Concerns," *Federal Times,* 25 December 2000, 3.

23. Paul Light, "To Restore and Renew," *Government Executive* (Special Report, November 2001), 9.

24. Bill Miller, "$37.7 Billion for Homeland Defense Is a Start, Bush Says," *Washington Post,* 25 January 2002, A15.

25. "Ridge Will Not Give Congress His Testimony," *USA Today,* 25 March 2002, 7A. See also Liza Porteus and Lisa Caruso, "Dems Continue to Rap Ridge for Failure to Testify on Hill," *GovExec.com,* 12 April 2002, 1.

26. Quoted in George C. Edwards III and Stephen J. Wayne, *Presidential Leadership* (New York: St. Martin's, 1985), 351.

27. *Humphrey's Executor v. United States,* 295 U.S. 602 (1935), is the classic example.

28. Angel Moreno, "Presidential Coordination of the Independent Regulatory Process," *Administrative Law Journal of the American University* 8 (1994): 461–516.

29. U.S. Office of Personnel Management, Office of Workforce Information, "Political Appointment by Type and Work Schedule," *Central Personnel Data File* (Washington, DC: U.S. Office of Personnel Management, September 2001).

30. Paul Light, *Thickening Government* (Washington DC: Brookings Institution, 1995), 7.

31. Ibid., 8–9.

32. Ibid., 95.

33. Richard Nathan, "The Reagan Presidency in Domestic Affairs," in Fred I. Greenstein, Ed., *The Reagan Presidency: An Early Assessment* (Baltimore: Johns Hopkins University Press, 1983), 71.

34. Ibid.

35. Joel Aberbach and Bert Rockman, *The Web of Politics* (Washington, DC: Brooking Institution, 2000), 38–39.

36. Gore, *From Red Tape to Results,* 75.

37. See Ellen Nakashima, "Bush View of Secrecy Is Stirring Frustration: Disclosure Battle Unites Right and Left," *Washington Post,* 3 March 2002, A4. Bush's Executive Order 13,233 (2001) relied on executive privilege to revise several provisions of the Presidential Record Act of 1978.

38. See Tom Shoop, "Bush Budget Rips Agencies' Management in Key Areas," *GovExec.com,* 4 February 2002; and Mitchell Daniels, "A Valuable Tool for Managers," *Federal Times,* 13 October 2002, 13.

39. Jason Peckenpaugh, "White House to Propose Increased Use of Pay Banding, Bonuses," *GovExec.com,* 17 December 2001.

40. Phillip J. Cooper, "The Duty to Take Care: President Obama, Public Administration, and the Capacity to Govern," *Public Administration Review,* 71 (January/February 2011): 7–18.

41. Robert La Follette, Jr., "Congress Wins a Victory over Congress," *New York Times Magazine,* 4 August 1946, 11; Estes Kefauver and Jack Levin, *A Twentieth-Century Congress* (New York: Essential Books, 1947), 5 and title of chap. 1.

42. See David H. Rosenbloom, *Building a Legislative-Centered Public Administration: Congress and the Administrative State, 1946–1999* (Tuscaloosa: University of Alabama Press, 2000), for an extended analysis.

43. *Congressional Record,* 79th Cong., 2d sess. 1946, 92, 5:10060.

44. Joel Aberbach, *Keeping a Watchful Eye* (Washington, DC: Brookings Institution, 1990), 198; and Aberbach, "What's Happened to the Watchful Eye?" *Congress & The Presidency* 29 (Spring 2002): 3–23.

45. Kefauver and Levin, *A Twentieth-Century Congress,* 10, 186.

46. See Paul Dwyer and John Pontius, "Legislative Branch Employment, 1960–1997" (Washington, DC: Congressional Research Service, June 6, 1997); and Bruce Oppenheimer, "Abdicating Congressional Power," 371–389 in Lawrence Dodd and Bruce Oppenheimer, Eds., *Congress Reconsidered,* 6th ed. (Washington, DC: CQ Press, 1997), 379–381. Norman Ornstein, Thomas Mann, and Michael Malbin, *Vital Statistics on Congress* (Washington, DC: Congressional Quarterly, annually) is an excellent source for statistics on Congress.

47. William Roth, Jr., and William Nixon, *The Power to Destroy* (New York: Atlantic Monthly Press, 1999).

48. Kenneth Cooper, "The House Freshmen's First Choice," *Washington Post,* 5 January 1993, A13.

49. Jock Friedly, "Pork: Highways in Canada, N.Y.," *The Hill,* 3 June 1998, 4.

50. Robert S. Kravchuk and Ronald W. Schack, "Designing Effective Performance Measurement Systems Under the Government Performance and Results Act of 1993," *Public Administration Review,* July/August 1996, 348–358.

51. Francis Rourke, "Whose Bureaucracy Is This, Anyway? Congress, the President, and Public Administration," *PS: Political Science and Politics* 26 (December 1993): 687–692.

52. See David H. Rosenbloom, Rosemary O'Leary, and Joshua Chanin, *Public Administration and Law,* 3rd ed. (Boca Raton, FL: CRC/Taylor & Francis, 2010); and James D. Carroll, "The New Juridical Federalism and the Alienation of Public Policy and Administration," *American Review of Public Administration* 16 (1982): 89–105.

53. See *Parrish v. Civil Service Commission,* 425 P.2d 223 (1967).

54. See Robert Vaughn, *The Spoiled System* (New York: Charterhouse, 1975), for an analysis of this problem.

55. Martin Shapiro, *The Supreme Court and Administrative Agencies* (New York: Free Press, 1968).

56. See David H. Rosenbloom, *Federal Service and the Constitution* (Ithaca, NY: Cornell University Press, 1971), chap. 6.

57. For a full discussion, see Rosenbloom, O'Leary, and Chanin, *Public Administration and Law.*

58. See *O'Hare Truck Service v. City of Northlake,* 518 U.S. 839 (1996) and *Board of County Commissioners, Wabaunsee County v. Umbehr,* 518 U.S. 668 (1996).

59. See Rosenbloom, O'Leary, and Chanin, *Public Administration and Law,* and the following cases: *Wyatt v. Stickney,* 325 F. Supp. 781 (1971); *Youngberg v. Romeo,* 457 U.S. 307 (1982).

60. *FTC v. Sperry & Hutchinson Co.,* 405 U.S. 233 (1972); *Motor Vehicle Mfg. Ass'n. v. State Farm,* 463 U.S. 29 (1983); *Citizens to Preserve Overton Park v. Volpe,* 401 U.S. 402 (1971); *Industrial Union Department, AFL-CIO v. American Petroleum Institute,* 448 U.S. 607 (1980).

61. *Chevron v. NRDC,* 467 U.S. 837 (1984); *Vermont Yankee Nuclear Power Corporation v. NRDC,* 435 U.S. 519 (1978); *City of Arlington, Texas v. Federal Communications Commission,* U.S. Supreme Court Nos. 11-1545 and 11-1547 (2013).

62. See Abram Chayes, "The Role of the Judge in Public Law Litigation," *Harvard Law Review* 89 (1976): 1281–1316; and Robert Wood and Clement Vose, *Remedial Law* (Amherst: University of Massachusetts Press, 1990).

63. Robert Turner, "Governing from the Bench," *Boston Globe Magazine,* 8 November 1981, 12 ff.

64. August 15.

65. *Brown v. Plata,* 131 S. Ct. 1910 (2011).

66. *Carlson v. Green,* 446 U.S. 14, 21 (1980).

67. See Rosenbloom, O'Leary, and Chanin, *Public Administration and Law,* chap. 8, for a more detailed discussion.

68. Among the key cases are *City of Canton v. Harris,* 489 U.S. 387 (1989); *Will v. Michigan Department of State Police,* 491 U.S. 58 (1989); and *Hafer v. Melo,* 502 U.S. 21 (1991).

69. *Owen v. City of Independence,* 445 U.S. 622, 669 (1980).

70. *Hope v. Pelzer,* 536 U.S. 730 (2002).

71. See Jeffrey Berry, *The Interest Group Society,* 2d ed. (Glenview, IL: Scott, Foresman, 1989). See also Samuel Krislov and David H. Rosenbloom, *Representative Bureaucracy and the American Political System* (New York: Praeger, 1981).

72. Henry J. Steck, "Politics and Administration: Private Advice for Public Purpose in a Corporatist Setting," in Jack Rabin and James Bowman, Eds., *Politics and Administration* (New York: Marcel Dekker, 1984), 159.

73. Ibid., 161.

74. Ibid.

75. See Cary Coglianese, "Assessing Consensus: The Promise and Performance of Negotiated Rulemaking," *Duke Law Journal* 46 (1997): 1255–1349.

76. Public Law 111-352, 124 *Statutes at Large* 3866, Section 306(d), 4 January 2011.

77. See Robert Salisbury et al., "Triangles, Networks, and Hollow Cores: The Complex Geometry of Washington Interest Representation," in Mark Petracca, Ed., *The Politics of Interests* (Boulder, CO: Westview Press, 1992), 130–149; and Robert Hrebener and Ruth Scott, *Interest Group Politics in America,* 2d ed. (Englewood Cliffs, NJ: Prentice-Hall, 1990), chap. 8.

78. Sabatier, Paul A., and Hank Jenkins-Smith, "An Advocacy Coalition Model of Policy Change and the Role of Policy Orientated Learning Therein," *Policy Sciences* 21 (1988): 129–68.

79. Salisbury et al., "Triangles, Networks, and Hollow Cores," 149.

80. Berry, *The Interest Group Society,* 150.

81. Grant McConnell, *Private Power and American Democracy* (New York: Knopf, 1966), chap. 4.

82. Jeffrey Berry, quoted in Krislov and Rosenbloom, *Representative Bureaucracy,* 170.

83. Tichakorn Hill, "Rules Are Roadblock to Agency Outsourcing," *Federal Times,* 30 October 2000, 1, 23.

84. Frank Camm, "Invest in New A-76 Rules," *Federal Times,* 13 January 2003, 21; Amelia Gruber, "GAO Criticizes Administration's Proposed Changes to A-76 Process," *GovExec.com,* 22 January 2003.

85. Valerie Ann Bailey Grasso, *Circular A-76 and the Moratorium on DOD Competitions* (Washington, DC: Congressional Research Service, January 16, 2013).

86. Woodrow Wilson, "The Study of Administration," *Political Science Quarterly* 56 (December 1941): 491 (originally published in 1887).

87. A thoughtful discussion in the U.S. context can be found in Herbert Storing, "Political Parties and the Bureaucracy," in Robert A. Goldwin, Ed., *Political Parties, USA* (Chicago: Rand McNally, 1964).

88. Edwards and Wayne, *Presidential Leadership,* 360.

89. Larry Sabato, *Goodbye to Good-Time Charlie: The American Governorship Transformed,* 2d ed. (Washington, DC: CQ Press, 1983).

90. Bonfield and Asimow, *State and Federal Administrative Law,* 3.

91. Burton A. Weisbrod, "Toward a Theory of the Voluntary Non-Profit Sector in a Three-Sector Economy," in Edmund Phelps, Ed., *Altruism, Morality, and Economic Theory* (New York: Russell Sage, 1975), 171–195.

92. Henry Hansmann, "The Role of Nonprofit Enterprise," *Yale Law Journal* 89 (1980): 835–901.

93. James Douglas, "Political Theories of Nonprofit Organizations," in Walter W. Powell, Ed., *The Nonprofit Sector: A Research Handbook* (New Haven, Conn.: Yale University Press, 1987), 43–54.

94. Publius. "The Federalist No. 10: The Utility of the Union as a Safeguard Against Domestic Faction and Insurrection," *Daily Advertiser* (November 22, 1787). See George W. Carey and James McClellan, *The Federalist* (Indianapolis: Liberty Fund, 2001).

95. *Walz v. Tax Commission of the City of New York* 397 U.S. 664 (1970).

96. Evelyn Brody, "The Legal Framework for Nonprofit Organizations," in Walter W. Powell & Richard Steinberg, Eds., *The Nonprofit Sector: A Research Handbook, 2nd Edition* (New Haven, CT: Yale University Press, 2006), 243–266.

97. Ibid., 245.

98. Ibid., 243.

99. Lester M. Salamon, "Of Market Failure, Voluntary Failure, and Third-Party Government: Toward a Theory of Government-Nonprofit Relations in the Modern Welfare State," *Nonprofit & Voluntary Sector Quarterly* 16 (Nos.1–2, 1987): 29–49.

Additional Reading

Aberbach, Joel, and Bert Rockman. *The Web of Politics.* Washington, DC: Brookings Institution, 2000.

Durant, Robert F. *The Oxford Handbook of American Bureaucracy.* New York: Oxford University Press, 2010.

Light, Paul. *Thickening Government.* Washington, DC: Brookings Institution, 1995.

Wilson, James Q. *Bureaucracy.* New York: Basic Books, 1989.

FEDERAL, STATE, AND LOCAL ADMINISTRATION WEB SITES

Developments in federal administration can be tracked through the federal government's portal at http://www.firstgov.gov. The text of laws, the U.S. Code, the *Federal Register,* judicial decisions, congressional bills, and presidential documents can be found on the U.S. Government Printing Office Web site at http://www.gpo.gov. The U.S. Government Accountability Office publishes reports on a variety of current aspects of federal administration. See http://www.gao.gov.

Consult the Council of State Government's Web site at http://www.csg.org for developments regarding state administration and the International City/County Management Association's site http://www.icma.org for local governmental matters. Local government administration is also tracked by the National League of Cities at http://www.nlc.org. Other useful state Web sites are those of the National Association of State Budget Officers at http://www.nasbo.org, the National Conference of State Legislatures at http://www.ncsl.org, and the National Governors Association at http://www.nga.org.

CHAPTER 3

FEDERALISM AND INTERGOVERNMENTAL RELATIONS

The Structure of the American Administrative State

Key Learning Objectives

1. Be able to define federalism and describe its legal, structural, and political characteristics in the case of the United States.

2. Understand how the division of functions between the federal government and the state governments has evolved since the founding of the republic.

3. Know the crucial role of the courts in determining the nature of federal–state relations, as well as the contemporary legal issues.

The American system of government is the longest-lived constitutional system on earth. Ratified by the states in 1789, the U.S. Constitution has been in effect for 225 years. The federal structure embodied in the Constitution adds stability to an otherwise complex, unwieldy system of governments. Three major characteristics are important. First, the United States is a system of *representative* governments rather than direct democracies. This stems from the Founders' distrust of the masses; they instituted elected representatives as a means to "refine the passions." Second, the separation of powers into executive, legislative, and judicial branches effectively fragments the power of majority rule via a system of checks and balances. This requires coordinated action so that the rights of minority interests will be protected, but at the same time enables public policy to be made. Third, and most important for this chapter, the United States is a *federal* system. The states and the national (or federal) government have separate spheres of (sometimes overlapping) sovereign powers. The powers of states limit those of the federal government, and the federal government limits the powers of the states. The basic system developed by the framers of the Constitution has proved flexible enough to adapt effectively to changing national needs, emergencies, and otherwise normal changes.

Governing the United States is one of the most complicated activities in the world. In 2012, the nation had some 89,000 governments within its borders. Their relationships are sometimes cooperative, sometimes competitive, and sometimes conflictual. Public administrators often face the challenging task of coordinating the programs of several governments with one another in a variety of related policy areas. This chapter explores federalism, intergovernmental relations, and the administrative structure of the major governments found in the United States. The maze of governments forms a substantial part of the political and legal environment in which public administrators work. Governmental authority and jurisdiction were divided in the 2012 U.S. Census of Governments among a national government, 50 state governments, the District of Columbia, 3,031 counties, 19,522 municipalities, 16,364 townships, 12,884 school districts, and 37,203 special districts (not to mention the territories and possessions of the United States).[1]

The management, politics, and laws of federalism and intergovernmental relationships are so perplexing that they have emerged as areas of activity and study to which some have devoted their entire professional lives. The typical citizen escapes with a lesser burden—on average he or she works until mid-April just to pay for federal, state, and local governments.[2] Obviously, governmental decentralization and fragmentation are key areas of concern for public administrators and a feature of governance that they sometimes find frustrating.

◆◆   WHY FEDERALISM? THE POLITICAL APPROACH

Federalism is a common feature of many contemporary nation-states. It refers to the division of political authority between a central government and state or provincial governments. Canada, Australia, Nigeria, and the United States are examples. In each of these nations there are states or provinces that have a substantial measure of legal or constitutional sovereignty (supreme political authority). However, in each case these units of government are also subordinate in many major legal/constitutional respects to a central government. Federalism stands in contrast to "unitary" political systems in which there are no quasi-sovereign governmental units coexisting with the national government. England and Israel are examples of unitary states. So is the Russian Federation, despite the country's formal name. In such nations all sovereignty is exercised by the national government, which in democracies is viewed as the agent of the people, who are the sovereign. Unitary governments may delegate administrative and political authority to municipalities or other governmental bodies, but these bodies have no inherent sovereignty or any authority other than that which is given to them by the national government. Delegations of this type constitute political and administrative "decentralization," but not federalism.

What Federalism Does

Federalism was developed as a political solution to the problem of *large* and *diverse* nation-states such as the United States. Many federal nations are "compound" political communities; that is, they are made up of *territorially based* and heterogeneous ethnic, tribal, racial, religious, linguistic, or other social groups imbued with different cultural values. Canada is a leading example, with distinct English, French, Scottish, Irish, German, Polish, Ukrainian, and Native peoples. In fact, numerous languages are spoken across Canada, including French in Quebec to Ukrainian in Saskatchewan and various cities. Federalism in compound nations provides a measure of representation and political autonomy for ethnic and other territorially based cultural groups. Yet a large nation might also turn to federalism as a means of making the national government sensitive to regional issues. The United States is a leading example.

In large part the United States relies on federalism because of the historical pattern of its early settlement by Europeans. Thirteen colonies were settled and separately chartered. Initially there was some important religious and linguistic diversity among them. But English became the common language, and over time a sense of being "American" developed. During the Revolutionary War, a *confederal* government was formed. Under this approach, the former colonies, now *states,* had a great deal of independent authority. The central government was relatively weak. The main impetus for abandoning the confederal government seems to have been a practical one. Coordinated public policy was difficult to achieve, so that trade among the states faced numerous barriers, and the national government seemed too weak to deal with military threats posed by various European nations and the new nation's conflicts with numerous Native American tribes.

From the revolution until the U.S. Constitution was ratified in 1789, the United States was governed according to the Articles of Confederation, our original constitution. The drive toward independence of the American colonies imparted to the United States a bias toward decentralization of authority. But the weak national government embodied in the Articles resulted in serious problems of governance. Under the Articles, the powers of the national government were largely limited to the conduct of foreign policy and were placed in a unicameral (one-house) legislature. National laws were unenforceable in state courts. With severe restrictions on its ability to conduct domestic policy and to raise money, the central government relied entirely on the states for its revenues. Domestic and foreign trade was regulated by the various states, which raised tariffs against one another, imposed customs duties at state border crossings, and engaged in other competitive and even outright discriminatory practices. Disputes arose between the states; some of them turned violent. The situation deteriorated so rapidly that a convention was called in Philadelphia to address the perplexing problem of recognizing and combining state interests, yet maintaining the identity of the United States as a single country. This has become known as the Constitutional Convention of 1787, or the "Grand Convention."

The Constitution's framers were concerned with the problem of how a large population could be represented by a single government. To be responsive, and effective, it was thought, elected or appointed representatives must know the people they are representing and share their lives. But how many people can one individual know? A single government seeking to represent a large population would be confronted with a dilemma. In principle, a large number of representatives would be required. But then the national legislature would have to be very large, perhaps too large to accomplish its work. Alternatively, a smaller number of representatives could be relied on. This would make the legislature manageable, but it would also tend to detract from the quality of representation because one individual would be responsible for representing a large number of citizens. To accommodate the preexisting sovereignty of the states and deal with the representational problem, the framers devised a form of federalism incorporating three central features: dual sovereignty, bicameralism, and multiple layers of representation.

Dual Sovereignty

First, the states would retain sovereignty in important spheres, and more states would eventually be created from the lands that would come under national control. The national government would also have sovereignty in some functional areas. This is the principle of dual sovereignty. The Constitution expressly identifies the powers vested in the national government, in Article I, section 8, referred to as the "enumerated powers" of the federal government. Originally, these powers were listed in order to limit carefully what powers would be vested in the national government. The U.S. system was to have a "state-centered federalism," as opposed to a "nation-centered federalism." As a means to protect states' rights, the powers granted to the federal government are few in number and well defined. The federal government derived its sovereignty directly from the people in the states rather than the state governments. Its sovereignty therefore was not to depend on the continued support of individual states, as some Southern states maintained before the Civil War. In the period leading up to that conflict, some states attempted to nullify or veto any national law that they believed to be in violation of the Constitution. Some Southern politicians went so far as to claim that any state had the right to withdraw from the Constitution (effectively, to secede from the Union) if it so desired. This question was settled only by the victory of the Union forces, which established definitively the concept of national supremacy.

Much of the pre–Civil War dispute concerned interpretation of the "residual powers clause" of the Tenth Amendment, ratified in 1791, which specifies that "The powers not delegated to the United States by the Constitution, nor prohibited by it to the States, are reserved to the States respectively, or to the people." This indicates that while the powers originally delegated to the national government are limited, the powers reserved to the states are broad and unspecified. The Tenth Amendment effectively endorses the concept of "dual sovereignty." But the powers retained by the states have varied with judicial interpretation of the commerce clause (see below). The consequence has been that a "nation-centered federalism" has dominated since the Civil War.

Dominant federal authority today derives from the Constitution's provisions in Article VI, section 2, which provides that the Constitution and national laws are "the supreme law of the land." But it is the combination of the "supremacy clause" of Article VI, section 2, with the Supreme Court's ruling in *McCullough v. Maryland* (1819)[3] that enables wide-ranging federal action in areas not specifically enumerated. In that case the Court ruled that, in addition to its enumerated powers, the federal government possesses broad-ranging "implied powers" under the "necessary and proper clause" of Article I, section 8. Since the mid-1800s, as a matter of practical necessity, Congress has used this clause as the legal basis for many laws only vaguely associated with its enumerated powers, especially the power to regulate commerce among the states. States do retain many protections under the Constitution, however. First, Article IV protects the territorial integrity of the states by prohibiting their division or combination without the consent of their legislatures (and Congress). (Some territorial boundaries have been subject to dispute. See Box 3.1.)

Bicameralism

Second, a bicameral Congress was created in which one chamber, the Senate, provides each state with equal representation regardless of geographic size or population. The Senate also has the power to ratify treaties, which in part manifests the sovereignty of the states. Even today the Senate can be viewed as a protector of state sovereignty. The House of Representatives, the lower chamber, apportions representation according to population, rather

3.1   ONE NATION, INDIVISIBLE, WITH MANY BORDERS

New Jersey v. New York
No. 120, Orig.
Decided May 17, 1999
526 U.S. 589

Decree

The Court having exercised original jurisdiction over this controversy between two sovereign States, the issues raised having been heard in an evidentiary proceeding before the Special Master appointed by the Court, the Court having heard argument on the Final Report of the Special Master and the exceptions filed by the state parties, the Court having issued its opinion on the issues raised in the exceptions, which is reported at 523 U.S. 767 (1998), and the Special Master having submitted his Report Upon Recommittal,

IT IS HEREBY ORDERED, ADJUDGED, AND DECREED AS FOLLOWS:

I

The State of New Jersey's prayer that she be declared to be sovereign over the landfilled portions of Ellis Island added by the Federal Government after 1834 is granted, and the State of New York is enjoined from enforcing her laws or asserting sovereignty over the portions of Ellis Island that lie within the State of New Jersey's sovereign boundary as set forth in paragraph 4 of this decree.

II

The sovereign boundary between the State of New Jersey and the State of New York is as set forth in Article First of the Compact of 1834, enacted into law in both States and approved by Congress.

III

The State of New York remains sovereign under Article Second of the Compact of 1834 of and over the original Ellis Island, to the low water mark, and the pier area built on landfill, as the Island and pier were structured in 1834, as more particularly depicted in the 1857 United States Coast Survey of New York Harbor.

IV

The boundary between the two States on Ellis Island is as depicted on the map of Ellis Island, Showing Boundary Between States of New Jersey and New York, dated December 1, 1998, which is appended hereto.*. . .

V

The Court retains jurisdiction to entertain such further proceedings, enter such orders, and issue such writs as may from time to time be considered necessary or desirable to give proper force and effect to this Decree or to effectuate the rights of the parties.

VI

The States of New Jersey and New York shall share equally in the compensation for the Special Master and his assistants, and for expenses of this litigation incurred by the Special Master in this controversy.

*The map and detailed coordinates have been omitted.

than states. However, an important feature of representation in this body is that no House district crosses any state borders. This means that all members of the lower house represent districts from only one state, and so the states are also represented—in indirect fashion—in the House.

Multiple Layers of Representation

Third, the national government would have direct power over citizens, rather than having to act upon them through the state governments; accordingly, the citizenry would be represented directly in the House of Representatives. Consequently, Americans possess a kind of "dual citizenship." They are citizens of the United States, and of the states in which they reside. (As yet another vestige of state sovereignty, prior to the ratification of the Seventeenth Amendment in 1913, the Senate was not directly elected by the population; instead, senators were appointed by the state governments.)

The framers' arrangement goes a long way toward resolving the representational dilemma. By vesting a good deal of political authority in smaller governmental units (the states), it enhances the likelihood that the federal government will concentrate on representing the will of the people on matters of national importance. It also enhances representation, responsiveness, and accountability at lower levels of government on regional and local matters. The states have constitutional authority to provide public education, public safety, and roads. They have authority to tax, to zone, to define crimes and punishments, to charter corporations, and to engage in a great many other functions. These kinds of powers are generally called **"police powers."** Today some of these functions are performed in conjunction with the federal government. They are also constrained by the Fourteenth Amendment's guarantees of due process and equal protection of the laws. But historically, the solution to the representational problem was thought to be allowing local people to control the governance of local matters. Sometimes this idea is discussed in terms of "grassroots" democracy.

The idea that smaller political jurisdictions are better able than larger ones to respond to the diverse preferences of their citizens has evoked great support throughout United States history. It is discussed further toward the end of this chapter. Interestingly, this approach held potential to provide a special cultural group with a considerable amount of autonomy if it were able to gain political dominance of a state. The Mormons in Utah are the leading example. However, because the national government can act directly on the people and seek to represent them, the chances for separatist movements to develop and be successful in a federal system such as that of the United States are greatly reduced. This has been especially true since the adoption of the post–Civil War constitutional amendments. The Fourteenth and Fifteenth, in particular, promoted national integration by giving the national government direct responsibility for protecting the civil rights and liberties of individuals against infringement by the states themselves.

◆◆ Administrative Decentralization: The Managerial Approach

Federalism is a form of *political* decentralization. It divides political authority and sovereignty between the national government and states, provinces, or similar governmental bodies. Hence, political authority is not centralized in the national government but shared with other governmental units. The reasons for this arrangement are overwhelmingly political, but they are also of administrative concern. Here the managerial perspectives on public administration exert their influence.

Administrative decentralization occurs when administrative responsibility, authority, and discretion are delegated to administrative units having jurisdiction over at least one program or function in a subnational geographic territory. The existence of a field office or regional office of an administrative agency is evidence of administrative decentralization. So is a neighborhood school. Administrative decentralization coincides with federalism when states or provinces serve as administrative districts of the national government. But other arrangements, such as regional districts spanning several states or provinces, are also possible. There are a variety of managerial reasons for encouraging administrative decentralization that have little to do with political concerns.

Traditional American public administrative theory recognizes that organization by "place" may be an appropriate basis for establishing administrative arrangements.[4] This is perhaps particularly true in large nations, especially if their physical characteristics, such as climate, topography, and hydrology, vary widely. Under such circumstances there is an ever-present likelihood that highly centralized administration will fail to adapt to local or regional conditions. National standards may fail to fit situations in vastly different geographic settings.

Centralized administration can also present the difficulty of becoming too extended and far-flung to ensure responsibility and compliance with national directives by local administrators. Here the concept of the **span of control**—that is, the number of subordinates directly reporting to a superior—becomes important. There is a limit to the number of subordinates any administrative official can effectively supervise. Administrative decentralization is one means of keeping the span of control manageable. The number of administrators reporting directly to the headquarters can be sharply reduced. At the same time, the regional, field, and installation levels might be able to adapt national guidelines to local conditions and coordinate the activities of local administrators in the same geographic area.

Federalism and administrative decentralization have different purposes. One promotes political values (representation, union, economic development, and perhaps military strength). The other promotes managerial values of efficiency, economy, administrative effectiveness, and responsiveness to clients and customers. But there is another difference. Administrative decentralization does not convey sovereignty to the subnational administrative units, whereas federalism does carry with it the notion that some subnational political units (states or provinces) are vested with a measure of sovereignty. We will return to these matters shortly.

◆◆   THE QUEST FOR UNIFORMITY: THE LEGAL APPROACH

Federalism and administrative decentralization raise the possibility that the extent of individual rights and the enforcement and implementation of administrative programs may vary widely from place to place. This is one of the advantages of these arrangements. But it can also be a drawback. Adapting to local conditions can stand in the way of integration of the nation's economy and economic development. It can also involve the violation of individual rights and standards of decency to which the political community is committed. In the United States, an example combining these two types of concerns was present prior to the adoption of the federal Civil Rights Act of 1964. In some states, by state law, individuals could be excluded from places of public accommodation, such as motels and restaurants, based on their race. African Americans, in particular, were also subject to segregation on common carriers (buses, trains) and in public buildings. Not only was this offensive to the national commitment to equal protection and decency, but, as the Supreme Court reasoned in *Katzenbach v. McClung* (1964),[5] it also impeded commerce by making it difficult for some people (African Americans) to travel.

This is where the legal perspective enters the picture most forcefully. Law, especially constitutional law, can be used to protect the most fundamental rights of individuals from infringement by states or administrative units. That federalism can enable local communities to have a good measure of political control over their lives is indisputable, but it does not necessarily protect minorities from repression by those communities. Consequently, it is often necessary that a line be drawn between local control and national protection. Typically, this is done on the basis that some rights are so fundamental that they must be given national recognition and protection. However, precisely what those rights are has varied over time and is often difficult to discern.

The Fourteenth Amendment

In the United States the courts are often called on to address this question. Historically, the Bill of Rights (the First, Fourth, Fifth, Sixth, and Eighth Amendments in particular) imposed restrictions on the federal government's treatment of individuals but did not place limitations on the states or their political subdivisions. During the late 19th century and throughout the 20th, however, constitutional theory held that the Fourteenth Amendment's guarantee that no state shall deprive any individual of life, liberty, or property without due process of law "incorporates" much of the Bill of Rights. Application of the Bill of Rights to the states through the Fourteenth Amendment after 1868 has expanded the civil rights and liberties of the citizenry immensely.

The Commerce Clause

The judiciary has also dramatically affected federalism through its interpretation of the **commerce clause.** The clause (Article I, section 8, clause 2) authorizes Congress "To regulate Commerce with foreign Nations, and among the several States, and with the Indian Tribes." Historically and at present, many court decisions have turned on the question of whether, in seeking to impose uniformity on commercial practices within the states, Congress had gone beyond its constitutional powers to regulate commerce. The clause was viewed as an improper basis for regulating commerce for social purposes, such as eliminating undesirable employment practices or conditions (e.g., the use of child labor) and for regulating activities that only indirectly affected the stream of interstate commerce. Today, however, the vast majority of economic activity in the nation is considered to be within the scope of Congress's reach. From 1942 until 1995, the scope of the commerce clause was governed by *Wickard v. Filburn.*[6] There the Supreme Court held that even a crop grown and largely consumed on a single farm within one state was subject to congressional regulation. The Court reasoned that crops grown for the farmers' personal consumption would have an impact on the national economy even though the crop never entered the commercial market directly.

Today, the federal government can regulate the channels of interstate commerce, such as motels and other places of public accommodation; persons, items, and the instrumentalities of interstate commerce, including vehicles and thefts from interstate shipments; and activities having a substantial relation to interstate commerce, either individually or in the aggregate, as in the case of farmers who exceed crop quotas. Based on these principles, the commerce clause gives to Congress power to enact landmark legislation such as the Civil Rights Act of 1964, which prohibits discrimination based on race, religion, sex, or ethnic origin. The commerce clause also supports federal law against discrimination based on age or disability. However, as broad as the commerce clause is, it does not give Congress power to regulate morality and social behavior in general. Under the Constitution's Tenth Amendment, such police power is reserved to the states.

Until the 1990s there appeared to be no clear limits to the federal government's powers under the commerce clause. However, in a series of cases the Supreme Court has emphasized that the acts being regulated must be *economic* in character. For instance, in *United States v. Lopez* (1995),[7] a slim majority of the Supreme Court held that Congress had exceeded its authority under the commerce clause when it enacted the Gun-Free School Zones Act of 1990, which prohibited knowingly bringing a firearm within 1,000 feet of a public, private, or parochial school anywhere in the United States.[8] According to the *Lopez* decision, as in *Wickard,* activity that falls into the scope of the commerce clause can be regulated by Congress even though it takes place wholly within a single state. By contrast, behavior that has little or no economic component cannot be regulated by Congress via the commerce clause. The importance of this limitation was demonstrated in *United States v. Morrison* (2000), in which a majority of the justices ruled that a provision of the federal Prevention of Violence Against Women Act of 1994 exceeded Congress's commerce clause powers because gender-motivated crimes are not economic activity.[9]

The commerce clause also places limits on state and local governments. By judicial construction there is a "negative" or "dormant" commerce clause. It rests on the view that "The Commerce Clause presumes a national market free from local legislation that discriminates in favor of local interests."[10] It prohibits (1) discrimination against interstate commerce, including regulations requiring that a local resource such as timber, raw milk, or shrimp be processed in-state; or (2) placing excessive burdens on interstate commerce, such as adopting regulations that conflict with those of other jurisdictions. By way of illustration, in *Carbone v. Town of Clarkstown* (1994), a majority of the Supreme Court held that a local "flow control" ordinance discriminated against interstate commerce by requiring that solid waste generated in or brought into Clarkstown, New York, be processed at a designated facility within the town. The ordinance made it impossible for other facilities to compete for processing the town's garbage and also for recyclers like Carbone to dispose of their nonrecyclable residual solid waste at other (and less expensive) facilities.[11] In a concurring opinion, Justice Sandra Day O'Connor argued that "[t]he increasing number of flow control regimes virtually ensures some inconsistency between jurisdictions, with the effect of eliminating the movement of waste between jurisdictions,"[12] and thereby excessively burdening interstate commerce.

The Tenth Amendment

By the late 1980s judicial interpretations of the commerce clause and limits on the states through incorporation of the Bill of Rights seemingly left the states with only limited vestiges of sovereignty. In the 1985 case of *Garcia v. San Antonio Metropolitan Transit Authority,*[13] the Supreme Court came close to holding that the Tenth Amendment was practically not enforceable. It reasoned that the states' chief protection against encroachments by the national government lay not in constitutional litigation but in the structure of Congress, which affords each equal representation in the Senate, regardless of population or other characteristics.

Some observers considered *Garcia* a death blow to federalism, but in the 1990s the Court breathed new life into Tenth Amendment jurisprudence. In *New York v. United States* (1992) and *Printz v. United States* (1997), it held that state sovereignty protects state (and local) governments or officials from being "commandeer[ed]" or "dragooned" into administering federal laws.[14] Significantly, in *Printz* the Court held that where "it is the whole object of the [national] law to direct the functioning of the state executive, and hence to compromise the structural framework of dual sovereignty, . . . a 'balancing' analysis is inappropriate."[15] Consequently, Congress's temporary and admittedly limited effort to compel local law enforcement officials to do background checks on gun purchasers as part of a federal handgun regulatory scheme violated the Tenth Amendment.

The Eleventh Amendment

In the late 1990s the Supreme Court also gave state sovereignty a strong boost in a series of Eleventh Amendment cases. The amendment, ratified in 1795, has always protected the states from being subject to some kinds of suits in federal court. It does not extend to local governments or to situations in which the states are allegedly acting in violation of the U.S. Constitution. But it does give the states immunity from a wide variety of suits involving commercial matters and personal injuries. By 2000, the Court had made it considerably more difficult for Congress to override this aspect of state sovereignty via the commerce clause and mapped out clear limitations on how it can be abrogated under the Fourteenth Amendment.

In *Seminole Tribe of Florida v. Florida* (1996), the Court ruled in a 5-4 decision that Congress is without power under the commerce clause to abrogate a state's sovereign immunity.[16] In so doing, the Court overruled an earlier decision in *Pennsylvania v. Union Gas* (1989) that recognized such authority.[17] The Court reasoned that only under the Fourteenth Amendment can Congress abrogate a state's sovereign immunity. In *Alden v. Maine* (1999), the Court, again by a slender 5-4 margin, extended constitutional protection to states that are sued in their own courts for violations of federal law.[18] Rather than base its decision on the Eleventh Amendment, which the Court admitted contains no such language, the majority concluded that the common law concept of sovereign immunity had been implicitly adopted by the framers of the Constitution, and was still in effect. Again in 2002, the Court ruled, in the case of *Federal Maritime Commission v. South Carolina State Ports Authority,* that the Constitution shielded states from having to answer private complaints brought before federal agencies.[19] This was the first time that the sovereign immunity doctrine was extended beyond the courts to proceedings in agencies of the executive branch. In his dissent, Justice Breyer argued that the majority had no support for its opinion "in any text, in any tradition, or in any relevant purpose."[20]

Congress can override state Eleventh Amendment immunity from suits for money damages by drafting legislation that is "congruent and proportional" to the states' infringement of individuals' equal protection rights. Using this formula, the Supreme Court held that state employees cannot sue their state employers in federal court for damages incurred by the states' violation of the federal Americans with Disabilities Act or Age Discrimination in Employment Act. In the Court's view, overriding Eleventh Amendment immunity for these violations is not congruent and proportional to the injuries caused by the states' discrimination against their disabled or older employees. By contrast, the Court upheld the Family and Medical Leave Act's Eleventh Amendment override because the act was intended to deal with gender discrimination by state employers, which is a much more serious affront to the equal protection clause.[21]

Because *Lopez, Morrison, New York, Printz,* and the Eleventh Amendment cases were decided by narrow 5-4 or 6-3 majorities and contained vigorous dissents, the balance between national power and state sovereignty can hardly be considered a matter of settled law, and things can change. At present Congress can get around some of the constitutional limitations on its powers by attaching conditions to the funding it grants to the states. Thus far, the Supreme Court has adhered to the legal principle that these conditions do not invade state sovereignty because the states are free to reject them—along with the federal funding to which they are attached. The political reality may be different, and a state's elected officials may have a hard time explaining to the voters why they are turning down millions of dollars in federal funds. For instance, the federal government was effectively able to establish a national drinking age of 21 by making states ineligible for federal highway funds if they allowed younger people to purchase alcoholic beverages.[22] Some states resisted the condition, but none was willing to forfeit the funds indefinitely.

◆→ EVOLVING MODELS OF AMERICAN FEDERALISM

The United States has evolved through several models of federalism. Change has taken place in response to political interests, administrative concerns, and the nation's desire to establish uniformity. These models are graphically depicted in Box 3.2. The first model, **dual federalism,** predominated in the American system from 1787 until around 1933 (the advent of President Franklin Roosevelt's New Deal). David Nice characterizes dual federalism as a system in which each level of government, national and state, "is supreme within its areas of responsibility. According to this model, neither level is dominant and neither level should intervene in the affairs of the other."[23] For instance, exclusive authority might be vested in the states for education and labor law, whereas foreign affairs is solely in the domain of the federal government. The federal and state governments are viewed as competitive in their relationship. Dual federalism is sometimes called "layer-cake federalism," or the "coordinated authority model." However, a black and white cookie would be a better metaphor than a layer cake because dual sovereignty does not establish a hierarchical relationship in which the states are always subordinated to the federal government. This period was characterized by a state-centered brand of federalism.

The New Deal marked the end of dual federalism—until the 1990s, at least. The expansion of federal powers to deal with the Great Depression of the 1930s gave rise to a more nation-centered federalism whereby the states and federal government would cooperate in certain critical areas, with the federal government playing a key coordinating role. To this end, large amounts of federal funding were provided to states and localities for job creation, social welfare, and infrastructure development (among other things). The period from roughly 1933 until around 1964 is thus characterized by **cooperative federalism,** although it is sometimes called "marble-cake federalism" or the "overlapping authority model." Nice refers to this model as one of "interdependency," "based on a sharing of power and responsibility, with the various participants working toward shared goals."[24] In this model, the states act primarily as the service delivery arm, while the federal government makes available its greater resources.

3.2 MODELS OF FEDERALISM IN U.S. HISTORY

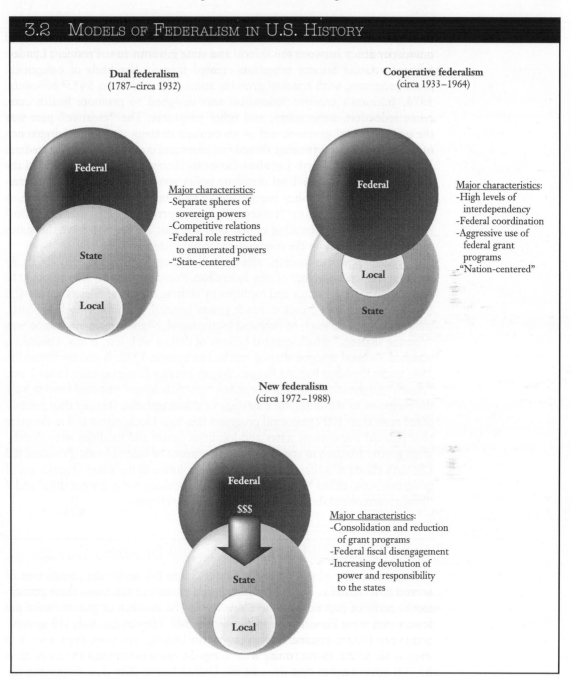

Dual federalism
(1787–circa 1932)

Federal

State

Local

Major characteristics:
-Separate spheres of
 sovereign powers
-Competitive relations
-Federal role restricted
 to enumerated powers
-"State-centered"

Cooperative federalism
(circa 1933–1964)

Federal

Local

State

Major characteristics:
-High levels of
 interdependency
-Federal coordination
-Aggressive use of
 federal grant
 programs
-"Nation-centered"

New federalism
(circa 1972–1988)

Federal

$$$

State

Local

Major characteristics:
-Consolidation and reduction
 of grant programs
-Federal fiscal disengagement
-Increasing devolution of
 power and responsibility
 to the states

Since 1964, however, the United States has been in another era, characterized in a number of ways that more or less describe the kind and degree of interdependency between the federal and state governments. President Lyndon Johnson's Great Society programs created literally hundreds of categorical grant programs, with funding growing some 540 percent to $41.7 billion by 1973. Johnson's **creative federalism** was designed to promote health care, crime reduction, antipoverty, and other programs. The "creative" part was the use of federal grants-in-aid as an explicit strategy and federal bypassing of the states, passing funding directly to cities and counties in some 70 federal programs. Former North Carolina Governor Terry Sanford characterized the federal presence in state-level domestic policy spheres as **picket-fence federalism,** wherein federal policy reaches down to subnational levels within major policy areas like so many "pickets."[25] This is perhaps not as useful a model today because of accelerating efforts over the past 30 years to have the states regain their primacy in the intergovernmental system.

Federal power in domestic affairs reached its apex during the early 1970s. At that time, under the banner of **new federalism,** President Richard Nixon sought to restore power to the states and localities by shifting the Great Society categorical (i.e., special-purpose) grants to block grants (general, fairly open-ended grants), subject to increased levels of state and local control. Nixon's main innovation was "revenue sharing," which granted billions of dollars with few, if any, conditions attached. General revenue sharing reached its apex in 1978. It was terminated in 1986 under President Ronald Reagan, largely because Congress came to see it as a "crutch" for the states. Reagan's brand of "new federalism" involved turning back the programs to the states via a strategy of disengagement. Reagan thus consolidated more than 500 categorical programs into nine block grants and at the same time reduced transfers to states and localities. States and localities were thereby given greater freedom to spend a declining amount of federal funds. President Bill Clinton's efforts at welfare reform and the devolution to the states of major social programs—also called "new federalism"—will be discussed in greater detail under "Intergovernmental Relations" (IGR), later in the chapter.

◆→ AMERICAN GOVERNMENT: THE BUILDING BLOCKS

The vast majority of people in the United States fall under the jurisdiction of several governments. The exact number and the mix of functions these governments perform depend on where one lives. The number of governments per state varies from Hawaii's 21 to Illinois's 6,968. Hawaii has only .15 governments per 10,000 residents, whereas North Dakota has more than 43.[26] It is impossible to do justice to the wide range of variation among the more than 89,000 governments that exist in the United States. Box 3.3, displaying the number of federal, state, and local employees allocated to various functions, provides an idea of the activities with which the federal, state, and local governments are most concerned. Box 3.4 shows the size and growth of public employment in the states (including local governments) from 1954 to 2008.

3.3 ALL GOVERNMENTS—EMPLOYMENT BY FUNCTION: 2011 (AT MARCH. COVERS FULL-TIME AND PART-TIME EMPLOYEES. LOCAL GOVERNMENT AMOUNTS ARE ESTIMATES.)

Function	Total	Federal (civilian)*	Employees (000s) State and local Total	State	Local
National defense†	806	806	n.a.	n.a.	n.a.
Postal Service	632	632	n.a.	n.a.	n.a.
Space research and technology	19	19	n.a.	n.a.	n.a.
Elementary and secondary education	7,541	n.a.	7,541	44	5,998
Higher education	1,506	n.a.	2,830	1,267	239
Other education	91	11	80	80	n.a.
Health	571	163	408	189	219
Hospitals	1,057	209	848	355	493
Public welfare	482	9	473	225	248
Social insurance administration	464	71	393	82	311
Police protection	1,072	189	883	100	783
Fire protection	320	n.a.	320	n.a.	320
Correction	743	38	705	457	248
Highways	501	3	498	218	280
Air transportation	92	48	43	3	41
Water transport/terminals	18	5	13	5	8
Solid waste management	101	n.a.	101	2	99
Sewerage	122	n.a.	122	2	120
Parks and recreation	212	27	185	28	157
Natural resources	348	188	160	124	36
Housing and community development	120	15	105	0	105
Water supply	164	n.a.	164	1	163
Electric power	84	0	84	4	80
Gas supply	11	0	11	0	11
Transit	220	n.a.	220	32	188
Libraries	93	4	89	1	88
State liquor stores	6	n.a.	6	6	0
Financial administration	494	128	366	156	210
Other government administration	265	25	240	48	192
Judicial and legal	463	64	399	167	232
Other and unallocable	610	199	411	180	231
Total	17,414	2,854	14,560	3,779	10,781

* Includes employees outside United States.
† Includes international relations.

Note: Numbers may not sum due to rounding.

Source: U.S. Census Bureau, Federal, State, and Local Governments, "Public Employment and Payroll Data"; Available online at: http://www.census.gov/govs/apes/

3.4   BUREAUCRATIC SIZE AND GROWTH IN THE STATES, 1954–2008

State	1954 Number of Employees*	1954 Bureaucratic Load†	2008 Number of Employees	2008 Bureaucratic Load	% Increase in Size	% Average Annual Growth	% Increase in Bureaucratic Load
Alabama	77,895	2.5	324,365	6.9	316	2.68	176
Alaska	(prior to statehood)		62,644	9.1	n.a.	n.a.	n.a.
Arizona	28,787	3.8	373,696	5.8	1,198	4.86	53
Arkansas	43,318	2.3	190,155	6.6	339	2.78	187
California	438,772	4.1	2,256,634	6.2	414	3.08	51
Colorado	51,539	3.9	320,650	6.5	522	3.44	67
Connecticut	(not available)		227,433	6.5	n.a.	n.a.	n.a.
Delaware	11,477	3.6	58,822	6.7	413	3.07	86
Florida	109,926	4.0	1,049,028	5.7	854	4.27	43
Georgia	89,680	2.6	604,002	6.2	574	3.60	138
Hawaii	(prior to statehood)		90,599	7.0	n.a.	n.a.	n.a.
Idaho	21,143	3.6	107,779	7.1	410	3.06	97
Illinois	251,288	2.9	800,539	6.2	219	2.17	114
Indiana	120,725	3.1	423,601	6.6	251	2.35	113
Iowa	90,611	3.5	232,004	7.8	156	1.76	123
Kansas	69,235	3.6	241,713	8.6	249	2.34	139
Kentucky	66,235	2.3	279,962	6.5	323	2.71	183
Louisiana	92,148	3.4	314,294	7.1	241	2.30	109
Maine	30,926	3.4	102,812	7.8	232	2.25	129
Maryland	69,651	3.0	339,137	6.0	387	2.97	100
Massachusetts	167,521	3.6	403,808	6.2	141	1.64	72
Michigan	221,332	3.5	600,755	6.0	171	1.87	71
Minnesota	114,543	3.8	360,790	6.9	215	2.15	83
Mississippi	57,043	2.6	218,186	7.4	282	2.52	185
Missouri	108,851	2.8	391,944	6.6	260	2.40	136
Montana	22,248	3.8	70,094	7.2	215	2.33	89
Nebraska	51,601	3.9	143,208	8.0	178	1.91	105
Nevada	8,213	5.1	135,957	5.2	1,555	5.33	2
New Hampshire	21,059	3.9	87,006	6.6	313	2.66	69

It leaves no doubt that much public administrative activity takes place at the subnational levels of government. Although there are great differences among governments at the subnational level, some common features can be described.

Municipalities

Municipalities are cities, towns, villages, or boroughs, legally defined as public corporations. Their objective is to provide governance and public administration

| State | 1954 | | 2008 | | % Increase in Size | % Average Annual Growth | % Increase in Bureaucratic Load |
	Number of Employees*	Bureaucratic Load	Number of Employees	Bureaucratic Load			
New Jersey	149,427	3.1	585,379	6.8	292	2.56	119
New Mexico	24,853	3.6	144,852	7.3	483	3.32	103
New York	540,075	3.6	1,410,211	7.2	161	1.79	100
North Carolina	108,903	2.7	655,598	7.1	502	3.38	163
North Dakota	24,905	4.0	60,528	9.4	143	1.66	135
Ohio	254,615	3.2	750,760	6.5	195	2.02	103
Oklahoma	76,676	3.4	249,724	6.9	226	2.21	103
Oregon	56,934	3.7	240,869	6.4	323	2.71	73
Pennsylvania	260,188	2.5	696,616	5.5	168	1.84	120
Rhode Island	22,836	2.9	59,761	5.6	162	1.80	93
South Carolina	58,783	2.8	290,428	6.4	394	3.00	129
South Dakota	25,308	3.9	60,891	7.6	141	1.64	95
Tennessee	87,188	2.6	369,578	5.9	324	2.71	127
Texas	230,232	3.0	1,522,294	6.5	561	3.56	117
Utah	28,604	4.2	179,899	6.6	529	3.46	57
Vermont	13,002	3.4	49,997	8.1	285	2.53	138
Virginia	96,109	2.9	562,602	7.2	485	3.33	148
Washington	94,193	4.0	427,078	6.5	353	2.84	63
West Virginia	50,600	2.5	117,327	6.5	132	1.57	160
Wisconsin	119,494	3.8	379,539	6.7	218	2.16	76
Wyoming	12,411	4.3	59,238	11.1	377	2.94	158
Total	4,771,194		19,643,836				

* Combined state and local (full-time equivalent employees), excluding Washington, D.C. (DC has 48,969 employees).
† Bureaucratic load = number of public sector employees per 100 persons in the state population. [Note: Excludes contract employees.]

Source: Data from Council of State Governments, *The Book of the States, 1954–56, 2010 Editions* (Lexington, Ky: Council of State Governments).

to local areas. Cities typically provide a greater range of functions than do other municipalities and may have special status under a state's constitution. At a minimum, all municipalities seek to provide for public safety and perform some amount of public works. Cities may provide not only these functions but also hospitals, libraries, elaborate zoning and planning, higher education, museums, jails, public parks, recreation, and various licensing and inspection functions.

Municipalities tend to fall into one of three types of governmental structure. The **mayor-council** form of government is especially prevalent in the nation's cities with 500,000 or more residents. Here the mayor has primarily executive functions, whereas the council has both executive and legislative functions. In what has been dubbed the "weak-mayor" variant, the heads of the city's departments may be directly elected, thereby limiting the mayor's control over their selection and activity. The council in such a form of government may be directly involved in executive decision making. Under the "strong-mayor" plan, department heads are directly appointed by the mayor, subject to council approval. Here, although the mayor and the council make policy jointly, it is the mayor's legal responsibility to execute it. It is large cities that mostly rely on the strong-mayor approach. In practice, each city is likely to have its own hybrid of the strong- and weak-mayor approaches. The mayor-council approach was created to assure a separation of executive and legislative powers and a system of checks and balances. Council members may be elected "at large," that is, citywide, by wards, or in some combination of the two.

At the other extreme, only about 3 percent of municipalities (generally with populations of less than 5,000) rely on the **commission plan** of governance. Here, a number of commissioners, frequently five, are elected at large, generally for a four-year term. One serves as chair of the commission. There is little separation of powers; the commission is a deliberative legislative body, yet each commissioner has executive responsibility for the operations of a specific department. The plan is convenient in politically and socially homogeneous jurisdictions. However, where there is marked political conflict, the commission can become deadlocked and administrative operations may not be coordinated with one another.

The **council-manager** plan is the third common form of municipal governance. It is found in nearly two-thirds of all cities with a population of 25,000 or more. Historically, the council-manager approach was last to evolve and was a part of the broader effort at administrative reform from the 1880s to the 1920s that included the establishment of merit systems for the selection of civil servants. The council-manager plan reflects the orthodox managerial approach to public administration in many respects. It presumes that the main problems of cities are administrative, not political. This was often captured in the aphorism that "there is no Republican and no Democratic way to pave a street." It also assumes that although the managers of cities should be responsible to elected officials, administration should not be infused with electoral concerns.

The council is generally elected at large on a nonpartisan basis. It has legislative authority for the city, passing ordinances, developing or sanctioning policy, and approving financial and budgetary proposals. Generally the council consists of five to nine members. It is presided over by a mayor, who may be one of its members. The mayor in this form of government has important ceremonial functions but no significant executive powers. The council hires a manager, who serves at its pleasure. The manager is the chief executive officer of the city and has the authority to appoint and dismiss the heads of administrative departments.

The council, in turn, is barred from involvement in administrative matters other than the selection and retention of the manager. City managers are considered professionals and often hold advanced degrees in public administration. Their jobs may be extremely difficult because it is often impossible for the manager to avoid becoming involved in political disputes—or even the object of them.

Townships

Townships are found primarily in the Midwest and mid-Atlantic states. Originally they were used to identify sections of federal lands. Today they often constitute civic units as well. They are characteristic in rural areas and provide a minimum of functions, sometimes having responsibility only for roads. Townships rely heavily on the commission form of government.

Counties

Counties are a comprehensive, general form of local government with a wide range of functions. Municipalities, townships, and other forms of government (school districts and special districts) are found within their boundaries. Counties are best considered to be arms of the state government for local administration and governance. Exceptions are in New England, where the states tend to rely on "towns" more than counties; Louisiana, which uses "parishes"; and Alaska, where "boroughs" provide some of the functions supplied by counties elsewhere. Their number varies widely from state to state, as does their size. On average, there are 65 counties per state. Some are highly urbanized, such as New York County (Manhattan), whereas others are rural. Counties have no sovereignty or inherent authority.

County functions vary widely, but with few if any exceptions, they include some law enforcement functions, tax functions, and record keeping. Many counties have important responsibilities for education, recreation, roads, and civic activities. The typical county is governed by a board of elected commissioners, frequently called a board of supervisors. About two-thirds of counties have boards of 3 to 5 members, but some have as many as 30 or more.[27] The board has policy and administrative functions. It oversees a number of appointive officials who carry out executive responsibilities. In addition to the board, voters typically elect a number of other county officials, including sheriffs, judicial officers, clerks, treasurers, assessors, and coroners. Some counties have professional managers and/or elected executives. In rural areas, the county may be the main focus of governance. In more urban settings, the coexistence of counties and municipalities may lead to a patchwork of overlapping functions and haphazard relationships.

School Districts and Other Special Districts

Special districts are "single-purpose" local governments. They deal primarily with such areas as water, sewage, recreation, highways, bridges, fire protection, cemeteries, libraries, and utilities. School districts are a special case. They were established to give local communities control over the education of their children. In the past, the independence of school districts was a guarantee of diversity. Today, however, school systems must meet so many state and federal requirements that a good deal of educational uniformity now exists. For the most part, school districts are governed by boards. Most of these boards are elected, but a substantial minority are appointed by municipal or county officials. Other special districts, sometimes called "authorities," are also headed by boards, but a higher proportion of the members may be appointed. Special districts often overlap several municipal and/or county governments, and a board may be composed of elected or appointed representatives of those units of government. Special districts frequently exercise considerable powers of taxation and authority to charge user fees and incur debt. Ease of debt issuance for specific purposes has, in fact, been one of the factors behind the rapid increase in the number of special districts. For the most part, however, the average citizen seems unconcerned with their composition and operations— at least as long as things are running smoothly. Historically, special districts have been considered a way of taking particular functions, such as cemeteries, water, and libraries, out of the political arena and of making it possible to manage them in a "businesslike" manner.

States

In many respects, the *structure* of state governments tends to parallel that of the federal government. The executive branch in all states is headed by an elected governor, some of whom have weaker formal powers than others. With the exception of Nebraska, all states have a bicameral legislature. The upper house is invariably called the *senate,* whereas the lower house may be called an *assembly* or *state house.* The states also provide for independent judiciaries having the power of judicial review. The highest court in most states is called the *state supreme court* (some call it the court of appeals). Despite these structural similarities, however, many states differ markedly from the pattern of political and administrative arrangements found at the national level. They also differ broadly from one another.

One of the most striking differences is the nature of state constitutions. Only those of Massachusetts (adopted in 1780) and New Hampshire (adopted in 1784) have had the longevity of the U.S. Constitution, adopted in 1789. Most states have had more than one constitution; Louisiana has had 11. Only those of Connecticut and Vermont are as concise as the federal Constitution; many are much wordier. Most have also been amended more frequently than has the U.S. Constitution. Some have been amended repeatedly, such as those of California and South Carolina, which have been changed 519 and 493 times, respectively.[28] These differences reflect a virtue of federalism in enabling each state to adapt its governmental powers and processes to its economic, political, and social conditions and needs.

They also reflect the ability of organized pressure groups to advance their interests by having provisions written into state constitutions. State constitutions are far more detailed than the federal Constitution, sometimes resembling ordinary legislation in spelling out provisions for roads, sewer systems, and zoos![29] Many of them are easier to amend than is the federal Constitution, which accounts in part for the tendency to treat them as vehicles for the expression of policy as well as statements of the fundamental law by which the state governments operate. In several states—including large ones such as California, Florida, Massachusetts, and Illinois—constitutional amendments can be initiated directly by the people.[30] All state constitutions provide for checks and balances, suffrage and elections, taxation and appropriations, local government, public education, state institutions, and law enforcement.[31]

The states also vary greatly in their administrative structures. Every governor is considered the head of state administrative operations, but the governor's power to appoint, engage in fiscal management, and supervise administrators varies considerably from one state to another. In several states six or more administrative officials are elected by the voters. In Connecticut, for example, the constitution provides for the separate election of the secretary of state, treasurer, comptroller, and attorney general. (These officials are often of different political parties.) Among those most frequently elected are attorneys general, lieutenant governors, treasurers, secretaries of state, auditors, and superintendents of education. Among other elective state administrators are agricultural commissioners; controllers; and commissioners for insurance, land, labor, highways, railroads, corporations, and charities. University regents and others may also be elected.[32] Generally speaking, the greater the number of elected administrative officials is, the less control the governor has over state public administration. Elected officials may be opposed to the governor's policies and administrative programs. The governor has no formal role in selecting these officials and cannot fire them. Their responsibility is to the voters, who may see no problem in electing administrative executives who are opposed to one another. Moreover, elected administrators may tend to develop closer relationships with the legislature than with the governor.

The governor's ability to oversee administrative matters is also complicated by the unwieldy structures of many state governments. In 2010, on average, a governor had more than 20 cabinet departments reporting directly to him or her.[33] But the number of separate agencies could reach well over 100. From a managerial perspective, the average governor's span of control is too large to be effective. Consequently, efforts have been made in several states to reform their administrative structures by consolidating the agencies into a few departments. In part, however, the fragmented administrative structures of the states reflect the competing concerns of public administration. Some independent boards and commissions are designed to exercise judicial functions and to be independent of the rest of the government to a considerable degree. Others provide political representation for the interests of distinct economic, social, or geographic groups. Still others are engaged in executive functions and are most likely to be placed more closely under the governor's control.

Finally, there are widespread variations in the patterns of state-level party politics; the professionalization and strength of state legislatures and administrative components; the scope of services and regulations states provide; and the mix of administrative responsibility among counties, local jurisdictions, and the state government. When taken together, these differences make administrative life different from state to state. They can also lead to serious complications in trying to draft federal legislation and programs that require state administration of a certain caliber. We will return to this problem after we briefly review the federal government's administrative structure.

Federal

We have already mentioned many of the salient features of the federal government's administrative component in our discussion of the rise of the contemporary American administrative state (Chapter 2). However, a summary of the federal administrative structure is in order (refer to Box 3.5). As in the states, the federal administrative structure is fragmented. It consists of departments, agencies, commissions, corporations, and a number of miscellaneous units. Departments are generally considered the most important and comprehensive administrative units. They enjoy the highest formal status. Today, there are 15 departments—the most recent addition being Homeland Security—although their number has varied over the years. There are marked differences in their sizes and budgets. The Department of Defense (DOD) overshadows all others in size and complexity. At the other end of the scale, the Department of Education and the Commerce Department are relatively small. The structure of these departments also differs considerably. Some are pyramidal, hierarchical organizations resembling a typical bureaucracy. Others are conglomerates of separate, somewhat autonomous units and may be thought of as types of "holding companies." The DOD is an example, being composed of the Army, Navy, and Air Force, among other units. Typically, departments are distinguished from other administrative organizations, such as agencies, by the comprehensiveness or national importance of their missions.

Independent agencies are administrative units outside the departments with responsibility for more limited areas of public policy. The Environmental Protection Agency, the Small Business Administration, and the National Aeronautics and Space Administration are examples. These agencies are called "independent" because they are not housed within departments. In practice, however, they may be more tightly controlled by the president than some departments are. Independent agencies may be large, though the scope of their mission is often limited, focusing on a particular group of people or sector of the economy. Some independent agencies, such as the General Services Administration and the Office of Personnel Management, engage in overhead administrative functions, including supply, security, and personnel.

Independent regulatory commissions are another kind of unit. These commissions are deliberately designed to be autonomous and removed from direct presidential control. Among the better known regulatory commissions

3.5 THE GOVERNMENT OF THE UNITED STATES

The Constitution

Legislative Branch

THE CONGRESS
Senate   House

Architect of the Capitol
United States Botanic Garden
Government Accountability Office
Government Printing Office
Library of Congress
Congressional Budget Office

Executive Branch

THE PRESIDENT
THE VICE PRESIDENT
Executive Office of the President

White House Office
Office of the Vice President
Council of Economic Advisers
Council of Environmental Quality
National Security Council
Office of Administration

Office of Management and Budget
Office of National Drug Control Policy
Office of Policy Development
Office of Science and Technology Policy
Office of the U.S. Trade Representative

Judicial Branch

THE SUPREME COURT OF THE UNITED STATES

United States Court of Appeals
United States District Courts
Territorial Courts
United States Court of International Trade
United States Court of Federal Claims
United States Court of Appeals for the Armed Forces
United States Tax Court
United States Court of Appeals for Veterans Claims
Administrative Office of the United States Courts
Federal Judicial Center
United States Sentencing Commission

DEPARTMENT OF AGRICULTURE

DEPARTMENT OF COMMERCE

DEPARTMENT OF DEFENSE

DEPARTMENT OF EDUCATION

DEPARTMENT OF ENERGY

DEPARTMENT OF HEALTH AND HUMAN SERVICES

DEPARTMENT OF HOMELAND SECURITY

DEPARTMENT OF HOUSING AND URBAN DEVELOPMENT

DEPARTMENT OF THE INTERIOR

DEPARTMENT OF JUSTICE

DEPARTMENT OF LABOR

DEPARTMENT OF STATE

DEPARTMENT OF TRANSPORTATION

DEPARTMENT OF THE TREASURY

DEPARTMENT OF VETERANS AFFAIRS

INDEPENDENT ESTABLISHMENTS AND GOVERNMENT CORPORATIONS

African Development Foundation
Broadcasting Board of Governors
Central Intelligence Agency
Commodity Futures Trading Commission
Consumer Product Safety Commission
Corporation for National and Community Service
Defense Nuclear Facilities Safety Board
Environmental Protection Agency
Equal Employment Opportunity Commission
Export-Import Bank of the United States
Farm Credit Administration
Federal Communications Commission
Federal Deposit Insurance Corporation
Federal Election Commission

Federal Housing Finance Board
Federal Labor Relations Authority
Federal Maritime Commission
Federal Mediation and Conciliation Service
Federal Mine Safety and Health Review Commission
Federal Reserve System
Federal Retirement Thrift Investment Board
Federal Trade Commission
General Services Administration
Inter-American Foundation
Merit Systems Protection Board
National Aeronautics and Space Administration
National Archives and Records Administration
National Capital Planning Commission

National Credit Union Administration
National Foundation on the Arts and the Humanities
National Labor Relations Board
National Mediation Board
National Railroad Passenger Corporation (Amtrak)
National Science Foundation
National Transportation Safety Board
Nuclear Regulatory Commission
Occupational Safety and Health Review Commission
Office of the Director of National Intelligence
Office of Government Ethics
Office of Personnel Management
Office of Special Counsel
Overseas Private Investment Corporation

Peace Corps
Pension Benefit Guaranty Corporation
Postal Rate Commission
Railroad Retirement Board
Securities and Exchange Commission
Selective Service System
Small Business Administration
Social Security Administration
Tennessee Valley Authority
Trade and Development Agency
U.S. Agency for International Development
U.S. Commission on Civil Rights
U.S. International Trade Commission
U.S. Postal Service

are the Federal Communications Commission, the Securities and Exchange Commission, the National Labor Relations Board, and the Federal Trade Commission. Such commissions are headed by a bipartisan group of commissioners appointed by the president with the advice and consent of the Senate. They hold staggered terms and are not removable by the president except for specified causes. The president may disagree with them on policy, but he or she cannot replace them for this reason until their terms expire. They are not subject to a number of executive orders or to the same Office of Management and Budget controls that apply to other departments and agencies. The regulatory commissions have quasi-legislative and/or quasi-judicial functions. They may make rules for regulation of some sector of the economy and enforce those rules; this often requires judicial-style hearings. The basic idea behind the regulatory commission is that taking an area out of the "tug and pull" of legislative politics makes it possible to weigh competing perspectives on a matter, such as the rates common carriers can charge or what constitutes an unfair labor or trade practice, and to arrive at decisions that are judicious, fair, and in the public interest. (Regulatory administration is the subject of Chapter 9.)

Federal corporations, such as the Tennessee Valley Authority (TVA) and the Federal Deposit Insurance Corporation (FDIC), differ from other federal units primarily in that they sell products or services. The U.S. Postal Service sells mail service; the TVA sells electricity; the FDIC sells insurance. A variant on federal corporations are Government-Sponsored Enterprises, such as the housing finance giants Fannie Mae and Freddie Mac. Such administrative units can be run more according to private sector methods than can other governmental activities. They generate their own revenues through sales and, as long as they do not run deficits, need not rely on budgetary appropriations. When successful, this gives the corporations a large measure of financial independence from the legislature and budgetary process. By contrast, when they are unsuccessful, federal corporations may turn to Congress for additional funds, or a "bailout." This occurred in the instances of both Fannie Mae and Freddie Mac during the real estate crisis period of the early years of the Great Recession (2008–2009). In most other respects, however, the legal status of corporations is similar to that of other agencies. Like all governmental agencies, they are subject to constitutional constraints.

In practice, federal administrative arrangements are somewhat more complicated than presented here. Hybrids can be found among the independent agencies and the regulatory commissions. There are a number of agencies called *boards,* and there are foundations, institutes, and institutions. Interagency committees and advisory committees are plentiful. Some executive branch units are in the Executive Office of the President (EOP), such as the Office of Management and Budget, whereas others having related functions, such as the Office of Personnel Management, are outside the EOP. Many of the reasons for these organizational arrangements are discussed in Chapter 4. They reflect the competing managerial, political, and legalistic perspectives on public administration. Their net result, however, is governmental fragmentation and a degree of complexity in trying to coordinate public policy. Not only does the American governmental and political structure make coordination among the different levels of government difficult, it also makes coordination within governments a considerable task. This can greatly complicate intergovernmental relations.

✦✦   INTERGOVERNMENTAL RELATIONS

Federal-State Relations and Fiscal Federalism

Federalism requires coordination and cooperation along two major dimensions. One is between the national government and state governments; the other is between or among the states. However, the central question has always concerned the extent of state sovereignty in the federal system. What, precisely, are the powers reserved to the states by the Tenth Amendment? As early as the 1790s, Virginia and Kentucky argued that the states possessed the sovereignty to declare acts of the federal government to be void on the grounds that they violated the U.S. Constitution. The Virginia and Kentucky "resolves" were in response to the federal Naturalization, Alien, and Sedition Acts of 1798. That the Virginia resolves were drafted by James Madison, who played a leading role in the drafting and ratification of the U.S. Constitution, and that Kentucky's statement was written by Thomas Jefferson gave this view of federalism some credibility. In the 1820s and 1830s, John C. Calhoun of South Carolina articulated the notion that the states possessed the right to nullify federal laws they viewed as unconstitutional. In 1832, South Carolina attempted this, but after President Jackson threatened to use military force against the state, a compromise was reached and the state repealed its nullification ordinance. The view that the states possessed broad rights to go their own way was one of the factors that led to the Civil War, when 11 states seceded from the federal union in 1861.

For the most part, the Civil War put to rest the theory that each state has an inherent right to define the scope of *federal* powers. Every now and then, however, a state may refuse to abide by a federal statute and may even make a dramatic show of the affair. These legal battles are fought out in the courts, and in the past several decades, until quite recently, the federal judiciary has not sided with the states. The federal courts have been so active in applying the U.S. Constitution to the states that a kind of "juridical" or "judicial" federalism has developed. For instance, it is not unusual for federal judges to be involved in the drawing of state legislative districts, the operation of public schools, or the reform of state and local prisons and jails.

Another fundamental question in federal-state relationships concerns equity. To what extent should each state be treated equally by the federal government? Should federal grants to the states follow a strict formula? Should they take state population, state size, and state need into account? As a practical matter, politics is frequently the motivating force behind federal allocations to states and their subdivisions. But this does not exclude other factors. There is considerable variation in (1) the federal presence in the states in the form of federal civilian and military employment, military bases, and federal contracts and (2) the total federal spending per capita within states. Sometimes the politics involved in federal allocations depends heavily on the memberships on various congressional committees and the relationship between these committees and the federal administrative units with which they deal. For instance, membership on the House Armed Services Committee has long been associated with disproportionately high military spending in one's district.[34]

Many contemporary federal-state relationships involve money. The basic pattern of expansion of federal relationships with state governments has involved federal grants as part of the federal government's attempt to achieve some national policy. This approach is not new; the Morrill Act of 1862 provided federal aid to state land-grant colleges in an effort to advance higher education. The Federal Aid Road Act of 1916 made federal funds available to the states for highway construction as part of a policy intended to modernize road transportation in the wake of the growing use of automobiles. What has changed is the scope of federal grants and the degree of cooperation and coordination that they require of the states.

From 1964 to 1980, federal contributions to state and local spending increased from about 14 percent of state and local spending to about 25 percent; they declined during the 1980s in both absolute and proportional terms but then began to rise again in the early 1990s. They totaled 20.9 percent in 2000, but in the aftermath of the Great Recession, have climbed dramatically. According to Scheppach and Hildreth, "History will write the two-year period of 2009 to 2010 as a watershed in the federal-state-local fiscal relationship. The outpouring of aid helped states to avoid cutting spending and increasing taxes in the depths of the Great Recession. Federal grants dramatically increased as a percentage of total state revenues, from 26 percent to 35 percent."[35] Today, there are over 900 grant programs administered in around 26 federal grant-making agencies, offering grants in 20 categories.[36] In recent years, the federal government has relied heavily on the three types of grants described in Box 3.6 to further national policies at the state level.

Grants can also be classified according to how the funds are distributed. *Formula grants* are based on a decision rule, such as *x* dollars per public school pupil in daily attendance. The rule is frequently written into the legislation creating the grant, though it could also be established by the administering agency. The purpose is to allocate money on the basis of general social conditions in the recipient government's jurisdiction. Block grants are always distributed on a formula basis.

Project grants require jurisdictions seeking funds to submit applications describing how they intend to use the money. The administrative agency makes allocations based on the merits of these proposals and the funds made available by the legislature. Consequently, project grants allow for considerable

3.6   THREE BROAD TYPES OF FEDERAL GRANTS

1. *Categorical grants* are provided for specific programs and may be used only for narrowly defined purposes. Welfare, airports, and highway programs are examples. Sometimes the states are required to participate in funding operations undertaken through such grants. As noted previously, the federal strings attached to such grants may involve matters that the states could legitimately consider to be within their sovereignty, such as speed limits, drinking age, public personnel, and collective bargaining regulations. Sometimes these grants are allocated based on a formula; others must be specifically applied for. The proportion of federal grant money that was categorical was 73 percent in 1978, had risen to around 90 percent by 1993, and remains at this level as of 2012.

2. *Block grants* are less tightly circumscribed by federal regulations. They provide federal funding for a general policy area of governmental activity, such as community development, education, health services, and crime control and leave a good deal of flexibility to the states in deciding how the funds should be used. An example is the Community Development Block Grant (CDBG). The intent is to give the recipient governments considerable flexibility in responding to their most pressing needs.

3. *Revenue sharing* began in 1972 as a process in which the federal government disbursed funds to state and local governments to use as they saw fit. The major restriction was that the recipient government must not engage in prohibited forms of discrimination. The amount of money transmitted to state and local governments through revenue sharing was predetermined by a complex formula. Most revenue-sharing funds were spent on equipment, streets, and roads rather than on social services and health programs. In part this was because such funds were so limited, but state and local officials were also apparently reluctant to use revenue-sharing grants in ways that would put pressures on their budgets in times of federal cutbacks.[37] A thing of the past, general revenue sharing was phased out in 1987. General-purpose grants now constitute only about 1 percent of federal grants.

administrative discretion and promote politicking after the legislature has established the general parameters and scope of funding. Categorical grants have historically been around two-thirds project-based.

Matching grants require the recipient to contribute some of its resources to the activity for which the funds are earmarked. Matching does not always require that a state or local jurisdiction put up one dollar for each dollar it receives.

The idea is to stimulate state and/or local expenditure in pursuit of federal policy goals and to be sure that the recipient government is serious. While some grants are fixed, others are open-ended. In the latter case, the amount allocated will depend on the number of individuals eligible for a program, the number treated by it, or on other factors.

Devolution in the 1990s

The grant system is a deeply entrenched feature of federalism. The Reagan administration sought to reorganize it to reduce paperwork, administrative costs, and the federal budgetary deficit, while at the same time encouraging the states to take on more responsibility. In particular, an effort was made to consolidate categorical grants into broad block grants, and general revenue sharing was terminated. However, despite some successes, Reagan's approach met considerable resistance in Congress. As an institution, the legislature demonstrated a powerful orientation toward protecting state, local, and private beneficiaries of existing programs funded by federal grants.

The Clinton midterm elections of 1994 brought to power in the 104th Congress not only a Republican Party majority but a body with a great deal of experience in state government. The Senate contained 17 former governors and 38 former state representatives; half of the House membership had previously served in state government. As an institution, this Congress was more prone to have confidence in the ability of the states than was the case previously. The states were also anxious to exercise new powers and authority. In the same election, the number of Republican governors increased from 19 to 31, bringing to the states leadership with much in common with their congressional delegations. Ironically, this Congress was more apt to work with the Democratic president—a former governor—to devolve greater authority and responsibility to the states.

The approach to federalism in the administration of President George W. Bush ran contrary to expectations for a Republican president. While it is true that Bush took steps to rein in federal Medicaid spending (which accounted for around two-thirds of all federal aid to states and localities), he also pursued policies and reforms from the center outwards to the states.[38] For example, he expanded and intensified the federal presence in educational policy, previously under the purview of state government, through the No Child Left Behind legislation (2001), which pushed states to perform more frequent student testing. He also proposed a "super waiver" for states to effectively take over administration of federal welfare aid, in order to permit states to reprogram and use federal aid for multiple social programs. These changes came at a very difficult time for the states, a consideration which Bush apparently ignored. In pursuing such measures, Bush also expanded greatly federal spending.

More in line with expectations for a Democrat, the administration of President Barack Obama initiated new policies and programs which have important consequences for federalism and intergovernmental relations, particularly in the areas of health care reform, education, economic recovery and renewal, and climate change. In pursuing this agenda, the administration employs money, federal mandates, and grants of state-level flexibility in new and innovative ways.[39] Not every state has been cooperative with the Obama program, however; and several have stood in defiance of important aspects of the Affordable Care Act (i.e., "Obama-care"), most notably, Texas. Thus, the states still possess political and institutional resources of their own, and some scholars have noted that resistance to Obama's initiatives on the part of some states may yet hamper the full implementation of his program. Overall, it seems to be too early to characterize Obama's approach as a new form of federalism. The complex relationship between the states and the federal government still needs to be worked out. Conlan and Posner put the matter well, writing that, "the nuanced federalism of Barack Obama cannot be pigeonholed as simple centralization. It is true that federalism concerns did not inform the decision about *whether* the federal government should play a role. Nonetheless, federalism issues played a prominent role in determining *how* such new national initiatives would be implemented."[40]

Unfunded Mandates Reform

A significant change in the intergovernmental relationship occurred in the mid-1990s, with reduced federal intervention in state policy making and operations under the Unfunded Mandates Reform Act (Public Law 104-4, UMRA) of 1995. Familiar examples of federal unfunded mandates imposed on the states are the Americans with Disabilities Act of 1990, the Clean Air Act of 1970, and the No Child Left Behind Act of 2001. By enacting UMRA, Congress and the president sharply rejected the long-standing federal practice of imposing new responsibilities on the states without concomitant federal funding, which had been a major problem.

In the mid-1990s, considerable sensitivity to *unfunded* federal mandates had developed. Federal environmental and education legislation in the 1980s imposed billions of dollars of annual costs on state and local governments. By 1992, there were some 172 federal mandates that obliged states or local governments to fund programs out of their own revenues, to some extent. The states complained about this, at times bitterly. By 1995, Congress had gained a clearer understanding of the issue and took legislative and other steps to make sure that the federal government did not lightly thrust extensive costs onto these governments. In the 1980s most of the states had already adopted measures intended to protect their local governments from state-level unfunded mandates.[41]

UMRA set a dollar cost limit for intergovernmental mandates at $50 million per mandate in 1996, adjusted annually for inflation. All federal agencies must document the estimated impact of any bill, amendment, motion, or conference report that would increase the costs of federal mandates more than the threshold, unless the federal government will make funds available to the states to cover the added costs. There are some obvious ways around the limit, such as splitting mandates into separate bills to minimize the impact(s) of any one of them. But to date, the states have compelled Congress to act fairly by providing their own estimates of proposed federal actions.[42]

Early analyses of the effects of the federal UMRA of 1995 indicate that it has had only a limited direct impact on federal agencies' rule making actions, which continue to impose new burdens and responsibilities on the states.[43] The problem is that UMRA leaves it to federal agencies to determine if their proposed rules and other requirements are not "economically significant"; in other words, if they are duplicative of actions already taken, or if accurate estimates of the effects cannot be made—in either case, UMRA's other provisions (including consultation with the affected governments) do not apply. The results were disappointing; in the first three years of the act, no more than three federal actions were judged to affect lower-level governments enough to trigger UMRA's provisions. At the time of this writing, the issue of unfunded federal mandates remains largely unresolved.

Welfare Reform

Another significant federalism development in the 1990s was the wholesale repudiation of the 60-year-old welfare system, with enactment of the Personal Responsibility and Work Opportunity Act of 1996. Under welfare reform, benefits, previously unlimited as to duration, would be subject to a five-year (lifetime) limit. All individuals able to work must do so. Food stamps were also subject to a limit of three months in any three-year period for adults with children, excepting the elderly. The intergovernmental component included a sharp change in the funding mechanism. States would receive a lump sum block grant based on a state's estimated caseload. States were also given greater flexibility to tailor their welfare programs to local needs and preferences. The national welfare system as we knew it before 1996 was gone. But devolution was left incomplete, and the debate continued to rage concerning other significant federal programs not turned over to the states. These included Medicaid, the medical assistance program for low-income persons, and the creation of new job training block grants.

Other Aspects of Federal-State Relations

Many federal objectives are promoted through grants and are dependent on state and local government implementation. However, these subnational governments may, in turn, rely on not-for-profit organizations and privatization to achieve the specific goals. The system combines federalism and administrative decentralization in a way that is managerially, politically, and legally complicated. So-called "third-party government" places a premium on maintaining accountability and monitoring implementation. Traditional management has relied on conformance with procedural requirements for these purposes. The new public management (NPM) contends that such controls tie public administration up in red tape. Instead, it favors establishing measures of performance and monitoring them.

Providing federal money is not the only means of achieving policy objectives. Cooperation between the states and the national government can be voluntarily established. State governors communicate with a state's representatives in Congress. An annual conference of governors also serves as a vehicle for expressing state concerns to the national government. Mayors engage in similar activities. A number of organizations, such as the Council of State Governments and the National League of Cities, engage in lobbying efforts to promote states' and cities' general interests. However, where cooperation of this nature fails, coordination can be imposed through congressional exercise of powers under the commerce clause. As noted earlier, this can go a long way toward regulating the treatment of any person, product, or substance that is part of an economic activity that bears a substantial relationship to interstate commerce, regardless of whether state lines are crossed.

Entitlements

Another aspect of federal-state relationships that should be considered is **entitlements**—federal programs, administered with state and local personnel, that provide benefits to private individuals. Unemployment insurance, health, education, and public housing are some of the major policy areas in which this practice is found. A state's participation in these programs may be voluntary, but a private individual's eligibility for the benefits may be established under federal regulations. Thus, once a state is involved in such a program, it may be confronted with a number of people "entitled" to benefits. Moreover, their number may grow over the years, adding not only to the expense of funding the benefits but also to the cost of administering the program. When states provide matching funds, the costs of a given program to the state may escalate rapidly, as has been the case with Medicaid costs. Yet the state is not free to reduce the number of beneficiaries at will by redefining eligibility. Under federal court rulings, it may be difficult for a state to cut off an individual's benefits without affording that person a good measure of due process, sometimes culminating in a judicial-style hearing.[44] Due process also costs money and adds to the fiscal burdens on the state. In a strange yet plausible outcome, it may even cost more than allowing ineligible people to continue to receive benefits!

Entitlements make it difficult to cut state budgets in some areas. They can also impose a heavy burden on the states when the federal government engages in reduced funding or program cuts. For example, if the federal government reduces welfare benefits, will the state have to make up the difference, if not as a matter of law, then as a matter of political necessity? If the state can also engage in program cuts, on what basis should it decide to reduce benefits or eligibility—and what will the federal courts say about this approach? These are hardly hypothetical questions. The federal contribution as a proportion of total state and local spending declined markedly during the 1980s. This imposed a considerable political, administrative, and financial burden on the states.

What the individual views as an "entitlement," the state or local administrator may consider a federally imposed "mandate" for which the state bears the cost. This is a feature of federalism that state administrators find especially problematic, as the following description of Medicaid indicates: "The mission of today's Medicaid manager is to control costs without cutting eligibility, benefits, or reimbursement, and despite numerous internal, environmental, and intergovernmental constraints. As a job description, this assignment leads inevitably to frustration. . . . [T]he managers are losing the war: Medicaid costs continue to escalate dramatically, the rising costs thrust enormous burdens on state budgets, and the vision of a decent yet cost-effective program slips further away."[45]

Shifting Federal-Local Relations

A final development has been a shifting relationship between the federal government and the nation's local governments, especially its large cities. Many of the Great Society programs of the Lyndon Johnson presidency were oriented toward the urban poor. Cities—even neighborhoods—forged direct financial relationships with the federal government. Since that time, the famous **Dillon's rule,** which holds that local governments possess only those powers expressly granted to them by the states, has frequently been circumvented, if not nullified, by direct federal funding of local administrative activities. But IGR is dynamic, and in the 1990s the situation changed dramatically. Federal funding was considerably reduced even as the number of programs targeted at urban areas was growing. Cities were competing for funding from a large number of relatively small programs. Consequently, cities were becoming more state-oriented in the early 21st century than they had been for some time.

"Horizontal Federalism": Interstate Relations

Interstate relations are another aspect of American federalism of importance to public administration. The states not only need to get along with the federal government but must find ways of coordinating their activities with one another in mutually beneficial ways. When necessary, they must also attempt to resolve disputes in a satisfactory manner. The range of problems that can arise is enormous. Coordinating road construction, establishing uniform drivers' licensing and drinking-age regulations, agreeing on means of rebating sales taxes collected from out-of-state residents to the state in which they live, agreeing on the types of vehicles (large trucks and tandem trucks) and equipment that can be operated on a state's roads, joint law enforcement activities and insect control programs, and many more matters are the stuff of everyday interstate relations. More complex matters concern border disputes and one state's discrimination against residents or former residents of another state with regard to such matters as jobs, welfare benefits, public housing, higher education, the issuance of occupational licenses, and the granting of permits to engage in commercial exploitation of a state's fisheries and other natural resources. Clearly, interstate relations carry with them potential for chaos and disarray.

Interstate Commerce

The U.S. Constitution fosters coordination among the states in several areas. The main one is commerce. The federal government not only has the authority to regulate commerce among the states, with foreign nations, and with Indian tribes, it also can establish legal-tender money, levy tariffs, enact maritime law, grant patents and copyrights, and set standard weights and measures. These powers cut deeply into state sovereignty. Once the federal government takes action in any of these areas, state policies contrary to federal regulations may be preempted and viewed as unconstitutional encroachments on the national government's authority. A wide range of state activities must comply with federal law. These include occupational health, safety, compensation, and collective bargaining matters; banking regulations; use of roads; transportation of products across state lines; and relationships with foreign nations and their political subdivisions, including Canada and Mexico. The Constitution's commerce clause has also been used as a vehicle for promoting civil rights through legislation prohibiting discrimination in employment, public accommodations, housing, banking, and insurance and on common carriers.

Interstate Cooperation

The Constitution also promotes cooperation among the states. Here the main means is the **full faith and credit clause.** It reads, "Full Faith and Credit shall be given in each State to the public Acts, Records, and judicial Proceedings of every other State," and that "A person charged in any State with Treason, Felony, or other Crime, who shall flee from Justice, and be found in another State, shall on Demand of the executive Authority of the State from which he fled, be delivered up, to be removed to the State having Jurisdiction of the Crime" (Article IV). Under this clause, one state is bound to recognize the legal acts of another, even though their policies may differ. For instance, a divorce decree of one state must be recognized by another even though the second state may have different requirements for divorce, which may vary considerably among the states. The same is true of wills and other civil instruments. The extradition of persons accused or convicted of crimes is also required.

However, the cooperation anticipated through Article IV has not been perfect. When residents of one state go to another as migrants for the purpose of gaining a divorce and then return to their native state, a jurisdictional issue may arise. Even when a divorce granted in one state is recognized by a second state, related child custody and property settlements may be subject to the jurisdiction of the second state. Extradition of wanted criminal suspects is usually smooth, but sometimes a state governor is reluctant or unwilling to return an individual to the state from which he or she fled. What is a crime in one state may be an act of heroism and virtue in another, as was true of civil rights protests in the 1960s. The unfair or harsh treatment that one accused of a crime is likely to receive in the state seeking extradition may also be a barrier to his or her return. In most instances the full faith and credit clause promotes cooperation, but there have been enough exceptions to generate a good deal of litigation and a whole area of study and adjudication called "conflict of laws."

Equal Protection

The Fourteenth Amendment's **equal protection clause** is also of importance to interstate relations. It prohibits a state from discriminating against nonresidents and new residents in some contexts. For instance, regulations requiring substantial residency in a state before becoming eligible for state welfare benefits have been challenged successfully under this clause.[46] Interestingly, in a major case, a state made an administrative argument that residency requirements facilitated budgetary planning and reduced fraud.[47] The Supreme Court, however, was less impressed with these concerns than with the free movement of individuals from one state to another and their equal treatment under the law. Nevertheless, in some circumstances, including public employment and higher education, states may treat established residents differently from nonresidents or newcomers.

States may also require new residents and nonresidents to take occupational tests prior to being permitted to practice a trade or profession within their jurisdiction. The full faith and credit clause does not require one state to recognize occupational licenses granted by another. Lawyers, for example, may be required to take a bar examination in every state in which they seek to practice. Ultimately, it is for the federal judiciary to decide whether state policies having a discriminatory impact on newcomers or nonresidents are constitutional. Generally speaking, in reaching their conclusions, the courts weigh the state's rationale or interest in propounding regulations of this nature against their infringement on the equal protection and other constitutional interests of individuals.

The constitutional validity of state residency requirements may also be affected by the "privileges and immunities" clauses in Article IV and the Fourteenth Amendment. These provisions guarantee that the federal government will afford the citizens of each state the same privileges and immunities as those of the other states and that no state will abridge the privileges and immunities of U.S. citizenship. The clauses protect an individual's rights to travel among the states and to reside in the one of his or her choosing. When sufficient governmental interests exist, nonresidents may be charged higher fees than residents for a benefit such as a fishing license or enrollment at a state university. However, state policies that seriously interfere with the freedom to travel or take up residence may be unconstitutional. For example, the clauses protect nonresidents seeking employment, medical services, access to a commercial activity such as shrimp fishing, and welfare benefits.[48]

Interstate Compacts

The Constitution specifically allows the states to cooperate with one another by drafting an "Agreement or Compact with another State," *provided* that Congress gives its consent. The Supreme Court has interpreted congressional consent to be pertinent only when such agreements or compacts increase the political power of the states and encroach on the powers of the federal government.[49] Interstate compacts have been important means by which two or more states can tackle a common problem, such as pollution, health, the protection of natural resources and wildlife, and dealing with traffic congestion and transportation in a metropolitan area. Compacts may include the national government as a party. They sometimes create governmental "authorities" such as the Port of New York Authority, established by New York State and New Jersey in 1921. Authorities of this nature are single-purpose governments, although they can be extensive. The Port Authority, for instance, is involved in the operation of airports, trains, buses, bridges, tunnels, and land and sea terminals. Although interstate authorities facilitate coordination among the states involved, they also fragment government responsibility and may make it difficult to coordinate the provision of municipal services.

States can also coordinate many of their policies without entering into formal compacts. For instance, in 1983, before the federal government became involved through highway grants, the governors of New York, New Jersey, New Hampshire, Connecticut, Massachusetts, Rhode Island, and Pennsylvania sought to coordinate state laws concerning the minimum drinking age.[50] They reasoned that a uniform drinking age would promote highway safety and save lives by reducing the number of people who drive from one state to another in search of a "legal beverage." The possibilities for states to agree to coordinate policies are endless. However, different economic and cultural interests in the states often dictate disparate policies. For instance, independent-minded Vermont was notably uninvolved in the northeastern governors' efforts.

Uniform Legal Codes

Another means of coordination among the states rests in the adoption of uniform laws. The most successful of these has been the Uniform Commercial Code, which covers a number of commercial transactions and is subscribed to by all the states except Louisiana. Other attempts at uniformity in the face of the diversity anticipated by federalism have fared less well. As noted in Chapter 2, about two-thirds of the states have adopted administrative procedure acts, but these are somewhat competing models.

Where it is envisioned that the states will need an ongoing organization to facilitate coordination, a regional commission may be established. Examples are the Appalachian Regional Commission for economic development and the New England Regional Commission for river basin planning.[51]

Relationships among Local Governments

The overwhelming proportion of the 89,000 governments in the United States are below the state level. A typical large metropolitan area includes several municipalities, school districts, and special districts or public authorities. It may overlap county and state lines (see Box 3.7). Although adjacent local governments and those in close proximity to one another clearly share many common interests, some aspects of their relationships are also competitive. Like states, municipalities compete with each other for business investments in offices, manufacturing facilities, shopping malls, and other forms of economic development. They also compete for federal and state grants and other public investments. They compete in the same labor markets for their public employees. Frequently, the actions of one jurisdiction will have problematic effects in neighboring ones. For example, it is not uncommon for municipalities or counties to locate landfills at the edges of their boundaries, leaving their neighbors to cope with the pollution, health hazards, and damage to property values that they cause. Local zoning decisions can affect other jurisdictions. A shopping mall in a newer suburb may pose threats to the retailers in downtown areas of central cities and older suburbs. Sporting events, rock concerts, and other mass spectator activities can create traffic jams and congestion across municipal lines. Suburban strip development may impede the flow of traffic into central cities.

At the same time, though, some of the activities in one jurisdiction are likely to have externalities and beneficial spillover effects on others. The same concert or sporting event that ties up traffic may bring patrons to the area's motels, restaurants, cafes, and shops. The location of hospitals, universities, and theaters in one town may improve the quality of life and desirability of locating in nearby ones. Coordinating and managing these relationships is a major political and administrative concern.

The traditional managerial perspective on relationships among local governments favors reduction of the number of independent municipalities through consolidation or the imposition of countywide or regional governance.[52] This managerial perspective is particularly critical of the overlapping and duplicative functions performed by adjacent municipalities and the high overhead costs they incur. Economies of scale may be lost, and coordination may be expensive. If regional problems are not treated on a regional basis, resources may not be expended in the most cost-effective manner. Consolidation has sometimes been achieved by transferring municipal functions to the encompassing county. Annexation of smaller jurisdictions by central cities also reduces the number of independent governments in an area. In Florida, the Miami–Dade County Metropolitan Government has sought to reassign governmental functions to reduce costs and increase effectiveness.

The political and NPM perspective on the plethora of local governments is different. It views small-scale governments as a means of enhancing political responsiveness and representativeness. Historically, general-purpose local governments have been a manifestation of grassroots democracy. The New England town meeting epitomizes the democratic and participatory self-government that can

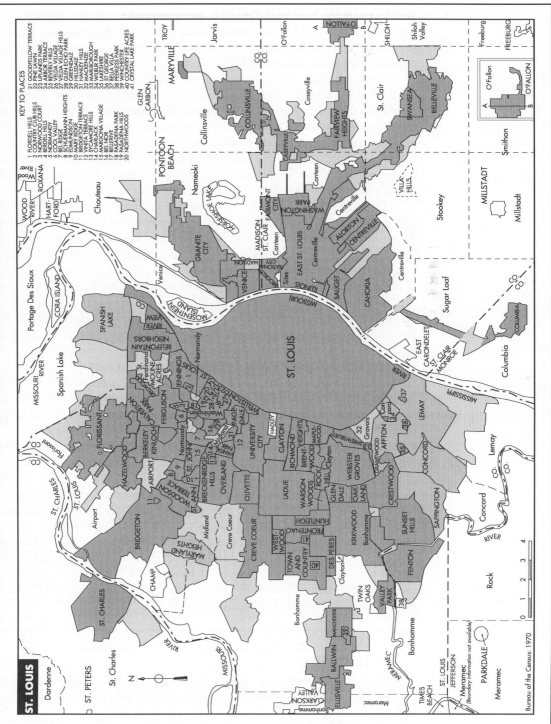

3.7   The Intergovernmental Maze: Counties, Cities, and Towns in the St. Louis Metropolitan Area

ST. LOUIS

KEY TO PLACES

1 FLORDELL HILLS
2 COUNTRY CLUB HILLS
3 NORWOOD COURT
4 BERDELL HILLS
5 NORMANDY
6 BEL-RIDGE
7 COOL VALLEY
8 SCHUERMANN HEIGHTS
9 EDMUNDSON
10 MARY RIDGE
11 BRIDGETON TERRACE
12 VINITA TERRACE
13 SYCAMORE HILLS
14 CHARLACK
15 MARGONA VILLAGE
16 BEL NOR
17 BELLERIVE
18 PASADENA PARK
19 PASADENA HILLS
20 NORTHWOODS

21 GOODFELLOW TERRACE
22 PINE LAWN
23 UPLANDS PARK
24 ARBOR TERRACE
25 BEVERLY HILLS
26 VELDA VILLAGE
27 VELDA VILLAGE HILLS
28 GLEN ECHO PARK
29 GREENDALE
30 HILLSDALE
31 HANLEY HILLS
32 MACKENZIE
33 MARLBOROUGH
34 WILBUR PARK
35 LAKESHIRE
36 ST GEORGE
37 BELLA VILLA
38 PEERLESS PARK
39 WINCHESTER
40 COUNTRY LIFE ACRES
41 CRYSTAL LAKE PARK

Bureau of the Census: 1970

PARKDALE
(Boundary information not available)

N

Meramec

0 1 2 3 4

be achieved at the local level. Residents are afforded a meaningful opportunity to express their views in a public forum and to approve or disapprove of proposed governmental activities. Such government may be viewed as an end in itself, but the contemporary public choice and NPM approaches take their logic further.[53]

The multiplicity of municipalities in a large urban area may offer residents choices among diverse combinations of public services. They may emphasize different educational, economic, developmental, crime control, and recreational policies. If considered analogous to an economic market, individuals (that is, the customers or consumers of public services) might choose to locate in the jurisdictions that suit their needs best. The presumed competition among municipalities for residents might impel them to be responsive to the public's demands for services. There is clearly merit to this perspective.

However, the dispute between the traditional administrative-management approach and the political/public choice perspective remains unresolved. Those who support consolidation question the virtue of self-government that causes problems for neighboring jurisdictions. One town's public choice to locate its dump near the water supply of another, whose residents have no say in the matter, hardly seems responsible. How responsive a small government is to its voters depends on a number of factors, including the citizens' interest in the local community, the degree of competition between candidates or parties, and the quantity of resources available. The extent to which individuals locate and *relocate* themselves in accordance with the mixes of services provided by different governments is generally unknown (and perhaps limited). Large jurisdictions may not achieve the economies of scale predicted by those favoring consolidation.[54] Given these divergent perspectives and the practical impediments to consolidation, "interlocal" governmental relations are certain to remain an area of challenge to public administrators for some time.

Whatever the fate of consolidation, there is strong interest in coordinating public services. From 1954 to the mid-1980s, the federal government promoted the creation of Regional Councils, also called Councils of Government, as a means of coordinating the administrative activities of subnational governments. By 1980 there were more than 660 such councils blanketing the country. They were involved in several policy areas, including planning, criminal justice, water quality, housing, and economic development. When President Ronald Reagan's administration reduced federal participation in local governmental affairs, their number dropped to about 530. Most states continue to sponsor coordination through the use of planning and development districts in which local governmental units participate.[55]

◆→ CONCLUSION: FEDERALISM AND INTERGOVERNMENTAL RELATIONS

One can see many forces at work in the structuring of public administration in the United States. The nature of the 89,000 governments and their interrelationships are so complex that it is often difficult for governmental officials and citizens to keep track of administrative authority and responsibility. Perhaps the best way of understanding the contemporary American administrative state is to view it as a contest or tension between fragmentation and diversity on the one hand and coordination and uniformity on the other.

Political, as opposed to administrative, judgment stands largely on the side of fragmentation and diversity. It favors federalism as the solution to the problem of developing a representative government in a large territory. It also favors political decentralization as a means of affording the population a good measure of influence over matters of local governance. But it was also a political judgment to establish a *national* government as a means of coordinating activities among the states and of promoting uniform policies for economic development, the common defense, and other purposes. This was accomplished through a constitution that clearly reflects the tensions between fragmentation and coordination. The Constitution protects state sovereignty in some respects and creates a national government that depends on the states in several others, including representation in the Senate. But it also gives the national government considerable power over commerce and has been interpreted to require state protection of many rights that are thought to be too fundamental to vary from jurisdiction to jurisdiction. Although constitutional law may promote uniformity in one sense, it frequently fosters diversity in another. When states are forbidden to abridge someone's free exercise of religion or freedom of speech, individual diversity is protected even though the same constitutional standard is imposed on all the states.

For the most part, administrative judgment stands on the side of coordination and uniformity. Federal administrators devote a great deal of time, money, effort, and thought to seeking ways of implementing national programs in conjunction and coordination with state and local governments. But public administration in the United States is fragmented and decentralized. Coordinating activities among the agencies of one government can be difficult—from the lowest level to the highest. This is not a reflection of poor management; rather, it is a consequence of the mix of political, legal, and managerial approaches that dominate our public administrative theory and practice. Ironically, managerially based efforts to take the administration of many local matters, such as schools, cemeteries, and transportation, out of politics have contributed to further fragmentation and made coordination more difficult. This has made some yearn for the days of old, before administrative reforms got hold of governments, when coordination was imposed by political machines and strong political parties, relying heavily on patronage. But must coordination come at the price of "dirty politics and corrupt government"?

Although historical analysis might lead one to answer with a resounding "yes," the student and practitioner of public administration should reject such a false trade-off. The system can work, it *does* work, and it can work well. It can still be improved. But improvement depends in part on public administrators who can integrate the competing values and perspectives found in public administration and coordinate administrative activities among different levels of government. The system often depends on such integration. As in so many other areas of American public administration, it is a matter of balancing the competing values among the managerial, political, and legal dimensions.

STUDY QUESTIONS

1. Some believe that the United States has too many governments, in the sense that governmental authority is too fragmented and that the cost of redundancies and loss of coordination is too high. Would you favor abolishing any levels or kinds of government? Why or why not?
2. What are some of the externalities and spillover effects that public universities cause for the municipalities and counties in which they are located? How might universities and local governments deal with these?
3. There have been periodic calls to realign the functions of government so that the national government would be responsible for, say, defense, foreign affairs, and health, whereas the subnational governments would have complete control over welfare and housing policy. Assuming such realignments were politically feasible, which functions would you place at the state level? Local level? Why?
4. In reading this chapter, it may have occurred to students that federalism has involved "pendulum swings" as between policies and programs that are state-centered, and those that are federally-dominated. Does the idea of a "pendulum swing" accurately describe the evolution of American federalism? Or, has there been a clear tendency towards federal domination over the past 150 years?

NOTES

1. U.S. Bureau of the Census, *2002 Census of Governments,* July 2012. Available online at http://www.census.gov/govs/cog2012/.
2. According to Alfred Malabre, "The Outlook," *The Wall Street Journal,* 5 August 1991, taxpayers had to work, on average, until May 8 of each year to meet the combined federal, state, and local tax bill. The date was April 28 during President Reagan's first term. Today it is around April 15th; by coincidence, that is the date that federal income tax returns are due.
3. *McCullough v. Maryland,* 4 Wheaton 316 (1819).
4. James W. Fesler, *Area and Administration* (University, AL: University of Alabama Press, 1949).
5. *Katzenbach v. McClung,* 379 U.S. 294 (1964).
6. *Wickard v. Filburn,* 317 U.S. 111 (1942).
7. *United States v. Lopez,* 514 U.S. 549 (1995).
8. Ibid., 564.
9. *United States v. Morrison,* 529 U.S. 598 (2000).
10. *Carbone v. Town of Clarkstown,* 511 U.S. 383, 393 (1994).

11. Ibid., 383.
12. Ibid., 407.
13. *Garcia v. San Antonio Metropolitan Transit Authority,* 469 U.S. 528 (1985).
14. *New York v. United States,* 505 U.S. 144 (1992); *Printz v. United States,* 521 U.S. 898 (1997).
15. *Printz v. United States,* 521 U.S. 898 (1997).
16. *Seminole Tribe of Florida v. Florida,* 517 U.S. 44 (1996).
17. *Pennsylvania v. Union Gas Co.,* 491 U.S. 1 (1989).
18. *Alden v. Maine,* 527 U.S. 706 (1999).
19. *Federal Maritime Commission v. South Carolina Ports Authority,* 535 U.S. 743 (2002).
20. Ibid.
21. *Board of Trustees of the University of Alabama v. Garrett,* 531 U.S. 356 (2001); *Kimel v. Florida Board of Regents,* 528 U.S. 62 (2000); *Nevada Department of Human Resources v. Hibbs,* 538 U.S. 721 (2003).
22. *South Dakota v. Dole,* 483 U.S. 203 (1987); *National Federation of Independent Business v. Sebelius,* 132 S.Ct. 2566 (2012).
23. David C. Nice, *Federalism: The Politics of Intergovernmental Relations* (New York: St. Martin's Press, 1987), 4–9.
24. Ibid.
25. Terry Sanford, *Storm over the States* (New York: McGraw-Hill, 1967).
26. U.S. Bureau of the Census, *2002 Census of Governments,* July 2012, Table 416.
27. Daniel R. Grant and H. C. Nixon, *State and Local Government in America,* 3d ed. (Boston: Allyn & Bacon, 1975), 380.
28. Robert Lorch, *State and Local Politics,* 2d ed. (Englewood Cliffs, NJ: Prentice-Hall, 1986), 15.
29. George Berkley and Douglas Fox, *80,000 Governments* (Boston: Allyn & Bacon, 1978), 40–41. New York's constitution has limited the width of certain ski trails.
30. Council of State Governments, *The Book of the States, 2007* (Lexington, KY: CSG, 2007), 13, Table 1.3.
31. Grant and Nixon, *State and Local Government in America,* 114.
32. Ibid., Table 12-1.
33. Calculations from Council of State Governments, *The Book of the States, 2007,* p. 173, Table 4.6.
34. R. Douglas Arnold, *Congress and the Bureaucracy* (New Haven, CT: Yale University Press, 1979).
35. Raymond C. Scheppach and W. Bartley Hildreth, "The Intergovernmental Grant System." *The Oxford Handbook of State and Local Government Finance* (New York: Oxford University Press, 2012), 937.
36. The 21 categories are: Agriculture; Arts; Business and Commerce; Community Development; Consumer Protection; Disaster Prevention and Relief; Education Regional Development; Employment, Labor, and Training; Energy; Environmental Quality; Food and Nutrition; Health; Housing; Humanities; Information and Statistics; Law, Justice, and Legal Services; Natural Resources; Science and Technology; Social Services and Income Security; and Transportation.
37. Nice, *Federalism,* 92.
38. See Tim Conlan and John Dinan, "Federalism, the Bush Administration, and the Transformation of American Conservatism." *Publius: The Journal of Federalism* (2007): 1–25.

39. Timothy Conlan and Paul L. Posner, "Inflection Point? Federalism and the Obama Administration." *Publius: The Journal of Federalism* (2011): 1–26.

40. Ibid., p. 23.

41. David Walker, *The Rebirth of Federalism* (Chatham, NJ: Chatham House, 1995), 266.

42. Janet M. Kelly, "The Unfunded Mandate Reform Act: Working Well for No Good Reason," *Government Finance Review* 19, no. 1 (February 2003), 28–31.

43. U.S. General Accounting Office, *Federalism: Previous Initiatives Have Little Effect on Agency Rulemaking* (Washington, DC: U.S. General Accounting Office, 1999).

44. See David H. Rosenbloom, Rosemary O'Leary, and Joshua Chanin, *Public Administration and Law,* 3rd ed. (Boca Raton, FL: CRC/Taylor & Francis, 2010), chap. 4; *Goldberg v. Kelly,* 397 U.S. 254 (1970); *Mathews v. Eldridge,* 424 U.S. 319 (1976).

45. Michael Sparer and Lawrence Brown, "Between a Rock and a Hard Place: How Public Managers Manage Medicaid," in Frank Thompson, Ed., *Revitalizing State and Local Public Service* (San Francisco: Jossey-Bass, 1993), 303.

46. *Shapiro v. Thompson,* 394 U.S. 618 (1969).

47. Ibid.

48. See *Hicklin v. Orbeck,* 437 U.S. 518 (1978); *Doe v. Bolton,* 410 U.S. 179 (1973); *Toomer v. Witsell,* 334 U.S. 385 (1948); *Saenz v. Roe,* No. 98-97 (1999).

49. *Virginia v. Tennessee,* 148 U.S. 503 (1893).

50. *New York Times,* 6 December 1983.

51. Ann O'M. Bowman and Richard C. Kearney, *The Resurgence of the States* (Englewood Cliffs, NJ: Prentice-Hall, 1986), 29.

52. See Nice, *Federalism,* chap. 8.

53. See Robert Bish and Vincent Ostrom, *Understanding Urban Government* (Washington, DC: American Enterprise Institute, 1973), for a classic discussion.

54. Nice, *Federalism,* 188.

55. Bowman and Kearney, *The Resurgence of the States,* 162; Walker, *The Rebirth of Federalism,* 274–276.

ADDITIONAL READING

Beer, Samuel H. *To Make a Nation: The Rediscovery of American Federalism.* Boston: Belknap Press of Harvard University Press, 1998.

Elazar, Daniel J. *The American Mosaic: The Impact of Space, Time, and Culture on American Politics.* Boulder, CO: Westview Press, 1994.

Gerson, Larry. *American Federalism.* Armonk, NY: M.E. Sharpe, 2007.

Greve, Michael. *Real Federalism: Why It Matters, How It Could Happen.* Washington, DC: American Enterprise Institute, 1999.

LaCroix, Alison. *The Ideological Origins of American Federalism.* Boston: Harvard University Press, 2010.

Walker, David. *The Rebirth of Federalism,* 2d ed. Chappaqua, NY: Chatham House, 2000.

Wildavsky, Aaron. *Federalism and Political Culture.* New Brunswick, NJ: Transactions Publishers, 1998.

Zimmerman, Joseph. *Contemporary American Federalism.* Albany, NY: SUNY Press, 2008.

FEDERALISM WEB SITES

An excellent time line on development of American Federalism from 1776 to 1997 can be found at http://usa.usembassy.de/etexts/gov/federal.htm.

The National Conference of State Legislatures chronicles the evolving state-federal relations at http://www.ncsl.org. At the NCSL home page, click on "State and Federal Committees."

The Urban Institute has posted research on new federalism at its Web site at http://www.urban .org/.

Publius: The Journal of Federalism is available for purchase online at http://www.oxfordjournals .org.

The American Constitution Society's Web site posts materials analyzing new developments in federalism at http://www.acslaw.org.

PART II

CORE FUNCTIONS

CHAPTER 4

ORGANIZATION

Structure and Process

Key Learning Objectives

1. Understand the critical ways in which public sector organizing approaches and internal processes influence and affect administrative performance.

2. Be able to enumerate and explain the key attributes of bureaucratic organization and the way that bureaucracy generally functions.

3. Describe the attributes of effective leaders, and explain how an administrator's leadership style can affect an organization's performance.

4. Differentiate between "orthodox" administrative theory and more modern approaches, and know the critical distinctions between the traditional managerial approach to public administration and the political and legal approaches.

5. Understand the ways in which networked organizations are becoming more important to the conduct of public administration.

Public administration concerns *organized* activity aimed at the provision of services and the application of constraints to individuals and groups. It requires *organization*. Organization can take many different forms. The *structure* of an organization affects the behavior of the organization as a whole and that of its individual members. The same is true of the *processes* through which organizations operate. The structure and process of an organization can also have important impacts on its clients and customers. Through the design of organizational structures and processes of one kind or another, different values can be maximized, different needs can be served, and different purposes can be achieved. Therefore, the organization of administrative activity ranks at the forefront of questions with which the student and practitioner of public administration must be concerned. As in other areas of public administration, though, there are few simple answers. Rather, there are competing responses to the basic question: How should public agencies be organized?

◆→   ORGANIZATIONS AND ORGANIZATION THEORY

What Are Organizations?

Organization coordinates human activity. Armies are a contemporary example that reaches back to antiquity. As human cultures developed from hunter-gatherer societies to the "postindustrial," technocratic ones found in advanced countries today, greater reliance was placed on organizations as a means of achieving social, economic, and political purposes. The 20th century was characterized by the development of an "organizational society"[1]—that is, a society in which a great deal of peoples' waking time is spent in organizations, such as schools, universities, workplaces, and places of worship, recreation, and health care. Frances Westley defines an organization in a very minimalist manner as "a series of interlocking routines, habituated action patterns that bring the same people together around the same activities in the same time and places."[2] As such, while it does not take much to be considered an organization, it also does not take much to stop being one either.[3] Karl Weick argues that the recipe for an organization to unravel is to: "Thrust people into unfamiliar roles, leave some key roles unfilled, make the task more ambiguous, discredit the role system, and make all of the changes in a context in which small events can combine into something monstrous."[4]

Inherent in modern organization theory is the notion that organizations should be rationally designed to achieve their purposes effectively and efficiently (i.e., rationally). It is perhaps above all the commitment to rationality that separates contemporary organizational society from earlier periods in human history. Unfortunately, the task of designing organizations that effectively and efficiently achieve their purposes can be extremely complicated. An "organizational society" may not mesh well with cultural and political values that emphasize individualism and individual rights. Bureaucracy may therefore, at times, come into conflict with constitutional values. So, "the problem of modern organizations is thus how to construct human groupings that are as rational as possible, and at the same time produce a minimum of undesirable side effects and a maximum of satisfaction."[5]

Working or participating in an organization can be frustrating and alienating. Rather than being tools for the rational attainment of goals, organizations can emerge as powerful masters that seek their own survival, aggrandizement, and maximization of power. Organizations can also infringe on the human rights of individuals to privacy, freedom of expression and association, peace, and love. They often also stand at odds with individual efforts at further occupational, professional, and psychological self-development. But this does not necessarily have to be so.

Organization Theory

Efforts to understand the rise of modern organizations led to the development of a self-conscious body of thought called "organization theory." Given its fragmented character, it might be more appropriate to speak in terms of *theories* of organization, but some premises underlie most of the thinking in this area.[6] Among these premises are the following:

1. The structure of an organization affects its behavior.
2. The structure of an organization affects the behavior of its workers, participants, and perhaps even casual members.
3. Organizational processes also affect organizational and individual behavior.
4. Organizations can be rationally (or scientifically) designed structurally and procedurally to achieve their goals in an effective and efficient manner.
5. Organizations can usefully be conceptualized as systems that respond to and affect their environments and seek to gain information about the efficacy of those responses.
6. Organizations may have cultures that partially define how their members conceptualize organizational activity and the environment.

In general, organizational theory is "generic" in the sense that it does not make distinctions between public and private organizations. All organizations share some characteristics, and nearly all significant ones are regulated by governments in one way or another.[7] Nevertheless, public sector (or governmental) organizations face legal-constitutional, political, and market conditions that distinguish them from most private organizations. Some theorists concentrate on these distinctions in an effort to develop better knowledge about public organizations.[8] To date, organization theory has made some important strides, but it remains true, as Charles Perrow, a leading theorist, observed, that "[w]e have probably learned more, over several decades of research and theory, about the things that do *not* work (even though some of them obviously *should* have worked), than we have about things that do work."[9] What are some of the lessons we have learned?

◆→ COMMONALITIES IN PUBLIC ADMINISTRATIVE ORGANIZATION

Certain aspects of organization theory are so commonplace and ingrained that they have become part of the society's culture.[10] They serve as a platform for almost all discussions of how public administration should be organized.

Bureaucracy

Some aspects of the concept of bureaucracy and the attributes of that form of organization were discussed in Chapter 1. But bureaucracy has been so central to public administration that we must continually return to it. Many organizations embody structural and procedural characteristics associated with bureaucracy. According to the highly influential theory developed by Max Weber, these characteristics, in turn, make bureaucracies behave in predictable ways.

Attributes of Bureaucracy

Max Weber (1864–1920) was a German sociologist who used an "ideal-type" approach to identifying the structure, process, and behavior of bureaucratic organization.[11] The "ideal type" was not intended to be an observed reality. Rather, it is a mental construct that purports to identify what would emerge if a phenomenon (such as bureaucracy) could develop into its most complete form; that is, what it would be like if there were no opposing forces to limit its full development. Weber does not purport to describe reality, but he does identify the essence of bureaucracy. (Examples of federal agencies that meet Weber's criteria are presented in Boxes 4.1 and 4.2.) In abridged form, bureaucracy in Weber's concept consists of the following structural elements:

1. Specialized jurisdictions, offices, and tasks, that is, a division of labor and authority regarding the achievement of the organization's goals.
2. A hierarchy of authority to coordinate the activities of the specialized offices and integrate their jurisdictional authority. In the most rational bureaucratic design, the organization is headed by a single authority.
3. A career structure in which individual employees of the bureaucratic organization move through various specializations and ranks. Movement is based on merit and/or seniority.
4. A bureaucratic structure that tends to be permanent. It remains intact regardless of the flow of members in and out of it. Society becomes dependent on the bureaucracy's functioning to the extent that chaos results if it is destroyed.
5. By implication, bureaucracies are large organizations.

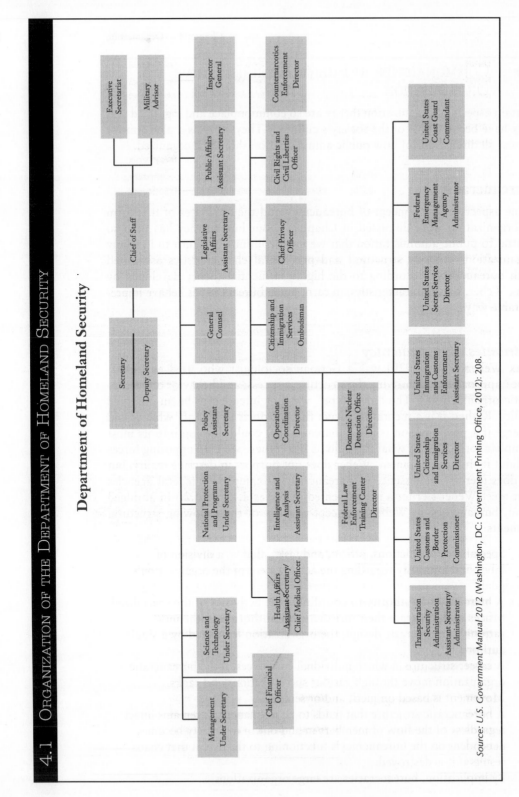

Department of Homeland Security

Source: U.S. Government Manual 2012 (Washington, DC: Government Printing Office, 2012): 208.

Corporation for National and Community Service

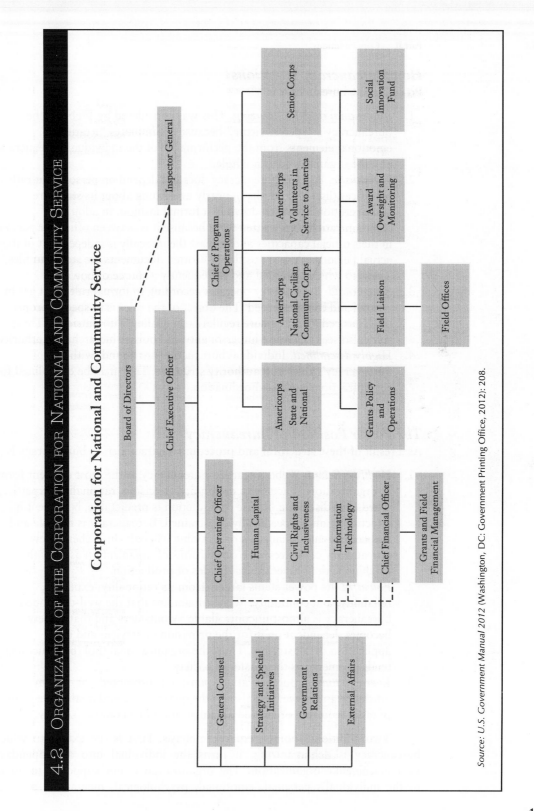

Source: U.S. Government Manual 2012 (Washington, DC: Government Printing Office, 2012): 208.

How Bureaucracy Functions

Procedurally, bureaucracy is

1. *Impersonal or dehumanizing.* This was considered by Weber to be bureaucracy's "special virtue" because it eliminates "irrational" emotional elements from the performance of the individual bureaucrats and the organization as a whole.

2. *Formalistic.* Because bureaucracy does not depend on persons but rather on offices (literally, "desks"), nearly everything about its structure and operation is written down in a formal fashion. In addition, communication is in written form because it is between offices or persons in their official capacities and at least theoretically is independent of the actual persons in those positions. Written documents are stored in files, access to which is limited and is frequently a source of power.

3. *Rule-bound.* Bureaucracy operates according to formal rules that are in writing and can be learned. The object of the rules is to specify proper office procedure and assure regularity in dealing with outsiders. These rules also seek to ensure impersonality and bolster hierarchical authority.

4. *Highly disciplined.* Individual bureaucrats are bound by the bureaucracy's rules and authority structure. They may be disciplined for rule infractions and insubordination.

The Power Position of Bureaucracy

As a result of these structural and procedural characteristics, bureaucracy is

1. *Highly efficient.* Weber regarded bureaucracy as the most efficient form of organization. It acts with continuity, precision, rationality, expertise, speed, and discipline. Its use of discretion is predictable, because it is structurally and procedurally constrained. Bureaucracy is reliable and reduces the emotional costs of attaining its goals. In Weber's view, bureaucracy compares with other forms of organization as does the machine with nonmechanical modes of production.

2. *Powerful.* Its power stems largely from its rationality, expertise, reliability, and continuity. Weber maintains that the well-developed bureaucracy is almost uncontrollable by outsiders and that society becomes dependent on it for the provision of services and the application of constraints. Thus, the organizational tool (bureaucracy) tends to emerge as the master of society.

3. *Ever-expanding.* Bureaucratic expansion is prompted not only by efficiency and power but also by the quantitative and qualitative growth of tasks requiring organized administration in a complex society.

Two additional points require emphasis. First is the extent to which bureaucracy is dehumanizing; it turns the individual into an appendage to a machinelike organization. The organization is not supposed to adapt to the individual's personal, emotional, psychological, mental, or physical idiosyncrasies. Rather, the individual is *standardized* to fit the particular organizational slot in which he or she is to be used. The organization revolves around positions and offices, not persons. Second, the power of bureaucratic organization not only is derived from its structural and procedural attributes but also flows from its *rationality*. People comply with bureaucratic orders and decisions because they accept them as legitimate. That legitimacy is based on the belief that they are rational, reflect trained expertise and not irrational whims, and are regulated by law or official directive. In the ideal-type bureaucracy—although not in its real-world counterpart—an arbitrary, capricious, or personally discriminatory decision or order is an impossibility.

Continuing Controversies

There has been a great deal of debate over the utility of Weber's concept and theory of bureaucracy. Although the current consensus appears to be that Weber provided a brilliant and useful statement, four points of contention remain. First, even though bureaucracy was conceived as an "ideal type," we live in a real world in which bureaucratic behavior seems markedly at variance with Weber's ideas. Warren Bennis seems to have captured this point best. He writes that real-world bureaucracy is characterized by

- bosses without (and underlings with) technical competence;
- arbitrary and zany rules;
- an underworld (or informal) organization that subverts or even replaces the formal apparatus;
- confusion and conflict among roles;
- cruel treatment of subordinates based not on rational or legal grounds but upon inhumanity.[12]

The new public management (NPM) is also critical of bureaucracy's rule-bound and hierarchical qualities. It views bureaucracy as obsessed with procedure but relatively uninterested in achieving results. It is so concerned with avoiding mistakes—and fixing accountability for them—that it fails to maximize its performance in any positive sense. In consequence, the NPM holds that bureaucracy is so tied up in red tape that it cannot respond effectively and efficiently to its citizen-customers.

A second criticism is that Weber failed to understand the extent to which specialized expertise is inherently at odds with formal hierarchical authority. The point is that the formal superordinate ("boss") becomes dependent on subordinates who have greater specialized technical expertise in various areas of the bureaucracy's operation. This gap between ability and authority can be the source of great anxiety for the "boss," who is responsible for operations over which he or she has far less than full control. The NPM emphasizes employee empowerment precisely because "Management too often is happily unaware of what occurs at the front desk or in the field. In fact, it's the people who work closest to problems who know the most about solving them."[13]

Third, as these two criticisms suggest, Weber may have overstated the extent to which bureaucrats can and do behave rationally. Herbert Simon, whose work in the 1940s and 1950s revolutionized public administrative thinking, reminded us that "human behavior in organizations is best described as 'intendedly rational. . . .'"[14] Complete rationality is frustrated by incomplete knowledge and information as well as by individuals' multiple, unranked preferences. Decision makers in organizations rarely know what all the consequences of an important decision will be. Nor are they always able to determine which course of action suits their preferences most fully. The concept of "bounded rationality," as Simon's view has come to be called, is now an important aspect of the study of human behavior and decision making in organizations. (Chapter 7 is devoted to decision making.)

Finally, Weber's ideal-type analysis is widely considered of limited utility in designing real-world organizations because it fails to take into account the vast cultural differences among societies. In some national bureaucracies there are strong service ethics and high degrees of formalism and impersonality. Elsewhere, these characteristics are weak and bureaucratic encounters involve a good deal of personalization, pleading, and bargaining. Further, whereas the authority and legitimacy of a bureaucrat in Germany, France, or Austria may be strengthened by the high social status accorded to such functionaries, in other societies, such as the United States, the bureaucrat may be more or less an object of derision. Recognition of cultural variations that bear on the operation of bureaucracies has prompted analysts to devote considerable attention to comparative public administration.

Still, these criticisms should not be taken as rendering the Weberian model useless. All one needs to do is to belong to an organization or, better yet, try to form one to realize how dependent American society is on the principles of bureaucratic organization. Specialization (often by committee), hierarchy (for coordination, often by a governing board or council of some type), and formalized procedures manuals and standard operating rules are well-known attributes of contemporary organizations, whether they are social clubs, university departments, or governmental units. Although sometimes contrasted with bureaucracy, successful market-driven firms can also be organized bureaucratically.

Scientific Management

Scientific management is a second aspect of organization theory that has worked its way into American popular thinking about organizations. This approach was popularized in the early twentieth century through the work of Frederick Winslow Taylor,[15] whose life span more or less coincided with Weber's. However, while Weber came to lament the transformation of employees into "cogs," Taylor embraced this transformation as a prerequisite for scientifically finding the most efficient way of accomplishing any given task. By contemporary standards, much of what Taylor had to say appears naive, paternalistic, inaccurate, and sometimes just plain silly. However, Taylorism became a worldwide movement and continues to have an important legacy in the public sector in the United States. Taylor developed four core principles of scientific management:

1. Management should study the mass of traditional knowledge possessed by workers and devise a way to accomplish each task, using time-and-motion studies that determine precisely the "one best way" of performing a specific work operation. For instance, Taylor developed a "science" of shoveling coal into blast furnaces.
2. Workers should be scientifically selected according to physical, mental, and psychological attributes. If the "one best way" of shoveling coal is to do it in 21-pound loads, a worker who has the physical strength and stamina to perform this operation will be selected.
3. The worker should be scientifically motivated to do as management instructs. Taylor stressed tying productivity to pay through "piece-rate" pay plans, in which the worker was paid according to how much he or she produced. Taylor also thought the frequency with which pay should be given could be scientifically determined in the interests of maximum motivation. He also recommended developing effective sanctions against workers who failed to do as they were told.
4. Work should be redivided so that management has more responsibility for designing work processes and work flow. This proposal fostered the rise of a "science" of efficiency engineering.

Taylor was optimistic that scientific management would yield greater cooperation between workers and management. He believed his system would lead to greater productivity and therefore a higher standard of living for any society in the long run. The greater productivity would yield more profit to go around and therefore would reduce conflict over the distribution of income. Scientific management holds that workers would lose some control over their work, but they would increase their standard of living. This seemed a fair trade-off.

Taylor's legacy has been pronounced in professionalized management, industrial engineering, industrial psychology, ergonomics, and contemporary personnel administration. In the public sector, position classification and job design continue to reflect many of the attitudes and ideas of scientific management (see Chapter 5). More generally, Taylorism strongly reinforced the idea that a worker should be treated as an appendage to a machine, should perform only the functions that a machine or animal—today we might add a robot or computer—could not perform more cheaply. Workers should not be encouraged to participate in the designing of work processes and work flow, because these were matters for scientifically trained managers. It also contributed to the still prevalent idea that productivity is the primary object of organization and that the "good" organization is the one that efficiently produces what it intended to.

For Taylor, the "bottom line" was output; what happens to the worker in the process—boredom, alienation, lack of personal growth, occupational disease—is of secondary concern. Work is to supply products and services, not to develop workers to their fullest capacity. When one lays bare the premises of Taylorism, it can sound dreadful. Yet as a society, the United States continues to define the workplace in terms of efficiency and productivity. The prevalent attitude is that good performance should be rewarded and inadequate productivity should be punished.

The Human Relations Approach

The dehumanization explicit in Weber's ideal-type bureaucracy and implicit in Taylorism has been considered by some to be dysfunctional because it runs counter to the needs of the human beings who make up organizations. Ironically, Taylorism also leads to reduced productivity. Proponents of the **human relations approach** work to develop ways of making organizations less socially and psychologically demeaning to employees. This approach accepts efficiency and productivity as legitimate values but seeks to maximize them by eliminating the dysfunctions caused by overspecialization, alienating hierarchical arrangements, and general dehumanization.

The Hawthorne Experiments

The human relations approach grew out of a rather elaborate set of experiments in the scientific management tradition. Elton Mayo, Fritz Roethlisberger, and others associated with the Harvard Business School conducted studies at the Hawthorne Works of the Western Electric Company in Chicago from 1927 to 1932.[16] The experiments started from the premise that the physical conditions of work would directly affect productivity. For instance, it was hypothesized that an increase in illumination would lead to greater production per worker. This turned out to be the case, but as the experiment proceeded and lighting was reduced to the original level, it was observed that productivity remained higher than it had been before the study began. From a scientific management perspective this was not the predicted result.

Eventually the experimenters concluded that to some extent the workers were responding to the experiment itself, that is, the attention being devoted to them, rather than to the levels of illumination. This phenomenon has been called the "Hawthorne effect." In the context of organization, it stands for the premise that social and psychological factors can play a major role in determining the productivity of workers. It was not management but the workers who controlled the pace and level of output. This conclusion was a radical departure from the Weberian and Taylorist traditions emphasizing dehumanization because it asserted that human factors are key contributors to organizational efficiency. Put simply, based on the illumination experiment, the Hawthorne researchers concluded that if greater attention were paid to the worker as a person, the worker would feel a greater degree of self-esteem and would consequently become more productive.

As the Hawthorne studies continued, the researchers observed that workers socialize with one another and may form groups or what Chester I. Barnard called in 1938 "informal organizations."[17] As a result, workers tend to respond to changes in the work environment or formal organization as groups rather than as individuals. The responses could promote greater productivity, or they could be dysfunctional by limiting productivity. A useful response would be, for example, that the production group would "cover" for a member having an off day and going slower than the norm. A "dysfunctional" response might be a mild, but symbolic, form of physical violence used against individual employees who exceed the group's norm for productivity. Such a collectively enforced limitation may be effectively imposed even though under the piece-rate pay plan it is in any given individual worker's economic interest to be as productive as possible. In short, the workplace may have a "culture" that affects both overall productivity and individual behavior.[18]

Basis of the Human Relations Approach

Several important conclusions were drawn from the Hawthorne experiments. These became the basis for further research and the development of the human relations approach to organization. Among them were that (1) productivity is strongly affected by social and psychological factors, not simply by physical ability and stamina; (2) noneconomic rewards and sanctions are significant determinants of workers' motivation and level of job satisfaction; (3) the highest degree of specialization is not necessarily the most efficient approach to dividing labor; and (4) workers may react to management, the organization, and work as members of groups or informal organizations rather than as individuals. The human relations approach, however, did not assert that the ultimate objective of an organization was to increase the workers' happiness—the end remained efficiency and productivity. But the human relations approach conceptually put the human being back into the organization.

Zone of Indifference

By the late 1930s a new view found its way into print in Chester Barnard's influential book *The Functions of the Executive*. Barnard was the successful president of the New Jersey Bell Telephone Company and, as a self-taught sociologist, had a keen understanding of the complexities of human motivation at work. He emphasized the obvious in reminding those imbued with the principles of scientific management that an organization depended on the willingness of its members to serve. Such willingness generally had to be cultivated by management and could be withdrawn by a participant at any time. Consequently, authority in organizations did not simply flow downward from the top; those on the bottom could exercise power by refusing to cooperate. In Barnard's view, there was a "zone of indifference" in which workers would follow the directives of management without question. But orders beyond this zone would be questioned and perhaps opposed, subverted, or circumvented. A key to effective management was to expand the zone of indifference.

The zone of indifference is notably *personalized*. In theory, it can vary with each subordinate–superordinate relationship. The human relations approach followed through on this insight by dealing with personal and interpersonal behavior in organizations. A new dimension was added to organization theory, which had previously focused on the organization, rather than on the behavior of its members. Attention could now be more profitably turned to such key subjects as leadership and motivation.

Leadership

Leadership is a process, not a position, and can take place at any level in an organization. At its core is the ability to influence a group toward the achievement of goals. Leadership is doing the right thing, whereas management is doing the things right.[19] The organization theory approach to leadership raises at least two broad concerns: What are the qualities of leadership? How is leadership exercised?

Qualities of Effective Leaders

Stephen Robbins organizes the development of leadership studies into three phases: trait theories, behavioral theories, and contingency theories. *Trait theories* derive from Max Weber's theorizing about "charismatic" authority.[20] In this phase of leadership studies, researchers attempted to find traits that differentiated leaders from nonleaders. However, they were unable to develop a consistent list of traits. Some leaders are introverted, shy, bland, and given to procrastination, whereas others are flamboyant, eccentric, and decisive.

Failure to identify a set of traits common to all leaders led the next generation of leadership scholars to attempt to identify a common set of behaviors exhibited by all leaders in all contexts. Unlike trait theories, which assumed that leaders are *born, behavior theories* of leadership attempted to discern those behaviors that could *make* individuals leaders. A number of important studies examined the relationship between leaders and workers in terms of the attention leaders gave to the relationship with the workers versus the amount of effort they focused on the work process.[21] As with the trait theories, there was not one profile of effective leadership behavior. Some effective leaders were very focused on their workers, some were very focused on production and the work process, and others were more balanced in their approach. But no behavioral approach may fully account for effective leadership.

The inability to identify either traits or behaviors led researchers to look for the *situational* factors that bring about effective leadership. The *contingency theories* approach to leadership attempts to identify the circumstances external to the individual leader that account for leadership. The *Fiedler leadership model,*[22] *leader-member exchange theory,*[23] *path-goal theory,*[24] and the *leader-participation model*[25] are all attempts to isolate the situational conditions that make a leader effective. While there is some empirical support for these approaches to leadership, identifying all of the relevant contextual conditions is a very complex process.[26] Although this approach may be useful, it can also be too mechanistic. It would suggest that President George W. Bush's personality had nothing to do with his high approval ratings during his first two years in office or that only the lack of progress in the Iraq War was responsible for his abysmally low approval ratings during his fifth year in office. Clearly, the personal qualities of someone in a position of leadership can make a difference, even though much of what leaders accomplish may be dictated by their circumstances.

Leaving aside the disputed ground of personality traits, are there any qualities and skills that seem to be prerequisites for effective leadership in a wide variety and large number of situations? Among the qualities and skills often mentioned are those found in Box 4.3.

4.3   COMMON TRAITS, QUALITIES, AND SKILLS OF EFFECTIVE LEADERS

1. *Belief in the possibility of success.* Leaders want to change or maintain some aspect of social, political, or economic life. They must believe that there is a significant, though possibly small, likelihood that their efforts will make a difference.

2. *Communication skills.* Leaders must effectively communicate with followers. This requires substantial verbal skill. Followers must have a reasonably clear picture of what is expected of them if they are to work in a coordinated way toward a common purpose.

3. *Empathy.* Leaders often have a deep understanding of the psychology, thought processes, aspirations, and fears of their followers. Empathy not only facilitates communication but also enables a leader to find successful ways of influencing people. Empathy is not sympathy. The leader may remain detached or aloof yet still be able to enter the mental processes of the followers.

4. *Energy.* Tales of the long hours put in by leaders are legion. The "workaholic" label probably fits many. To cite only a few examples, Eugene Lewis observes that Hyman Rickover, "father" of the U.S. nuclear navy, and Robert Moses, who oversaw the building of more roads, bridges, tunnels, and parks than perhaps anyone in recent history, devoted tremendous time and attention to gaining detailed understanding of the projects and technologies that might be appropriate for their organizations.

5. *Sound judgment.* Continuing leadership may depend substantially on the exercise of sound, reasoned judgment. Emotional, arbitrary, or capricious responses to situations are not the hallmark of long-lasting leadership—at least where the followers are free to abandon the leader. It is considered important for leaders to maintain an unbiased, disinterested (but not uninterested) posture with regard to the organization's members. This helps the leader keep matters in perspective.

6. *Constancy.* Leaders need to manage the trust placed in them by their followers. They must make it clear where they stand and avoid waivering capriciously, for self-aggrandizement, or opportunistically. Although followers may disagree with a leader's specific position, they need to know he or she can be counted on to act in reasoned, consistent ways.

7. *Self-management.* Leaders must be aware of their strengths and weaknesses and act accordingly. Leaders do not have to do everything themselves. There is no reason to expect leaders to master all the specializations found in large, complex organizations. They must remain focused on what they can achieve and contribute best.

Source: Derived from Eugene Lewis, *Public Entrepreneurship: Toward a Theory of Bureaucratic Political Power* (Bloomington: Indiana University Press, 1984); and Warren Bennis, *Why Leaders Can't Lead* (San Francisco: Jossey-Bass, 1989).

There are a number of other qualities that leaders often possess but which appear to be less essential. Intelligence is one. Certainly the "best and the brightest" are often in a position of leadership. But many leaders are not the most intelligent people. Nor does it appear crucial that leaders have technical proficiency in the work performed by their organizations, though many do. Finally, leadership is sometimes defined in terms of decision making, but some effective leaders have avoided decisions whenever possible.

Exceptional Public Administrators

In view of the generality of contemporary knowledge about leadership, some have sought to learn more by studying the organizational careers of individuals who were exceptionally successful public administrative leaders. For instance, Eugene Lewis's book *Public Entrepreneurship: Toward a Theory of Bureaucratic Political Power* (1984) considers in depth the "organizational lives" of Hyman Rickover, J. Edgar Hoover, and Robert Moses. These men were eccentric in many respects, but Lewis found some common keys to their leadership.

First, each saw organizations as tools for the achievement of his goals. These goals were not simply rising to the top but rather accomplishing something substantive through the organization. Hoover thoroughly improved the Federal Bureau of Investigation (FBI), Rickover brought the U.S. Navy into the atomic age by demonstrating the desirability and feasibility of submarines driven by nuclear power, and Moses pursued his vision of the public good by building parks and improving transportation in the greater New York City area.

Second, Lewis finds that "the [highly successful] public entrepreneur typically 'owns' all or some of the reality premises of the society in one or more areas of specialized concern."[27] Such entrepreneurs dominate media accounts, legislative hearings, and various meetings pertinent to their area of specialization and interest. In this way, the leader comes to "own" some aspect of public policy. Hoover "owned" statistics pertaining to crime, Rickover "owned" nuclear power in the Navy, and Moses "owned" the construction of parks and bridges in metropolitan New York.

Third, successful public administrative leaders grasp the potential impact that effective organizations can have. As Lewis puts it, "The public entrepreneur, somewhere during his career, comes to understand that *the large, complex public organization is the most powerful instrument for social, political, and economic change in the political universe.*"[28] Public organizations can provide a base of political power that protects the leader from opponents and serves as a lever for exercising influence on important external political actors, such as legislators. At the height of their influence, Hoover and Moses were untouchable by their political opponents.

Another important characteristic is that "each entrepreneur conveyed to his listeners the impression that he possessed a knowledgeability and a capacity to carry out monumental tasks that no other element in the political system seemed able to accomplish."[29] Rickover introduced a new technology to submarine warfare that would make for a "true submarine," that is, one that could remain submerged for extended periods. Hoover reduced both crime and subversion. Moses mobilized the resources for huge projects such as New York City's Triboro Bridge.

Finally, public entrepreneurs like Hoover, Rickover, and Moses expand their "ownership" of areas of public policy. They extend the boundaries of their organizations to bring more under their control. In classic organization theory, this reduces uncertainty and maximizes autonomy, though it may eventually undercut the democratic processes of representative government.[30] Perhaps Hoover is the best example. He expanded the FBI's role in society from combating narrowly defined federal crimes to working with local police forces throughout the nation to combat the alleged threat of subversion by communists and other radicals. The FBI grew from a small, ineffective adjunct of the Department of Justice to an autonomous police agency with a presence throughout the nation.

Not all leaders in public agencies operate on the scale of Lewis's entrepreneurs. Norma Riccucci studied six federal senior executives who worked within their agencies to make major contributions in promoting human rights, health, environmental safety, and public integrity. She found that they had the following in common:

1. *Political skills,* or the "ability to maneuver effectively within their policy environment"
2. *Management and leadership skills,* including the "ability to plan, organize, communicate clearly, motivate staff, and set realistic goals and to be honest, fair, understanding, knowledgeable of agency politics, and expert in their fields"
3. *Technical expertise* in their various fields
4. *Strategies* for achieving their goals

In summarizing their personalities, Riccucci frequently used the following terms: "integrity," "morality," "honest," "trustworthy," "ethical," and "good sense of humor."[31]

Moral Leadership

The factors that Riccucci cites are consistent with the findings of another study of personal excellence in the public service. In a series of case studies of "exemplary public administrators," Terry Cooper and Dale Wright cite virtue and moral character as the critical factors that distinguish excellent from mediocre leadership.[32] In addition to the individuals cited by Lewis and Riccucci, the Cooper and Wright study includes former Comptroller General of the United States Elmer B. Staats for his promotion of governmental ethics and administrative morality; former Deputy U.S. Attorney General William D. Ruckelshaus for his refusal to fire the special prosecutor in the Watergate scandal investigation of President Richard M. Nixon; and former

U.S. Surgeon General C. Everett Koop for his singular dedication to the legal duty of the surgeon general to advise the American public concerning serious health risks, particularly smoking and AIDS. All these individuals—and others in their study—distinguished themselves and brought honor to their positions by exhibiting a constancy of moral principle and purpose that inspired others by example. This sums up the essence of the **moral approach to leadership.**

Choosing a Leadership Style

A thoroughly developed analysis of "How to Choose a Leadership Pattern" was presented by Robert Tannenbaum and Warren H. Schmidt in the *Harvard Business Review* in 1958. In 1973 they added a "Retrospective Commentary" to their classic article.[33] They emphasize the desirability of congruence between "forces" in the manager and those in the subordinates. The original article posited a continuum from a **boss-centered** leadership style to a **subordinate-centered** style. As the leadership style changed from highly boss-centered to more subordinate-centered, subordinates were given greater freedom and opportunities for participation in organizational decision making. Although drawn more complexly in their article, the basic continuum, moving progressively from boss-centered to subordinate-centered leadership, is given in Box 4.4.

This scheme was modified by the authors in 1973 in response to a number of social and work-related changes that had occurred in the 1960s.

4.4   THE CONTINUUM FROM BOSS- TO SUBORDINATE-CENTERED LEADERSHIP STYLES

BOSS-CENTERED LEADERSHIP

1. The manager makes a decision and announces it.
2. The manager "sells" the decision to subordinates.
3. The manager presents ideas and invites questions.
4. The manager presents a tentative decision subject to change.
5. The manager presents a problem, obtains suggestions, and makes the decision.
6. The manager defines the restrictions pertinent to a decision and asks subordinates to make the decision as a group.
7. The manager permits subordinates to make decisions within broad limits defined by the manager.

SUBORDINATE-CENTERED LEADERSHIP

Source: Robert Tannenbaum and Warren H. Schmidt, "How to Choose a Leadership Style," *Harvard Business Review* 36 (March/April 1958): 95–101.

Especially important were greater opposition to the exercise of hierarchical authority, demands for participation in the workplace, and increasing concern with the quality of work life. In the 1973 version, subordinates were called "nonmanagers" and the labels on the continuum were changed. The boss-centered end was called "manager power and influence," whereas the other end was "nonmanager power and influence." There was also greater recognition that managers were dependent on the willingness of nonmanagers to accept their decisions and that an organization's environment could impose constraints on its decision making.

Tannenbaum and Schmidt reasoned that the most suitable leadership styles in any given context would depend on the managers, the subordinates or nonmanagers, and the organizational situation. For managers, the main concerns would be their personal beliefs in the desirability of participation and their willingness to tolerate risk and uncertainty. For the subordinates, the main forces would be their willingness to participate in decision making, their understanding of and identification with the goals of the organization, and their tolerance for ambiguous direction as opposed to highly specific instruction from hierarchical authorities.

An important conclusion is that the leadership style should be determined by the congruence of forces in the manager and those in the subordinates. A subordinate-centered leadership style would be inappropriate where subordinates did not want to share authority and participate in decision making. Conversely, where the subordinates do want greater freedom and participation, a boss-centered leadership style would be inappropriate. Nor could a manager who is uneasy when exercising authority or one who is opposed to subordinate participation simply change his or her style to make it congruent with the outlook of the subordinates.

A serious criticism of subordinate-centered leadership would be that organizational performance needs ought to be driven by customers, and not by the preferences and desires of rank and file workers. The purpose of employees in the first place is to serve the objectives of the organization which, presumably, point to customer and client service. Thus, the modern manager must seek to strike a balance between customers' and the organization's performance requirements, and the active participation of employees in devising the most effective and professionally-rewarding means to fulfill the organization's requirements. That said, subordinate-centered leadership is predicated on the understanding that leadership may emerge at any level in the organization, a topic to which we now turn.

Leadership throughout an Organization

Most approaches to administrative leadership tend to assume that the leader is in a hierarchy, often at or near the top. However, our discussion of leadership indicates that as we move from trait and behavioral theories of leadership to more contingent theories of leadership, opportunities arise for individuals throughout organizations to exercise leadership.

The NPM takes a normative view on this matter. It downplays hierarchy and puts considerable emphasis on teams and teamwork. Teams are formal work groups that may be composed of employees at all levels—managerial, supervisory, and front-line workers. Team leaders are not necessarily the highest-ranking employees. They may be formally designated, or they may emerge out of circumstances. Use of teams to address organizational and policy problems is becoming more characteristic of public organizations.

Leaders in collaborative governance relationships require different mindsets and skills than those in traditional hierarchical administrative organizations. They need to:

1. Know when to lead and when to follow
2. Be "authoritative, without being authoritarian"
3. Encourage "followers to lead"
4. "[K]now when to give direction and when to allow the collaboration members to take charge of the situation"
5. See "both the forest and the trees"
6. "[A]pproach collaborative situations with an assumption that, by using divergent thinking, it may be possible to have everyone's needs fully met, but that this is more likely to happen if the reasoning behind each party's views is made explicit"
7. Understand that "the more that stakeholders fundamentally distrust each other, the more leadership must assume the role of honest broker. However, when incentives to participate are weak or when power is asymmetrical, the leader must often intervene to help key stakeholders at the table or empower weaker actors."[34]

One concern with collaborative governance is that when governmental and nongovernmental actors collaborate, the importance of the rule of law and constitutional values in the overall endeavor can become ambiguous. Because private for profit and nonprofit organizations are not constrained by constitutional and administrative law, they can use means prohibited to public agencies and may even be encouraged to do so. Consequently, leaders in collaborative governance should be cognizant of the potential need to focus on maintaining democratic-constitutional norms and values and the rule of law when engaged in collaborative governance.

Leadership is only part of the equation. There are also those who are led, followers who are willing to serve. Consequently, any discussion of leadership must be complemented by a consideration of motivating followers.

Motivation

Understanding what motivates people in the workplace requires understanding their needs. Therefore, the willingness of an individual to do something is conditioned by the organization's ability to satisfy some need for that individual. Scientific management theory assumed that workers were motivated by monetary rewards and sanctions. Heavy emphasis was placed on piecework, under the assumption that if a worker could earn more by producing more, he or she would be motivated to work harder. Similarly, if productivity and pay could be increased through the introduction of highly specialized work tasks, Taylorism assumed the worker would perform them, however boring, mind-numbing, and physically uncomfortable they might be. This approach to motivation was dealt a severe blow by the Hawthorne experiments and the human relations approach. More recently, researchers have developed a concept called Public Service Motivation (PSM), which indicates that workers in public agencies are motivated by different needs than workers in the for-profit sector.[35]

Maslow's Hierarchy of Needs

An important breakthrough occurred in 1943, when Abraham Maslow introduced "A Theory of Human Motivation."[36] Maslow hypothesized that there is a hierarchy of human needs, that humans are satisfaction-seeking by nature, and that they are therefore motivated in a never-ending quest for greater satisfaction of their needs. In Maslow's scheme, human beings first seek to satisfy their physiological needs, such as hunger and thirst; then, once these are met, they seek to fulfill safety and shelter needs. Next, they focus on social needs and seek a sense of belonging. At the fourth level of needs, they want self-esteem and social status; finally, they seek "self-actualization," or true self-fulfillment (see Box 4.5).

When viewed in the light of the human relations approach, it is not difficult to see some immediate implications of Maslow's theory. First, if "a happy worker is a productive worker," then work should satisfy the

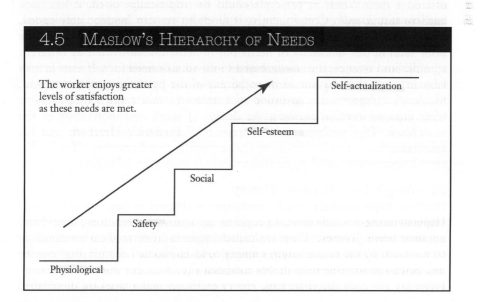

4.5   MASLOW'S HIERARCHY OF NEEDS

The worker enjoys greater levels of satisfaction as these needs are met.

Self-actualization

Self-esteem

Social

Safety

Physiological

workers' needs at whatever level they may be. If workers seek social activity, the organization should provide opportunities for it. If they seek self-esteem or self-actualization, they will probably need some control over the structuring of their jobs and some opportunity to participate in decision making. At the least they cannot be ordered around like dumb beasts in the Taylorist tradition.

In practical terms, several elements of bureaucratic organization may be at odds with human needs. Certainly hierarchy and specialization militate against self-actualization, self-esteem, and the social needs of those denied control over their work processes and social interactions on the job—meaning a lot of employees other than those at the top. The lack of opportunity to complete an entire unit of output, such as a report or an automobile, is also problematic in terms of self-esteem and self-actualization. Formalization and impersonality would seem seriously to undercut the fulfillment of social needs. The entire sense of being but a mere "cog" in the machinery of government deflates one's sense of self-esteem.

An important second implication is that bureaucratic organization is somewhat out of date. It is possible that as a society develops economically and politically, the plurality of public employees may be seeking to satisfy needs at the top levels of Maslow's hierarchy. They may want meaningful work (status, self-esteem) and influence over the directions their agencies are taking (self-actualization through public policy making).[37] Unless bureaucracies can respond to these needs, their employees will be somewhat dissatisfied and organizational efficiency may consequently suffer.

Despite the enthusiasm of some for Maslow's theory and its implications, others have remained unconvinced. At least two general criticisms are frequently directed at Maslow's hierarchy. First, although Maslow offered a theory that in principle could be empirically tested, it has been hard to test it well. Consequently, it tends to remain inadequately tested. Moreover, some people find it counterintuitive. Many of us may be at the same level in our hierarchy of needs but nonetheless motivated by different stimuli. For instance, the *strength* of an individual's need for self-esteem may vary in ways that do not seem to be explained by the hierarchy. Second, Maslow's categories are so broad that unless further refined they seem to offer little connection between the design of work and motivation in the workplace. This problem was addressed by Frederick Herzberg and his associates.[38]

Herzberg's Two-Factory Theory

Herzberg hypothesized that job satisfaction is affected by two types of factors. Hygiene factors include working conditions, supervisory relations, salary, and administrative policies. They are called **hygienes** after medical terminology to connote that they are environmental and contextual factors that can be attained by preventing undesirable conditions (such as dirt in drinking water). Hygienes are considered to have the capacity to make workers dissatisfied if they are inadequately met. However, they do not lead to job satisfaction. In contrast, **motivators,** including advancement, responsibility, the job, recognition, and achievement, could produce greater job satisfaction and therefore lead to greater productivity.

The implications of the Herzberg model are similar to those of Maslow's hierarchy. Motivation depends more on opportunities for advancement, responsibility, recognition, and achievement than on the type of hygiene factors that were of greater concern to the scientific management approach. Even more important, Herzberg turned attention to the nature of the job as a motivator. This led _____ _____ _____ ghest degree of specialization, _____ _____ _____ mployee's motivation. It also _____ _____ hanced by allowing them to _____ e Maslow's theory, however, _____ ptance. Empirical tests of its _____ a debate continues as to its

_____ and psychological variation _____ assume that all workers can _____ nple, based on the work of _____ some people are far more _____ tivated by the opportunity _____ e same level of Maslow's _____ iliation.[39] The same could _____ l by Herzberg.

_____ eliminates some of the _____ theory.[40] It assumes that workers have a variety of goals and that the strength of their preferences for those goals varies. Moreover, it proposes that their motivation on the job will depend on the extent to which they expect a certain activity to lead to some degree of satisfaction of these goals. For instance, if they want higher pay and think greater productivity will lead to it, the workers will be more productive. But the same is true if they want recognition or a sense of achievement and believe that these goals can be attained through greater productivity. According to this approach, the key to motivation is affording workers some opportunity to achieve their desired goals and making clear what activities or efforts on the job they can reasonably expect to lead to attainment of these goals.

Based on expectancy theory, organizations should emphasize recruiting personnel whose personal goals can be fulfilled while serving the needs of the organization. Additionally, rewards and sanctions must be clearly linked to performance. There is no coherent body of theory about individual personality type and motivation in organizations. However, people do vary widely in their approach to work. Some possibilities are set forth in Box 4.6.

Handwritten note:

Milestones - Board meeting
- E+F current market size, segments, pricing, process
- How many non-discretionary, discretionary, vs OCIO in mkt as a whole
- 4 yrs - how many E+F RFPs responded to, how many won

4.6   ORGANIZATIONAL PERSONALITIES: A SAMPLING

According to Anthony Downs:

1. CLIMBERS—A "climber seeks to maximize his own power, income, and prestige, he always desires more of these goods." Climbers seek to increase the power, income, and prestige of their positions in ways that will create the least effective resistance.

2. CONSERVERS—"Conservers seek to maximize their security and convenience. . . . [They] are essentially change avoiders. In this respect, they are the opposite of climbers."

3. ZEALOTS—officials who "act as though pursuit of the public interest means promotion of very specific policy goals . . . regardless of the antagonism they encounter or the particular positions they occupy."

4. ADVOCATES—"are basically optimistic, and normally quite energetic. . . . [T]hey are strongly subject to influence by their superiors, equals, and subordinates. Nevertheless, they are often quite aggressive in pressing for what they believe best suits their organizations."

5. STATESMEN—are loyal to the nation or the society as a whole. They "can persist in maintaining a generalized outlook even when their responsibilities are quite particular. However, they do not like conflict situations and seek to reconcile clashes of particular viewpoints through compromises based upon their broad general loyalties."

According to Robert Presthus:

1. UPWARD-MOBILES—have "the capacity to identify strongly with the organization, permitting a nice synthesis of personal rewards and organizational goals." They make "special efforts to control situations and people." They "stress efficiency, strength, self-control, and dominance. [Their] most functional value is a deep respect for authority."

2. INDIFFERENTS—reject the values of status and prestige. Their "aspirations are based on a realistic appraisal of existing opportunities. Escaping the commitments of the 'true believer' and the anxiety of the neurotic striver, he receives big dividends in privacy, tranquility, and self-realization through his extravocational orientation."

3. AMBIVALENTS—have a fear of authority and an inability to accept the organization's collective goals, "which violate his need for personal autonomy. His 'tender minded' view of human relations disqualifies him for the 'universalistic' decision making required for success on organizational terms. Since his preferences include a desire for creativity and for a work environment that permits spontaneity and experiment, the structured personal relations, stereotyped procedures, and group decision making of big organization prove stifling. . . . If his values did not include prestige and influence, a happier accommodation might be possible."

According to Leonard Reissman:

1. FUNCTIONAL BUREAUCRATS—are "oriented towards and [seek] recognition from a given professional group outside of

Contemporary Approaches to Organization Theory

Organization theory is a diverse, interdisciplinary enterprise. If there is any unifying paradigm, it is methodological rather than substantive. Contemporary organization theory seeks to develop and test empirical propositions pertaining to all important aspects of organizational behavior, including structure, change, and psychology. Unlike some earlier approaches, it tries to separate facts from values and to use empirical social scientific methods for determining relationships rather than within the bureaucracy." For this group, bureaucracy is just another place to practice their profession.

2. SPECIALIST BUREAUCRATS—display "a greater awareness of an identification with the bureaucracy." They seek both professional and bureaucratic recognition and therefore can be "overly meticulous about the rules and regulations" of the organization.

3. SERVICE BUREAUCRATS—enter "civil service primarily to realize certain personally held goals which center about rendering service to a certain group." The service bureaucrat's task is using the bureaucratic mechanism to achieve these goals.

4. JOB BUREAUCRATS—are "immersed entirely within the structure" of the bureaucracy. They seek "recognition along departmental rather than professional lines," and strive for the "improvement of the operating efficiency of the bureau. His aspirations consist of achieving material rewards and increased status through promotions. He strongly adheres to the rules and the job constitutes his full center of attention and the end to be served."

According to Michael Maccoby:

1. THE CRAFTSMAN—displays "the work ethic, respect for people, concern for quality and thrift. . . . [H]is interest is in the process of making something; he enjoys building. . . . Although his virtues are admired by everyone, his self-containment and perfection do not allow him to lead a complex and changing organization."

2. THE JUNGLE FIGHTER—"The jungle fighter's goal is power. He experiences life and work as a jungle (not a game), where it is eat or be eaten, and the winners destroy the losers. . . . There are two subtypes of jungle fighters, lions and foxes. The lions are the conquerors who when successful may build an empire; the foxes make their nests in the corporate hierarchy and move ahead by stealth and politicking."

3. THE COMPANY MAN—is "the well-known organization man, or functionary whose sense of identity is based on being a part of the powerful, productive company. His strongest traits are his concern with the human side of the company, his interest in the feelings of the people around him and his commitment to maintain the organization's integrity."

4. THE GAMESMAN—is a new type. "His main interest is in challenge, competitive activity where he can prove himself a winner. . . . [H]e likes to take risks and to motivate others to push themselves beyond their normal pace. He responds to work and life as a game."

Sources: Anthony Downs, *Inside Bureaucracy* (Boston: Little, Brown, 1967), chap. 9; Robert Presthus, *The Organizational Society* (New York: Knopf, 1962), 203, 218, 285–286; Leonard Reissman, "A Study of Role Conceptions in Bureaucracy," *Social Forces* 27 (March 1949): 305–310; Michael Maccoby, *The Gamesman* (New York: Simon & Schuster, 1976), 42–45, copyright © 1976 by Michael Maccoby, reprinted by permission of Simon & Schuster, Inc.

among observable aspects of organizational behavior. To a large extent, it relies on systems theory to aid in the conceptualization of such relationships.

The Systems Approach

The systems approach can be elaborate, but at its core is the concept that an organization (or other functional entity) constitutes a system distinct from its environment.[41] It is a system because its parts are interrelated. The system responds to stimuli from the environment and obtains feedback (information) concerning the impact of its responses. Another way of thinking about a system is that it is an organization that converts inputs (stimuli) into outputs. For public agencies the inputs could be demands for the development or improvement of programs (e.g., crime control), while the conversion could be the combination of these demands into a change in public policy, such as more police patrols or community policing, which would be the output. The conversion process concerns the way the organization responds to demands for changes in its programs and operations. Inputs can also be in the form of support for the organization and its policies and programs.

Some systems are treated as closed, which means it is assumed that everything is known about their internal functioning and their relationship to the environment. A heating device controlled by a thermostat is an example. The system puts out heat predictably with changes in the temperature of the environment. The environment responds to this output, the thermostat provides feedback on the response, and the outputs cease when a certain temperature is reached. Closed-systems theory, which includes Taylorism, tends to focus on stability (equilibrium), control mechanisms, and predictable responses. Some relatively simple public administrative operations can be viewed as closed systems. For instance, the operations of a motor vehicle bureau in renewing automobile registrations might be treated in this fashion. The registrant submits the required payment and documentation of insurance and inspection (inputs); the bureau processes these inputs (conversion) and issues the registration (output). Should something in the environment change, such as the sale of the car, the bureau receives notification (feedback) and responds according to its regulations.

Open systems, by contrast, are viewed as too complex to be so predictable. It is recognized that the relationships between the parts of the system and the system and its environment are not fully comprehensible, especially as internal and external environmental conditions change. Both the environment and the internal operations of the open system are viewed with an expectation of uncertainty. Many believe that the open-systems concept is more useful for analyzing most public organizations. By way of illustration, many of the operations of the U.S. Department of Agriculture fit this model. Inputs often depend on such diverse and relatively unpredictable matters as the weather, pest control, consumer preferences, the relative strength of the dollar against other currencies, foreign policy, and the trade preferences of other nations. Feedback about the impact of outputs can be difficult to read or interpret where so much uncertainty and complexity prevail. Politics and individual preferences, as well as intraorganizational rivalries and other factors, come into play. The great benefit of the open-systems model is that it can help organize our thoughts about the operations of public agencies or other organizations under such circumstances.

Open-systems theory has focused greater attention on organizations as cooperating with and adapting to their environments. They adjust to its pressures, which enhances their ability to persist. For instance, public sector organizations are often required by legislators and political executives to take on new functions. How well an organization can assimilate and integrate new tasks is likely to have a bearing on the organization's long-term prospects for survival. The U.S. Civil Service Commission (1883–1979) is an excellent example of an organization that failed to adapt to a rapidly changing environment, and, consequently, was disbanded. Between 1965 and 1978, it struggled to combine new equal opportunity and affirmative action functions with traditional personnel administration. It also sought to be responsive to political appointees while protecting the somewhat competing interests of career civil servants. In 1973, these pressures led the commission's chairman, Robert Hampton, to ask, "What is our identity?" "What is our purpose?" And, "Why do we exist?"[42] By 1979, it didn't! It had failed to adapt.

The concept that public organizations either adapt to their environment or perish fits the normative tenet of democratic constitutionalism that public administrators ought to be responsive to elected and politically appointed policy makers, including judges, and, perhaps in some areas, directly to constituencies and clientele groups as well. But organizational theorists such as Charles Perrow[43] and William Scott[44] argue that organizations may sometimes be more oriented toward *controlling* their environment than adapting to it. In Scott's words, "Organizations must ingest those necessary elements in their environment that enable them to survive."[45] Perrow reminds us that the environment can be conceptualized in strategic terms on the basis of network and ecological models—both having an environmental focus.

The systems approach focuses attention on the organization as something that reacts to internal and external change. Many organizational systems theorists believe that this behavior is a kind of rational action. James D. Thompson, whose *Organizations in Action* (1967) is a leading work in the systems tradition, viewed organizational rationality as produced by an appropriate relationship among three types of activities: input, technology, and output. This approach also enables us to think in terms of "subsystems" and their relationships with one another, as well as to the organization as a whole and the environment.

Daniel Katz and Robert Kahn identify some common subsystems as "production subsystems," "supportive subsystems" (procurement, etc.), "maintenance subsystems" (personnel management), "adaptive subsystems" (concerned with organizational change), and "managerial subsystems" (controlling the other subsystems).[46] These subsystems are likely to have different and somewhat competing priorities and ideologies supporting them. The managerial subsystem seeks control in order to regulate the system, while a production subsystem may seek autonomy, in order to enhance its performance (perhaps at the expense of other subsystems). Often, it is the subsystems that interact with the environment and with subsystems of other organizations. Recognizing subsystems' existence and interaction often yields a more nuanced and sophisticated understanding of agencies and their relationships with other organizations.

Network Organizations

Networks are constituted by the external organizations with which an organization routinely deals *and* some of the other organizations that interact with those external organizations.[47] For example, organization A may deal with organizations B and C, which, in turn, deal with organizations D, E, and F. Organization A might be a city bus system, whereas B and C might be transportation systems in the surrounding suburbs and counties. B and C might bring A a substantial number of its rush-hour riders. D and E might be the labor unions representing B's and C's employees. F might be an organization that supplies B and C with new buses from time to time. Thinking about these relationships as networks makes it evident that A's ridership can be affected by B's and C's operations, which depend on D's and E's activities to some extent. A has no direct relationship with D and E, but they can disturb its environment. F, by contrast, is only remotely related to A's operations. This is only a simple example, but it is clear that a great many interdependencies and threats to organizational stability can emerge from a relatively small number of factors. Network analysis helps us see and understand how all the pieces "fit together." Box 4.7 provides as an example a network "map" of the interrelationships among U.S. Defense Department major weapon acquisition projects in 2007. Note how closely the largest network cluster [see inset box in Box 4.7] resembles a "spider web" of links.

4.7   COMPLEX FISCAL RELATIONS AMONG U.S. DEFENSE DEPARTMENT MAJOR WEAPONS ACQUISITION PROGRAMS, 2007

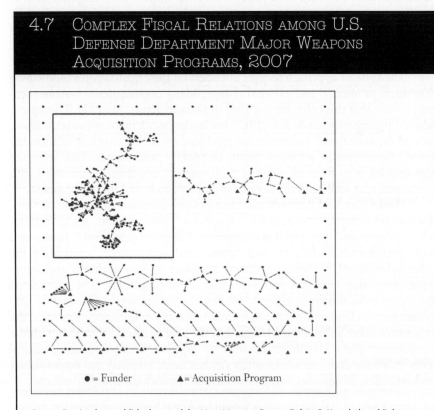

● = Funder   ▲ = Acquisition Program

Source: Previously unpublished research by Mary Maureen Brown, Robert S. Kravchuk and Robert Flowe on the financial interdependencies among major defense acquisition programs (MDAPs). For more information on this ongoing project, contact author Kravchuk at Indiana University.

The Ecology of Organizations

The *ecological model* also considers the environment to be of critical importance to organizations. Its focus is on change. As Perrow describes it,

> The ecological model identifies three stages in a process of social change. First is the occurrence of *variations* in behavior. They may be intended or unintended; it doesn't matter. In organizations, a production crew might gradually vary its techniques, or a shortage of gasoline might lead to a variation in truck-delivery practices. Second, natural *selection* occurs as some variations are eliminated because they are undesirable and others are reinforced because they work. The criterion of effectiveness is survival. Third, there is a *retention* mechanism that allows those "positively selected variations" to be retained or reproduced. Since nothing ever stands still, either for those in the organization or for its environment, over the long run positively selected variations that become stable activities will be subject to further variation.[48]

Organizations as Complex Adaptive Systems

In *Time, Chance, and Organizations* (1985), Herbert Kaufman seemingly builds on the ecological approach but reaches the rather different conclusion that "the survival of some organizations for great lengths of time is largely a matter of luck."[49] He argues that randomness rather than rationality may explain organizational survival because when all is said and done, organizations can change only marginally, whereas environmental changes are volatile. Furthermore, the flexibility of organizations required for change has disadvantages for their coherence and persistence. Kaufman sees real advantages to the demise of some organizations and their replacement by newer ones, just as one would expect evolution to advance an animal or plant species. He writes, "Instead of striving to *lower* organizational death rates and *extend* organizational longevity, we should, according to the implications of the evolutionary hypothesis, concentrate on *maintaining* birth rates and organizational diversity."[50] Put simply, there is no particular reason to resist change.

In the modern literature on organizational adaptation and complexity, Kaufman's views appear underdeveloped, and perhaps even a bit naïve. Complex adaptive systems (CAS) are those which demonstrate the usual attributes of open systems, but which also manifest a capacity to learn from experience and to adapt to changing internal and external conditions; and they do so in a manner that makes overall system behavior difficult or impossible to predict from the behaviors of its subsystems. That is, they exhibit emergent properties and behaviors. Most common examples would be CAS that emerge—spontaneously, as it were—in the natural and social worlds. A leading example of an emergent biological system would be any living organism; an example from the social world would be Adam Smith's competition market model, wherein the separate motivations and behaviors of many individuals, households, firms, and governments interact in ways that produce an efficient allocation of scarce economic resources, to the benefit of everyone.

An instance of a complex organization—one that exhibits emergent behavior of an efficient nature—may be found by returning to Box 4.7. The complicated web in the inset box in that exhibit emerged—in an unplanned manner—over time, from 2004 to 2007, involving nearly every military service and dozens of different commodities under development (weapons and other material requirements). The number of funding sponsors and program linkages in the entire network grew from 135 in 2004 to 319 in 2007; the non-clustered programs had remained fairly stable in terms of their funding relationships. (There were 80 MDAPs [major defense acquisition programs] sampled during the period of study.) The most important consideration here is that, while the participating MDAPs understood that they had "partner programs," none had even the slightest clue that they had spontaneously organized into a larger cluster. That is, they did not know that they were involved in a network web, let alone an increasingly dense one.

The existing literature suggests that task interdependency may influence program performance, and in a negative fashion.[51] Historically, organizations have often sought to compartmentalize their operations in a manner that minimizes external dependencies. However, in the present era, the strategy of minimizing interdependencies is rapidly eroding, because many of the public's most pressing problems demand multi-disciplinary solutions that cross organizational boundaries. In the research project that is depicted in Box 4.7, Maureen Brown and her collaborators tested whether membership (among other variables) in the largest "network cluster" was important in explaining the various member programs' budget and schedule performance. It turns out that membership in the network is, in fact, an important positive factor in explaining performance. All of the projects which have linked into the rather dense network cluster in the inset box in Box 4.7 are under budget and ahead of schedule; that is, they are efficient, and their efficiency is not predictable from the attributes of the programs.

Such developments hold great potential for positively impacting public system performance. In summary, the key implications of Brown's research are:

1. Complex behavior—in the form of network efficiency—is observed at the network level, and not at the subsystem level.
2. Network complexity demonstrates emergent attributes, as MDAP projects became more efficient as the network became denser.
3. The emergent network cluster (inset box in Box 4.7) emerged in an unplanned manner; not all public networks are guided by previous intent.
4. Complex networks, or network clusters, are not necessarily inefficient, in contradiction to some previous studies.[52]
5. Therefore, it cannot be assumed that increasing network complexity will lead to decreased organizational performance; quite the contrary is observed, in this instance.

The more complex networks in Brown's study demonstrate superior performance over their non-cluster counterparts in meeting performance expectations. In short, it is membership in the network itself, and not particular attributes of the individual member programs, that influenced performance. Spontaneous emergence of complex networks that exhibit many and varied task interdependencies may achieve greater efficiency levels than was originally believed.

Neo-Institutional Theory & Organizational Rigidities

Some scholars[53] argue that organizations do not adopt structures, routines, and procedures for rational reasons (i.e., to make an organization more efficient, or effective, or adaptive), but for institutional reasons. In order to develop, enhance, and preserve organizational legitimacy, organizations adopt those structures and procedures that their organizational fields have defined as important. Looking like a legitimate organization is equally, if not more, important in determining access to resources than producing quality programs and services in the most efficient manner.

In this theory, the concept of the organizational field is important. An organizational field is defined as "those organizations that, in the aggregate, constitute a recognized area of institutional life: key suppliers, resource and product consumers, regulatory agencies, and other organizations that produce similar services or products."[54] Organizations face three different types of institutional pressures that drive them to adopt structures and procedures, ultimately causing organizations in the same field to look alike. These three pressures are:

1. *Coercive* isomorphism that stems from political influence and the problem of legitimacy;
2. *Mimetic* isomorphism resulting from standard responses to uncertainty; and,
3. *Normative* isomorphism, associated with professionalization.[55]

While giving in to these pressures may increase an individual organization's legitimacy and access to resources, the long-term implication of this theory is that these isomorphic pressures will reduce the variety of organizational structures, thus reducing an organizational field's ability to adapt to dramatic changes in the environment, leading to an unhealthy rigidity.

The Organizational Culture Perspective

The above approaches to organizational theory assume that organizations are rational. Any claim that an organization is rational implies that organizations can think, which immediately seems at odds with the commonsensical view that inanimate things lack mental processes. However, Mary Douglas, one of the 20th century's great anthropologists, so argued in a book titled *How Institutions Think* (1986).[56] The essence of her claim is that a social institution serves as a "suprapersonal cognitive system"[57] that confers identity, remembers and forgets, classifies, and makes life-and-death decisions. Further, she argues that "the individual's most elementary cognitive process depends on social institutions."[58] In this formulation, not all social institutions are organizations (momentary instruments are an example), but some, like bureaucracy, are.

Douglas's theory is complex and controversial. Further analysis and discourse will be required before its potential for effectively enlightening us about the activities of public administrative organizations will be determined. However, the extreme quality of Douglas's argument can serve to allay doubts that, whether organizations actually "think," they certainly can have an impact on the cognitive processes and value systems of their members. This is the organizational culture perspective.

Organizational culture stands in contrast to approaches emphasizing the importance of structure and the systems framework. As Steven Ott explains, the organizational cultural school

> assumes that many organizational behaviors and decisions are almost predetermined by the patterns of basic assumptions existing in the organization. Those patterns of assumptions have continued to exist and influence behaviors because they have repeatedly led people to make decisions that usually worked for the organization. With repeated use, the assumptions slowly drop out of peoples' consciousness but continue to influence organizational decisions and behaviors—even when the organization's environment changes. They become the underlying, unquestioned—but virtually forgotten—reasons for "the way we do things here.[59]

Controls on individual members' thinking and behavior consist primarily of beliefs, assumptions, norms, and values that constitute the organization's culture.

The cultural perspective makes several important contributions to thinking about organizations. First, as Douglas's theory suggests, it can help explain how organizations can be said to "do the thinking." Organizational culture both conditions and reflects the ways individuals in organizations define issues, challenges, and phenomena; sort them out; evaluate; and decide. Thus the organizational culture perspective helps explain the impact of professionalism on the behavior of individuals in organizations.

Second, the organizational culture perspective helps explain why organizations that have similar structures may nevertheless behave differently. Bureaucratic structure is common, but individual bureaucracies often behave differently and the behavior of public administrative bureaucracies in different countries can be strikingly different. Moreover, though structurally similar, sometimes the contents of organizational cultures fit the expectations of the larger society well, and sometimes they are out of sync with it. For instance, there is sometimes a public outcry when a single incident of police brutality is attributed to an organizational culture in which racism, excessive force, and other illegal practices are considered normal within a department's culture.

Third, variations among organizations and within the same organization over time can be partly explained by differences or changes in the strength of organizational cultures. Some organizations have strong cultures that serve to unify and focus the behavior of their members. This was true of the FBI under Hoover and NASA during the Apollo period. In other organizations, culture is a weak force. According to some analysts, NASA's significant number of operational failures during the 1980s, including the explosion of *Challenger* and the death of its crew, were in part due to a shift from an organizational culture that valued sound engineering above all else to one in which the values of effective management took on greater importance.

Fourth, the organizational culture perspective helps explain why organizations once considered rational (in some sense) act in inappropriate ways. For instance, the culture of the U.S. Civil Service Commission emphasized policing the personnel system to prevent partisan political encroachments long after new concerns, including equal employment opportunity, became of much greater national concern.

Feminist Theories

Some modern theories challenge certain outmoded concepts of organization that reinforce masculine role models and thereby rigidify organizations in ways that work to the disadvantage of women.[60] For instance, Jean Lipman-Blumen specifically calls for reexamining the myths of female leadership: that women make poor leaders, that people dislike working for them, and that acknowledged female leaders are perceived as masculine.[61] Based on studies of male and female interpersonal skills, she concludes that women have advantages over their male counterparts insofar as the skills required for success turn on what women do well—informal relationship building and interpersonal communications— but that men's gameplaying skills are better suited to the "paying one's dues" at subordinate levels required to reach senior management levels.

The upshot is that leadership is individualized, not by nature gender-specific, but to the detriment of many organizations, more than half of the best-suited individuals are not reaching the top. Feminist approaches call for study of the ways in which gender relations are produced, reproduced, and reinforced in organizations. In the early twenty-first century, it appears vitally necessary to the future of many organizations to examine critically the "gendered substructure" of the organization in order to effect positive change. It is ultimately in the interest of all organizations to do so, in that failure to employ the full potential of all their employees maximally will cause them to underperform and, perhaps, to fail.

Sorting It Out

What are we to make of this diversity of organization theory? Organizations are highly varied, and many are complex. Therefore, it is not surprising that no one theory or approach explains everything about all organizations. Rather, the various theoretical approaches and frameworks reviewed provide tools for analyzing organizational activity. Sometimes these tools can be used in complementary fashion; at other times the use of one may preclude the use of another. But in all cases one or another of them should help explain why organizations do what they do.

Contemporary organization theory includes both private and public organizations. However, there are some key differences between the public and private sectors. When we focus specifically on public agencies, the distinct perspectives of the managerial, political, and legal approaches to public administration should be considered in some detail.

Managerial Perspectives on Public Organization

Orthodox Public Administration: POSDCORB

The traditional managerial perspective in public organization grows largely out of the "classical" approaches of Weber and Taylor. It is sometimes considered an extension of those approaches, and with them is referred to as the public administrative "orthodoxy." It has been said that 1937 was the high noon of this orthodoxy—and that the clock stopped![62] It was in that year that the orthodoxy's principles were codified in a volume called *Papers on the Science of Administration,* edited by Luther Gulick and Lyndall Urwick.[63] Gulick's article, "Notes on the Theory of Organization," has been of particular importance in the managerial tradition.[64]

The orthodox managerial perspective emphasizes efficiency, economy, and effectiveness as the values that should inform the structure and process of public administrative organizations. It views the division of labor (specialization) as the fundamental key to economic rationality and productivity. But once the work is divided, coordination of effort becomes necessary. Coordination can be by (1) *organization,* "that is, by interrelating the subdivisions of work by allotting them to men who are placed in a structure of authority, so that the work may be coordinated by orders of superiors to subordinates, reaching from the top to the bottom of the entire enterprise,"[65] and (2) *idea,* "that is, the development of intelligent singleness of purpose in the minds and wills of those who are working together as a group, so that each worker will of his own accord fit his task into the whole with skill and enthusiasm."[66] Gulick thought that an enterprise could not be truly effective without using both these bases of coordination, but he tended to stress organization for its reliability, predictability, and economy.

Gulick repeated many of Weber's observations, but he turned them into prescriptions. He believed that the organization coordinating the specializations should be hierarchical and culminate with "one master."[67] Hierarchical authorities should be in control in fact as well as in theory. Their control should be ensured by limiting their span of control, that is, the number of subordinates directly responsible to any single superordinate. Gulick and others in this tradition believed that the appropriate span of control could be determined scientifically. The work of executives was aimed at maintaining coordination and control. It consisted of POSDCORB, an acronym that may well continue to describe the core curriculum of many public administrative master's degree programs: Planning, Organizing, Staffing, Directing, Coordinating, Reporting, and Budgeting (not necessarily in that order!).

POSDCORB activities were thought to include all functions of the chief executive and the heads of organizational subdivisions. Importantly, Gulick averred that some of them could be undertaken by *staff* employees, employees who are not in the *line* (or chain) of direct authority, but rather act as assistants or advisers to those in such positions. The distinction between line and staff became important in the orthodox tradition, which admonished that the two functions should not be mixed, as this blurs the assignment of responsibility.

The orthodoxy held that there was essentially one most efficient way to organize any given governmental function. Organization could be by *purpose* (e.g., education, health, welfare); *process* (engineering, accounting); *clientele or materiel* (farmers, veterans, the poor, or a natural resource); or *place* (state, region, city, rural areas). Each of these bases of organization had advantages and disadvantages in terms of the relevant organizational values of efficiency, economy, and effectiveness. A listing of these developed by the authors is set out in Box 4.8.

4.8   SCIENTIFIC ADMINISTRATION: ADVANTAGES AND DISADVANTAGES OF DIFFERENT ORGANIZATIONAL BASES

Organization by Purpose (such as education, health, welfare):

Advantages:
- Serves purpose better
- Public prefers it
- Elicits more energy and loyalty from employees

Disadvantages:
- Requires substantial overlaps
- Ignores new technologies
- Loses sight of subordinate parts of work

Organization by Clientele or Materiel (farmers, the poor, veterans):

Advantages:
- Simplifies and allows coordination of contact with consumer
- Eliminates duplication
- Centralizes information

Disadvantages:
- Clientele may take over
- Sacrifices specialization
- May be hard to apply (citizens fall into overlapping categories)

Organization by Process (teaching, law, engineering, accounting):

Advantages:
- Uses technical skill maximally
- Uses automation maximally

- Permits coordination
- Fosters professionalism, career service

Disadvantages:
- May be difficult to apply
- Process may hinder purpose
- Fosters arrogance, resistance to democratic control

Organization by Place (state, region, rural, urban areas):

Advantages:
- Allows greater coordination
- Adapts total program to area served
- Cuts red tape in dealing with other governmental units (state, local)
- Cuts costs for travel, etc.

Disadvantages:
- Makes it difficult to maintain uniformity
- Encourages short-sighted management geared to local problems
- May make it difficult to specialize
- May be vulnerable to local pressure groups

Source: Compiled by the authors, based on L. Gulick and L. Urwick, Eds., *Papers on the Science of Administration* (New York: Institute of Public Administration, 1937).

Challenges to the Orthodoxy

The purpose/process/clientele/place scheme has been severely criticized for not even approaching the level of scientific exactness that it purports to possess. The most devastating attack on the orthodoxy in this context came from Herbert Simon, who dismissed the purpose/process/clientele/place scheme as no more than a set of "proverbs."[68] And like proverbs, he argued, its premises come in twos. "Haste makes waste" is balanced out by "He who hesitates is lost." The scheme suggests that, for example, organization by process promotes professionalism on the one hand and unresponsiveness on the other. Simon went on to argue that a science of administrative organization was possible, but that it would have to separate out facts from values with great care.

In intellectual terms, the orthodox approach was dealt a devastating blow by Simon's critique. It was also impaled by Dwight Waldo's influential *The Administrative State*.[69] Waldo attacked the classical approach on its own terms. He demonstrated that "efficiency" and "economy" could not be treated as values in an operational sense because they did not provide sufficient direction for public administrative action to be useful in practice. Moreover, far from being apolitical, Waldo showed that the traditional approach contained an implicit political theory. In a related development, Paul H. Appleby's *Policy and Administration* directly challenged the notion of a policy-neutral science of administration, by showing that unelected administrators make many decisions affecting the lives of American citizens.[70] These authors stressed that hierarchy and centralization are at many points in conflict with democratic politics. This cast doubt on the very idea of a strict separation of politics and administration, because, as Waldo argued, any comprehensive public administrative theory is likely also to have an embedded theory of politics.

Together, Simon, Waldo, and Appleby destroyed the intellectual underpinnings of the orthodox approach. Their critiques were successful in discrediting the earlier claims that orthodox theory was "scientific." Certainly none would deny that it contained a great deal of common sense; equally, however, few would continue to accept its advocates' claim to scientific, apolitical, and value-free knowledge of public administration. But as valuable as their critiques of the earlier theoretical paradigm were, Simon, Waldo, and Appleby were not successful in replacing it with a new one. They are not to be faulted for this, because in the roughly 65 years since they wrote their groundbreaking books, no one else has been able to develop a unified general public administrative or organization theory that has gained anywhere near the following that the orthodoxy once had.

What Will Replace POSDCORB?

One of the important consequences of the failure to develop a new theoretical paradigm for public organization theory has been a continuing reliance on the orthodox approach in practice. Practitioners and political leaders who must contend with public administrative practice on a day-to-day basis need some principles and values to inform their actions. They must have some reasons for doing what they do. They must also be able to explain these reasons in terms acceptable to the public. Although many now embrace the NPM, many others are more likely to fall back on the orthodoxy for its commonsense wisdom: who can argue with "efficiency," after all?

Contemporary managerial perspectives on organization emphasize the importance of being results-oriented, however. The NPM and related approaches reject the orthodox view that structure is the key to cost-effective performance. They argue that successful administration requires clear objectives and flexible processes for achieving them. Structure should be designed to facilitate performance rather than to control employees, information, and resources. Organization should be designed more from the bottom up than from the top down. It should flow from the needs of service delivery. Decentralization and the reduction of hierarchy are typically favored.

Several results-oriented organizational strategies have been deployed in recent decades. **Operations management** seeks to identify the specific operational responsibilities of government agencies and to design their organizations and work flows to maximize productivity.[71] This approach does not deny or belittle the importance of politics and law in the public sector. But it does concentrate on the obvious need to perform governmental functions productively within the parameters set by politics and law. The many functions of government that may be suitable for the operations management approach include those that are highly routine, such as: issuance of drivers' licenses and vehicular registrations; the maintenance of highways and roads; sanitation; water supply; and processing Social Security payments.

An example of a highly complex administrative process badly in need of simplification is diagrammed in Box 4.9. The benefits of systematically studying complex work processes and procedures are obvious. Operations management also encourages the gathering of information about each step as a means of planning workloads and allocating the organization's resources more efficiently. Coupled with the analysis of organizational networks, it can also identify potential disturbances in the environment.

Management by objectives, or **MBO,** is a common results-oriented approach. MBO can be outlined as follows: setting goals, objectives, and priorities at the organizational, unit, and manager levels; developing plans to achieve results; allocating resources; tracking or monitoring progress toward goals and objectives; evaluating results; and generating improvements based on the results achieved.[72]

MBO appears to be underappreciated in public administration's academic literature. It was emphasized at the federal level during President Richard Nixon's administration but then fell out of favor—perhaps as a result of guilt by association. However, surveys of cities suggest that its popularity has been sustained in urban administration, with well over half reporting its use in the 1980s. Evidence shows that MBO produces large productivity gains when top management is committed to it.[73]

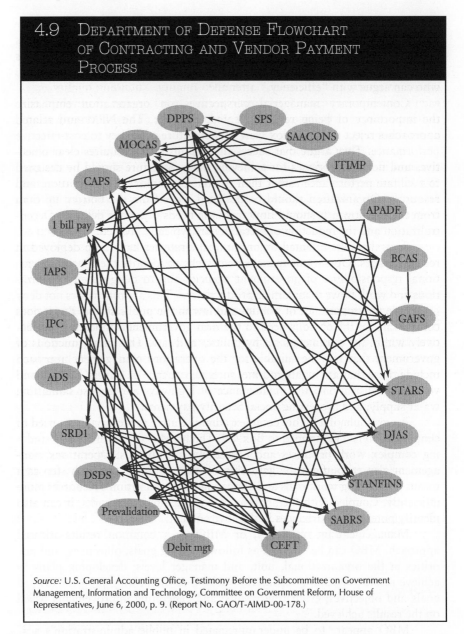

4.9　DEPARTMENT OF DEFENSE FLOWCHART OF CONTRACTING AND VENDOR PAYMENT PROCESS

Source: U.S. General Accounting Office, Testimony Before the Subcommittee on Government Management, Information and Technology, Committee on Government Reform, House of Representatives, June 6, 2000, p. 9. (Report No. GAO/T-AIMD-00-178.)

Total quality management, or **TQM,** attracted great attention in the public sector during the late 1980s and into the 1990s. TQM was initially developed by W. E. Deming.[74] Deming's version emphasizes the need to build quality into an organization's products rather than to weed out defects later. His approach involves analyzing defect rates and finding ways of reducing them. Other advocates of TQM, such as Philip Crosby and Joseph Juran, advocate instilling in employees an intolerance for any defects or deviations from the letter of product specification requirements.[75] Although these approaches are sometimes viewed as poles apart, TQM has been so widely used that a working synthesis has developed. Its main elements are customer-driven and customer-determined quality, "building quality in" at each stage of production, controlling variations in output, teamwork, continuous improvement, strong worker participation, and total organizational commitment.[76]

TQM has been employed at all levels of government, in many universities, and in private firms. But public sector interest in it peaked by the mid-1990s. Budget constraints and NPM pressures for downsizing, privatizing, and achieving results may have been factors. Another factor, as James Swiss contends, is the imperfect fit between TQM and government. TQM was developed for the production of products, not services. First, most customers do not care about the personal qualities of the workers who produce their DVDs and toasters. However, the characteristics of their social workers, police, waiters, and waitresses may be part of the overall service. Variability is less controllable in service delivery than in manufacturing.

Second, defining customers is not always easy for government agencies that do not sell anything. Based on the mission statement of the Department of the Interior printed in Box 4.10, who are the department's customers? They even include future generations. But no one in the department will be around to see if four or five generations from now these customers will be delighted with what was done today. There are also multiple customers with competing objectives and perspectives. How are they to be prioritized? Because government is overwhelmingly not market-driven, the market cannot be expected to determine how its scarce resources and services are allocated.

Finally, "Orthodox TQM depends on an extremely strong organizational culture with an almost single-minded commitment to quality. In order to shape that culture, the managers must be continuously involved in improving management."[77] The turnover among political executives in government may be too rapid, abrupt, and jarring for TQM to operate well. Despite these limitations, TQM is often appropriate for some governmental organizations.

4.10   MISSION STATEMENT FOR THE U.S. DEPARTMENT OF THE INTERIOR

The mission of the Department of the Interior is to protect and provide access to our Nation's natural and cultural heritage and honor our trust responsibilities to Indian Tribes and our commitments to island communities.

Source: www.doi.gov/secretary/mission.html (accessed February 23, 2007).

Benchmarking is a useful tool that can be used in conjunction with TQM to improve organizational performance dramatically. It essentially consists of scanning the "best practices" in a particular functional area (production management, order processing, accounts payable processing, inventory management, etc.) to uncover potential improvements in an organization's ways of doing things. An example of the benefits of benchmarking is the U.S. Air Force process for acquiring landing gear components for its jets compared to that of a commercial airline. The opportunity for improvement is so vast (117 days versus 12 days) that the benefits of the comparisons that emerge from benchmarking are clear. Consequently, public organizations at all levels now employ forms of benchmarking as a means of routinely checking on how they are doing compared to those who do it best.

Business process reengineering (BPR) is closely related to TQM but maintains that, in many circumstances, organizational structures and procedures have become so ossified that a radical redesign is more appropriate than TQM's more deliberate process of gradual, incremental improvement. Developed by MIT Professor Michael Hammer in the early 1990s, BPR emerged from the observation that many organizations focus on doing the wrong things better! His prescription is therefore not to make business processes more efficient but to look toward new ways of accomplishing the organization's purpose.[78] An important dimension of BPR is the aggressive use of information technology to leverage the talents and skills of employees at all levels of the organization. BPR is somewhat critical of benchmarking, insofar as benchmarking may work against business improvement by restricting thinking to what already is being done in other organizations rather than "thinking outside of the box" in the direction of dramatic breakthroughs and innovations. The basic idea is to use information technology to unleash the latent, untapped potential that exists in most organizations.

Performance-based organizations (PBOs) are a results-oriented organizational format promoted by the NPM. The idea is to place core governmental "factory" operations into units that resemble private firms. PBOs are highly deregulated, but they are not privatized because they perform functions considered to be inherently governmental. The government corporation model is also considered unsuitable either because of the PBO's functions or because of its inability to generate sufficient revenues through the sale of a service or product. The Federal Aviation Administration (FAA) became a flagship model in 1996, and the Patent and Trademark Office followed soon thereafter. Being freed from much regulation by law and the Office of Personnel Management, the FAA was able to reduce 1,069 pages of internal regulations to 41 and drop the number of position descriptions it uses from 155,000 to 2,000.[79] Whether these agencies are more cost-effective as a result of these changes is somewhat hard to establish, however.

Organizational culture change is a prerequisite for MBO, TQM, BPR, and PBOs to work. Traditional attitudes toward employees and organizational attributes must change. Two main approaches have been widely discussed: organizational humanism and organizational development.

Organizational humanism is an approach rooted in *The Human Side of Enterprise,* in which Douglas McGregor developed a contrast between two managerial approaches.[80] "Theory X" (scientific management) was based on the presumption that the average worker was indolent, found work distasteful, lacked ambition and creativity, was largely indifferent to organizational needs, and he or she was in favor of close and continuous supervision. By contrast, "Theory Y" assumed that people can find work natural and enjoyable, that they can be creative and exercise self-control, and that "[t]he motivation, the potential for development, the capacity for assuming responsibility, the readiness to direct behavior toward organizational goals are all present in people . . . *It is the responsibility of management to make it possible for people to recognize and develop these human characteristics for themselves.*"[81]

Organization development (OD) is an example of an approach for improving organizations that embraces and builds on Theory Y assumptions. Originally developed by Kurt Lewin and his associates at the National Training Laboratories, OD theory emphasizes human interactions as the key to organizational success or failure.[82] It assumes that organizations will be more effective at problem solving and coping with their environments when there is more trust, support, and cooperation among their members. OD involves the use of "change agents," or consultants, to increase one or more of the following: trust, confrontation of organizational problems, openness among employees, personal enthusiasm and satisfaction, group and self-responsibility, and creativity. OD relies on psychological theory to help members of an organization understand and change their attitudes toward themselves, their roles, other employees, and the organization.[83]

Critics of the organizational humanism approach argue that many workers fit the assumptions of Theory X more than those of Theory Y. Additionally, critics such as H. Roy Kaplan and Curt Tausky charge that organizational humanism lacks empirical grounding.[84] Consequently, some view Theory Y as highly ideological. Yet ideologies as well as technological and scientific developments have the potential to change relationships in the workplace. As indicated by MBO, TQM, and the NPM's commitment to employee empowerment, there is reason to believe that interest is growing in making organizations more participatory.

◆◆ THE POLITICAL APPROACH TO PUBLIC ORGANIZATION

Since the end of World War II, several observers have noted the extent to which politics pervades the organization of public bureaucracies. Today this may sound obvious—but it must be remembered that since the 1880s, theorists of public administration in the United States had been claiming that politics should be kept almost distinct from administration. The federal reinvention efforts of the 1990s continued to insist that public administration should be businesslike and market-oriented and that its factory operations can be separated from its policy functions. Those who view public organization as a question of politics start off from three very different premises.

Government Is Different. First, this perspective assumes that government is different from private organization. In other words, the prospects for generic organization theory are limited, and consequently distinctions must be made between public organization and private organization. Paul Appleby, in *Big Democracy* (1945), wrote, "In broad terms the governmental function and attitude have at least three complementary aspects that go to differentiate government from all other institutions and activities: breadth of scope, impact, and consideration; public accountability; political character."[85]

Government Involves Sovereign Power. Second, whereas orthodox theory is concerned with hierarchical authority in an administrative sense and the NPM is concerned with customer-driven organization, the political approach emphasizes the development, maintenance, and location of political power—that is, the authority to make political decisions concerning policies, means of implementation, and general operations of public administrative agencies. According to the political approach, power is a central facet of administrative organization and public agencies can be neither efficient nor effective without cultivating it. Norton Long drew attention to this in a 1949 essay titled "Power and Administration":

> The lifeblood of administration is power. Its attainment, maintenance, increase, dissipation, and loss are subjects the practitioner and student can ill afford to neglect. . . .
>
> The power resources of an administrator or agency are not disclosed by a legal search of titles and court decisions or by examining appropriations or budgetary allotments. Legal authority and a treasury balance are necessary but politically insufficient bases of administration . . .
>
> It is clear that the American system of politics does not generate enough power at any focal point of leadership to provide the conditions for an even partially successful divorce of politics from administration. . . [A]dministrative rationality demands that objectives be determined and sights set in conformity with a realistic appraisal of power position and potential.[86]

Diverse Interests Must Be Represented. The third premise of the political approach is that representation is a major concern in the organization of public agencies. Long stated that "the bureaucracy is recognized by all interested groups as a major channel of representation."[87] Consequently, in practice a great deal of effort is exerted by groups, political officials, and others who want to see a particular set of values represented in the missions and programs of public agencies. This often makes for an untidy situation in which agencies have highly diverse, overlapping, and conflicting goals. Yet to the extent that representation is present, "[e]xecutive branch structure is in fact a microcosm of our society. Inevitably it reflects the values, conflicts, and competing forces to be found in a pluralistic society. The ideal of a neatly symmetrical, frictionless organization structure is a dangerous illusion."[88]

The political approach's interest in representation also leads it to consider the public sector workforce in a radically different way than does the managerial approach. The concept of **representative bureaucracy**[89] holds that the social backgrounds and statuses of public administrators can affect their performance on the job. Members of different racial and ethnic groups, men and women, and individuals from different economic backgrounds may have disparate perspectives based on their experience and socialization. These different outlooks can lead them to define problems and design solutions in dissimilar ways. The concept also maintains that the social composition of government agencies is related to their performance and legitimacy among members of the public. For example, an all-white police force might be considered less legitimate in African American neighborhoods than would an all-African American or racially integrated one.

In emphasizing these three premises, the political approach to public organization holds that "established organization doctrine [the orthodoxy], with its emphasis on structural mechanics, manifests incomplete understanding of our constitutional system, institutional behavior, and tactical and strategic uses of organization structure as an instrument of politics, position, and power. Orthodox theories are not so much wrong when applied to the central issues of executive branch organization as largely irrelevant."[90] Here again, then, we find that to an extent the political and traditional managerial approaches, starting from different premises, end up talking past one another.

The political approach is based on a number of observations that are not necessarily linked to each other in a coherent fashion. Among these are the following.

Pluralism

The organization of public agencies and governmental executive branches should be pluralistic. In other words, they should be highly representative of the competing political, social, and economic groups in the society as a whole. Agencies should provide representation to these interests, and public policy should be made through the political competition among agencies. This approach requires that organizational missions be compound rather than unified or that there be many separate organizations. Overall, the public sector must address a number of different concerns without establishing any formal set of priorities. The mission statement of the U.S. Department of the Interior presents a classic example (see Box 4.10). Diverse missions of this kind generate broad support for agencies and enable administrators to shift emphasis from one aspect of their program to others in conjunction with the need to maintain and strengthen support among their constituencies and to minimize opposition.

Pluralism is also generated by overlapping missions among agencies. Perhaps the best current example is found in federal personnel administration. Each of the following is directly involved, but each has a different focus, as their names imply: the Office of Personnel Management, the Merit Systems

Protection Board, the Federal Labor Relations Authority, Office of Government Ethics, and the Equal Employment Opportunity Commission.

Autonomy

Pluralism requires that government structure reflect the diverse interests of the society. Representation further demands that there be a high degree of autonomy among the many organizational units in a governmental administrative structure. Autonomy enables different units to focus on providing representation to their constituencies or clienteles. Sometimes autonomy evolves under political pressure and administrative leadership; at other times it is built into law. Constitutionally, independent regulatory commissions (IRCs) are not considered part of the executive branch. Independent agencies, such as the EPA, and even some units within the departments, such as the FBI, can also achieve a high degree of autonomy. Organizational autonomy may be politically desirable to foster greater representation, but may also make executive coordination and control of public administration difficult.

The Legislative Connection

The political approach to public organization also stresses the connection between legislative committees and administrative agencies. Many consider public agencies to be key adjuncts of legislative committees and subcommittees. According to this view, organizational hierarchy within the executive branch does not capture the entire structure of authority, which would have to include at the least the chairpersons of committees and subcommittees in the legislature, and perhaps their staffs as well. To a large extent the organizational structure of the federal executive branch and committees and subcommittees of Congress are directly related. The proliferation of executive branch organizational units went hand in hand with the growth of subcommittees. Moreover, agencies and subcommittees will develop mutually supportive relationships. The Government Performance and Results Act of 1993 and the Government Performance and Results Act Modernization Act of 2010 formalized the link between (sub)committee and administrative programs by requiring federal agencies to formulate and prioritize specific program goals in consultation with Congress. A public administrator may thus be accountable and politically responsible to members of the legislature, as well as to executive branch officials.

Decentralization

The orthodox approach to public organization addresses the question of centralization versus decentralization from the perspective of efficiency and economy. Decentralization in the sense of establishing field offices and regional offices is considered useful in making government services available to the citizenry. But decentralization also complicates coordination and control of administrative units. Hence, the managerial approach maintains that a balance must be struck at some point. Once again, the political approach asks a different question and reaches a different conclusion.

From the political perspective, decentralization cannot be considered apart from representation. For instance, Herbert Kaufman observed that "while [decentralization] is sometimes defended on grounds of efficiency, it is more frequently justified in terms of effective popular participation in government."[91] At the federal level, about 15 percent of employees are located in the metropolitan Washington, DC, area. The others are located in agency field and regional offices, domestic or abroad. There is a certain logical order in the location of federal agencies' regional offices in ten major cities, including San Francisco, Denver, Boston, New York, and Atlanta. But the location of field offices for various administrative operations often appears haphazard. Within a given region, the separate bureaus of a single department may locate their field offices in different cities. If an individual wants to deal with one administrative unit in the field, he or she may have to go to a different city than will be necessary if he or she wants to deal with another unit of the same department. Prior to the consolidation and elimination of some of its 1,200 field offices in the 1990s, the Department of Agriculture had as many as 20 or more "regional maps," that is, ways of dividing up the country in terms of the location and jurisdiction of the field offices of their various bureaus.

A major explanation for this approach to organizational decentralization is political. As Kaufman points out, it may facilitate representation.[92] Another factor is the relationship between a bureau and a member of the legislature. Field offices are affected by pork-barrel politics. Agencies can also locate them in an effort to gain or maintain legislators' support. It may well be helpful to place a field office in the home district of a legislator with whom the bureau wants particularly to cooperate. Here the bureaus (agency subsystems) seek to adapt to or control their environment in ways that may detract from the organization's overall coherence.

A Checklist of Political Questions on Administrative Organization

Harold Seidman examined the political approach to public organization in great detail in his book *Politics, Position, and Power: The Dynamics of Federal Organization.* In his conclusion he provides a checklist of the issues that must be addressed in any proposed reorganization. His questions serve as a useful summary of the considerations discussed previously. They can be paraphrased or quoted as follows:

1. "What is the nature of the constituency that is being created or acquired, and to what extent will it be able to influence policies and program administration?"
2. How broad is the constituency? Does it represent narrow interests opposed to some aspects of the administrative program?

3. What committees in Congress will have jurisdiction over the administrative program, and what is their attitude likely to be in view of their constituencies?

4. What is the tradition of the department in which a program is to be placed? Will it be supportive, hostile, or indifferent?

5. "What are the constituencies to whom the administering agency responds? Would there be any obvious conflicts of interest?"

6. "Where are the loci of power with respect to program administration: the President, the agency head, the bureaus, congressional committees, professional guilds, interest groups . . .?"

7. What are the limitations on access to those with decision making responsibility for the program?

8. "Does the program design foster dominance by a particular professional perspective and will this result in distortion of program goals?"

9. Will the organization of the program be designed so as to facilitate cooperation with other governmental units having overlapped or related responsibilities?

10. "What safeguards are provided to assure that no group or class of people is excluded from participation in the program and an equitable share in program benefits?"

11. Will the form of organization engender status, visibility, and public support to the extent appropriate for the program function?

12. How do the structural and procedural arrangements affect the definition of responsibility and accountability for the program? Do they encourage "buck passing"?[93]

To Seidman's list could be added questions about the supervision of the program within the executive branch. Of particular interest would be whether the political executives in charge of it will require senatorial confirmation, whether they will be appointed directly by the president, or whether they will be appointed by department heads. No doubt other issues could also be raised. However, these considerations should provide a reasonably comprehensive guide to the political approach to organization.

◆→ THE LEGAL APPROACH TO PUBLIC ORGANIZATION

The legal approach to public organization is rarely discussed as a coherent body of principles and premises. Rather, it must be inferred from the writings of legal scholars, decisions of judges, and relevant legislative enactments. Its main thrust is to establish a structure in which fair adjudication or resolution of conflicts can take place. At a minimum, such a structure must enable opposing sides to be given notice of the issues to be contested, to be afforded an opportunity to present evidence or information supporting their interpretation of rules or laws, and to have a chance to explain their behavior and intentions. But most important, perhaps, adversary procedure must afford each side a fair forum in which to challenge the evidence, claims interpretations, and information presented by the other. Traditional adjudication uses adversary procedure, as is best exemplified by courtroom procedure, replete with complex rules of evidence. Alternative dispute resolution (ADR) relies more heavily on settling conflicts through negotiation, mediation, or arbitration. (These dispute resolution techniques are discussed in the context of labor relations in the next chapter.)

Independence

It has long been asserted by those supportive of the legal approach to public organization that administrative agencies exercising adjudicatory functions must enjoy a good deal of independence from the rest of the government. Some legal scholars thought that any adjudication by administrative agencies would imperil adherence to the rule of law.[94] The idea that agencies could combine legislative functions (rule making), enforcement (execution), and adjudication was particularly disturbing to many. This helps explain why IRCs, which often rely heavily on adjudication, evolved. The key concept was that administrative adjudication could be vested safely in nonpartisan, politically insulated independent regulatory commissions. At the federal level, the first of these, the Interstate Commerce Commission (ICC), was created in 1887 and authorized to regulate transportation, especially the railroads, in the public interest. Over the years several other independent regulatory commissions, boards, and agencies were created largely under the rationale that "just as we want our judges to be independent of political influence, so we want agencies that exercise judicial functions to be similarly independent. The larger the judicial function, the stronger the reasons for independence."[95] In other words, where agency operations are concerned with adjudication, they should not be subjected to partisan and other political pressures. The effort to establish such independence involves several structural arrangements, as discussed in the following sections.

The Commission Format

Frequently agencies that exercise quasi-judicial functions are headed by a board of commissioners rather than a single political executive or other hierarchical authority, as would generally be dictated by managerial and political approaches to public organization. As Kenneth C. Davis, one of the 20th century's leading administrative law scholars, explains, "just as we want appellate courts to be made up of plural members, to protect against the idiosyncrasies of a single individual, we want agencies that exercise judicial power to be collegial."[96] Moreover, because the missions of these agencies are defined as regulation in the *public* interest, they should not be controlled by one political party or another. Rather they should be allowed to develop a long-term, nonpartisan perspective.

There are typically limits on the number of commissioners who can belong to the same political party. Such arrangements guarantee minority party members some degree of participation and an opportunity to voice their opinions. If necessary, they may file dissenting opinions, which may sway courts on appeal. In addition, commissioners typically appointed by the chief executive with legislative consent generally hold their offices during staggered, fixed terms and are protected from removal solely on political grounds. This prevents the president or a governor from replacing all the commissioners at will. Depending on the context, the commission format may reach deep into the administrative structure of such an agency. Staff may be responsible and accountable to individual commissioners, thereby fragmenting authority. The commission may also become politically divided along partisan or policy lines.

Insulation from *Ex Parte* Influences

It stands to reason that if the commissioners of an agency with judicial functions are to be independent in their decision making, they must be insulated from pressures applied by the legislature and perhaps other groups. Yet it appears equally true that the views of legislators and others may be helpful in determining what is in the public interest. The legal approach tries to resolve this dilemma by encouraging widespread participation in the *rule making* procedures of such agencies while at the same time prohibiting one-sided contacts with agency decision makers when they are engaged in adjudication. Such one-sided contacts are called **ex parte,** and they are considered an unfair breach of the requirement that each side have a fair opportunity to present its case. The legal approach has been so insistent on this that in at least one case, *D.C. Federation of Civic Associations v. Volpe* (1972),[97] a federal court of appeals ordered a district court to require the secretary of the Department of Transportation to establish a decision making process that would enable it to act free "from extraneous pressures unrelated to the merits of the question."[98] The point of such procedures was to exclude pressure from a member of Congress!

Independent Hearing Examiners–Administrative Law Judges

Just as the legal approach favors the independence of agency heads who engage in adjudication and their insulation from ex parte communications, it holds that others making adjudicatory decisions within the agency should be similarly autonomous. Again, this approach stands in stark contrast to the orthodox managerial insistence on hierarchy. It also contravenes the emphasis on representation and widespread participation encouraged by the political approach to public organization. Hearing examiners, who may also be called administrative law judges (ALJs), preside over administrative hearings involving issues of compliance with agency rules and laws, eligibility for benefits, license granting, some forms of rule making, and rate setting.

At the federal level, the Administrative Procedure Act of 1946, as amended, provides that the central personnel agency, the Office of Personnel Management, select ALJs through competitive merit procedures and establish their pay. The Merit Systems Protection Board protects them from discipline or dismissal for reasons other than "good cause." ALJs are exempt from agency performance appraisals and are prohibited from performing any duties inconsistent with their adjudicatory responsibilities. In principle, if not practice, contrary to the notion of specialization found in managerial approaches, these civil servants may be rotated from agency to agency so that they do not become overly supportive of the policy perspectives of one agency or another.

In addition to these provisions for independence, the ex parte rule is strictly interpreted. Officials in the agency to which a hearing examiner is assigned are prohibited from discussing matters under adjudication with the hearing examiner. So are agency employees performing prosecutorial and investigatory functions except as part of the hearing.

These provisions for independence would make little sense if the agency were free to override the hearing examiner's recommended decision with impunity. Consequently, through custom, practice, and law, a tendency has developed for the administrative law judge's opinion to be upheld unless it appears to "(1) be flatly unjustifiable in light of the facts; (2) be obviously contrary to and disruptive of agency policy objectives; (3) have been reached in a procedurally reckless manner destined to elicit court review; (4) be unnecessarily harsh on a party; and (5) be likely to attract unwanted political reprisals."[99] However, to guard against a misguided decision by a single hearing examiner, procedures may provide for an appeal within an agency. This adds another adjudicatory process and structure to the agency's organization.

Staffing for Adjudication

The legal approach toward public administration holds that the adjudicatory activities of public agencies will often follow trial-like procedures. This approach is buttressed by constitutional requirements for procedural due process under certain circumstances. The adjudicatory model contains an implicit structure that goes beyond the existence of independent hearing examiners. It also includes other types of organizational positions, including investigatory and prosecutorial units. Investigators have been identified as key functionaries in many regulatory contexts.[100] Because they must exercise a good deal of discretion, their supervision and training become critical considerations for the proper functioning of the agency. This introduces the need for hierarchical positions to oversee their behavior and staff units to keep them fully cognizant of changes in agency policy, law, and technique. Prosecutors also require supportive arrangements, including staff to do research; analyze private parties' requests for rate increases, licenses, and other benefits; and help prepare cases and briefs for adjudication.

Alternative Dispute Resolution

Alternative dispute resolution (ADR) offers much greater flexibility than does traditional adjudication and is strongly supported by the NPM. The Negotiated Rulemaking Act (1990) and the Administrative Dispute Resolution Acts

(ADRAs) of 1990 and 1996 provide new frameworks for dispute resolution by federal agencies. The Negotiated Rulemaking Act allows agencies to develop proposed rules on a consensus basis through negotiation. The main purposes are to improve the timeliness and content of rules (see Chapter 9) and reduce the number of lawsuits challenging agency rule making. Theoretically, agencies should negotiate as equals with other interested parties. Ultimately, though, they are responsible for the content of rules. Mediation or other means of facilitation may be used. The ADRAs require agencies to have dispute resolution specialists on their staffs and promote ADR in contract and other legal conflicts. The 1996 Act permits binding arbitration as a means of resolving disputes.

All three acts look toward a sharing of authority with outsiders, including mediators, and greater administrative responsiveness. They conflict with orthodox management's emphasis on unity of command and clear lines of authority. They also pose a challenge to organizational cultures that view negotiation as unprofessional and a devaluation of technical expertise.[101] Although the responsiveness they may afford is favored by the political approach, it comes at the price of obscuring accountability.

In sum, there is a legal approach to public organization that differs substantially from the managerial and political approaches. It emphasizes independence rather than hierarchy, procedural fairness and regularity rather than efficiency, and individual rights rather than group representation. In the ADR version it favors sharing authority and responsiveness even at some cost to accountability and reliance on specialized expertise. Although it probably achieves many of its goals, it is not surprising that the legal approach to public organization is frequently attacked by those seeking to promote managerial and political objectives and values. Once again, therefore, we find the tendency for public administrative practices to confirm Miles's law: "Where one stands depends on where one sits." What are the prospects for a synthesis of the approaches to public organization?

❖❖   CONCLUSION: THE FUTURE

Many believe that public organizations in the future will look considerably different from those reflecting the managerial, political, or legal perspectives of today. But it is possible that they will synthesize many of the characteristics of contemporary organizations based on these approaches. Certainly there are widespread tendencies toward change, but they point in somewhat different directions.

Fundamental Assumptions

At the root of the general claim that public organization will look different in the future is the notion that contemporary administrative agencies are rapidly becoming outmoded. This is a central tenet of the NPM. According to a

U.S. Government Accountability Office (GAO) study, to keep pace with a rapidly changing environment, federal agencies will need to embrace:

1. a demonstrated leadership commitment and accountability for change;
2. the integration of management improvement initiatives into programmatic decision making;
3. thoughtful and rigorous planning to guide decisions, particularly to address human capital and information technology issues;
4. employee involvement to elicit ideas and build commitment and accountability;
5. organizational alignment to streamline operations and clarify accountability; and,
6. strong and continuing congressional involvement.[102]

These elements are broadly consistent with the requirements of the Government Performance and Results Act of 1993 and the Government Performance and Results Act Modernization Act of 2010, which form the legislative basis of the federal effort to measure agency performance, allocate resources on the basis of meeting performance targets, and take corrective action where there are shortfalls. Put more starkly, agencies must adapt or they will fail in their public service missions.

However, for a variety of reasons, traditional organizations seem slow or unable to adapt to the rapid pace of change in contemporary life. Many agencies remain highly centralized, rigid, defensive, unable to use their human resources effectively, alienating, and even repressive in some respects. In short, they lack the flexibility to keep up with the constantly changing technological, political, economic, and social environments with which they must interact. Hierarchy, in particular, is unable to tap the full talents and use the perspectives of employees in the lower and middle ranks. Moreover, it tends to overemphasize the authority and overstate the ability of those at the top in an age when a person's "knowledge and approach can become obsolete before he has even begun the career for which he was trained."[103] In this view, the era has passed when a "great leader," dominated by a single idea—such as assembly-line production—can effectively run an organization for very long. Change appears inevitable, but in which direction?

There are three emergent models, each with deep roots in American culture—**democratic organization**, market-based organization, and the networked organization.

Democratic Organization

"Democracy becomes a functional necessity whenever a social system is competing for survival under conditions of chronic change."[104] Democracy in this view will include:

1. Full and free *communication,* regardless of rank and power.
2. A reliance on *consensus,* rather than the more customary forms of coercion or compromise to manage conflict.

3. The idea that *influence* is based on technical competence and knowledge rather than on the vagaries of personal whims or prerogatives of power.

4. An atmosphere that permits and even encourages emotional *expression* as well as task-oriented acts.

5. A basically *human* bias, one that accepts the inevitability of conflict between the organization and the individual, but which is willing to cope with and mediate this conflict on rational grounds.[105]

Moreover, a scientific attitude of inquiry and experimentation will prevail, loyalty to organizations will decline as those who are less committed are likely to be more able to take advantage of change, and structural arrangements will be flexible and task-oriented rather than based on fixed specializations, rigid jurisdictions, and sharply defined levels of hierarchical authority.

Employee Participation

Participative organizations, according to this look into the future, will encourage the participation of employees at all levels in decisions affecting their work and, perhaps, in the formulation of broad agency policies. The idea of employee participation is not new. Contemporary "agency theory," which grows out of economic assumptions concerning individuals' proclivity toward "self-regarding" behavior directed at maximizing their utilities (preferences), put the desirability of participation in a new light. Agency theory "assumes that social life is a series of contracts. Conventionally, one member, the 'buyer' of goods or services, is designated the 'principal,' and the other, who provides the goods or services, is the 'agent.' . . . The principal-agent relationship is governed by a contract specifying what the agent should do and what the principal must do in return (e.g., . . . pay a wage and benefits . . .)."[106] In the abstract, each employee of an organization could be considered an agent, free to attempt to write the terms of his or her contract with it. This calls attention to the prospect that self-regarding behavior will lead to shirking and other forms of cheating.

One response to such potential behavior is to try to minimize the organizational characteristics that would foster undesirable self-regarding activity. Minimizing self-regarding behavior in the public sector calls for "debureaucratizing" organizations, transforming the exercise and distribution of authority within them. In other words, greater equality and participation among employees in running an organization could check undesirable self-regarding behavior to an extent.[107] To the extent that agency employees have a high degree of public service motivation, that, too, should check self-regarding behavior. Yet, the precise scope and structure of employee participation necessarily remain vague when we engage in speculation about the future. One aspect does seem certain, however: Such participation, if it occurs at all, will go well beyond collective bargaining as currently constituted.

Advocacy Administration

Organizational democracy in the future may include an increased reliance on **advocacy administration,** which involves "the passionate commitment of those with professional skills and official standing to use these assets on behalf of the least powerful and wealthy members of the community."[108] Advocacy can take at least three forms: (1) advocacy from outside the government, which we will discuss in the next section; (2) "advocacy from within a government agency established to act in a manner adversary to other public agencies and programs,"[109] such as a public defender's office; and (3) advocacy by administrative officials on behalf of their clientele or constituency groups.

At the root of the advocacy concept is the belief that the adversary model of adjudication can be generalized to provide effective representation to all elements of the political community, including those who face special difficulties in organizing. Governmental structure would continue to be pluralistic, but to provide comprehensive representation, government may have to organize disadvantaged groups or at least place spokespersons who can effectively identify and represent their interests within the governmental structure.

Advocacy administration also would require a changed view of hierarchical authority. Advocates' right to advocate, that is, to oppose the policies and programs of administrative hierarchies, must be protected. The notion of "insubordination" has little relevance in this context, as does the managerial approach's desire to eliminate duplication, overlap, and conflictual lines of authority and responsibility. Finally, advocacy would differ from adjudication in that the policy decisions would be made by elected bodies and political executives rather than by independent hearing examiners.

Citizen Participation

Citizen participation is a form of advocacy from outside the government that is a long-standing feature of public administration in the United States. It may become an even more important factor in the future. Such participation can take place through advisory committees, citizen boards, or similar arrangements and can also be directly built into administrative decision making. This approach has been evident in the controversial use of "community action programs," which "offer citizen participation in and control of public administration. Local neighborhood representatives are held to be more truly spokesmen of the disadvantaged citizens, of the spirit of the local community, than the politicians of city hall and city council."[110]

Community action approaches may be used to control or influence schools, public housing developments, zoning, police conduct, and other aspects of local neighborhood administration. In some cases, citizen participation may be facilitated by governmental provision of professional planners, lawyers, or others to the citizen groups. New York State's Department of Environmental Conservation employs full-time "citizen participation specialists" whose job is to facilitate citizen involvement in environmental policy decision making. Citizen participation can be encouraged through open hearings on matters being considered by administrative agencies, such as changes in utility rates, zoning changes, and the building of roads or housing developments. Such hearings are often sparsely attended, but they afford public administrators an opportunity to hear what some interested citizens have to say.

Electronic government, or "e-government," opens entirely new prospects for involving the public in public administration. Agency Web pages can solicit suggestions for improving service delivery, infrastructure, and policies. Electronic "town meetings" are now possible. As access to and use of the Internet grow, electronic government should provide a highly effective tool for increasing citizen participation.

Citizen participation is obviously based on the notion that one does not need to be an expert in technical matters of public policy to be able to form a valuable opinion about the desirability of pursuing one course or another. Though the idea of citizen participation has been around for centuries, recently there has been a revitalization of the study of civic duty, in which scholars argue that public administrators should be more responsive to citizens and "should focus their responsibility to serve and empower citizens as they manage public organizations and implement public policy."[111] This "new public service" paradigm advocates the concept of "authentic citizen participation," in which the citizen is positioned closest to the issue and the administrative structures and processes are the furthest away.[112] Additionally, empowerment is a central focus of this unconventional method of participation. "Empowering citizens means designing processes where citizens know that their participation has the potential to have an impact where a representative range of citizens are included, and where there are visible outcomes."[113]

While conventional methods of citizen participation remain an integral part of democracy, especially at the local level, discovering new ways to increase citizen participation (i.e., e-government, authentic citizen participation) is critical in developing solid policies to produce a strong social and economic future. This approach poses a threat to hierarchy, specialization, and the belief that trained expertise should provide the dominant basis for participation in public policy making. In some forms, such as open hearings and community action programs, it also tends to challenge the political perspective's reliance on established groups and formal organizations as the basis for representing the views of the citizenry in public administration. (The public and public administration are the subjects of Chapter 10.)

Market-Based Organization

Market-based public administration is another model for administrative organizations of the future. It is strongly advocated by the NPM. At its core is the belief that marketlike competition leads organizations to be efficient and responsive to customer preferences. The NPM vision shares some of the elements of democratic organization just discussed. It strongly favors employee empowerment and disfavors hierarchy. Empowerment would enable those who deliver services to the public to decide how to do so. The empowered employee is held accountable for his or her performance, that is, for results. Management's main job is not to control employees but to be entrepreneurial in creating and marketing valued services or products for customers. Organizations will be successful if they satisfy their customers. Customers will drive public agencies to be efficient and responsive.

The market model is based on the same politics-administration dichotomy embraced by the orthodoxy. Like the orthodoxy, it is overwhelmingly managerial and places a high premium on efficiency or a variant of it, such as cost-effectiveness. Administration is business, not policy. Ideally, the NPM would institutionalize the dichotomy by privatizing and separating factory operations from political ones, as in the case of PBOs. Presumably, PBOs will be flat, rather than hierarchical, for the sake of flexibility, and will afford a great deal of employee participation for the intelligence and efficiency it yields.

The market model does not provide for direct citizen participation in public administration. It serves customers, not citizens.[114] Individuals participate as customers; perhaps groups can do the same (e.g., group fares or discounts). One risk, already present in bureaucratic politics, is that agencies may be responsive to their customers at the expense of the wider public's interests. Farmers, slaughterhouses, food processors, shippers, supermarkets, and restaurants are the customers of agencies engaged in food safety. They tend to resist regulation as unnecessary until a tragedy occurs and the public loses confidence in their products.

Market-based public administration is so new that it is difficult to see how it will deal with three key questions. First, how can politics be separated from administration? Orthodox administration insisted that separation was possible and tried to take politics out of personnel and the management of cities, ports, bridges, parks, and other infrastructure. But personnel remained infused with policy issues. Similarly, city managers often have a difficult time avoiding politics. Cost-effectiveness is only one criterion for distributing services. Who benefits and who pays may be of more interest to residents and their elected representatives.

Second, how appropriate are markets for allocating public goods and services? Markets register customer preferences and thereby allow stratification according to ability and willingness to pay. There are niches and boutiques. People who can afford better services and products are apt to buy them. Can the same principle be applied to public sector programs? Express mail costs more. Should there be express lines at motor vehicle departments or Social Security offices for those who are willing to pay for quicker service? Inequality is already a fact of life in the United States; would market-based public administration increase it? Perhaps.

Finally, how will market-based administrative organizations be held accountable? The NPM is certainly correct that traditional accountability mechanisms focus on processes rather than results and can strangle public administration in red tape. But accountability for results alone is also problematic. Inevitably, the results orientation will have to be blended with and tempered by the values of the political and legal approaches. But how can this be done without *re*regulating the agencies and processes the NPM has struggled so hard to *de*regulate?

Addressing these issues does not disparage the market-based model. No approach to organizing public administration has yet been able to satisfy our three general perspectives or maximize all our competing goals. The movements toward democratic organization and market-based public administration embrace responsiveness and employee participation, though not necessarily through collective bargaining. These values have already had a major impact on revamping public personnel management, central to all public administration.

The Networked Organization

In contemporary public administration, many programs are organized and operate in collaborative governance models or in other ways that span the boundaries between the public and private sectors (as in the case of nonprofit organizations providing direct social services under contract with state government agencies), and involving levels of government (as when state governments use federal grant monies to coordinate programs involving many local governments and non-governmental organizations). It seems that public-private policy and administrative networks are here to stay.

Robert Agranoff discusses four types of networks distinguished according to their purposes, studying such diverse areas as economic and rural development, wastewater management, watershed conservation, and transportation:[115]

1. *Informational Networks*—partners voluntarily organize to collaborate in sharing information, ideas, and data about policies, programs, technologies, and problem solutions.
2. *Developmental Networks*—partners seek actively to increase and expand their service capacity through technical and informational exchanges, as well as education and member service.
3. *Outreach Networks*—partners pool information, technologies, client contact lists, and other resources, and will sequence their programming efforts in order to access and create opportunities for new programming activities.
4. *Action Networks*—partners formally collaborate in interagency programming through more or less formal agreements, involving perhaps mutual service delivery efforts that coordinate and lever their separate strengths and capabilities.

Somewhat unlike the rather opaque, hidden networks that Brown and her collaborators study in the Defense Department, Agranoff's networks are transparent; that is, network partners are all known and/or are accessible to each other through the network itself. Further, they are consciously created as means to leverage the strengths of the partners. In contrast to traditional hierarchies, networks substitute information and expertise for authority structure and established administrative routines. They must be *governed* more than they are managed, and often the governing arrangements will be more informal than they are formal.

Among the important lessons he draws from Agranoff's research are that the highest-performing networks will mobilize and leverage information and knowledge to the mutual benefit of the partners; they may adopt common approaches to shared problems or common clients, and collaboratively execute the adopted approaches. In so doing, the partners assist one another with problem identification, exchanging information as they do. They will work together to identify and assess existing technological solutions, and work to develop and adapt new, emergent ones. In the process, they improve their collective knowledge base, its supporting informational infrastructure, and experiment with management approaches and new techniques for knowledge management. The overall thrust of the research in the new network management literature is that networks, when employed skillfully, can be a valuable asset; they can be formed collaboratively or spontaneously—with or without the conscious design of the network partners—and that their advantage rests in the ability to mobilize a diverse array of intelligence, information, and expertise in the solution of common problems. This area of study and practice is as yet at a nascent stage of development. Suffice it for now that most public administrators of the future will work at least in part through networked organizations.

STUDY QUESTIONS

1. Consider the university or college you attend from an organizational design perspective. What values does its organizational form emphasize? What objectives appear to be promoted by these values and the design? Are there any values or objectives that you think are appropriate to the institution but suffer as a result of its organizational design? Does the organizational design cause you any problems personally?
2. Can you identify some public administrative organizations that should not be considered "bureaucratic" from a Weberian perspective?
3. Choose any public administrative function with which you are familiar. How could it be organized to *maximize* efficiency, representativeness, and equity?
4. Draw up a list of the potential advantages and disadvantages of organizing public schools to be market-based. On balance, do you support or oppose such organization? Why? What does your conclusion suggest about making other types of public organizations market-based?

NOTES

1. Amitai Etzioni, *Modern Organizations* (Englewood Cliffs, NJ: Prentice-Hall, 1964), 1.
2. Frances R. Westley, "Middle Managers and Strategy: Microdynamics of Inclusion," *Strategic Management Journal* 11 (1990): 339.
3. Karl E. Weick, "The Collapse of Sensemaking in Organizations: The Mann Gulch Disaster," *Administrative Science Quarterly* 38 (1993): 628–652.

4. Ibid., 638.

5. Etzioni, *Modern Organizations,* 2.

6. A classic volume on organization theory is James G. March, Ed., *Handbook of Organizations* (Chicago: Rand McNally, 1965). See Gareth Morgan, *Images of Organization,* rev. ed. (Thousand Oaks, CA: Sage, 2006) for an alternative grouping of organization theories.

7. Barry Bozeman, *All Organizations Are Public* (San Francisco: Jossey-Bass, 1987).

8. Harold Gortner, Julianne Mahler, and Jeanne Nicholson, *Organization Theory: A Public Perspective* (Chicago: Dorsey, 1987).

9. Jay M. Shafritz and Philip Whitbeck, Eds., *Classics of Organization Theory* (Oak Park, IL: Moore, 1978), 322.

10. Dwight Waldo, "Organization Theory: An Elephantine Problem," *Public Administration Review* 21, no. 4 (1961): 210–225, at 220.

11. Max Weber, *From Max Weber: Essays in Sociology* (New York: Oxford University Press, 1958), Trans. and Ed. H. H. Gerth and C. W. Mills, especially chap. 8; Max Weber, *The Theory of Social and Economic Organization* (New York: Free Press, 1947), Trans. and Ed. A. M. Henderson and Talcott Parsons, especially chap. 3.

12. Warren Bennis, "Beyond Bureaucracy," *Transaction* 2 (July/August 1965): 32.

13. Al Gore, *From Red Tape to Results: Creating a Government That Works Better & Costs Less: The Report of the National Performance Review* (Washington, DC: U.S. Government Printing Office, 1993), 67.

14. Herbert Simon, *Models of Man* (New York: Wiley, 1957), 196.

15. See Frederick Winslow Taylor, "The Principles of Scientific Management," in Shafritz and Whitbeck, *Classics of Organization Theory,* 9–23. For a fuller discussion see Frederick W. Taylor, *Principles of Scientific Management* (New York: Norton, 1911).

16. For a good review, see George C. Homans, "The Western Electric Researches," in Amitai Etzioni, Ed., *Readings on Modern Organizations* (Englewood Cliffs, NJ: Prentice-Hall, 1969), 99–114.

17. Chester I. Barnard, *The Functions of the Executive* (Cambridge, MA: Harvard University Press, 1938).

18. For a classic discussion of different approaches to the study of organizational culture, see Linda Smircich, "Concepts of Culture and Organizational Analysis," *Administrative Science Quarterly* 28 (1983): 339–358.

19. Warren Bennis, *Why Leaders Can't Lead* (San Francisco: Jossey-Bass, 1989), 18.

20. Stephen P. Robbins, *Essentials of Organizational Behavior,* 8th ed. (Upper Saddle River, NJ: Pearson Prentice Hall, 2005), 157–171.

21. For a discussion of the Ohio State Studies, see C. A. Schriesheim, C. C. Cogliser, and L. L. Neider, "Is It Trustworthy? A Multiple-Levels-of-Analysis Reexamination of an Ohio State Leadership Study with Implications for Future Research," *Leadership Quarterly* (Summer 1995): 111–145. For the University of Michigan Studies, see R. Kahn and D. Katz, "Leadership Practices in Relation to Productivity and Morale," in D. Cartwright and A. Zander, Eds., *Group Dynamics: Research and Theory,* 2d ed. (Elmsford, NY: Row Peterson, 1960). For a discussion of the Managerial Grid, see R. R. Blake and J. S. Mouton, *The Managerial Grid* (Houston, TX: Gulf, 1964).

22. See F. E. Fiedler, *A Theory of Leadership Effectiveness* (New York: McGraw-Hill, 1967).

23. For a discussion of this theory, see G. B. Graen and M. Uhl-Bien, "Relationship-Based Approach to Leadership: Development of Leader-Member Exchange (LMX) Theory of Leadership over 25 Years: Applying a Multi-Domain Perspective," *Leadership Quarterly* (Summer 1995): 219–247.

24. R. J. House, "A Path-Goal Theory of Leadership Effectiveness," *Administrative Science Quarterly* (September 1971): 321–338.

25. V. H. Vroom and P. W. Yetton, *Leadership and Decision Making* (Pittsburgh, PA: University of Pittsburgh Press, 1973).

26. For example, Vroom and Jago, working with a revised version of the leader-participation model, needed to develop a computer program to guide managers through all of the choices in the decision tree in the model. V. H. Vroom and A. G. Jago, *The New Leadership: Managing Participation in Organizations* (Upper Saddle River, NJ: Prentice Hall, 1988).

27. Eugene Lewis, *Public Entrepreneurship: Toward a Theory of Bureaucratic Political Power* (Bloomington: Indiana University Press, 1984), 109.

28. Ibid.

29. Ibid., 240.

30. James Thompson, *Organizations in Action* (McGraw-Hill, 1967).

31. Norma Riccucci, *Unsung Heroes* (Washington, DC: Georgetown University Press, 1995), 226–231.

32. Terry L. Cooper and N. Dale Wright, Eds., *Exemplary Public Administrators: Character and Leadership in Government* (San Francisco: Jossey-Bass, 1992).

33. Robert Tannenbaum and Warren H. Schmidt, "How to Choose a Leadership Pattern," *Harvard Business Review* 36 (March/April 1958): 95–101; Tannenbaum and Schmidt, "Retrospective Commentary," *Harvard Business Review* 51 (May/June 1973): 1–10.

34. One through six are from David Connelly, Jing Zhang, and Sue Faerman, "The Paradoxical Nature of Collaboration," pp. 17–35 in Lisa Blomgren Bingham and Rosemary O'Leary, Eds., *Big Ideas in Collaborative Public Management* (Armonk, NY: M.E. Sharpe, 2008), pp. 24, 29, 31–32; seven is from Chris Ansell and Alison Gash, "Collaborative Governance in Theory and Practice," *Journal of Public Administration Research and Theory* 18 (No. 4, 2008): 543–571 at p. 555.

35. For a foundational reading on this concept, see James L. Perry and Lois R. Wise, "The Motivational Bases of Public Service," *Public Administration Review* 50 (May/June 1990): 367–373.

36. Abraham Maslow, "A Theory of Human Motivation," *Psychological Review* 50 (July 1943): 370–396.

37. See Cary Hershey, *Protest in the Public Service* (Lexington, MA: Lexington Books, 1973), for further theoretical development and examples.

38. Frederick Herzberg, B. Mausner, and B. Snyderman, *The Motivation to Work* (New York: Wiley, 1959); Frederick Herzberg, *Work and the Nature of Man* (Cleveland, OH: World Publishing, 1966).

39. See David McClelland, *The Achieving Society* (Princeton, NJ: Van Nostrand, 1961); David McClelland, "That Urge to Achieve," in Walter E. Natemeyer, Ed., *Classics of Organizational Behavior* (Oak Park, IL: Moore, 1978), 88–94.

40. John P. Campbell et al., *Managerial Behavior, Performance, and Effectiveness* (New York: McGraw-Hill, 1970); V. H. Vroom, *Work and Motivation* (New York: Wiley, 1964).

41. David Easton, *A Framework for Political Analysis* (Englewood Cliffs, NJ: Prentice-Hall, 1965); Thompson, *Organizations in Action*; Daniel Katz and Robert L. Kahn, *The Social Psychology of Organizations,* 2d ed. (New York: Wiley, 1978).

42. Robert Hampton, "The Basic Question," *Civil Service Journal* 13 (January–March 1973): 2–5.

43. Charles Perrow, *Complex Organizations,* 3d ed. (New York: Random House, 1986).

44. William Scott, "Organicism: The Moral Anesthetic of Management," *Academy of Management Review* 4 (No. 1, 1979): 21–28.

45. Ibid., 23.

46. Katz and Kahn, *The Social Psychology of Organizations,* 52.

47. Perrow, *Complex Organizations,* 192–208.

48. Ibid., 210.

49. Herbert Kaufman, *Time, Chance, and Organizations* (Chatham, NJ: Chatham House, 1985), 67.

50. Ibid., 134.

51. James D. Thompson, *Organizations in Action.*

52. See Philip O. Selznick, *TVA and the Grassroots* (New York: Harper and Row: 1949); see also James Q. Wilson, *Bureaucracy* (New York: Basic Books, 1989).

53. P. J. DiMaggio and W. W. Powell, "The Iron Cage Revisited: Institutional Isomorphism and Collective Rationality in Organizational Fields," *American Sociological Review* 48 (1983): 147–160; P. J. DiMaggio and W. W. Powell, "Introduction," in W. W. Powell and P. J. DiMaggio, Eds., *The New Institutionalism in Organizational Analysis* (Chicago: University of Chicago Press, 1991), 1–33; J. W. Meyer and B. Rowan, "Institutionalized Organizations: Formal Structure as Myth and Ceremony," *American Journal of Sociology* 83, no. 2 (1997): 340–363.

54. DiMaggio and Powell, "The Iron Cage Revisited," 148.

55. Ibid., 150.

56. Mary Douglas, *How Institutions Think* (Syracuse, NY: Syracuse University Press, 1986).

57. Ibid., x.

58. Ibid., 45.

59. Steven Ott, *The Organizational Culture Perspective* (Chicago: Dorsey, 1989), 2–3.

60. For an excellent summary of the issues, see Joan Acker, "Gendering Organizational Theory," in *Gendering Organizational Analysis* (New York: Sage, 1992), 248–260.

61. Jean Lipman-Blumen, "Female Leadership in Formal Organizations: Must Female Leaders Go Formal?" in M. Horner et al., Eds., *The Challenge of Change* (New York: Plenum, 1983).

62. Harold Seidman, *Politics, Position, and Power* (New York: Oxford University Press, 1970), 9.

63. Luther Gulick and Lyndall Urwick, Eds., *Papers on the Science of Administration* (New York: Institute of Public Administration, 1937).

64. Ibid., 3–13.

65. Ibid.

66. Ibid.

67. Ibid.

68. Herbert Simon, *Administrative Behavior,* 2d ed. (New York: Free Press, 1957), 20–36 (originally published in 1947).

69. Dwight Waldo, *The Administrative State* (New York: Ronald Press, 1948); see also Waldo, "Development of the Theory of Democratic Administration," *American Political Science Review* 46 (March 1952): 81–103.

70. Paul H. Appleby, *Policy and Administration* (University, Alabama: University of Alabama Press, 1949).

71. See Stephen R. Rosenthal, *Managing Government Operations* (Glenview, IL: Scott, Foresman, 1982).

72. Chester A. Newland, "Policy/Program Objectives and Federal Management: The Search for Government Effectiveness," *Public Administration Review* 36 (January/February 1976): 20–27, at 26.

73. Robert Rodgers and John Hunter, "A Foundation of Good Management in Government: Management by Objectives," *Public Administration Review* 52 (January/February 1992): 27–39. The classic work on MBO is George S. Odiorne, *Management by Objectives: A System of Managerial Leadership* (New York: Pitman, 1965).

74. See W. Edwards Deming, *Out of the Crisis* (Cambridge, MA: MIT Center for Advanced Engineering Study, 1986).

75. P. Crosby, *Quality Is Free* (New York: McGraw-Hill, 1979); J. Juran, *Managerial Breakthrough* (New York: McGraw-Hill, 1964).

76. James Swiss, "Adapting Total Quality Management (TQM) to Government," *Public Administration Review* 52 (January/February 1992): 356–362.

77. Ibid., 359.

78. The seminal article is Michael Hammer, "Reengineering Work: Don't Automate, Obliterate," *Harvard Business Review* 68 (July/August 1990): 104–112. It was followed by the more elaborate Michael Hammer and James Champy, *Reengineering the Corporation: A Manifesto for Business Revolution* (New York: Harper Business, 1993).

79. Editorial: "The New Flight Path Plan for the FAA," *Washington Post,* 31 March 1996, C6.

80. Douglas McGregor, *The Human Side of Enterprise* (New York: McGraw-Hill, 1960); see also Douglas McGregor, *The Professional Manager* (New York: McGraw-Hill, 1967).

81. Douglas McGregor, "The Human Side of Enterprise," in H. J. Leavitt and L. R. Pondy, Eds., *Readings in Managerial Psychology* (Chicago: University of Chicago Press, 1973), 748.

82. For a detailed study of Kurt Lewin's contributions, OD theory, and the National Training Laboratories, see Art Kleiner, *The Age of Heretics: Heroes, Outlaws, and the Forerunners of Corporate Change* (New York: Currency Doubleday, 1996).

83. See Wendell French, "Organization Development: Objectives, Assumptions and Strategies," in Natemeyer, *Classics of Organizational Behavior,* 348–362.

84. H. Roy Kaplan and Curt Tausky, "Humanism in Organizations: A Critical Perspective," *Public Administration Review* 37 (March/April 1977): 171–180.

85. Paul Appleby, *Big Democracy* (New York: Knopf, 1945); the quoted passage can be found in Jay Shafritz and Albert Hyde, Eds., *Classics of Public Administration* (Oak Park, IL: Moore, 1978), 105.

86. Norton Long, "Power and Administration," *Public Administration Review* 9 (Autumn 1949): 257–264; quoted from reprinted essay in Francis E. Rourke, Ed., *Bureaucratic Power in National Politics* (Boston: Little, Brown, 1965), 14–16.

87. Ibid., 17–18.
88. Seidman, *Politics, Position, and Power,* 13.
89. Samuel Krislov and David H. Rosenbloom, *Representative Bureaucracy and the American Political System* (New York: Praeger, 1981); Julie Dolan and David H. Rosenbloom, Eds., *Representative Bureaucracy* (Armonk, NY: M. E. Sharpe, 2003).
90. Seidman, *Politics, Position, and Power,* 13.
91. Herbert Kaufman, "Administrative Decentralization and Political Power," in Shafritz and Hyde, *Classics of Public Administration,* 356. Originally published in *Public Administration Review* 29 (January/February 1969): 3–15.
92. Shafritz and Hyde, *Classics of Public Administration,* 353–356.
93. Seidman, *Politics, Position, and Power,* 284–285; and Harold Seidman and Robert Gilmour, *Politics, Position, and Power,* 4th ed. (New York: Oxford University Press, 1986), 340.
94. Roscoe Pound, "Justice According to Law," *Columbia Law Review* 14 (1914): 1–26, at 1.
95. Kenneth Culp Davis, *Administrative Law and Government,* 2d ed. (St. Paul, MN: West, 1975), 17.
96. Ibid.
97. 459 F.2d 1231 (1972). For a discussion, see Kenneth F. Warren, *Administrative Law in the American Political System* (St. Paul, MN: West, 1982), 211.
98. As quoted in Warren, *Administrative Law,* 212.
99. Warren, *Administrative Law,* 289.
100. Eugene Bardach and Robert Kagan, *Going by the Book* (Philadelphia: Temple University Press, 1982), especially chaps. 5 and 6. See also Pietro S. Nivola, *The Urban Service Problem* (Lexington, MA: Lexington Books, 1979).
101. Nancy Manring, "ADR and Administrative Responsiveness," *Public Administration Review* 54 (March/April 1994): 197–203.
102. U.S. General Accounting Office, *Management Reform: Elements of Successful Improvement Initiatives* (Washington, DC: General Accounting Office, 1999), 1.
103. Philip E. Slater and Warren Bennis, "Democracy Is Inevitable," *Harvard Business Review* 42 (March/April 1964): 51–59; quoted from reprinted article in Shafritz and Whitbeck, *Classics of Organization Theory,* 306.
104. Slater and Bennis, "Democracy Is Inevitable," in Shafritz and Whitbeck, *Classics of Organization Theory,* 305.
105. Ibid., 304.
106. Perrow, *Complex Organizations,* 224.
107. Ibid., 224, 233.
108. Lewis C. Mainzer, *Political Bureaucracy* (Glenview, IL: Scott, Foresman, 1973), 132.
109. Ibid.
110. Ibid., 139.
111. Robert Denhardt and Janet Vinzant Denhardt, "The New Public Service: Serving Rather Than Steering," *Public Administration Review* 60, no. 6 (2000): 549–559, at 549.
112. Cheryl S. King, Kathy Feltey, and Bridget O'Neill Susel, "The Question of Participation: Public Participation in Public Administration," *Public Administration Review* 58, no. 4 (1998): 317–326.
113. Ibid., 323.

114. Gore, *From Red Tape to Results,* 6.
115. Robert Agranoff, *Managing Within Networks: Adding Value to Public Organizations* (Washington, DC: Georgetown University Press, 2007): 10.

ADDITIONAL READING

Agranoff, Robert. *Managing Within Networks.* Washington, DC: Georgetown University Press, 2007.

Agranoff, Robert, and Michael McGuire. *Collaborative Public Management: New Strategies for Local Governments.* Washington, DC: Georgetown University Press, 2003.

Ban, Carolyn. *How Do Public Managers Manage?* San Francisco: Jossey-Bass, 1995.

Cohen, Steven, William Eimicke, and Tanya Heikkila. *The Effective Public Manager,* 4th edition. San Francisco: Jossey-Bass, 2008.

Cooper, Terry L., and N. Dale Wright, Eds. *Exemplary Public Administrators: Character and Leadership in Government.* San Francisco: Jossey-Bass, 1992.

Lynn, Laurence, and Carolyn J. Hill. *Public Management: A Three-Dimensional Approach.* Washington, DC: CQ Press, 2008.

Ott, Steven. *The Organizational Culture Perspective.* Chicago: Dorsey, 1989.

Rainey, Hal. *Understanding and Managing Public Organizations,* 4th ed. San Francisco: Jossey-Bass, 2009.

ORGANIZATION THEORY AND BEHAVIOR WEB SITES

The National Center for Public Productivity has an array of interesting materials available at http://www.ncpp.us.

The Aspen Institute specializes in promoting and developing executive-level leadership skills. Its Web site is http://www.aspeninstitute.org.

The United Nations studies and consults on matters of administrative reform around the world. The relevant U.N. Web site is http://www.undp.org/governance/sl-par.htm.

The World Bank promotes administrative capacity building and civil service reform among its member countries. A variety of useful and interesting documents are available at http://web.worldbank.org/WBSITE/EXTERNAL/TOPICS/EXTPUBLICSECTORANDGOVERNANCE/0,,contentMDK:20206128~pagePK:210058~piPK:210062~theSitePK:286305,00.html.

CHAPTER 5

Public Personnel Administration and Collective Bargaining

Key Learning Objectives

1. Understand how and why the federal civil service system developed as it did.

2. Know the federal government's merit principles.

3. Be familiar with the core aspects of public personnel management, including position classification, selection, performance appraisal, pay, and collective bargaining.

4. Understand the overlaps and tensions among the managerial, political, and legal approaches to public personnel administration.

This chapter discusses the history of public personnel administration in the United States, emphasizing how the three major historical phases of public personnel administration maximized certain values but failed to deal adequately with others and revealing how those failures subsequently led to reforms. The historical phases have been (1) the era of "gentlemen" (1789–1828), (2) the "spoils system" (1829–1882), and (3) the "merit system" (as it has evolved since 1883). The federal civil service reform of 1978 is discussed, as are the new public management (NPM) reforms of the 1990s and recent trends. The chapter then explores the managerial, political, and legal perspectives on public personnel administration. The process and politics of public sector collective bargaining are also examined.

About 22 million people are employed by the 89,000 governments in the United States. If you were in charge of managing them, according to what criteria and under what organizational arrangements would you select, assign, train, discipline, promote, and pay these public employees? How would you motivate them to provide the highest levels of performance? How would you ensure their loyalty to the nation and their willingness to cooperate with their jurisdictions' political leadership? Would you engage in collective bargaining with them? These are among the central questions of contemporary public personnel management. They raise perplexing issues that seem to defy permanent resolution. The nation's ability to achieve its goals through public administrative action depends heavily on the performance, honesty, and motivation of public employees. Although we think in terms of institutions and principles, in the final analysis, organizations and governments are not charts and words on pieces of paper or screens; they are made up of people, and it is necessary somehow to organize the conditions of their employment. Today no one seriously disputes the central importance of public personnel administration. Some prefer to call it human resources management (HRM)—a term that emphasizes the importance of people, who are increasingly referred to as human capital. As in other areas of public administration, personnel policy can be analyzed from the different perspectives provided by the managerial, political, and legal approaches.

◆▶ HISTORICAL BACKGROUND

Sometimes public personnel administration seems to be in such a mess that we are tempted to ask how it ever arrived at such a state. In 1993, the National Performance Review (NPR) complained, "[T]alk to a federal manager for 10 minutes: You likely will hear at least one personnel horror story. The system is so complex and rule-bound that most managers cannot even advise an applicant how to get a federal job. . . . The average manager needs a year to fire an incompetent employee, even with solid proof."[1] But such charges were hardly novel; public personnel administration's historical development in the United States has been largely in response to successive calls for reform. In this area of public administration, therefore, it is particularly necessary to understand the past to comprehend the present and anticipate the future.[2]

Public Personnel Administration According to "Gentlemen"

It is possible to divide the evolution of public personnel practice in the United States into three broad periods. Each was characterized by a different style of politics, of which public personnel was an integral part. First was the era of "gentlemen," which began with President Washington's first administration in 1789 and ended with the inauguration of President Jackson in 1829. Washington wanted to get the fledgling administrative system off to a sound start, realizing the importance of his administration in setting precedents. For Washington, the primary criterion in making appointments was "fitness of character." Fit characters were those with high standing in the community and personal integrity. They tended to be members of the upper class. Some lacked any apparent technical qualifications for the jobs to which they were appointed, but they did bring a measure of greater prestige to the new government. They were also capable of learning what they needed to know on the job.

Washington hoped his fit characters would perform honestly and efficiently, but he also sought effectiveness. This brought forth another and somewhat competing criterion for selection. By 1795, when the division between the Hamiltonian and Jeffersonian visions of how active the federal government should be became apparent, Washington realized that politics could be important in the selection and assignment of public personnel. He considered appointing a public administrator who opposed his policies to be a sort of "political suicide."[3] In other words, he sought political loyalty as well as social and administrative fitness.

Washington's precedents were carried forward by his successors, though with a differing emphasis. President John Adams began to stress politics to a greater extent, although he still made appointments from the upper class. In addition, the federal government's first political dismissals have been attributed to him. It was Jefferson, however, who first developed a reasonably clear theory about the role politics should play in public personnel administration.

Upon entering office, Jefferson complained that Adams had stocked the federal government's administrative apparatus with members of the opposition Federalist Party. He thought that this situation could be remedied primarily in two ways. First, he sought to forbid federal administrators from taking an active part in electioneering. This was the federal government's earliest attempt to develop **political neutrality** in the administrative branch. By taking federal employees out of politics, Jefferson would be neutralizing the Federalist influence that could be waged against his Republican Party. But his vision of political neutrality may have gone well beyond that. He argued that electioneering was inconsistent with the spirit of the Constitution and administrative officials' responsibility to it. Public administrators were seen as exercising a public trust in the public interest rather than playing a partisan political role.

Like Washington, however, Jefferson recognized that public administrators did have a political role in terms of public policy. Consequently, he sought to appoint Republicans until the balance between them and Federalists in the administrative branch roughly matched the balance between the two parties among the electorate at large. In other words, he sought to make the federal service politically *representative* of the partisanship of the nation as a whole. In practice, however, Jefferson overwhelmingly appointed Republicans throughout his tenure.

Over time, the tenure of federal administrators became secure, and several remained in their jobs well into old age. There was even a tendency for civil service positions to be informally "bequeathed" to the incumbents' male heirs when death made the ultimate removal. The federal service during this period was well managed, honest, efficient, and effective. Historical consensus holds that it reflected the highest ethical standards in the nation's history.

Public Personnel Administration According to "Spoils"

All this was changed by the inauguration of President Jackson in 1829. There has been historical debate about whether it was Jefferson or Jackson who made the first significant patronage dismissals and patronage appointments.[4] However, Jackson institutionalized the spoils system by developing a politically convincing rationale for it. Upon becoming president, Jackson declared that public sentiment was strongly in favor of "reform" of federal personnel administration. Why? What was wrong with public personnel during the era of "gentlemen"? Jackson's views were as follows:

1. The long tenure of federal administrators in office made them unresponsive to the public and the public interest. In Jackson's well-known words, "The duties of all public officers are, or at least admit of being made, so plain and simple that men of intelligence may readily qualify themselves for their performance; and I cannot but believe that more is lost by the long continuance of men in office than is generally to be gained by their experience."[5]

2. The upper-class bias of the federal service was intolerable in a democratic (republican) nation such as the United States. Jackson's constituency was largely from the western and frontier areas and of middle- or lower-class status. His supporters were mostly without formal education, and a high proportion were illiterate. It is reputed that Jackson was unable to read fluently. Jackson thought such people ought to have an opportunity to participate in government by becoming public administrators. As he put it, "in a free government the demand for moral qualities should be made superior to that of talents."[6] By making appointments from among his constituents, Jackson would be able to reward his loyal supporters and strengthen himself politically. However, he may also have believed that "rotation" in office constituted "a leading principle of the republican creed" and was good for the political system.[7]

3. The long tenure of federal administrators had contributed to the aging of the public service. Jackson believed that this hurt the government's

performance. It also encouraged the notion that a government job was a kind of property to which the incumbent civil servant had a right. Jackson and his political following found this position wholly antithetical to democratic principles.

Jackson's reforms were straightforward. He sought to establish a maximum term of four years in office for federal administrators. Previously, the Tenure of Office Act of 1820 set a four-year term for some federal employees, but it allowed their appointments to be renewed and few removals were made. Jackson's proposed term would coincide with presidential administrations, thereby allowing the newly elected president to distribute "the spoils of victory"[8] among his supporters without facing the unpleasant necessity of dismissing incumbents, whose appointments would expire as a matter of law and/or custom. Unlike Jefferson, no pretense of creating partisan balance would be made. The victorious political party would feast on federal administrative jobs.

Jackson's program was severely opposed by the opposition party, the Whigs, until 1840. In that year, sometimes called the year of the great "Whig sellout," the Whigs embraced the spoils system with a vengeance.[9] From then until the administration of President Andrew Johnson (1865–1869), the spoils system thrived. Among its chief effects were the following:

1. *A serious decline in administrative ethics, efficiency, and performance.* The spoils period was racked with scandals, petty and large. A plethora of superfluous administrative jobs was created to pay off the party faithful. Incumbents, recognizing their limited tenure, often sought to make the most of their positions through embezzlement, bribery, and extortion.
2. *A thorough intermixing of public administration and partisan politics.* Sometimes administrative appointees had nothing to do except engage in partisan acts and electioneering. Some never showed up at their federal offices, reporting to party headquarters instead. One of the more notorious practices was for the parties to levy "political assessments" of roughly 1 to 6 percent on the salaries of federal administrators. This practice, called an indirect robbery of the federal treasury, enabled the finances of the government and the political party in power to merge to an extent.
3. *A high degree of political competition.* This is something of a mystery because one would assume that the advantages accruing to the party in power would be sufficient to ensure its victory in future elections. Logically, spoils should have encouraged the development of a one-party state. In practice, however, the partisanship of the president changed in 1841, 1845, 1849, and 1853. In 1857 there was a marked change in the dominant faction within the Democratic Party, and in 1860 the modern Republican Party achieved its first presidential victory with the election of Abraham Lincoln. The 20 years from 1841 to 1861 were a period

of great popular participation (at least among the eligible electorate) in politics and vigorous partisan competition. One explanation is that the party in power could distribute only so many jobs and inevitably made enemies by disappointing some of its supporters; in contrast, the party out of power could generate a great deal of support by promising a massive amount of patronage should it be elected (only to cause disappointment later).

4. *A reduction in the social class status of federal administrators.*
    The federal service became more representative of the social class composition of the population as a whole. This was an important change, ending the possibility of the development of an elite civil service.

Public Personnel Administration According to "Merit"

The development of the administrative state spelled the doom of spoils, at least in theory and practice, if not in each jurisdiction. Patronage has fallen so out of favor under contemporary public personnel and constitutional theory that in 1976, 1980, and again in 1990 the Supreme Court handed down decisions that make such firings unconstitutional in the vast majority of circumstances.[10] (See Box 2.8.)

Commitment to a merit system began to develop at the federal level in the 1860s and 1870s. By 1883, it had been written into law—a law, the Pendleton Act (Civil Service Act), that eventually was superseded by the Civil Service Reform Act of 1978. From the 1880s to the turn of the century, several states and cities followed suit in adopting "merit" as the basis of public personnel administration.

We have been using the term "merit" in quotation marks because in some respects it is a misnomer. The cornerstone of the merit system has been the open, competitive examination as a tool for selecting public servants. There have been important political and administrative reasons for the heavy reliance placed on such examinations. However, many merit examinations were inadequately validated, which means that it could not be demonstrated that they predicted much, if anything, about a candidate's on-the-job performance. At the same time, such examinations frequently exhibited a bias against or disparate impact on applicants belonging to minority groups, including those of African American and Latino backgrounds. In some respects the merit system was a major barrier to equal employment opportunity. We will have much more to say about this issue shortly. First, though, it is desirable to review briefly the chief causes of and arguments for the adoption of the merit system as part of the civil service reform of the 1880s.

Along with other upper middle-class activists, the civil service reformers of the 1870s and 1880s were intent on replacing the spoils politicians, who tended to be responsive to lower-class and ethnic interests—the urban poor and immigrants were the mainstay of the most powerful political machines.

In the revealing words of Dorman B. Eaton, a leading reformer, "We have seen a class of politicians become powerful in high places, who have not taken (and who by nature are not qualified to take) any large part in the social and educational life of the people. Politics have tended more and more to become a trade, or separate occupation. High character and capacity have become disassociated from public life in the popular mind."[11] Carl Schurz, also a reform leader, was even more blunt in claiming that the point of civil service reform was to "rescue our political parties, and in great measure the management of our political affairs, from the control of men whose whole statesmanship consists in the low arts of office mongering, and many of whom would never have risen to power had not the spoils system furnished them with the means and opportunity for organizing gangs of political followers as mercenary as themselves."[12]

Like Jackson's introduction of the spoils system, then, merit-oriented civil service reform was premised largely on the desire to attain broad political change. But that does not mean that the reform movement was devoid of administrative objectives. By the 1880s, the spoils system had become a relatively soft target for change.

The spoils system was rapidly becoming viewed as anachronistic—a harmful legacy of simpler preindustrial times. In his inimitable style, Schurz squarely addressed this matter: "There are certain propositions so self-evident and so easily understood that it would appear like discourtesy to argue them before persons of intelligence. Such a one it is, that as the functions of government grow in extent, importance and complexity, the necessity grows of their being administered not only with honesty, but also with trained ability and knowledge."[13] As the government became more heavily engaged in regulatory policy and administration, it seemed inevitable that the spoils system would have to be replaced.

The spoils system was also vulnerable because its corrupt practices interfered with industrialization. In its heyday, spoils turned the nation's custom houses into hotbeds of graft. Vast overstaffing, bribery, and extortion were common. By the late 1870s, the rising industrialists and proponents of industrialization had become opposed to patronage politics because it was harming international commerce.

There is a persistent thread running through this opposition to the spoils system. Both the reformers and the industrialists stood to gain by diminishing the impact of the lower-class and immigrant population in politics. The reformers thought the participation of those groups in machine politics tended to reduce the influence of middle-class Anglo-Americans—a category to which many of the reformers belonged.

Woodrow Wilson, often considered the founder of self-conscious American public administration, had this to say about the rising tide of immigrants:

> [The] character of the nation . . . is being most deeply affected and modified by the enormous immigration which year after year pours into the country from Europe: our own temperate blood, schooled to self-possession and to

the measured conduct of self-government, is receiving a constant infusion and yearly experiencing a partial corruption of foreign blood: our own equable [tranquil] habits have been crossed with the feverish habits of the restless old world. We are unquestionably facing an ever-increasing difficulty of self-command with ever-deteriorating materials, possibly with degenerating fibre.[14]

A new class of industrialists was especially fearful of the rise of socialist labor unions and political parties, which in all likelihood would find both leadership and support among immigrant workers. In addition, politically perceptive industrialists might have understood that once the political parties could no longer raise money through political assessments or count on patronage as a means of winning votes and inducing political participation, they would inevitably turn to the wealthy sector of society to finance their operations and campaigns. Political historians note that popular participation in politics crested in the 1890s and at the same time the U.S. Senate began to emerge as a "millionaires' club."[15] Politically, there is no doubt that the chief battle lines concerning reform were drawn between industrialists and upper middle-class Anglo-Americans on the one hand and the lower-class, immigrant populations and spoils politicians on the other.

Politics aside, however, the spoils system did have serious administrative drawbacks. In the reformers' view, these drawbacks could be remedied by adopting the following public personnel program:

1. *Selection of public employees based on open competitive examinations.* Open examinations can be taken by anyone with the requisite background qualifications, such as age, literacy, and citizenship. They prevent politicians from selecting a group of the party faithful and administering the examination to them only. Competitive examinations require that appointments be made in the order of examination scores; that is, those who score highest are appointed first. This also prevents politicians from making placements based on politics.

    Open, competitive examinations are a highly effective means of preventing patronage appointments, but they also have an administrative logic. Assuming that the examination scores are an adequate predictor of the level of on-the-job performance, which is not always the case, such examinations promise to select the most competent and efficient applicants for the public service. As the spoils system receded into the political past, this was viewed by public personnel administrators as the chief virtue of the merit system. The examinations are relatively inexpensive to administer and use as selection devices.

2. *Depoliticization of the public service.* The reformers believed that the fundamental principle informing the public service should be politically neutral competence. Public employees should function on the basis of their trained ability to accomplish the governmental tasks at hand. Their authority and legitimacy flow from their professional

and technical competence rather than their partisan activities. This line of reasoning required the reformers to insist that the vast majority of administrative positions were not political in either a partisan or a policy making sense. The public service should be organized like a business, according to this view. The Civil Service Act of 1883 contained some provisions aimed at abolishing political assessments and political coercion.

3. *Tenure in office.* The spoils system was based on the premise that the rotation of public servants in and out of office was a desirable practice in a democratic nation. The reformers preferred tenure to be based on the competence of public employees and not be subject to political or partisan considerations. Originally, the reformers thought this could be accomplished by merit selection. Hiring officials would lose the opportunity to engage in political favoritism, and this, in the reformers' view, would eliminate the incentive for making dismissals based on political grounds. However, beginning in the 1890s it was viewed as desirable to provide public employees with a measure of legally protected tenure. After some earlier efforts, the Lloyd–La Follette Act of 1912 assured that dismissals from the federal service would only be for such cause as would promote the efficiency of the service. Some procedural protections were included in the act, but by today's standards, they were limited.

4. *A civil service commission.* The reformers thought that public personnel administration should be policed by a central personnel agency. A strong, independent agency could protect the public service against incursions by patronage-oriented politicians. The Civil Service Act of 1883 provided for a three-person, bipartisan Civil Service Commission (CSC) appointed by the president with the advice and consent of the Senate. The act gave the commission rule-making and investigative authority.

The reformers achieved lasting success in 1883 with the passage of the Pendleton Act (Civil Service Act), largely written by Eaton. Two factors determined the timing of its enactment. First, President James Garfield suffered a lingering death after being shot by a disappointed office seeker in 1881, and public opinion was quick to blame the spoils system rather than the demented assassin. Second, the Republican Party suffered substantial setbacks in the congressional elections of 1882 and was seeking to protect itself against the Democrats' spoils, should that party go on to win the presidency in 1884.[16] There is little doubt that reform-oriented public personnel administration would have been adopted sooner or later in any event. Several cities, including New York, Albany, Buffalo, Syracuse, Chicago, Evanston, and Seattle, introduced merit systems during the 1880s and 1890s. New York was the first state to adopt such a program (1883), but it was another two decades before the next state, Massachusetts, followed. Today, some merit provisions exist in the overwhelming number of jurisdictions. (A summary of federal merit principles is presented in Box 5.1.)

5.1   FEDERAL MERIT SYSTEM PRINCIPLES

Federal personnel management should be implemented consistent with the following merit system principles:

1. Recruitment should be from qualified individuals from appropriate sources in an endeavor to achieve a work force from all segments of society, and selection and advancement should be determined solely on the basis of relative ability, knowledge, and skills, after fair and open competition which assures that all receive equal opportunity.

2. All employees and applicants for employment should receive fair and equitable treatment in all aspects of personnel management without regard to political affiliation, race, color, religion, national origin, sex, marital status, age, or handicapping condition, and with proper regard for their privacy and constitutional rights.

3. Equal pay should be provided for work of equal value, with appropriate consideration of both national and local rates paid by employers in the private sector, and appropriate incentives and recognition should be provided for excellence in performance.

4. All employees should maintain high standards of integrity, conduct, and concern for the public interest.

5. The federal work force should be used efficiently and effectively.

6. Employees should be retained on the basis of the adequacy of their performance, inadequate performance should be corrected, and employees should be separated who cannot or will not improve their performance to meet required standards.

7. Employees should be provided effective education and training in cases in which such education and training would result in better organizational and individual performance.

8. Employees should be:

   A. protected against arbitrary action, personal favoritism, or coercion for partisan political purposes, and

   B. prohibited from using their official authority or influence for the purpose of interfering with or affecting the result of an election or a nomination for election.

9. Employees should be protected against reprisal for the lawful disclosure of information which the employees reasonably believe evidences:

   A. a violation of any law, rule, or regulation, or

   B. mismanagement, a gross waste of funds, an abuse of authority, or a substantial and specific danger to public health or safety.

Source: 5 U.S. Code, Sec. 2301.

The reform of 1883 established an institutional and conceptual framework for federal personnel administration that lasted until 1978. During that period, several additional personnel concepts were developed and implemented. By the 1920s, federal personnel officers were less obsessed with combating patronage and more concerned with achieving greater efficiency in the public service. Prior to the 1930s, the CSC was primarily an examining agency. In 1931, it embarked on a program of centralizing personnel functions under its authority. Soon the commission had taken on responsibilities for position classification, efficiency ratings, and retirement administration. As it became a more centralized personnel agency, the commission retained its "policing" outlook, though now this was aimed at other agencies as well as at politicians.

By the late 1930s, the CSC had come to be viewed as an obstacle to effective personnel management because it was so concerned with enforcing restrictive rules and statutes. This was partly redressed by the Classification Act of 1949, which made the agencies directly responsible for position classification, evaluation, promotion, and many other personnel functions.

Decentralization of federal personnel administration made the CSC's concern with "policing" inappropriate. But it had difficulty changing its focus from enforcement and inspection to the development of broad policies for the improvement of federal personnel management. By the 1970s, many personnel specialists, political executives, and some members of Congress considered it an inappropriate administrative structure for contemporary personnel management. The commission format also lost favor at the state and local levels. Many of these governments moved to place the major personnel functions in a department or division directly responsible to the chief executive. This approach was followed by the federal government in the Civil Service Reform Act of 1978.

◆→ MANAGEMENT, POLITICS, AND LAW IN PUBLIC PERSONNEL ADMINISTRATION

Each of the three approaches to public administration discussed in the first chapter can be found in the historical development of public personnel administration. Managerial principles and premises were most evident in the period of administration by "gentlemen," during the reform program of the 1880s and 1890s, and during the 1930s and 1940s. Assignments were made on the basis of fitness and merit; tenure was based on good behavior and competent, efficient performance. The public service was viewed as largely nonpolitical and in the service of the nation as a whole. Efficiency, honesty, and morality were highly valued. Although some political removals were made, there was no widespread practice of spoils or rotation in office.

Politics was most clearly manifested in the spoils system. Here it was believed that the public service should be politically and socially representative of the dominant political party first and technically competent second. Representation and political responsiveness rather than efficiency and economy were the fundamental values behind public personnel practices at this time. Rotation in office was valued as a means of promoting popular participation in government.

Legal considerations were most clearly evident in the civil service reform movement, although as a means of promoting managerially oriented personnel administration. The Pendleton Act and subsequent reform-oriented practices place much public personnel management in a law-bound environment. Advocates of the new public management (NPM) often charge that public personnel administration has become so legalistic that it is too rigid to be effective and that political executives lack the flexibility to handle personnel in a productive way. This is precisely the state of affairs that the 19th century reformers sought.

As one reformer explained, "We consider that fixed rules, however imperfect, are better than arbitrary power."[17] Since the 1950s, the judiciary has placed constitutional restraints on the handling of public personnel as a means of protecting employees' rights. This approach favors fair procedure and equal treatment, which can turn public personnel management into an adversary, legalistic procedure.

Historically, the chief problem of public personnel administration in the United States has been an inability to establish a satisfactory, stable mix of the managerial, political, and legal approaches. A series of federal reforms beginning in 1978 illustrates this difficulty. These reforms contribute to a disaggregation of the federal personnel system; one set of policies no longer applies to all federal employees.

Civil Service Reform, 1978

The Civil Service Reform Act of 1978 was hailed by President Jimmy Carter as the centerpiece of his efforts to reorganize the federal government to make it more manageable, efficient, effective, and politically responsive.[18] His administration was candid in proclaiming that the act had managerial and political goals. The president said that "there is not enough merit in the merit system. There is inadequate motivation because we have too few rewards for excellence and too few penalties for unsatisfactory work."[19] Alan Campbell, chairman of the CSC, which was terminated by the 1978 reform, put forward the political perspective: "Every new administration feels the negative aspects of the bureaucracy's pressure for continuity. New policy makers arrive with mandates for change and find that though they can change structures and appearances, it is very difficult to make dramatic changes in direction."[20] But how could managerial and political goals be achieved simultaneously? And could this be accomplished without wholesale reduction of the legal rights of federal employees?

The reform act was accompanied by massive politicking in Congress. Employee unions, veterans' groups, civil rights and minority interest groups, congressional committees and subcommittees, and officials in the presidential administration brought a variety of perspectives to bear on the question of what should be done to improve federal personnel management. The final statute was necessarily a compromise.

The major conceptual achievement of the reform act was the separation of many of the managerial, political, and legal aspects of federal personnel administration from one another. The effort made by the CSC to combine these diverse perspectives contributed to its lack of direction and ultimate demise. Under the reform, to a considerable extent, separate functions were housed in separate agencies. The Merit Systems Protection Board (MSPB) was created to deal with many of the legalistic concerns of federal personnel management. The MSPB included an Office of the Special Counsel, which subsequently became an independent administrative entity. The Special Counsel's function is to assure that personnel laws and regulations are followed and that merit system principles and requirements are not violated. It investigates the activities of agencies, federal managers, and officials. The MSPB can levy sanctions against federal employees who violate personnel regulations. The agency also hears appeals of adverse actions, such as demotions and dismissals, against federal employees. It is considered the watchdog of the federal merit system and the protector of the legal rights of federal employees. The MSPB has specific authority to protect whistle-blowers, who expose waste, fraud, or abuse, against reprisals. The MSPB has done a number of in-depth studies of various subjects of importance to federal personnel management, such as surveys of sexual harassment in the federal service and analyses of why employees leave the government.

A second agency created by the reform, the Federal Labor Relations Authority (FLRA), also embodies the legalistic approach to public personnel. It oversees the process of collective bargaining in the federal service (though not in the postal service). The FLRA makes a variety of rulings concerning fair and unfair labor relations practices and the aspects of employment that can be collectively bargained. It also has authority to resolve questions concerning the representation of federal employees by labor unions and can play a role in the resolution of disputes between unions and the government. Collective bargaining in the public sector is addressed later in this chapter.

A more clearly political mission was vested in the Equal Employment Opportunity Commission (EEOC). The EEOC was created by the Civil Rights Act of 1964, but it did not have authority over federal employment practices at that time. The federal equal employment opportunity (EEO) function was vested in a number of agencies, including the CSC. The decision to give the EEOC this authority for federal EEO was highly political, made at the urging of civil rights and minority groups who believed that the EEO program could not be successfully implemented under a personnel agency that viewed its primary mission in managerial terms. Those groups saw a conflict because the merit system and merit examinations emerged as major barriers to the achievement of a high degree of minority employment in the upper levels of federal service. The 1978 reform act seeks a federal service socially representative of the nation's workforce as a whole. The act defines "underrepresentation" of EEO target groups and outlines procedures for overcoming it. Part of the EEOC's mission is to promote the representation of minorities and women in the federal workforce. Although much of the EEO process is legalistic, the ultimate objective of representation is political.

The reform act assigned the CSC's managerial functions to an Office of Personnel Management. This agency was designed to serve as the president's arm for positive, effective personnel management. It inherited from the CSC such managerial functions as responsibility for testing, training, operating benefits and retirement systems, and general oversight of the personnel operations of federal agencies. In addition to placing the managerially oriented personnel agency closer to the president than was the more independently organized bipartisan CSC, the reform act mandated the use of some new management

5.2   SES Executive Core Qualifications (ECQs)

ECQ 1: Leading Change
Creativity/Innovation
External Awareness
Flexibility
Resilience
Strategic Thinking
Vision

ECQ 2: Leading People
Conflict Management
Leveraging Diversity
Developing Others
Team Building

ECQ 3: Results Driven
Accountability
Customer Service

Decisiveness
Entrepreneurship
Problem Solving
Technical Credibility

ECQ 4: Business Acumen
Financial Management
Human Capital Management
Technology Management

ECQ 5: Building Coalitions
Partnering
Political Savvy
Influencing/Negotiating

Source: http://www.opm.gov/policy-data-
oversight/senior-executive-service/executive-
core-qualifications/ (accessed June 4, 2012).

tools, including a merit pay system and a performance appraisal system, discussed later in the chapter.

Another central feature of the reform act bears mention. The top career managerial positions in the federal service were largely converted into a Senior Executive Service (SES). The theory behind the SES is largely an effort to combine the political and managerial approaches to public administration. It rests on the belief that (1) there is a body of skill or professionalism called "public management" that can be transferred from organizational setting to organizational setting, (2) it is politically desirable for top federal managers to move among administrative units to develop a more comprehensive view of the public interest, and (3) political executives need greater flexibility in assigning and directing these top career officials to implement their policy mandates. Box 5.2 lists the core qualifications for membership in the SES.

Today, OPM's main operational responsibilities are the federal employees' health and retirement benefits programs. Overall, it now functions largely as a policy advisory body and advocate for the president's HRM initiatives.

There are four types of appointments in the SES, which currently includes about 7,000 personnel. **Noncareer appointments** can constitute up to 10 percent of the total number of positions allocated to the SES. These are political appointees who assist the political executives at the top levels of departments and agencies, implementing their policies and programs. No more than 25 percent of the SES positions in a single agency can be filled with noncareer appointees. **Limited-term appointments** can also be purely political. They can serve nonrenewable terms of up to three years. **Career appointees** constitute the largest group in the SES. These federal servants have often spent many years in the government and may have worked their way up the ranks to the top of the career service. **Limited emergency appointments,** who can serve for up to 18 months, are the fourth category, but to date one that has not been important. In addition to the four types of appointments, there are two types of positions: **career reserved** and **general.** Only career appointees can be assigned to the former; any type of appointee can be placed in the latter.

Finally, the Civil Service Reform Act provided for "personnel research programs and demonstration projects." It allows the OPM to suspend the application of many personnel regulations to experiment with new approaches and techniques. Projects can involve up to 5,000 employees (not including any who may be in a control group) and last up to five years. Successful projects can become permanent.

HRM Reform in the 1990s and 2000s

The NPR considered federal personnel administration a disaster area ripe for reinvention. In its view, personnel administration was overregulated, too centralized, and inadequately tailored to the agencies' specific needs and missions. It reported one statistic that spoke volumes: In 1993 the Department of Agriculture gauged the total weight of the personnel regulations affecting it, including case law, at 1,088 pounds![21] Embracing NPM principles, the NPR's vision for a new federal HRM included the following:

- Deregulation, freeing the agencies from centralized OPM and other controls
- Decentralization, making federal executives and managers responsible and accountable for personnel management
- "Ownership" by executives and managers, who would help design HRM systems, buy into their principles, and make them work
- Incorporation of HRM specialists into management teams, rather than functioning as outsiders policing the systems
- Adaptation of HRM systems to fit an agency's organizational culture
- Transformation of personnel offices from paperwork processors to expert advisers and consultants[22]

Several of the NPR's HRM achievements were noted in Chapter 2. It was especially proud of scrapping the notoriously complex, voluminous *Federal Personnel Manual* as the authoritative rulebook for federal personnel. Less dramatically, through the use of research and demonstration projects and special statutory authority from Congress, about 50 percent of the federal workforce was incrementally "liberated" from the government's traditional "one-size-fits-all" legal framework for personnel (Title 5 of the U.S. Code). The Federal Aviation Administration, the Patent and Trademark Office, the Internal Revenue Service, and several units within the Department of Defense were prominent examples. To a considerable extent, by the end of the 1990s the NPM had changed the language, organization, and underlying concepts of federal personnel. The Homeland Security Act of 2002 required federal agencies to designate "chief human capital officers" (CHCOs) for HRM supervision, coordination, and proactive planning. Along with other provisions, the CHCOs' (pronounced, "cheekos") role is to elevate the importance of HRM in agencies' strategic planning and general managerial decision making. Agencies also gained flexibility in hiring and buying out employees, compensating executives, and paying for employees' higher education.

We have discussed the historical development of public personnel administration in the United States and the conceptual problems presented by its organization in some detail so that the reader will not fall victim to a pervasive tendency to place "technique over purpose" in the area of public personnel.[23] We now turn to a more techniques-oriented review of the major public personnel functions. This discussion is organized according to our threefold categorization of public administration into managerial, political, and legalistic approaches.

♦♦   MANAGERIAL PUBLIC PERSONNEL ADMINISTRATION

Both orthodox and NPM public personnel administrations seek to maximize the values of efficiency, economy, and administrative effectiveness through the recruitment, selection, placement, pay, training, and general treatment of public employees at work. The underlying assumption behind managerial public personnel administration is that the public service should be apolitical and businesslike. Employees should be selected, placed, promoted, and paid on the basis of their competence to perform governmental work. There should be adequate protection of public employees from political encroachments.

Orthodox managerial doctrine envisions the public service as a career in which employees serve the public interest by developing long-term expertise in government operations and programs. It favors career growth and development through training. It also relies on retirement systems that encourage public employees to remain in the government throughout their work lives. By contrast, the NPM considers many government jobs as essentially interchangeable with those in private businesses. Employees should transfer freely from one sector to the other. Accordingly, public employees should participate in general social security systems and should be able to take the retirement funds they accrue while in government with them when they leave. Logically, the NPM is more apt than traditional management to consider training a cost or short-term investment than a means of upgrading government's human resources. Unlike traditional management, the NPM is open to eliminating civil service protection for public employees as has been done in several U.S. states—Florida, Texas, and Georgia being leading examples. It is important to recognize that no public employees in the U.S. are truly "at will" because they cannot be dismissed for reasons violating their constitutional rights to freedom of speech, religion, association, privacy, equal protection, and other protected rights and liberties. However, in the absence of civil service or contractual tenure or other property interests in their jobs, they lack an automatic right to procedural due process in adverse actions. Both managerial approaches believe that employees should be appraised periodically as a means of indicating how their performance could be improved.

Position Classification

Position classification is one of the most important aspects of traditional public personnel management. In a sense, the entire traditional personnel program rests upon it. Position classification is the system of designing jobs, organizing them into useful managerial and career categories, and establishing their rates of pay. A good position classification system provides a convenient inventory of everything that government workers do. The "position" is the work done. According to rules first established as early as 1923, the classification system should be based on the following principles:

1. Positions and not individuals should be classified. In other words, unlike the military, rank is vested in the position, not in the individual who happens to occupy that position. Membership in the SES is a major exception to this rule at the federal level.
2. The duties and responsibilities pertaining to a position constitute the outstanding characteristics that distinguish it from or make it similar to other positions. Among the classification factors frequently used are the nature and variety of the work; the nature of supervision received by whoever is occupying the position; the nature of available guidelines for performance of the work (that is, is the work routine or does it require flexible responses to ever-changing situations?); the originality required; the purpose and nature of person-to-person work relationships; the scope and nature of decision making; the nature and extent of supervision over other employees; and the qualifications required. Sometimes, these considerations are grouped into four categories: the difficulty of duties, supervisory responsibility, nonsupervisory responsibility, and requisite qualifications.
3. The individual characteristics of an employee occupying a position should have no bearing on the classification of the position.
4. Persons holding positions in the same class (level of position and kind of duties and responsibilities) should be considered equally qualified for any other position in that class.

In trying to grasp what is involved in position classification it may prove useful to think in terms of categories of positions, such as executive; administrative, professional, and technological; clerical, office machine operator, and technician; and trade, crafts, and manual labor. Within each of these broad categories would be a number of positions such as receptionist, keyboarder, file clerk, and stenographer. Each of these positions would bear a classification and a rank. The rank would be related to pay. For the sake of a relatively simple example, consider a file clerk position in the federal government's National Institutes of Health. The position is classified as File Clerk GS 0305-03.

The grade is GS 3; the classification is 0305, which is the code for file clerk in the clerical series at this level. There is a position description explaining the file clerk's duties and responsibilities and a list of factors that determine the level of the position. A more senior file clerk might be a GS-4 or higher and would have broader responsibilities. In theory, unless a special security clearance is required, any file clerk GS 0305-03 in one agency would be suitable for employment in the same class of positions in another agency. Each of the grades in the General Schedule would be paid at a different rate. Thus, GS-1s, at the bottom of this classification system, on average receive the lowest rates of pay, and GS-15s, who are now in the highest general grade, receive the highest. (Most GS 16 through 18 positions, known as "supergrades," were phased out when the SES was created.)

There is no doubt that position classification is a valuable managerial tool. How else might a large workforce be organized? Classification tells managers and employees what the occupants of positions are supposed to do. It makes it possible to design career ladders for advancement. It facilitates testing applicants for competence. It provides a basis for evaluating the performance of government workers.

However, position classification can be problematic. Among the most serious complaints about the practice of position classification is that it is dehumanizing for the employee. In essence, the job is designed and classified without regard to the employee who holds it. The organization is viewed as a set of positions (specializations) coordinated in some fashion, typically through hierarchy. An employee may be able to contribute more to the organization than the position he or she is in allows. For example, a keyboarder may have the ability and willingness to take dictation or transcribe tapes, but that would require classification as a stenographer and higher pay. Hence, allowing a typist to function as a stenographer would be prohibited by position classification principles. The employee can neither go beyond the level of work required in the position nor fall short of it. Working "out of class" is particularly opposed by unions, especially when employees are doing higher-level work without receiving more pay. These problems are particularly evident where classifications are narrow and specific, as opposed to broadly banded into categories such as clerical or technical.

Position classification practices, associated with Frederick Taylor's scientific management (see Chapter 4), have also tended to design jobs in a stultifying fashion (see Box 5.3). They have stressed the need for order and conformity in governmental positions, sometimes at the expense of the interest the job could possibly hold for the incumbent. This has led to boredom and alienation among employees. There is growing concern that job design take the following considerations into account:

1. Job rotation, that is, developing a classification and career system that enables employees to move through several positions. This enables an employee to use several skills and avoid the boredom that comes with the repetitive performance of routine tasks.

5.3 POSITION CLASSIFICATION STANDARDS

Series: Grade:

GS 0305   GS 3

FILE CLERK

GS-0305-03
National Institutes of Health

I. Introduction

This position is located in the Office of Grants Support Services (OGSS), NIH, as part of the Government's Most Efficient Organization (MEO) responsible for extramural support in the development of grant-and-contract-supported research and training programs on a wide variety of biomedical and behavioral diseases and disorders. The incumbent is responsible for providing filing and other clerical services to Task Unit members, Program Directors, Grants Management Officers/Specialists, and Scientific Review Administrators NIH wide. Supported NIH employees are located in all the extramural activities and components of the NIH Institutes and Centers. Major duty and responsibility is to provide office filing services; and may assist in other clerical and mail delivery tasks as needed. May be assigned to any of the various MEO Hubs, Task Units, or Institutes and Centers (ICs) and may perform any of the following duties. (Percentages of time may vary depending on workload and scheduling requirements.)

II. Duties and Responsibilities

PERFORMS FILING TASKS 80%
Performs filing and clerical duties associated with the assembly, retention, maintenance, disposition, and control of records in both a 13-digit numeric and an alphabetic file system used throughout the NIH MEO.

Receives requests for documents to be withdrawn from files, refers to classification guides, index registers, index cards, or other finding media to locate appropriate document locator number or other identification in order to obtain documents from files (or to abstract requested information), inserts charge-card for all materials withdrawn, re-files returned materials, and withdraws charge-cards.

Routes requests requiring special search (e.g., other work areas within the organization) to appropriate operating elements. Where necessary, returns incomplete requests for additional information required to identify material requested.

Consolidates, attaches, and cross-references new material with previously filed material, utilizing searching, withdrawing, filing, or re-filing procedures.

ASSISTS IN OTHER CLERICAL AND MESSENGER SERVICES 20%
Assists others in performing repetitive or standard clerical tasks. Coordinates with supported employees to verify items to be transported. Before calling the NIH Transportation Office to pick up items, ensures all items are in a covered box and taped.

As needed, the incumbent may collect, sort, and deliver a variety of documents from various locations in the NIH Campus and Rockville, as well as outlying buildings. In addition to the cited campus sites, incumbent may be required to go to offices in Bethesda, the Rockledge area, and on Democracy Boulevard as well as in various office buildings located

2.   Job enlargement, or placing more tasks within a position description.
3.   Job enrichment, or vesting greater authority, responsibility, and autonomy in positions.
4.   Empowerment, or providing employees with discretion to resolve work flow and other work process problems that impede their job performance.

on Executive Boulevard. Copies, faxes, answers telephone, routes email inquiries to correct destinations. Performs other related duties as assigned.

III. Factors

Factor 1: Knowledge Required

—Knowledge of the numerical and the alphabetical filing systems used throughout the NIH, and knowledge of the functions and organizational structures of the units serviced.

—Knowledge of subject files, cross-reference files, classification guides, and indexes maintained within the immediate unit and procedures related to their use.

—Skill to identify the proper sequential location of material to be filed, withdrawn, or re-filed.

Factor 2: Supervisory Controls

Supervisor assigns work, advises of procedural changes, and is available for assistance when required. Normal work is performed independently following prescribed procedures. Work is reviewed in terms of accuracy, adequacy, and timeliness of service provided.

Factor 3: Guidelines

A number of procedural guides and instructions pertain to the work. Requesters may provide inadequate information, however, and a large number of locations are possible, so that employee must select most appropriate guide or search procedure in locating materials sought.

Factor 4: Complexity

The work involves filing and clerical duties associated with a wide variety of documents. Searching assignments occasionally involve such characteristics as incorrect, indefinite, or incomplete information, requiring reference to guides, indexes, or other finding media to locate materials requested.

Factor 5: Scope and Effect

Purpose of the work is to maintain working documents and provide an efficient reference service. Timely and proper disposition of records affects the work of offices waiting for the records.

Factor 6: Personal Contacts

Contacts are with coworkers of the unit and with employees throughout the NIH requesting materials.

Factor 7: Purpose of Contacts

Contacts are for the purpose of obtaining and supplying information in relation to filling requests or filing of materials.

Factor 8: Physical Demands

Work requires prolonged standing, walking, and bending to perform required filing and searching duties.

Factor 9: Work Environment

Work is performed in an office setting.

Source: National Institutes of Health; http://oma.od.nih.gov/ms/a76-fair/EXTRAMURAL%20PDs/Extramural%20PDs/File%20Clerk%20(GS-0305-03).pdf (accessed June 4, 2013). The position description was prepared in 2003. The designation of Most Efficient Organization (MEO) is related to the federal competitive sourcing practices at the time.

Another problem with position classification is that position descriptions can become rapidly outdated as technology and the work of governmental agencies change. Position classifiers may not be able to keep pace with all the constant changes, but agency managers are not likely to favor limiting the introduction of new technologies and tasks to enable the classifiers to catch up. Then, too, there has been a problem of "grade creep," or a tendency for positions constantly to be reclassified at a higher level. Collective bargaining also presents a problem for position classification. Unions contend that classification levels and pay should be subject to bargaining and that more positions should be created to take account of workers' increased seniority. For example, to return to the case of Supply Clerk GS-3, a union might want to see a classification system that would create a position of Senior Supply Clerk GS-4 (or higher) so that someone who has held the position for, let's say, 15 years would not be paid at the same rate as a newcomer (even though they do the same work). Finally, as a practical matter, position classification systems are seldom as neat in practice as they are in theory. For instance, the federal government has not only a General Schedule but also a wage board system for industrial-type jobs, a foreign service classification system, a postal classification system, the SES, a system denoted "GM" for managers and supervisors at the GS 13 through 15 ranks, and an executive-level system for political executives.

Contemporary thinking holds that complex classification systems should be simplified. The number of classifications should be reduced, and positions should be classified in broad bands such as clerical, administrative, technical, managerial, and executive. Broad banding enhances flexibility in assigning functions to employees and in moving employees among positions. It also requires less paperwork and effort to classify positions. The NPM strongly favors broad banding at the discretion of individual agencies.

Recruitment, Selection, and Promotion

Recruitment, selection, and promotion are among the core functions of public personnel management. The managerial approach dictates that cost-effectiveness be the ultimate value in performing these functions. The NPM also embraces these values, but in the United States it adds a concern that employees reflect the nation's social diversity.

Recruitment is the process of encouraging individuals to apply for government positions. The critical elements of a successful traditional management recruitment program aimed at procuring the most efficient, effective employees, consists of (1) governmental efforts to upgrade the image of public employment; (2) efforts to recruit for careers rather than single jobs; (3) efforts to give examinations at convenient times and convenient places; (4) the elimination of pointless background requirements, such as age or non-job-related training requirements; and (5) efforts to reach all segments of the population. The value of economy dictates that government spending on these functions vary with its needs for personnel. The NPM prizes flexibility, decentralization, multiple means of entry, and recruitment for specific jobs rather than careers.

Selection is the process of choosing among applicants. In the United States a wide variety of approaches is used, but the dominant pattern stems from the 19th-century reform period. It relies on an open, competitive examination or ranking system of some kind, which can potentially generate the greatest degree of competition among applicants. Competitive examinations are those in which the hiring of individual test takers is in accordance with their exam scores. In a purely competitive examination system, the person who achieved the highest score would be hired first, whereas the person who scored the lowest passing grade would be hired last if enough positions were available. In practice, the best person for the job does not necessarily score the highest on a competitive exam. Therefore, most jurisdictions modify this approach by allowing selection from among groups of applicants, such as those obtaining the three or ten highest scores. The latter approaches are called the "rule of three" or "ten" or any other number. The rationale is to provide the hiring authority with some discretion in making selections but nevertheless assure that the selection process is open and competitive.

Selection by examination may involve the use of an **eligibles register,** a list of those who passed an examination, ranked in the order of their scores. Under the "rule of three" approach, for example, if a vacancy occurred for the position described in Box 5.3, the appropriate eligibles register would be consulted and selection would be from among the top three scorers on the list. If another vacancy occurred, selection would be from among the remaining two highest scorers, plus whoever scored fourth highest (that is, ranked fourth on the eligibles register). If someone is passed over a number of times (typically three), he or she will be deleted from the register despite his or her score. Contemporary information technology makes it possible to create an eligibles register for any particular job from among applicants who have passed a relevant examination.

The NPM objects to the rigidity and delay often caused by the construction of eligibles registers and the rule of three. It favors the flexibility of two approaches that have gained increasing use in recent years. **Direct hiring** enables agencies to hire any qualified applicant. It is particularly useful when agencies have critical staffing needs and/or a shortage of qualified applicants. **Categorical ranking** permits agencies to place all eligible candidates into groups according to their qualification levels, such as very highly qualified, highly qualified, and qualified. Selection begins with the top-ranked group and can be from among everyone in it rather than only the top three. There are several types of examinations:

1. *Performance examinations.* These are devices intended to determine whether an applicant can perform the tasks required in the position for which a hire is being made. Word processing and equipment operation are functions in which performance examinations are used. Such an examination might determine, for example, how many words a minute a person can process accurately.

2. *Written examinations.* These may stress achievement, aptitude, or both. They are typically of the multiple-choice, machine-scored variety. Some jurisdictions purchase them commercially rather than developing their own. A major virtue of such examinations is that they are inexpensive to administer.

3. *Oral examinations.* These are often considered more practical for upper-level positions involving discretionary authority or positions

for which there are few applicants. Generally, an oral examination is administered by a panel that has an established set of criteria for making a judgment. The candidate may appear before the panel alone or with a group of other applicants.

4. *Assessment centers.* Assessment centers try to duplicate some of the approaches of performance examinations, but for positions in which the tasks are less concrete and are evaluated more subjectively. Individuals may be put through a series of activities that simulate some of the critical aspects of the job for which someone is being hired. Such activities may consist of getting along with others, engaging in leadership, or exercising discretion. Ratings are usually made by a panel, with predetermined criteria for assessment.

No matter which kind of examination is used, the selection device should be *valid*. In other words, the score on the examination should predict the level of performance on the job. Yet for many positions this is difficult to achieve and demonstrate. The chief problems in validating examinations are three-fold. First, it is difficult to construct an examination that truly reflects on-the-job conditions. This is especially true for positions involving the exercise of interpersonal skills, policy making, and discretion. However, it can also be a problem in performance examinations, because the environment in which an individual works can affect productivity. Sometimes this problem is addressed by distinguishing between **job proficiency,** that is, the ability to do the work, and **job performance,** the reality of how much work gets done. An example is a typist who, although proficient, performs far better in a cubicle alone than in an open room where he or she is easily distracted. Although it may be possible to test for this, it may be expensive or impractical to do so. Aspects of the work environment—such as noise, degree of privacy, and the extent of time pressures—that can affect performance are called **situational factors.**

A second problem is that there may be little variation in the scores of those who are selected for governmental positions. There are often many more applicants than position openings. There have been cases of some 15,000 individuals applying for fewer than 100 jobs. Under such circumstances it is highly likely that those selected will have virtually the same high scores on the examinations. When this occurs, it is difficult to validate an examination because there is no way of knowing how well someone with a much lower score would have performed. Those with lower scores cannot be hired, of course, because of the rule of three or a similar approach. An exam may be valid, but the problem is that this cannot be demonstrated statistically. This is a serious legal problem under equal employment opportunity law when the average scores of members of minority groups taking the exam are lower than those of non-minorities, which may signal that the exam is culturally biased (see Box 5.8). By bringing in candidates with a wider range of scores, categorical ranking should make it easier to validate exams.

Third, to validate an examination, the level of performance by employees who took it must be measured. Again, the objective is to show a relationship between examination score and performance level on the job. If the latter cannot be measured well, validity cannot be demonstrated. Performance appraisal is possible for some jobs but extremely difficult in any systematic fashion in others. We will have more to say about this momentarily.

Despite these problems, there is a well-developed set of approaches to merit examination validation. The best is the **criterion-related** approach. It seeks to relate examination scores to on-the-job performance in one of two ways. First, it may be **predictive;** that is, it takes the scores of those selected and associates them statistically with these employees' on-the-job performance at some later time. Predictive validation is difficult to establish for the reasons discussed previously. **Concurrent validation** is a technique that administers the examination to those already employed and then seeks to determine the statistical relationship between their scores and their performance appraisals. The chief virtue is that there may be more variation in scores among those taking the examination. However, performance remains difficult to measure objectively, and this approach also runs the risk that extraneous factors may contribute to an employee's score *and* performance level. For instance, an employee who is well-liked personally and consequently has a high degree of self-esteem may obtain a higher score and higher performance appraisal than will one who is isolated in and alienated from the workplace—even though under neutral social conditions both might score or perform equally.

By the 1970s, so-called merit examinations were frequently challenged in court on the basis that they had disparate racial and ethnic impacts and consequently violated equal opportunity law and/or the constitutional right to equal protection of the laws. The examinations' discriminatory impact stems in part from the inequality of opportunity in society at large, especially in education. Such an impact thus flies in the face of equal opportunity and the political approach's emphasis on representative government. It may be legally tolerable only if the examinations truly are highly predictive of job performance.

The traditional managerial approach also stresses efficiency and productivity as the basis for *promotion.* According to this approach, promotions are usually made on the basis of written examinations and/or performance appraisals. The promotional examination resembles the merit entrance examination except that it is open only to those employees who qualify for consideration for promotion. Performance appraisals are discussed in the next section.

Promotions remain a controversial aspect of public personnel management. In hierarchical organizations, there are fewer positions at the top than at the bottom. Therefore, there is a limit on how high up an employee can rise. Promotions tend to be "zero-sum"; that is, one employee's gain (promotion) is another's lost opportunity. The competition can be fierce and can lead to discord among employees. This is one of the virtues of a written promotional examination. As long as the examination is accepted as legitimate and fair, it settles the issue without any possibility of favoritism or office politics playing a role. Similarly, promotion by seniority, a principle often stressed by unions in collective bargaining, tends to minimize discord. However, seniority is not necessarily the best indicator of productivity, and consequently the managerial approaches tend to discourage it. Sometimes merit-oriented promotion and seniority are combined by restricting the opportunity for promotion to those who have been on the job for a given number of years. Presumably, in the flexible, flatter (e.g., less hierarchical) organizations and broad-banded classification systems favored by the NPM, employees (or teams) can be rewarded for the results they produce without having to be promoted to new positions.

Performance Appraisal

Performance appraisals have gained greater attention since the 1970s, as governments at all levels have been under public pressure to be more efficient, economical, effective, and responsive. The federal Civil Service Reform Act of 1978 provided for individual performance appraisals. The NPM has a strong performance orientation, though where the once pervasive TQM (total quality management) is still used performance is not viewed as a product of individual ability or effort. Although there is a wide variety of performance appraisal techniques, evaluating employee productivity remains problematic. The main difficulties are that appraisals reflect varying degrees of subjectivity, that it is often impossible to quantify the output of public employees in a meaningful fashion, and that there tends to be limited variability in the level of appraisal. In the past, 98 percent of federal employees routinely obtained a "satisfactory" efficiency rating. Today, many performance appraisal techniques stress a combination of self-appraisals, peer ratings, and group or external ratings. The more tangible an employee's work product, the greater the probability of designing a performance appraisal approach that truly serves to indicate the level of that employee's productivity.

To some extent, public sector performance appraisal is a "process in search of a technique."[24] Typically, appraisals are concerned with the performance factors and employee traits displayed in Box 5.4. However, there are several ways of assessing these characteristics. Appraisals are usually done by supervisors, peers, the employees themselves, groups, external evaluators, or some combination of these. When appraisal is by supervisors, co-workers, subordinates, and customers, it is called a "360" (degree) evaluation. The techniques strive for objectivity, but where an employee's work is essentially qualitative (e.g., writing reports, supervising others, evaluating grant applications, procuring supplies/weaponry), appraisal will inevitably contain subjective judgments. Among the major techniques are:

1. *Rating scales,* as in Box 5.4, which are easy to administer, relatively inexpensive, clear, and in widespread use. Customer surveys can easily use rating scales to assay individual (and/or organizational) responsiveness, promptness, politeness, and so forth.
2. *Essay reports* focusing on an employee's need for further training and his or her potential and ability to obtain results. This technique is time-consuming.

5.4 PERFORMANCE APPRAISAL BY GRAPHIC RATING SCALE

Person evaluated _____ Position _____
Location _____

Performance Factors	Outstanding	Very Good	Satisfactory	Unsatisfactory	Unknown
1. Effectiveness					
2. Use of time and materials					
3. Prompt completion of work					
4. Thoroughness					
5. Initiative					
6. Perseverance					

Ethical Considerations					
7. Loyalty to department					
8. Loyalty to peers					
9. Loyalty to subordinates					
10. Sense of ethics					
11. Cooperativeness					
12. Responsibility					
13. Commitment of service					
14. Open-mindedness					

Abilities, Skills, and Faculties					
15. Technical skills					
16. Communication skills					
17. Judgment					
18. Analytical ability					
19. Ability to organize					
20. Ability to inspire and influence staff					
21. Ability to inspire and influence others than staff					
22. Flexibility and adaptability					
23. Imaginativeness and creativity					
24. Ability to develop subordinates					
25. Breadth of concepts					

Date evaluated _____ Evaluator _____
The above appraisal was reviewed with me on _____

_____

(Signature of Person Evaluated)

Comments _____

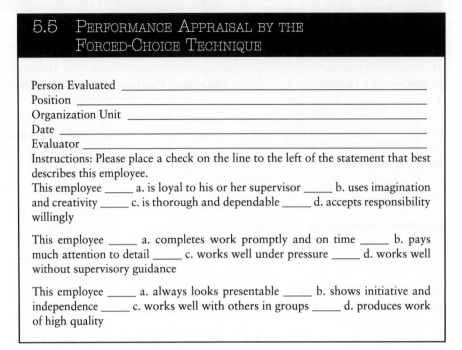

5.5   PERFORMANCE APPRAISAL BY THE FORCED-CHOICE TECHNIQUE

Person Evaluated _____

Position _____

Organization Unit _____

Date _____

Evaluator _____

Instructions: Please place a check on the line to the left of the statement that best describes this employee.

This employee _____ a. is loyal to his or her supervisor _____ b. uses imagination and creativity _____ c. is thorough and dependable _____ d. accepts responsibility willingly

This employee _____ a. completes work promptly and on time _____ b. pays much attention to detail _____ c. works well under pressure _____ d. works well without supervisory guidance

This employee _____ a. always looks presentable _____ b. shows initiative and independence _____ c. works well with others in groups _____ d. produces work of high quality

3. *Checklists* consisting of statements about the employee's performance. The rater checks the most appropriate statements. Some of these may be given greater weight than others in reaching an overall appraisal.

4. *Critical incidents,* an approach requiring the supervisor to keep a log of employees' performance, indicating incidents of both good and poor performance.

5. *Forced choice,* requiring supervisors to rate employees on the basis of descriptive statements. The statements are constructed so that the supervisor cannot be certain which ones are most indicative of employee performance that the personnel office will deem most desirable. An example is presented in Box 5.5. Forced choice enhances objectivity but results in evaluations that are difficult for supervisors and employees to interpret and use as a means of improving performance.

6. *Ranking* or comparing employees to one another.

7. *Forced distribution,* requiring the rater to place employees in categories such as top 5 percent, next 10 percent, next 25 percent, and so on.

These techniques have pros and cons in terms of objectivity, usefulness, cost, and ease of administration. None is best for all positions and circumstances. The search for better performance appraisal techniques retains a high priority in the managerial approach. The NPM seeks to augment customer satisfaction surveys with quantitative, results-oriented performance measures. It views most, if not all, of the factors in Box 5.4 as inadequate because their relationship to the achievement of results is indirect and unclear.

Because there is a tendency for organizations to get what they measure, caution is warranted in constructing performance appraisal instruments. For instance, if postal clerks are evaluated on courteousness but not on how rapidly they complete transactions, productivity may suffer. One approach for dealing with this type of problem is to use a "balanced scorecard," which rates performance on a variety of factors without ranking their relative importance.[25] Using this approach, postal clerks could be rated for courtesy, speed, accuracy, and other key dimensions of their jobs. A clerk who rated high on courtesy, but not on speed, would be advised to complete transactions politely, but more quickly.

There is no consensus on whether employees should be evaluated in comparison to one another, as part of groups or teams, or against their own past performance. Evidence suggests that federal employees are more likely to be motivated by performance appraisal systems when 1) they believe that performance standards are fair, 2) better work will be rewarded, and 3) employees have higher satisfaction with their supervisors.[26] Evidence further indicates that linking performance and pay to increased productivity is a complex process.

Pay

The managerial approaches stress economy and productivity in determining the pay levels of public employees. Pay systems are typically linked to position classification systems, but they tend to be problematic and controversial for a variety of reasons. First, it is held that pay systems should seek to motivate employees to be more productive. However, an emerging body of research around the concept of Public Service Motivation (PSM) finds that public employees are motivated by more than money.[27] In this construct, public employees have motivations for their choice of employment that are 1) *rational* (e.g., working for the government is the most effective way to achieve a change in a public policy issue), 2) *normative* (e.g., a family tradition of military service), and 3) *affective* (e.g., a deep belief that public service is a worthy career that sates an emotional attachment to being involved in a policy area). Public employment is not merely a means to the end of receiving a paycheck. Therefore, similar to Herzberg's Two-Factor Theory (see Chapter 4), to motivate employees managers may need to focus on issues of employee advancement, responsibility, and job enrichment and not just focus on pay (a hygiene factor that decreases job dissatisfaction).

To the extent that pay is a motivator, governments should seek to establish a clear link between an employee's performance rating and his or her level of pay. In some jurisdictions, efforts are made to grant increases in the pay of public employees largely on the basis of increased productivity. The major difficulties in this regard seem to be twofold. On the one hand, merit pay or pay for greater productivity is most suitable to positions where the worker's output is tangible and measurable. Benchmarking, revenue production, and other measures can be more readily used in these contexts. Word processing and a variety of other governmental jobs lend themselves to productivity measurement.

But jobs involving a qualitative output and the exercise of discretion tend to be unsuited to meaningful productivity measurement. For instance, how can the productivity of administrative law judges and hearing examiners be assessed? Although we could measure the time it takes them to reach and write opinions, what we are interested in is the quality of those decisions in terms of justice and the public interest. Within broad limits, we care little whether one such employee hears more cases per year than another does. We would probably be more concerned if one administrative law judge is overturned on appeal to a higher level reviewing body or court far more frequently than others are. However, that is something that would have to be evaluated over a period of several years and, consequently, could not be the basis for annual pay decisions. The NPM favors evaluating employees based on their customer service ratings and contributions to achieving results considered central to an agency's goals as established by strategic planning or other means. It is often good managerial practice for an employee and his or her supervisor to discuss appropriate performance goals and ways of assessing progress toward them. Various peer review systems also help assess performance.

Pay is also complicated by the desire to make it comparable with pay in the private sector. An employee in the public sector should earn what he or she would earn if doing the same work in the private sector. In the federal government, **comparability** is assessed on the basis of a survey done by the Bureau of Labor Statistics. The survey presents some challenging technical problems, but the main difficulty is that there are not true private equivalents for a large number of public sector jobs. Again, the problem is the qualitative aspect. Many of the features of a typical bureau chief's job can be compared to those of private sector executives—but the public sector job is ultimately different because for the most part it does not sell products or services and it involves qualitative questions about public policy and the public interest. Unlike the private sector, it is also bound by constitutional law in dealing with its employees and customers. To pay a bureau chief on the basis of the number of employees he or she supervises rather than on the basis of his or her development and implementation of effective public policies in the public interest according to the rule of law is to miss the main dimension of the job. Comparability also encompasses the variation in costs-of-living and labor costs from locality to locality. Employees in expensive areas can be compensated at a higher rate than others in identical positions.

Comparability refers to wage and salary rates among different employers and in different regions. **Comparable worth** concerns the pay rates for different occupations by the same employer. The Equal Pay Act of 1963 prohibits pay differentials based on sex for employees performing similar jobs under similar working conditions. However, it does not prohibit different rates of pay to men and women if they are not in the same jobs. The concept of comparable worth seeks to extend the principles of comparability and equal pay to situations in which men and women are performing dissimilar jobs that nonetheless could be considered of equal value to an employer. The concept

5.6 GENERAL SCHEDULE PAY BY GRADE AND STEP FOR 2012

Grade	Step 1	Step 2	Step 3	Step 4	Step 5	Step 6	Step 7	Step 8	Step 9	Step 10	Within Grade Amounts
1	17803	18398	18990	19579	20171	20519	21104	21694	21717	22269	Varies
2	20017	20493	21155	21717	21961	22607	23253	23899	24545	25191	Varies
3	21840	22568	23296	24024	24752	25480	26208	26936	27664	28392	728
4	24518	25335	26152	26969	27786	28603	29420	30237	31054	31871	817
5	27431	28345	29259	30173	31087	32001	32915	33829	34743	35657	914
6	30577	31596	32615	33634	34653	35672	36691	37710	38729	39748	1019
7	33979	35112	36245	37378	38511	39644	40777	41910	43043	44176	1133
8	37631	38885	40139	41393	42647	43901	45155	46409	47663	48917	1254
9	41563	42948	44333	45718	47103	48488	49873	51258	52643	54028	1385
10	45771	47297	48823	50349	51875	53401	54927	56453	57979	59505	1526
11	50287	51963	53639	55315	56991	58667	60343	62019	63695	65371	1676
12	60274	62283	64292	66301	68310	70319	72328	74337	76346	78355	2009
13	71674	74063	76452	78841	81230	83619	86008	88397	90786	93175	2389
14	84697	87520	90343	93166	95989	98812	101635	104458	107281	110104	2823
15	99628	102949	106270	109591	112912	116233	119554	122875	126196	129517	3321

Source: http://federaljobs.net/salarybase.htm (accessed June 4, 2013).

of comparable worth is especially important to an employer whose workforce has a high degree of occupational segregation by sex. Los Angeles and the states of Minnesota, New York, New Mexico, Iowa, and South Dakota were among the first jurisdictions to institute comparable worth.

"Pay caps" are another complication. At the federal level Congress has been loath to allow civil servants' pay to exceed its own (about $174,000 per year for rank and file members; the leadership positions receive $20–50 thousand more). Because Congress is skittish about raising its own pay, this can effectively cap the pay of SES members at one level for years. A table of General Schedule pay for 2012 is presented in Box 5.6. GS levels have 10 pay steps, which allow for pay increases and differences within grades. In many state and local governments and in some federal agencies, such as the U.S. Postal Service, pay is set primarily through collective bargaining (discussed later in this chapter).

Determining levels of public sector pay is complicated much further by politics. Politicians' electoral campaigns and taxpayers' dissatisfaction with government have often focused on the "bloated, unproductive" public sector. When inflation is rampant or budgets seem to defy balance or cities tread on the verge of bankruptcy, freezing or cutting the pay of public employees has become almost a reflexive response. Such freezes or reductions serve as indicators of the politicians' toughness and seem to offer the taxpayers some relief. Yet it is unclear why public employees should bear the brunt of fighting inflation or be penalized for providing services—such as police and fire protection and education—clearly in the public's interest. Whatever the sensibility of the "bash the bureaucrat" syndrome, however, public employees' pay is vulnerable in difficult economic times.

Finally, in considering the pay of public employees, calculations should include fringe benefits and pensions, both of which are often substantially greater in the public sector than among comparably salaried employees in the private sector. Recent presidents have favored basing public employees' comparability on "total compensation," which includes fringe benefits.

Workforce Planning

It was anticipated that between 2006 and 2010, more than 18 percent of the federal workforce would retire.[28] Such a departure of personnel leads to the loss of much "institutional memory" in many government agencies and places great financial stress on federal employee retirement benefit programs. And this is just the tip of the iceberg. In 2007, it was predicted that "Over the next 10 years, 60% of people in the federal workforce will be eligible to retire. More than likely, 40% of these individuals will retire when they are first eligible."[29] Can their skills be replaced, and if so, how?

Workforce planning is an effort to match an agency's projected need for various categories of skills with the availability of employees and applicants who can supply those skills. Assessing the future need for skills is especially precarious in the public sector. Agency budgets are generally controlled by legislatures on an annual or biennial cycle and are difficult to predict. Unforeseeable political and economic changes can have a major impact on agency spending. Agencies may also be required to take on new functions and drop or outsource older ones with little warning. For many agencies, projections of more than 12 months are impractical.

Workforce planning can focus on specific skills or look toward wider needs, such as succession into top-level career managerial or executive positions. It is obviously complex and subject to miscalculation. However, workforce planning is now a core HRM function, embraced by both the traditional managerial and NPM approaches as a substantial contributor to cost-effective public administration.

Cutbacks

From the late 1970s to the present, the desire to reduce the public sector payroll in an effort to reduce taxes, avoid deficits, and stimulate economic growth in the private sector has led to periodic widespread reductions-in-force (RIFs) in the public service. The managerial approaches stress the need to cut the least productive employees and services first and to outsource or terminate functions that can be supplied as well or better by the private sector. In addition, the NPM favors cutting managers and supervisors in the interest of empowering employees.

Like promotions, cutbacks are controversial and problematic because there are clear winners and losers. The main approaches to cutbacks involve (1) providing some employees with greater protection than others, such as veterans or more senior employees; (2) relying on attrition; (3) offering "buyouts" and "early" retirements as incentives for employees to leave the public sector voluntarily; and (4) employing "across-the-board" cuts among all levels of employees and all governmental functions. "Job sharing," or splitting one position between two or more part-time employees, has also gained attention. As the managerial approach argues, the main problem with these processes is that they may not lead to cuts where they are most desirable from an organizational standpoint. There have even been instances where early retirements have led to the separation of highly valued and necessary employees who subsequently had to be replaced or rehired on contracts, netting the government little, if any, savings.

Quality of Work Life (QWL)

Contemporary HRM is highly cognizant of the desirability of helping employees integrate their work lives with their personal lives. QWL programs and benefits seek to make public sector workplaces family-friendly, promote employee wellness, and provide employee assistance for alcohol and substance abuse and similar problems. Interest in QWL is largely driven by the problems governments face in competing with the private sector for employees and the changing nature of the workforce—particularly increased participation by women, which is sometimes referred to as the feminization of the workforce.[30] America's aging population also puts new pressures for elder care on middle-aged and older employees who are likely to make up the ranks of senior-level managerial and executive positions.

The federal Family and Medical Leave Act of 1993 allows eligible employees to take up to 12 weeks of unpaid leave a year for personal health problems, childbirth, adoption, and care of children, elderly parents, or ill spouses. Additional QWL measures include the following:

- Flexible work schedules
- Telecommuting
- On-site day care
- Job sharing
- Health and fitness programs
- Counseling for substance abuse and other antisocial or self-destructive behaviors.

The NPR promoted family-friendly policies through OPM, including encouraging employees to use up to five days of their paid sick leave annually to devote to family care.

Political Neutrality

Running throughout the managerial approaches to public personnel administration is the concept that the civil service should be politically neutral in a partisan sense. Managerially oriented public administration holds that to a large extent the public sector faces the same kinds of organizational and managerial conditions and problems that the private sector faces and that partisanship has no legitimate place in the vast majority of public personnel and managerial decisions. The notion that functions such as street paving and sanitation are inherently nonpartisan is illustrative. The functions of the public sector in this view have much to do with the public interest and little to do with the immediate electoral interests of political parties. To a large extent, the contemporary concept of political neutrality grew out of the 19th-century civil service reform movement and was a reaction to the abuses of the spoils system. Not only can the mixing of partisanship and personnel be seen to impede efficiency and foster corruption, it also can symbolize a perversion of the public interest, leading the citizenry to believe that the public service is engaged in the promotion of its own narrow partisan interests.

At the federal level, regulations for political neutrality are embodied in the Hatch Act. The original act, passed in 1939, prohibited employees from taking an active part in political management or partisan political campaigns. In 1993, the act was revised at the urging of federal employee unions, which considered it too restrictive. Most employees are now allowed to engage in a wide variety of campaign activities, including giving speeches, holding offices in political organizations, stuffing envelopes and making telephone calls, and distributing campaign literature. The main remaining restrictions deal with soliciting money for partisan political purposes. The 1993 revision does not apply to the Senior Executive Service; administrative law judges; several law enforcement positions; and agencies with defense, intelligence, or other missions that could be compromised by public displays of partisanship, such as the MSPB and the Federal Election Commission. Many state and local governments also have political neutrality regulations.

The main difficulty with political neutrality regulations is that they do not specify precisely what they prohibit. Some of the restrictions are clear, but it is not always evident when a political statement crosses a forbidden line. For instance, under the original Hatch Act, federal employees were disciplined for such behavior as stating "unsubstantiated facts about the ancestry of a candidate" (calling him an SOB?), failing to "discourage a spouse's political activity," and voicing "disapproval of treatment of veterans while acting as a Legion officer at a closed [American] Legion meeting."[31] Uncertainty may tend to inhibit public employees' freedom of speech more than is necessary to promote the value of partisan neutrality in the public service. Although political neutrality regulations place substantial limitations on public employees' political rights, they also protect employees from being coerced by elected officials and political executives to engage in partisan activities.

Despite their interference with public employees' constitutional rights under the First and Fourteenth Amendments, the Supreme Court has upheld the constitutionality of regulations for political neutrality in no uncertain terms.[32] In its view, legislatures have the power to establish such restrictions because they promote the legitimate objectives of creating and maintaining an efficient and nonpartisan civil service.

◆→ THE POLITICAL APPROACH TO PUBLIC PERSONNEL ADMINISTRATION

The political approach to public personnel administration stresses radically different values than do the managerial approaches and leads to an emphasis on different techniques and considerations. Its underlying value is to maximize the responsiveness of the public sector workforce to political officials and to the public at large (not as individual customers). The political approach deemphasizes the analogy between public and private employment and stresses the extent to which the public service is *public*. According to this approach, what is most significant about the public sector is that it makes and implements public policy, provides public goods and services that cannot or should not be supplied by the private sector, and is an integral part of a constitutional system of government.

Responsiveness

The quest for responsiveness has taken several forms. The central idea is that public employees should use their positions to advance the general political goals being pursued by the elected component of government and the political community as a whole. Concern with responsiveness reflects the view that public administration is not a politically neutral, technical, managerial endeavor but rather has to be considered in terms of the political choices facing the nation.

The most outstanding effort to ensure responsiveness was reliance on the widespread use of political patronage in recruiting, selecting, and promoting public employees. Patronage does much to ensure the responsiveness of public administrators to the public: The people elect political officials who espouse a political program outlined in a party platform, and then the elected officials appoint public administrators sympathetic to the party's policies. This promotes administrative responsiveness to elected officials and, by extension, to the public. Moreover, in patronage systems public employees have no civil service or other job tenure and the ability of elected officials to fire, reassign, or promote public administrators almost at will comes close to assuring that the administrators will not oppose or resist the programs of the political officials. In other words, patronage can be used to instill accountability. But today in the United States, as noted earlier, patronage-based personnel actions are generally unconstitutional abridgments of public employees' freedom of belief and association. Still, the Supreme Court's patronage decisions summarized in Box 2.8 do not take politics out of the public service completely.

Some of the arrangements in the Federal Civil Service Reform Act of 1978 seek to bring a permissible amount of political responsiveness into the federal personnel system. The Senior Executive Service is composed predominantly of top-ranking career civil servants. By law, 10 percent of allocated positions in the SES can be purely political (patronage) appointees. Members of the SES can be reassigned, voluntarily transferred from agency to agency, given different kinds of work, and reduced in grade with far greater flexibility than can most federal career civil servants. They are subject neither to the position classification system nor to the normal adverse action system for demotions based on poor performance. The rationale behind the SES was in large part to make these high-ranking administrative officials responsive to political executives. In addition, it was thought that moving SES members from bureau to bureau and possibly from agency to agency would enable them to develop a broader concept of the public interest, one that was not overly supportive of the aims of any particular interest group. Aside from affording these administrators new opportunities and challenges, the act made them eligible for financial bonuses in return for sacrificing some of the job security they had previously held.

The 1978 reform act also seeks to ensure some continuity in the higher civil service by prohibiting the involuntary reassignment of members of the SES within 120 days of the appointment of a new political executive in a supervisory position over them. The act also requires that 70 percent of the positions in the SES be filled with individuals with not less than five years of current, continuous administrative service.

The effort to assure responsiveness has also led to other kinds of ideological and political screening. At various times in the nation's history, for instance, the loyalty of public employees to the United States has been the subject of investigation. The most elaborate loyalty-security program existed in the late 1940s and early 1950s, a period referred to as "McCarthyism" after Senator Joseph McCarthy of Wisconsin. During part of that time, the loyalty of *every* federal employee and applicant was subject to question. Loyalty was defined largely in terms of adhering to an uninformed anticommunism, a rather repressive, limited political vision. In retrospect, had not so many lives been damaged by the program and had not the creativity of the federal service suffered so badly, the fetish with loyalty-security would be easily dismissed as aberrant. After all, seeking social equity, engaging in premarital sex, supporting racial integration and the recognition of "red" (mainland) China, and reading high-quality newspapers are no longer considered even remote indicators of disloyalty, though they were subject to investigation then.[33] However, at the time there was a real fear in Congress and the society at large that federal employees were not responsive to the dominant values of the American political community and that they would use their positions to undermine the goals being sought by elected officials.

Representativeness

The political approach to public administration stresses the value of representativeness. Administrative agencies are considered to be political, policy-making institutions that exercise governmental power. One line of thought is that this power can be controlled and channeled in the public interest if public employees and agencies are representative of the political community at large. Representativeness is related to responsiveness because it is assumed that a representative public service will have perspectives on questions of public policy similar to those of the majority in the legislature and in the electorate.[34] In public personnel administration, the quest for representativeness historically has centered on the need to select public administrators socially and/or politically representative of the nation's general population. The Pendleton Act of 1883 even included a provision for apportioning civil service appointments in the District of Columbia by the appointees' state of residency and according to the relative size of the states' populations. The political approach's emphasis on representation sometimes brings it into conflict with the traditional managerial perspective.

Today the quest for representativeness in public bureaucracies is manifested to the greatest extent in a concern with equal employment opportunity (EEO). One justification for such programs is that equal opportunity contributes to distributive and social justice; EEO is fair and ought to be practiced for that reason. Another justification notes a connection between the social representativeness of a public bureaucracy and its representativeness in a political and policy sense. Although the existing links between social background and the policy behavior of public administrators are not fully understood, some governmental policy makers have sought greater social representation in the federal bureaucracy on the assumption that there is a close connection between the two.[35] Another aspect of the theory of representative bureaucracy stresses that the allegiance of various social groups to the government can be enhanced by including their members in all institutions of public power, including administrative agencies. Finally, it is sometimes argued that government serves as an example (or model employer) for the society at large and that therefore its behavior has widespread ramifications for private personnel practices and the general treatment of groups. The federal government and many states prize social diversity in their civil services and want their governments to "look like America" in President Bill Clinton's memorable phrase.[36] Consequently, EEO has emerged as a central element of public personnel administration.

Equal employment opportunity began to emerge as a major personnel concern in the 1940s, when the first program for nondiscrimination was established in the federal government. The program was introduced against a background of rampant racial discrimination and segregation in the federal service. By the 1960s EEO was a central programmatic effort in the personnel field. The Civil Rights Act of 1964 placed the policy of establishing EEO in federal personnel management on the basis of statute. The Equal Employment Opportunity Act of 1972 strengthened this commitment and extended it to state and local governments, many of which had their own programs earlier. The Federal Civil Service Reform Act of 1978 further strengthened the commitment to EEO by making a socially representative federal workforce a policy objective.

The main reason why an EEO program is necessary is that traditional managerially oriented public personnel administration neither produced socially representative bureaucracies nor prevented racial, ethnic, gender, and religious discrimination. The managerial quest for efficiency and a smoothly functioning public administration sometimes served as a rationale for blatant discrimination. When Woodrow Wilson extended the practice of racial segregation in the federal service, he claimed that it would reduce social "friction" that interfered with administrative operations.[37] More important, merit examinations for a wide range of careers, including police, fire, sanitation, and general administration, all too frequently manifested an adverse disparate impact on African Americans, Hispanics, and perhaps Native Americans. Many civil rights activists considered the merit system to be the major barrier to equal opportunity and a socially representative public workforce.

Women, too, have faced a host of barriers to equal employment opportunity. In the past they were excluded from many positions in law enforcement and from positions requiring travel with male coworkers. The latter exclusion was based on a fear of "moral dangers." Until the 1970s, pregnancy could legally be a basis for discrimination. MSPB studies in 1980 and 1994 found high levels of sexual harassment of women in the federal service. More than 40 percent of women and 15–20 percent of men reported being sexually harassed in the workplace. Only recently have women, like minorities, gained substantial representation in the SES.

Equal employment opportunity and representativeness also encompass those with disabilities. The Americans with Disabilities Act of 1990 is a landmark in this regard.[38] It covers individuals who have physical or mental impairments that substantially limit at least one of life's major activities or who are regarded as having such impairments. The act's basic principle requires employers to make reasonable accommodations for qualified individuals to whom it applies. This can include making workplaces accessible, restructuring jobs, modifying schedules, adjusting or acquiring equipment, and providing interpreters and readers. Under federal Equal Employment Opportunity Commission regulations, employers may not initiate discussions about disabilities with job applicants. Employers should begin processing requests for reasonable accommodations as soon as they are made, must provide reasons in writing for denials, and should use dispute resolution procedures to address contested denials. In July 2000, President Bill Clinton directed the agencies collectively to hire 100,000 people with disabilities during the next five years.[39] Overall, about 7 percent of all federal workers have disabilities. On the tenth anniversary of Clinton's directive, President Barack Obama issued Executive Order 13548,[40] mandating "Increasing Federal Employment of Individuals With Disabilities" and charging the Office of Personnel Management, Equal Employment Opportunity Commission, Department of Labor, and Office of Management and Budget with developing strategies, including the use of numerical targets, for so doing.

Since the 1960s public personnel programs have made a commitment to and efforts at establishing greater EEO. For the most part, this commitment is manifested in personnel activities intended to (1) reach all segments of the population in recruitment efforts; (2) eliminate artificial barriers to equal opportunity, such as height and weight requirements; (3) eliminate racial or ethnic bias from merit examinations; (4) establish upward-mobility training programs for minority and female employees; and (5) eliminate all vestiges of discriminatory thinking and practice from the entire gamut of personnel actions, including promotions, assignments, and position classifications. Although these principles are usually focused most on women and members of minority groups (primarily African Americans, Hispanics, indigenous North American peoples, Asian Americans, and Pacific Islanders), they also apply to persons with disabilities. About a dozen states also prohibit discrimination based on sexual orientation.

Two broad techniques have emerged to achieve these objectives. One is the EEO Complaint System and related opportunities for litigation in the courts. Contemporary complaint systems seek to provide a quick resolution of problems related to prohibited discrimination. They stress informal resolution and corrective action. However, when neither of these is forthcoming, a complaint system is likely to provide for elaborate adjudicatory hearings at which both sides can present evidence, testify, and seek to rebut the other. To be credible, complaint systems must also offer sufficient remedies, including back pay, promotion, desired training, and other personnel actions. Moreover, discriminatory supervisors must be disciplined.

Although in the abstract complaint systems often appear eminently fair, in practice they tend to be problematic and to generate anxiety. The most vexing difficulty has been resolving complaints on a timely basis. Supervisors also contend that they are inadequately protected against frivolous or misguided complaints and cannot do their jobs under the threat of such actions. Complainants have frequently voiced the view that complaint systems are not truly impartial, but rather tend to favor management.[41]

The second technique for achieving EEO has been the use of **affirmative action.**[42] This has been far more controversial and continues to divide American society. Philosophically, affirmative action represents a departure from traditional concepts of equal opportunity. Rather than seeking to assure equal opportunity to compete for civil service positions, affirmative action seeks to assure equality in the outcome of the competition for those positions. Proponents of affirmative action usually argue that, at the least, members of groups that were thoroughly discriminated against in the past should be entitled to special, compensatory treatment until the effects of earlier practices have been eliminated. Such preferences may include special recruitment and promotion efforts, preferential allocation of training opportunities, and reevaluation of position classification systems to facilitate the upward mobility of people belonging to those groups. Opponents of affirmative action usually argue that it constitutes "reverse discrimination" against white males and undercuts the merit system.

Public sector affirmative action is now substantially constrained by the Fourteenth Amendment's equal protection clause. Contemporary equal protection analysis subjects all racial and ethnic classifications to strict judicial scrutiny, regardless of whether the intent is to help minorities.[43] A heavy burden of persuasion falls on the government involved to show a compelling interest for using the classifications and to demonstrate that they are narrowly tailored to serve that interest. Gender classifications are constitutional if they are substantially related to the achievement of important governmental objectives, a somewhat weaker test. (Equal protection analysis is discussed in greater detail in Chapter 11.)

To date the Supreme Court has held that quotas (more drastic than goals and timetables) can be used to remedy egregious past, proven, illegal, and/or unconstitutional racial discrimination in public sector hiring.[44] Quotas favoring minorities in layoffs and reductions-in-force are likely to be illegal and/or unconstitutional because they are not narrowly tailored; they cause nonminority employees to be dismissed according to racial or ethnic criteria.[45] The Court has upheld the legality (but not the constitutionality) of affirmative action that is voluntary (that is, not imposed as a remedy for past proven discrimination) in promotions.[46]

In recent years, public displays of religion have become common in American life, including among public employees. Civil rights law and EEO regulations prohibit religious discrimination, but some religious practices can be disruptive of office routines. The courts have not yet developed a comprehensive set of guidelines for determining which religious behavior in the workplace is protected and which is not. President Clinton issued a memo that may provide useful guidance to administrators in jurisdictions without comprehensive rules (see Box 5.7).

◆→   THE LEGAL APPROACH TO PUBLIC PERSONNEL ADMINISTRATION

The legal approach to public personnel administration places the constitutional relationship between citizen and government above the relationship between public employer and employee. It focuses on and values highly the rights and liberties of individual public employees and applicants for civil service jobs. It particularly emphasizes the need for fair and equitable procedures in adverse personnel actions and other situations in which an employee or applicant stands to lose or be denied something valuable to him or her. Moreover, the legal approach emphasizes the need for equal protection of the laws and consequently opposes racial, ethnic, gender, and some other forms of discrimination. By and large, this approach to public personnel administration stands in contrast to the managerial and political approaches. Its expansive

5.7 MEMORANDUM ON RELIGIOUS EXERCISE AND RELIGIOUS EXPRESSION IN THE FEDERAL WORKPLACE, AUGUST 14, 1997

Guiding Principles:

1. Federal agencies should permit employees to engage in personal religious expression in the workplace to the greatest extent possible, consistent with efficiency and the requirements of law.
2. Agencies may not discriminate in any aspect of employment on the basis of religion. Agencies are obligated to prevent supervisors or employees from engaging in harassment based on religion or creating a hostile environment through insult or ridicule of religious beliefs or practices.
3. Agencies must reasonably accommodate employees' religious practices. The need for accommodation arises in many circumstances—for example, when work schedules interfere with Sabbath or other religious holiday observances or when work rules prevent an employee from wearing religiously compelled dress. Once again, governmental interests in workplace efficiency may be at stake in such cases. But an agency . . . must always accommodate an employee's religious practice in the absence of nonspeculative costs and may need to accommodate such practice even when doing so will impose some hardship on the agency's operations.

Source: Weekly Compilation of Presidential Documents, vol. 33: 1246–1248.

view of employee rights and due process weakens the traditional managerial approach's reliance on hierarchical control and direction of public employees. It may also confound NPM efforts to deregulate public personnel management. Supreme Court decisions have also created constitutional barriers to patronage practices and affirmative action that have undercut the value of representation as asserted by the political approach. The courts have also handed down decisions making loyalty-security programs, such as those of the 1940s and 1950s, difficult to establish within constitutional grounds. At some points, however, the political and legal approaches are in greater agreement, such as in the realm of EEO and equal access to civil service jobs.

The Constitutional Rights of Public Employees and Applicants

In the early 1950s some federal civil servants were dismissed from their employment on the grounds that a reasonable doubt existed as to their loyalty to the United States. Prior to dismissal, an employee might have gone through a hearing before a Loyalty Review Board. The members of the board would be furnished, by the FBI or the CSC, with information impugning the loyalty of the employee. The information would come from informants unknown to the board, and the statements might be unsworn. The employee was not afforded a right to confrontation and cross-examination of these adverse "witnesses." In one case that reached the Supreme Court, part of the evidence against an employee was that she had written a letter to the Red Cross protesting the segregation of blood by race for social—not medical—reasons. A lower court decision, affirmed by an equally divided Supreme Court, held that although justice seemed to have been compromised, "the plain hard fact" was that there was no constitutional prohibition on the dismissal of public employees because of their political beliefs, activities, or affiliations.[47] In other words, public employees had few constitutionally protected civil rights and liberties, and consequently, it was not necessary to develop elaborate procedures to protect them against misguided and damaging dismissals.

By the 1970s the Supreme Court indicated that it had "fully and finally" rejected "the concept that constitutional rights turn upon whether a governmental benefit is characterized as a 'right' or as a 'privilege.'"[48] Instead, the Court declared that public employees do indeed have constitutional rights and that these rights cannot be "chilled," abridged, violated, or denied simply because the individual works for the civil service (see Chapter 11). However, governments have greater leeway in regulating employees than citizens at large because "the government's interest in achieving its goals as effectively and efficiently as possible is elevated from a relatively subordinate interest when it acts as a sovereign [in dealing with ordinary citizens] to a significant one when it acts as employer."[49] Where there is some infringement on the constitutional rights of public employees today, such as in the area of political neutrality, the government is required to demonstrate that such limitations are directly related to the necessities of the workplace or serve some overriding value, such as good, nonpartisan government.

A comprehensive treatment of the contemporary constitutional rights of public employees as they affect public personnel management would take volumes. Here we will identify some of the most outstanding instances of judicial involvement in public personnel. One of these is in the area of procedural due process, which addresses the fairness of the procedures under which a public employee is subjected to an adverse personnel action. Today public employees are likely to have a *constitutional* (not only statutory or administrative) right to a hearing in adverse actions if (1) the basis of those actions is the exercise of an ordinary constitutional right, such as freedom of association; (2) the action is likely to damage the employee's reputation, such as labeling him or her dishonest or immoral; (3) there is something about the employee (age perhaps) or the job (possibly highly specialized) that would drastically reduce the civil servant's future employability if dismissed; or (4) the employee holds a contractual, tenure, or other "property interest" in the job.[50]

The legal approach to public personnel administration places a strong emphasis on adversary procedure. Hearings are usually before impartial examiners and may be so elaborate that they resemble courtroom procedure.

Appeals may go to independent boards such as the MSPB and EEOC. Employee and employer (supervisor) are pitted against one another at the hearing, yet at the same time, or in the future, they may have to work together. In some respects, elaborate hearings are inappropriate from managerial perspectives. They seriously compromise control and direction through the exercise of hierarchical authority, and they exaggerate the adversary relations between superordinates and subordinates. The extent to which the legal approach dominates the procedure for dismissals is evident from the fact that managers need to build their cases for dismissal, rather than only assert that in their judgment dismissal is warranted. Removals can also be complicated by EEO antidiscrimination regulations and by grievance procedures negotiated through collective bargaining.

Freedom of expression is another area in which the courts have dramatically changed the nature of public personnel administration. Today public employees have a broad constitutional right to engage in "whistle-blowing"; that is, they are relatively free to speak out as citizens on matters of public concern, including waste, abuse, fraud, corruption, dangers to the public health or safety, or misguided policy in the public service. The major limitation is that employees' speech or written reports and documents that are part of a work assignment lack First Amendment protection.[51] Their right to disseminate whistle blower information to the public is protected even if their statements are inaccurate (unless the employee knows they are false or displays a reckless disregard for truth or falsity). The right to "whistle-blow" recognizes that a public employee's ultimate loyalty should be to the public rather than to a specific agency or manager. Consequently, it places strains on efforts to promote efficiency through loyalty to the organization and strict obedience to agency leadership.[52]

Developments in the area of freedom of association have also been revolutionary. The courts have declared that public employees have a constitutional right to join organizations, including labor unions. This reversed a policy followed by some states that outlawed public sector labor organizations. Moreover, it has fostered the development of elaborate collective bargaining in the public sector—a development that radically changes public personnel management, as we will soon consider. Further, the Supreme Court has held that public employees cannot constitutionally be compelled to join organizations, including political parties and labor unions.

The judiciary has handed down a number of decisions that protect the broad constitutional liberties of public employees. Among the most important are those dealing with mandatory maternity leaves. The traditional managerially oriented practice required a woman to begin a maternity leave well before the expected date of birth of her child. This made it possible to plan for a replacement employee for her and also was thought to assure that her physical condition would not interfere with her ability to perform her job. However, the Supreme Court found such rationales to be unsatisfactory.[53] It held that unless the maternity leave is geared to the woman's medical condition, that is, her ability to do her job, or begins late in the term of a normal pregnancy, it constitutes an unconstitutional infringement on a woman's liberty to choose whether to have a child.

The courts have also been active in determining the constitutionality of random drug testing of public employees. In *National Treasury Union v. Von Raab* (1989),[54] the Supreme Court found no Fourth Amendment barrier to testing customs agents, who are involved in drug interdiction, among other activities. A related decision upheld the constitutionality of drug testing for those in public safety positions.[55] Today random drug testing is widespread not only among law enforcement and public safety personnel but also among those who work in sensitive policy areas or even in close proximity to the president and perhaps other top-level officials at all levels of government. In 2001 the State Department placed about half its 26,000 employees in its random testing pool. Overall the federal government conducted 257,576 tests, which yielded 1,345 positive results for a hit rate of 0.52 percent. The cost was almost $32 million, or $23,637 per positive test result.[56]

The legal approach has had an important impact on equal employment opportunity. The judiciary has played a significant role in establishing standards for determining what kinds of personnel practices constitute unconstitutional violations of the right to equal protection of the laws. Today, under Supreme Court rulings, a personnel practice having an adverse impact on a specific social group will *not* be unconstitutional unless it manifests a discriminatory purpose. However, where courts have found discriminatory treatment to be unconstitutional, they have sometimes responded with far-reaching intervention in public personnel administration. They have found several merit examinations to be unacceptable and have required jurisdictions to develop new procedures for hiring, promoting, and laying off employees.[57] Box 5.8 illustrates how complex contemporary EEO can be from a legal perspective.

The Liability and Immunity of Public Employees

The mere declaration of constitutional or legal rights does not ensure their enforcement. Independent enforcement mechanisms may be necessary when new legal or constitutional rights are established. This is especially true when these rights stand in contravention of long-standing administrative, political, or social practice. The constitutional barrier to patronage dismissals is a good example. Thus far, the judiciary has tended to promote enforcement of employees' constitutional rights through two types of approaches. One, as discussed earlier, is the requirement of procedural due process in adverse actions. The other can be described briefly but has far-reaching ramifications.

In the 1970s the Supreme Court expanded the scope of public employees' liability in civil suits for damages for violating an individual's constitutional rights. These are known as **constitutional tort** suits, that is, civil suits seeking compensation for injuries to constitutional rights. But the individual whose rights have been violated may be another public servant. At the state and local levels, if a supervisor, public personnel administrator, or other official violates a subordinate's "clearly established . . . constitutional rights of which a

5.8   "Damned If You Do and Damned If You Don't": The Complexity of Public Sector Equal Employment Opportunity Law

Ricci v. DeStefano (2009) presented the Supreme Court with a case that illustrates the complexity of public sector equal employment opportunity law. As the Court explained:

> In 2003, 118 New Haven [CT] firefighters took examinations to qualify for promotion to the rank of lieutenant or captain. Promotion examinations in New Haven . . . were infrequent, so the stakes were high. The results would determine which firefighters would be considered for promotions during the next two years, and the order in which they would be considered. Many firefighters studied for months, at considerable personal and financial cost.
>
> When the examination results showed that white candidates had outperformed minority candidates, the mayor and other local politicians opened a public debate that turned rancorous. Some firefighters argued the tests should be discarded because the results showed the tests to be discriminatory. They threatened a discrimination lawsuit if the City made promotions based on the tests. Other firefighters said the exams were neutral and fair. And they, in turn, threatened a discrimination lawsuit if the City, relying on the statistical racial disparity, ignored the test results and denied promotions to the candidates who had performed well. In the end the City took the side of those who protested the test results. It threw out the examinations.
>
> Certain white and Hispanic firefighters who likely would have been promoted based on their good test performance sued the City and some of its officials. Theirs is the suit now before us. The suit alleges that, by discarding the test results, the City and the named officials discriminated against the plaintiffs based on their race, in violation of both Title VII of the Civil Rights Act of 1964 . . . and the Equal Protection Clause of the Fourteenth Amendment. The City and the officials defended their actions, arguing that if they had certified the results, they could have faced liability under Title VII for adopting a practice that had a disparate impact on the minority firefighters. . . .
>
> We conclude that race-based action like the City's in this case is impermissible under Title VII unless the employer can demonstrate a strong basis in evidence that, had it not taken the action, it would have been liable under the disparate-impact statute. The [City], we further determine, cannot meet that threshold standard. As a result, the City's action in discarding the tests was a violation of Title VII. In light of our ruling under the statutes, we need not reach the question whether respondents' actions may have violated the Equal Protection Clause.

During oral argument in the Court, Justice David Souter observed that New Haven could be construed to be in a "damned if you do, damned if you don't situation." Other than litigation, there was no obvious way to resolve the dispute. The Court's decision was 5–4 with two concurring opinions and one dissent, indicating how difficult New Haven's dilemma was.

Sources: Ricci v. DeStefano, 557 U.S. 557 (2009) and Robert N. Roberts, "Damned If You Do and Damned If You Don't: Title VII and Public Employee Promotion Disparate Treatment and Disparate Impact Litigation," *Public Administration Review*, 70 (No. 4/July/August 2010): 582–590.

reasonable person would have known," the subordinate may file a civil suit seeking damages.[58] The same is true of applicants whose constitutional rights have been violated. The suit may be against the official as an individual and may seek punitive damages, that is, more money than the amount of damage caused by the unconstitutional action. For instance, a supervisor who fires a subordinate for joining a union or another association may be vulnerable to such a suit. So may an official whose actions are unconstitutionally discriminatory. Liability may be incurred if the evolving constitutional law gives the employee "fair warning" that his or her actions would violate someone's rights.[59] If so, he or she may be liable, regardless of intent. The point of liability is not only to compensate individuals for wrongs done to them but also to deter public officials from violating individuals' constitutional rights. Consequently, it becomes an important enforcement mechanism that strongly encourages public officials to scrupulously avoid abridging the constitutional rights of others.

In *Bush v. Lucas* (1983), the Supreme Court held that federal employees cannot sue supervisors for damages for breach of their First Amendment rights because Congress had established an elaborate alternative protective scheme, including appeals to the MSPB.[60] This decision recognizes another remedy; it does not increase or reduce the scope of federal employees' constitutional rights.

Municipalities may also be found legally liable when their policies result in the violation of constitutional rights. Here the sole issue is whether a municipality's policies led to an unconstitutional abridgment of individual rights.[61] Because public employees have a wide array of First, Fourth, Fifth, and Fourteenth Amendment rights, civil suits are common.

◆ COLLECTIVE BARGAINING AND LABOR-MANAGEMENT PARTNERSHIPS

The managerial, political, and legal approaches to public personnel administration emphasize different values and frequently conflict with one another. This has the tendency to fragment personnel practice, making it somewhat incoherent. For instance, merit, EEO's interests in a socially representative workforce, and veteran preference coexist on uneasy terms, as do traditional hierarchical managerial authority, the NPM's effort to deregulate personnel practices, and constitutional procedural due process. Political patronage and the rights of public employees clash even more directly. These tensions and conflicts raise the question running throughout much public administration of whether it is possible to synthesize or combine the three approaches in some fashion. At the moment, in public personnel administration, the answer is: to some extent, but not completely. For the most part, progress toward this end has been made through the rise of a model of public personnel administration—one that stresses **codetermination** of policy through the process of collective bargaining and labor-management partnerships.

Collective Bargaining

Until the 1960s, collective bargaining in the public sector was frequently considered a threat to constitutional democracy in the United States. It was thought absurd that organized public employees could bargain with the government as a coequal or that matters of public policy would be determined in any forum other than the legislature, elected and appointed executives, or courts. In particular, strikes were feared because they represented a breakdown of the public order and could lead to chaos. Many states viewed collective bargaining as a threat to sovereignty, and the federal government had no general policy or practice for collective bargaining by its employees.

All this changed with remarkable rapidity. In large part, the rise of collective bargaining has been related to the growth of public employment and the political pressure exerted by unions. Many unions viewed the public sector as a promising recruiting ground in the face of declining private sector union membership. Today public sector collective bargaining is found in the federal government and at one level or another in almost all the states. Yet to a large extent it remains a patchwork of practices. There is no national law on the subject, and state laws and practices vary widely in their coverage and content. Nonetheless, a common pattern has emerged. Public personnel policy is now largely determined through a framework of labor-management relations that incorporates substantial parts of the managerial, political, and legal approaches to personnel administration.

Collective bargaining is based on the following general pattern: Employees in the same occupations (teachers, police, firefighters, clerks, etc.) or performing similar kinds of work (general administrative work, for instance) organize into **bargaining units.** Through an election or submission of union membership cards to the employer, a majority of the employees in the unit can designate a single union to bargain on behalf of *all* the employees in the unit. This is known as **exclusive recognition** (of the union). Precisely what can be bargained over is called the **scope of bargaining.** It may be relatively comprehensive and include wages, hours, fringe benefits, position classification, promotion procedures, training, discipline, grievances, holidays, sick leave, seniority preferences, overtime assignments, and other working conditions. Conversely, it may be narrow, confined largely to matters of discipline and the issuance of safety clothing, coffee breaks, and parking spaces. It is useful to think of the scope of bargaining as items over which bargaining is mandatory, items over which it is permitted, and items over which it is prohibited. When labor and management cannot reach agreement on matters subject to mandatory bargaining, an impasse results. Resolution of the impasse can take many forms, including mediation, fact finding, and arbitration. Once there is agreement among the parties or a binding arbitration award is handed down, a contract is signed and goes into effect. Some states, including Alaska, California, Hawaii, Minnesota, Montana, and Pennsylvania, allow strikes when an impasse persists. Again, depending on the scope of bargaining, this may amount to codetermination by labor and management of the conditions of employment.

The collective bargaining approach outlined here readily takes advantage of managerial, political, and legal perspectives. It is no accident that the first federal executive order on the subject declared that labor-management relations could foster efficiency and democracy.[62] From a traditional managerial perspective, the emergent collective bargaining model promotes the following. First, it clearly defines the rights of management and makes these rights non-bargainable. Examples would be the right to direct employees and determine the budget of an agency. Second, it facilitates communication between management and employees, which provides supervisors and other officials with valuable information as to how efficiency and economy can be improved. A closely related benefit is that it facilitates the participation of employees in determining the conditions under which they work. Within limits, such participation may create greater job satisfaction, loyalty to the organization, and, therefore, efficiency. Finally, the employee grievance system (discussed later in this chapter) negotiated through collective bargaining serves to alert management to serious problems and unfit supervisors. Yet collective bargaining is not primarily a management tool, and it clearly presents challenges to managers who cling to traditional practices and notions of hierarchical authority.

The political approach is also evident in the collective bargaining model. On the one hand, the value of representation is fundamental to public sector collective bargaining. Part of the purpose of organized labor relations is to provide civil servants with a voice in determining the nature of working conditions in government employment. Apart from actual bargaining sessions, public employees are to be represented by unions in many personnel matters and unions are frequently consulted on changes in public policy that may affect their jobs.

At the same time, however, the political approach demands that public sector collective bargaining practices serve the public interest and not undermine the responsiveness of government to the electorate. Consequently, certain limitations have been placed on public sector labor relations that make the collective bargaining process different from private sector practices. Most notably in this context are comprehensive restrictions on the scope of bargaining and the prohibition or regulation of strikes. Many jurisdictions have enacted a strong management rights clause that severely limits the items over which collective bargaining can take place. Frequently, agency missions, budgets, public policies, technologies, recruitment, selection, and sometimes the basis for disciplinary proceedings are outside the scope of bargaining. Within the ambit of these limitations lie fundamental conditions of work. For instance, in some jurisdictions teachers cannot bargain over the number of pupils per class or the school calendar; similarly, police may not be able to bargain over deployment (one- or two-person patrols), weapons, and defensive gear. Some employees, including most nonpostal workers in the federal government, are prohibited from bargaining over wages and hours. These restrictions are a legacy of the concept of sovereignty. The main point of a limited scope of bargaining is to ensure that matters of public policy are determined by representative governmental institutions rather than through a special process that shares political authority with private organizations.

Some prohibitions or limitations on the right to strike are found in all the states and in the federal government. Although not always effective, these restrictions raise the cost of strikes to employees and unions and probably serve as a deterrent to them. Many view the strike as fundamental to any serious collective bargaining process. However, by and large the political approach to public administration has ruled it out not only because it could lead to chaos, but also because it tends to provide organized public employees with a means of compromising the responsiveness of government to the citizenry. For example, teachers and parents have an interest in school calendars and the curriculum. Providing teachers with the right to bargain over these matters and use the strike in an effort to compel the government (school board) to accept their will gives the teachers leverage over public policy that is not available to parents. The parents can neither collectively bargain nor strike. They can vote for school board members and lobby, but so can teachers. According to the political approach, if government is to be responsive to the public interest, public policy cannot be the outcome of labor negotiations and strikes. The public interest cannot be held hostage by striking public employees or bargained over in negotiating sessions.

These restrictions on the public sector collective bargaining model reduce its coherence and limit its effectiveness. It is clear that the model cannot work well or be meaningful if the scope of bargaining is too narrow to serve as a vehicle for employees to affect their working conditions. It may also be true that management will not take public employees seriously in bargaining sessions unless the employees have a weapon such as the strike. The absence of the right to strike requires some other means of resolving impasses. This brings us to the legal approach.

Overwhelmingly, the public sector collective bargaining model has moved in the direction of arbitration as a means of resolving impasses. **Arbitration** can be over *interests* such as wages and hours or over *grievances* involving the mistreatment of an employee or another violation of a contract. It can take many forms. The most forceful interest arbitration is compulsory and binding. This compels the parties to enter into arbitration when an impasse occurs and requires them to accept the arbitrators' award. Arbitration is a judicial-style process. The individual arbitrator or panel hears the views and proposals of both sides in what amounts to an adversary proceeding. The facts are then weighed, principles according to which a judgment will be made are considered, and a decision is handed down. In **final offer arbitration** the arbitrator is limited to choosing from the contract proposal made by each side. This format puts pressure on management and labor to make reasonable offers lest the arbitrator select the other's proposal. In *whole package* final offer arbitration, the arbitrator is limited to selecting one offer in its entirety. *Item-by-item* final offer arbitration allows the arbitrator to select from among the two sides' proposals. For instance, the arbitrator may choose management's wage proposal and labor's proposal for protection against layoffs.

Grievance arbitration often involves discipline and work assignments. It can be similar to adverse action hearings. It is common and places challenges and constraints on public managers, who find their flexibility in dealing with employees to be severely limited.

Because collective bargaining favors negotiation and agreement by the parties, arbitration is generally viewed as a last resort for resolving impasses. Less intrusive approaches include mediation, fact finding, and med-arb (mediation-arbitration). Mediators work with the parties to reduce the distance between their proposals. They generate "supposals": suppose management does this, will you do that? They also keep the negotiators focused on the issues rather than allowing personalities and the desire to win for the sake of winning get in the way of settlement. In med-arb, the mediator works with the parties to resolve as much as possible and then arbitrates the remaining disputed issues. Fact finders are used when the parties disagree over an empirical matter such as increases in the cost of living since the last contract was signed and matters of pay comparability.

Interest and grievance arbitration make much of the collective bargaining model look like a quasi-judicial process. By regulating strikes the public sector model has taken conflict off the streets and away from the collective bargaining table and placed its resolution in the hands of arbitrators who act like judges.

Comprehensive programs for collective bargaining provide for Public Employment Relations Boards (PERBs) or equivalent agencies, such as the Federal Labor Relations Authority. These agencies adjudicate or oversee the adjudication of unfair labor practice charges, disputes over the authorized scope of bargaining, the appropriateness of the bargaining units that employees seek to organize, and other matters. PERBs may also have rule making authority regarding labor relations.

The judiciary's concern with constitutional rights and values has led to a number of decisions that have had a major impact on public sector collective bargaining. One, already mentioned, is that public employees have the right to join unions, though there is no constitutional right to engage in collective bargaining. Another is that the "union shop," that is, an arrangement whereby all employees in a collective bargaining unit must join the exclusively recognized union, is an unconstitutional abridgment of public employees' right to freedom of association.[63] However, an "agency shop" requiring all employees to pay fees to a union for its services as a collective bargaining agent is permissible. Just how far the legal approach penetrates collective bargaining is evident from the Supreme Court's holding in *Chicago Teachers Union v. Hudson* (1986) that "the constitutional requirements for the Union's collection of agency fees include an adequate explanation of the basis for the fee, a reasonably prompt opportunity to challenge the amount of the fee before an impartial decision maker, and an escrow for the amounts reasonably in dispute while such challenges are pending."[64] The Supreme Court has also refused to allow the principle of exclusive recognition to stifle the ability of public employees to express their views on matters of public policy in public forums.[65]

Labor-Management Partnerships

The NPM argues that traditional public sector labor relations create rigid and rule-bound personnel practices, militate against performance, and promote adversary relationships between workers and managers. The NPR advocated a new model for the federal government that would rely on labor-management partnerships. The partnership approach embodies the following principles:

1. Federal workers are valued as full partners in substantive and procedural decision making. They have a role in transforming agency structures and work processes.
2. Consensual methods should replace adversarial ones in resolving problems.
3. Collective bargaining promotes the public interest when it embraces "[t]he elements of a good government standard [that include] . . . the promotion of increased quality and productivity, customer service, mission accomplishment, efficiency, quality of work life, employee empowerment, organizational performance, and, in the case of the Department of Defense, military readiness."
4. Dispute resolution should be "fair, simple, determinative, and inexpensive."
5. "Union effectiveness is one of the cornerstones of the productive workplace partnership."[66]

Many bargaining units quickly formed partnership councils to develop the new model. However, after the 1994 congressional elections, labor's enthusiasm flagged in the face of its inability to obtain the right to set up agency shops, continuing pressure for deep cutbacks in personnel, and furloughs caused by a protracted budget dispute between Congress and the president. Toward the end of the 1990s, the partnership model seemed to be making limited progress in a few agencies, but in February 2001, President Bush rescinded President Clinton's executive orders regarding partnerships.

CONCLUSION: THREE POSSIBLE FUTURES FOR HRM

Since their rudimentary beginnings in the 1880s, modern American public personnel systems have moved from relative simplicity to considerable complexity. But a countertrend is under way. Today a comprehensive public personnel program would address merit testing, information systems, planning, classification and position audits, compensation, recruitment, selection, performance evaluation, promotion, training, health (including wellness and assistance programs), equal opportunity, labor relations, retirement, family policies, attitude surveys, and perhaps drug testing. A central personnel agency has to deal with elected and appointed executives, legislators, courts, unions, and veterans and a variety of other groups. The pressure on such agencies and personnel systems to perform well is intense—in many cases too intense to be satisfied. The NPM contends change toward simplification is inevitable. Assuming, without necessarily agreeing, that is correct, what directions will it take?

Three broad approaches are apparent. First, personnel systems will continue to be decentralized and made more flexible. Central personnel agencies will be called on to do less, and individual agencies to do more. If the federal government's actions signal a direction, one-size-fits-all regulations will be abandoned in favor of laws and rules tailor-made for specific agencies based on their missions. As part of overall deregulation, employees will gain more responsibility but will have less legal (though not necessarily constitutional) protection in the workplace. Quality of work life policies will take on greater importance.

If labor relations partnerships can substitute for traditional collective bargaining approaches, rigid work rules, grievances, and complaints of unfair labor practices should be reduced and less adversarial methods of problem solving should be adopted. Traditional personnel systems designed for unskilled industrial workers are not the best fit for today's well-educated, information-age public employees. Government can be a model employer, but not while saddled with a convoluted, century-old personnel system.

A second approach to simplification is also available: privatization. As early in the reinvention movement as 1993, a survey of state agencies for general administration, corrections, education, health, mental health, social services, and transportation indicated that about 78 percent of such organizations contracted out for some services, functions, or goods.[67] Privatization remains controversial. Public sector employees and their unions oppose it. It can obscure accountability. Whether (and when) it promotes significant cost savings for comparable service is frequently disputed. However, privatization does enable governments to avoid many of the costs of their personnel systems. When a function is contracted out, the government does not have to recruit, test, select, promote, discipline, provide direct benefits, bargain, or otherwise deal with the workers who perform it. From a personnel standpoint, contracting out simplifies in the extreme. The temptation to do so is often great, even when the potential cost savings may be negligible or marginally negative. Every government will define some functions as "core" and, therefore, not subject to privatization.

A third possible way of simplifying public personnel administration is to "blow it up,"[68] that is, abandon traditional civil service systems altogether. To some extent this is what Texas, Florida, and Georgia have done. Georgia's approach is the most extreme and perhaps is illustrative of this path to change in governmental HRM. In 1996, Georgia undertook a civil service "meltdown." By 2012, the proportion of its employees covered by civil service had declined from 82 percent to just 12 percent.[69] Its strategy is to give agencies responsibility for their own HRM, including recruitment and selection, promotion, position classification, dismissal, discipline, downsizing (for those hired or promoted after July 1, 1996), and some aspects of compensation. A survey of human resources professionals in 2006 indicated some negative aspects of the reform: there was a perception that they opened the door to "spoils," made employees feel less secure, diminished trust in management, and increased apprehension about whistle-blowing.[70] Whether Georgia's reform brings higher productivity, better results, and greater cost-effectiveness is not amenable to definitive analysis because much else has changed since 1996, including technology and a considerable proportion of its workforce. However, initial evaluations were largely positive and Georgia-style reforms have spread to other states.[71] Consequently, "blowing it up" remains a significant possibility. It is impossible to know which of these approaches—or a mix of them—will dominate future developments. Nevertheless it is safe to say that change is inevitable.

STUDY QUESTIONS

1. Many observers believe that contemporary public personnel systems are too complicated to be efficient or fair. Based on the chapter and your experiences, if you could recommend one change to a state legislative or U.S. congressional committee dealing with personnel, what would it be? Why?

2. The issue of whether public employees should be allowed to strike has been a concern of public personnel administration. Do you think all strikes by public employees should be prohibited? Why or why not? If you favor a right to strike, should any limitations be placed on it? What would these be, if any? Why?

3. Having read the chapter on personnel, what aspects of contemporary public personnel management would attract you to the public sector? Which, if any, would you find objectionable?

4. What elements, if any, would you add to or delete from the SES ECQs in Box 5.2? Why? Try to categorize the ECQs according to whether they predominantly reflect the concerns of the traditional managerial, NPM, political, or legal approaches to public administration. What conclusions do you draw?

NOTES

1. Al Gore, *From Red Tape to Results: Creating a Government That Works Better & Costs Less* (Washington, DC: Government Printing Office, 1993), 22.

2. There are several excellent histories of the federal service that emphasize personnel administration. See Frederick Mosher, *Democracy and the Public Service,* 2d ed. (New York: Oxford University Press, 1982); Paul P. Van Riper, *History of the United States Civil Service* (Evanston, IL: Row, Peterson, 1958); Leonard D. White's four-volume series, *The Federalists, The Jeffersonians, The Jacksonians,* and *The Republican Era* (New York: Free Press, 1965), paperback editions; and Stephen Skowronek, *Building a New American State* (Cambridge, UK: Cambridge University Press, 1982).

3. David H. Rosenbloom, *Federal Service and the Constitution* (Ithaca, NY: Cornell University Press, 1971), 36.

4. See ibid., 38–41 and chap. 2, for a discussion of Jefferson's appointment policy and that of Jackson.

5. Quoted in ibid., 49.

6. Ibid., 56.

7. Ibid., 49.

8. See Jay M. Shafritz et al., *Personnel Management in Government* (New York: Marcel Dekker, 1978), 16.

9. Rosenbloom, *Federal Service and the Constitution,* 55.

10. *Elrod v. Burns,* 427 U.S. 347 (1976); *Branti v. Finkel,* 445 U.S. 506 (1980); *Rutan v. Republican Party of Illinois,* 497 U.S. 62 (1990).

11. Rosenbloom, *Federal Service and the Constitution,* 73.

12. Ibid.

13. Ibid., 71.

14. Quoted in John A. Rohr, *To Run a Constitution* (Lawrence: University Press of Kansas, 1986), 72.

15. Matthew Josephson, *The Politicos* (New York: Harcourt, Brace & World, n.d.), 438.

16. Ari Hoogenboom, *Outlawing the Spoils* (Urbana: University of Illinois Press, 1961).

17. Rosenbloom, *Federal Service and the Constitution,* 80.

18. *New York Times,* 3 March 1978. See also David H. Rosenbloom, Ed., "Public Administration Forum: Civil Service Reform, 1978: Some Issues," *Midwest Review of Public Administration* 13 (September 1979): 171–188.

19. *New York Times,* 3 March 1978.

20. Alan K. Campbell, "Civil Service Reform: A New Commitment," *Public Administration Review* 38 (March/April 1978): 102.

21. Al Gore, *Creating a Government That Works Better & Costs Less: Reinventing Human Resource Management* (Washington, DC: Government Printing Office, 1993), 1.

22. Ibid., 3–4.

23. Wallace Sayre, "The Triumph of Techniques over Purpose," *Public Administration Review* 8 (Spring 1948): 134.

24. Charlie B. Tyer, "Employee Performance Appraisal: Process in Search of a Technique," in Steven Hays and Richard Kearney, Eds., *Public Personnel Administration* (Englewood Cliffs, NJ: Prentice-Hall, 1983), 118–136. The discussion in this paragraph is based on Tyer's essay.

25. Robert Kaplan and David Norton, *The Balanced Scorecard* (Boston: Harvard Business School Press, 1996).

26. S. S. Oh and G. B. Lewis, "Can Performance Appraisal Systems Inspire Intrinsically Motivated Employees?" *Review of Public Personnel Administration* 29 (No. 2, 2009): 158–167.

27. The seminal reading in this theory is James L. Perry and Lois Wise, "The Motivational Bases of Public Service," *Public Administration Review* 50, no. 3 (1990): 367–373. For a more complete review of research on motivating public employees see James L. Perry, Debra Mesch, and Laurie Paarlberg, "Motivating Employees in a New Governance Era: The Performance Paradigm Revisited," *Public Administration Review* 66, no. 4 (2006): 505–514; Oh and Lewis, "Can Performance Appraisal Systems Inspire Intrinsically Motivated Employees?"; K. Yang, "The Sisyphean Fate of Government–wide Performance Accountability Reforms: Federal Performance Management Efforts and Employees' Daily Work, 2002–2008," *Public Performance and Management Review* 35 (No. 1, 2011): 149–176. Major questions are whether linking pay to performance can weaken public employees' intrinsic motivation to do their jobs well and how to construct pay for performance systems that employees perceive as fair. It is important to

note that the connection between public service motivation and *organizational performance*, if any, is uncertain. See Nicolai Petrovsky, "Does Public Service Motivation Predict Higher Public Performance?" Martin School of Public Policy and Administration, University of Kentucky, September 24, 2009; http://www .ifigr.org/workshop/fall09/petrovsky.pdf.

28. U.S. Office of Personnel Management; www.opm.gov/feddata/retire/rs2004.pdf.

29. Linda Springer, Director, U.S. Office of Personnel Management; http://www .opm.gov/rsm/index.asp (accessed 8 March 2007).

30. Evan Berman, James Bowman, Jonathan West, and Montgomery Van Wart, *Human Resource Management in the Public Service* (Thousand Oaks, CA: Sage, 2001), 197.

31. *National Association of Letter Carriers v. Civil Service Commission,* 346 F. Supp. 578 (1972), at 581.

32. *Civil Service Commission v. National Association of Letter Carriers,* 413 U.S. 548 (1973).

33. Rosenbloom, *Federal Service and the Constitution,* chapter 6.

34. See Samuel Krislov and David H. Rosenbloom, *Representative Bureaucracy and the American Political System* (New York: Praeger, 1981), for a comprehensive discussion. See also, Julie Dolan and David H. Rosenbloom, Eds. *Representative Bureaucracy: Classic Readings and Continuing Controversies* (Armonk, NY: M.E. Sharpe, 2003).

35. See U.S. Commission on Civil Rights, *The Federal Civil Rights Enforcement Effort—1974,* vol. 5 (Washington, DC: Commission on Civil Rights, 1975), 6.

36. Katherine C. Naff, *To Look Like America* (Boulder, CO: Westview, 2001).

37. Arthur Link, *Wilson: The New Freedom* (Princeton, NJ: Princeton University Press, 1965), 251.

38. Federal employees' disability coverage is based on the Rehabilitation Act of 1973 (Public Law 93–112; 87 *Statutes at Large* 355 [September 26, 1973]), section 501.

39. Lisa Daniel, "Directive Taps into Disabled as Hiring Resource," *Federal Times,* 6 November 2000, 12.

40. 75 *Federal Register* 45039 (July 26, 2010).

41. See David H. Rosenbloom, *Federal Equal Employment Opportunity* (New York: Praeger, 1977), 126–138. See also Robert Vaughn, *The Spoiled System* (New York: Charterhouse, 1975); and M. Weldon Brewer, *Behind the Promises* (Washington, DC: Public Interest Research Group, 1972).

42. See Rosenbloom, *Federal Equal Employment Opportunity,* chap. 5, for a discussion.

43. *Adarand Constructors v. Peña,* 515 U.S. 200 (1995).

44. *United States v. Paradise,* 480 U.S. 189 (1987).

45. *Wygant v. Jackson,* 476 U.S. 267 (1986).

46. *Johnson v. Transportation Agency,* 480 U.S. 624 (1987).

47. *Bailey v. Richardson,* 182 F2d 46, 59 (1950); 341 U.S. 918 (1951).

48. *Sugarman v. Dougall,* 413 U.S. 634, 644 (1973); *Board of Regents v. Roth,* 408 U.S. 564, 571 (1972).

49. *Waters v. Churchill,* 511 U.S. 611, 674 (1994).

50. *Board of Regents v. Roth,* 408 U.S. 564, 571 (1972). See also *Cleveland Board of Education v. Loudermill,* 470 U.S. 532 (1985).

51. *Garcetti v. Ceballos,* 547 U.S. 410 (2006). The Supreme Court drew a distinction between public employees' speech on matters of public concern as citizens

and as employees. The result is that "work product" speech does not enjoy constitutional protection. Part of the Court's reasoning was based on a desire not to intrude into ordinary matters of public management.

52. See Robert Vaughn, "Statutory Protection of Whistleblowers in the Federal Executive Branch," *University of Illinois Law Review,* no. 3 (1982): 615–667; and "Public Employees and the Right to Disobey," *Hastings Law Journal* 29 (November 1977): 261–295. Although the legal right to whistle-blow is well established, whistle-blowers often face their employer's wrath for appearing to be disloyal to their organizations. Reprisals against whistle-blowers, though illegal, are common and difficult to prevent.

53. *Cleveland Board of Education v. LaFleur,* 414 U.S. 632 (1974); argued and decided with *Cohen v. Chesterfield County School Board.*

54. *National Treasury Employees Union v. Von Raab,* 489 U.S. 656 (1989).

55. *Skinner v. Railway Labor Executives' Association,* 489 U.S. 602 (1989).

56. Ellen Nakashima, "Group Protests Drug Testing Policy," *Washington Post,* 1 June 2001, A29.

57. For more extensive treatment of public employees' constitutional rights see David H. Rosenbloom, Rosemary O'Leary, and Joshua Chanin, *Public Administration and Law,* 3rd ed. (Boca Raton, FL: CRC/Taylor & Francis, 2010), chapter 6.

58. *Harlow v. Fitzagerald,* 457 U.S. 800, 818 (1982). This is true at present for state and local public employees under 42 U.S. Code section 1983. It does not apply to federal employees whose right of freedom of speech has been abridged; it may not apply in instances of violation of other constitutional rights of federal employees. See *Bush v. Lucas,* 462 U.S. 367 (1983). State and federal agencies cannot be sued in federal court for money damages for constitutional torts; by contrast, local governments and their agencies are subject to such suits. Public employees at all levels of governments and agency hierarchies are vulnerable to constitutional tort suits, though when engaged in adjudicatory functions, such as serving as administrative law judges, they have absolute immunity from such suits.

59. *Hope v. Pelzer,* 536 U.S. 730 (2002). See also *Harlow v. Fitzgerald,* 457 U.S. 800 (1982).

60. 462 U.S. 367.

61. See *Owen v. City of Independence,* 445 U.S. 622 (1980).

62. Executive Order 10988 *Federal Register* vol. 27, 17 January 1962, 551.

63. *Abood v. Detroit Board of Education,* 430 U.S. 209 (1977).

64. *Chicago Teachers Union v. Hudson,* 475 U.S. 292 (1986).

65. *City of Madison, Joint School District No. 8 v. Wisconsin Employment Relations Commission,* 429 U.S. 167 (1976).

66. National Partnership Council, *Partnership Handbook* (Washington, DC: Government Printing Office, 1994), 3.

67. Council of State Governments, *Book of the States, 1994–1995* (Lexington, KY: Council of State Governments, 1995), 411.

68. Jonathan Walters, *Life After Civil Service Reform: The Texas, Georgia, and Florida Experiences* (Arlington, VA: IBM Endowment for the Business of Government, 2002), 7.

69. Heather Kerrigan, "Civil service reform: Lessons from Georgia and Indiana," *Governing The States and Localities,* June 13, 2012; http://www.governing.com/topics/public-workforce/col-civil-service-reform-lessons-from-georgia-indiana.html.

70. R. Paul Battaglio, Jr. and Stephen Condrey, "Reforming Public Management: Analyzing the Impact of Public Service Reform on Organizational and Managerial Trust," *Journal of Public Administrative Research and Theory*, 19 (2009): 689–707; http://faculty.cbpp.uaa.alaska.edu/afgjp/PADM601%20 Fall%202010/Reforming%20Public%20Management.pdf.

71. Ibid. and Jonathan West, Ed., "Symposium Issue: Civil Service Reform in the State of Georgia," *Review of Public Personnel Administration* 22 (Summer 2002): 79–166. See also D. Goodman and P. French, "Assessing the Temporary Use of At-will Employment for Reorganization and Workforce Reduction in Mississippi State Government," *Review of Public Personnel Administration* 31 (No. 3, 2011): 270–290.

ADDITIONAL READING

Battaglio, R. Paul, Jr., and Christine B. Ledvinka. "Privatizing Human Resources in the Public Sector: Legal Challenges to Outsourcing the Human Resources Function," *Review of Public Personnel Administration*, 29 (No. 3/September 2009), 293–307.

Hays, Steven, Richard Kearney, and Jerrell Coggburn, Eds. *Public Personnel Administration: Problems and Prospects,* 6th ed. New York: Longman, 2014.

Ingraham, Patricia. *The Foundation of Merit.* Baltimore: Johns Hopkins University Press, 1995.

Naff, Katherine. *To Look Like America.* Boulder, CO: Westview, 2001.

Riccucci, Norma, Ed. *Public Personnel Management,* 5th ed. New York: Longman, 2011.

_____, Katherine Naff, and Siegrun Fox Freyss, *Personnel Management in Government,* 7th ed. Boca Raton, FL; CRC/Taylor & Francis, 2013.

Van Riper, Paul P. *History of the United States Civil Service.* Evanston, IL: Row, Peterson, 1958.

PUBLIC PERSONNEL WEB SITES

A great deal of current information regarding federal personnel administration can be found on the following Web sites:

U.S. Office of Personnel Management: http://www.opm.gov

U.S. Merit Systems Protection Board: http://www.mspb.gov

U.S. Equal Employment Opportunity Commission: http://www.eeoc.gov

American Federation of Government Employees: http://www.afge.org

The Brookings Institution: http://www.brookings.org

The American Federation of State, County, and Municipal Employees, AFL-CIO, has information on current developments, concerns, and initiatives in state and local human resources, at http://www.afscme.org.

CHAPTER 6

BUDGETING AND THE PUBLIC FINANCES

Key Learning Objectives

1. Understand the crucial importance of budgets and budgeting to modern public administration.

2. Explain the stages in the federal budgetary process in relation to the budget calendar.

3. Develop a working knowledge of the strengths and weaknesses of the various possible budget formats.

4. Be able to explain the various sources of revenue available to and used by governments at the federal, state, and local levels.

5. List and explain the general criteria for evaluating alternative sources of revenue, as well as the advantages and disadvantages of each source.

6. Understand the relationship between federal budget deficits, surpluses, and the growth of the national debt.

7. Explain the controversy about whether the national debt is a burden on future generations, or not.

Governmental finances today are receiving public attention as never before. Three decades of chronic federal deficits, at times accompanied by serious state budget deficits (not to mention several prominent cities that went or nearly went broke), have focused considerable attention on budgets at all levels of government. By 2013, the U.S. national debt had grown to unprecedented levels, mainly in response to unfunded new programs and deep cuts in federal income taxes, but also aggravated by efforts to reverse the effects of the Great Recession of 2007–09. Perceptions of waste, fraud, and abuse—real or imagined—have propelled efforts to reform budgets, their structures, and their procedures in ways that have involved actions by all three branches of government.

The public, it appears, wants many things from their governments' budgets. Citizens are concerned that their taxes be used in the wisest, most effective ways. Legislators want budgets responsive to society's needs. Executive branch officials are concerned with promoting managerial efficiency. And the courts have become involved in cases where lack of adequate funding threatens rights or benefits provided to individuals by law. These budget "players," and the competing values they embrace and serve, make public budgeting and finance a complex and interesting subject.

This chapter discusses various theories and ideas about how budgets should be formulated and executed, including the strengths and weaknesses of these approaches. We will see that, as in other aspects of public administration, budgeting and finance have managerial, political, and legal dimensions that lead to conflict and, at times, confusion. In the budgetary arena, these dimensions often come into sharp, almost irresolvable conflict. To learn how, we begin by discussing budgets and budgetary growth in general terms. We will then proceed to some of the more critical problems and the reforms that have been proposed from time to time to deal with them.

Budgeting is a public administrative activity of preeminent importance. Money is crucial to public administration. It is also scarce in that not all legitimate needs can be fully funded. Consequently, budgeting is usually surrounded by controversy and calls for reform. In view of the competing perspectives on public administration, no single budgetary process can satisfy everyone. Moreover, budgeting tends to be so complex in its political and economic ramifications that in many respects it defies understanding. This chapter explores just why this is so.

In essence, a governmental budget is a statement of social priorities. It indicates how much money a government proposes to spend. Equally important, it provides a record of a society's changing priorities. But this definition is a bit too simple. The budget also has a revenue dimension, which raises important questions: Will revenues be generated through taxes? If so, what kinds? Sales taxes, income taxes, corporate taxes, general consumption taxes, property taxes, excise taxes, luxury taxes? What will the mix be? What should it be? Will funds also need to be raised through borrowing? On the expenditure side, budgets indicate how governmental activity will be classified. Will expenditures be categorized by "objects," such as equipment, supplies, and salaries of government employees? Will they be categorized by function, such as health and defense? By program, such as equal employment? How will allocation decisions be made? Finally, with a growing national debt to be passed on to future generations, what are the intergenerational implications of shifting tax and debt burdens? These are the chief concerns of the politics and economics of the budgetary process. Although we cannot provide all the answers in this chapter, we can at least help the reader understand the theoretical and practical issues in the formulation of budgets and the selection of various budgetary strategies or techniques. We will start by mapping out some general considerations and then proceed to a discussion of managerial, political, and legal approaches to budget making.

◆✦ THE SIZE AND GROWTH OF BUDGETS

Governmental spending is an indicator of the extent of governmental involvement in the life of society. But like the administrative state generally, the vastness of its scope is difficult to comprehend. How does one comprehend a federal budget of some $3.8 trillion (FY 2014)? It is staggering to think that this amounts to spending more than $120.5 thousand per second, every second of the year. (The size of the federal budget is projected to grow to $5.9 trillion by fiscal year 2023.)[1] Some suggest that the best indicator of the size of the budget is the proportion of all spending that is governmental. This expresses government expenditures as a percent of the gross domestic product (GDP), defined as the monetary value of all goods and services produced in the nation in a given year. In 2012, the combined spending of all governments in the United States was nearly 35 percent of GDP (see Box 6.1). In 1929, by contrast, it was only about 10 percent. The federal government's budget accounts for about 22.7 percent of GDP. Its receipts in 2012 were about 15.8 percent of GDP. (This is actually the fourth lowest overall tax burden since 1950! The other three lower years were 2009, 2010, and 2011.) Governments raise and spend a great deal of money. This reflects the fact that the scope and intensity of governmental activity have been changing.

Greater clarity could be achieved by looking at how the money is spent. But here we run into a fundamental problem. Should we monitor expenditures on such things as the number of pencils, pens, and paper clips bought by governments? The miles of highway built? Or the broad categories of governmental activity, such as transportation? Shall we include "tax expenditures," which, as explained in Box 6.2, constitute spending only in the sense that they are funds not collected in the first place because of special provisions in the tax code? We can categorize spending in many ways, and this has been a subject of considerable controversy over the years. We will return to this problem later in the chapter. For now, it is helpful to mention the relative proportion of federal, state, and local budgetary expenditures that go to broad, general functions.

Despite a good deal of overlap, governments in the United States are somewhat specialized. The federal government allocates a large proportion of

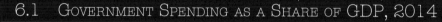

6.1   GOVERNMENT SPENDING AS A SHARE OF GDP, 2014

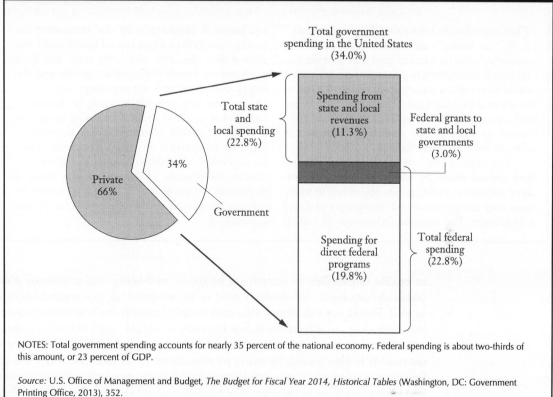

NOTES: Total government spending accounts for nearly 35 percent of the national economy. Federal spending is about two-thirds of this amount, or 23 percent of GDP.

Source: U.S. Office of Management and Budget, *The Budget for Fiscal Year 2014, Historical Tables* (Washington, DC: Government Printing Office, 2013), 352.

its budget to defense, income security, and health programs (Social Security and Medicare in particular); the states spend a higher proportion on highways and education; and local governments spend the greatest proportion of their funds on education and utilities. The proportion of dollars allocated to the salaries of public employees is highest at the local level and lowest at the federal level, with the states falling somewhere in between. Box 6.3 presents a broad categorization of the proportion of federal revenues coming from different sources and expenditures going to different functions. Box 6.4 displays similar information for the states.

This provides some idea of the size of governmental budgets in the United States but does not tell us much about what causes the growth of governmental expenditure. It is believed that governmental spending grows as a result of the same factors that give rise to the administrative state (see Chapter 2). As the society and economy become more complex, government intervenes in an effort to protect and promote the public interest. Antisocial behavior and harmful economic practices are regulated; governmental services are provided

6.2   WHAT ARE TAX EXPENDITURES?

Tax expenditures (also called "tax preferences," or "tax breaks") are features of the individual and corporation income tax laws that provide special benefits or incentives in comparison with what would be permitted under the general provisions of the Internal Revenue Code. They arise from special exclusions, exemptions, or deductions from gross income or from special credits, preferential tax rates, or deferrals of tax liability.

Tax expenditures are so designated because they are one means by which the federal government carries out public policy objectives; in many cases they can be considered alternatives to direct expenditures. For example, investment in capital equipment is encouraged by the investment tax credit; a program of direct capital grants could also achieve this objective. Similarly, state and local governments benefit from direct grants and the ability to borrow funds at tax-exempt rates.

Because tax expenditures can be viewed as alternatives to direct federal spending programs, it is desirable that estimates of tax expenditure items be comparable to outlay programs. Thus, tax expenditures are shown as outlay equivalents—that is, the amount of budget outlays required to provide the same level of after-tax benefits by substituting a direct spending program for the tax expenditure.

to enable individuals to contribute to social well-being and continued economic development. Yet budgets tend to be wrapped up in electoral politics as well. Funds are sometimes allocated to help incumbents win reelection or, less commonly, to unseat them. For instance, so-called "pork-barrel" projects are undertaken to bring funds, jobs, and capital improvements to a legislator's district.[2] It is also politically easier to allocate more funds rather than less to functions supported by powerful interest groups or important constituencies and voting blocs. As in the area of personnel, cutbacks and decline are painful, whereas growth can be used to resolve or smooth over conflicts. It is especially for these political reasons that some politicians and analysts believe that the federal budget process has gotten out of control and that serious reforms are necessary if the political community is to cure its tendency toward deficit spending.

Sources of Revenues

Governments have three main ways to pay for the goods and services they consume and those they provide: taxes, borrowing, and printing money. There are limits to all three. For instance, governments cannot print as much money as they want and expect that it will retain its value. Inflation is the inevitable result, and it can ruin even the strongest economy. Borrowing money—either from its citizens or from foreigners—requires that the market rate of interest be paid on the funds. That increases the budget dollars that must be used in the future to repay the debt, thereby diverting funds away from other priorities, such as education and environmental protection. Too much debt also raises the possibility of a default, which can destroy citizens' confidence in a government. This leaves taxation as the most preferred (or, in the view of

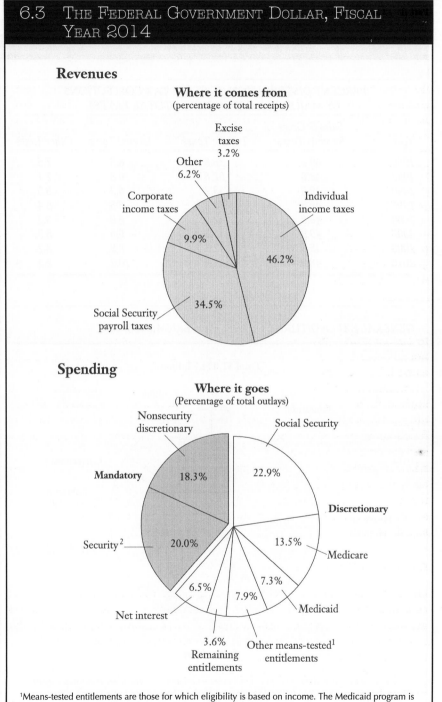

Revenues

Where it comes from
(percentage of total receipts)

Excise taxes 3.2%

Other 6.2%

Corporate income taxes 9.9%

Individual income taxes 46.2%

Social Security payroll taxes 34.5%

Spending

Where it goes
(Percentage of total outlays)

Nonsecurity discretionary

Social Security 22.9%

Mandatory 18.3%

Discretionary

Security[2] 20.0%

13.5% Medicare

Net interest 6.5%

7.9%

7.3% Medicaid

3.6% Remaining entitlements

Other means-tested[1] entitlements

[1]Means-tested entitlements are those for which eligibility is based on income. The Medicaid program is also a means-tested entitlement.
[2]This category includes funding for the Department of Defense, as well as government-wide homeland security activities (including the Department of Homeland Security), and funding for international affairs.

Source: U.S. Office of Management and Budget, *The Budget for Fiscal Year 2014, Historical Tables* (Washington, DC: Government Printing Office, 2013), 34, 153, 161.

6.4   STATE TAXES AND EXPENDITURES

PERCENT DISTRIBUTION OF STATE TAX COLLECTIONS BY MAJOR TAX CATEGORY (% TOTAL TAXES)

Year	Sales & Gross Receipts Taxes	Income Taxes	License Taxes	Other Taxes
1980	49.4	36.8	6.3	7.5
1985	48.8	37.8	6.3	7.1
1990	49.0	39.2	6.3	5.5
1995	49.3	38.8	6.5	5.4
2000	46.8	42.0	6.0	5.2
2003	49.9	38.3	6.5	5.3
2008	45.8	42.1	8.9	3.2
2010	48.9	38.8	10.2	2.1

GENERAL EXPENDITURE OF STATE GOVERNMENTS, 2008

Total $1,024.7 billion

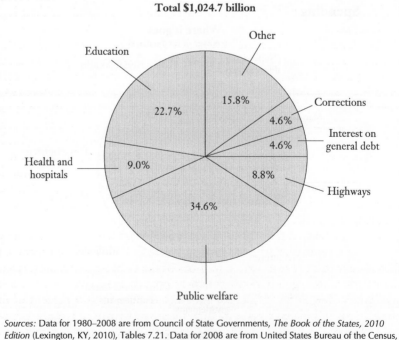

Sources: Data for 1980–2008 are from Council of State Governments, *The Book of the States, 2010 Edition* (Lexington, KY, 2010), Tables 7.21. Data for 2008 are from United States Bureau of the Census, *Statistical Abstract of the United States, 2011* (Washington, DC: 2012), Table 436.

many, the least distasteful) means of generating funds. There are also limits on a society's "tax tolerance"; most citizens see the need for taxes if society is to function. It is too simplistic to say that taxpayers would rather not pay taxes. Rather, there is an unseen "upper limit" on most taxpayers' *willingness to pay* (probably different for different taxpayers) and on their *ability to pay* (based on how financially well off one is). Limitations on willingness and ability to pay also vary considerably according to the type of tax. As a result, a broad assortment of taxes have been devised over the years, though most Americans are usually subject to just three general types.

Individual and Corporate Income Taxes

Taxes levied on the income individuals earn from wages, salaries, and some forms of investment are called **income taxes.** Income taxes can be progressive, regressive, or proportional. A progressive tax claims a larger proportion of an individual's gross income at higher income levels than at lower levels. This is based on the notion that those with a greater ability to pay should pay more. For instance, in a progressive system, a family with income of $90,000 might pay $30,600 in income taxes (34 percent of their gross), whereas a family with a more modest income of $30,000 might be required to pay $6,000 (20 percent of their gross). A regressive system has the opposite effect. It takes a higher proportion of the gross income of those at lower rather than higher income levels.

In determining whether a particular tax is progressive or regressive, the important relationship to look at is the amount of tax paid as a percentage of gross income, not the statutory rate. This can be clearly seen in the case of an income tax system that places a reduced tax rate on capital gains income (income from the appreciation in value of stocks and bonds), which is more likely to be earned by higher-income taxpayers. For example, if the family earning $90,000 a year derived half its income from capital gains, which let's say are taxed at 50 percent of the ordinary income tax rate, its tax bill would be reduced to $22,950 (25.5 percent of its gross), proportionately lower than that of a family with only one-third of its income! Finally, tax systems that result in an equal proportion of one's income paid in taxes, regardless of income level, are termed proportional tax systems.

Several concerns must be addressed in taxing income. Equity is important, as are incentives. Most Americans would probably find an income tax system unfair if it did not tax the incomes of the wealthy *at all*. Stories about millionaires who pay no taxes routinely receive media coverage. Equally evident, however, is that if people were taxed close to 100 percent of their income, they would have no economic incentive to work. We are left with the problem of determining, between these extremes, what is equitable in the setting of rates, and where do incentives to work fall off intolerably? These questions are inherently debatable, but the answers arrived at by a society at any given time do set limits on the utility of the income tax. High rates place a premium on reducing one's *taxable* income through deductions and "under the table" practices, such as working on a "cash only" basis, and bartering. Consequently, actual tax rates probably are considerably lower than nominal ones. The federal government places heavy reliance on the personal income tax, which accounts for about 46 percent of its total receipts. It also levies a corporate income tax, accounting for about 10 percent of receipts.[3] Some form of income tax also was employed by 41 states in 2013, making it the second most relied on tax among state governments.[4]

Sales and Use Taxes

Taxes levied on the sale and use of goods and services in states and/or localities are called **sales and use taxes.** Sales and use taxes are forms of consumption taxes. There is no national sales tax. Instead, sales taxes have traditionally been the bedrock of state tax systems. In 2013, 45 of the 50 states employed sales and use taxes, with rates ranging from a low of 4.0 percent (seven states) to a high of 7.5 percent (California).[5] Thousands of local governments also levy general sales taxes (usually "piggybacked" on the state sales tax levy). Retail sales taxes are the single largest source of state and local tax revenue, accounting in 2008 for nearly one-half of the states' general tax revenue and 10.3 percent of local general tax revenue.[6]

The main advantages of sales taxes are their broad tax base—all retail sales—capable of producing plentiful revenue, and the fact that they are relatively easy to collect. Governments can raise ample revenues at relatively low administrative cost compared with other taxes. To meet equity goals, there is considerable flexibility for governments to exempt certain items as matters of policy, such as food purchased at grocery stores or children's clothing. There are some potential drawbacks, however. First, sales taxes are highly visible precisely because nearly everyone pays them. This makes sales tax rates politically difficult to raise. Second, sales taxes tend to be highly regressive taxes, with the burden falling disproportionately on lower-income families. Third, high sales tax rates can encourage residents to shop elsewhere, especially where there are lower tax rates "just across the state line." This not only works against the revenue-raising purpose of the tax but also may do damage to the economic health of a state or community. Despite these drawbacks, however, sales taxes remain an important pillar of state tax systems.

The Internet Sales Tax Controversy

A current controversy concerns the congressional moratorium on taxation of sales transactions over the Internet. The volume and value of Internet transactions is expected to grow exponentially. As this occurs, both cash-only and face-to-face credit card purchases are declining rapidly. The states therefore have an important interest in taxing Internet sales if many of them are to maintain the integrity of their revenue systems. As a consequence, this has become one of the crucial state tax issues.

The United States Supreme Court in two cases, *National Bellas Hess v. Illinois*[7] and *Quill v. North Dakota,*[8] exempted most mail order firms from having to collect state and local sales taxes, citing as the reason its adverse impact on interstate commerce. However, the Court specifically noted that Congress can require mail order taxation by statute, if it chooses to do so. Rather than give states the right to sales taxes on mail order transaction, Congress has specifically exempted all Internet sales from taxations. The 1998 Internet Tax Freedom Act was signed into law on October 21, 1998 by President Bill Clinton in order to promote growth of Internet commerce. The law specifically barred federal, state, and local governments from taxing Internet access. Nor could they impose discriminatory taxes on Internet usage, such as bit taxes, bandwidth taxes, or e-mail taxes. The law also barred taxes on electronic commerce, which is of obvious concern to the states. The bill has been renewed and extended three times, the last time on October 30, 2007, extending until 2014.

According to Donald Bruce and William F. Fox, the ban on Internet sales taxation affects the states in at least three adverse ways:

1. It gives companies domiciled in other states an approximately 4 to 8 percent price advantage over local vendors.
2. It seriously reduces tax revenues for local schools and public services, a loss estimated at between $21.5 billion and $33.7 billion for 2003.[9] The state revenue losses alone totaled over $11.4 billion in 2012.[10]
3. It aggravates the regressivity of the sales tax, insofar as only those with Internet access and credit cards are able to take advantage of the tax break.

The states have responded in three ways: lobbying Congress for relief, simplifying sales taxes, and intensifying efforts to collect "use taxes" as a substitute for sales taxes. Lobbying efforts focus on urging Congress to enact the Marketplace Fairness Bill, which would require e-commerce enterprises to collect sales taxes on behalf of those jurisdictions that charge them. A version of the Marketplace Fairness Bill was passed by the U.S. Senate in May 2013. However, as of January 1, 2014 it had not been passed by the House of Representatives.

Regarding sales tax simplification, in 2002 state governments organized an initiative known as the Streamlined Sales & Use Tax Agreement. Under it, some 40 states and the District of Columbia committed to simplify their sales tax codes in order to facilitate sales tax collections. Even so, the collection of sales tax remained voluntary. A more aggressive effort is that of the National Governors Association (NGA). NGA initiated its Streamlined Sales Tax Project in an effort to overcome the burdens that companies face in collecting taxes for many jurisdictions, thereby eliminating one of Congress's principal objections to Internet taxation. By June 2011, some 24 states had approved legislation that conforms to the Streamlined Sales and Use Tax Agreement that specifies uniform sales tax rules and definitions. Under the agreement, states and cities retain authority to determine sales tax rates and the goods subject to taxation, but they must adhere to new rules governing, for instance, how and when they can change tax rates. It is hoped that this will prompt Congress to enact the Marketplace Fairness Bill.

The final strategy relies on existing state authority to levy "use" taxes on items that are purchased for use within a jurisdiction. The informational burdens that this imposes on state tax administrators are so onerous as to effectively limit the attractiveness and practicality of this approach. Bruce and Fox note that some states have tried to encourage mail order and Internet suppliers to collect and pay the use tax by purchasing goods and services only from companies that collect and pay all sales taxes, including those for mail order and Internet transactions. North Carolina and South Dakota are two states that have followed this approach.

A related problem is "entity isolation." It is widely known that a number of national retail chains have established Internet sales operations. If a mail order or Internet firm has a physical presence (which the Court has termed a "nexus") within the state, then it must collect and remit sales taxes. However, many national chains contend that their e-commerce operations are distinct legal entities, unrelated to their retail store operations.

Some states have amended their sales tax nexus laws to address entity isolation. The courts in three states (Ohio, Pennsylvania, and Connecticut), however, have held that entity isolation is a legally valid mechanism of tax avoidance. There is no uniform national policy, however, as the U.S. Supreme Court has never agreed to decide a case on the issue. In mid-2013, it is safe to say that taxation of Internet sales remains an open dispute between the federal government and the states.

Real Property Taxes

Taxes on real estate of various kinds are called **property taxes**—the mainstay of local governmental revenues. But as in the case of sales taxes, there is considerable variation among local governments in the extent to which they rely on property taxes. In some states, such as those in New England, almost all local governmental revenues may come from property taxes. Elsewhere, it is typical for local governments to raise only about one-half or less of their revenues in this fashion (Alabama, Louisiana). Again, there may be competition among jurisdictions with regard to property tax rates. When the rates in one city or town are high compared with those in neighboring jurisdictions, some people may choose to reside in the areas with lower taxes. This can serve to depress real estate market values, leading to a stagnant or declining tax base in the locality with higher rates, and could eventually be a factor in a serious financial crisis. The financial crisis in Bridgeport, Connecticut, in the early 1990s is an example. Of course, local jurisdictions with high property tax rates may provide better services, including education, public safety, and sanitation.

Among the major problems with the property tax is the tendency for it to be inequitably administered over time. The tax assessments on similar dwellings may vary considerably, especially if a particular parcel has been bought and sold more frequently during periods of high inflation. Sometimes, too, the property tax acts as a deterrent to improving one's dwelling. The addition of rooms, porches, swimming pools, and so on, can lead to a higher tax assessment.

It is also possible that when property values and tax assessments rise, families or individuals with stable incomes will find the increasing tax burden too great. Property taxes may be regressive, insofar as richer people tend to spend a lower proportion of their wealth on housing than do poorer people. In addition, as the value of real property—such as farmland near urban and suburban areas—increases, so too may the tax on it, although the incomes of those living on or farming the land remain relatively constant.

Additional Taxes and Sources of Revenue

There is a great variety of other sources of governmental revenues, including *excise taxes, motor fuel taxes, business taxes, inheritance taxes, capital gains taxes, license fees, user fees, lotteries, sale of utilities* such as water or electricity, and the *operation of liquor stores*. Governments can also raise funds by borrowing money through the sale of bonds and other forms of loans. (Borrowed funds must be repaid and therefore cannot, in a technical sense, be classified as "revenue.") The sources of federal revenues are displayed in Box 6.3; those of local governments and states are given in Box 6.4.

Revenue Evaluation Criteria

Equity and Political Feasibility

Any consideration of raising governmental revenues must take several general concerns into account. An inequitable taxing arrangement can promote a popular tax revolt, as was witnessed in California through Proposition 13 (1978), in Massachusetts through Proposition 2½ (1980), and elsewhere. Equity is related to political feasibility. Some forms of taxation are too unpopular with the general public or with powerful constituencies to be applied or raised beyond certain levels. For example, some sober voices have urged that the federal government place a heavy tax on the sale of gasoline—perhaps as much as a dollar a gallon. This would raise the cost of fuel and presumably encourage conservation, as well as raise funds that could be used for the development of other energy sources and cheaper means of transportation. However, under normal conditions, the political feasibility of such a high tax is low. Consequently, the federal motor fuels tax remains at levels that do not promote conservation on a sufficient scale to make a genuine difference.

Administrative Capability

The administrative feasibility of different forms of taxation must also be considered. Can a particular tax be administered, or will it be evaded on a widespread basis? For instance, property taxes that base assessments on aspects of the interiors of houses may be difficult to apply. To do so, assessors must gain entry to dwellings and be able to snoop around in them. Aside from questions of individual privacy and taxpayer resentment of such administrative intrusion, this system could take a great deal of time to administer on an equitable basis.

It would be much easier to base assessments on the exteriors of houses, their last sales price, or their estimated market value. Similarly, in societies where cash registers are not usually used, applying the sales tax can be difficult. Income taxes can be problematical in some service areas of the economy where payment of fees in cash may be the norm. Taxing restaurant tips has been a long-standing problem. Administrative feasibility is also concerned with the efficiency with which the funds can be collected. For instance, it is usually more efficient to collect taxes through payroll withholding than by billing individuals once or twice a year. It is also more effective, so taxpayers do not have to "stretch" to come up with the money all at once. One of the arguments in favor of a flat income tax is that it would be simple to file and inexpensive to administer.

Economic Effects

Governments must also consider the economic effects of a particular means of raising revenue. As previously noted, some forms of taxation can be counterproductive; that is, raising the tax or user fee may provide less revenue because it will encourage individuals to move from one jurisdiction to another, shop elsewhere, or avoid publicly provided services such as transportation that are considered too costly. Eventually, all tax and revenue-raising devices can reach their limits of efficacy by draining too much from the private sector and reducing private incentives to work. Although we are sometimes accustomed to believe that governments can raise as much money as they want, in truth there are substantial limitations on the ability of the public sector to finance itself. These limits must be taken into account in developing governmental budgets.

Governmental Fiscal Policy Making

State and local governments cannot run substantial budgetary deficits indefinitely. Many are constitutionally or legally required to have balanced operating budgets. They can fund developmental projects through capital budgets, which do permit long-term borrowing for building public works that will have long service lives (bridges, sewers, tunnels, roadways). But they do not typically treat budgets as a tool for encouraging or discouraging short-term economic growth. By contrast, however, at times the federal government has planned for deficits as a means of managing the nation's economy. This is another development that coincides with the expansion of the contemporary administrative state. Prior to the 1930s, the "balanced budget" norm predominated. A federal budget that *planned* to spend more than it anticipated in revenues would have been taken as a sign that the government was profligate and out of control. The government's credit, or at least so it was thought, would falter and an economic panic might ensue. Such deficits as did occur were unplanned, and soon reverted to balance.

By the mid-1930s, another approach began to emerge. This is commonly called the **Keynesian approach** after the British economist who developed it, Lord John Maynard Keynes.[11] In its simplest form, Keynesian economics holds that once the government's role in the economic life of a capitalist society becomes substantial, government spending can be used to counteract the normal boom-and-bust tendencies of the business cycle. In other words, if governmental spending is a considerable proportion of a nation's GDP, government should have substantial leverage over business cycle fluctuations in that nation. Deficit spending—that is, spending more than is raised in revenues—can be used to stimulate the economy out of recession or depression. A government surplus—that is, raising more revenues than are to be spent—can be used as a means of regulating economic growth and limiting inflation.

To the extent that a government subscribes to the Keynesian approach, budgeting has great ramifications for the economy. It is no longer simply a matter of deciding what kinds of activities government should engage in, what they will cost, and how revenues may be raised to finance them. Rather, the budgetary process ought to take into account the government's role in trying to keep the economy on a long-term growth track. This being the case, governmental spending and revenue raising must be related to the economy generally, as opposed to the funding of governmental programs alone. In the United States, this role for government was legally adopted in the Employment Act of 1946, which created a policy that the federal government should promote full employment to the extent "practicable" in the society. This statute is often considered a landmark in the political and economic development of the United States because it signified the weakening of an ideology of laissez-faire capitalism, and called for governmental intervention in the economy.

Despite the Employment Act, however, Keynesian economics has been difficult to practice, especially when the economy is good. The main problem may be less in the theory than in practice; it is difficult to apply. First, it is hard to analyze the economy and coordinate the analysis with a lengthy budget-making process. It takes 18 months to two years to formulate a federal budget for one year. The fiscal assumptions on which a budget is built may fail to match a fast-changing economy. Second, the intended effects of governmental spending and tax policy changes may take months. Third, the politics of budgetary process make it difficult to generate surpluses—required by the Keynesian countercyclical approach. The electoral interests of members of Congress often dictate federal spending on projects in their districts in election years. Deficit spending also tends to be inflationary, which can produce pressures for higher interest rates. Higher rates, in turn, can dampen borrowing for business investment and slow economic growth. Slower growth is likely to have a negative impact on government's ability to raise revenues through taxation. Consequently, under such conditions, reducing the deficit or balancing the budget becomes even more difficult. Countercyclical fiscal policy requires delicate economic balancing that has often been upset by the realities of budgeting cycles and electoral politics.

Largely as a result of Congress's inability to satisfy its appetite for spending, the United States has witnessed some three decades of huge, persistent budgetary deficits. Box 6.5 graphically displays a history of federal surpluses and deficits since 1940. Deficits increased sharply in the 1980s, but by the

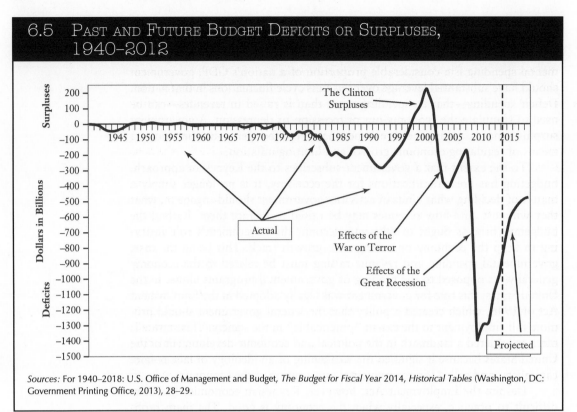

6.5 Past and Future Budget Deficits or Surpluses, 1940–2012

Sources: For 1940–2018: U.S. Office of Management and Budget, *The Budget for Fiscal Year* 2014, *Historical Tables* (Washington, DC: Government Printing Office, 2013), 28–29.

mid-1990s they were beginning to decline and were eliminated in 1998—two years ahead of schedule—as a result of extraordinary spending restraint. Due to the war on terrorism, the overthrow of the Taliban in Afghanistan and the lingering war in Iraq, however, deficits returned to record-high levels in 2003. According to the Congressional Budget Office (CBO), with the advent of the Great Recession in 2007, and the Obama stimulus package and its aftermath, federal deficits are likely to persist, and even grow through at least 2023.[12] Deficits have become commonplace in Washington, and have been a fairly permanent piece of the federal fiscal landscape for quite some time: the federal budget has been in deficit in all but eight years since 1931.

The National Debt: Is It a Burden?

The gross federal debt stood at $8.4 trillion in 2006, and $16.0 trillion in 2012 (including $11.3 trillion held by the public—which is the number that really matters; the rest is held in U.S. Government accounts, such as the Social Security Trust Fund). Economists remain uncertain about the impact of a national debt of such magnitude.[13] The 2012 figure is 103.2 percent of annual GDP (and 72.6 percent for the debt held by the public), and costs the federal government $220.4 billion a year in net interest payments, and this figure is projected to grow considerably (especially if world interest rates begin to rise in the next few years). The national debt would have cost even more, except that interest rates have fallen considerably in the last decade. The unprecedented long period of national economic growth in the 1990s—combined with genuine spending restraint and tax increases—by 1998 produced budget surpluses of such size that there was optimism that the national debt would be retired before the end of the first decade of this century. However, for reasons already mentioned, record-high deficits have returned. Consequently, the debt is expected to grow again in the coming years, reaching around $25.2 trillion by 2023. This will drive net interest payments to an estimated $823 billion in that year (but this figure could be higher still, depending on the interest rates that prevail at that time). To put these figures in perspective, the interest payments would come to overwhelm the budget, becoming larger than the projected budgets for the Departments of Agriculture, Education, Housing and Urban Development, Interior, Commerce, and Homeland Security combined!

Of the total 2013 debt of $16.0 trillion, around 71 percent was owed to the public (including about 56 percent in the hands of foreigners), with the rest owed by the government to other U.S. government agencies—primarily the Social Security Trust Fund. The U.S. Treasury has historically "borrowed" any Social Security surpluses to offset general government spending, replacing these funds with "IOUs" in the form of nonmarketable government bonds. U.S. Government bonds held in the accounts of the Social Security Trust Fund may be thought of as future tax increases that will pay for benefits when they come due. After all, when needed, these bonds will have to be redeemed for "hard cash."

The increasing level of government debt has spurred discussion among economists about whether it is a burden on future generations. Those who argue that the debt does burden future Americans argue that they will have to pay taxes to retire the debts that have financed present spending. Those economists who argue that the debt is not a burden assert that the debt is offset by the assets (both in the form of necessary infrastructure and the bonds themselves) that the next generation will inherit from the present generation. The answer to the general question of the burden of the debt, however, appears to be a little of both. First, the debt represents an asset to those who hold the government's bonds, who will tend to be wealthier Americans. If the U.S. economy is viewed as a closed economy, where the lenders (investors) and taxpayers are all American citizens, then there is likely to be no intergenerational burden. There will likely be an internal transfer of wealth in the future; that is, among all Americans. Second, since the debt is increasingly owed to foreign creditors, the U.S. economy must be viewed as an open economy. To the extent that the debt is owned by foreigners, the interest payments that go abroad constitute a transfer of future wealth out of the United States. This concern is particularly acute in the case of China, which has accumulated some $1.3 trillion, or about 12 percent of the debt held by the public.

There are several problems with both of these two points, however. First, regarding the internal transfer of wealth, the perspective ignores economic growth and labor productivity improvements—which have historically manifested themselves in rising household incomes. If the size of the debt grows at rates that are less than the rates of growth of the economy, and especially of household income, then the debt may grow in size, yet constitute less of a burden on future generations. Second, not all debt is the same. Borrowings in foreign currency and short-term debt maturities are pro-cyclical, and expose a country to risks of adverse exchange rate fluctuations and dramatic interest rate changes.[14] Fortunately, U.S. sovereign debt held by foreigners is denominated in our own currency, unlike the debts of many countries that are in distress today (such as Greece, Spain, Portugal, and Italy). The U.S. is not susceptible to dollar devaluations or inflation in its own currency. Devaluations would reduce the real value of U.S. debt, which would thereby lessen the burden on Americans. Further, the U.S. Treasury has moved toward lengthening the maturities on its debt portfolio, which serves to lock in for the longer term the lowest interest rates in the past half century. Finally, U.S. government debts in the Great Recession are occurring in the face of a dwindling capacity of households to maintain their consumption levels with private debt. The entire picture would change if the U.S. dollar were to devalue significantly relative to the Chinese renminbi (or if the renminbi were to strengthen against the dollar, which would have the same effect)—say, by around 30 percent.[15]

The most serious consideration with a growing debt burden in the near term is the growing periodic interest payments that it must make on the outstanding debt. As mentioned above, affordability of the debt is tied directly to the size and strength of the economy. For example, at the end of 2012 the federal debt held by the public was about 72.6 percent of GDP. By historical comparison, that was not particularly high. It stood at 109 percent of GDP at the end of World War II. It then fell to 24 percent in 1974 but climbed to 49 percent in the mid-1990s before declining again in the remainder of that decade as economic growth outpaced borrowing. Thus, another important indicator of affordability is the rate of growth of the debt versus that of the national income. By 2000, the trend had tipped in favor of increasing affordability. In 2001, the debt held by the public was much smaller—just 32.5 percent of GDP. But the economic downturn of 2002–2003 decreased tax revenues and the unanticipated expenses associated with the war on terrorism and the Great Recession caused government spending, and with it, the debt, to rise again.

Despite the problems posed by deficit spending and the national debt, however, many believe that the government should be required to balance the budget on an annual basis. This is considered a pillar of sound financial management in government, just as it is in households. Some members of Congress have proposed a constitutional amendment for this purpose. Though never actually passed, the movement to enact a **balanced budget amendment** represents an expression of real concern over whether government is prone to runaway spending. The deficit problem has been a focal point of much political concern to the federal government over the past 40 years.

◆◆   THE FEDERAL BUDGETARY PROCESS

The development of the contemporary federal budgetary process has its roots in the recommendations of the Taft Commission of 1912, which sought to unify federal spending in a single "executive budget" to be developed by the president. The executive budget process was introduced in 1921, when the Bureau of the Budget was created as a unit within the Treasury Department. Prior to that time, the budget was a somewhat haphazard and largely congressional function. There was little coordination in the process, and no rigorous effort was made to connect revenues to expenditures in the budget. In 1939, as part of the development of the modern presidency, the Bureau of the Budget was placed in the newly created Executive Office of the President. This reorganization solidified the president's roles as "administrator-in-chief" and manager of the economy. It also emphasized the president's responsibility for developing a comprehensive budget for transmittal to Congress.

In 1970, the Bureau of the Budget's functions were expanded to include greater responsibility for the way federal agencies were managed, and it was accordingly renamed the Office of Management and Budget (OMB). (See Box 6.6 for a chart of OMB's organization.) Throughout this time, the federal government has adhered to an annual budget. However, in 1974 it was decided to begin the fiscal year on October 1 rather than July 1. (The fiscal year [FY] is numbered according to the year in which it ends; e.g., FY 2014 ends on September 30, 2014.) In 1974 Congress also created the Congressional Budget Office (CBO) to provide it with an independent source of economic and fiscal analysis. In a sense, the CBO was intended to balance the influence of the OMB. This demonstrated the tendency to try to control one agency with another one, giving testimony to the continuing relevance of the separation of powers and the application of checks and balances.

One of the problems with the budget process after the 1974 reforms was the development of "multiple budgets."[16] The president proposed one, but so did Congress. Disagreement between the two has sometimes led to failure to enact a budget by the beginning of the fiscal year. Especially in the modern era; starting in 2009, there has been no annual congressional budget enacted, as the term "congressional budget" is ordinarily understood. Instead, "continuing resolutions" (CRs) are passed to keep the doors of the government open while Congress deliberated on the budget. It has also become common to handle additional spending in the form of supplemental appropriations, which have recently been justified as so-called "emergency" spending measures. Such practices were considered extraordinary, even in the not-so-distant past. Political rancor often accompanied enactment of CRs. For instance, in FY 1996, failure to enact a budget or CRs led to two partial government shutdowns. "Off-budget" items, establishment of separate "trust funds," "backdoor spending," supplemental appropriations, and projected expenditures are also practices that threaten the concept of a unified annual budget. These spending vehicles make it hard to determine what financial commitments the government is making from year to year.

6.6 ORGANIZATION OF THE U.S. OFFICE OF MANAGEMENT AND BUDGET

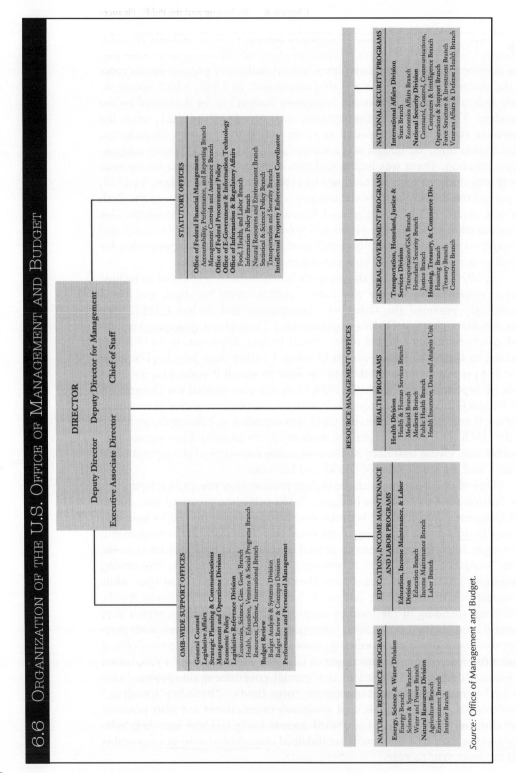

DIRECTOR

Deputy Director   Deputy Director for Management
Executive Associate Director   Chief of Staff

OMB-WIDE SUPPORT OFFICES

General Counsel
Legislative Affairs
Strategic Planning & Communications
Management and Operations Division
Economic Policy
Legislative Reference Division
  Economics, Science, Gen. Govt. Branch
  Health, Education, Veterans & Social Programs Branch
  Resources, Defense, International Branch
Budget Review
  Budget Analysis & Systems Division
  Budget Review & Concepts Division
  Performance and Personnel Management

STATUTORY OFFICES

Office of Federal Financial Management
  Accountability, Performance, and Reporting Branch
  Management Controls and Assistance Branch
Office of Federal Procurement Policy
Office of E-Government & Information Technology
Office of Information & Regulatory Affairs
  Food, Health, and Labor Branch
  Information Policy Branch
  Natural Resources and Environment Branch
  Statistical & Science Policy Branch
  Transportation and Security Branch
  Intellectual Property Enforcement Coordinator

RESOURCE MANAGEMENT OFFICES

NATURAL RESOURCE PROGRAMS

Energy, Science & Water Division
  Energy Branch
  Science & Space Branch
  Water and Power Branch
Natural Resources Division
  Agriculture Branch
  Environment Branch
  Interior Branch

EDUCATION, INCOME MAINTENANCE AND LABOR PROGRAMS

Education, Income Maintenance, & Labor Division
  Education Branch
  Income Maintenance Branch
  Labor Branch

HEALTH PROGRAMS

Health Division
  Health & Human Services Branch
  Medicaid Branch
  Medicare Branch
  Public Health Branch
  Health Insurance, Data and Analysis Unit

GENERAL GOVERNMENT PROGRAMS

Transportation, Homeland, Justice & Services Division
  Transporation/GSA Branch
  Homeland Security Branch
  Justice Branch
Housing, Treasury, & Commerce Div.
  Housing Branch
  Treasury Branch
  Commerce Branch

NATIONAL SECURITY PROGRAMS

International Affairs Division
  State Branch
  Economics Affairs Branch
National Security Division
  Command, Control, Communications, Computers & Intelligence Branch
  Operations & Support Branch
  Force Structure & Investment Branch
  Veterans Affairs & Defense Health Branch

Source: Office of Management and Budget.

The hallmark of the federal budgetary process is its complexity. (Box 6.7 provides a glossary of budgetary terms, many of which are unique to the federal budget.) Even during "normal" times, there are usually several activities going on at once: the budget for one year is being executed; the budget for the next may be under legislative consideration; the budget for the year after the one being considered by Congress is simultaneously being developed in the executive branch; and, in many instances, agencies are engaged in a consideration of the likely costs of their programs five years into the future. The fiscal results of past years may also be subject to audit and/or evaluation. But these activities only begin to tap the surface of the budgetary activity that is going on. The Council of Economic Advisers, some officials in the OMB, some of the president's aides on fiscal policy, and parts of the Treasury and Labor Departments simultaneously work to develop information and projections that will accurately describe the performance of the economy during the fiscal year for which the budget is being developed. This is necessary if spending is to be matched to revenue, as an emphasis on avoiding deficits requires. At the same time, the CBO may also be evaluating many aspects of the budget proposal for the next fiscal year. At any given time, there is a great deal of budget activity under way—even if it does not conclude in the actual enactment of a federal budget!

As a result of concern with the federal debt, the budgetary process has undergone change so frequently in recent years that describing it is like trying to hit a rapidly zigzagging target. The current approach, framed by OMB Circular A-11, "On the Preparation, Submission, and Execution of the Budget," contains a host of technical provisions, complex procedures, and deadlines for enacting the budget. Until 2002, the budget process was controlled by both Circular A-11 and the Budget Enforcement Act (BEA) of 1990, and subsequent amendments. The BEA was devised as a means to limit discretionary spending while ensuring that new entitlement programs and/or tax cuts would not worsen the deficit. To accomplish this, the BEA set annual limits on total discretionary spending for defense, international affairs, and domestic programs.

The BEA expired at the end of 2002, but its operation was widely considered to be very effective. Here's how it worked: If any of the three limits were to be "breached," the BEA would trigger an automatic spending reduction, called a "sequester." Sequesters could occur at any time during the fiscal year. This means that Congress could not authorize new spending after the budget was enacted and escape the BEA requirements. The limits were adjusted each year to account for forecasted inflation, technical changes, and other similar factors. Another key feature of the BEA was enactment of so-called Pay-as-You-Go (PAYGO) rules. This was the most innovative (and controversial) aspect of BEA. The PAYGO rules applied to the budget in total and required that any new spending proposals or tax cuts be offset by cutting other programs or raising other taxes. If this requirement was not met, politically painful sequester was required in mandatory spending programs—something Congress would do all that it could to avoid.

1. AUTHORIZING LEGISLATION—Legislation enacted by Congress to establish or continue the operation of a federal program or agency. Prior statutory authorization is normally a prerequisite for subsequent appropriations but does not provide budget authority (see *Budget Authority*).

2. BUDGET—A plan of proposed revenues and spending outlays for the coming fiscal year or longer. It sets forth the financial plan for allocating resources and indicates the policy priorities of the government.

3. BUDGET AUTHORITY—Authority provided by Congress to enter into obligations that will result in immediate or future outlays. The basic forms of federal budget authority (described in the text) are appropriations, contract authority, borrowing authority, entitlements, and loan or loan-guarantee authority. In contrast to the federal practice, state and local governments do not normally distinguish between budget authority and appropriations.

4. BUDGET RECEIPTS—Income, net of refunds, collected from the public by the federal government through the exercise of its governmental or sovereign powers. Also includes gifts and contributions. Excludes amounts received from business-type transactions (such as sales, interest, and loan repayments) and payments between U.S. government accounts.

5. BUDGET SURPLUS OR DEFICIT—The difference between budget receipts and outlays. It may refer to either the on-budget, off-budget, or unified budget result.

6. CAP—Refers to the legal limits placed on the budget authority and outlays for discretionary appropriations for each fiscal year under the Budget Enforcement Act (BEA) of 1990 and other legislation.

7. CONCURRENT RESOLUTION ON THE BUDGET—A resolution passed by both houses of Congress that sets outlays and receipt targets for Congress in its subsequent budget deliberations. It does not require the president's signature.

8. CONTINUING RESOLUTION—Legislation enacted by Congress for specific ongoing activities when a regular appropriation for those activities has not been enacted at the beginning of the fiscal year. It usually provides for spending to continue at the level of the immediately preceding fiscal year.

9. CREDIT BUDGET—A plan of proposed direct loan obligations and guaranteed loan commitments. Budget authority and outlays associated with the credit budget are included in the on-budget totals.

10. CROSSWALK—An accounting device that transforms the spending limits in the 21 functional categories of the Concurrent Budget Resolution into spending ceilings for individual congressional committees.

11. CURRENT SERVICES ESTIMATES—Estimates of receipts, outlays, and budget authority for coming fiscal years that assume no policy changes from the current year. The estimates do make allowance for impacts of expected changes in economic conditions, beneficiary levels, pay increases, and changes required under existing law.

12. DEFERRAL—Executive branch action that temporarily delays obligating the government to spend money. Deferrals may be overturned at any time by an act of Congress.

13. FEDERAL FUNDS—Monies collected and spent by the government other than those designated as trust funds. The major federal fund is the general fund, derived from general taxes and borrowing. Other forms of federal funds are special funds, public enterprise funds, and intragovernmental funds.

14. FISCAL YEAR—A government's yearly accounting period. The federal fiscal year begins October 1 and ends on the following September 30. States and municipalities may have fiscal years that begin on other dates (such as January 1 or July 1). The fiscal year is generally designated by the calendar year in which it ends; e.g., fiscal year 2009 begins on October 1, 2008, and ends on September 30, 2009. (From 1844 to 1976 the fiscal year began on July 1 and ended on the following June 30.)

15. IMPOUNDMENT—Any action or inaction by an officer or employee of the federal government that precludes the obligation or expenditure of budget authority provided by Congress (see also *Deferral* and *Rescission*).

16. OBLIGATIONS—Legally binding agreements made by the federal government that will result in outlays immediately or in the future. At the state and local levels, these are sometimes called commitments; unexpended portions of longer-term municipal obligations are generally termed encumbrances.

17. OFF-BUDGET—Transactions of governmental entities excluded from the on-budget totals by law. At the federal level, under current law, the off-budget totals include the Social Security trust funds (Federal Old-Age and Survivors Insurance and Federal Disability Insurance Trust Funds) and the Postal Service Fund. The budget combines both on-budget and off-budget totals to derive the unified budget results for all federal activity (see *On-Budget*).

18. OFFSETTING RECEIPTS—Collections deposited in receipt accounts offset against budget authority and outlays rather than being counted as budget receipts. These monies are not authorized to be credited to expenditure accounts. These collections are derived from business-type or market-oriented activities.

19. ON-BUDGET—All transactions of governmental entities except those specifically excluded (off-budget) by law.

20. OUTLAYS—Payments made to liquidate obligations of the government. Outlays are the basic measure of federal government spending. Such payments are normally made in cash (including checks), net of refunds, reimbursements, and offsetting collections or receipts but are also recorded for cash-equivalent transactions, such as subsidy costs of loans and loan guarantees and interest accrued on the public debt.

21. PAY-AS-YOU-GO (PAYGO)—Refers to the requirements of the Budget Enforcement Act (BEA) of 1990 that result in a sequestration if the estimated combined result of new legislation that affects mandatory spending or receipts will be a net cost for a given fiscal year.

22. RECONCILIATION—Refers to provisions in the Concurrent Budget Resolution that calls on various congressional committees to recommend legislative changes that reduce outlays or increase receipts by specified amounts. A reconciliation bill would contain these changes.

23. RESCISSION—An executive action that cancels budget authority previously provided by Congress.

24. SEQUESTRATION—A legislative process whereby specific automatic spending cuts are required if discretionary spending exceeds the discretionary spending caps or if the combined result of legislation affecting mandatory programs is a net cost. It was first devised under the Gramm-Rudman-Hollings Balanced Budget and Deficit Reduction Act of 1985 and then embodied in the Budget Enforcement Act (BEA) of 1990 (and subsequent amendments).

25. SUPPLEMENTAL APPROPRIATION—An appropriation enacted subsequent to a regular annual appropriations act. Supplemental appropriations provide additional budget authority for programs or activities (including new programs authorized after the date of the original appropriations act) for which the need for funds is too urgent to be postponed until the next regular appropriation.

26. TAX EXPENDITURES—Provisions of the federal income tax laws that permit a special exclusion, exemption, or deduction from gross income or that provide a special credit, preferential tax rate, or deferral of tax liability. Tax expenditures frequently have results similar to those of spending programs, loan guarantees, or regulations.

27. TRUST FUND—A type of account that receives funds collected and expended for carrying out specific purposes and programs according to a statute or trust agreement and specified by law as being trust fund money. Prime examples are the Social Security and unemployment trust funds. Trust fund receipts not needed immediately usually are "loaned" to the general fund, with nonmarketable U.S. Treasury securities substituted for them.

28. UNOBLIGATED BALANCE—The cumulative amount of budget authority that has not been obligated and that remains available for obligation and expenditure under existing budget authority.

In general, the BEA process accomplished what it was designed to do. It limited discretionary spending and forced new spending proposals to be offset by cuts in other areas or new revenues. However, as a result of an economic recession, the deficit continued to rise in the early 1990s. In 1993, the president and Congress agreed on a five-year program to cut spending and raise taxes. But the entire system broke down in 1995, when Congress and the president could not agree on a complete budget until April 1996—about halfway through the fiscal year—but not before a general government shutdown had sent some 800,000 government employees home for a week. The primary bone of contention was disagreement between the president and Congress over cuts to education, job training, and Medicare. The 1997 Balanced Budget Act (BBA) appeared to resolve most issues over spending cut priorities. Congress also got its way with the Taxpayer Relief Act of 1997. The real story behind the recent success in balancing the budget was the strength of the economy, which, combined with the effects of the BEA, provided four years of budget surpluses under President Bill Clinton. But economic growth began to soften in 2000 and grew worse by the end of 2002. More recent deficits have been aggravated by the federal tax cuts of 2001 and 2002, and expenditures on the Global War on Terror. Today OMB Circular A-11 continues to provide guidance to agencies regarding the formulation of their annual budgets. Instructions include information on the "Federal performance framework" and performance reporting related to the Government Performance and Results Act Modernization Act of 2010.[17]

Stages in the Budgetary Process

The federal budgetary process can be divided into five stages: (1) formulation of individual agencies' budgets; (2) preparation of the executive budget by the central budget agency (OMB), in consultation with the president and/or his or her advisers; (3) presentation of the budget to the legislature; (4) legislative action on the proposed budget and enactment of legislation appropriating funds; and (5) execution of the budget by the executive branch. State government budget processes more or less follow the same pattern. There is much about what goes on in each stage that is highly technical, but the process can be described in broad terms as follows. Box 6.8 diagrams much of the federal budget process as it is supposed to work under current law and regulations. (As noted previously, it has changed from time to time.)

Agency Budgets

In July of each year the OMB calls on the agencies to submit their budget proposals by September. In practice, agencies may begin preparing their budgets much earlier. The president begins the process by setting general budget and fiscal policy guidelines at least nine months before the budget is transmitted to Congress, and around 18 months prior to the start of the fiscal year. Those responsible for formulating each agency's budget requests typically ask bureau chiefs and

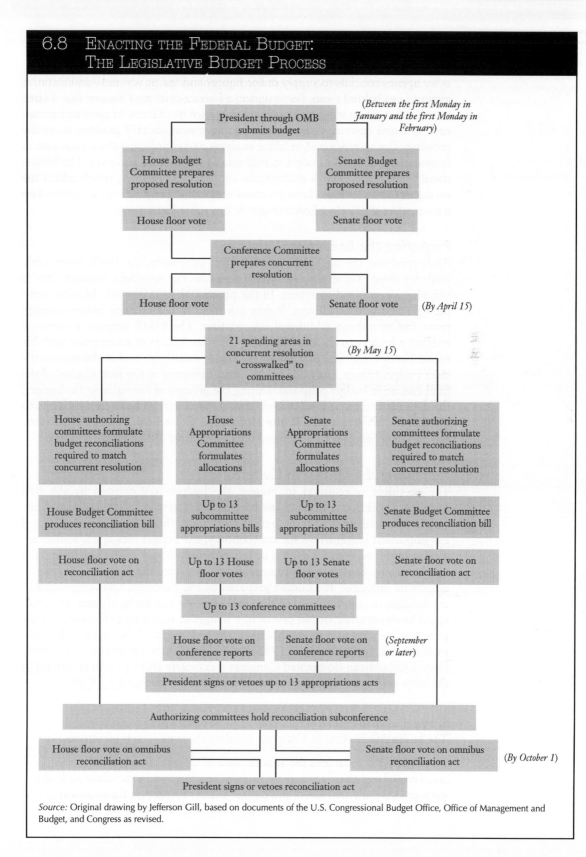

Source: Original drawing by Jefferson Gill, based on documents of the U.S. Congressional Budget Office, Office of Management and Budget, and Congress as revised.

other agency officials to supply dollar figures and the policy and administrative assumptions behind them. For instance, a bureau chief may assume that a large increase in funding will be necessary if the size of its clientele or customer group, such as senior citizens, veterans, or individuals who are HIV-positive, is rapidly growing. The agency's budget office analyzes and coordinates these responses in formulating a tentative budget in response to the OMB's directives. The budget should reflect the OMB's instructions and policy guidelines, which reflect the president's assumptions about priorities within the spending caps established by a statute like the Budget Enforcement Act or other legislation.

Preparing the Executive Budget

After receiving the agencies' initial budget proposals, the OMB thoroughly analyzes them. Generally, the OMB seeks to cut spending requests, but it can also recommend increases. In the process, the OMB holds hearings with the agencies' budget officers. It may ask them to defend their policy assumptions and to submit additional information. The OMB submits a tentative executive budget to the president and then finalizes it in accordance with his recommendations. The director of the OMB, usually viewed as the president's chief budget officer, generally wields great influence in the formulation of the final executive budget proposal. During the process of formulating the budget, the director and other OMB administrators are likely to be in contact with the president's advisers at the White House, the Council of Economic Advisers, the National Security Council, and other Executive Office units.

Presenting the Budget to Congress

The president is required to present the budget to Congress by the first Monday in February. Because the budget is a statement of governmental priorities, affects everyone in the nation (and many throughout the world), and has important implications for the economy, the budget message is sometimes a major political event. It should be remembered, though, that constitutionally speaking, only Congress can appropriate money from the Treasury. Therefore, despite its influence, the budget prepared by the executive and transmitted to the legislature is nothing more than advisory—it has no legal force or standing. The importance of the president's budget is based on perceptions of the president's ability to obtain what he or she has proposed. Sometimes this ability is limited. For example, in 1995, the budget Clinton presented to the newly elected Republican-dominated Congress was clearly DOA ("dead on arrival"); the same was essentially true of President Obama's budget for FY 2013.

Congressional Action

The budgetary process in Congress involves three main sets of actors:

- The CBO examines the assumptions of the president's budget and works out alternative projections of revenues and expenditures. It also provides an analysis of the budget's likely impact on the economy.

It may engage in a discussion of the priorities inherent in the president's budget and how these priorities may be at odds with its sense of Congress's desires.

- The *House and Senate Committees on the Budget* work with the CBO in examining the president's proposal. These committees formulate a budget resolution intended to establish the budget's maximum spending authority.
- The *Appropriations and Authorizations Committees in the House and Senate* develop appropriations bills and bring them to the floor of each legislative chamber for consideration by the legislature as a whole. The appropriations committees work within a framework of requirements generated by the budget committees. The annual appropriations bills pertain to discretionary spending and a limited number of mandatory programs (such as food stamps). Less than half of annual federal spending is covered by the annual appropriations process; the rest of federal spending takes place automatically and includes mainly entitlements (e.g., Medicare, Medicaid, and Social Security). Recently, Authorizations Committees have been slipping spending measures into authorizing legislation, thereby blurring the traditional lines of distinction between themselves and the Appropriations Committees.

In its broadest terms, the congressional budgetary process works in the following way. After receiving the president's budget, congressional committees develop spending and revenue plans for the coming fiscal year. These plans are transmitted to the budget committee in each house. Working with these plans and information about the economy provided by the CBO, the budget committees prepare the congressional budget resolution. The resolution establishes the level of revenues, budget authority, and projected outlays. If the assumptions behind the resolution are correct and the resolution is adhered to, it sets the level of deficit or surplus that the government will have in the coming fiscal year. The congressional budget resolution should be adopted by Congress by April 15, but this usually happens later.

After the resolution establishes the parameters of the budget, the appropriations committees work with the various congressional committees in formulating the annual appropriations bills (in a typical year, there would be 12 such bills, to be enacted in sequence). Because Article I, section 7 of the Constitution requires that "All Bills for raising Revenue shall originate in the House of Representatives," the House Appropriations Committee takes the leading role in this aspect of the process. However, because both houses must pass identical appropriations bills, activity in the Senate is equally important. In June, the House Appropriations Committee should report its version of the spending bills to the whole House, which is supposed to pass final versions by the end of the month. All appropriations legislation should be passed by both houses by October 1.

The Distinction between Authority and Appropriations

The result of the congressional action phase of the federal budget process is enactment of *budget authority*. There are several kinds of budget authority, each permitting federal departments and agencies to make commitments that obligate the federal government to make outlays (or expenditures), either for the current fiscal year, or in the future. Box 6.9 lists the various types of budget authority, which are as follows:

- *Appropriations authority* pertains to all discretionary spending and a small number of mandatory programs. It sets upper limits on budget authority and actual outlays (expenditures of funds) for federal agencies and programs, usually for a single fiscal year.
- *Borrowing authority* permits an agency to incur and liquidate debts. Such authority may appear either in an appropriations act or in another statute and may permit borrowing from the Treasury, from the Federal Financing Bank, or directly from the public. The amount that can be borrowed annually is limited to that provided for in annual appropriations acts.

6.9   RELATIONSHIP BETWEEN BUDGET AUTHORITY, APPROPRIATIONS, AND OUTLAYS

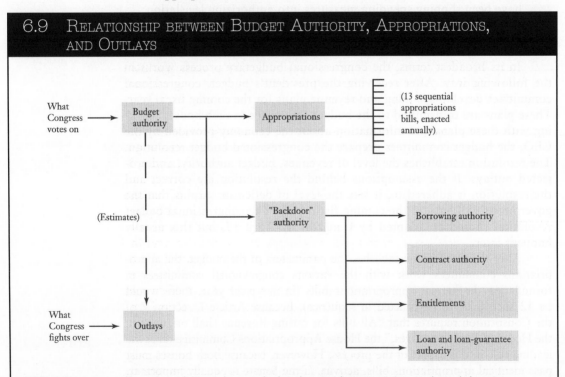

NOTE: Today contract and borrowing authority can be enacted only to the extent that appropriations are also made for a given fiscal year. For loan and loan-guarantee authority, commitments made after 1990 now require estimations of long-term costs (as to delinquencies, defaults, etc.). As a consequence, these are no longer strictly classified as "backdoor" spending. However, since these authorities span two or more fiscal years, such spending may have the effect of compelling the government to continue spending.

- *Contract authority* permits agencies to enter into binding agreements for work to be performed before appropriations are made to compensate contractors for their work. As with borrowing authority, new contract authority is limited to annual appropriations.
- *Entitlement authority* takes place almost entirely outside of the annual appropriations process. It permits agencies to commit the government to make expenditures where no budget authority has been provided in advance. Important examples are the large entitlement programs: Social Security, Medicare, and Medicaid. Such authority, in effect, represents *permanent budget authority*. These programs make payments according to formulas contained in the authorizing legislation, so that spending is relatively automatic; Congress need not act explicitly for expenditure to take place.
- *Loan and loan-guarantee authority* constitutes what has become known as the federal "credit budget." This consists of authority to make pledges that bind the government to pay all or part of the principal and interest to some lender if the borrower defaults. This creates contingent liabilities for the government; there is no obligation to pay unless the borrower fails to make payments.

As indicated in Box 6.9, some of this authority has traditionally been considered (somewhat impolitely) as "backdoor authority." This term generally applies to budget authority provided in legislation outside the normal appropriations process (the "front door"). It usually involves advance commitments to expend funds that haven't been appropriated yet (and that may not be voted on for several years). This is not all budgetary "trickery," however. For instance, there are many legitimate managerial reasons to permit government officials to enter into long-term contracts (e.g., building a nuclear aircraft carrier spans several fiscal years). Long-term borrowing is also appropriate to finance infrastructure projects (highways, bridges, tunnels, etc.) that will benefit the public for decades. In the case of interest payments on the national debt, a permanent appropriation is in place that permits funding without any current action by Congress. As a general rule, however, to avoid abuse of such mechanisms, any authority to commit the government to expend funds outside the formal appropriations process is to be made somewhat reluctantly, insofar as it tends to bind future Congresses to decisions made by a current one. It also pushes the full cost of current spending decisions onto future Congresses and taxpayers, with clear intergenerational equity implications.

State governments make no such distinction between budget authority and appropriations. At the state and local levels, authority to spend generally is granted when appropriations are made. (Even long-term contracts may be made contingent on future appropriations.) In the case of the federal government, however, the distinction between budget authority and actual expenditures is crucial to understanding the pattern of federal expenditures (or outlays). Outlays can be made only on the basis of budget authority. Both are necessary

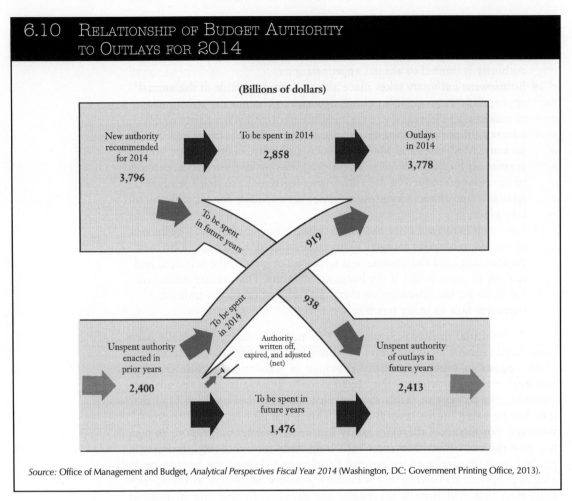

6.10   RELATIONSHIP OF BUDGET AUTHORITY TO OUTLAYS FOR 2014

(Billions of dollars)

| New authority recommended for 2014 **3,796** | To be spent in 2014 **2,858** | Outlays in 2014 **3,778** |

To be spent in future years

919

To be spent in 2014

938

| Unspent authority enacted in prior years **2,400** | Authority written off, expired, and adjusted (net) -4 | Unspent authority of outlays in future years **2,413** |

To be spent in future years **1,476**

Source: Office of Management and Budget, *Analytical Perspectives Fiscal Year 2014* (Washington, DC: Government Printing Office, 2013).

for good budgetary management, however, because many federal activities span several fiscal years, and it is important to know not only the current cost (outlay) but also the estimated total cost (budget authority). This means that in a given fiscal year, new outlays and authority are enacted for the current and future fiscal years. At the same time, unspent authority from prior years may be expended in the current year or future years. This can be one of the most confusing aspects of federal spending; it is most easily understood with the help of a diagram. Box 6.10 graphs the relationship of budget authority to outlays for fiscal year 2014. We are now ready to consider the execution phase of budgeting.

The Continuing Saga of the Budget: Execution

As lengthy and complex as adopting the federal budget may be, its enactment is only the beginning. It must also be executed. Execution is the aspect of budgeting that most affects the performance of government, and in that sense it is the most critical phase of the budget process. Yet execution is subject to all kinds of pitfalls. First, suppose that for one reason or another the budget's projection of revenues falls short. Perhaps the economy has performed worse than anticipated and consequently revenues from income taxes have fallen off because of higher than anticipated unemployment and slower than anticipated growth in personal and corporate income. Under those conditions, if the government spends at levels authorized by the budget, it may run a deficit considered too large and/or too inflationary. Under such circumstances, a number of actions are possible.

Sequesters

Under BEA, if either the budget authority cap or the outlay cap were to be breached, discretionary funds could be sequestered to bring spending into line with the caps. Sequesters were imposed by the OMB, except in the case of supplemental appropriations passed by Congress after June 30. In that case, the cap in the program category for the coming fiscal year would be reduced by the amount appropriated over the cap for the current fiscal year.

As mentioned previously, BEA expired at the end of 2002. However, in its FY 2008 budget submission, the George W. Bush administration proposed extending provisions of BEA in order to subject entitlements and other mandatory spending to control.[18] Bush proposed legislation to require that all legislation that changes mandatory spending in total should not increase the deficit. Any legislation that would increase the deficit would trigger a sequester of direct spending programs, but that proposal failed. There is a good reason that President Bush's proposal targeted mandatory spending specifically. Whereas discretionary spending requires that Congress enact a law, mandatory spending will occur unless Congress does so. Mandatory spending is considered "uncontrollable" (in a sense) because it represents the financial impact of programs and commitments already established. For instance, "entitlements," such as payments under Medicare or to veterans, are available to all eligible individuals who apply. As the number of such individuals increases or if the payments are indexed to inflation, the costs of entitlements will increase. Permanent appropriations to pay interest on the national debt are another example of mandatory, or uncontrollable, spending. Such spending is also subject to sequesters, but under a different process. Even if sequestration is unnecessary, the president may want to reduce or revise spending during the current fiscal year through a variety of techniques.

Direct Budgetary Control

In a very recent development, as part of the 2011 debt ceiling deal, the Obama Administration agreed to enact a "weak" version of BEA in the form of the Budget Control Act of 2011,[19] signed into law by President Barack Obama on August 2, 2011. The Act brought to a conclusion the 2011 United States debt-ceiling crisis. The 2011 law is but a shadow of the original BEA of 1990, however, as it sets hard limits on spending, and calls for firm budget reduction targets. Such rigidities were excluded from the original BEA, and this accounted for the original law's successes. The BEA of 1990 brought spending under control by aligning spending flows with revenue flows, resulting in four successive balanced budgets, beginning in 1998 (the so-called "Clinton Surpluses"). The Budget Control Act of 2011, on the other hand, was the result of a partisan political battle whereby each side sought—not budgetary control per se (bringing back the original BEA mechanism would have handily accomplished that goal)— but rather a postponement of the budget battle until after the 2012 presidential election, and, potentially, the political embarrassment of the other side. Like the Gramm-Rudman-Hollings Acts of 1985 and 1986, the 2011 law only affirms the historical lesson that direct controls are not effective; the BEA of 1990 demonstrated that a flexible approach has great potential to be very effective, however.

Hiring Freezes

The president can refuse to fill vacant federal positions. Such a **hiring freeze** probably does not amount to much of a savings relative to the entire budget. However, it is a symbolic act that may be politically desirable. It is also true that agencies may not be able to spend the funds appropriated to them if their programs are drastically understaffed.

Impoundments

An **impoundment** occurs when the president refuses to allow an executive agency to spend the funds that have been allotted to it. Impoundments can take two forms. **Rescissions** are terminations of funds for an agency or program. In essence, previously appropriated funds will not be spent. **Deferrals** are delays in the spending of appropriated funds. In the case of rescission, if Congress does not vote to rescind the funds within 45 days (of continuous legislative session, rather than calendar), the president is obligated to release funds. Deferrals can be made upon notification of Congress, unless Congress specifically rejects such deferral.

The constitutionality of impoundments has long been in doubt. The first impoundment occurred during Thomas Jefferson's presidency, but the exercise of impoundments seems not to have reached crisis proportions until recent times. In the early 1970s, President Richard Nixon impounded some $12 billion earmarked for highway, health, education, and environmental projects. Nixon thereby attempted to circumvent Congress on important matters of domestic policy. This provoked a number of lawsuits, most of which the president lost. It also encouraged the 1974 Budget and Impoundment Control Act. Under this legislation, the president was authorized to impound funds, but subject to congressional approval. However, the provision for deferrals relied on a type of "one-house veto" declared unconstitutional in *Immigration and Naturalization Service v. Chadha* (1983).[20] Subsequently, several members of Congress and some cities brought suit against deferrals on the basis that Congress would not have granted deferral authority to the president had it known that it would not be able to exercise a legislative veto over the president's actions.[21] Under current legal interpretation, deferrals cannot be made for policy reasons, but only for efficiency, savings, dealing with contingencies, or other reasons specified by statute.

As a result of this litigation, the president's executive power under Article II of the Constitution cannot be said to include impoundments. Legislation passed in 1996 granting the president a "line-item veto" held promise to enhance his or her ability to cut spending up front. More than 40 state governors have some form of line-item veto power, enabling them to take a more central role in the legislative bargaining on the budget through the judicious use of threats to veto specific spending items. Proponents thought, therefore, that similar veto powers would strengthen the president's ability to protect the whole budget. However, several prominent House members and senators thought that the presidential line-item veto violated the constitutional separation of powers by shifting much of an essentially legislative function—budget making—to the executive. The opponents were right; in 1998, the United States Supreme Court struck down the federal line-item veto as an unconstitutional exercise of legislative power by the president (see Box 6.11).

6.11   CLINTON V. CITY OF NEW YORK (1998): THE SHORT LIFE OF THE PRESIDENTIAL LINE-ITEM VETO

The Line-Item Veto Act of 1996 gave the president power to cancel three types of budgetary provisions *after* they had been enacted into law (and most likely signed by the president). These included (1) any dollar amount of budget authority; (2) any item of new direct spending; and (3) any limited tax benefit (e.g., a targeted tax expenditure). The act required the president to consider the legislative history of the provisions being vetoed and to determine that his or her action would reduce the federal budget deficit and not impair governmental functions or the national interest. The act required the president to notify Congress of every veto within five days. It provided for congressional nullification of the president's action by a disapproval bill passed by simple majorities in the Senate and House. The disapproval bill was subject to the normal constitutional provisions for presidential veto and congressional override by a two-thirds majority in each chamber.

The constitutionality of the Line-Item Veto Act was tested after President Bill Clinton canceled spending and tax benefit measures in 1997. By a 6–3 majority, the Supreme Court found the act constitutionally defective. The Court reasoned,

"In both legal and practical effect, the President has amended two Acts of Congress by repealing a portion of each," which violates the Constitution because "there is no constitutional authorization for the President to amend or repeal" statutes after they are enacted. The power to modify laws is one that the framers denied to the president.

The Court was undeterred that the Line-Item Veto Act was strongly supported by a majority of the members of Congress and had been signed by the president. Its opinion issues a strong call for constitutional integrity that appears to foreclose establishing a federal line-item veto by statute. According to its holding, "If this Act were valid, it would authorize the President to create a law whose text was not voted on by either House or presented to the President for signature. That may or may not be desirable, but it is surely not a document that may 'become law' pursuant to Article I, section 7. If there is to be a new procedure, in which the President will play a different role, such change must come through Article V amendment procedures."

Source: Clinton v. City of New York, 524 U.S. 417 (1998).

A second set of problems associated with the execution of budgets occurs at the agency level. Agencies need flexibility in administering their programs. They need to be able to respond to changes in the environments of their programs, to new demand levels, and to unexpected success in accomplishing their purposes. After all, one of the chief reasons for the creation of administrative authority is to enable government to react more rapidly and flexibly than is generally practical through coordinated congressional and presidential action. So what happens when an agency has funds earmarked for one program that it feels should be spent elsewhere in view of new circumstances? Remember, the agency may have formulated its initial budget request two or more years earlier. Two devices are commonly used to shift funds around within agencies. One is called **transfers.** Money can be transferred from one purpose to another if Congress has authorized this process in advance. Transfers are particularly common in the field of foreign affairs, where depending on regime changes abroad, government agencies may want to spend more or less on aid and military assistance. Closely akin to the transfer is **reprogramming.** Under this process an agency is not authorized in advance to switch funds from one program to another but must consult first with the relevant committees in Congress to obtain permission to do so. Despite all the attention paid to funding agencies at the stage of formulating the budget, relatively little attention is paid to these devices, which can result in the movement of billions of dollars from one purpose to another.

One additional process at the agency level bears mention. It is commonly assumed that if an agency fails to spend its entire appropriation, it must return the leftover portion to the Treasury. However, some agencies are authorized to retain the money and apply it to the next year's budget. Again, the sums accumulated in the "pipeline" of "no year" money can be substantial, reaching several hundreds of millions of dollars for the government as a whole.

When one puts all these elements together, the budget as enacted may differ from the budget as executed. Substantial sums can be involved in supplemental appropriations, deferrals, rescissions, transfers, reprogramming, and in the "pipeline." These procedures are often used to promote political ends, as opposed to administrative economies. They open the prospect for continuing controversy over funding even after appropriations have been authorized. But this is only one of several problems associated with the federal budgetary process.

Continuing Problem Areas

Among the major problems with the federal budget process that we have not yet emphasized are the following.

The Length of the Budget Cycle

The entire budget cycle from its start in agencies to the finish of the fiscal year takes about 30 months. This often means that the assumptions about the economy and the needs of any given program present at the start of the cycle need to be revised later. It is one reason that flexibility in execution is so desirable. The interdependence of the United States economy and foreign economies, the rapidly changing character of international relations, and even the unpredictability of the weather's impact on agriculture and energy consumption all make even one-year predictions somewhat unreliable.

The length of the budget cycle has an impact on presidential transitions. A newly elected president, who may have run against the incumbent, spends January 20 to September 30 under the budget established by his or her predecessor and already being executed by the agencies. The presidential budget proposal that would go through the next fiscal year (that is, from October 1 of the year of presidential inauguration to September 30 of the next calendar year) has already been worked on in the executive branch for some nine months or so. The new president is in a position to modify this budget somewhat, though a radical refashioning is politically and administratively difficult.

A new president elected in 2016, taking office in January 2017, would not be able to work with a budget wholly of his or her proposing until October 1, 2019—almost a full two years after the electoral campaign that may have provided a mandate for change. It is no wonder presidents often find administrative matters so exasperating. A positive feature of the length of the budget cycle, however, is that it makes for administrative continuity.

It is sometimes proposed that the government move away from the annual budget to a two-year budget. Twenty-two states employ some form of two-year (or biennial) budget, with some enacting a true two-year spending plan, while others enact two one-year budgets consecutively. Variations on these approaches also permit some states to adjust budgets based on updated revenue and expenditure forecasts. Some states also require five-year projections of major spending categories based on current legislative requirements. The advantage of two-year budgeting is that it permits closer scrutiny of expenditure program changes beyond the current fiscal year. The states have recently been moving toward annual budgeting, however. Local governments usually have no tradition of multiyear budgeting, because municipal councils have made a fairly standard practice of adjusting appropriations, as necessary, throughout the fiscal year (called "rebudgeting"). A biennial budget process would not alleviate the problems associated with a long time frame, however, and probably would only lengthen the budget cycle.

Budgetary Politics

Sometimes budgeting takes on the aura of a game, with the various agency players trying to increase their shares and elected officials trying, at least ostensibly, to keep taxes down and promote administrative economy. A number of agency strategies are common. One is to threaten to cut the most popular or politically desirable functions first. Thus a school district will frequently threaten to cut football and basketball programs if the voters do not approve higher taxes. So, too, federal agencies threaten to cut popular services unless their full funding requests are met. The National Park Service once threatened to close the Washington Monument in such a game! (Such a closure—along with many others—did occur in FY 1996, when at considerable expense to the taxpayers, the government was partly shut down for lack of a budget. Due to a legislative impasse resulting in a sequester in November–December 2013, about 800,000 federal employees were furloughed and closures included such iconic sites as the National World War II Memorial in Washington DC. A chronology of the FY 1996 shutdown is presented in Box 6.12.)

6.12   NO GOVERNMENT TODAY! ANATOMY OF A SHUTDOWN

From November 14 to November 19, 1995, and then again from December 16, 1995, to January 6, 1996, the federal government was partly shut down. There was no natural disaster, no subversion, no attack by a foreign foe. Rather, the constitutional separation of powers was hard at work: Congress and the president were unable to come to terms on a budget. Here's what happened:

November 13: President Clinton vetoed a bill that would have provided funds for continuing government operations because it included cuts in educational and environmental programs and an increase in Medicare premiums.

November 14: No agreement is reached, and about 800,000 federal workers throughout the nation are dismissed until further notice. National monuments, museums, and the National Zoological Park close. About 340 White House staffers are barred from work, and about 90 remain on duty. "Essential" federal employees, including air traffic controllers and safety personnel, continue to work, as do military personnel and about two-thirds of the Department of Defense's civilian employees. (The term "essential" causes a stir among pundits and public employees. Is the partially closed Office of Government Ethics essential? Eventually other terms are adopted.)

November 15: The shutdown spreads to government contractors who are told to stop working on agency projects. The Treasury loses an estimated $15 to $25 million because of the Securities and Exchange Commission's inability to charge a fee. The Secretary of the Treasury says he will use billions of dollars from government retirement accounts to keep the government from defaulting on its debt payments.

November 16: The Grand Canyon is closed; steps are taken to close the nation's largest national parks. Congress, also without appropriations, keeps its staff hard at work.

November 17: No progress.

November 18: Concern grows that the shutdown will prove very costly and, if continued, will jeopardize the Department of Veterans Affairs' hospitals, federal prisons, and benefit payments to the public.

November 19: The president and Congress agree to balance the budget by 2002. Legislation is passed putting federal employees back to work. Plans are made to fund the government until December 15 in the hope of enacting a budget for fiscal 1996 by then.

December 16, 1995–January 6, 1996: Redux on a smaller scale. About 284,000 federal employees are furloughed. The public seems fed up, and Congress gets most of the heat. Government is reopened, but there is still no agreement to fund it through the remainder of the fiscal year.

April 25, 1996: After the two shutdowns and 13 stopgap funding measures, the nation has a budget. The president appears victorious in preventing deep cuts in the administration's favored programs. The congressional Republicans, so seemingly invincible after their spectacular victories in the 1994 elections, appear to be in disarray.

The total cost of the two shutdowns was estimated at $1.4 billion, leaving many to wonder whether this is any way to run a government already strapped for cash.

Sources: Christy Harris, "Clinton, Congress Finalize 1996 Budget," *Federal Times,* 6 May 1996, 3; "Shutdown Chronology," *Washington Post,* 20 November 1995, A19; authors' interviews and observations.

Agencies also pad their requests in the expectation that they will subsequently be reduced. This promotes a budgetary ritual that involves a lot of noise, activity, hand-wringing, and newspaper headlines—and no significant change. Agencies can play the "camel's nose" game and seek to obtain seed money—limited funds for a one-year program—with the expectation that, like a camel, once they get their nose under the budgetary "tent," more is sure to follow. Finally, **repackaging** is a common ruse used to seek increased funding. Under this approach, an existing program is explained in terms that seem to fit with a president's new priorities. Although it is difficult to become irate about these games, they are inherently dishonest and can hardly raise the levels of public debate and voter information about the way the government operates.[22] Such game playing may be complicated by deep disagreements between the executive and legislative branches.

Raising the Debt Ceiling, or Eliminating It?

The American public has never fully accepted the idea that long-term deficits are legitimate. There is something psychologically pleasing about the notion of a balanced budget. It is viewed as "tidy" or something that reflects sound management. Consequently, it has been thought that there should be a statutory limitation on the size of the federal government's accumulated deficit (the national debt). But Congress and the president have found it impossible or undesirable to live within the confines of these debt ceilings, and so with routine frequency they vote to raise the ceiling and increase the debt. When Congress failed to raise the ceiling in FY 1996, the Secretary of the Treasury kept the government from defaulting by borrowing from various funds to escape the statutory debt ceiling. This prompted calls for his impeachment among some seemingly irate members of Congress. In the end, though, whatever leverage the ceiling may have given, the legislature lost when public opinion turned against the Republican-led Congress. The ceiling was lifted in return for a presidential promise to achieve a balanced budget within seven years. Consequently, the debt ceiling is not much of a genuine limit.

As previously noted, the debt ceiling crisis of 2011 ended with enactment of the Budget Control Act of 2011. Essentially a political dispute between the president and congressional Republicans, the debt ceiling crisis threatened to force the U.S. Government into sovereign default by around August 3, 2011. As it turned out, the bond ratings agency Standard & Poor's subsequently reduced the U.S. Government's credit rating from the highest possible rating of "AAA," to "AA+," citing not the country's ability to pay its debts—which remained unquestioned—but the Congress's willingness to jeopardize the stability of world credit markets for political purposes.[23] In the wake of the 2011 downgrading of U.S. Treasury securities, economists began to raise important questions about the economic effectiveness of having any debt limit at all. The limit is always raised, and almost always on time. Thus, as a check on debt levels, it may be argued that it is ineffective. Quite to the contrary, it can prove to be harmful, as the Standard & Poor's action demonstrates. As the U.S. debt levels continue to rise, the issue of retaining the debt limit appears likely to arise again.

"Uncontrollable" Spending

Perhaps these problems point in the direction of what seems to have been the most serious problem with federal budgeting since the early 1970s. To a large extent, perhaps involving over two-thirds of the budget, federal spending has been uncontrolled in the sense that funds have been committed in advance. Such commitments take three main forms. First, there is payment of the federal debt, generated by the borrowing that accompanies deficit spending. Payment cannot legally or constitutionally be avoided, and real as opposed to technical default by the federal government would surely spell disaster for the nation. Net interest payments on the debt alone accounted for about 6.4 percent of budget outlays in 2011.[24] A second kind of uncontrollable spending involves entitlements. Entitlements arise out of governmental commitments to groups of citizens. Social Security, Medicare, Medicaid, and veterans' benefits are examples. The expense of entitlements tends to rise over time as the number of people in the eligible group expands. For instance, as the proportion of the population that is elderly expands, so too expands the number of individuals entitled to Medicare and Social Security benefits. In addition, cost-of-living adjustments (COLAs) may be granted to beneficiaries to compensate for inflation. Finally, uncontrollable spending may result from contractual obligations entered into by the government. Often these are multi-year and involve cost overruns and adjustments for inflation that become substantial. However, despite the label "uncontrollable," these costs can be reduced over time. As part of a general reaction to the "uncontrollable" problem, federal agencies now make five-year projections of the cost of their programs.

◆→ A BUDGET THEORY OR THEORIES ABOUT BUDGETING?

For the most part, the mixture of political, managerial, and legal dimensions of public budgeting and finance makes it difficult to develop a budgetary process that is coherent and that satisfies all governmental needs. Although most of our focus in this chapter has been on the federal level, the same is true for the states. The main differences are that state governments are under far greater pressure to avoid annual deficits, do not engage in countercyclical fiscal policy, and are far more subject to the discipline of the public debt market.

State-level deficits and surpluses do not necessarily coincide with similar fiscal results at the federal level. State finances are much more sensitive to the national and regional business cycles. In the 1980s, for example, many states had great surpluses, standing in sharp contrast to the federal government's Reagan-era deficits. By the early 1990s, both the federal and state governments were running serious deficits, although the magnitudes did vary somewhat by region of the country. By 2000, as a direct result of the unprecedented economic expansion of the Clinton years, governments at all levels were enjoying surpluses. In the mid-2000s, however, state and federal finances had softened again, as a consequence of revenue falls in the Great Recession.

Unlike the federal government, states draw distinctions between operating budgets, which encompass the costs of running the business of government, and capital budgets, money used for longer-term projects such as investments in infrastructure. Consequently, state surpluses or deficits better reflect the match between current year revenues and expenditures than does the federal budget. Today only 19 states employ various forms of two-year budgets. States also vary in the extent to which they rely on county governments to deliver public goods and services, making comparisons across states a tricky business. Hence, some care must be exercised when comparing budgetary results between the federal and state levels and among the several states.

One might look to the states as "laboratories" in which different approaches to budgeting have been undertaken. There is enough variation among them to provide a fruitful field of investigation. The ways in which they raise revenues differ widely, as do their spending patterns. Some states rely heavily on income taxes and fund huge educational programs or welfare programs, whereas others rely on sales taxes and provide a much reduced program of public services. The behavior of local governments also varies substantially with respect to raising and spending revenues. However, despite these "laboratories" and variations, the United States has not worked out a dominant theory of public budgeting that can answer what has long been considered the most basic question on the expenditure side: "On what basis shall it be decided to allocate x dollars to activity A instead of activity B?"[25] We can study the variety of budgetary processes, sources of revenue, and allocation of expenditures ad nauseum without finding an answer to this question. As usual, however, part of the reason is that different perspectives generate different answers. Those who view budgeting as a managerial endeavor stress one set of values, those who see it as political emphasize another, and those imbued with legalistic concerns emphasize still others. Therefore, there are several theories of budgeting rather than a single budget theory. And as in other areas of public administration, there is a vigorous contest among these theories for influence and dominance.

The Managerial Approach to Public Budgeting

The orthodox managerial perspective on public administration seeks to develop an approach to budgeting that promotes the values of efficiency, economy, and effectiveness. It seeks to use budgeting to cut waste, encourage the highest level of productivity, and strengthen managerial control over the operations of government. The new public management shares some of these goals but puts greater emphasis on performance and responsiveness. It favors financing agencies through user fees where feasible and making programs compete for customers. In this view, market forces are the best way of promoting efficiency and customer satisfaction.

The first major step in the development of the traditional managerial approach to budgeting occurred in 1912, when the Taft Commission first proposed a unified executive budget for the federal government, to be proposed by the president. This was followed in 1914, when the New York Bureau of Municipal Research called for the development of a "performance budget." The executive budget was instituted with the Budget and Accounting Act of 1921. The performance budget would have to wait until 1949, when the influential First Hoover Commission recommended the use of performance budgeting in the federal government.

To understand the importance of the performance budget one must appreciate that it was preceded by lump-sum appropriations and the **line-item budget.** Lump-sum budgets gave agencies funds to expend more or less as they saw fit, with little political control over how the funds were used. The lump-sum approach was chaotic and left the activities of public administrators beyond the scrutiny of elected officials. The line-item budget was adopted in order to rectify this situation. It requires that appropriations be linked to objects of expenditure (salaries, benefits, travel, supplies, grants, etc.). Although these objects could be defined in different ways, the tendency was to place every significant expenditure on a separate line in the agency's budget. For instance, the salary of each employee might be listed separately, as might the cost of pencils, paper, pens, and so forth. The chief executive or legislature could then go down the list of agency requests for appropriations and cross out, reduce, or, less likely, augment an agency's funding request for any of the items. This provides a great deal of control of *how* money is spent, but it tells elected officials little about what the agency is supposed to accomplish. In other words, what are all those pencils for? What is it that the agency does? And how much does it cost? The **performance budget** was intended to address questions like these.

The Performance Budget

The performance budget seeks to answer these questions without losing control over expenditures. At a minimum, it involves the following:

1. "The *formulation* and adoption of a plan of activities and programs for a stated time period." In other words, what is the agency intending to do, why, how much of it, and when?
2. *Funding,* that is, relating program costs to resources, or determining what kind of agency performance can be obtained within the confines of the resources available.
3. *Execution,* or the achievement of the authorized plan, within the time frame and resources allocated to it.[26]

Performance budgeting is the foundation of all modern managerially oriented public budgeting strategies. A performance budget does not do away with line items entirely, however; it is best thought of as being layered on top of traditional line-item budgets. It fits in well with specialized organizational designs, as the subunits of agencies could be considered the "activities" for which funding is targeted. For example, in a public hospital, "food service," "x-rays," "surgery," and "housekeeping" might be considered budget activities and might also form separate administrative organizational units. Performance budgeting promotes the managerial goal of allowing evaluation of administrative performance because it often requires that "performance reports" accompany budget requests. Consequently, performance budgeting has a concrete meaning to public managers: activities and organizational units tend to coincide; performance is measured and evaluated (in some fashion); and budgetary requests and appropriations are connected to performance levels.

The use of performance budgeting has made considerable headway in American government at all levels. However, even though most states use it in some aspects, only a few could be considered to adhere rigorously to the performance concept. Among the common complaints about performance budgeting are that (1) it does not afford the legislature the same level of participation and control as does the line-item budget, and (2) it is not refined enough to deal with the complexity of administrative operations. Overcoming these specific limitations was the thrust in development of the **program budget** approach.

The Program Budget

Program budgeting is often considered interchangeable with performance budgeting, but there is a significant difference. Whereas performance budgeting concentrates on activities and tends to overlap organizational units, program budgeting looks at the purpose (not activities) of governmental administration and seeks to relate funding to the achievement of these purposes. Program budgeting may tend to "cross-cut" administrative organizational units, but it does not necessarily do so. It is also prospective in the sense of seeking to adopt policies based on the prospects for the achievement of goals at given levels of cost. In other words, it incorporates a "cost-effectiveness" approach while exploring various administrative means to obtaining a given level of benefit at the lowest cost.

Returning to our example of performance budgeting in a hospital may help clarify the difference between these two systems of budgeting. Listing costs by activities does not provide us with an idea of what the purpose of a hospital is. It tells us what it does but not what its ultimate goal is. Program budgeting, in contrast, would identify the goals of the hospital and seek to relate funding to these goals. For instance, "housekeeping" might be redefined in terms of providing "sanitation," and an appropriate level of sanitation might be defined. Next, different ways of obtaining that sanitary level might be mapped out, along with their projected costs. Then the approach providing the desired level at the lowest cost would presumably be selected and funded. Such an exercise can involve interesting choices. For instance, the performance budgeting activity of taking x-rays could be redefined in program budget terms as part of a wider objective of "diagnosing." The success of the operation of the radiology department at this point would be related to the utility of using x-rays to diagnose medical problems, and the cost of x-rays would be compared to the cost of other diagnostic techniques. This would have obvious implications for the purchase and use of different types of radiological equipment and for the decision about who should operate it—technicians, medical doctors, or teams of both.

Perhaps policing provides a more familiar example of the distinction between the performance budget and the program budget. "Patrolling" under the performance budget could become "crime control" under a program budget. Then different types of crimes could be targeted for reduction, and police officers and other resources could be assigned accordingly.

These examples should help clarify the difference between performance budgeting and program budgeting, but they are not intended to suggest that program budgeting is not without substantial problems. These problems were made evident by the introduction of a particular type of program budgeting into the federal government in the 1960s. The federal experience with the Planning Programming Budgeting System (PPBS) provides so many lessons that it should be considered in some detail.

PPBS was once hailed as a revolutionary approach to budgetary and administrative decision making with almost messianic qualities.[27] It promised to solve many of our budgetary problems, many of our administrative ones, and many of our political conflicts over how governmental funds should be spent. It was used by Secretary of Defense Robert McNamara in the early 1960s to select weapons systems based on delivering more "bang for the buck." In 1965, President Lyndon Johnson made PPBS mandatory for most federal departments and agencies. But by 1971 it was discontinued as a requirement for all agencies. The core elements of PPBS were the following:

1. Analyze program goals in operational terms. For example, instead of saying the goal of a program is to promote highway safety, the goal would be presented as averting x number of deaths through traffic accidents, averting y number of serious injuries, averting z number of lesser injuries, and reducing property damage by w percent.
2. Analyze the total costs of programs over one year and several years.
3. Analyze alternative ways of achieving the goals. This would be done from a cost-effective approach. In the example, how much does it cost to avert a death through the use of seat belts versus the cost per death averted through better driver training?
4. Develop a systematic way of considering the costs and benefits of all governmental programs in a comparative fashion. In other words, what is the cost of a death averted through driver training versus the cost through public health activities or the cost through promotion of world peace? What are the total benefits of each approach?

At first glance, this sounds eminently reasonable. What does it cost the government to do what it seeks to do? How could it do it for less? Certainly these are important questions. However, PPBS was hard to apply and did not always determine how funds should be appropriated. Why did PPBS not work out in practice?

First, the goals of governmental programs may be unclear and lacking in any operational content. For example, how does one operationally define "promoting world peace" or "winning the Global War on Terror" (GWOT) called for by President George W. Bush in 2001? To some, these goals mean avoiding the death of members of the U.S. armed forces in combat. To others, they mean promoting international security through the use of military force. Even more complicated is the situation in which a program, such as food stamps, is put together by a coalition of diverse and economically antagonistic interests.[28] Under such conditions, an operational definition of the objectives of the program would threaten to destroy the coalition and the program. While PPBS cannot work without operational goals, in some policy areas the U.S. political system may not be able to work well *with* them, because they exacerbate conflict and make it difficult to build majority coalitions.

Also, because "what you measure is what you get," choosing the right goals to measure is essential. This may be a serious problem for implementing the Government Performance and Results Act Modernization Act of 2010 as well because it requires agencies to formulate specific goals. (This act is discussed further later in this chapter.)

Second, cost-benefit analysis can be exceedingly difficult to perform, even when goals are clear. This is especially true when there are many program overlaps. Some costs and benefits cannot be quantified. Yet, at least in government, these may be of great political importance. For example, what is the benefit derived from a public park? From a strong civil rights policy? From intervening in the Middle East or the Balkans to promote peace? How does one assess the costs and benefits of any specific course of activity on the reputation of the president and his or her ability to exercise the functions of that office effectively?

Third, projecting the costs and benefits of different administrative means of obtaining objectives can be highly speculative or even impossible. In short, often not enough is known about how government can achieve its goals to enable us to predict the consequences of one particular strategy versus another.

Finally, even when the analysis was undertaken with sufficient rigor, although the PPBS approach could inform political decision makers, it could not necessarily resolve the key issues in choosing policy alternatives. Returning to our macabre example of deaths averted, we can illustrate this point through the following example. In an article called "HEW Grapples with PPBS," Elizabeth Drew found that the Department of Health, Education, and Welfare (HEW, later split into the Department of Health and Human Services and Department of Education) had programs intended to avert deaths caused by disease and through traffic accidents.[29] The cost of averting a death by promoting the use of seat belts was $87; the cost of averting a death by attacking cancer of the cervix was $3,470. In cost-benefit terms (assuming each death averted to be of equal benefit), the greatest benefit for the least cost would have had HEW allocate its resources to programs in the following order:

> Seat belt use
> Automotive restraint devices
> Avoiding pedestrian injury
> Motorcyclist helmets
> Arthritis
> Reducing driver drinking
> Syphilis
> Cancer of the cervix
> Lung cancer
> Breast cancer
> Tuberculosis
> Driver licensing
> Cancer of the head and neck
> Colorectal cancer

Suppose you have limited resources to give HEW for these worthy objectives (as taxpayers and legislatures do). Are you willing to allocate funds to motorcyclist helmets over cancer of the cervix or breast cancer? What would the National Organization for Women say about a decision to follow the logic of cost-benefit analysis in this case? What might it say it to members of Congress seeking reelection? How do motorcyclists feel about being required to wear helmets? What would philosophers say about the choice available to those who die in motorcycle accidents for failure to wear a helmet versus the "choice" available in getting cancer of the breast or cervix? Should these differences affect one's budget allocations?

The point is not that PPBS cannot be useful in providing an indication of the costs and benefits of various programs. However, it should be evident that it cannot answer the question, "On what basis shall it be decided to allocate x dollars to activity A instead of activity B?" Although PPBS was conceived as a managerial system of budgeting, the unfortunate experience with PPBS tends to illustrate the fundamentally political nature of budgeting. If one could use PPBS to resolve the matter of policy choice, the political priorities of the nation would be clear.

PPBS died in the federal bureaucracy largely for the reasons discussed—and also because it was difficult to apply where programs overlapped several agencies, as is so often the case in federal administration.[30] But that does not mean it is not appropriate for some types of budgetary decisions. It is still used in the U.S. Department of Defense, and in some state and local governments, apparently with satisfactory results. Still, its failure to be fully implemented at the federal level sparked interest in other managerial approaches to budgeting. Perhaps most important among these has been **zero-base budgeting (ZBB)**.

Zero-Base Budgeting

ZBB is intended to give budgetary decision makers a choice among different funding levels for different programs and activities. It starts from the intellectual premise that the budgeting process should be used to review the political desirability and administrative effectiveness of governmental programs. The concept of zero basing is that existing programs and activities should not automatically be funded, but rather should have to justify their continuation as part of the annual budget cycle. In theory, each program and activity is vulnerable to zero funding in each new fiscal year.

The main elements of ZBB are as follows:

1. The identification of *decision units*. These are the lowest-level organizational or programmatic units for which budgets are prepared.[31] Each decision unit must have a manager identified as responsible for the operation of that administrative entity as a whole.

2. The formulation of *decision packages*. These are derived from a comprehensive yearly review of each decision unit's purposes and functions. This review considers such questions as what would happen if the decision unit were not funded at all; what would happen with 50 percent funding, 75 percent, and so on; how can its operations be improved; and can a greater benefit-cost ratio be developed? Once the review is completed, the decision unit's operations are ranked according to the perceived importance of its activities. Those activities of top priority are in the first decision package, those of secondary importance in a second decision package, and so on. The operations, costs, and benefits of these packages are presented in a comprehensive fashion to budgetary decision makers.

3. The *ranking* of decision packages by top-level managers. This establishes organization-wide priorities and seeks to coordinate the agency's choice of level of activity with the amount of funding likely to be forthcoming. The key to ranking decision packages is not simply choosing from among different activities but also deciding on different levels of activity within any given package.

Like other budget processes, ZBB can be complex and difficult to understand in the abstract. Consequently, an example is in order. Peter Pyhrr, the developer of the ZBB concept, provided the following illustration.[32] For "residential refuse collection" in a city, the decision unit is the administrative operation responsible for collecting and transporting all residential solid waste for disposal. The decision package would evaluate different ways of performing this function and different levels of activity. Different means would include such approaches as the following:

1. Requiring residential users of the service to purchase 13 gallon plastic bags and place their garbage in them
2. Using neighborhood dumpsters
3. Collecting from garbage cans rather than plastic bags

4. Using "barrel" trucks rather than conventional trucks with the capacity to crush (compact) the garbage
5. Contracting out to private firms for refuse collection

The cost of each of these means would be assessed, and this assessment would go a long way in dictating the choice of which would be used.

Different levels of activity would then be considered. For instance, these might involve pickup once a week or twice a week for trash and different levels of activity for brush collection. When the decision packages were ranked, the most desired means would be linked with the most desired level of activity. In this fashion it might turn out that pickups twice a week could be afforded when dumpsters were used but that otherwise pickups would have to be limited to once a week.

As in the case of almost all known budgetary strategies, ZBB has some serious limitations. The analysis can become too complex, time-consuming, or cumbersome to be useful. The identification of decision units runs into the problem of specifying objectives in clear operational terms. Assessing costs can be difficult or impossible. In addition, as the example suggests, shifting the cost of a function may pose difficult problems for analysis. Requiring residents to purchase plastic bags pushes some of the costs from the city onto the private citizens and raises concerns for environmental protection agencies. Anytime costs are shifted onto individuals equity issues are likely to arise. Is the cost of plastic garbage bags substantial enough to pose an economic hardship for the city's poorest residents? When we try to apply ZBB at the federal level, such shifting of costs from one party or agency to another may be a substantial concern. ZBB also does not "start from zero," but applies mainly to those discretionary functions whose costs may be reduced without significantly affecting service levels.

Despite these problems, several jurisdictions have reported success with ZBB or some adaptation of it. However, it seems to have been misapplied in the federal government during the Carter administration (1977–1981). The main difficulties were that (1) perhaps out of political and organizational necessity, decision units were identified to coincide with agencies and bureaus rather than programs and activities and (2) the ZBB approach was applied government-wide rather than selectively. Pyhrr called Carter's approach "absolute folly."[33] Others detected a note of shrewdness: ZBB became little more than an overlay on traditional budgeting processes; consequently, it was easy to apply, engendered little controversy, and enabled Carter to take credit for a major reform!

PPBS and ZBB are leading examples of the managerial approach to budgeting. Although they do improve the budgeting process and generate much information pertinent to budgetary choices, neither has been fully satisfactory in reducing the budgetary process to a purely managerial endeavor. In truth, they are probably not intended to do so entirely, but they do tend to downgrade the political nature of budgets and the political choices inherent in budgetary decisions.[34]

New Performance Budgeting

Advocates for federal budgetary reform have long endorsed the notion that budget decisions should be more clearly informed by performance. New performance budgeting has been under development at the state and local levels for some time, going by such names as entrepreneurial budgeting, results-oriented budgeting, and outcome-based budgeting. A critical aspect of this approach is providing sufficient flexibility to public managers to take advantage of opportunities for cost savings and innovative uses of new technologies and techniques in service delivery. The basic idea is that focusing on results will prompt governments to become more responsive to the needs and interests of their citizens and more efficient and effective in service delivery. At the federal level, the Government Performance and Results Act of 1993 (GPRA) began the latest effort to strengthen the links between managerial performance and budgetary resource allocation. A congressional initiative, GPRA enjoyed wide support from the executive branch and endorsements from the National Performance Review (NPR). Implementation of GPRA was designed to be a multi-year-long process, ending in fiscal year 2000.[35]

According to GPRA, agencies were to formulate five-year **strategic plans** in conjunction with the OMB and Congress. The plans were required to include performance goals related to the achievement of specific, measurable outcomes. Beginning with fiscal year 1999, each federal agency was to prepare an annual performance plan containing annual performance goals covering the program activities in its budget requests. In addition, to line up performance plans with programs, the OMB required that agencies' performance plans display funding levels to achieve performance goals by program activity. This ensured a systematic presentation of performance information alongside budget amounts. In cases where there are overlapping performance goals or specific program activities that reinforced each other (not uncommon in the federal government), the links between program activities and annual performance goals were made through aggregation, disaggregation, or consolidation, as depicted in Box 6.13. This was a distinct improvement over past federal performance budget attempts in which the presentation of performance information was largely unconnected to the budget structures and budget decision making procedures employed by Congress.

Past performance budgeting initiatives failed because executive branch agencies selected goals, developed plans, and devised performance measures without direct congressional involvement. GPRA corrected this by assuring Congress a pivotal role insofar as performance goals, measures, and plans were the result of negotiations involving agencies, interested members of the public, and appropriations subcommittees. This meant that the structure of program activities would not be consistent across the federal government, but tailored to the management needs of particular agencies. This avoided a "cookie cutter" approach to budgeting across agencies and added an element of flexibility to the GPRA process. Another source of flexibility was the option that agencies had to propose changes to their budget structures, subject to OMB and congressional approval.

6.13   NEW PERFORMANCE BUDGETING—LINKING ANNUAL PERFORMANCE PLANS, BUDGET ACCOUNTS, AND PROGRAM ACTIVITY UNDER THE GPRA OF 1993

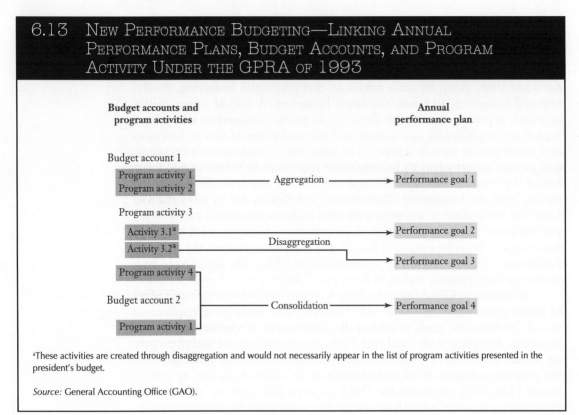

aThese activities are created through disaggregation and would not necessarily appear in the list of program activities presented in the president's budget.

Source: General Accounting Office (GAO).

Budget and activity structures can be complex in some agencies, and aligning the two was one of the greatest challenges in implementing GPRA. The budgetary account and planning structures in agencies were not developed as unified, integrated approaches. Each evolved over time in response to specific needs. This naturally led to a variety of approaches in linking up budget and performance plan information. Box 6.14 partially displays the effort of one agency to link the two in a way that indicated how spending for discrete activities may support the accomplishment of multiple goals and objectives. Other challenges included making agency goals more results-oriented, developing outcome-oriented performance measures, taking steps to ensure that performance data were accurate and reliable, and developing approaches to prioritize performance goals and objectives. Especially when it came to using performance measures, too many agencies continued to rely on outputs (e.g., number of clients contacted) rather than outcomes (e.g., clients who become economically productive).

There is no doubt that GPRA's new performance budgeting approach provided useful information about government programs to budget makers. However, it did not coordinate strategic plans with the presidential term of

6.14   New Performance Budgeting—Linking Program Activities that Support Common Goals and Objectives under the GPRA of 1993

ACF* budget accounts and program activities

Family support payments to states account

1. State child support administrative costs ($2,749)

2. Federal incentive/hold harmless payments to states ($469)

3. Access and visitation grants ($10)

4. Payments to territories

5. Repatriation

6. Aid to families with dependent children benefit payments

7. Emergency assistance

Children's research and technical assistance account

1. Federal parent locator service ($30)

2. Training and technical assistance

3. Child welfare study

4. Welfare research

5. Evaluation of welfare to work

6. Evaluation of abstinence education

ACF strategic goals, strategic objectives, and performance goals

Strategic goal:
Increase economic independence and productivity for families.

Strategic objective:
Increase parental responsibility ($3,257)

Performance goals:
• Increase the paternity establishment percentage among children born out-of-wedlock to 96 percent
• Increase the percentage of cases having child support orders to 74 percent
• Increase the collection rate for current support to 70 percent
• Increase the percentage of paying cases among arrearage cases to 46 percent
• Increase the cost-effectiveness ratio (total dollars collected per dollar of expenditures) to $5.00

Note: Dollars in millions. Numbers may not total due to rounding.
*Administration for Families and Children

Source: General Accounting Office (GAO). Based on the Administration for Children and Families fiscal year 1999 performance plan and the *Budget of the United States Government Fiscal year 1999-Appendix* (Washington, DC: Government Printing Office, 1998).

office, promoted tension between the OMB and congressional committees concerning the role of each in the strategic planning process, and, for reasons that are not entirely clear, was not used by Congress as much as anticipated in supervising the agency programs and making budget decisions. The Government Performance and Results Act Modernization Act of 2010[36] was enacted to overcome these limitations.

The GPRA Modernization Act contains a number of innovative features. In addition to coordinating strategic planning with the presidential term, it requires agency quarterly performance reports and establishes agency performance improvement officers and a Performance Improvement Council. Strategic plans must cover at least four years and be made available on a public website no later than the first Monday in February after the beginning of the president's term. The president and Congress must be notified when these plans are posted. The plans must contain a mission statement, identification of general and priority goals and objectives, information on how the agency proposes to achieve them, as well as *how the plan incorporates perspectives gained through consultation with Congress*. Consultation is specifically required with the majority and minority parties on the relevant authorizing, appropriations, and oversight congressional committees. The plans must also identify external factors that could affect achievement of agency goals and objectives. In this age of outsourcing, it is notable that the act specifically identifies drafting the strategic plans as an inherently governmental function that must be performed by federal employees. Performance goals and objectives should be "objective, quantifiable, measurable" unless the agency and OMB agree that this is infeasible. The agency's deputy agency head or equivalent is designated chief operating officer (COO) with responsibilities for overseeing agency strategic planning and performance improvement. The COO is assisted by the performance improvement officer. The director for management of the OMB and the performance improvement officers constitute the Performance Improvement Council, which is charged with coordinating agencies' goals, objectives, and performance efforts.

The GPRA Modernization Act's requirements for consultation with Congress and stakeholders point directly to the possibility of congressional micromanagement and the impact of organized interests on the strategic planning process. The act also has a number of provisions intended to improve transparency in agency strategic planning and performance reporting. This brings us to the politics of public budgeting.

The Political Approach to Public Budgeting

The political approach to public budgeting emphasizes several concerns: representation, consensus and coalition building, and the locus of power in allocating funds. Incrementalism has been the favored political approach to public budgeting in the United States. This approach tends to treat last year's appropriation to an agency or program as a base level of funding that should be diminished only under unusual and highly controversial circumstances. With the base being more or less fixed, the real discussion is over the increment that will be allocated to an agency or program during the next fiscal year. Moreover, incrementalism shies away from comprehensive analysis, the specifications of clear goals, and program evaluation.

Incrementalism is politically comfortable for several reasons. The gradualism of the incremental approach makes it possible to provide widespread representation to groups and interests in the society.[37] Any socially and economically diverse society, including the United States, is made up of antagonistic interests. Incrementalism allows these sectors to be represented in government even though they are at cross-purposes. This is true because it does not demand a comprehensive statement of the objectives of governmental activity and because it does not rigorously question the base appropriation to existing agencies and functions. Consequently, it is possible to have governmental programs that conflict without giving serious consideration to the issue of whether the failure to make fundamental choices among them is in some sense irrational. For instance, the federal government has subsidized tobacco growers and at the same time tried to discourage smoking by the public.[38] The growers are represented in the Department of Agriculture. Public health interests are represented in the Department of Health and Human Services. Each can be funded in the budget process, and until deficits were considered a major problem, neither was concerned about having its level of appropriation reduced from that of the past fiscal year.

Another factor favoring incrementalism is that it allows the building of consensus and coalitions by providing funding to diverse interests. Coalitions make it possible for political parties to exist and for politicians to be elected. Consensus is fostered when conflict is muted. And conflict can be avoided when the objectives of government are stated in terms that can be universally accepted. Again, "nutrition," "defense," "health," "justice," and "peace" are examples. Almost everyone in the society might agree that these are desirable governmental objectives in the abstract. However, the reaction may be different when they are translated into specific programs with specific objectives—to subsidize farmers, avert deaths in one way or another, deploy nuclear weapons and build military bases, require school desegregation through busing, represent the interest of the fetus in court, and destabilize foreign regimes through covert activities. A primary difficulty with comprehensive approaches such as PPBS and ZBB is that they exacerbate conflict, break down consensus, and make it difficult for the political system to work well at the national level. That may also prove true of the GPRA Modernization Act of 2010. Incrementalism, in contrast, allows funding for a variety of activities that enable different groups and citizens to define and conceptualize them in favorable terms.

Similarly, incrementalism enables parties and politicians to build broad coalitions by providing governmental funding to diverse and competing interests. The classic example of such a coalition was put together in the 1930s by President Franklin D. Roosevelt. He was able to gain widespread support of southerners, unions, urbanites, and members of minority groups. This "New Deal Coalition" remained the backbone of the Democratic Party well into the 1960s.[39] It was routine for Democrat to oppose Democrat on civil rights issues, but the basic coalition held together at least until the election of 1968. The typical legislator does not have to develop such a grand coalition. He or she has to be more concerned with voters in a specific district.

One way of building a majority coalition is to engage in pork-barrel allocations, getting as much public funding into the district as possible. This promotes the economic health of the community and is likely to provide more jobs. Pork barreling can be done without regard to ideology. For example, even communities in which there is strong support for reducing military appropriations usually want military bases in their states kept open. Incrementalism fits this approach to coalition building because it does not threaten existing governmental facilities and spending, but rather promises more and more. If a legislator's district is large and diversified enough, as in the case of senators from states such as California and New York, the incremental approach can also be used to support conflicting interests within the electoral constituency. It is not unusual for rural-urban conflicts to be diminished in this fashion in an effort to build statewide support. Simultaneous subsidies for mass urban transportation and spending for rural highway development are common examples.

Congressional support for the incremental approach also stems from incrementalism's tendency to place the locus of power for budgetary decisions in the legislature. Although GPRA and the GPRA Modernization Act push in the opposite direction, most managerial approaches strengthen the executive's role in the budgetary process. Some of them, such as PPBS, have had a marked centralizing bias within the executive branch.[40] They have militated against administrative decentralization and administrative responsiveness to the legislature. Under such circumstances, the "budget bureau" displaces the legislative appropriations committees as the key organizational participant in the budgetary process. This also tends to place power over budgetary decisions in the hands of unelected administrators as opposed to elected legislators.

If one views budgets as political statements, incrementalism has the benefit of placing the locus of power in the hands of the citizenry's elected representatives. Presumably legislators are held accountable to their constituencies and presumably will therefore be responsive to them, at least in the areas where the electorate has identifiable and salient interests. In addition to potentially enhancing the representative qualities of government in this fashion, incrementalism helps maintain the viability of checks and balances by maintaining the legislative power of the purse intact.

The nature and advantages of incrementalism have been summarized by Aaron Wildavsky and Arthur Hammond in a passage worth quoting at length:

> Whatever else they may be, budgets are manifestly political documents. They engage the intense concern of administrators, politicians, leaders of interest groups and citizens interested in the "who gets what and how much" of governmental allocations. Participants in budgeting use its political components as aids to calculation. They drastically simplify their task by concentrating on the relatively small portion of the budget that is politically feasible to change. The previous year's budget, the largest part of which is composed of continuing programs and prior commitments, is usually taken as a base needing little justification beyond that offered in the past. Attention is normally focused on a small number of incremental changes, increases and decreases, calling for significant departures from the established historical base of the agency concerned. Parts of the total budget are given to various administrative agencies, appropriations subcommittees, Budget Bureau divisions, and other interested parties for special attention. This fragmentation is increased because all budgetary items are not evaluated together, but are dealt with in sequence by the various participants, so that only a small number of items need to be considered by any participant at any one time.[41]

Although this approach maximizes important political values, it also has limitations. Budgets are political documents, but they are also economic documents and managerial documents. Incrementalism makes it difficult to avoid waste and promote administrative efficiency. The natural tendency is to spend more and avoid cuts. At the same time, raising taxes is so politically unpopular that the tendency is for the budget to be unbalanced and for deficits to grow. It is politically more popular to spend more than to cut programs. If taxes were raised to match the ever-continuing incremental increases in spending, it might cause problems for the economy. Eventually government might collect and reallocate a great deal of money from the private sector, which could seriously sap the economy's vitality.

By avoiding a clear identification of governmental objectives and priorities, incrementalism also makes public administration difficult to carry out. How do you manage an agency whose goals are unclear and contradictory? What do efficiency and economy mean in this context? More than one top-level administrator has found these questions frustrating in the extreme.

These problems of incrementalism are so profound that drastic measures are being considered to limit its negative impact on the economy. As mentioned, one such measure that has gained some credence has been a balanced budget amendment. Although there have been several variants, the basic idea is to force the federal government to balance the budget on an annual basis, unless a clear emergency were present and an extraordinary majority of the Congress agreed to let it be unbalanced. To some extent, balancing the budget is a matter of accounting practices. The federal government would show a far smaller deficit if it used a capital budget. Programs such as Social Security can also be put "off budget" by converting them into trust funds (see the glossary in Box 6.7). Consequently, a constitutional amendment might fail to accomplish its intended purpose, while at the same time expanding the political power of a minority in each congressional chamber.

Sunset provisions are another approach to keeping incrementalism in check. Sunset legislation provides for the termination of programs at some future date, often five years, unless they are reauthorized by statute at that time. This means that the programs will go out of existence if no legislative action is taken, and consequently, the burden is placed on those administrators and political actors who favor their continuance to justify the need for such programs. The sunset concept is integral to zero-base budgeting, because there is a presumption that each agency should justify all the budgetary allocations to it (not only the increment) on an annual basis. Sunset provisions are common in the states. Although they were popular when first enacted some 30 years ago, experience with sunset provisions has been mixed. They seem to work least well in programmatic areas where there are narrow and strongly organized interest groups, such as occupational licensing administration. Where there are broad and well-articulated conflicting interests involved, sunset provisions can promote better accountability and evaluation of the performance of agencies and programs. (Sunset provisions are discussed further in Chapter 8.)

The Legal Influence on Budgeting

In the past 35 years, the courts have assumed an increasingly important influence on budgets. The legal approach to public administration seeks to protect constitutional integrity and individual rights, assure equal protection under the law, and promote procedural fairness and equity. In some instances, seeking to promote or maximize these values can lead to sizable and identifiable costs for the political community. This is especially true where the judiciary finds that wide-ranging institutional reforms are necessary to protect individuals' rights. Such cases often involve prison reform, the reform of public mental health institutions, and school desegregation involving major changes in the operation of entire public educational systems.[42] Some courts have been involved in statewide reforms in each of these areas. As mentioned in Chapter 2, in the early 1980s, about half of Boston's budgetary appropriations were "presided over" by federal and state judges.[43] In one case, *Missouri v. Jenkins* (1990, 1995), a federal district court effectively imposed a local property tax to pay for a school desegregation plan involving lavish spending on magnet school facilities until the Supreme Court eventually said its remedy was inappropriate.[44]

There are two key aspects of judicially mandated reforms of this nature. First, generally speaking, the courts do not *require* a legislature to spend money on a function such as incarceration or public mental health care. Rather, the judicial logic is essentially stated to the legislature as follows: "You don't have to run prisons, mental health facilities, or public schools, but if you choose to do so, then you must not violate the constitutional rights of prisoners, patients, and students in the process."[45] Thus, the legislature is given a way out—it does not have to maintain the function or appropriate money to bring it up to constitutional standards. But the choice is often a hollow one. States may curtail some public mental health care or educational programs, but they are highly unlikely to stop imprisoning or institutionalizing dangerous persons or to terminate the public role in education. Nevertheless, by framing the issue in this fashion, the courts avoid the necessity of forcing the states to provide funds for any specific function.

Second, the judiciary is cognizant of the costs of its decrees, but overall, it does not consider limited resources to be a legitimate excuse for failing to protect someone's constitutional rights. As one court put it, "Inadequate resources can never be adequate justification for the state's depriving any person of his constitutional rights."[46]

In the abstract this approach may not present any particular issues in terms of budgeting. However, in concrete terms genuine problems of resource allocation do arise. For instance, one court decreed that the state's mental health facilities would have to have at least one shower or tub for each 15 patients, at least one toilet for each eight patients, no single room with less than 100 square feet of floor space, and a temperature range between 68 and 83 degrees Fahrenheit.[47] In addition, it ordered that more staff be hired. These reforms cost money; where will it come from? This is a question that the judges do not have to address directly. They do not know if the funds will come from housing programs for the elderly, nutrition programs for malnourished elementary school pupils, or the taxpayers in general. By seeking to define the rights of some groups in isolation from all the competing potential claims on the public treasury, the courts do not have to balance the constitutional rights of some against the economic needs of others. In short, the courts do not consider the possibility of more floor space for the mentally ill leading to reduced subsidies for the elderly. This fits the judiciary's historical role in protecting members of the political community who are inadequately protected or represented by the other branches of government.

But judicial involvement also fragments the budgetary process even further, because in a practical sense the judges are allocating money for some groups of people without assessing their claims relative to those of other groups or functions. The judiciary is inclined to rely on a contractarian, as opposed to utilitarian, basis for fundamental rights. The legislature, in turn, may victimize other politically weak groups that remain without meaningful judicial protection. This would occur, for example, if a state raised the temperature in its mental health facilities with money that previously would have gone into public housing or other benefits for the poor. No doubt an administrator in charge of such a housing program would find it frustrating to see appropriations earmarked for that function shifted to upgrading conditions in the public mental hospitals.

Yet the judicial influence on budgeting does not have to be so dramatic. There are countless public administrative activities and programs that tend to spend more money in one neighborhood than another. Schools, streets, lighting, sanitation, building inspection, police, and fire protection are some of the leading examples. Would unequal allocations be unconstitutional and in violation of equal protection where neighborhoods evidenced a great deal of residential segregation by race or ethnicity, age, or wealth? The answers to these questions depend on interpretation of the federal or state constitutions, the precise nature of the functions, the administrative intent in providing them on an unequal basis, and the nature of the social divisions among the neighborhoods. In some cases involving schools and public works, however, courts have found that the equal protection rights of the residents were violated by unequal spending. In such instances, judicial decisions force a reallocation of funds that can have a substantial impact on the budgets of local governments or even states.[48] Judicial decisions regarding local governmental liability and public personnel practices have also had significant price tags.

Conclusion: The Search for a Synthesis

The managerial, political, and judicial approaches identify important concerns in the area of public budgeting. The approaches are at odds with one another in many respects. What are the prospects for synthesis? The judicial influence does not seem to lend itself readily to integration with executive and legislative budgetary processes. Managerial and incremental budgeting can be combined to some extent, but performance budgeting and program budgeting appear to be at odds with the incremental approach. GPRA and the GPRA Modernization Act processes can potentially provide a bridge, but they may also enhance opportunities for enlarged stakeholder influence, congressional micromanagement, and conflict between the executive and legislative branches. Managerial orientations are clearly appropriate for some governmental functions but not for others. Many of the functions of local governments are particularly subject to improvement using program budgeting, zero basing, and new performance budgeting. For a variety of reasons, these strategies have been more successful at that level than in the federal government. However, incremental approaches are useful when it is politically difficult to establish clear objectives and priorities without denying some groups representation and weakening consensus and political coalitions. One approach to synthesis therefore is to "fudge" the issue somewhat. This pertains to circumstances where a hybrid of both incremental and rationalistic approaches is employed, such as in the Department of Defense. Another possibility is to admit that there cannot be a single budgetary process and to treat agencies and programs differently. The GPRA Modernization Act of 2010 provides some flexibility by recognizing that some agency programs may not have measurable objectives.

The current federal budgetary crisis may lead to other reforms and the development of new budgeting techniques. Whatever course is taken in the future, however, one thing is certain—budgeting will remain an area of controversy for public administrators, elected officials, political executives, interest groups, commercial interests, and the public at large. The way in which budgetary questions are framed has a great deal to do with the outcome of contests for public dollars. Both the budget *process* and *allocations* will continue to be of critical political, economic, and organizational importance in the modern administrative state.

STUDY QUESTIONS

1. Some people advocate a constitutional amendment that would require the federal government to balance its budget on an annual basis. What would be the chief advantages and disadvantages of such an amendment? Do you favor it? Should such an amendment have a clause allowing an unbalanced budget in times of emergency?

2. New performance budgeting has been attempted at the local level in recent years. What attributes of new performance budgeting make it particularly suitable to local government budgeting? Will the same attributes be as useful at the federal level? Do you think that Congress or the executive branch will find the performance budgeting process under the original GPRA and/or the GPRA Modernization Act of 2010 more useful? Why?

3. Think of a recent political campaign that involved the issue of government spending. Evaluate the candidates' remarks and positions on matters of spending, taxation, and budgeting. Whose position would you support, and why?

4. What are the fundamental differences between the budgetary process in the federal government and that in the state where you reside? What are some of the major consequences of these differences?

NOTES

1. Congressional Budget Office, "Updated Budget Projections: Fiscal Years 2013 to 2023." Washington, DC: Congressional Budget Office, May 2013.
2. See Morris P. Fiorina, *Congress: Keystone of the Washington Establishment*, 2d ed. (New Haven, CT: Yale University Press, 1989); Edward R. Tufte, "Determinants of the Outcomes of Midterm Congressional Elections," *American Political Science Review* 69 (1975): 812–826.
3. Office of Management and Budget, *Budget of the United States Government, Fiscal Year 2014* (Washington, DC: Government Printing Office, 2013), Table S-7; available online at http://www.whitehouse.gov/omb/budget/fy2014.
4. National Governor's Association and National Association of State Budget Officers, *Fiscal Survey of the States* (Washington, DC: June 2007), 39, Table A-6, indicates that 45 states had income taxes in 2008. In 2013, the U.S. Internal Revenue Service indicated that nine states did not levy them (Alaska, Florida, Nevada, New Hampshire, South Dakota, Texas, Tennessee, Washington, and Wyoming). See: http://www.irs.gov/uac/States-Without-a-State-Income-Tax.
5. Tax Foundation, "State and Local Sales Tax Rates in 2013." Fiscal Fact No. 357. Washington, DC: Tax Foundation, February 11, 2013.
6. United States Bureau of the Census, *Statistical Abstract of the United States, 2012* (Washington, DC: Government Printing Office, 2007), Table 442; available online at: http://www.census.gov/compendia/statab/2012edition.html.
7. *National Bellas Hess, Inc. v. Department of Revenue of the State of Illinois*, 386 U.S. 753 (1967).
8. *Quill Corp. v. North Dakota*, 504 U.S. 298 (1992).
9. Donald Bruce and William F. Fox, *State and Local Sales Tax Revenue Losses from E-Commerce: Estimates as of July 2004* (Knoxville: University of Tennessee, College of Business Administration, Center for Business and Economic Research, July 2004).
10. "Who Would Win or Lose on Internet Sales Tax," *USA Today,* May 6, 2013. Available online at: http://www.usatoday.com/story/money/business/2013/05/06/winners-losers-online-sales-tax/2139681/.
11. John Maynard Keynes, *The General Theory of Employment, Interest, and Money* (New York: Harcourt, Brace, and World, 1935).
12. Congressional Budget Office, "Updated Budget Projections: Fiscal Years 2013 to 2023." Washington, DC: Congressional Budget Office, May 2013.
13. A useful place to start on this issue is Charles Schultze, *The Politics and Economics of Public Spending* (Washington, DC: Brookings, 1968). See also Pete Peterson, *Facing Up* (New York: Simon & Schuster, 1993). For an alternative view, see Robert Eisner, *The Great Deficit Scares* (New York: Century Fund Press, 1997).
14. Michael Pettis, *The Volatility Machine* (New York: Oxford University Press, 2001).

15. Michael Pettis, *The Great Rebalancing* (Princeton University Press, 2013).

16. Jonathan Fuerbringer and Nathaniel Nash, "Seven Ways to Reinvent the Budget Process," *New York Times,* 27 September 1987, quoting Louis Fisher.

17. See Office of Management and Budget, Circular A-11 (2012), Part 6, sections 200 and 210, "Preparation and Submission of Strategic Plans, Annual Performance Plans, and Annual Program Performance Reports," http://www.whitehouse.gov/omb/circulars_a11_current_year_a11_toc.

18. Office of Management and Budget, *Budget of the United States Government, Fiscal Year 2008* (Washington, DC: Government Printing Office, 2007), chap. 15, "Budget Reform Proposals," 209–220.

19. *Public Law* 112–25 (S. 365); 125 *Stat.* 240 (*August* 2, 2011).

20. *Immigration and Naturalization Service v. Chadha,* 462 U.S. 919 (1983).

21. *City of New Haven v. United States,* 809 F.2d 900 (1987).

22. For a comprehensive discussion, see Aaron Wildavsky, *The Politics of the Budgetary Process,* 4th ed. (Boston: Little, Brown, 1984).

23. Standard & Poor's, "United States of America Long-Term Rating Lowered To 'AA+' On Political Risks And Rising Debt Burden; Outlook Negative" (New York: Standard & Poor's. August 5, 2011).

24. U.S. Government Accountability Office, *Budget and Federal Debt.* Interest payments accounted for 15.3 percent of federal outlays in 1995. See http://www.gao.gov/special.pubs/longterm/debt/budgetdebt.html.

25. V. O. Key, Jr., "The Lack of a Budgetary Theory," *American Political Science Review* 34 (December 1940): 1137–1140.

26. Catheryn Seckler-Hudson, "Performance Budgeting in Government," in Albert Hyde and Jay M. Shafritz, Eds., *Government Budgeting* (Oak Park, IL: Moore, 1978), 80–93, esp. 81. See also Robert D. Lee, "Developments in State Budgeting: Trends of Two Decades," *Public Administration Review* 51 (May/June 1991): 254–262.

27. Hyde and Shafritz, *Government Budgeting,* includes several works on this subject. See section III.

28. By creating artificial "money" and therefore greater demand, food stamps benefit farmers, ranchers, food processing companies, trucking companies and railroads that transport farm and ranch foodstuffs as well as processed food ready for sale, supermarkets and grocery stores, and stamp recipients. Recently, in response to the nation's obesity crisis several governors urged excluding sugary soft drinks and similar food products lacking significant nutritional value from the items available for purchase with the stamps. This would surely cause the producers of those products to be less supportive of the program.

29. Elizabeth Drew, "HEW Grapples with PPBS," *The Public Interest* 8 (Summer 1967): 9–27.

30. Allen Schick, "A Death in the Bureaucracy: The Demise of Federal PPB," *Public Administration Review* 33 (March/April 1973): 146–156.

31. See Graeme M. Taylor, "Introduction to Zero-Base Budgeting," in Hyde and Shafritz, *Government Budgeting,* 271–284, esp. 273; and Peter A. Pyhrr, *Zero-Base Budgeting* (New York: Wiley, 1973).

32. Peter A. Pyhrr, "Zero-Base Approach to Government Budgeting," *Public Administration Review* 37 (January/February 1977): 1–8.

33. *Houston Post,* 8 April 1977. See also Robert Anthony, "Zero-Base Budgeting Is a Fraud," *Wall Street Journal,* 27 April 1977.

34. Aaron Wildavsky, "The Political Economy of Efficiency: Cost-Benefit Analysis, Systems Analysis, and Program Budgeting," *Public Administration Review* 26 (December 1966): 292–310.

35. For a thorough description of GPRA's requirements and a discussion of implementation challenges, see Robert S. Kravchuk and Ronald W. Schack, "Designing Effective Performance Measurement Systems under the Government Performance and Results Act of 1993," *Public Administration Review* 56 (July/August 1996): 348–358.

36. Public Law 111-52; 124 Statutes at Large 3866 (January 4, 2011).

37. Aaron Wildavsky and Naomi Caiden, *The New Politics of the Budgetary Process,* 3d ed. (New York: Longman, 1997).

38. A. Lee Fritschler, *Smoking and Politics,* 4th ed. (Englewood Cliffs, NJ: Prentice-Hall, 1989).

39. For some of the dynamics, see Samuel Lubell, *The Future of American Politics* (Garden City, NY: Doubleday Anchor, 1955).

40. Wildavsky, "The Political Economy of Efficiency," 26.

41. Aaron Wildavsky and Arthur Hammond, "Comprehensive versus Incremental Budgeting in the Department of Agriculture," in Hyde and Shafritz, *Governmental Budgeting,* 236–251 at 237.

42. David H. Rosenbloom, Rosemary O'Leary, and Joshua Chanin, *Public Administration and Law,* 3d ed. (Boca Raton, FL: CRC/Taylor & Francis, 2010); and Donald Horowitz, *The Courts and Social Policy* (Washington, DC: Brookings, 1977).

43. Robert Turner, "Governing from the Bench," *The Boston Globe Magazine,* 8 November 1981, 13.

44. *Missouri v. Jenkins,* 495 U.S. 33 (1990); 515 U.S. 70 (1995). See Rosemary O'Leary and Charles Wise, "Public Managers, Judges, and Legislators: Redefining the 'New Partnership,'" *Public Administration Review* 51 (July/August 1991): 316–327.

45. In one case, a Virginia county was required to maintain a public school system because in abandoning it, the county was seeking to prevent racial integration; *Griffin v. County School Board of Prince Edward County,* 377 U.S. 218 (1964). See also Richard Lehne, *The Quest for Justice* (New York: Longman, 1978).

46. *Hamilton v. Love,* 328 F. Supp. 1182, 1194 (1971).

47. *Wyatt v. Stickney,* 325 F. Supp. 781 (1971), et seq. See also "The *Wyatt* Case: Implementation of a Judicial Decree Ordering Institutional Change," *Yale Law Journal* 84 (1975): 1338–1379.

48. *Hawkins v. Town of Shaw,* 437 F.2d 1286 (1971); *San Antonio Independent School District v. Rodriguez,* 411 U.S. 1 (1973); Lehne, *The Quest for Justice;* Horowitz, *The Courts and Social Policy,* chap. 4.

ADDITIONAL READING

Eisner, Robert. *The Great Deficit Scares: The Federal Budget, Trade, and Social Security.* New York: Century Foundation Press, 1997.

Forsythe, Dall W., and Donald J. Boyd. *Memos to the Governor: An Introduction to State Budgeting,* 3d ed. Washington, DC: Georgetown University Press, 2012.

Ippolito, Dennis S. *Why Budgets Matter: Budget Policy and American Politics.* University Park, PA: Pennsylvania State University Press, 2003.

Ippolito, Dennis S. *Deficits, Debt, and the New Politics of Tax Policy.* New York: Cambridge University Press, 2012.

Mikesell, John L. *Fiscal Administration: Analysis and Applications for the Public Sector,* 9th ed. Boston, MA: Wadsworth Cengage, 2014.

Rubin, Irene S. *The Politics of Public Budgeting,* 6th ed. Washington, DC: CQ Press, 2010.

Schick, Allen. *The Federal Budget: Politics, Policy, Process,* 3d ed. Washington, DC: Brookings Institution, 2007.

BUDGETING WEB SITES

Extremely useful information, data, and analyses concerning the federal budget can be found at the Web site of the U.S. Office of Management and Budget (OMB) at http://www.whitehouse.gov/omb.

Another valuable federal Web site, providing an interesting counterpoise to the OMB, is that of the Congressional Budget Office (CBO) at http://www.cbo.gov.

State budget data and information about formats, calendars, and other dimensions of budgeting and public finance in the various states can be found at the Web site of the National Conference of State Legislatures (NCSL) at http://www.ncsl.org.

The National Association of State Budget Officers (NASBO) provides further information, analyses, and detail about the current status of state finances at http://www.nasbo.org.

A national professional association of professors who study budgeting and financial issues at all levels of government is the Association for Budgeting and Financial Management (ABFM) at http://www.abfm.org.

CHAPTER 7

DECISION MAKING

Key Learning Objectives

1. Be able to explain the traditional managerial approach to decision making, known as the rational-comprehensive method, and show how the essential features of bureaucratic organization tend to support it.

2. Understand the key criticisms of the traditional approach and the features of the major alternative models, especially the incremental and adjudicatory approaches.

3. Know the limits of the alternative decision-making approaches and understand how many public decisions may be made according to processes that incorporate features of two or more of them.

4. Understand the type of approach that may be best suited to various decision situations.

This chapter reviews varied approaches to decision making, which many view as the essence of public administration and the key to governmental effectiveness. The traditional managerial approach to decision making relies on bureaucratic organization to promote rationality. It favors a rational-comprehensive approach to decision making that specifies objectives and identifies the most satisfactory means of achieving them. Many believe that this approach does not fit the U.S. political system well. The new public management (NPM) favors decentralized decision making based on market criteria and ample amounts of employee discretion. The political approach favors a kind of pluralistic "give-and-take" in decision making. This permits coalition building but usually leads to incremental decisions that modify past policies only relatively slightly. The legal approach favors an adjudicatory model to assess the reasonableness of decisions. An alternative approach called "mixed scanning" is a partial synthesis of these approaches. No matter what approach is taken, however, there are important pitfalls to be avoided in making administrative decisions; a list of common ones is considered toward the end of the chapter. Finally, a major issue for the future is raised: How profoundly will the use of modern information technology (IT) affect our thinking about administrative decision making and the actual deciding?

Public administration involves the formulation and implementation of public policies intended to provide services and/or impose regulations on individuals, groups, and organizations in the political community. Consequently, a large part of the job of some public administrators requires that they make decisions defining the objectives of public policies and choose appropriate means for achieving them. In essence, administrative decision making is the choice from among competing alternatives of the ends and means that an administrative program or organization will pursue and employ. But how should public administrators go about the business of deciding among these alternatives? How, in practice, do they decide? How can administrative decision making be improved? What are the inherent limitations on administrative decision making? These are important questions that should be considered by students and practitioners of public administration. This chapter will address them by considering the managerial, political, and legal approaches to administrative decision making and by considering a technique that can serve as a partial synthesis.

◆→ THE TRADITIONAL MANAGERIAL APPROACH TO DECISION MAKING

The traditional managerial approach to public administration stresses the need for rationality in decision making. It seeks to enable public administrators to make decisions in the most efficient, economical, and effective manner. One way to introduce rationality into the decision making process is to design a system that helps a public administrator choose from among competing alternatives by (1) reducing the number of alternatives that need to be considered,

(2) reducing the number of values that must be assessed in making a choice from among the alternatives, (3) assuring that the administrator knows how to make a rational choice, and (4) providing the administrator with sufficient information to select from among the alternatives. Such an organizational design will incorporate many features of bureaucratic organization.

Specialization

Specialization is the preeminent means of reducing the number of alternatives a public administrator may consider when making a decision. Jurisdictional specialization among public agencies confines the authority of public adminis-trators to relatively well-defined areas of public policy. For instance, the public administrator in the Department of Agriculture does not have to be concerned with issues of national security under the jurisdiction of the Department of Defense. Nor do public administrators in different agencies need to determine the social value of the various programs they administer compared with the value of those implemented by other agencies. Specialization within agencies has a similar effect. Some public administrators will formulate policies and rules, whereas others will enforce them. Although the two acts are obviously and intimately connected (or at least should be), the individual engaged in enforcement may be in a position to make some choices over means but is usually not in a position to consider the objective of the rule or policy. For example, a human resources manager engaged in the enforcement of an equal employment opportunity program may be able to make decisions regarding the appropriateness of an agency's efforts to hire and promote women and members of minority groups. If resources are scarce, such an administrator may also have to decide which units and what grade levels should be most closely monitored. This official may have to make a wide variety of additional decisions. However, being charged with enforcement, the public administra-tor in question will not have jurisdictional authority to decide whether equal opportunity should be a component of the personnel system.

Many cases are much more mundane, as occurs when a public manager in charge of a particular unit is concerned solely with the internal operating efficiency and effectiveness of that unit. Specialization divides the functions of public agencies into manageable units; the questions, issues, problems, and alter-natives facing any individual public administrator will be limited accordingly.

Specialization also limits the values a public administrator must take into account in making choices from among competing alternatives. Public admin-istrators must be concerned with promoting the public interest as it relates to their authority. They are not free to choose from among policy alternatives in an unfettered fashion. Sometimes, acting on their own, the political heads of agencies do try to depart radically from an agency's historical values, but this almost always causes turmoil in the administrative structure and is seldom fully successful. Thus, for the public administrator, the question in decision making is, "Within the set of values embodied in my official authority, what should and can be done?"

Answers may be narrowed by an agency's culture generally and by "premise controls." Specifically, specialization can affect the cognitive premises and thought patterns of individuals. Being socialized into and working in an agency, a skilled trade, or a profession often has an impact on the way people define situations. The decision maker "voluntarily restricts the range of stimuli that will be attended to ('Those sorts of things are irrelevant,' or 'What has that got to do with the matter?') and the range of alternatives that would be considered ('It would never occur to me to do that')."[1] The importance of premise controls varies not only with the nature of specialization but also with the character and level of work. Charles Perrow explains:

> Premise controls are most important when work is nonroutine . . . and this is one reason scientists and other professionals have such latitude in organizations. Their premises are well set in their training institutions and professional associations. Premise controls are also most important near the top of the organization because managerial work there is less routine, [and] the consequences of decisions are hard to assess immediately. . . . But . . . premise controls exist at all levels, created and reinforced by schools, the mass media, and cultural institutions in general.[2]

Hierarchy

The hierarchical nature of bureaucratic organizations also narrows the range of choices available to decision makers. Hierarchy defines the authority of public administrators. Typically, those with less authority have more limited choices confronting them. Some public administrators make almost no important decisions, but rather handle a large number of repetitive, routine tasks. An example would be an employee in a motor vehicle department who administers a vision test. Criteria for passing are established elsewhere in the organization, and the employee at the testing station observes whether a particular individual has met those criteria.

Even as one goes up the organizational ranks to positions with substantial authority over specific programs, hierarchy continues to limit the responsibility of officials and thus helps define the values with which they must be concerned. This is not to say that midlevel public administrators have no difficult choices to make. But it is only when one reaches the top levels of an organizational structure that it is typically necessary to consider choices from among a wide variety of competing and conflicting values. Street-level administration, discussed later in this chapter, is an important exception.

To some extent, as this discussion suggests, specialization and hierarchy tend to overlap one another in the sense of limiting authority. But the distinction is within the kind of authority being limited: Specialization limits jurisdictional authority, whereas hierarchy limits managerial authority. The difference is somewhat subtle but can be conveyed in the distinction between the following two statements: "I'm not responsible for what they do in that operation" (specialization) and "I don't make the rules" (hierarchy). In sum, hierarchy enables those with superior authority to define and limit the value choices available to subordinates.

Formalization

Formalization is particularly important in facilitating decision making. Standard operating procedures are produced to reduce the alternatives available by specifying precisely the factors and information to be taken into account in exercising choice. As the term "formalization" suggests, standardized forms may be used to solicit the information deemed by the public agency to be relevant to its decision making. Certain information is included; other information is excluded. Exclusion, in particular, tends to simplify decision making because it limits what must be considered. However, exclusions may prevent individuals from presenting mitigating information. For example, at one time, several states had long residency requirements for those seeking welfare benefits. These requirements were intended to prevent individuals from moving into a state to receive benefits that were higher than those available elsewhere. But the application processes did not ascertain the individual's intent or reasons for migrating to the state, which could have involved family matters such as moving in with one's parents or other relatives. Rather, the regulations and formal process assumed that newcomers were drawn by higher benefits and attributed this motive to all of them. Eventually such residency requirements were declared unconstitutional,[3] but they remain a vivid illustration of how formalization is used to ensure that if an organization does not anticipate its relevance, some information will be ignored. In a case like the one described, formalization is used to attain the goals of impersonality and procedural equality (see Chapter 1).

Formalization may also include a more direct statement of values. It can indicate to a decision maker the relative weight to be assigned to different factors when there is a potential conflict among them. A clear statement of this can be found in the old U.S. Civil Service Commission's (CSC) early set of instructions on affirmative action: "Agency action plans and instructions involving goals and timetables must state that all actions to achieve goals must be in full compliance with merit system requirements."[4] This clearly placed the value of merit above that of diversity in federal personnel administration. For those making decisions on the implementation of affirmative action, the CSC's statement of values acted as a constraint that substantially reduced the alternative courses of action permissible.

Merit

The traditional managerial approach to public administration also affects the decision making process by seeking to assure that public administrators have the technical ability to make the most rational choices. It also seeks to guarantee that they will use this ability free of partisan political considerations. The quest for technical expertise and nonpartisanship is embodied in the merit system.

Competent employees are defined as those who can understand the jobs they are hired to do, process the information before them, and grasp such concepts as specialization and hierarchy. They are further expected to perform their functions efficiently. Their actions are to be governed by the agency's hierarchy, rules, and values, as well as by the rule of law. They are not supposed to take their personal political beliefs or affiliations into account when implementing the will of the legislature or that of their superordinates.

The constraints of the traditional managerial approach on decision making are frequently reinforced by the development of organizational cultures that characterize agencies. These develop as agencies begin to express a consistent set of values, as they recruit individuals for their highest career positions who reflect these values, and as the values become expressed through procedural mechanisms and formalization. According to Harold Seidman, a longtime analyst of federal administration: "Each agency has its own culture and internal set of loyalties and values which are likely to guide its actions and influence its policies." Therefore, "institutional responses are highly predictable."[5]

In the ways described, the traditional managerial approach promotes an organizational design that has an important impact on public administrative decision making. The approach necessarily accepts the reality of "bounded rationality" (see Chapter 4), because not all the consequences of a complex decision are likely to be known in advance. However, it attempts to enhance rationality through specialization, hierarchy, formalization, and technical competence.

The effort to structure decision making for rationality sometimes takes the form of "grid regulations" ("grid regs"). Grid regs display the intent of written rules in tabular form. Box 7.1 presents an example of the grid regs developed for the Social Security Disability Insurance (SSDI) program. The agency's rules made SSDI available when there was no job in the national economy that an impaired individual could perform on a sustained basis. The regulations in Box 7.1 categorized work as "light" (Rule 202) and "medium" (Rule 203). Age, education, and previous work experience were taken as the determinants of disability. Rule 202.01 stated that an impaired worker of advanced age (55 and over) who had limited education and was unskilled would be considered disabled. By contrast, Rule 202.03 placed an individual of the same age and education but with transferable skills in the category of "not disabled."

Grid regs clearly reduce the discretion of individual administrators and hearing examiners in determining the status of the individuals whose cases are before them. They clarify policy and promote uniform treatment. They prevent decision makers from taking into account factors that the rules consider extraneous. At the same time, though, the regulations make it difficult or impossible for hearing examiners to assess the personal situation of each claimant. Consequently, an individual closely approaching advanced age (50 to 54) will sometimes be treated differently from one who is 55, even though for all

Residual Functional Capacity: Maximum Sustained Work Capability Limited to Light and Medium Work as a Result of Severe Medically Determinable Impairment(s)

Rule	Age*	Education	Previous Work Experience	Decision
		Light Work		
202.01	Advanced age	Limited or less	Unskilled or none	Disabled
202.02	do†	do	Skilled or semiskilled—skills not transferable	do
202.03	do	do	Skilled or semiskilled—skills transferable	Not disabled
202.04	do	High school graduate or more—does not provide for direct entry into skilled work	Unskilled or none	Disabled
202.05	Advanced age	High school graduate or more—provides for direct entry into skilled work	Unskilled or none	Not disabled
202.06	do	High school graduate or more—does not provide for direct entry into skilled work	Skilled or semiskilled—skills not transferable	Disabled
		Medium Work		
203.01	Closely approaching retirement age	Marginal or none	Unskilled or none	Disabled
203.02	do	Limited or less	None	do
203.03	do	Limited	Unskilled	Not disabled
203.04	do	Limited or less	Skilled or semiskilled—skills not transferable	do
203.05	do	do	Skilled or semiskilled—skills transferable	do
203.06	do	High school graduate or more	Unskilled or none	do
203.07	do	High school graduate or more—does not provide for direct entry into skilled work	Skilled or semiskilled—skills not transferable	do
203.08	do	do	Skilled or semiskilled—skills transferable	do
203.09	do	High school graduate or more—provides for direct entry into skilled work	Skilled or semiskilled—skills not transferable	do
203.10	Advanced age	Limited or less	None	Disabled
203.11	do	do	Unskilled	Not disabled
203.12	do	do	Skilled or semiskilled—skills not transferable	do

*Advanced age = 55 and over; closely approaching advanced age = 50–54; younger individual = 18–49.
†do = ditto.

Source: U.S. Department of Health and Human Services, Social Security Administration; regulations in *U.S. Federal Register,* vol. 43, 55369-53370, 28 November 1978.

other intents and purposes there is no significant physical or mental difference between them. A 54-year-old's mind and body may have aged more than those of someone who is 55 or older. Thus, the rationality of grid regs depends on the appropriateness of the categories they incorporate.[6]

Two of Graham Allison's three models of organizational decision making[7] map nicely onto our concepts of managerial, political, and legal approaches to public administration. Allison's discussion of the "rational actor model" complements the managerial approach to public administration. This model, a rational-comprehensive approach to decision making based on the scientific method, is discussed in the following section. The "organizational process model" informs our understanding of the political approach to public administration. The give-and-take of political negotiation and bargaining, constrained by organizational rules and processes, defines this model of decision making. We address this model in the next major section of this chapter. Allison's third model of decision making, the "governmental politics model," does not fit neatly into our three-part approach to understanding public administration. However, this stochastic, "garbage can" model of decision making describes the reality of many individuals in organizations and warrants a brief discussion at the end of this chapter.

The Rational-Comprehensive Model

In simplified form, the rational-comprehensive model consists of the following steps:

- Determine the objectives.
- Consider the means to achieve the objectives.
- Choose the best alternative.

Let us discuss each one in turn.

Determining Objectives

In making decisions, a public administrator must first determine the objectives of public policy. These objectives should be identified in operational terms, in ways that can be observed and, better still, measured. Again, equal employment opportunity (EEO) as applied to the public sector provides a good example. If the objective is defined as equal opportunity in public employment, the objective will necessarily remain vague and difficult to implement. Equal opportunity may be undefinable. (Is it nondiscrimination, or is it equalizing opportunity by equalizing education, nutrition, housing, etc., or is it compensating for the disadvantages placed on groups by the society?) Nor can EEO be seen or measured directly, though some surrogate indicators can be developed. If, however, equal opportunity is defined as the social representation of groups in the public sector workforce, there will be an objective that can be readily observed and measured. Social representation is far more tangible than opportunity. However, as discussed, a public administrator does not have a free hand in establishing objectives. He or she is constrained by authority, specialization, hierarchy, law, and political factors. If the legislature is completely clear about what it wants, it will severely reduce the alternatives available to the public administrator trying to interpret its will.

Considering the Means

Once the objectives of public policy are established, various means for accomplishing them must be considered. If the requisite comprehensiveness is to be achieved, nearly all the potential means that can be identified must be scrutinized. This may require heavy reliance on theory, because it is highly unlikely that all the potential means have at one time or another been tested and evaluated in practice. According to the rational-comprehensive model, in considering the potential means to the objectives, a public administrator is required to try to project *all* the consequences of each of the means on all the various areas of governmental concern. This can be a tall order.

Continuing with the equal employment opportunity (EEO) example, several means could be identified. Assuming that the objective is defined in terms of social representation, as is the case in federal employment, trying to recruit and later promote members from all segments of the population and eliminating barriers that some groups may face in competing for employment may be viewed as appropriate means. Similarly, protections might be afforded members of underrepresented groups in reductions-in-force. In addition, various special training programs to promote their upward mobility in the civil service could be developed. Other potential means include governmental programs, similar to those used by the military, to fund students' college and graduate educations in return for the students' commitment to join the civil service for a specified number of years. The elimination of veteran preferences would still be a means of promoting the employment of women. The objective of social representation could also be achieved by firing non-minorities (white males) to make room for African Americans, Hispanics, women, and other EEO target groups. Another possibility would be eliminating competitive merit examinations and the "rule of three" (see Chapter 5) in favor of pass examinations that would yield a more diverse pool of eligibles. One could go on identifying potential means in this context, and that is precisely what the rational-comprehensive model seeks to assure.

Choosing the Best Alternative

Once all the potential means for achieving an end are identified, it is necessary to choose among them. According to the traditional managerial approach, this choice should be made to maximize efficiency, economy, and effectiveness. Where these three values are not fully in harmony with one another, an appropriate balance is to be struck among them. Although that may prove difficult, there is no doubt that these values can serve as helpful guides. For instance, in terms of EEO, they would probably rule out establishing programs to pay

for the higher education of women and members of minority groups in return
for a commitment on their part to work for a relatively short period. Affording large-scale training to minorities and women might also prove expensive.
Aside from potential political and legal problems, firing white males could lead
to widespread demoralization, inefficiency, and political backlash. However,
relying solely on broad recruitment efforts might prove ineffective in bringing about change. To choose the most desirable means under such circumstances, a program might be developed using training, aggressive recruitment
of women and members of minority groups, and the modification of veteran
preference and various personnel devices to relax the disparate effects of competitive examinations and the rule of three. The result, at least in theory, is a
comprehensive program designed to operate within the confines of what is
acceptable in terms of efficiency, economy, and effectiveness. Whether such a
program can be immediately applied in practice, given political and legal constraints, however, is another matter.

Critique of the Rational-Comprehensive Model

The rational-comprehensive model, derived from the traditional managerial
perspective on public administration, has some important benefits. It is comprehensive and provides a good deal of direction in the choice of potential
means to identified policy objectives. It encourages a public administrator to
think a problem through and apply his or her technical expertise in identifying the best solution. If we look on public administrative decision making as a
problem solving endeavor, the rational-comprehensive model is often useful.
Nevertheless, in practice this model is not always suitable to the nature of governmental decision making.

Unclear Objectives

As discussed earlier in other contexts, efficiency, economy, and effectiveness are not necessarily dominant values in government. Many agencies are
charged with doing one thing or another "in the public interest." Although it
is probably necessary for the political community to believe that there *is* a public interest, it may be impossible to identify what the public interest requires
in operational terms. This is because as soon as we become specific, we tend
to generate conflict. For instance, veterans may agree that equal employment
opportunity is in the public interest, but they are likely to disagree that the
public interest requires the elimination of preferences for their own group.

Political Pluralism and Consensus Building

In pluralistic politics, consensus is sometimes built by developing inclusive
coalitions that tend to offer something to many significant political groups
without being specific concerning the aims of a policy and the priorities
within it. Looking at EEO in the federal government, we can see the effect

of this tendency. The program was established with a clear focus on black employment; subsequently, women and Hispanics were included within its ambit; today, it includes not only these groups but also Native Americans, Pacific Islanders, Asian Americans, veterans, and individuals with disabilities. In some localities gays and lesbians have sought specific protection against discrimination in public employment and domestic partner benefits to make such employment more attractive to them.

This approach builds broad coalitions supporting a public administrator's programs, but it makes it difficult to say precisely what a program's goals are in operational terms or to establish priorities. Thus, veteran preference has an adverse impact on the employment interests of women. Nor are the employment interests of African Americans and Hispanics identical. Gains for one group are not necessarily associated with greater employment opportunity for the other group.[8] Latinos, Mexican Americans, Cuban Americans, and Puerto Ricans, often lumped together for statistical purposes in EEO reports, may all have different employment interests.

Time Constraints

An additional problem with the rational-comprehensive model is that it assumes that public administrators have the time to approach problems in a dispassionate way, identify comprehensively all the potential means of achieving identified objectives, and assess all these means in terms of efficiency, economy, and effectiveness. Although circumstances in which a public administrator is truly proactive in this fashion sometimes exist, many practitioners of public administration would find such a scenario alien to their work environment. To a large extent, public administration in the United States is not proactive, but rather reactive. It requires that public administrators deal relatively quickly with problems, deadlines, or crises. Many hardly have enough time to identify even one potential means toward an end, much less to try to identify all potential means and then determine which is best in terms of efficiency, economy, and effectiveness.

Specialization

Another difficulty with the rational-comprehensive approach is that the specialization of which it makes such strong use may also become a liability. We are familiar with the image of the government's right hand not knowing what the left one is doing. This is because the hands operate in different spheres, under different time constraints, and with different objectives. But modern government has more than two hands; it has almost countless tentacles. The public administrator operating one of these is bound, on occasion, to be at odds with the actions of another. This is how the State Department came to back one side in the 1971 India-Pakistan war while the Department of Defense backed the other![9] Or how one agency seeks to preserve wilderness and wetland areas while another fights to develop them.

Groupthink

Groups can also create problems for the rational-comprehensive model. Irving Janis systematized the concept called *groupthink*.[10] The basic idea behind groupthink is that individuals choose to minimize conflict within the group by striving for consensus in decision making without going through all of the elements of the rational-comprehensive model of critically questioning and examining the objectives, means, and alternatives to the decision at hand. Janis developed eight "symptoms" of groupthink:

1. A feeling of invulnerability that creates excessive optimism and encourages risk taking
2. Discounting of warnings that might challenge assumptions
3. An unquestioned belief in the group's morality, causing members to ignore the consequences of their actions
4. Stereotyped views of enemy leaders
5. Pressure to conform against members of the group who disagree
6. Shutting down of ideas that deviate from the apparent group consensus
7. An illusion of unanimity with regard to going along with the group
8. Mindguards—self-appointed members who shield the group from dissenting opinions

A classic public administration example of groupthink involves the decision to launch the Space Shuttle *Challenger* in 1986.[11] Despite personal concern by Morton Thiokol engineers that previous data used to develop launch criteria were flawed and that the "O" rings on the solid rocket booster might fail if the temperature did not rise above 53° Fahrenheit, they succumbed to group pressures to sign off on the launch. In this extreme case, groupthink led to the deaths of the seven crew members of the *Challenger*.

Cost Shifting

To some extent, specialization also makes it difficult to assess the full costs of any particular governmental course of action. An agency making decisions in a complex policy area may create new problems for other agencies. For instance, the Department of Defense's decisions to close or downsize military bases can create significant costs for federal and state employment and social welfare programs and deeply upset the finances of local economies and governments. For the rational-comprehensive model, the problem is that these shifted costs are difficult to assess because they tend to get lost in the system of specialized jurisdictions. The problem is compounded as the administrative state grows and less is truly external to governmental concerns, so that even costs that are shifted from government to society tend eventually to become a public policy concern.

A final criticism of the rational-comprehensive model is that because it relies on theory and abstract expertise, it can produce decisions that are inappropriate in practice. This allegedly is one reason why centralized planning has not worked out as well as anticipated in a variety of political communities.[12]

It also partly explains why various budgeting techniques, such as PPBS and ZBB, have not worked out as well as anticipated in the United States (see Chapter 6).

◆◆ THE POLITICAL APPROACH TO DECISION MAKING:
THE INCREMENTAL MODEL

Critics of the rational-comprehensive model of decision making argue that it is unrealistic, that its values do not necessarily match those of the polity, that it does not fit the nature of contemporary administrative operations, and that it requires administrators to exercise a degree of rationality and comprehensive expertise beyond their ability.[13] These critics suggest that another process is more suitable to the public sector in the United States—a process dubbed the **incremental model**.[14] Proponents of this model develop a dual argument: first, that the incremental approach is more characteristic of public administrative operations in the United States, and second, that it is the model that *should* be relied on to the greatest extent. Further, they claim that it fits the nature of United States politics and political institutions well and that it is a model that public administrators can apply.

The incremental model of decision making comports with the political approach to public administration. It emphasizes the need for public administrators to be responsive to the political community, to be politically representative of the groups that constitute it, and to be accountable to elected officials. Together, these values dictate that administrative decision making should involve public participation, that public administration should be based on the development of political coalitions and political consensus, and that it should allow nonexpert political officials not only to give direction to public administrators but also to exert pressure on them to decide in favor of one policy application or another.

Its proponents argue that the incremental model recognizes the vagueness of many stated objectives of public policy. Such vagueness is considered natural in a pluralistic political community and often seems to be the price of building a consensus strong enough to support administrative programs. Politics, in this view, often requires that the objectives of public policy not be expressed in operational terms. Here lies the difference between EEO and affirmative action (AA), for example. It is easier to build a consensus in favor of EEO, because in the abstract anyone can support the principle of equality of opportunity. However, if it is operationalized by using goals and timetables for the purpose of hiring members of specific social groups, support for the program may decline drastically, and legal challenges will be more likely. Specific goals and timetables identify some groups as beneficiaries and others as potentially subject to heavy burdens. Consequently, some who can support EEO in the abstract may oppose a particular AA program that uses goals and timetables.

A similar phenomenon occurs in terms of agency mission statements to serve "the public interest," assure "equity," and so forth. As long as these

terms remain ill defined in an operational sense, a broad coalition can support
the programs designed to administer them. (This point is illustrated by the case
study of benzene in the workplace presented later in this chapter.)

There is some merit in going slowly. If the price of precisely defining
an objective is loss of political support and the demise of an administrative
program, public administrators will be reluctant to express their missions or
objectives in comprehensive or operational terms. Rather, they will prefer
to move slowly, step-by-step toward a somewhat improved state of affairs,
although this may require some backtracking and constant modification of
policies and means of implementing them. In other words, such an approach
will be *incremental* and will be considered by many to be in step with the style
of U.S. politics.

Components of the Incremental Model

Procedurally, the incremental model specifies the following general process for
administrative decision making:

- Redefining the ends
- Arriving at a consensus
- Making a satisfactory decision

Redefining the Ends

Means and ends are not treated as distinct from one another. The model recognizes that policy objectives may be too unclear to serve as ends in any operational sense. Consequently, the ends of government policy are often defined by
the means available to an agency for moving in some general policy direction.
In the EEO example, for instance, this required that, if used at all, hiring or
promotional goals and timetables, always constitutionally suspect in the public sector, would be in addition to merit examinations, veteran preference, the
rule of three, and so forth. It recognizes that it is politically impracticable to
reform the personnel system in one fell swoop, but eventually greater equality
of opportunity or social representation can be achieved by developing limited
programs toward those ends.

If the means to achieve full social representation of all ethnic and racial
groups in the society are not available without such major reform, the end of
social representation may be redefined. Thus, it may be defined as the proportional representation of minorities and women of working age. This too might
be unattainable, and the end might be further redefined as proportional representation of these groups in the workforce. Such an objective might be further
scaled down to be the proportional representation of the groups in the workforce in the occupations in which government personnel engage. A still further
modification might be that any given agency's staff should be proportionally
representative of minority groups and women in the workforce in the occupations *and* in the geographic area in which the agency recruits its personnel.
In such a situation, the means available eventually determine what the end

of public policy will be—at least until it is possible to employ other means or build a consensus for other ends.

Arriving at a Consensus

The test of a good decision is agreement or consensus in favor of the policy and its method of implementation. Means and ends are treated as packages more or less acceptable to relevant communities of interest. The package that is most acceptable—that has the greatest support behind it—is typically considered the "best" approach. In this sense, representativeness and responsiveness dominate efficiency, economy, and effectiveness as the values to be sought in choosing means. The traditional managerial values are not treated as inconsequential by the incremental model, but they are not weighed as preeminent. A program that does *less* and costs *more* may be more acceptable in the incremental model than one that is more economical and efficient. This view implies several additional points:

1. Because the test of a good policy is the level of political support it generates, decisions are not tested against their impact in producing a change in a given area of social, economic, or political life. Rather, the test is the maintenance of political support, often expressed through increases in budgetary allocations. Consequently, even a program that is overwhelmingly *symbolic* and has no discernible impact on society other than generating support can be considered successful.
2. Because the test of a good policy is not its impact on some economic or social problem but rather the support it generates, to oppose a program it is generally necessary to demonstrate what would be better. It is not enough to say that the program doesn't work; one has to indicate what *will* work.
3. This procedure for judging administrative decisions tends to be an obstacle to policy evaluation and to make performance evaluation difficult. Here again, the disjuncture between the political and managerial approaches to public administration is evident. (Policy evaluation is discussed in the next chapter.)

Making a Satisfactory Decision

In the process of incremental decision making, analysis tends to be more limited than it is in the rational-comprehensive approach. Administrative decision makers taking the incremental approach will consider a few means-ends packages and select one that is *satisfactory*. Little or no effort is made to reach an optimum decision that maximizes the pertinent values. According to Herbert A. Simon's concept of "satisficing," it is not rational even to attempt to maximize any given set of values.[15] Rather, decisions are guided by past practice and tend not to rely heavily on theory. However, a substantial degree of comprehensiveness may be built into the incremental decision making model by encouraging the participation of relevant interest groups, other agencies, members of the legislature, and stakeholders in the process of deciding on a policy.

To some extent this approach is embodied in the federal Administrative Procedure Act of 1946 and many similar state statutes. Under such legislation, when an agency is considering adopting a new policy through informal rule making, it usually must publish its proposed rule changes and an explanation of them in a public forum. It may explain the rationale behind its proposals in considerable detail. Interested parties are given a chance to respond in writing and sometimes through hearings, and the agency is supposed to take these responses into account before issuing its final rules. Often advisory committees are created or authorized to participate in agency policy making. More elaborate rule making, called "formal" rule making or "rule making on the record," provides a quasi-judicial forum in which many informed interested parties can present their perspectives to administrative law judges or other presiding officials.

When such pluralistic representation is provided, a degree of comprehensiveness is developed in an agency's consideration of what can and should be done. This is an area in which the political approach's emphasis on a fragmented administrative structure reinforces its approach toward decision making. Overlapping agency missions require the participation of several administrative units in making major decisions, and these units are likely to express differing perspectives. Compromises will be developed in the interests of maintaining cooperation and support. In general, radical departures from past practices and policies will be limited. This is seen as reinforcing stability and consistency in public administration.

A Critique of the Incremental Model

The incremental approach has some major advantages in representation and responsiveness, but its limitations are perhaps equally clear. First, it is inherently conservative to the extent that it may become extremely difficult for government to respond effectively to changes in society. Pluralism tends to be self-reinforcing. Every interest seeks its own governmental spokesperson (bureau or agency). The greater the number of administrative units involved, the more difficult coordination becomes. Consequently, more interagency coordinating committees are created. Policy judged by consensus will place a heavy emphasis on building and maintaining political support. As a result, conflict resolution and conflict avoidance will be stressed. Lawyers will work out acceptable lines of turf for the overlapping programs of different agencies or bureaus. Budgeters will seek to assure that relative levels of funding remain constant. "Hyperpluralism" or gridlock can lead beyond conservatism to immobilism.

A second difficulty with the incremental model is that because it relies on the taking of small steps in modifying policy, it is possible eventually to end up with undesirable and unforeseen consequences. One well-documented example of this was the "Bay of Pigs" invasion of 1961. A military force of anticommunist Cuban exiles was formed and trained in the United States and some Central American countries. The force was created for potential use in overthrowing the regime of Fidel Castro. Step by step, the force was enlarged and strengthened. Eventually, President Kennedy was confronted with the question of what to do with it. He did not want to turn it loose in the United States, nor were other countries willing to accept it. There seemed only one alternative: to let it invade Cuba. It did so, with the help of the United States, and was destroyed by Castro's forces. In discussing this sorry episode, Theodore Sorensen wrote:

> This plan was now or never, for three reasons: first, because the brigade was fully trained, restive to fight and difficult to hold off; second . . . because his only choice was to send them back to Cuba or bring them back to this country, where they would broadcast their resentment; and third, because Russian arms would soon build up Castro's army.[16]

A related limitation of the incremental model is that it can produce *circularity* in policy making. Taking step after step without a clear objective or a comprehensive plan can lead administrators to perpetuate existing processes and organizational arrangements even though they may need modification because of their perceived defects. For instance, the federal government's EEO program was shifted into its central personnel agency twice and out of it twice. Each second shift was accompanied by a well-worn rationale.[17] In other words, the incremental approach is particularly susceptible to failure to maintain an "organizational memory."

Finally, the incremental model of decision making does not support decisions intended to redirect the society or commit it to some large-scale venture. Likewise, it may actually be a hindrance in emergency situations, when time is of the essence. Despite its limitations in practice, comprehensive planning seems more appropriate in such cases. It is partly for this reason that societies seeking rapid economic development have tended to avoid incrementalism. However, because incrementalism requires a pluralistic political system and fragmented administrative organization to be comprehensive, rejecting incrementalism can reduce a political community's emphasis on developing and maintaining representative political institutions. Much depends on the degree of heterogeneity in the society. To some extent, then, the debate over rational-comprehensive planning versus incrementalism is also a controversy over the nature of political systems.

◆→ The Legal Approach to Decision Making

The legal approach to public administrative decision making relies on adjudicatory procedure in an effort to assure (1) that individuals, groups, corporations, or other parties are not denied their rights or otherwise treated contrary to law and (2) that decision making is reasoned and based on sound information. Adjudication is a special form of incrementalism, one bounded by an elaborate, formalized procedure and rules intended to identify the facts of a situation, the interests of opposing parties, and the balance between these interests that best fits legal requirements and/or best serves the public interest.[18] It is assumed that by going through adjudicatory procedures in a large number of instances dealing with essentially the same area of public policy, it will be possible eventually to build a body of principles that defines the public interest.

It is useful to think of adjudication as falling into two broad categories: prospective and retrospective. **Prospective adjudication** frequently involves requests by regulated utilities, transportation companies, radio and television broadcasters, and so forth, for the right to modify some aspects of their service, such as their rates, routes, or programming. It may also concern requests for licenses to operate a business or provide a service in a regulated sector of the economy. Formal rule making under the Administrative Procedure Act (APA) is prospective and uses an adjudicatory format.

Prospective adjudication also occurs when one applies for a variety of social welfare benefits. It frequently requires that the private party file a request for some kind of change and supply information and a rationale for its request. Typically, the public agency undertakes an analysis of the request. Assuming there is some controversy involved, such as whether the applicant is eligible or granting the request is in the public interest, a hearing before an impartial administrative law judge or hearing examiner may be held. During the hearing the party requesting the change will be afforded an opportunity to present more information relevant to the request. The staff of the regulatory agency may present countervailing information pertaining to its view of what the public interest requires, as outlined in the relevant statutes. Both sides may be able to present witnesses and confront and cross-examine witnesses for the other side. Third parties may be invited to submit comments either orally or in writing. The hearing examiner may play an active role in trying to clarify the issues, information, and opinions before the agency. This stage of adjudication will end when the hearing examiner issues a decision. Usually the decision will be subject to review at a higher level in the agency, often by a commission of some kind. It may be ratified, rejected, or amended at this stage. The process will be legalistic in the sense of being bound by established rules of procedure (that is, the order of the proceeding, who can appear as a witness, the form cross-examination takes, and the nature of the information that can be presented at the hearing). Administrative adjudication makes use of adversary procedure, but it is usually more flexible than courtroom procedure, especially in regard to rules of evidence and the more active role frequently played by the hearing examiner.

A second type of administrative adjudication is **retrospective.** Here an alleged wrongdoing comes to the attention of an administrative agency. This may occur through the filing of a complaint against an individual, corporation, or other party. Such a complaint may allege unfair competition, deceptive advertising, an unfair labor or personnel practice, or another form of behavior that violates law or agency regulations. Sometimes the agency becomes aware of the alleged wrongdoing through its preliminary investigations, monitoring of reports, audits, and similar means.

Once a wrongdoing is alleged, the agency is likely to undertake an elaborate investigation to determine what occurred. If agency officials in a "prosecutorial" role believe that the situation warrants further action, notice is given to the party charged with the wrongdoing. That party is then afforded a formal opportunity to respond either orally or in writing. In many cases this response will be in the form of a hearing presided over by an administrative law judge or independent hearing examiner. Again, the hearing will resemble a judicial trial, although it is likely to be more flexible. The party charged with the wrongdoing is likely to have the right to be represented by counsel and perhaps to present witnesses, and to confront and cross-examine adverse witnesses. Adversary procedure is used to establish the truth of what occurred and varying interpretations of the rules governing the action. The hearing examiner will issue a decision, which will probably be subject to review at some later stage within the agency or by another governmental body.

Advantages of Adjudication

Adjudication is an important means of making administrative decisions in several policy areas, especially regulation, personnel administration, and the granting or termination of social welfare benefits. Its best advantage is considered to be that it enables administrative bodies to act in a judicial fashion detached from political pressures. This encourages them to develop an independent view of the public interest informed by their expertise, to make decisions in an incremental fashion supporting that view, and to develop a body of law or precedent that helps identify the public interest on a continuing basis. Adjudication is especially useful when the legislature cannot agree or establish a comprehensive policy; when there is a need to make adjustments on a continual basis, as in the setting of rates for public utilities; and when flexibility is desired. It is also a useful process when decisions must turn on idiosyncratic factors, such as the intent, financial status, or physical condition of a party or the extent to which a party was acting in good faith or reasonably. Adjudication is especially suitable when the enforcement of a rule, law, or policy requires the weighing of several criteria in the context of a specific situation.

Adjudication goes a long way toward assuring that decisions are made on the basis of adequate information and are reasonable. Rules of evidence screen out unreliable information. Confrontation and cross-examination test the validity of the information on which the adjudicative decision is made. The APA authorizes judicial review of agency decisions that are allegedly arbitrary, capricious, or an abuse of discretion. It requires that formal rule making be supported by substantial evidence. The Fourth Amendment, important in street-level administration, prohibits "unreasonable" searches and seizures. At the least, it requires that administrators be able to articulate a reasonable basis for their actions involving searches or seizures. For instance, intuition alone is an insufficient basis for a police officer to stop a motorist to check on his or her license or the vehicle's registration.[19] Public administrators' liability for violations of individuals' constitutional rights depends on whether they reasonably should have known better. (The role of the Constitution in American public administration is the subject of Chapter 11.)

Critique of Adjudication as a Decision Making Model

Adjudication also has serious limitations. Adjudication is a form of incrementalism. It shares the major pitfall of that approach to decision making. It is possible to make a series of incremental decisions in a policy area without being fully cognizant of the resultant state of affairs toward which those decisions are ineluctably leading. One might find examples of this problem in several areas of adjudicative decision making. A case of intimate concern to public administrators involves the rights of public employees. Through a series of judicial decisions and administrative hearings, the constitutional and legal protections afforded public employees in adverse actions evolved from being minimal prior to the 1950s to being extremely comprehensive by the early 1970s.

Decisions involving substantive rights, equal protection, and procedural due process built on one another to the point where it appeared to many that the public service was becoming unmanageable. Sanctions could not be levied effectively against public employees whose performance or behavior was inadequate in some respect. For instance, by 1987 a constable in Harris County, Texas, found he could not constitutionally fire a probationary employee who, upon hearing of an assassination attempt on President Reagan, exclaimed, "Shoot, if they go for him again, I hope they get him." It is difficult to imagine that a court looking at a clean slate would have reached the conclusion that the First Amendment protects a probationary employee in a law enforcement office who makes such a statement at work. But to a majority of the Supreme Court, that result seemed to be compelled by past decisions, although many—including four dissenting justices—would find that the decision "boggles the mind."[20]

Adjudication has other limitations as well. It is time-consuming. It can lack uniformity, as occurs when different hearing examiners reach different conclusions in similar cases. The content of the decisional **case law** (that is, the legal principles that can be derived by analyzing decisions in previous cases) is not readily accessible to the public or to interested outside parties. It may even be obscure to the public administrators who are governed by it. Adjudications of federal equal employment opportunity complaints and labor-related issues are examples of this problem. In neither area is the content of the case law highly publicized or particularly clear in its principles, yet supervisors and employees are supposed to abide by the content of the rulings.[21] Adjudication also limits outside participation. Individuals and organizations can file the equivalent of "friend of the court" briefs under some circumstances, but there is no provision for the general, open participation of the public or interest groups in such proceedings. In addition, adjudicatory decisions can be tied to an eclectic set of facts that may tend to distort the principles underlying decisions. "Hard cases make bad law" precisely because there are at least two opposing and seemingly equally valid sets of principles on which they can be decided. In such instances, decisions may turn more than usual on the way the cases are presented to the hearing examiner or judge, on the personal sense of justice or view of the public interest held by such officials, or on their biases.

A final criticism of adjudication is that it places public administrators and individuals or organizations in an antagonistic, adversary position when such a relationship may be inappropriate to the public policy ostensibly being promoted. Examples include the public service supervisor and public employee, teacher and pupil, and social welfare caseworker and welfare recipient. In each of these instances, cooperative and supportive relationships are considered more appropriate than hostile ones. Yet when such parties enter adjudication, their relationship becomes adversarial. Moreover, adversary procedure encourages each side to present the strongest, most forceful case. This often results in exaggerated allegations that place the opposing party in the worst possible light. Behavior and motives are portrayed in black-and-white terms. This leads each party to distrust the other even more, and conflict is exacerbated. In sum, adjudication is generally a better dispute resolution process than a problem solving exercise.

◆→   THE CASE OF BENZENE IN THE WORKPLACE

We have been discussing the managerial, political, and legal approaches to public administrative decision making as though they were easily separable or came in distinct packages. In practice, public administrators are forced to combine these approaches in their day-to-day decision making. This may lead to "public management by groping along," as Robert Behn suggests.[22] But sometimes, perhaps frequently, the decision making approaches converge in one area of public administration in a way that clearly highlights their advantages and disadvantages. The effort by the federal Occupational Safety and Health Administration (OSHA) to reduce the hazards of benzene in the workplace provides an excellent illustration.

The Occupational Safety and Health Act of 1970 states that the secretary of labor

> in promulgating standards dealing with toxic materials or harmful physical agents . . . shall set the standard which most adequately assures, to the extent feasible, on the basis of the best available evidence, that no employee will suffer material impairment of health or functional capacity even if such employee has regular exposure to the hazard dealt with by such standard for the period of his working life.

Benzene is a rapidly evaporating, aromatic liquid produced by the petroleum and petrochemical industries for use in manufacturing motor fuels, solvents, detergents, pesticides, and other organic chemicals. It is known to be associated with leukemia, a cancer attacking white blood cells. No safe level of benzene, measured in its airborne state in parts per million (ppm), is known.

Following what he understood to be the legislative mandate, the secretary of labor issued standards reducing the allowable levels of benzene from 10 ppm to 1 ppm in the rubber, petroleum refining, and petrochemical industries. The costs to the industries were projected to range from $1,390 to $82,000 per worker (in physical plant changes and first-year costs). The American Petroleum Institute sued the secretary, partly on the grounds that he exceeded his statutory authority because the reduction from 10 ppm to 1 ppm was not feasible. The case reached the Supreme Court level as *Industrial Union Department, AFL-CIO v. American Petroleum Institute* (1980).[23] Part of the issue was what "feasible" meant in the context of the statute.

To answer this question, one might turn to the legislative record and attempt to discern the intent of Congress. Supreme Court Justice Rehnquist did this and concluded:

> I believe that the legislative history demonstrates that the feasibility
> requirement . . . is a legislative mirage, appearing to some Members
> [of Congress] but not to others, and assuming any form desired by the
> beholder. . . .
>
> In sum, the legislative history contains nothing to indicate that the
> language "to the extent feasible" does anything other than render what
> had been a clear, if somewhat unrealistic, standard largely, if not entirely,
> precatory. There is certainly nothing to indicate that these words . . . are
> limited to technological and economic feasibility. [Concurring opinion.]

The words "to the extent feasible" may not mean anything specific in the context of the statute, as Rehnquist argues, but the mirage they conjured up was crucial to Congress's decision making. They were offered as a substitute for the original language of the OSHA bill as a means of forming a coalition in support of greater regulation of workplace health and safety. The words may have had different meaning to different members of Congress, but they reduced opposition to the bill and generated greater support for it.

This is an example of incremental decision making. It is accepted that eliminating toxic substances from the workplace is a desirable policy objective. Such a policy is viewed as a step forward in improving American life. But it is a small and tentative step because the statute does not identify the substances deemed toxic and the standards for determining the feasibility of eliminating them. Were it to do so, it would face so much political controversy and opposition that it might be entirely impossible to move in the desired policy direction of creating safe workplaces. For example, identifying benzene as a toxic substance in the bill would have provoked opposition from the petroleum, rubber, and petrochemical industries, as well as their lobby organization, the American Petroleum Institute. Because benzene is used in pesticides, agricultural groups might also have become involved, and so on. But benzene would not be the only toxic substance identified in the bill, and consequently opposition from other industries and economic sectors would have been forthcoming. Members of Congress whose districts included the industries that would clearly be adversely affected might well oppose the bill. Politically, the way around this problem is to do what Congress did, that is, to form a broad coalition in favor of a desired policy objective by avoiding taking any specific regulatory steps. The bill was neither comprehensive in its identification of toxic substances nor particularly rational in its language. But it was passed, and it did establish a process for making America's workplaces safer.

A more rational-comprehensive approach was left to OSHA and the secretary of labor. OSHA developed the following standard: "Whenever a carcinogen is involved, OSHA will presume that no safe level of exposure exists in the absence of clear proof establishing such a level and will accordingly set the exposure limit at the lowest level feasible." Feasibility here was defined by the technologies available for eliminating the toxic substance, the devices available for measuring its presence, and the costs likely to be incurred. In the case of benzene, technology and measurement dictated 1 ppm. OSHA did consider the costs to the industries, but it "did not quantify the benefits to each category of worker in terms of decreased exposure to benzene." It reasoned that because the costs were bearable by the industries, the new standard was feasible. From a market perspective, the American Petroleum Institute considered the costs too high for many American companies to bear under the pressure of global competition. OSHA's assumption was that 1 ppm of benzene was the lowest level feasible and therefore the one that was safest. This assumption was a key issue in the subsequent adjudication in the federal courts.

This case study of decision making concerning benzene in the workplace juxtaposes the rational-comprehensive approach, incrementalism, market considerations, and adjudication, a particular variant of incrementalism, as noted earlier. It suggests that the legislature and the courts face serious institutional limitations on decision making. Public administrators are also constrained by institutional barriers, but sometimes their tasks are further complicated by the likelihood that their implementation of vague legislative mandates will be overturned by the courts, as ultimately happened in the benzene case. The case shows how the managerial, political, and legal styles of decision making can be opposed to one another—how what is acceptable reasoning under one is unacceptable under another.

◆▸   THE NEW PUBLIC MANAGEMENT
     AND DECISION MAKING

Market Criteria

The NPM strongly favors basing public administrative decisions on market criteria. In general, NPM embraces entrepreneurial organizations, considers customer satisfaction of key importance, and seeks to set up performance-based organizations to mirror private corporations in performing government's "factory" operations.[24]

Markets promote two types of efficiencies. First, they allocate goods and services efficiently in terms of matching production to consumer demand.

Organizations dependent on market transactions for their revenues or incomes are impelled by economic incentives to offer what customers want. In free, competitive markets, firms that fail to do so will suffer economically and eventually will fail. This stands in contrast to traditional bureaucracies or other nonmarket operations that use hierarchical command as a means to determine which goods and services will be offered. To return to an earlier example, agencies are more likely to satisfy their training needs if they can select programs in an open market as opposed to being required to rely on what is prescribed and offered by a central personnel agency.

Second, markets foster technical efficiency, sometimes called X efficiency. Technical efficiency is typically calculated by the inputs used to produce outputs. The less input per output, the greater the efficiency. All things being equal, more technically efficient organizations have an advantage in competitive markets. The proposition that organizations in competitive markets will necessarily be more technically efficient than nonmarket administrative operations is less widely accepted than the belief that they will have greater allocational efficiency. However, it is an article of faith in the NPM. And, undeniably, "bureaucracy" is used in most quarters to denote technical as well as allocational inefficiency.

In the NPM's view, therefore, requiring administrative units to respond to market forces causes their decision making to be more concerned with customer satisfaction and technical efficiency. It also holds that empowering frontline employees to make decisions in response to customers' needs and to solve production and other problems will enhance both types of efficiency. Further, entrepreneurial organizations, which the NPM assumes will be less hierarchical, develop goods and services that customers demand. They are proactive in serving the public and creating value. In sum, markets are better than rules—especially centralized controls—in providing public services efficiently.

There is expansive literature on the market theory that underlies the NPM.[25] However, empirical evidence is beginning to raise doubt about the translation of these theories into practice. Kenneth Meier and Laurence O'Toole subject the "proverbs" of NPM to an evidence-based test. They "find that management certainly matters, but in definite ways and often not as enthusiasts for contracting, or entrepreneurial approaches, or adaptive organizations, or other popular ideas might expect."[26]

Employee Empowerment

Street-level administrators have long been "empowered" in the sense in which the NPM uses the term. These are public employees who interact directly with segments of the public in a variety of service and regulatory capacities.[27] They include police, social workers, parole officers, teachers, and housing and health inspectors, among others. They can be considered empowered because:

1. They exercise a great deal of discretion in frequent face-to-face encounters with clients, customers, and those whom they regulate.

2. They have considerable independence within their organizations and do not work under direct visual or close proximate supervision.
3. Frequently, limited resources require that they provide services or enforce the law selectively.
4. In the aggregate, their decisions constitute the policy outputs of the agencies for which they work.

Police are probably the best example. They have tremendous discretion in determining when and how to act upon individuals. In many places, without broad discretion they probably could not survive. They often work alone or in pairs, without immediate hierarchical supervision. Selective enforcement or nonenforcement of the law is a necessity. They cannot possibly ticket every jaywalker, speeder, litterer, or person whose dog is unleashed. To a large extent, their actions determine what the police force does. Does it treat people fairly and reasonably? Does it mediate, ignore, or squelch domestic disputes? Does it make the acceptable speed limit 5 or 10 miles per hour higher than the posted limit? Does it discriminate against members of minority groups and treat them harshly?

Although street-level administrators have a great deal of discretion, they are not wholly unconstrained or without official guidance.[28] They rely on law, agency guidelines, and the expertise and training required for their jobs. In many situations, they also use intuition to assess the actions of those with whom they are interacting. Court cases reveal that sometimes police officers cannot explain how they correctly determined that someone was transporting illegal drugs; they just knew it.[29] Research indicates that street-level administrators' personal values and those of their fellow employees have a great impact on their decision making.[30] Personal values may act as a filter through which law, guidelines, principles derived from training, and intuition are either embraced and acted upon or resisted. Failure to enforce the rules always raises issues where the rule of law is highly valued. However, American society seems willing to tolerate nonenforcement when it is reasonable and involves everyday behavior of minor consequence. Problematic patterns of practice arise when the law is applied more harshly to some groups than to others. For instance, it is well documented that African Americans, Hispanics, "hippie types," and Asians are disproportionately stopped by law enforcement personnel along the southern border, on highways, and in airports.[31] Indeed, during summer 2012, a federal judge approved a class-action lawsuit against the New York Police Department for its "stop-and-frisk" policy in which officers stop people they reasonably believe are committing or about to commit a crime. In 2011, the NYPD recorded over 680,000 stops with more than 80 percent of those stopped being black or Latino.[32] Blacks with out-of-state license plates are particularly likely to be stopped by state and local police.[33] Critics of racial profiling derisively call the "infraction" DWB, or driving while black.[34]

Concern that street-level administrators may abuse their discretionary authority has led to efforts to constrain them with rules. This diminishes the flexibility sometimes necessary for successful street-level administration. Compliance with the rules can become an end in itself rather than a means to a public policy goal. A popular stereotype is the housing or Occupational Health and Safety Administration (OSHA) inspector who writes up tons of minor violations of minimal (or no) importance instead of helping solve real problems.

The NPM rejects the rule-bound approach. It favors letting administrators in virtually every capacity in public organizations rely on "common sense" to a greater extent. The empowered public administrator will have greater discretion but will be held more accountable for policy outcomes. Based on what is known about street-level administrators, the success of the NPM model for public administration in general will depend on recruitment and socialization that ensure decision making that is fair-minded and technically, politically, and legally correct. Performance measures and benchmarks (see Chapter 1) are tools that can aid in evaluating the impact of this decision making.

◆→ THE IMPACT OF CONTEXT ON DECISION MAKING

Individual Level: Recognition-Primed Decision Model

There are growing literatures in emergency/disaster management and forensic science[35] that study how decisions are made in the field. Many of these experienced street-level bureaucrats are continuously making high-stakes decisions characterized by uncertainty and time pressures. In Recognition-Primed Decisions (RPD) cues from the environment are matched to their past experiences to make instantaneous decisions. However, RPD is not the same as making a decision by analogy. Most contexts are too complex with too many variables to be simply matched to a previous experience. Rather, in assessing a situation, the decision maker is considering four aspects of the situation: 1) the types of goals that can be reasonably accomplished, 2) the relevant cues within the context of the situation, 3) developing expectations that can check the accuracy of the situation assessment, and 4) identifying typical actions.

Decision makers are not comparing alternatives; they go with the first action that comes to their mind. This is a linear process, where, before a course of action is chosen, it is evaluated on likeliness that it will succeed in the given context, not on relative advantages/disadvantages of different dimensions of the decisions. In a study of fireground commanders, Gary A. Klein[36] states, "They saw themselves acting and reacting on the basis of prior experience; they were generating, monitoring, and modifying plans to meet the needs of the situation. We found no evidence for extensive option generation. Rarely did fireground commanders contrast even two options." Effective solutions are what decision makers are after, not necessarily optimal solutions. This description of how decisions are made in the real world argues that decisions are made based on the experiences of the decision maker rather than through lengthy deliberations and use of analytic strategies to arrive at optimal solutions.

Organizational Level: The Governmental Process Model and Accountability for Decisions: Inside the "Garbage Can"

Most theories consider managerial decision making to be a process or activity that takes place mainly at the level of the individual manager. But individual managers work in an organizational setting that forms the context of the decision making activity. A moment's thought and reflection will reveal that most of the problems that managers make decisions about are the organization's problems. They may affect an individual manager's career, stand in the way of his or her fulfilling some critical goal or objective, or appear (for functional or jurisdictional purposes) to be "his or her problem." But despite who is directly responsible for resolving them, organizational problems tend to emerge fairly continuously. That is, they come as part of a kind of "problem stream"—an admixture of problems, big and small, including some that the organization has yet to confront. The problem stream mixes in fairly unpredictable ways with a loosely corresponding "solutions stream"—a set of proposals to solve problems, some of which are not solutions at all but are representative of the sorts of things the organization can do well. (The latter may include "solutions in search of problems.") When the various interests and constituencies within and without the organization are included, the decision making context becomes complex. Consequently, some authorities have described organizations as "garbage cans," or collections of problems, solutions, policies, and constituencies that make them disorganized and chaotic.[37]

How are decisions to be reached in such a chaotic internal context? In an innovative study of how decisions are reached within large organizations, John Kingdon has challenged dominant models of decision making by arguing that decisions are not so much "made" as they *emerge* from an organizational "primeval soup" of factors that mix together in ways that are somewhat organized and somewhat anarchic.[38] If this sounds confusing, it becomes clearer when we consider that in Kingdon's framework, problems, solutions, participants, opportunities, and choice criteria are so intertwined that it is difficult to sort out the separate influences of each. Kingdon builds on the earlier work of Michael Cohen and James March, which focused on organizations (like universities) that suffer from ambiguity as to purpose (What is the goal?), experience (What events can we learn from?), judging success (How do we know we are succeeding?), and using power (What can we realistically hope to accomplish?).[39] Decisions in these types of organizations tend to be as much the result of inertia as that of rational choice. "Standard operating procedures" are often used as a rational means to deal with problems of complexity even if they do not fit the problem, with the result that individual decisions are not optimal.

The decision rules that an organization requires managers to follow may routinely fail to achieve the optimal choice. This can occur, for instance, when there is a rule that the requested budgets of all programs must be cut by some fixed percentage, say, 10 percent, across the board. This simple rule will tend to reward "fat" programs at the expense of those that have been well managed. Because resources may not be allocated rationally in these circumstances

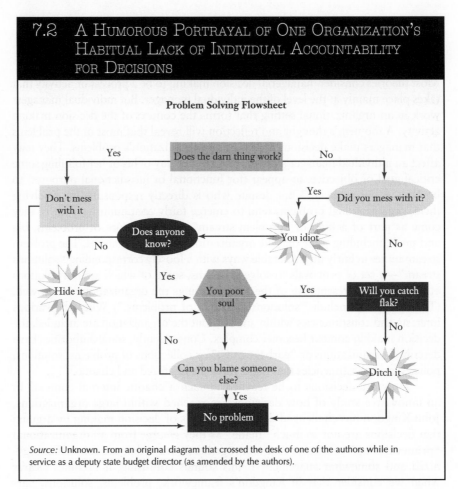

Problem Solving Flowsheet

Source: Unknown. From an original diagram that crossed the desk of one of the authors while in service as a deputy state budget director (as amended by the authors).

(i.e., cuts will hurt the well-managed programs more than others), a great deal of energy may be devoted to avoiding blame for poor results of decisions. Box 7.2 takes a humorous look at one organization in which individual managers habitually look for ways to duck responsibility for results. When unwillingness to take responsibility becomes ingrained in an organization's culture, no theory or model of decision making will save the organization from poor decisions and even poorer results. The critical point for present purposes is that organizational context will affect how effectively any decision making approach can and will be applied.

CONCLUSION: SYNTHESIZING DECISION MAKING APPROACHES

Each of the decision making approaches reviewed here has advantages and disadvantages. None is fully suitable for all decision situations. Therefore, as in other aspects of public administration, it becomes necessary to attempt a synthesis through which the advantages of each of the managerial, political, and legal approaches can be maximized and their limitations minimized. The most comprehensive approach to accomplishing this in the context of decision making has been the **mixed-scanning approach.**[40]

Mixed scanning attempts to combine incrementalism, including adjudication, with the rational-comprehensive approach. It can accommodate market-based decision making as well. This approach to decision making was developed by Amitai Etzioni, who illustrates it as follows:

> Assume we are about to set up a worldwide weather observation system using weather satellites. The rationalistic approach would seek an exhaustive survey of weather conditions by using cameras capable of detailed observations and by scheduling reviews of the entire sky as often as possible. This would yield an avalanche of details, costly to analyze and likely to overwhelm our action capacities (i.e., "seeding" cloud formations that could develop into hurricanes or bring rain to arid areas). Incrementalism would focus on those areas in which similar patterns developed in the recent past and, perhaps, on a few nearby regions; it would thus ignore all formations which might deserve attention if they arose in unexpected areas.
>
> A mixed-scanning strategy would include elements of both approaches by employing two cameras: a broad angle camera that would cover all parts of the sky but not in great detail, and a second one which would zero in on those areas revealed by the first camera to require a more in-depth examination. While mixed-scanning might miss areas in which only a detailed camera could reveal trouble, it is less likely than incrementalism to miss obvious trouble spots in unfamiliar areas.[41]

Mixed scanning requires that decision makers differentiate between fundamental decisions pertaining to long-range goals and more limited decisions made within the context of those goals. This distinction between fundamental and limited decisions is akin to the distinction made by the managerial approach between politics and administration. However, Etzioni recognizes that public administrators may make fundamental and limited types of decisions and argues that they ought to be clear about what it is they are doing. Moreover, he argues that through clarification of the relationship among types of decision making, the shortcomings of each can be substantially reduced. The approach also appears to fit well within a wide variety of internal organizational decision making contexts—from the stable to the chaotic.

Several examples of the utility of mixed scanning can be found in federal administration in the United States. The Executive Office of the President, in particular, contains a number of units essentially charged with taking a long-range view of a particular policy area and evaluating policy options. The Council of Economic Advisers is responsible for analyzing the national economy and its various segments, advising the president on economic developments, evaluating governmental programs, and recommending policies for economic growth and stability. It keeps track of markets and alerts the president to failures, threats of failure, or problems. The National Security Council has somewhat more complex operating responsibilities, but its main function is to advise the president with respect to the integration of domestic, foreign, and military policies relating to the security of the United States. Presidential commissions in various policy areas, including Social Security, Central America, and nutrition, are also used as mixed-scanning devices. In addition, various administrative operations can include a mixed-scanning function, as when agencies make five-year budget projections that try to develop a realistic appraisal of where they should be headed. All these devices can serve as checks on administrative "drift" through incrementalism and on the overly complicated and unrealistic qualities of the pure rational-comprehensive decision making model.

Mixed scanning often involves organizations charged with taking a long-range view of policies, programs, and environmental changes. Another way of achieving the benefits of mixed scanning is to engage in periodic exercises in strategic planning. Strategic planning is a deliberate attempt to force important organizational and/or policy changes in response to any number of foreseeable environmental shifts, such as changing demographics or technologies. For instance, much of the discussion of Social Security and health policy issues in recent presidential campaigns has been spurred by the impending retirement from the workforce of many 1940s and 1950s baby boomers.

Strategic planning involves several steps: developing a strategy for doing the planning; surveying trends, forces, clients, customers, competitors, and networks in the organization's environment; surveying internal resources, capabilities, and strategies; identifying alternative ways of adapting mandates and values to projected changes; developing a step-by-step approach for adjusting to the future; and describing the organization's "vision of success" to its members and other relevant groups.[42]

There are several hurdles to successful strategic planning, but like institutionalized mixed scanning it can help correct the limitations of the rational-comprehensive, short-term market-based, and muddling-through approaches. At a minimum, success requires a strong sponsor and constant effort to keep the planning exercise on track, on time, and realistic.[43]

What to Avoid

Whichever administrative decision making approach is employed, there are several pitfalls that should be avoided. As a public administrator, it is too easy to make mistakes. There are many sources of pressure; time, interest groups, members of the legislature and their staffs, the media, chief executives and their staffs, personal advancement, and personal goals are among the more common. Specialization may limit a public administrator's view and definition of reality, and administrative jargon may obscure matters. Furthermore, group decision making carries within it a tendency toward conformity, the stifling of dissent, and constant reinforcement of the agency's traditional view of matters. It is also difficult to know precisely when to decide and when to await further development before adopting new policies and new procedures.

Among some of the more commonly identified obstacles to sound administrative decisions are the following:

1. *Lack of goal clarity.* As the incremental decision making model suggests, sometimes the political price of having an administrative program is the absence of clear goals. Public administrators also display a tendency to confuse ends and means: the agency's continued existence and growth may become the true end, and its programs merely a means for justifying that end, rather than vice versa. The development of administrative ideologies touting the importance of the agency and its programs is often a sign of this ends–means inversion. When decision makers take such ideologies at face value, misplaced priorities are likely to become a problem.

2. *Confusion of the public interest with that of a customer, clientele group, or constituency.* The nature of bureaucratic politics in the United States places emphasis on the formation of alliances among bureaucratic agencies, legislative (sub)committees, and interest groups (see Chapter 2). Such relationships can easily distort a public administrator's view of the public interest. There is also a tendency to confuse the reaction of interested parties (that is, constituencies) with the view of the public more generally. This has commonly been apparent in the decision making process of regulatory agencies.

3. *Rigid conservatism (in the sense of strict adherence to rules, procedures, and past practices).* For various reasons discussed in Chapter 4, bureaucratic organization—especially hierarchy—can cause public administrators to feel personally insecure. Under such circumstances, rigidity is often a favored course of action. It is less likely that one will be disciplined or affected adversely when "going by the book" than when taking risks to further one's vision of the public interest.

4. *The tendency to oversimplify reality.* It is likely that any social or economic problem is the result of several factors and will have several effects. Specialization may confine the vision of any group of public administrators to one or a few of these causes and effects, and, hence, an appreciation of the whole problem is lost. For example, a former head of the U.S. Equal Employment Opportunity Commission, engaged in designing a better EEO complaint system, once told one of the authors that *all* racial and sexual discrimination in the federal service was interpersonal. Yet the evidence is overwhelming that much discrimination, probably most, was built into the system of examinations, position classification, and job design at the time.

5. *"Overquantification" and a tendency to deemphasize or ignore qualitative factors.* As the NPM complains, pressures for accountability, political neutrality, and job security, as well as an emphasis on objective technical expertise, make public administrators reluctant to exercise "subjective" judgment. Consequently, they seek quantitative indicators of qualitative performance. Sometimes these indicators are satisfactory, but at other times they lead administrators to decide in favor of what will look best in terms of quantity. For instance, a social agency may define successful services to needy children in terms of the number of hours spent counseling such children, despite the real outcomes of the counseling. When emphasis on quantitative compliance detracts from qualitative performance—as it could in the above example—the relationship between the two is *pathological,* because it measures the wrong things.

6. *Reluctance to engage in policy and program evaluation.* It is axiomatic that decision makers need information about the impacts of their decisions in order to make improvements. However, largely for political reasons, administrative agencies may be reluctant to gather information and engage in analysis that makes their past decisions and program implementation look seriously inadequate. Such analysis also facilitates the ability of outsiders to review and understand an agency's operations. Consequently, there is sometimes a tendency to engage in only the most perfunctory and superficial kind of policy and program evaluation. Administrative culture tends to be intolerant of internal and external criticism. Thus public administrators often fall into a highly defensive posture when confronted with challenges to their internal hierarchies, past decisions, and present procedures.

Impact of Information Technology (IT)

New technological developments in the use of information are occurring at a rapid pace. Computers and management information systems are now permanent fixtures in most organizations. Like other decision making tools, computers assist in the process of gathering and organizing information. In the view of some early observers, such as Herbert Simon, the advent of the computer and attendant information systems had the potential to revolutionize public administration.

In the years since Simon's prophetic vision, it has become clear that information technology holds the key to maximizing managerial, political, and legal values across the entire administrative landscape.[44] IT enables public administrators to cope with the complexity of the programs and policies they implement. IT makes the rational-comprehensive model more usable by enabling a public administrator to compare and project the likely consequences and costs of alternative means of implementing public policies.

IT can also facilitate employee empowerment. "Informating" the workplace in the late 20th century was as dramatic a change as was automating it earlier. In the past, managerial authority was justified and bolstered in part by control of information. IT—and especially use of the World Wide Web and social media (e.g., Facebook and Twitter among many others)—facilitates the dissemination and sharing of information. Shoshana Zuboff, a leading analyst of "informated" work, concluded in the late 1980s:

> As the new technology integrates information across time and space, managers and workers each overcome their narrow functional perspectives and create new roles that are better suited to enhancing value-adding activities in a data-rich environment. As the quality of skills at each organizational level becomes similar, hierarchical distinctions begin to blur. Authority comes to depend more upon an appropriate fit between knowledge and responsibility than upon the ranking rules of the traditional organizational pyramid.[45]

IT enhances individual employees' problem solving capabilities and reduces the relevance of traditional managerial control functions.

IT can also be beneficial to the incremental and adjudicatory models. Incrementalism is deeply concerned with making decisions that gain political support among relevant communities and constituencies. IT can assist in this effort by making it possible to analyze rapidly information gained by public opinion polls, in community surveys, and from election results. IT makes it easier for the interested public to comment on agencies' proposed rules and other actions. IT can also aid in the analysis of the limited means-ends packages under consideration. IT can help provide a better "organizational memory" to incremental decision makers. Computerized legal information systems have the ability to bring previous decisions and principles to the attention of lawyers, who, in turn, may raise them in presenting their cases before judges and administrative law judges.

No matter which decisional approach is taken, computers and information technology can help clarify thinking. They cannot resolve value conflicts among the managerial, political, and legal perspectives, but they can help us foresee the consequences of choices made within the framework of these perspectives. As in the case of many new technologies, IT also carries some risks. IT can be used to reduce individuals' privacy.[46] It sometimes promotes excessive impersonality and reliance on inappropriate quantifiable indicators of qualitative performance.

As in other areas of public administration, when considering decision making, the student and the practitioner should avoid the once common tendency to believe that there is always "one best way" and that technological and organizational processes can automatically resolve policy conflicts over competing values. Certainly, the different managerial, political, and legal approaches are more useful in some circumstances than in others. The problem is to improve them and to determine when each should be used alone or combined with one or another.

STUDY QUESTIONS

1. How are decisions made at the college or university you attend? What values are maximized by this approach? In your opinion, what are its advantages and disadvantages?
2. How do you make decisions when
   a. You think about your career plans?
   b. You are involved in a social activity?
   c. You are called on to resolve some disagreement between friends, co-workers, fellow students, or relatives?

   Does your decision making process differ in varied contexts? If so, how?
3. "Interactive TV" enables the viewer to send electronic signals instantaneously to the broadcaster. These signals can indicate agreement or disagreement with statements or propositions made on the TV program. Elaborate interactive systems would also enable the viewers to indicate the general level of intensity of their preferences.

   Some believe that interactive TV is a way of improving government decision making by allowing the public to register its preferences on matters of public policy. Do you think interactive TV or similar technologies would have any utility in improving public administrative decision making? Why or why not?

NOTES

1. Charles Perrow, *Complex Organizations,* 3d ed. (New York: Random House, 1986), 129.
2. Ibid., 130.
3. *Shapiro v. Thompson,* 394 U.S. 618 (1969).
4. See David H. Rosenbloom, *Federal Equal Employment Opportunity* (New York: Praeger, 1977), 113; Robert Hampton, Chairman, U.S. Civil Service Commission, "Memorandum for Heads of Departments and Agencies," 11 May 1971.
5. Harold Seidman, *Politics, Position, and Power* (New York: Oxford University Press, 1970), 18.
6. The Supreme Court upheld the legality of grid regs in *Heckler v. Campbell,* 461 U.S. 458 (1983).
7. Graham Allison, *Essence of Decision: Explaining the Cuban Missile Crisis,* (Boston: Little Brown, 1971). Graham Allison and Phillip Zelikow, *Essence of Decision: Explaining the Cuban Missile Crisis,* 2d ed. (New York: Longman, 1999).
8. See *Personnel Administrator v. Feeney,* 422 U.S. 256 (1976); and David H. Rosenbloom and Peter Grabosky, "Racial and Ethnic Competition for Federal Service Positions," *Midwest Review of Public Administration* 11 (December 1977): 281–290.
9. Peter Woll and Rochelle Jones, "Bureaucratic Defense in Depth," in Ronald Pynn, Ed., *Watergate and the American Political Process* (New York: Praeger, 1975), esp. 216–217.
10. Irving L. Janis, *Victims of Groupthink* (Boston: Houghton Mifflin, 1972).
11. Diane Vaughan, *The Challenger Launch Decision: Risky Technology, Culture, and Deviance at NASA* (Chicago: University of Chicago Press, 1996).

12. For an interesting discussion from the perspectives of individual administrators, see David Granick, "The Red Executive," in Gerald Bell, Ed., *Organizations and Human Behavior* (Englewood Cliffs, NJ: Prentice-Hall, 1967), 218–230. See also, a classic in the field, Joseph LaPalombara, Ed., *Bureaucracy and Political Development* (Princeton, NJ: Princeton University Press, 1963).

13. See Deborah Stone, *Policy Paradox: The Art of Political Decision Making* (New York: Norton, 1997).

14. Charles Lindblom, "The Science of 'Muddling Through,'" *Public Administration Review* 19 (Spring 1959): 79–88; Amitai Etzioni, "Mixed-Scanning: A 'Third' Approach to Decision-Making," *Public Administration Review* 27 (December 1967): 385–392, reprinted in Alan Altshuler and Norman Thomas, Eds., *The Politics of the Federal Bureaucracy,* 2d ed. (New York: Harper & Row, 1999), 139–146; and Amitai Etzioni, "Mixed Scanning Revisited," *Public Administration Review* 46 (January/February 1986): 8–14.

15. See Herbert Simon, *Administrative Behavior,* 2d ed. (New York: Free Press, 1965 [original copyright 1945]).

16. Theodore Sorensen, *Kennedy* (New York: Harper & Row, 1965), 296.

17. See Rosenbloom, *Federal Equal Employment Opportunity,* chaps. 3 and 4.

18. Kenneth Warren, *Administrative Law in the American Political System,* 2d ed. (St. Paul, MN: West, 1988), chap. 7.

19. *Delaware v. Prouse,* 440 U.S. 648 (1979); *Whren v. United States,* 517 U.S. 806 (1996).

20. *Rankin v. McPherson,* 483 U.S. 378 (1987).

21. See Patricia Ingraham and David Rosenbloom, Eds., *The Promise and Paradox of Civil Service Reform* (Pittsburgh, PA: University of Pittsburgh Press, 1992), chaps. 7 and 11.

22. Robert Behn, "Management by Groping Along," *Journal of Policy Analysis and Management* 7 (Fall 1988): 643–663.

23. *Industrial Union Department, AFL-CIO v. American Petroleum Institute,* 448 U.S. 607 (1980).

24. Al Gore, *From Red Tape to Results: Creating a Government That Works Better & Costs Less* (Washington, DC: Government Printing Office, 1993), chap. 2; and Al Gore, *Common Sense Government Works Better & Costs Less* (Washington, DC: Government Printing Office, 1995).

25. A good overview of the salient questions can be found in Charles Lindblom, *Politics and Markets* (New York: Basic Books, 1977). Among the more influential critiques of market theory are Stone, *Policy Paradox;* and Amitai Etzioni, *The Moral Dimension* (New York: Free Press, 1988).

26. Kenneth J. Meier and Laurence J. O'Toole, Jr. "The Proverbs of New Public Management: Lessons from an Evidence-Based Research Agenda," *The American Review of Public Administration* 39 (1, 2009): 4–22 at p. 18.

27. Michael Lipsky, *Street-Level Bureaucracy* (New York: Russell Sage, 1980).

28. See David Rosenbloom, Rosemary O'Leary, and Joshua Chanin, *Public Administration and Law,* 3rd ed. (Boca Raton, FL: CRC/Taylor & Francis, 2010), chap. 6.

29. *New Mexico v. Bloom,* 561 P.2d 925 (1976); *Delaware v. Prouse,* 440 U.S. 648 (1979).

30. See Rosenbloom, O'Leary, and Chanin, *Public Administration and Law,* chap. 6, for a review of the literature.

31. S. Duke and A. Gross, "Casualties of War," *Reason* 25 (February 1994): 20–27.
32. Ray Rivera, "Pockets of City See Higher Use of Force During Police Stops," *New York Times* (August 16, 2012): A17.
33. S. Duke and A. Gross, "Casualties of War," *Reason* 25 (February 1994): 20–27.
34. Jennifer Larrabee "DWB (Driving While Black) and Equal Protection: The Realities of an Unconstitutional Police Practice," *Journal of Law and Policy* 6, no. 1 (1997): 291–328.
35. Ira Helsloot and Jelle Groenedaal, "Naturalistic Decision Making in Forensic Science: Toward a Better Understanding of Decision Making by Forensic Team Leaders" *Journal of Forensic Sciences* 56 (No. 4, 2011): 890–897.
36. Gary A. Klein, "A Recognition-Primed Decision (RPD) Model of Decision Making," in Gary A. Klein, Judith Orasanu, Roberta Calderwood, and Caroline E. Zsambok, Eds., *Decision making in action: Models and Methods* (Norwood, NJ: Ablex, 1993), 139.
37. James G. March and Johan P. Olsen, "Garbage Can Models of Decision Making in Organizations," in J. G. March and R. Weissinger-Baylon, Eds., *Ambiguity and Command* (White Plains, NY: Pitman, 1986).
38. John W. Kingdon, *Agendas, Alternatives, and Public Policies,* 2d ed. (New York: Longman, 2003).
39. Michael D. Cohen and James G. March, "Leadership in an Organized Anarchy," in Jay M. Shafritz and J. Steven Ott, Eds., *Classics of Organization Theory,* 4th ed. (Belmont, CA: Wadsworth, 1996), 385–399.
40. Etzioni, "Mixed-Scanning."
41. Ibid., reprinted in Altshuler and Thomas, *The Politics of the Federal Bureaucracy,* 143.
42. For the basic principles of strategic planning, see Arnoldo C. Hax and Nicolas S. Majlut, *Strategic Management: An Integral Perspective* (New York: Prentice-Hall, 1984); or Robert Boyden Laueb, Ed., *Competitive Strategic Management* (New York: Prentice-Hall, 1984).
43. See John Bryson and William Roering, "Initiation of Strategic Planning by Governments," *Public Administration Review* 48 (November/December 1988): 99–104.
44. Herbert Simon, "Applying Information Technology to Organization Design," *Public Administration Review* 33 (May/June 1973), esp. 276. Other, more recent observers predict sweeping changes in the way citizen and consumer preferences are expressed to government and in the market. See Bill Gates, *The Road Ahead* (New York: Viking, 1995); and Esther Dyson, *Release 2.0* (New York: Broadway Books, 1997).
45. Shoshana Zuboff, *In the Age of the Smart Machine* (New York: Basic Books, 1988), 6.
46. See Alan F. Westin, *Privacy and Freedom* (New York: Atheneum, 1967).

Additional Reading

Allison, Graham, and Phillip Zelikow. *Essence of Decision: Explaining the Cuban Missile Crisis,* 2d ed. New York: Longman, 1999.
Kahneman, Daniel. *Thinking, Fast and Slow.* New York: Farrar, Strauss, and Giroux, 2011.

Lindblom, Charles. "The Science of 'Muddling Through,'" *Public Administration Review* 19 (Spring 1959): 79–88.

March, James. *Decisions and Organizations.* Oxford: Blackwell, 1989.

Murray, Michael. *Decisions: A Comparative Critique.* Marshfield, MA: Pitman, 1986.

Simon, Herbert. *Administrative Behavior,* 3d ed. New York: Free Press, 1976.

Wilson, David. *Top Decisions.* San Francisco: Jossey-Bass, 1986.

DECISION MAKING WEB SITES

A useful lexicon of decision making is available through the Decision Analysis Society at http://decision-analysis.society.informs.org/Field/FieldLexicon.html.

The Society for Judgment and Decision Making has an extensive set of hot links to many specialized decision making Web sites at http://www.sjdm.org.

PART III

The Convergence of Management, Politics, and Law in the Public Sector

CHAPTER 8

POLICY ANALYSIS AND
IMPLEMENTATION EVALUATION

Key Learning Objectives

1. Know the difference between policy outputs and policy outcomes or impacts.

2. Understand the three different research designs for analyzing policy outcomes or impacts.

3. Understand the managerial, political, and legal perspectives on evaluating policy implementation.

Public administration's myriad impacts on the economy and society have fostered concern about how well public policies work and how their implementation could be improved. This chapter focuses on two ways of judging policies: policy analysis and implementation evaluation. Policy analysis can be prospective or retrospective. It seeks to determine how social, economic, and other problems will be affected by different governmental policy choices. It also considers the extent to which a policy achieves its objectives and why it is successful or falls short. Implementation evaluation focuses on whether implementation maximizes appropriate values. The traditional managerial, political, and legal perspectives tend to agree that implementation can be problematic if it gives too much discretionary authority to individual administrators. However, the new public management favors broad discretion. Each of these perspectives may be more suitable for evaluating policy in a particular area of public administration, such as overhead administrative functions, sociotherapy, or regulation.

Public administration is an activist part of government. It is a means by which government seeks to intervene in aspects of the economy, society, and polity. When called on to be the arm of governmental intervention in these spheres of life, public administrators are required to *implement* policy. The question of how successfully public policy is being implemented inevitably arises. And, if the answer is, "Not successfully enough!" is the problem with the implementation, the policy, or both? In essence, seeking answers to such questions is *policy analysis* and *implementation evaluation*. However, in an age of hollowed out government, these questions are increasingly difficult to answer as nonprofit and for-profit organizations are increasingly being contracted by government to deliver public services. Public administrators not only need to be substantive policy experts, they must also be good at contract management.

◆◆ THE GROWING CONCERN WITH POLICY ANALYSIS

Although these questions seem normal enough, systematic policy analysis became a standard public administrative function only in the 1960s and 1970s. In part this was due to a shift in the nature of administrative intervention in the 1960s that made public administration more salient in the workplace, in neighborhoods, in families, and in society. President Lyndon Johnson's "Great Society" program, for instance, rested on the premise that public administration could intervene successfully in a wide range of aspects of life to promote greater equality of opportunity among the citizenry. However, assessments of implementation tend to depend on one's perspectives. What one person considers a *service* provided by public administration, another may consider a *constraint*. Whereas an employee may view public administrative intervention to protect him or her from toxic substances in the workplace as a valuable governmental service, the employer may view it as administrative interference in legitimate business considerations.

As public administration provides more services to people, it also engages in more extensive regulatory activities.

By the 1970s it was evident that many individuals and groups thought that the administrative state had gone too far in regulating their activities. Some policies for broad social change, conceived in hope in the 1960s, appeared to fail. Perhaps even worse, they seemed to linger on well after their inadequacies were widely understood. In truth, many of the policies being implemented by public administrators were established by legislatures, but nonetheless opposition often focused on "the bureaucrats."

Public administrative intervention in the economy, society, and polity makes policy analysis more salient. The more resources the administrative state consumes, and the more it intervenes in our lives, the more we want it to adopt successful strategies and to know about the effects it is having. The growing desire to evaluate policy design and implementation coincided with the rapid development of analytic techniques, especially in the social sciences, that could be used to assess the impacts of administrative interventions and ascertain the costs and benefits associated with public administrative implementation of policies. In one sense, the basic question is at least as old as Woodrow Wilson's call in the 1880s for a new study of administration that could "discover, first, what government can properly and successfully do."[1] The development of new analytical approaches, statistical techniques, and social scientific methodologies gave impetus to the development of public policy analysis as an area of study and applied research. Some broad aspects of these methodologies are outlined later in this chapter.

By way of introduction, it should also be mentioned that in a practical sense retrospective policy analysis was strengthened by a number of related administrative developments. Among these developments were a congressional requirement that in many policy areas a percentage of a program's budget be set aside for program evaluation; the enactment of the Freedom of Information Act of 1966, which facilitated greater public access to information that makes policy analysis feasible; the development of program budgeting; and the growing tendency to place "sunset" clauses in enabling legislation. Policy analysis can help by showing whether a program is having the intended impact in a cost-effective manner and with a favorable benefit-cost ratio. By the 1980s, policy analysis had become central to much federal rule making as well.

◆→ APPROACHES TO ANALYZING PUBLIC POLICY

It is sometimes useful to distinguish between two aspects of public policy. One is called **policy output,** the other **policy impact** or **policy outcome.** They are linked, but they can be separated for analytical reasons to avoid confusion. (See Box 8.1 for a description of the different components of this linkage.)

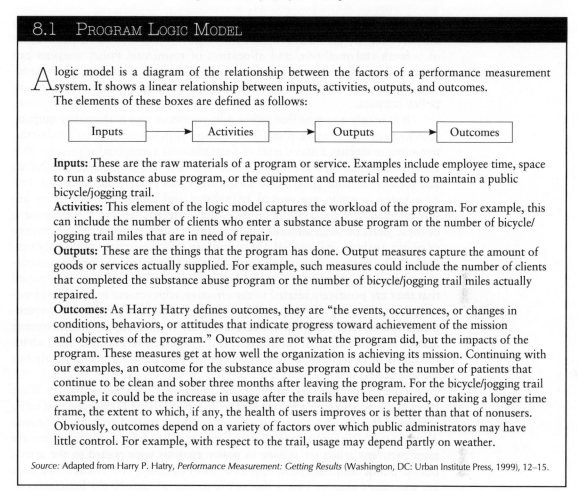

8.1   PROGRAM LOGIC MODEL

A logic model is a diagram of the relationship between the factors of a performance measurement system. It shows a linear relationship between inputs, activities, outputs, and outcomes. The elements of these boxes are defined as follows:

Inputs ⟶ Activities ⟶ Outputs ⟶ Outcomes

Inputs: These are the raw materials of a program or service. Examples include employee time, space to run a substance abuse program, or the equipment and material needed to maintain a public bicycle/jogging trail.

Activities: This element of the logic model captures the workload of the program. For example, this can include the number of clients who enter a substance abuse program or the number of bicycle/jogging trail miles that are in need of repair.

Outputs: These are the things that the program has done. Output measures capture the amount of goods or services actually supplied. For example, such measures could include the number of clients that completed the substance abuse program or the number of bicycle/jogging trail miles actually repaired.

Outcomes: As Harry Hatry defines outcomes, they are "the events, occurrences, or changes in conditions, behaviors, or attitudes that indicate progress toward achievement of the mission and objectives of the program." Outcomes are not what the program did, but the impacts of the program. These measures get at how well the organization is achieving its mission. Continuing with our examples, an outcome for the substance abuse program could be the number of patients that continue to be clean and sober three months after leaving the program. For the bicycle/jogging trail example, it could be the increase in usage after the trails have been repaired, or taking a longer time frame, the extent to which, if any, the health of users improves or is better than that of nonusers. Obviously, outcomes depend on a variety of factors over which public administrators may have little control. For example, with respect to the trail, usage may depend partly on weather.

Source: Adapted from Harry P. Hatry, *Performance Measurement: Getting Results* (Washington, DC: Urban Institute Press, 1999), 12–15.

The formulation of public policy involves establishing the objectives to be attained and at least sketchily outlining the general means to be used in seeking to achieve these objectives. For instance, to return to a familiar example, if a legislature decides that equal employment opportunity is a desirable objective, it may enact a statute intended to regulate the behavior of employers to facilitate the achievement of this aim. The statute may also vest responsibility for implementing or enforcing its provisions in an administrative agency, such as an equal employment opportunity commission. Presumably, if the legislature is serious in its intentions, it will allocate sufficient financial and personnel resources to the administering agency and also grant it the legal powers to accomplish its mission.

The formulation of public policy is often highly politicized and may involve hotly contested elections, votes in the legislature, and extensive lobbying activities. The outgrowth of policy formulation is the policy output—that is, an official statement of governmental intent, delineation of powers and methods, and allocation of resources. Policy outputs can involve tangible and/or symbolic activity. Statutes, congressional resolutions, presidential proclamations, and the allocation of staff and funds are policy outputs.

It is widely accepted that public administrators also make policy outputs, such as rules and strategic plans. The creation of policy outputs by administrative agencies violates a major tenet of the traditional managerial approach—that administration be separate from politics. The new public management (NPM) also focuses on "*how* government should work, not *what* it should do."[2]

Policy outputs are central to politics and administration. They are statements of the goals of the polity and are prerequisites to the attainment of these goals through administrative action. However, from the perspective of policy analysis, it is crucial not to confuse policy outputs with policy outcomes. The outputs do not tell us much about performance or the achievement of stated objectives. The outputs are essentially *activities*. It is hoped that they are positively related to the effective achievement of a policy objective. But today, only a naive political observer would assume that a governmental purpose is achieved because a statute is enacted, an administrative agency is empowered, or funds are spent. Too much has been learned about the limits of governmental action to assume that the output necessarily has the intended outcome.

Policy outcomes, by contrast, are concerned with performance: What effect is the policy output having on the intended target? Is the objective being achieved? If not, why not? If so, is achievement related to administration? At what cost? With what side effects? These are the types of questions that are most pertinent when we engage in policy analysis with regard to the activities of public administrative agencies. Unfortunately, the answers we seek are sometimes elusive. This is due partly to several factors: the limitations of analytical techniques, problems of measurement, lack of information, and the complexity of so many governmental programs.

Outcome Analysis

Before the outcome of a policy can be ascertained, it is necessary to identify the content of that policy in operational terms. In other words, the policy must have some specific content that lends itself to observation. Many policies do that. For instance, a policy of reducing taxes to stimulate economic growth is something that can be analyzed. But many policies are too vague in their objectives or too resistant to measurement to be systematically observed. Policies to promote some aspects of the public interest or justice, where there are competing visions of what the public interest is or justice requires, are examples. Such policies may be extremely important—after all, they are the stuff of which politics is made and over which wars and revolutions are fought—but their content may not be suitable for the policy analysis techniques and methods available to us. Other policies fall somewhere in between these two categories. In principle their impact can be evaluated; in practice it becomes difficult to separate the impact of the policy from other factors. To what extent did the Troubled Asset Relief Program (TARP) prevent a second great depression in 2008 relative to the impact of growing U.S. exports of goods and services to Brazil, Russia, India, and China (also known as the BRIC nations)? This type of problem is not inconsequential, for often specific policy outcomes are related to very complex political, economic, or social phenomena.

Assuming that the objectives of the policy outputs are suitable for it, an **impact analysis** or **outcome analysis** may be undertaken. Impact or outcome analysis can be defined as being "concerned with examining the extent to which a policy causes change in the intended direction."[3] The idea behind impact analysis is causality. Does the policy cause change? Or is the change, if any, or some of it, independent of the policy?

Answering such questions can often be complex in the context of public administration. There are three basic models that policy analysts use to assess the impact or outcome of a particular policy: **pure experimental design, quasi-experimental design,** and **nonexperimental design.** Pure experimental design is the "gold standard" of research design. Participants are randomly selected from a population and are put into one of two groups. Those who receive the treatment are in an experimental group; those who do not are in a control group. Using various statistical tools, analysts try to determine whether the treatment is correlated with the desired impact. However, quasi-experimental and nonexperimental designs are more frequently used because opportunities for pure experimentation are often limited.

Limited Opportunities for Experimentation

Opportunities for experimentation are frequently limited by political, moral, and/or legal concerns. For example, suppose you are in the public health service and you want to analyze the impact of treating people for syphilis. Can you treat some while creating a control group by withholding treatment from others in similar condition even though ample resources are available to treat everyone? In essence, this was done over a period of four decades by the U.S. Public Health Service in Tuskegee, Alabama, with tragic outcomes (see Box 8.2).[4] What about constructing experiments to provide welfare, food stamps, free medical assistance, sex education, school vouchers, transportation, or zero-tolerance police protection to some but not others in an effort to assess the impact of policies? Although some creative approaches to experimentation are politically, morally, and legally feasible in these areas, sometimes technically appropriate approaches are ruled out.

8.2   EXPERIMENTAL RESEARCH DESIGN: THE CASE OF "BAD BLOOD"

From 1932 to 1972, the United States Public Health Service (PHS) conducted a study on the effects of *untreated* syphilis on African American men in the area around Tuskegee, Alabama. The "Tuskegee Study" involved 399 men with syphilis; 201 others were used as controls. The Public Health Service's primary interest was in learning about the impact of the disease on blacks in its final stages. They found that untreated syphilis can cause skin tumors and ulcers, mutilating bone destruction, heart damage, paralysis, insanity, and blindness. Apparently, the dominant view of the PHS was that, "There was nothing in the experiment that was unethical or unscientific." Once the experiment became highly publicized in 1972, much of the nation was not so sure.

According to James H. Jones, "Journalists tended to accept the argument that the denial of penicillin [to the untreated group] during the 1940s was the crucial ethical issue." Earlier forms of treatment were ineffective, painful, and in some respects as bad as the disease.

However, the men may have benefited greatly from penicillin, and withholding it from them condemned the untreated men to a painful life with a very debilitating disease. But some observers thought a moral problem was inherent in the experiment from the outset. The *St. Louis Post-Dispatch* argued, "The fact is that in an effort to determine from autopsies what effects syphilis has on the body, the government from the moment the experiment began withheld the best available treatment for a particularly cruel disease. The immorality of the experiment was inherent in its premise." Jones's book, *Bad Blood,* makes it clear that the study was also inherently racist.

Eventually, a lawsuit was filed on behalf of the untreated men and their heirs. The case was settled out of court, with the government agreeing to pay $37,500 to each of the "living syphilitics," $15,000 to the heirs of each of the "deceased syphilitics," $16,000 to each living member of the control group, and $5,000 to the heirs of each of the "deceased controls."

Source: James H. Jones, *Bad Blood: The Tuskegee Syphilis Experiment* (New York: Free Press, 1981), 8, 9, 217.

Assuming Causality in Nonexperimental Analyses

The limited opportunities for experimentation in the public sector force policy analysts to rely on other approaches. Some of these approaches can be convincing at best but misleading at worst. A nonexperimental approach assumes a connection between the availability or level of a program and a condition in the target population. For instance, one can analyze the nutrition of children who receive school lunches through governmental programs. One might find that their nutrition is adequate, but one should not assume on that basis that this is due to the availability of the lunches alone. Perhaps other information could be brought to bear on the situation in an effort to ascertain causality. For instance, are the lunches the *only* food consumed by some of the students? What do the others eat? Still, without a control group, one cannot be sure what the students would do for nutrition in the absence of the lunch program.

A similar problem arises in what is called a **preprogram-postprogram analysis.** Here the condition of the target population or phenomenon prior to the implementation of the program is compared with the condition afterward. Comparison can be of any number of criteria that seem relevant. For instance, if one wants to assess the impact of affirmative action on patterns of federal employment, one could look at the employment of a group, such as African Americans, prior to the use of affirmative action. Salary, grade, and occupation could be some of the aspects of employment considered. The patterns observed could be compared with patterns after the implementation of affirmative action. One might find changes or the absence of change, and one might be tempted to attribute such change to the use of affirmative action. Without further information, however, that could be a serious mistake. A wide variety of factors—including job-market conditions and demographic and general attitudinal change—could have contributed to changing employment patterns independently of the use of affirmative action. Moreover, even if there were no changes, does this mean that the program does not work in terms of maintaining and preventing deterioration of the present level of equality of opportunity? Without more to go on, this question cannot be answered within the framework of the nonexperimental research design.

One way of improving on preprogram-postprogram comparisons is to establish the rate of change before the introduction of a new policy such as affirmative action. By projecting this rate of change into the postprogram period, we can obtain a rough idea of what would have been expected had the new policy not been adopted. Then the projections could be compared with the observed reality. This approach remains vulnerable to variations in confounding conditions. But in the absence of these variations, focusing on the rate of change may often provide a better basis for assessing the impact of an alteration in policy.

Quasi-Experimental Research Designs
The opportunity for truly experimental research designs is often limited in public administration. Nonexperimental designs are not likely to be satisfactory, especially in complicated policy areas where the political and administrative salience of solid policy analysis is often greatest. Sometimes it is possible to bridge this gap somewhat by developing a quasi-experimental design. Such designs often try to determine the impact of policies by contrasting performance between groups exposed to the policy and those not exposed while statistically controlling for confounding conditions.

Federalism, which allows for such great variation among governmental policies, often facilitates such comparisons. For example, one state may rigorously enforce mandatory seat belt laws whereas neighboring states do not. Subsequently, one could compare motorist fatalities or serious injuries in these states. If the state enforcing the use of seat belts had fewer fatalities or serious injuries, it would *suggest* that the policy was responsible. That is the idea of quasi-experimental designs. However, elaborate precautions have to be taken in such research to assure that the conclusion is valid. The analysis should control for differences among the states. In the foregoing example, it would probably be advisable to compare fatalities or serious injuries per mile driven on the states' roads, because one state may have a much greater number of drivers than the other. The topography of the state; the number of miles of roads in urban and rural areas; the nature of licensing procedures; maximum speed limits; the demographic character of drivers, such as average age and percent over 70 or under 20; and several other factors would probably have to be taken into account before one could be relatively sure that the seat belt policy was having the intended effect.

Interpreting Results

Taking so much into account makes for a difficult analysis that may be time-consuming and expensive. Moreover, the results of such a study may be equivocal. It is unlikely that analysis will lead to such conclusions as "Spending x dollars to convince drivers to use seat belts saves y lives per year." One of the great problems of policy analysis is that so many studies are unable to ascertain what kind of effect, if any, a policy is having. It is important that a public administrator not draw the wrong lesson from this. The fact that the impact or outcome of a policy cannot be satisfactorily determined through our available methods of policy analysis does not mean that the policy is not working. It may be working, and working well, although we are unable to demonstrate, in an analytically satisfactory way, that it is doing so. By contrast, even where policy analysis suggests that a policy is working well, a public administrator should always bear in mind that there may be some factor not taken into account in the analysis that explains the seeming success. For instance, reorganizing and redeploying a police force may coincide with a reduction in crime rates. However, the reduction could stem from a number of other factors, including economic, demographic, environmental, and social changes.

Moreover, although policy impacts may be observable in the short run, strong policy analysis must also consider the long run. It must be concerned with the target group in the future, the policy's impact on nontarget groups ("spillover" effects), and the options created or foreclosed by the policy. For instance, a welfare policy aimed at providing aid to poor children may successfully accomplish that while simultaneously increasing delinquency among adolescent youth who are unsupervised because the policy requires their parents to work or receive job training. Policy analysis should also be sensitive to the symbolic importance of governmental actions. Even if a policy has no discernible impact, it may be an important political indicator of a government's interest in dealing with a problem or group interest.

Process Analysis and Implementation Studies

Successfully predicting and ascertaining the outcomes of public policies is often difficult or impossible. However, policy analysis should not be confined to considering impacts; it can also be used to assess the *process* through which a policy is being implemented. **Process analysis** concerns the way in which a particular policy or program is implemented.[5] Its importance can be succinctly stated: "The content of a particular public policy and its impact on those affected may be substantially modified, elaborated, or even negated during its implementation. Obviously, it is futile to be concerned with the impact of a particular policy if it has not been implemented."[6]

Surprisingly, however, policy analysis often neglects process analysis. In part this may be because it calls for a different type of approach than does impact or outcome analysis. Whereas the latter tends to deal with aggregate data, such as crime rates or traffic fatalities, process analysis requires that the analyst become intimately aware of the administrative process through which the policy is implemented. For instance, if the policy is mandatory use of seat belts, one would have to look at the process of getting people to buckle up. Do police officers issue tickets for nonuse? Are penalties applied? If so, are they substantial? Why or why not? Just as the enforcement of other traffic laws may vary widely, so might that be the case with a mandatory seat belt law. In that event, it would be not only the policy but also the enforcement that one would expect to have an impact on the area of behavior (driving).

Much process analysis has taken the form of "implementation" studies. These often rely on qualitative techniques, including case studies, historical analysis, participant observation, and extensive interviewing. Implementation studies have identified some key factors affecting the execution of policies. One is the number of points at which different administrators must make decisions concerning implementation. The more decision points there are, the less likely it is that the policy will be implemented as those who formulated it intended. Serious underfunding of programs is another barrier to successful implementation. Sometimes the goals or objectives of policies are so unclear that different agencies and public administrators adopt disparate approaches to defining and implementing them. For instance, during the early years of affirmative action in the federal personnel system, some agencies adopted goals and timetables that, if implemented, would have left their workforces *less* socially representative of the nation's working population. One agency even sought to increase occupational segregation by sex by establishing a 100 percent hiring goal for women in clerical positions! This may have provided more jobs for women, but it was a peculiar—though plausible—interpretation of the policy of using affirmative action to achieve equal employment opportunity.[7]

Implementation studies have focused attention on the design of public policies. **Policy design** should maximize the likelihood that implementation will be successful (as defined by the policy makers). In a discussion of "The Deadly Sins in Public Administration," Peter Drucker, a leading expert on management, identifies the following conditions as fatal to effective implementation: (1) lack of clear, preferably measurable, goals; (2) several objectives addressed at once, with no clear priorities; (3) assumption that personnel and funds will solve complex problems; (4) policies or programs tried out on a grand scale; (5) failure to learn from feedback; and (6) inability to abandon policies or programs when they become unnecessary or fail to achieve the desired results.[8]

Implementation studies suggest that a process analysis may be the place to begin policy analysis. If the implementation is such that there is no logical reason to expect a policy to have much or any impact, there is no need to go further. Nevertheless, process analysis is sometimes neglected because it may require access to public administrators and the ability to monitor aspects of their behavior over a substantial period. But administrators may perceive such access as a potential source of conflict, for in the area of process analysis, evaluation of administrative behavior is seldom far beneath the surface.

◆◆   IMPLEMENTATION EVALUATION

Implementation evaluation depends on policy analysis, but it is a different enterprise. In public administration, the question is whether the implementation of the policy is appropriate, rather than whether it has the intended impact. Because a consensus on normative questions is often missing, just what we are likely to view as "good" public administration depends on our perspective. What we consider properly executed policy will often depend on whether we adopt a managerial, political, or legal perspective.

◆◆   MANAGERIAL PERSPECTIVES ON IMPLEMENTATION

Assuming that a policy has some traceable impact in the intended direction on its target, how can we determine if its execution is "optimal," or whether it is "satisfactory" or "not good enough"? The traditional managerial and NPM perspectives present distinctive sets of answers to this question.

Traditional Management

The traditional managerial perspective values effectiveness, efficiency, and economy in implementation. It places much less importance on such other concerns as customer satisfaction, public participation, and procedural due process.

Effectiveness

In this context, effectiveness will focus on the process of implementation. Among the major questions likely to be asked are the following: Is the administering agency effectively (that is, rationally) organized? Is the behavior of the public administrators involved *predictable*? Are patterns of authority and responsibility clear? Is feedback within the agency sufficient? Is communication adequate? Are enough resources being devoted to the policy? In short, does the organization of the effort to implement the policy follow the principles of effective management with regard to structure, personnel, budgeting, decision making, and so on? From this perspective, some policies are more suitable for implementation than others. Those relatively unsuitable will not be considered to be policies that work well, even though they may achieve their intended objectives. They will not be considered "good" policies because their administrative costs will be judged excessive, and they will be thought to be too resistant to "good" (effective) management.

From this perspective, many policies will not work well. Policies that require "street-level" interactions between administrators who are, at the time, unsupervised and clients or other individuals will inevitably have an unpredictable quality about them. For example, no matter how explicit the formal rules seem to be, one housing inspector, police officer, member of the border patrol, teacher, or other street-level administrator may treat similar situations, cases, or individuals differently than another administrator does.[9] The exercise of discretion is necessary in many of these interactions. Actions may turn on individual administrators' judgments of the motives of the people with whom they come into contact, or with assessments of their behavior. What is "suspicious" behavior to one police officer may not appear so to another.

Because street-level administrators have so much discretion, their personal motives can have a major impact on their decision making. Some will have a high degree of "public service motivation,"[10] which will impel them to promote the public interest as commonly understood in the policy area in which they work. However, they may lack the resources to apply the rules uniformly to all cases. Their response might be to engage in "triage," that is, to invest their time and other resources where they can do the most good. For example, a parole officer may decide some of his or her cases are career criminals so likely to be recidivist that anything more than pro forma intervention will be pointless. The same will be true for parolees who made a one-time mistake, paid their debt to society, and are highly unlikely ever to commit another criminal offense. However, in between these groups, there may be a number of individuals who can be helped by the parole officer's attention and assistance in finding jobs, joining productive social networks, and going straight.

By contrast, other street-level administrators will be more self-interested than motivated to serve the public interest. Here they may engage in "creaming." They will devote their efforts to the cases that are easiest to deal with and will make their performance look best. Where this occurs, for example, parole officers will try to have those parolees least likely to commit additional crimes assigned to them. Their intervention will do little to promote the public interest, though it may serve their self-interests well.

Although triage seems more productive than creaming, in both cases it is the street-level administrators who determine how policy will be implemented and, to a large extent, what its effect is likely to be. From the traditional managerial perspective, the possibility of these patterns of enforcement arising and the unpredictability of others that may develop present a serious problem.

Street-level administrators may be acting in ways that deviate from the organization's formal guidelines. Consequently, the organization may be deviating somewhat from its intended role within the framework of the public policy being implemented. Teachers may be babysitting or controlling students rather than educating them. Police may be punishing suspects by using excessive force rather than arresting them and leaving punishment to the courts and prisons. Housing inspectors may be making judgments that have the tendency to allow some areas of a city to deteriorate far more rapidly than others. Moreover, because the individual street-level administrator is so difficult to supervise—and is often the main source of information about his or her activities—the management of the organization may not even be aware of how discretion is being used or abused.

The traditional managerial approach, in turn, will try to develop performance measures that constrain the street-level administrator more to the formal guidelines and expectations of the organization. Where these measures are indicative of what it is the street-level administrator is supposed to be doing, this will be a helpful response. However, in many cases solid indicators cannot be developed. Sometimes quantitative indicators of qualitative performance can be counterproductive, as when teachers pass students on to the next grade although they have not shown satisfactory learning. (In other words, a teacher whose pupils fail to learn is likely to be judged a poor teacher. Consequently, he or she may exaggerate the students' achievements.)

Policies requiring or involving hearings of some sort to determine eligibility for a government program are also likely to be considered less effective from the traditional managerial perspective. Again, the problem is largely one of predictability. Hearings lead to idiosyncratic assessments by examiners or administrative law judges and to unplanned allocations of resources. Their outcomes may be unpredictable and inconsistent.

Policies may also be judged as undesirable from a managerial perspective because their goals are too amorphous. The traditional managerial emphasis on effectiveness favors policies with clear, identifiable goals so that formal organizational arrangements and guidelines can be formulated toward their achievement. In addition, the clearer the goal is, the more likely it is that meaningful performance measures with regard to its achievement can be developed. From a traditional managerial perspective it is difficult to have an effective implementation process unless there are clear objectives and performance measures.

The traditional managerial approach favors techniques for evaluating implementation that allow evaluation to remain under the control of an agency's hierarchy. Four common techniques of this kind are the following:

1. *Site visits* by teams of high-ranking administrators and other experts in the agency's employ can be used to assess operations at various installations. As Thomas Dye notes, "These teams can pick up impressionistic data about how programs are being run, whether programs are following specific guidelines, whether they have competent staffs, and sometimes whether or not 'clients' (target groups) are pleased with the services."[11]
2. *Process measures,* such as the number of claims processed, pupils matriculated, or arrests made, are often a useful gauge of activity on a year-to-year or month-to-month basis.
3. *Comparison with professional standards* is useful in some areas where such standards have been established independently by engineers,

educators, health professionals, or others. For example, civil service examinations may be evaluated for "construct validity" (see Chapter 5) through comparison to standards set by professional organizations of psychologists or personnel specialists.

4. *Benchmarking* identifies a level of actual past or current performance to which future performance may be compared. The benchmark may be based on the performance of the administrative unit under evaluation or that of some other comparable organization.

Cost-effectiveness combines concern with efficiency, economy, and effectiveness. For cost-effectiveness the central question is, given that a policy achieves a certain level of success, could another means achieve the same or a higher level at the same or less cost? For instance, if the policy is to have clean streets, will it be cost-effective to use mechanical street sweepers to replace human labor? Would adopting and enforcing antilitter laws be more cost-effective? Is outsourcing street cleaning to a private sector organization more cost-effective than public servants providing the service? The traditional managerial perspective is likely to favor the approach that achieves the most outcome per unit of cost (input).

Evaluating implementation from the perspective of cost-effectiveness can become complicated. The best approach to implementation may be considered the one that is most cost-effective, but cost-effectiveness can depend on the level of application of the policy. This is the matter of **marginal costs,** embodied in the simple-sounding question "How much will it cost to treat one more case?" Generally speaking, the marginal cost of treating the first case is high and then the cost decreases until we approach a point where treating each additional case theoretically becomes more expensive than treating the one immediately preceding it. In other words, implementation faces diminishing marginal returns. To place the principle in more concrete terms, suppose the public policy is to immunize all children in the United States between the ages of two and five against a variety of diseases. Suppose further that the policy is premised on the use of public administration to administer inoculations directly (perhaps to those children not provided with them by private doctors). To accomplish the public goal a public health service of some type would be set up. It would occupy physical space and employ medical practitioners as well as administrative staff to manage such functions as personnel, budgeting, and organizational design; it would also have clerical staff to assist management and aid in record keeping. In addition, staff for security and transportation might be necessary. These arrangements cost money: for salaries and supplies of the frontline service providers (the medical practitioners), for the physical plant, for administrative overhead. If such a system were put in place to treat only two or three cases, the cost per case would be very high. However, the cost per case would probably come down dramatically if thousands or perhaps millions of children were inoculated by the system. Here economies of scale would result from the ability of the same medical practitioners to inoculate more children for the same salary, from the ability of relatively fewer managers (per case treated) to oversee the operation, and from relatively fewer clerical and other staff. No matter how well the system was designed, however, at least two problems could lead to diminishing marginal returns. First, universal enforcement can lead to rising costs. Some children would be difficult to inoculate. Perhaps they live in remote areas, drift from place to place, or have parents opposed to inoculation. Tracking down such cases for inoculation is probably possible, but the costs of doing so would be much greater than the cost for the majority of children brought into a public health center by a parent for inoculation. In other words, achieving 100 percent compliance would probably be *disproportionately* more expensive than achieving only 80 percent compliance. Theoretically, depending on the precise circumstances, gaining compliance from the last 10 or 20 percent might cost as much as or more than treating the rest of the cases.

This is a common phenomenon in cost-effectiveness analysis and can be applied to a wide range of examples. How much will it cost to pick up the last ton of garbage scattered around in the form of litter in an urban area? How much will it cost to educate the slowest student to an eighth-grade reading level, compared with the average student? How much more will it cost to achieve 100 percent health insurance coverage as opposed to 85 or 90 percent?

Second, congestion can cause diminishing marginal returns. The number of cases to be treated can overwhelm an administrative system's capacity. If the number of children needing inoculation rapidly increased in a particular area due to migration, immigration, or a markedly greater birth or illness rate, the system might incur higher staffing, overtime, and perhaps contracting-out costs per child treated. Congestion is a common problem for public school systems in high population growth areas. Additional costs include more staff, supplies, and space, often including portable classrooms. Ideally, public agencies would be flexibly organized so that they could continually "right size" themselves. In practice, it is often very difficult for them to adjust rapidly to unpredicted fluctuations in workload.

The traditional managerial approach tends to evaluate policy implementation as not working well, in terms of cost-effectiveness, if its marginal costs or average marginal costs are rising. If they are decreasing, the managerial perspective may support the treatment of still more cases; if they are level, this perspective may look for additional ways to reduce them (by cutting administrative overhead, for example). However, if no means of saving are evident at the point where marginal costs begin to rise, the managerial perspective will tend to conclude that the policy is being applied to too many cases, that it is too comprehensive, and that another approach should be developed. For example, garbage collection can be augmented by antilitter laws and deposits on beverage containers.

Alternatively, the traditional managerial perspective may conclude that the policy is too comprehensive in its objectives and cannot be soundly implemented as a consequence. In a sense, the question is, "How much is enough?" And the managerial answer is often, "As much as will reduce marginal costs to their lowest plausible level." An exception is cases in which universal or highly comprehensive treatment is necessary to make the policy work, as might be true in eradicating diseases such as polio and smallpox, or the health insurance mandate portion of the Patient Protection and Affordable Care Act (Affordable Care Act or Obamacare).

The traditional managerial approach raises a number of questions from political and legal perspectives. The criterion of cost-effectiveness may need to be augmented by cost-benefit analysis. Whereas the cost-effectiveness approach assumes that the value of each unit or case treated is constant, cost-benefit analysis requires assessment of potential differences among these units or cases. It also assumes that greater or lesser application of a policy may have disproportionate benefits. For instance, the economic benefit of reducing crime or litter in a city's commercial or entertainment districts might be greater than that of doing the same thing in an outlying residential neighborhood. Additionally, those adopting a legalistic approach will augment concerns with cost-effectiveness with constitutional values. For example, is there disinvestment in minority neighborhoods? Or because land is less expensive in them, are they a preferred site for processing toxic waste?

In short, when one is applying a cost-effectiveness approach, the cases or units for treatment must be identical. This was the problem we observed in relation to budgeting in Chapter 6. The cost of averting a death by promoting the use of seat belts or motorcycle helmets is less than that of treating or curing cancer of the cervix. From a managerial perspective the "case" is the death averted, and aside from costs, it does not matter much how it is averted (by buckling up or treating cancer). From political and legal perspectives, however, it may matter a great deal *whose* death is being averted.

Cost-benefit analysis can often augment or substitute for cost-effectiveness studies. It enables us to compare the benefits of different policy and implementation approaches. Comprehensive cost-benefit analysis would also assess **opportunity costs.** That is, when one policy is adopted, what is the cost of the lost opportunity to pursue others? However, even basic cost-benefit analysis may founder when it becomes necessary to put a dollar figure on intangible values. Deborah Stone, a leading critic of cost-benefit analysis, notes, "When the consequences of an action are intangibles such as death, damaged political reputation, decline of a city, or destruction of a wilderness area, they must still be measured and valued in order to be used in cost-benefit analysis."[12] An even deeper problem is identifying and agreeing on what constitutes benefits worthy of consideration.

Stone reminds us that "reasoned analysis is necessarily political. It always involves choices to include some things and exclude others and to view the world in a particular way when other visions are possible."[13] For instance, it is common for politics and law to focus more on the *distribution* of burdens and benefits, and somewhat less on the cost of distributing them, than does the traditional managerial approach.

Economy is also central to the traditional managerial perspective, which will consider a policy to be executed well when its administrative costs and loss through mistakes, fraud, or waste are minimal. For the most part, this aspect of the traditional managerial approach to evaluating implementation is not controversial. It tends to focus on a process analysis, though it is also concerned with impact in the sense that a policy should not be constructed in such a way as to facilitate fraud by its beneficiaries. Sometimes, however, this perspective does raise interesting questions from political and legal standpoints.

Passing Costs on to Clients

One classic way of reducing administrative costs is to pass them on to the recipients of services. Often this is simple and may involve no more than making would-be recipients apply for a benefit rather than using the administrative apparatus to go out and find them. This pattern is followed in welfare and Social Security programs. Those believing that they are eligible for benefits must apply for them at an administrative office. Sometimes the passing on of costs is more subtle and can have serious consequences (see Box 8.3).

8.3   PASSING COSTS ON TO OTHERS

Walter Little, Appellant

v.

Gloria Streater

452 U.S. 1, 68 L Ed 2d 627, 101 S Ct 2202

[No.79-6799]

Argued January 13, 1981. Decided June 1, 1981.

SUMMARY

An unmarried woman gave birth to a child, and, as a requirement of the Connecticut Department of Social Services stemming from the child's receipt of public assistance, identified the putative father. The Department then provided an attorney for the mother, who commenced a paternity suit against the putative father in a Connecticut state court. The putative father moved the trial court to order blood grouping tests on the mother and the child pursuant to a Connecticut statute. The statute provided, in part, that the costs of such blood tests shall be chargeable against the party making the motion. Although the putative father asserted that he was indigent and asked that the state be ordered to pay for the tests, the trial court granted the motion only insofar as to order the blood tests, but denied the request that the state pay for the tests. Consequently, no blood grouping tests were performed because the putative father could not

afford their cost. After hearing testimony, the trial court found that the putative father was the child's father, and ordered him to pay child support. The Appellate Session of the Connecticut Superior Court affirmed the trial court's judgment in an unreported per curiam opinion. It held that the statute does not violate the due process and equal protection rights of an indigent putative father, and found no error in the trial court's denial of the putative father's motion that the cost of blood grouping tests be paid by the state. . . .

On appeal, the United States Supreme Court reversed and remanded. In an opinion by BURGER, CH. J., expressing the unanimous view of the court, it was held that the application of the statute to deny the putative father blood grouping tests because of his lack of resources, where the statute requires that the costs of such tests be chargeable against the party requesting them, violated the due process guarantee of the Fourteenth Amendment.

Making the potentially eligible apply for the benefit may deter some people. But even greater deterrence may be accomplished by forcing applicants to wait in line for long periods under unpleasant conditions. For instance, a site visit by one of the authors to a large urban welfare bureau revealed that applicants had to stand in a long line that snaked around a dingy, poorly ventilated, hot, and crowded corridor. Many applicants were holding babies or toddlers. It could take several hours to move from the end of the line to the proper administrative official. Seating was nonexistent, and closing time was scrupulously guarded, thereby forcing some who may have waited considerable time to return. Certainly, such conditions deter some individuals from applying for benefits even though they may be eligible to receive them. Precisely how many is impossible to say. A study in the 1970s concluded that about one-third of the population eligible for some administrative services fail to use them for one reason or another, including unpleasant administrative conditions.[14] In theory, perhaps, those deterred most are those whose eligibility is most questionable. In practice, however, this may not be the case.

Another means of passing on costs is to rule individuals ineligible for benefits, such as Social Security disability, pending decision of their appeals in administrative hearings.[15] If an individual subsequently wins, retroactive benefits may not necessarily be awarded. In any event, many individuals elect not to pursue the opportunity for a hearing, although they may be eligible.

Residency requirements are another potential way of passing costs on to would-be clients. For instance, until the Supreme Court ruled such an approach unconstitutional in violation of equal protection and the right to travel in *Shapiro v. Thompson* (1969),[16] several states had long residency requirements for welfare benefits. Connecticut, for example, had a one-year requirement, which it argued would accomplish a number of laudable administrative objectives. It would facilitate planning the welfare budget; it would reduce the number of individuals fraudulently receiving payments from two or more states; it would encourage individuals to seek work (rather than welfare) upon arrival in the state; and it would ensure that recipients of the benefits were bona fide residents of the state. Although the residency requirement may have made sense from a traditional managerial perspective, the Supreme Court considered the cost passed on to the individual to be a sacrifice of an essential right and liberty. More recently, the Supreme Court invalidated a similar effort by California to avoid becoming a welfare magnet by limiting benefits to indigent newcomers to the amounts they would have received in the states from which they migrated.[17]

Passing Costs on to Employees

Employees can also be made to bear some of the costs of implementing an administrative program. For example, employees may have to supply uniforms, transportation for official purposes, or continued training through refresher courses and the like as a condition for continued employment. More controversially, employees may bear the costs of occupational disease and exposure to harmful substances in the workplace. In recent years, for example, public employee unions have been protesting against the continued presence of asbestos in public buildings.

Controlling Misuse

The reduction of costs may be controversial when it involves an effort by public administrators to assure that clients do not misuse funds allocated to them. For instance, efforts to assure that welfare funds to families with dependent children are used for the children's benefit can raise difficult issues. Can a caseworker insist on entering a dwelling on pain of cutting off the funds?[18] Is advance notice necessary? Are unannounced "midnight raids" allowed?[19]

The New Public Management

The NPM favors implementation by "steering" rather than "rowing."[20] It favors discretion over rules and measures success in terms of customer satisfaction and performance.

Alternative Service Delivery

A major premise of the NPM is that, wherever reasonable, government should arrange for the provision of public services rather than deliver them directly. In short, it should concentrate on steering, not rowing. This approach, derived from business practices, enables government to focus on its core responsibilities and, presumably, to reduce its costs. For example, the primary function of a university, state or private, is to educate. But it also has a payroll and provides a broad range of services, such as food service. In many cases, these services can be delivered more cost-effectively by firms specializing in them and providing them on a regional, national, or international basis. When a university relies on Marriott, Aramark, or a similar firm for food service, it also drastically reduces the amount of time the central administration has to devote to making sure the students can eat on campus. Presumably, then, the administration can devote more time to educational matters.

The rowing, sometimes called "third-party government," can be arranged in several ways, as explained by E. S. Savas in *Privatization: The Key to Better Government:*[21]

1. Governments often contract with private parties (both nonprofit and for-profit) or other governments. Contracts are used for a wide range of activities: public works, transportation, safety, health and human services, prisons, recreation, and support functions. Trash collection, street repair and cleaning, building inspection, fire and police communication, landscaping, building and vehicle maintenance, and payroll are among the functions most commonly contracted out by local governments.
2. Franchising is also common. It provides private firms with a monopoly right to provide services for the government. Taxi and bus

transportation are common examples, as are telephone and cable TV services as well as concessions at public parks and zoos. Franchises can be awarded to more than one company, but they limit competition by nonfranchisees. Consequently, they are valuable and may be a significant source of revenue when governments sell them.

3. Grants are used by governments to subsidize third parties that produce desired services. Examples include health services, museums, and performing arts. If tax expenditures (see Chapter 6) are included, a wide range of private production is subsidized by grants.

4. Vouchers are used to subsidize consumers rather than producers. Food stamps are probably the leading example, but vouchers are also used for medical services, education, and low-income housing.

5. Voluntary services often augment the governmental provision of public goods. Recreation, ambulance service, fire protection, and neighborhood patrols are examples. Government may cooperate with the private groups providing the services by including them in planning and other relevant activities.

6. Self-service relies on private individuals to produce desired conditions, such as low fire and crime rates. Savas claims, "The family as a self-service unit is the original and most efficient department of housing, health, education, welfare, and human services, and it provides a wide range of vital services to its members."[22] The term "coproduction" is often used to denote cases in which self-service is combined with governmental action. One example is alerting firefighters to where children may be sleeping by putting "tot finder" stickers in appropriate windows.

7. Markets are often juxtaposed to government in the production of goods and services. However, government can regulate markets to foster desired social and economic conditions. For example, equal employment opportunity law seeks to promote economic and social equality while reducing the acceptability and incidence of discrimination. Laws dealing with child labor, minimum wages and hours, and labor relations are also broadly aimed at protecting widely shared social values.

Savas points out that these arrangements can be used in multiple, hybrid, and partial forms. For instance, a city may rely on several approaches for providing ambulance service; tax exemptions for nonprofit organizations help subsidize their voluntary activities; and services can be partitioned, as in the case of public education where an array of voluntary PTA/PTO activity augments instruction.

Discretion

The NPM also favors less rule-bound and more discretionary public administration. It welcomes the deregulation of public employees as empowerment to find commonsense responses to situations not fully anticipated even by voluminous sets of rules. It often prefers negotiation to rule-bound regulation. Negotiation can be used to obtain acceptable outcomes and avert lawsuits. In one example, the Army Corps of Engineers used the partnership approach "to accelerate hazardous and toxic waste cleanup projects, resolve conflicts over the operation of multi-purpose dams, handle wetland permits, acquire real estate, even handle internal labor disputes."[23] It reduced its legal caseload by 70 percent and saved millions of dollars in the process.

The NPM differs dramatically from the traditional managerial perspective by not being concerned with uniformity and not fearing that employees will abuse their discretion. By definition, the outcomes of negotiations will depend on the bargaining positions and skills of the parties involved. Some public employees will be better at using discretion than others, and accordingly, some outcomes will be more in the public interest than others. The NPM's claim is that overall, or on balance, discretionary government will work better and cost less despite some inevitable mistakes. Similarly, the NPM reflects the belief that in results-oriented public administration, discretion will not breed corruption.

Monitoring and Measuring Performance

It is axiomatic that if government relies on third parties and empowered employees to achieve public purposes, it will have to monitor their performance. A variety of contract monitoring approaches have been used.[24] The first step is to develop a strategy for monitoring before the contract is written, negotiated, and signed. Where feasible, specific observable and measurable performance requirements should be included in the contract. For instance, a contract may specify the maximum amount of time a third party has to fill potholes after being notified of them. It may require the contractor to periodically submit its work records to an agency for inspection. Additionally, bonuses may be paid for completing work early or penalties assessed for missing deadlines. Citizen and customer surveys are also useful in some cases, though to develop and implement meaningful ones may be expensive. There is also some risk that if such surveys become as ubiquitous in public administration as in the use of service rating cards in fast-food restaurants, customers will lose interest in them. Scheduled and surprise inspections can be useful. It is best for government to provide for these inspections in the contract to reduce potential legal problems under the Constitution's prohibition of unreasonable searches and seizures (see Chapter 11). Agency complaint and whistle-blower "hot lines" are also useful means of obtaining information on a third party's performance.

Performance measuring is relevant to third parties and empowered public employees. The most general measure of performance is customer service. The Clinton administration required federal agencies to set customer service standards and to measure results against them. Agencies were also instructed to benchmark their standards against business practices, use customer surveys, and set up systems for dealing with customer complaints. Box 8.4 presents several examples of federal customer service standards.

8.4   SAMPLE CUSTOMER SERVICE STANDARDS

OPM'S FEDERAL EMPLOYMENT INFORMATION SYSTEM

OPM has established the following service standards for job seekers using the Federal Employment Information System:

- We will provide you with courteous and timely service.
- We will update our nationwide job listings every business day.
- We will have Employment Information Specialists available to answer your questions.
- We will provide 24 hours a day, seven days a week access to nationwide job information and application request services through a variety of electronic media.
- We will respond to your requests for applications and/or routine information within one business day.
- We will use your suggestions and complaints to improve our service continually. We will always remember we work for you, the American public.

DEPARTMENT OF STATE

The Department of State issues passports for U.S. citizens and provides information and guidance to U.S. travelers. The State Department offers these services for international travelers:

- You will receive timely and accurate information on travel safety and conditions in foreign countries 24 hours a day, seven days a week.
- You will receive your passport within 25 days after receipt of your application. Service will be provided in a courteous manner and, whenever possible, we will try to meet your travel needs.
- You will receive timely and courteous responses to requests for American citizen services, and services will be provided by knowledgeable and professional personnel.
- Service to persons seeking visas to legally visit or reside in the United States will be provided by knowledgeable, professional, and courteous personnel.

OCCUPATIONAL SAFETY AND HEALTH ADMINISTRATION

OSHA is making these commitments to business:

- Focus OSHA inspections on the most serious hazards.
- Be respectful and professional during inspections.
- Help them identify and control workplace hazards.

U.S. POSTAL SERVICE

- Your First Class Mail will be delivered anywhere in the United States within three days.
- Your local First Class Mail will be delivered overnight.
- You will receive service at post office counters within five minutes.
- You can get postal information 24 hours a day by calling a local number.

Source: Al Gore, Putting Customers First: Standards for Serving the American People (Washington, DC: Government Printing Office, 1994), 18, 25, 52, 54, 83.

The NPM is somewhat divided over whether other performance measures should focus on outputs, outcomes, or both. Assessing outputs provides no measure of a program's effectiveness in achieving its goals. But concentrating on outcomes or impacts, typically the product of multiple actors and programs, fails to assess the contribution of each administrative unit to the government's overall performance. The NPR was explicit in favoring a results-oriented approach that measures outcomes, not internal processes. Holding empowered employees accountable demands nothing less. New Zealand and Great Britain favor output measurement, whereas Canada and Australia look at outcomes as well as outputs. The Government Performance and Results Act of 1993 and the Government Performance and Results Act Modernization Act of 2010 also elected the dual approach.[25]

The U.S. Office of Management and Budget defines an outcome as "an assessment of the results of a program compared to its intended purpose."[26] An output measure is "a tabulation, calculation, or recording of activity or effort that can be expressed in a quantitative or qualitative measure."[27] Several examples for different kinds of administrative concerns are presented in Box 8.5.

Performance measurement is eminently logical. But it is not new and has had limited success in the past. Measuring outputs alone can drive agencies to concentrate on processes without knowing their relationships to outcomes. But, agreeing on what program outcomes should be is sometimes politically difficult. The legislative coalitions that enact and support programs often depend on vagueness; they are jeopardized by specific, prioritized goals. Consequently, defining goals is easier in some governments, agencies, and programs than in others. The Oregon Benchmarks program offered an example that works at the state level; however, given the budget crisis Oregon faced beginning in 2008, the program was defunded beginning in 2009.[28]

If performance measures are going to be useful to public administrators, there must also be standards with which to judge how well government is performing. As David Ammons suggests, making relevant comparisons with similar governmental units is one means to achieve this end.[29] This process, called *benchmarking*, identifies a point of reference for comparison. With the right mind-set (realizing you are probably not the best at everything you do) and selection of appropriate benchmarking partners (a place that is getting good results), Ammons argues that public officials should focus on adapting how they do business to improve performance. If benchmarking is going to be useful, public administrators need to be realistic about the changes they can make and should focus on improving performance and not necessarily on being the best performer.

In order to improve the federal government's ability to judge program effectiveness and hold public agencies accountable for outcomes in a systematic and transparent manner, the George W. Bush administration introduced the Program Assessment Rating Tool (PART) in 2002. The goal of this program was to use high quality evidence to direct budget allocations to effective programs. Carolyn Heinrich's evaluation of the program finds that while some programs were able to generate rigorous and useful data, there was

8.5   OMB EXAMPLES OF VARIOUS TYPES OF PERFORMANCE MEASURES

Workload
(not otherwise categorized):

Output	Annually *inspect* 3,200 grain elevators.
Outcome	Through *periodic* grain elevator *inspection,* reduce the incidence of grain dust explosions resulting in catastrophic loss or fatalities to zero.

Production:

Output	*Manufacture and deliver* 35,000 rounds of armor-piercing 120-mm projectile shells in FY 1997.
Outcome	*Produce sufficient* 120-mm armor-piercing *projectiles* to achieve a 60-day combat-use supply level by 1999 for all Army and Marine Corps tank battalions.

Transactions:

Output	*Process* 3.75 million payment *vouchers* in FY 1995.
Outcome	*Ensure* that 99.25 percent of *payment vouchers are paid* within 30 days of receipt.

Records:

Output	*Update* earnings *records* for 45 million employee contributors to the Social Security Trust Fund.
Outcome	*Ensure* that all earnings *records are posted and current* within 60 days of the end of the previous quarter.

Utilization rates:

Output	*Operate* all tactical fighter aircraft simulator training *facilities at not less than 85 percent of rated capacity.*
Outcome	*Ensure* that all active duty tactical fighter aircraft *pilots* are fully qualified having *received a minimum of 32 hours of simulator training* and flown 400 hours in the previous 12 months.

Frequency rates:

Output	Issue 90-day national temperature and precipitation forecasts *every six weeks.*
Outcome	Provide users of meteorological forecasts with *advance information sufficiently updated to be useful* for agricultural, utility, and transportation planning.

Timeliness:
  Response times:

Output	Adjudicative *decision* on all claim disallowances will *be made within 120 days* of appeal hearings.
Outcome	*Provide* every claimant with *timely* dispositive *determination* on claims filed.

Adherence to schedule:

Output	*Operate* 95 percent of all passenger trains *within 10 minutes of scheduled arrival times.*
Outcome	*Provide* rail *passengers* with reliable and *predictable* train *service.*

Continued

8.5   OMB Examples of Various Types of Performance Measures   *Continued*

Out-of-service conditions:

Output   All Corps of Engineers *locks* on river basin *x* shall be *operational during at least 22 of every consecutive 24 hours.*

Outcome   *Ensure no significant delays* in traffic transiting through river basin *x.*

Defect rates:

Output   *Not more than 1.25 percent* of 120-mm armor-piercing projectiles shall be *rejected as defective.*

Outcome   *No armor-piercing ammunition projectiles* fired in combat *shall fail to explode* on impact.

Mean failure rates:

Output   *Premature* space shuttle main engine *shutdown shall not occur more than once in every 200 flight cycles.*

Outcome   Space shuttle shall be maintained and operated so that *99.95 percent of all flights safely reach orbit.*

Accuracy:

Output   The *position* of 300,000 navigation buoys shall be *checked monthly.*

Outcome   All navigational buoys shall be *maintained within 5 meters of the charted position.*

Inventory fill:

Output   *Store* a minimum of 3.5 million barrels of *petroleum* stock.

Outcome   Petroleum *stocks* shall be maintained at a level sufficient to *provide a 60-day supply* at normal daily drawdown.

Complaints:

Output   Not more than *2.5 percent* of individuals seeking information *will subsequently re-request the same information because the initial response was unsatisfactory.*

Outcome   *99 percent* of all requests for information *will be satisfactorily handled with the initial response.*

Customer satisfaction levels (Output and outcome measures may often be indistinguishable):

Output   *In 1998,* at least *75 percent* of individuals receiving a service *will rate the service delivery as good to excellent.*

Outcome   At least *90 percent* of recipients will *rate the service delivery* as good to excellent.

Efficiency:

Output   Annual transaction costs/production costs/delivery of service costs projected on a per unit basis. *Produce 35,000 rounds of armor-piercing ammunition at a cost of $17.75 per round.*

Outcome   (Not commonly measured as an outcome.)

Milestone and activity schedules:

Output | *Complete 85 percent of required flight-worthiness testing* for Z-2000 bomber *by July 30, 1999.*

Outcome | The Z-2000 *bomber* will be flight-certified and *operational by December 1, 2000.*

Design specifications:

Output | Imaging *cameras* on Generation X observational satellite will have *resolution of 0.1 arc second.*

Outcome | Generation X observational satellite will *successfully map 100 percent terrain of six Jovian moons to a resolution of 100 meters.*

Status of conditions:

Output | In 1995, *repair and maintain 1,400 pavement miles* of Federally-owned highways to a *rating of "good."*

Outcome | By 2000, *35 percent of all Federally-owned highway pavement miles* shall be *rated* as being in *good condition.*

Percentage coverage:

Output | Provide *doses of vaccine to 27,000 preschool children* living on tribal reservations.

Outcome | *100 percent* of children living on tribal reservations will be *fully immunized* before beginning school.

Effectiveness:

Output | *Not more than 7,000 in-patients* in military hospitals will be readmitted, postdischarge, for further treatment of the same diagnosed illness at the time of initial admission.

Outcome | *Initial treatment* will be therapeutically *successful for 85 percent* of all hospital admissions.

Notes: For the purpose of these examples: Some of the outcome measures are much more narrowly defined than would otherwise be appropriate or expected. Some of the outcome measures are not inherently measurable, and would require use of supplementary performance indicators to set specific performance targets and determine whether these were achieved. Some measures include several aspects of performance; italics are used to feature the particular characteristic of that example. Many of the examples of output measures are process or attribute measures.

Source: U.S. Office of Management and Budget, "Primer on Performance Measurement," 23 September 1994, 4-7 to 4-9.

no relationship between PART performance ratings and changes in funding allocations.[30] This finding hints at the likelihood that the Obama administration's efforts to use evidence-based practices to improve government performance may meet similar problems, which can be best understood through the political perspective on implementation.

❖❖ THE POLITICAL PERSPECTIVE ON IMPLEMENTATION

As we have been suggesting, a political perspective on whether a policy is being successfully implemented may differ from a managerial perspective. Again, assuming that the policy has been determined to have some impact, evaluating its execution will depend on how well it fits the values inherent in the political approach. For even if a policy achieves its objectives, the means it uses and the values it embodies may be evaluated as either satisfactory or unsatisfactory.

Representation

The political approach tends to view a policy as appropriately executed, within the parameters of the policy having a discernible impact on the target, if it affords representation to those individuals and interests most affected by it. Representation is often valued in two contexts: participation in decisions and representation of demographic constituencies.

Participation in Decisions about Implementation

Several administrative programs in the United States have emphasized the idea that those most directly affected by a program be granted a voice in deciding how it will be implemented. The Federal Advisory Committee Act of 1972, as noted in Chapter 1, seeks to assure representation of interests through the participation of advisory committees in administrative decision making. During the 1960s, the poverty program sought to make use of local participation through the election of some members of community action agencies. The Model Cities Program of the same decade sought the representation of local communities in urban renewal and revitalization decisions. The poverty program went somewhat beyond other approaches by encouraging the participation of representatives of the local population directly in the implementation of policy.[31] More recently, researchers have begun examining the use of deliberative democracy[32] and dialogue[33] as means of involving citizens in the development and implementation of public policy. From the perspective of the political approach, a domestic policy that does not allow the participation of those most affected by it may be considered undesirable.

Representation of Demographic Constituency Interests

The political perspective is also concerned that public administrative implementation be deemed to substantively serve the interest of demographic groups in legislative constituencies. For instance, an immunization program that fails to include rural children may be judged inadequate from a political perspective. This is true even though a cost-effectiveness approach might show that it is dysfunctional in terms of administrative efficiency to try to reach large proportions of that group. Similarly, locating undesirable infrastructure, such as incinerators, in minority neighborhoods is likely to be challenged from a political perspective. Passing on costs to an identifiable constituency may also be opposed. There are many regulatory and service activities of public administrators that may potentially affect demographic groups differentially. It has even been argued by some legislators that raising the federal tax on cigarettes to pay for the expansion of health insurance under the Affordable Care Act is unfair to low income smokers.

Responsiveness

The political perspective's value of responsiveness is related to considerations of representation. However, it sometimes goes beyond the representation of relatively specific interests to a sense of being in step with what the community seems to want. For instance, in the early 1980s, a grassroots movement against drunken driving developed in several states. Mothers' and students' groups against drunken driving sprang up. Some laws were rewritten in response to the public's pressure. Police began enforcing driving under the influence (DUI) laws more stringently and vigorously. In some states, New York for one, police roadblocks, at which all drivers are stopped as potentially DUI, became common. This redeployment of police is an inconvenience to the sober public and criticized as a waste of fuel by others. However, DUI initiatives are probably responsive to the concerns of the majority of citizens who care about the matter.

Sometimes the issue of responsiveness acts as a check on administrative logic that, although internally sound, is not in touch with reality. In other words, it can be invoked to counteract the "tunnel vision" that sometimes develops as a result of administrative specialization.

An example occurred in 2002, when the Department of Justice (DoJ) was forced to retract its Terrorism Information and Prevention System ("TIPS") in the face of a public outcry from right to left. Charged with combatting terrorism, the DoJ saw nothing wrong with calling on workers who have opportunities to look inside clients' homes and offices to report anything suspicious to it. The thought of delivery drivers, appliance repair technicians, postal carriers, and similar workers acting as "government-sanctioned Peeping Toms," in Texas Republican Richard Armey's words, was too much for Congress.[34] It passed legislation specifically prohibiting implementation of the program. TIPS was also denounced by an American Civil Liberties Union official as epitomizing "the government's insatiable appetite for surveillance of law-abiding citizens."[35] The minting of the Susan B. Anthony dollar coin in the 1970s was another example. Administrators in Washington, DC, were convinced that the coin would be useful. Apparently, serious consideration was given to its size, shape, and design. But as far as the public was concerned, there was no need for the Anthony dollar, and people would not use it. The "Golden (Sacagawea) Dollar" did not do much better. The use of focus groups can help avoid blunders, but sometimes the conclusions drawn from them are misleading.

Decentralization of administrative operations is another aspect of responsiveness that can lead the political and traditional managerial perspectives to diverge on what constitutes proper implementation. It may often be more expensive for administrative agencies to maintain a large number of field offices or satellite facilities. Individuals wanting something from the administrative agency or compelled to interact with it may be required to travel to its headquarters or less conveniently located field offices. At one time in the state of Vermont, for example, to register a new car brought in from outside the state, one had to travel to the capital, Montpelier, which might be a substantial distance away. There were no local offices in towns to deal with this administrative operation. From a political perspective, such an arrangement is not responsive to the needs of individuals who live in areas remote from the administrative offices. If these remote areas coincide with legislative districts, there is every likelihood that pressure will be placed on elected representatives to require the administrative agencies to maintain more convenient field offices in order to be more *responsive* to the needs of the legislators' constituencies. This is one reason why states with large geographic areas and low population densities tend to have more public administrators per capita than do other states.[36]

Accountability

Accountability is a final value that should be considered in addressing the political perspective's evaluation of the implementation of public policy. That perspective demands that public administration be held accountable to elected officials, particularly legislators. Accountability is addressed in greater detail in Chapter 12. Here, however, it is desirable to indicate how the execution of some policies can pose a challenge to it.

Sunshine

In 1933, Supreme Court Justice Louis Brandeis claimed that sunlight is the best of disinfectants.[37] Since the mid-1960s, federal policy and that of several states has emphasized the desirability of promoting "freedom of information" about the operation of administrative agencies. Some laws require that certain types of meetings and hearings within agencies be open to the public and the press. Although these **sunshine laws** hardly provide any citizen with a right to every bit of administrative information, they do serve to *open* the administrative process to public and legislative scrutiny to a substantial extent. From this perspective, an administrative program that operates in secret may be judged not to be working well, even though it achieves its objectives at a reasonable level and cost. Covert CIA operations have been opposed on this basis. Supreme Court Justice William O. Douglas once said that if the public was not told how the CIA spent its money, "a secret bureaucracy is allowed to run our affairs."[38] In 2013, a leak regarding the National Security Agency's monitoring of Americans' phone calls and emails created a political controversy even as the agency claimed its activity thwarted numerous terrorist plots.

Sunset

Sunset provisions, as noted earlier, are another manifestation of the desire to hold public administrators accountable and to prevent agencies or programs that are not providing politically valued outcomes from continuing. From the managerial perspective, all the periodic reporting and justifying involved when agencies operate under a sunset provision (and desire to be continued) can be serious diversions from or barriers to customer satisfaction, monitoring third parties, and/or efficient, economical, and effective operations. Yet from the political perspective, administrative programs that do not labor under such conditions may not be considered policies that work well. For the policy to work well, a review by the legislature at some fixed time is sometimes deemed essential.

General Legislative Oversight

Legislatures in the United States use a committee and subcommittee system partly to exercise "oversight" of administrative operations. They may also create administrative agencies of their own such as the federal General Accountability Office and offices such as Inspector General to aid in oversight. In general, a policy that eludes effective oversight, perhaps because it overlaps too many committee jurisdictions, may be judged a policy whose implementation is inherently risky. Even if its objectives are achieved, a policy resistant to oversight may be evaluated as a poor means of using public power to intervene in the economy or society because such a policy would be largely beyond the control of elective officials. This was one of the major concerns with the original Office of Homeland Security (OHS). As an advisory unit in the White House Office, it was subject to far less legislative oversight than are executive branch agencies. Congress objected and successfully pressured President George W. Bush to support reorganizing homeland security functions in a regular executive department, subject to normal oversight.

Casework

Legislative casework, discussed in Chapter 2, can be a means of promoting the accountability of public administrators to elective officials. Consequently, from a political perspective, a means of policy execution that prohibits the administrators from responding to casework inquiries could be judged undesirable. Sometimes resistance to legislative involvement in administrative routines is understandable because it is desirable to insulate public administration from political pressures. For instance, the IRS may not want to divulge what triggers a tax audit. Other times, though, casework, like process analysis, suggests how implementation can be improved.

◆ THE LEGAL PERSPECTIVE ON IMPLEMENTATION

The legal approach to public administration also asks a distinctive set of questions in evaluating the implementation of public policies. Its focus tends to be on constitutional integrity, equal protection, fairness (procedural due process), and protection of the rights of those individuals who come into contact with public administrative operations. Consequently, because the questions asked by the legal perspective differ from those asked by either of the other perspectives, the answers it reaches may also be different. Here it is impossible to consider in detail all the fine points that the legal perspective would take in evaluating policy, but some of the more central aspects can be briefly reviewed. Chapter 11 devotes more space to public administration and democratic constitutionalism.

Constitutional Integrity

Sometimes public policies are in conflict with constitutional provisions for the separation of powers or federalism. For instance, during the 1980s the Supreme Court found that the federal government's policy for deporting illegal aliens incorporated an unconstitutional "one-house legislative veto." In the complicated case of *Immigration and Naturalization Service v. Chadha* (1983),[39] the Court held that allowing the House of Representatives to overrule (that is, to exercise a legislative veto over) the attorney general's decision to suspend an order to deport an individual violated two aspects of constitutional integrity. First, it infringed on the "presentment clauses," which require Congress to present legislative actions such as bills and resolutions to the president for approval or veto. Because "legislative vetoes" are not presented to the president, and therefore cannot be blocked by a presidential veto, they violate the integrity of constitutional process. Second, the one-house veto defeats the Constitution's provision for a bicameral (two-house) Congress. In the Court's view, bicameralism could not be dismissed as a mere formality or redundancy because the Senate provides representation by state, whereas the House does so by population within the states, and each chamber can serve as a check on the other.

The Court was cognizant that the legislative veto is a convenient shortcut, but it emphasized its commitment to constitutional integrity: "There is no support in the Constitution or decisions of this Court for the proposition that the cumbersomeness and delays often encountered in complying with explicit constitutional standards may be avoided, either by the Congress or by the President."

The *Chadha* decision was not an aberration. Constitutional procedure and the separation of powers have been invoked in other cases involving contemporary policies, including the line-item veto.[40] So have a variety of federalism issues. In *Seminole Tribe of Florida v. Florida* (1996),[41] the Supreme Court held that Congress cannot use its powers under the commerce clause to undermine the states' Eleventh Amendment protection against being sued in federal court by their citizens for alleged violations of federal laws.* Nor can Congress use the enforcement clause of the Fourteenth Amendment to authorize state

---

*Citizens may continue to sue a state in which they reside in federal court for violations of some provisions of federal civil rights laws and the U.S. Constitution.

employees to sue their state employers in federal court for violations of federal age and disability discrimination legislation.[42]

In *U.S. Term Limits v. Thornton* (1995),[43] the Court narrowly held that the states could not constitutionally impose term limits on their members of Congress. In part, the prevailing argument rested on the belief that allowing term limits would enable the states to change the characteristics of the national government's legislature, thereby substantially altering the federal government's relationship to the people.

Equal Protection

As we have seen, distributional issues often arise in the administrative implementation of public policy. Who shall receive a benefit and where? Who shall be subject to a regulation, and will there be discernible patterns of enforcement? The traditional managerial approach to public administration tends to address such issues from a cost-effectiveness or economizing approach. The NPM centers on customers. The political perspective is concerned with the representation of identifiable groups or constituencies and responsiveness to these groups. The legal approach adds yet another dimension.

It focuses more on whether individuals or groups are afforded equal protection of laws. In other words, does the policy place members of some social groups at a disadvantage? If so, is the policy rationally formulated and implemented to achieve a legitimate, important, or compelling governmental purpose? Does the policy intentionally discriminate against groups that have historically been subject to discrimination and disadvantage in the United States?[44] Answers to questions such as these will determine whether the legal perspective will view a policy and/or its execution as appropriate or inappropriate.

In practice, two types of problematic cases arise. One is where public policy allocates resources differentially to different racial or ethnic groups or to men and women. Here the issue is likely to be whether such a policy, even if otherwise rationally related to a legitimate governmental purpose, has an unconstitutional or illegal discriminatory intention. For instance, in one case, the town of Shaw, Mississippi, managed to pave streets and put in sewers, streetlights, and other infrastructure improvements in the white section of town but not in the black neighborhood.[45] Its actions were found to be unconstitutional by the federal courts even though the racism involved was implicit rather than explicit. In another case, the school system in San Antonio, Texas, allocated far greater funds per student to a school attended primarily by "Anglos" as opposed to one with a large number of Hispanic students. The city argued that the classification, or basis for distribution of funds, was based on wealth, not ethnicity, and that it rationally served a legitimate purpose. The U.S. Supreme Court agreed.[46] (Equal protection analysis is discussed in Chapter 11.)

A second type of problem is the use of social characteristics, such as race, as proxies for some other attribute. Racial or ethnic profiling is a clear threat to equal protection. "Driving while black" cannot be a legitimate cause for being pulled over by a police officer.[47] Gender profiling presents a similar problem. To be constitutional, laws or administrative practices that treat males and females differently must be substantially related to the achievement of important governmental objectives, and the burden is typically on the government to provide an exceedingly persuasive justification for them.[48]

Procedural Due Process and Protection of Individual Rights

The legal perspective toward public administration also favors providing those dependent on administrative services or subject to administrative regulation with procedural protections against an adverse action. Thus, whereas the traditional managerial perspective might support immediately cutting off a benefit to a client suspected of fraud and the NPM favors great discretion in dealing with customers, the legal perspective might favor continuing the benefit until the individual is given the opportunity to answer the allegations that he or she had engaged in fraudulent behavior.[49]

The legal approach also takes an expansive position on the importance of individual rights and liberties. Consequently, it may view administrative implementation as not working well if it tends to infringe on these rights. An example already mentioned is the imposition of residency requirements for eligibility for welfare benefits. Other intriguing instances have been such requirements as being available for work on Saturday, despite one's religious beliefs to the contrary, for unemployment insurance;[50] exclusion from extracurricular high-school activities for being married;[51] and a variety of conditions in prisons and public mental health facilities.

Estoppel

The legal approach aligns with the traditional managerial approach and stands in stark contrast to the NPM in the increasingly important area of estoppel. In legal jargon, "to estop" means to prevent. The law of estoppel determines when agencies are bound by the advice or information that their personnel give to customers. For instance, a Social Security claims agent or an IRS employee, whose job is to advise customers, may provide incorrect information. Should the agencies be held responsible for their employees' errors? Put differently, should an applicant eligible for benefits be deprived of them because a claims agent inappropriately dissuaded her or him from filing a written claim? Should a taxpayer have to pay a penalty fee for relying on incorrect advice from the tax agency? The traditional managerial perspective does not favor allowing lower-level employees to bind an agency because it would violate the principle of hierarchy. It could also create disarray in administrative systems for determining eligibility for benefits or tax breaks. In addition, some regulations, including Social Security rules and the tax code, are so complicated that errors are inevitable—especially by lower-level customer service personnel who do not have advanced legal training. In the aggregate, such errors could prove costly to an agency. By contrast, the NPM's emphasis on customer service and employee empowerment logically requires that no customer be left worse off because of an agency representative's mistake. The political approach has no fixed view on such matters, but would handle them through legislative "casework."

As the law stands, customers are at a serious disadvantage when relying on incorrect official advice or information. They have to show not only that they were made worse off by the agency's poor guidance but also that there was no other way they could have obtained the correct information. The latter requirement effectively holds every applicant or taxpayer responsible for knowing the laws and published regulations that govern his or her interactions with public agencies. This is true even where the rules are arcane and inaccessible to almost anyone without technical training. Agencies are able to release benefits and waive penalties even when they are not estopped (prevented) from withholding or applying them. Presumably, an agency administered according to NPM principles would place service to the customer above other values and would rarely penalize someone for following its instructions.

◆◆   USING ANALYSIS AND EVALUATION

Policy analysis and implementation evaluation are intended to be useful to political officials and public administrators. At the least, they should contribute to knowledge about the design and effects of public policies. Ideally, retrospective analysis and evaluation would also lead to direct improvements in policy implementation in the short run. But there are barriers to the effective use of such research. First, as Aaron Wildavsky observed, administrative organizations may not be set up to digest evaluation. He wrote:

> Evaluation and organization may be contradictory terms. Organizational structure implies stability while the process of evaluation suggests change. Organization generates commitment while evaluation inculcates skepticism. Evaluation speaks to the relationship between action and objectives while organization relates its activities to programs and clientele.[52]

Second, even if administrative organizations were amenable to analysis and evaluation research, they would still face problems in interpreting such studies. Many evaluations are inconclusive. Some studies are unable to ascertain any significant impact of public policy. Others show limited effects. The failure to discern impacts may lie in any of the following or some combination thereof: (1) the policy, (2) implementation, (3) the evaluation design and methodology, or (4) errors in carrying out the research.

When analysis and evaluation fail to find a policy impact, supporters of the program may argue that *more* funding and authority are needed to make the policy work. Opponents, by contrast, may assert that the policy is misconceived or that implementation is unworkable. Both can speculate about the likelihood of the policy working better in the long run. In essence, the political debates concerning public policies are frequently left largely unresolved by evaluation studies.[53]

Arnold Meltzner has identified "The Seven Deadly Sins of Policy Analysis," all of which detract from use.[54] He suggests that there is enough experience with policy analysis to identify the "sins," but not necessarily enough to avoid them. The sins are (1) "being in a rut," or unable to recognize that circumstances have changed significantly in ways that make former analytical perspectives inappropriate; (2) being too distant, either geographically or conceptually, to have a firm grip on the reality of how a policy is operating; (3) lacking timeliness; (4) offering superficial analysis that misses the roots of problems; (5) providing topical advice, or policy analysis that stems from a crisis and is reactive, that tends to crowd out other policy analysis on less visible or pressing concerns; (6) offering capricious advice, or advice that advocates change for its own sake; and (7) giving apolitical advice that ignores political constraints or opportunities.

On a more basic level, policy analysis does not take place in a vacuum. Politicians and other policy makers deal with multiple streams of information feeding into their decision making process. Many competing interests and values are at stake. Even using the latest economics-based tools to carry out evaluation, as Giandomenico Majone argues, is ultimately value laden.[55] The recommendation of the policy analyst is only one piece of information in this decision making stream. If this recommendation does not conform to a policy maker's ideological beliefs, the information may be discounted or discarded.

In the past, the use of policy analysis and evaluation was often limited by the difficulty analysts had in speaking to politicians and policy makers. Analysts using economics-based paradigms found "It was not possible to find a common denominator for very diverse values and players."[56] Beryl Radin sees a brighter future. Not only has the quality of analysis and evaluation improved in terms of scope and technique, but "it is now a profession with multiple voices that reflect the diversity of American society."[57] It is "speaking multiple truths to multiple powers."[58] And the proponents of results-oriented public administration, as well as executives and legislators eager to improve governmental performance, are ready to listen and participate in the conversations generated by contemporary policy analysis and evaluation. It is precisely because the conversation is now broader that performance evaluation and policy analysis may succeed even though earlier efforts along the same lines were disappointing.

Conclusion: The Complexity of Policy Design

The diverse managerial, political, and legal perspectives on implementation can make policy design a complex endeavor. There is little agreement concerning the basic criteria on which implementation should be judged. Cost-effectiveness, customer satisfaction, political accountability, procedural due process, and other relevant values often conflict with one another—in the abstract and in day-to-day administrative practice. The traditional managerial, political, and legal approaches all favor strictly limiting administrative discretion, especially at the street level. By contrast, the NPM favors broad employee empowerment. No overall synthesis is possible, but one or another of the perspectives might be more suitable to different types of policy.

Overhead Policy

Overhead policies are those concerned with keeping public administrative operations running on a day-to-day basis. They include disbursing and accounting for money, personnel functions such as compensating and retiring employees, and the maintenance and interior design of the physical plant of agencies. They do not include levels of budgeting, the allocation of personnel, or the nature of missions. For the most part, traditional managerial concerns are most appropriate in judging overhead policies. There is little doubt that efficiency, effectiveness, and economy have been valued since the managerial perspective was first developed.

Sociotherapeutic Policies

These policies—such as the war on poverty and the Model Cities Program— seek to treat an undesirable condition that has become associated with a particular group. The group could have various attributes: it could be economic, urban, elderly, or rural, for example. To a large extent, sociotherapeutic policy coincides with the idea "welfare" in the label "welfare state." Traditionally, such policies seemed to favor the political perspective in their administrative arrangements. The participation of their beneficiaries and responsiveness to their needs were considered of great importance in their relative success. In the absence of participation and representativeness, these policies become paternalistic; they become regulatory in the sense of controlling individuals' behavior without affording them a voice in the process. The NPM's insistence on customer satisfaction and employee empowerment offers great promise in redesigning sociotherapeutic policy because it emphasizes the individualized or customized treatment of beneficiaries.

Regulatory Policy

Regulation through administrative action comes in many guises. However, some programs are clearly "regulatory" in a classical sense. These are programs engaged in such functions as rate setting for public utilities and common carriers; zoning; assuring purity or healthfulness of substances such as food, water, and air; and promoting fair economic competition and eliminating deceptive marketing practices. Regulatory policies rely heavily on a legal perspective. Because the rights of private parties are being determined through public administrative action, it has been considered highly desirable to assure the private parties protection against untoward infringements on those rights. In practice, this often means that an adjudicative hearing format is used. Due process is stressed, as is the impartiality of the hearing examiner. There are some good reasons why the legal perspective seems most appropriate to regulatory policy. Traditional managerial perspectives could easily lead to the squelching of the rights of private parties and to harming their legitimate interests. The NPM's partnership approach can clearly lead to inconsistent and less than optimal outcomes. The political approach's emphasis on responsiveness to the general public could easily facilitate a kind of "tyranny of the majority" against the interests and rights of the private parties. The legal perspective, by contrast, seeks to balance the public and private interests in each instance, affording adequate protection to both.

Perhaps this does not take us far enough. After all, public policy does not come neatly packaged with clear labels, and there are many other types of policy, including those related to foreign affairs, national security, macroeconomic policy, economic redistribution, energy, and distribution of the nation's resources. It is not possible in this volume to assess which of the perspectives, if any, would be most suitable in any of these areas. Quite possibly, different aspects of each of these policy types would most properly be organized according to one or another of the perspectives. Perhaps one perspective could dominate a whole policy area. Still, without answering or addressing these speculations, we hope that our suggestions for analyzing these problems will be helpful. Awareness of what different perspectives demand should help us evaluate policy more comprehensively and eventually may lead us to formulate better means of implementation.

STUDY QUESTIONS

1. Can you think of a policy attaining its objectives, but through an implementation to which you are opposed? Consider the use of police roadblocks to combat DUI and random urinalysis drug testing of public employees and high school students.
2. During the early and mid-1980s, many states raised their drinking age to 21 in response to federal prompting and as a means of promoting traffic safety. How would you go about analyzing the impact of this policy? What kind of approach would you take, and what kinds of information would you seek and use? Suppose your analysis discerned no policy impact; how do you think different political groups would react?
3. At least 27 states have taken some initiatives to reduce obesity among their residents, particularly children. The states are concerned with both health and health care costs. One cardiologist involved in the policy area suggested that every taxpayer be weighed at a post office once a year, when filing his or her tax return. Those whose weight is normal or who have lost weight over the past year would get a tax break from the IRS; those who are significantly overweight would pay the standard rates. Do you favor such a policy? Why or why not? If it were enacted, how would you evaluate its impact?
4. Issuing the Susan B. Anthony dollar was clearly a blunder. The Sacagawea dollar did not fare much better. What seems to account for these mistakes? What steps might be taken to avoid them and similar ones? What do you think has made the 50 State Quarters Program a success?

NOTES

1. Woodrow Wilson, "The Study of Administration," *Political Science Quarterly* 56 (December 1941): 481.
2. Al Gore, *From Red Tape to Results: Creating a Government That Works Better & Costs Less* (Washington, DC: Government Printing Office, 1993), ii.
3. See David Nachmias, *Public Policy Evaluation* (New York: St. Martin's, 1979), 5.
4. James H. Jones, *Bad Blood* (New York: Free Press, 1981).
5. Nachmias, *Public Policy Evaluation,* 5.
6. Ibid.
7. David H. Rosenbloom, *Federal Equal Employment Opportunity* (New York: Praeger, 1977), chap. 5.
8. Peter Drucker, "The Deadly Sins in Public Administration," in Frederick Lane, Ed., *Current Issues in Public Administration,* 2d ed. (New York: St. Martin's, 1982), 421–426.
9. Michael Lipsky, *Street Level Bureaucracy* (New York: Russell Sage, 1980); Pietro S. Nivola, *The Urban Service Problem* (Lexington, MA: Lexington Books, 1979); Eugene Bardach and Robert A. Kagan, *Going by the Book: The Problems of Regulatory Unreasonableness* (Philadelphia: Temple University Press, 1982).
10. See Katherine Naff and John Crum, "Working for America," *Review of Public Personnel Administration* 19 (Fall 1999): 5–16.
11. Thomas R. Dye, *Understanding Public Policy,* 6th ed. (Englewood Cliffs, NJ: Prentice-Hall, 1987), 356. The remainder of this paragraph draws heavily from this source.
12. Deborah Stone, *Policy Paradox* (New York: W. W. Norton, 2002), 235.
13. Ibid., 378.
14. Daniel Katz et al., *Bureaucratic Encounters* (Ann Arbor: University of Michigan, Institute for Social Research, 1975).
15. *Mathews v. Eldridge,* 424 U.S. 319 (1976).
16. *Shapiro v. Thompson,* 394 U.S. 618 (1969).
17. *Saenz v. Roe,* 526 U.S. 489 (1999).
18. *Wyman v. James,* 400 U.S. 309 (1971).
19. *Parrish v. Civil Service Commission,* 425 P.2d 223 (1967).
20. David Osborne and Ted Gaebler, *Reinventing Government* (Reading, MA: Addison-Wesley, 1992), chap. 1.
21. E. S. Savas, *Privatization: The Key to Better Government* (Chatham, NJ: Chatham House, 1987), esp. chap. 4, on which much of the following discussion in this section is based.
22. Ibid., 81.
23. Al Gore, *Common Sense Government Works Better & Costs Less* (Washington, DC: Government Printing Office, 1995), 81.
24. See Savas, *Privatization,* 270–272.
25. Donald Kettl, "Performance Measurement, Benchmarking, and Reengineering," testimony before the Subcommittee on Government Management, Information, and Technology, Committee on Government Reform and Oversight, U.S. House of Representatives, 20 June 1995, 5; U.S. Office of Management and Budget, "Primer on Performance Measurement," 23 September 1994, 4–2.
26. U.S. Office of Management and Budget, "Primer on Performance Measurement," 4–1.
27. Ibid.

28. http://www.hg.org/oregon-government.html.

29. David N. Ammons, "Overcoming the Inadequacies of Performance Measurement in Local Government: The Case of Libraries and Leisure Service," *Public Administration Review* 55 (No. 1, 1995): 37–47; David N. Ammons, "A Proper Mentality for Benchmarking," *Public Administration Review* 59, no. 2 (1999): 105–108.

30. Carolyn J. Heinrich, "How Credible Is the Evidence, and Does It Matter? An Analysis of the Program Assessment Rating Tool," *Public Administration Review* 72 (2012): 123–134.

31. See Daniel P. Moynihan, *Maximum Feasible Misunderstanding* (New York: Free Press, 1970).

32. Edward C. Weeks, "The Practice of Deliberative Democracy: Results from Four Large-Scale Trials," *Public Administration Review* 60 (No. 4, 2000): 360–372.

33. Nancy C. Roberts, "Keeping Public Officials Accountable through Dialogue: Resolving the Accountability Paradox," *Public Administration Review* 62 (No. 6, 2002): 658–669.

34. Dan Eggen, "Proposal to Enlist Citizen Spies Was Doomed from Start," *Washington Post,* 24 November 2002, A11.

35. Ibid.

36. David H. Rosenbloom and Frank Bryan, "The Size of Public Bureaucracies," *State and Local Government Review* 13 (September 1981): 115–123.

37. Brandeis's statement retains great influence. See Justice Sandra Day O'Connor's opinion in *Buckley v. American Constitutional Law Foundation,* 525 U.S. 182, 223 (1999).

38. *U.S. v. Richardson,* 418 U.S. 166, 201 (1974).

39. *Immigration and Naturalization Service v. Chadha,* 462 U.S. 919 (1983).

40. *Bowsher v. Synar,* 478 U.S. 714 (1986); *Buckley v. Valeo,* 424 U.S. 1 (1976); *Clinton v. City of New York,* 524 U.S. 417 (1998).

41. *Seminole Tribe of Florida v. Florida,* 517 U.S. 44 (1996).

42. *Kimel v. Florida Board of Regents,* 528 U.S. 62 (2000); *Board of Trustees of University of Alabama v. Garrett,* 531 U.S. 356 (2001).

43. *U.S. Term Limits v. Thornton,* 514 U.S. 779 (1995).

44. *Washington v. Davis,* 426 U.S. 229 (1976).

45. See *Hawkins v. Town of Shaw,* 437 F2d 1286 (1971).

46. *San Antonio School District v. Rodriguez,* 411 U.S. 1 (1973).

47. Jennifer Larrabee, "DWB (Driving While Black) and Equal Protection: The Realities of an Unconstitutional Police Practice," *Journal of Law and Policy* 6 (No. 1, 1997): 291–328.

48. *United States v. Virginia,* 518 U.S. 515 (1996); *Craig v. Boren,* 429 U.S. 190 (1976).

49. *Goldberg v. Kelly,* 397 U.S. 254 (1970).

50. *Sherbert v. Verner,* 374 U.S. 398 (1963).

51. *Cochrane v. Board of Education,* 103 NW 2d 569 (1960); *Starkey v. Board of Education,* 381 P.2d 718 (1963).

52. Aaron Wildavsky, "The Self-Evaluating Organization," in David Nachmias, Ed., *The Practice of Policy Evaluation* (New York: St. Martin's, 1980), 441–460, at 443.

53. Stone, *Policy Paradox.*

54. Arnold Meltzner, "The Seven Deadly Sins of Policy Analysis," in Frederick Lane, Ed., *Current Issues in Public Administration,* 4th ed. (New York: St. Martin's, 1990), 429–439.

55. Giandomenico Majone, *Evidence, Argument, and Persuasion in the Policy Process* (New Haven, CT: Yale University Press, 1989).

56. Beryl Radin, *Beyond Machiavelli: Policy Analysis Comes of Age* (Washington, DC: Georgetown University Press, 2000), 115.

57. Ibid., 186.

58. Ibid.

ADDITIONAL READING

Bardach, Eugene. *A Practical Guide for Policy Analysis: The Eightfold Path to More Effective Problem Solving.* New York: Chatham House/Seven Bridges, 2000.

Dye, Thomas. *Understanding Public Policy,* 14 ed. Upper Saddle River, NJ: Pearson Higher Education, 2013.

Levy, John. *Essentials of Microeconomics for Public Policy Analysis.* Westport, CT: Praeger, 1995.

Radin, Beryl. *Beyond Machiavelli: Policy Analysis Comes of Age.* Washington, DC: Georgetown University Press, 2000.

Shadish, William R., Cook, Thomas D., & Campbell, Donald T. *Experimental and Quasi-experimental Designs for Generalized Causal Inference.* Boston, MA: Houghton Mifflin, 2002.

Stone, Deborah. *Policy Paradox,* 3rd ed. New York: W. W. Norton, 2011.

POLICY ANALYSIS WEB SITE

The National Center for Policy Analysis has a wealth of information on its Web site at http://www.ncpa.org.

CHAPTER 9

REGULATORY ADMINISTRATION

An Illustration of Management, Politics, and Law in the Public Sector

Key Learning Objectives

1. Understand the different types of regulatory administration and know why they developed.
2. Understand the politics of regulatory administration according to James Q. Wilson's framework.
3. Be familiar with regulatory reform measures, including deregulation.
4. Know the traditional managerial, new public management, political, and legal approaches to regulatory administration.

Regulation, the subject of this chapter, has become a major and controversial public administrative activity. Regulatory administration provides a good illustration of how the managerial, political, and legal perspectives can converge and conflict in a major policy area. The roots of governmental regulation are economic, political, and social. Regulatory structure and process often involve a combination of executive, legislative, and judicial functions. The challenges facing regulatory administration tend to parallel those of public administration more generally. There is a strong need to recognize the relevance of managerial, political, and legal concerns and also to strive for a synthesis of them that is in the public interest.

Regulation has emerged as an area of distinctive concern in public administration. Because regulatory administration encapsulates much of the challenge that contemporary public administration poses for the United States political system, it can be used to illustrate the convergence and clashing of different perspectives. It represents a direct use of governmental authority to penetrate spheres of life once left primarily to the workings of private social and economic controls. For instance, regulatory agencies are engaged in rate setting for utilities; they seek to ensure that products sold on the open market are not injurious to the health and safety of consumers; they have the authority to prohibit the use of technologies and industrial, mining, and agricultural processes deemed damaging to the environment or potentially dangerous to workers or people in proximate areas; they regulate landowners and farmers to protect the environment and ecosystems; and they are involved in seeking to protect workers from discrimination and unhealthy or unsafe conditions in employment.

Regulatory administration tends to vest a great deal of authority in agencies that are designed to be considerably independent of elected officials. These agencies also tend to combine legislative, executive, and judicial authority. They make rules that constrain the conduct of individuals, corporations, governments, and other organizations; they implement or enforce these rules; and they often adjudicate the application of the rules should a challenge to or breach of such regulations arise. Much regulatory administration makes use of judicial processes. But regulatory agencies are not courts, nor are they part of the judicial branch. Regulatory administration is an area of administration in which judicial review has been of exceptionally great importance.

As the scope of regulatory administration has grown, greater attention has been paid to its economic, political, and social costs and benefits—and many have come to believe that the costs are too high and that regulatory reform or deregulation is often desirable. In this chapter we will consider the development and growth of regulatory administration, the problems it presents, and managerial, political, and legal perspectives on improving the quality of governmental regulatory activities. The reader should bear two things in mind: first, that regulatory administration is illustrative of many of the broader problems and challenges confronting public administration, and second, that a great deal of what takes place on the federal level is matched by the operation of state and local regulatory agencies. These are especially important in regulating utilities, occupational licensing, consumer affairs, housing, land use, day care and nursing home facilities, and health centers.

◆→ THE DEVELOPMENT AND GROWTH OF REGULATORY ADMINISTRATION

Origins of Government Regulation

Today much of American economic and social life is the direct subject of administrative regulation by the federal government. The number of rules issued by federal agencies annually far outpaces the legislative output of Congress. It is debatable when federal regulatory activity began in earnest. Some might date it from the 1850s, when the federal government created a Steamboat Inspection Service; others, from 1883, when the Civil Service Commission was created to regulate federal personnel administrative practices; still others, from 1887, when the Interstate Commerce Commission was created to regulate railroad service. However, it is hardly debatable that regulation continues to have a very broad sweep, despite significant deregulation and regulatory reform beginning in the 1970s. The table in Box 9.1 lists the main regulatory agencies that were created since the 1880s, their subject matter, the date of their creation, and their location within the government's administrative structure. The table conveys a good deal of information to which we will be referring throughout this chapter. Some of these regulatory activities have fallen by the wayside in the effort to eliminate unnecessary regulation. Especially notable in this context has been the demise of the Civil Aeronautics Board and the Interstate Commerce Commission and deregulation of some aspects of truck, bus, and rail transportation; and the natural gas and oil industries. Perhaps the most immediate question raised by the table is, "Why so much regulation?"

The general origin of federal regulatory activities is associated with the tendency of industrialization to cause greater economic, technological, and social complexity of life since the 1880s. The increasing division of labor and greater specialization make us highly dependent on one another but less able to assess the predictability and reliability of each other's behavior. For example, we are dependent on farmers, food handlers, and processors whom we do not know personally. They are anonymous, and so traditional channels (families, religious organizations, and communities) for exercising social control over their behavior and assessing their reliability are unavailable to us. Lacking social controls, we have to rely on other means for ensuring the availability and safety of food and other goods on which we depend. Some of these means are non-governmental. For example, we can still exercise some personal judgments about the safety of foods, drugs, products, and modes of transportation. Such private organizations as Consumers Union and Underwriters' Laboratories might also help inform us of dangerous or hazardous products. Liability law affords protection too. It gives producers an incentive to produce

9.1 SOME REGULATORY AGENCIES OF THE FEDERAL GOVERNMENT

Agency*	Present Organization	Year of Origin	Responsibility†
Comptroller of the Currency	Dept. of Treasury	1863	National banks
Fish and Wildlife Service	Dept. of Interior	1871	Preservation of fish and wildlife
Interstate Commerce Commission	Abolished (1995)	1887	Prices, entry in rail, trucking, buses, and inland and coastal waterways
Forest Service	Dept. of Agriculture	1905	Management of resource use
Employment Standards Administration	Dept. of Labor	1913	Wages, hours, and discrimination in employment
Federal Reserve System	Independent	1913	Interest rates, national banks, and banking
Federal Trade Commission	Independent	1914	Consumer information, advertising, business practices
Coast Guard	Dept. of Homeland Security	1915	Ship and port safety, antiterrorism and drug interdiction, environmental protection
International Trade Commission	Independent	1916	International "dumping," industry relief, protection of intellectual property
Food Safety and Quality Service	Dept. of Agriculture	1916	Food inspection, grading, and standardization
Federal Energy Regulatory Commission (formerly, Federal Power Commission [FPC])(FERC)	Dept. of Energy	1930	Prices for natural gas, interstate electricity, oil by pipeline
National Transportation Safety Board	Independent	1926	Recommends safety improvements in air, rail, highway, and shipping transportation, and in pipelines
Food and Drug Administration	Dept. of Health and Human Services	1931	Food and drug safety
Federal Home Loan Bank Board	Succeeded by the Federal Housing Finance Board (1989) Independent	1932	Interest rates and entry into savings-and-loan industry
Commodity Credit Corporation (CCC)	Dept. of Agriculture	1933	Farm commodity pricing
Federal Deposit Insurance Corp. (FDIC)	Independent	1933	Insurance of bank deposits
Farm Credit Administration	Independent	1933	Agricultural credit and banks
Federal Communications Commission (FCC)	Independent	1934	Entry into broadcasting, aspects of telecommunications
Securities and Exchange Commission	Independent	1934	Information and trading conditions of securities
National Labor Relations Board	Independent	1935	Labor contracts and collective bargaining
Civil Aeronautics Board	Abolished	1938	Prices, entry into airline industry
Bureau of Land Management	Dept. of Interior	1946	Management of public lands
Animal and Plant Health Inspection Service	Dept. of Agriculture	1953	Food inspection

Continued

9.1 Some Regulatory Agencies of the Federal Government (Continued)

Agency*	Present Organization	Year of Origin	Responsibility†
Federal Aviation Administration	Dept. of Transportation	1958	Airline, airport safety
Federal Maritime Commission	Independent	1961	Shipping
Agricultural Stabilization and Conservation Service (reorganized into Consolidated Farm Service Agency, 1994)	Dept. of Agriculture	1961	Farm acreage allotments
Equal Employment Opportunity Commission (EEOC)	Independent	1964	Ending prohibited employment discrimination
Federal Railroad Administration	Dept. of Transportation	1966	Rail safety and transportation policy
Federal Highway Administration (FHA)	Dept. of Transportation	1967	Truck and bus safety; transportation planning
National Oceanic and Atmospheric Administration (NOAA)	Dept. of Commerce	1970	Management of marine resources and protection of marine mammals
National Highway Traffic Safety Administration (NHTSA)	Dept. of Transportation	1970	Motor vehicle safety and fuel economy
Environmental Protection Agency (EPA)	Independent	1970	Environmental protection of air, water, and land
Occupational Safety and Health Administration (OSHA)	Dept. of Labor	1970	Worker safety
Postal Rate Commission	Independent	1970	Recommends prices of U.S. Postal Service; reviews post office closure decisions
National Credit Union Administration	Independent	1970	Credit unions
Federal Election Commission	Independent	1971	Federal elections
Agricultural Marketing Service	Dept. of Agriculture	1972	Standardization, grading, inspection
Consumer Product Safety Commission (CPSC)	Independent	1972	Safety of consumer products
Bureau of Alcohol, Tobacco, Firearms and Explosives	Dept. of Treasury	1972	Firearms, explosives, alcohol, tobacco, commercial arson
Mine Safety and Health Administration	Dept. of Labor	1973	Miner safety
Economic Regulatory Administration	Dept. of Energy	1974	Petroleum pricing and allocation, coal conservation, temperature limits for buildings, energy standards for new buildings
Commodity Futures Trading Commission	Independent	1975	Information and trading conditions of commodity futures
Nuclear Regulatory Commission	Independent	1975	Licensing and regulation concerning nuclear reactors
Federal Grain Inspection Service	Dept. of Agriculture	1976	Grain inspection
Office of Surface Mining Reclamation and Enforcement	Dept. of Interior	1977	Environmental effects of surface mining

Agency	Type	Year	Function
Federal Mine Safety and Health Review Commission	Independent	1977	Adjudicates disputes under the Mine Act
Office of Government Ethics	Independent	1978	Ethics in the federal executive branch
Federal Labor Relations Authority	Independent	1979	Federal labor relations
Merit Systems Protection Board (MSPB)	Independent	1979	Federal personnel administration
Defense Nuclear Facilities Safety Board	Independent	1988	Dept. of Energy nuclear facilities
Chemical Safety Hazard Investigation Board	Independent	1990	Recommends safety improvements in the handling and transportation of chemicals; works with EPA and OSHA
Public Company Accounting Oversight Board	Nonprofit corporation aligned with SEC	2002	Oversight of public company auditing
Financial Stability Oversight Council	Dept. of Treasury	2010	Identify risks to the U.S. financial system and issue corrective rules
Bureau of Consumer Financial Protection (often abbreviated CFPB)	Federal Reserve System	2010	Regulates consumer financial products and services

*Some agencies listed have been phased out or subsumed by others in the movement toward deregulation.
†Some agencies have nondomestic regulatory or nonregulatory functions as well.

Source: Derived from Lawrence J. White, *Reforming Regulation* (Englewood Cliffs, NJ: Prentice-Hall, 1981), Tables 3-1, 3-2; updated according to the *United States Government Manual*, 2013 Edition (Washington, DC: Government Printing Office, 2013).

safe products and retailers not to sell dangerous ones by enabling consumers to obtain compensation if they are injured by products determined to be unsafe. We can also rely on economic markets to provide incentives for producers to supply what consumers want and to ensure the safety of their products so that demand for them will not falter. However, in the real world, markets are imperfect.

Market Failure

In the United States our first preference is usually to rely on market forces, rather than agencies, to regulate economic practices. However, markets sometimes fail. Consequently we may want some economic practices to be made predictable, reliable, and perhaps stable through regulation.

The public tends to favor regulation when it learns from private sources of how undesirable some industrial processes are, even though they may pose no immediate danger. For instance, the publication of Upton Sinclair's *The Jungle* (1905), which described the filthy conditions in the meatpacking industry, was a catalyst in the passage of the Pure Food and Drug Act of 1906. The book turned President Theodore Roosevelt into an advocate of the regulation of some aspects of the food and drug industries.[1] To some extent the issue was not that the meat depicted in *The Jungle* was dangerous to one's health after being thoroughly cooked but rather that it was so unsanitary as to be repulsive—that is, even if it wouldn't hurt them, after knowing how it was handled, people did not want to eat it. But the danger is often real. In 1938, drug regulations were expanded to require testing of new drugs *prior* to marketing after some 107 people were killed by sulfanilamide, a new sulfa drug that had been initially hailed as promising. Similarly, just as once the safety of steamboats was of great concern to passengers not in a position to make a sound evaluation, today few of us are able to evaluate the safety of different types of commercial airplanes or that of railroad trestles and trackbeds. Consequently, we may turn to the government to regulate these transportation services.

Product safety regulation to protect us from harmful goods, services, processes, and technologies is handled by the FDA, FAA, CPSC, NHTSA, NRC, and a variety of other agencies. It is largely based on science and engineering and tends to rely on inspections and testing for enforcement. A special variant of this type of regulation involves occupational licensing, mostly at the state level, in a number of fields to assure the public that practitioners are competent. Product safety regulation compensates for information asymmetry that often puts consumers at a disadvantage because they know less about the safety of products than do those who produce them.

Rate setting regulation provides a similar example. In the 1880s, farmers in some areas were dependent on railroads to transport their produce to markets. Some railroads sought to take advantage of their monopolies on various routes by charging rates that bore little relationship to the actual cost of transporting the farmers' shipments. If allowed to continue indefinitely, this most likely would have depressed the agricultural sector of the economy, at least in some geographic areas, and/or have driven up prices for food in urban areas. It was also viewed as fundamentally unfair. In 1887, the ICC was set up to avoid these consequences by regulating railroads in the public interest.

Regulation of this type is intended to create a surrogate for the market. It concentrates on setting prices (or rates) and/or controlling entry into a field of economic activity. It has been most common in transportation (rail, bus, trucking, shipping, and air), the field of public utilities, and some aspects of the FCC's regulation of radio and television broadcasting. Deregulation of some of these areas has been substantial. Surrogate-market regulation is characterized by economic analysis of costs, rates of return, and distribution of services. Sometimes it is used to subsidize an industry, as when past ICC regulations enabled truckers to compete with railroads on long hauls even though their real costs were higher. More commonly, surrogate-market regulation creates **cross subsidies** through which one set of customers (residential water users) pays prices that are intended to subsidize another (agricultural users).

Market functioning regulation addresses problems in markets that keep them from operating properly. Antitrust and fair-trade regulations are preeminent examples. The Sherman Antitrust Act of 1890 was intended, in part, to assure that markets did not become noncompetitive through monopolization. The Federal Trade Commission and Clayton Acts of 1914 were concerned with competition but became the basis of regulatory activity also intended to curb trade practices that distorted market forces, such as false advertising and price fixing. The Securities and Exchange Act of 1934 established the SEC to regulate stock markets and trading practices to protect against a host of problems associated with insider trading, false and misleading information, and inadequate disclosure. After the Enron debacle fully unfolded in 2001, the SEC was given greater authority to regulate accounting practices. Market functioning regulation tends to be legalistic and to rely heavily on legal processes, such as administrative adjudication and judicial trials.

The list of regulatory activities does not stop there. There has also been great concern with *environmental regulation*. Like Upton Sinclair's *The Jungle,* Rachel Carson's *Silent Spring* (1962) helped crystallize demands for regulation by increasing public awareness of the long-term dangers confronting the environment through chemical pollution and various agricultural, mining, and building practices and deterioration of wetlands and other ecosystems. Some of these dangers have already materialized, such as "air inversions," dangerous levels of smog, and acid rain, which can be factors in individuals' deaths and cause major damage to lakes and forests. Others, such as global warming and the depletion of the earth's ozone layer, threaten to wreak havoc on the ecology of vast geographic areas. Greater regulation of shipping practices has been a direct result of a number of spectacular oil spills by supertankers and a growing realization that the ecology of the oceans is vulnerable to pollution.[2]

One reason regulation of the environment appears sensible and desirable to many is that the forces of the marketplace do not always seem to work as an adequate check on the practices of a broad range of economic concerns. For instance, it may be cheaper for utilities and manufacturers in the Midwest to pass off sulfur dioxide pollution as a negative externality rather than change their processes or install "scrubbers" to reduce it. An externality is a positive or negative aspect of a product or its production that is not accounted for in the economic transaction between buyer and seller. In this case, it is a part of production that returns in the form of acid rain and is paid for by the Northeast and parts of Canada.

Environmental regulation relies on engineering, agronomy, hydrology, biology, and a host of other sciences, as well as economic analysis. It makes use of "environmental impact statements," or analyses of the likely ecological effects of economic development, production processes, and product uses. Inspections and monitoring are also used as enforcement techniques. Today, environmental regulation frequently involves health concerns, as in the case of the disposal and cleanup of hazardous wastes or the regulation of arsenic in drinking water.

Employment regulation is another area of comprehensive regulatory activity. Because it consists of human effort, labor differs from other commodities or factors of production bought and sold in markets. Some economic and production practices have such undesirable and major social consequences that they are prohibited through regulation. Child labor and unsafe "sweatshops" are classic cases. Collective bargaining practices, including union organizing, are regulated by the NLRB. The EEOC was created to prevent employment and union practices that illegally discriminate against individuals on the basis of race, color, religion, national origin (ethnicity), or sex. Discrimination based on age or disability is also under its jurisdiction. Congress has considered discrimination along these lines to be *unfair* and also an impediment to interstate commerce and harmful to the nation's economy. Occupational safety and health regulation has grown immensely since OSHA was established in 1970. In part, this has been a response to the growing awareness that the individual worker may be unable to make a sound judgment as to the safety of some substances, such as benzene and lead, found in the modern workplace. More specialized regulatory activities exist in some occupations, such as mining.

The regulation of employment practices is so broad and prone to overlap other forms of regulation that it necessarily involves a variety of techniques. The NLRB and the EEOC rely heavily on adjudicatory processes. Accordingly, their operations are largely informed by legal analysis. OSHA, by contrast, relies far more on rule making and inspections. Much of its activity is based on health sciences and engineering.

Regulatory Federalism

Although these are the main types of regulatory administration in the United States, they do not encompass all of it. There is also the Federal Election Commission, which regulates some aspects of election campaigns for federal office. Several federal and state agencies are engaged in regulatory activity to protect individuals' civil rights in voting, in places of public accommodation, on common carriers, and in educational facilities. Some federal regulations apply to state and local jurisdictions, as in civil rights and some aspects of employment and environmental regulatory administration. This creates a kind of "regulatory federalism" in which subnational governments are regulated by the national government. Finally, a great deal of federal regulatory activity is augmented by state and local agencies, especially in the fields of health, safety, employment, the environment, and fair trade practices.

Regulatory Policy and Administration

The scope and complexity of regulatory administration make it difficult to generalize about regulatory policy. Some analysts use categories such as "old style" or "economic" regulation (surrogate market, market functioning, and/or single industry) as distinct from "new style" or "social" regulation (health, safety, environment, employment, across industries).[3] Such simplifications are convenient for some purposes, but they must be used with caution: Some environmental and health regulation is older than some forms of economic regulation, and some unfair-practice regulation, including discrimination, in labor markets is both "social" and "economic." Some analysts contend that regulatory activity should be strictly limited to "market failures," as discussed in Chapter 2. To the extent that this approach suggests that governmental regulation is justified only when markets fail, it states a policy position, rather than a proof, that is contestable in the political system.

The Constitution's commerce clause allows federal regulation of economic activity to promote the general welfare, not solely to address market failure. Markets do not necessarily produce the social outcomes favored by political majorities. Economists consider workers' reluctance to relocate geographically to be a market failure called "labor immobility"; sociologists are more likely to refer to it as "community." Markets are also limited in their capacity to take the interests of future generations into account, but political leaders may sometimes be concerned precisely about the nation's future. Conservation policies, governmental hoarding of strategic reserves, and the systems of national and state forests are examples of political decisions not to cede the allocation of scarce, limited, and even renewable resources to the here-and-now workings of the market.

Perhaps regulatory administration is best understood as part of a web of controls—economic, social, and legal—over activity considered antisocial or otherwise undesirable. Therefore, an important question is: Given all the mechanisms for exercising such controls, how is the choice for different types of regulatory administration made?

Political Patterns

Regulatory administration is established as a political response to a problem, real or imagined, in the economy, society, polity, or ecology. It will have costs and produce benefits that may be distributed in a variety of ways. Hence, inevitably there is a "politics of regulation."[4] In considering the origins of regulatory administration, James Q. Wilson identified several types of political conditions associated with the creation of specific regulatory agencies and statutes.

Majoritarian Politics

When the costs and benefits of a governmental policy or activity are widely distributed, we see **majoritarian politics** occurring. "All or most of society expects to gain; all or most of society expects to pay."[5] Wilson believes that the passage of the Sherman Antitrust Act (1890) and the Federal Trade Commission Act (1914) are examples. Neither was aimed at a specific industry; both promised to eliminate unfair, harmful, or unscrupulous economic practices without specifying what these were. Neither was strongly supported nor strongly opposed by business.

Interest Group Politics

When both costs and benefits are narrowly concentrated, **interest group politics** results. "A . . . regulation will often benefit a relatively small group at the expense of another comparable small group. Each side has a strong incentive to organize and exercise political influence. The public does not believe it will be much affected one way or another; though it may sympathize more with one side than the other."[6] Perhaps the best single example in the regulatory realm is the Shipping Act of 1916, which since 1961 has been administered by the Federal Maritime Commission. The competition was between those who shipped goods by sea and the shipping companies. Although the public interest was involved in a general sense, the public and others not directly or immediately affected were relatively uninvolved in the issues posed. The National Labor Relations Act of 1935, which created the NLRB, was another example. It pitted organized labor against industry.

Client Politics

At those times "when the benefits of a prospective policy are concentrated but the costs are widely distributed,"[7] **client politics** prevails. Here some relatively small and easily organized group stands to benefit, while the costs are "distributed at a low per capita rate over a large number of people." Consequently, there may be little incentive to organize substantial opposition. Wilson finds that the creation of the CAB and many public utility commissions at the state level more or less fits this pattern. He suggests that occupational licensing boards probably do also. However, he notes that sometimes opposition may develop to what would otherwise be a case of "client politics" when public interest groups become involved. Wilson also notes that despite the widespread distribution of relatively low costs, many business or other groups may become involved in discussion of the policy when it is first proposed.

The "client politics" model makes clear that despite the popular view that private enterprise thoroughly opposes government regulation, there is reason to believe that some industries have sought to be regulated. George Stigler, a Nobel Prize recipient in economics, promoted an influential theory about this. In his view, "regulation is acquired by the industry and is designed and operated primarily for its benefit."[8] This is especially true where the industry sees the opportunity of using governmental power to keep new entrants (would-be competitors) out. To accomplish its ends, the industry may seek to "capture" the regulatory agency, often an independent commission. Such a strategy was first propounded by Attorney General Richard Olney in the early 1890s with regard to the probable future of the ICC. He wrote: "The Commission . . . is, or can be made, of great use to the railroads. It satisfies the popular clamor for a government supervision of railroads, at the same time that the supervision is almost entirely nominal. Further, the older such a commission gets to be, the more inclined it will be found to take the business and railroad view of things."[9]

The capture theory was rigorously developed by Marver Bernstein, who hypothesized that regulatory agencies go through predictable "life cycles."[10] At birth they avidly regulate the industries under their jurisdiction on behalf of consumers, rate payers, or the public interest more generally. The second stage is reached when the agency has either eliminated the worst abuses it was created to correct or, alternatively, becomes frustrated with its inability to do so and the lack of public concern with its activities. At this point, agencies begin to compromise more with the regulated industries and begin to view the industries as an important part of their constituency. In the final stage, the regulatory agency becomes protective of the status quo and often is a de facto "captive" of the industry. In the latter case, the industry gains informal but real political control over the appointment of regulatory commissioners and uses the commission's public power for private gain.[11] Such a pattern is frequently descriptive of client politics but is not necessarily confined to it.

Entrepreneurial Politics

When "a policy may be proposed that will confer general (though perhaps small) benefits at a cost to be borne chiefly by a small segment of society,"[12] we encounter **entrepreneurial politics.** Wilson points to antipollution and auto-safety bills as examples. What is peculiar about this type of politics is the inability of the small segment on which the burden falls to block the regulatory policy at issue. Wilson attributes this primarily to the work of people he calls **entrepreneurs,** such as Ralph Nader, whose work was instrumental in the passage of the Auto Safety Act of 1966. An earlier example was Dr. Harvey Wiley, who helped mobilize support for the Food and Drug Act of 1906. This type of policy entrepreneur effectively represents groups not directly involved in legislative policy making.

In sum, Wilson concludes that the politics of regulatory policy "follows different patterns, mobilizes different actors, and has different consequences depending, among other things, on the perceived distribution of costs and benefits of the proposed policy."[13]

Wilson's scheme is useful in gaining an understanding of regulatory policy. Although his categories do not coincide perfectly with the types of regulation discussed, some *tendencies* are evident. Client politics describes much surrogate-market regulation; entrepreneurial politics pertains to much health, environmental, and safety regulation; majoritarian politics, as noted, is associated with the regulation of the market's functioning; interest group politics is descriptive of much but not all employment regulation. Wilson's discussion encompasses the politics and some of the economic bases of regulation. It is necessary to consider social factors, as well, to have a more complete picture of the growth of regulatory administration.

Social Factors

Sometimes the contemporary administrative state is referred to as the "welfare state," and it is said that government has placed a safety net underneath nearly everyone in the population to protect those unable to care for themselves. Whereas some argue that the safety net is already too broad, others maintain that it needs to be enlarged to encompass some individuals and circumstances for whom or which there is inadequate protection. Whatever one's stance on the desirability of the "safety net," it does seem evident that as a society the United States has developed two characteristics in this regard that bear heavily on regulatory administration and public administration in general.

First, this society has frequently sought to augment personal responsibility with government regulation. The variety of state mandatory seat belt laws provides a good example. The federal government has long required that new cars sold in the United States be equipped with seat belts. There are now very few cars on the roads without them. So the belts are there for anyone to fasten. It is a matter of personal responsibility, requiring but a few seconds and little effort to accomplish. However, for one reason or another, the states reasoned that it was *their* responsibility to make sure that everyone buckles up. It is now a regulation that is enforced by the police and courts—not something left up to the individual. The same tendency to use regulation to override (and diminish) personal responsibility can be found in consumer affairs. Here state agencies and the FTC seek to protect the consumer from being deceived or cheated. Laudable though this may be, in the past it was primarily the consumer's personal responsibility. Similarly, some of the OSHA regulations tend to treat workers as though they were incapable of judging how to use equipment safely and move about in the workplace. In the past, a cheated consumer or an injured worker might have had recourse after the fact at common law. Much regulation today is by administrative agencies and seeks to prevent harm in the first place.

The new public management (NPM) may be part of a larger trend in the United States to reemphasize personal responsibility. Employee empowerment, deregulation of the public service, and the NPM's strong emphasis on results place greater responsibility on public servants. They make it more difficult for administrators and organizations to blame failures on procedures and red tape.

As its title suggests, the Personal Responsibility and Work Opportunity Reconciliation Act of 1996 is another manifestation of this trend. It seeks to strengthen welfare recipients' sense of personal responsibility for their economic status. Similarly, the Department of Homeland Security urges Americans to take a significant measure of personal responsibility for their safety by having survival supplies in their homes to deal with a biological, chemical, radiological, or other terrorist attack that disrupts electricity, water, communications, commerce, and other aspects of day-to-day life. The 1998 federal Assessment of Regulations and Policies on Families Act requires agencies to consider whether new regulations and policies might undermine family responsibility and functionality.

Second, it has been observed that, "wholly aside from objective changes in risk, cultural changes in the past two decades [1960s–1970s] have increased our *intolerance of risk,* resulting in greater expectations of security from physical hazards, illness, environmental degradation, and even from being cheated in the marketplace."[14] Greater affluence, sensitivity to power relationships and exploitation, and a growing concern with the quality of life seem to have coincided with the rise of opportunities for entrepreneurial politics, as described by Wilson. Public interest groups and policy entrepreneurs both in and out of government have taken it upon themselves to represent and mobilize support for what they perceive to be the public's interest in reducing risks. In retrospect, many readers may find it amazing that prior to 1938 there was no general requirement that drugs be tested before being sold to the public in large quantities. The growing intolerance of risk and the diminished reliance on personal responsibility are factors in the shifting focus of much regulation from surrogate market to environmental and health and safety (both generally and in employment).

◆→ THE STRUCTURE AND PROCESS OF REGULATORY ADMINISTRATION

Independent Regulatory Commissions (IRCs)

Regulatory administration can take several organizational forms. Perhaps the independent commission format is the best known. This approach to administrative organization was discussed briefly in Chapter 3. Its most distinctive feature is that it is headed by a number of commissioners who form a bipartisan group and typically hold fixed and staggered terms of office. The purpose of this arrangement is to insulate the workings of the regulatory commission from electoral politics. It provides a degree of stability and continuity in the commissions and protects them from rapid changes in leadership when the partisanship of the presidency or the majority in Congress changes. Political detachment of this type has been deemed desirable, as it is thought that the commissions' missions are to regulate sectors of the economy and society or aspects of commerce in the public interest in the long run. They are not intended to engage in rapid ideological shifts in striking balances among the competing interests they must consider. Rather, they are designed to develop a clear vision of the public interest by making highly specific rules and adjudicating cases that may arise under them. Regulatory commissions occupy a peculiar place in the separation of powers. They are not considered part of the executive branch, but neither are they part of Congress or the courts.

When the ICC, the prototypical federal regulatory commission, was set up in 1887, Congress clearly believed that the policy area of railroad rate regulation ought to be taken out of partisan politics and that the commission was capable of ascertaining the public interest with little direct guidance from the legislature. Eventually, Congress established some commissions with broad missions and no genuine guidance as to what policies should be adopted.

The FCC is a good example. It was set up in 1934 "to regulate interstate and foreign communications by wire and radio in the *public interest*."[15] This broad, undefined mission gave the commission a great deal of freedom to initiate policy. It also bespeaks Congress's unwillingness or inability to formulate policy more forcefully in this area. (See Box 9.2.)

Regulatory Agencies

Regulatory agencies may be free standing within the executive branch or housed as relatively independent units within cabinet departments. When they are not part of a department, as is the case with the EPA, they are generally called "independent regulatory agencies." Those located within departments are typically referred to as regulatory agencies even though by virtue of their functions they are apt to enjoy considerable independence within the larger organization. For instance, as Box 9.1 indicates, this is true of the FDA (Health and Human Services), OSHA (Labor), NHTSA (Transportation), and some others. In either case, they are headed by a single director, whose title may vary, and are subject to greater presidential authority and control than the IRCs.

Rule Making

However organized, regulatory administrators use several processes. As noted earlier, they make *rules* according to procedures set forth in the Administrative Procedure Act of 1946, the Negotiated Rulemaking Act of 1990, and a complex web of additional statutes and executive orders. These are too voluminous and complex to review here, but the key point is that rulemaking is heavily encumbered by procedural and substantive requirements.[16] For example, the FDA has made a number of rules regarding the labeling of drugs and foods. It requires that drug advertising include a statement of side effects, contraindications, and appropriate precautions and warnings. It has also issued rules for "standards of identity" of products such as fish sticks, ice cream, and hot dogs. In one celebrated case, it took two years or so to determine whether a new type of potato chip, now marketed as a "potato crisp," could

9.2 THE FEDERAL COMMUNICATIONS COMMISSION AND "FLEETING EXPLETIVES"

The Federal Communications Commission has been in an ongoing legal tussle with Fox Television Stations, Inc. Federal law prohibits the broadcasting of indecent language, defined as relating to sexual or excretory activity or organs, over airwaves regulated by the FCC. On the live 2002 Billboard Music Awards Cher noted that she has had critics for "the last 40 years saying that I was on my way out every year. Right. So F*** 'em" (as the Supreme Court printed it). At the awards program in 2003, Nicole Richie found occasion to ponder: "Why do they even call it 'The Simple Life?' Have you ever tried to get cow s*** out of a Prada purse? It's not so f***ing simple." In 2006, the FCC released Notices of Apparent Liability for these broadcasts and others. The agency's chief concern was that approximately 2.5 million minors heard these fleeting expletives. Seeking to establish the authority to fine Fox TV for Cher and Richie's words was a change of policy. In the past, the Commission let "isolated or fleeting expletives" pass without taking action. Now, it was concerned that audiences would be exposed to them 24/7 if it didn't clamp down. The legal issue in the case was whether the FCC had provided a "reasoned explanation" for its policy change. In *Federal Communications Commission v. Fox Television Stations* (2009), the Supreme Court held that:

> To be sure, the requirement that an agency provide reasoned explanation for its action would ordinarily demand that it display awareness that it is changing position. An agency may not, for example, depart from a prior policy *sub silentio* or simply disregard its rules that are still on the books. And of course the agency must show that there are good reasons for the new policy. But it need not demonstrate to a court's satisfaction that the reasons for the new policy are better than the old one; it suffices that the new policy is permissible under the statute, that there are good reasons for it, and that the agency believes it to be better, which the conscious change of course adequately indicates. This means that the agency need not always

provide a more detailed justification than what would suffice for a new policy created on a blank slate.

Finding that the FCC "knew it was making a change" and that its reasoning was rational, the Court's majority had little trouble holding that the Commission was legally entitled to adopt the new policy. The Court also noted that the FCC had declined to levy sanctions against the TV stations because it was enforcing a policy change without clear prior notice.

But there was a hitch. Is banning the F-word constitutional? Certainly, treating it as always referring to sexual activity is peculiar—after all, Cher was decidedly not asking for sex with her detractors. And notwithstanding Richie's proper usage, always taking the S-word literally is also a stretch. Enter *Federal Communications Commission v. Fox Television Stations* (2012), or *Fox II*. This sequel to *Fox I* also included an episode of NYPD Blue in which a woman's buttocks and the side of her nude breast were briefly shown on ABC as well as an NBC Golden Globe Awards program in which Bono proclaimed winning an award was "really, really, f***ing brilliant."

Does banning fleeting or prolonged iteration of the F- and S-words or brief nudity violate the First Amendment guarantee of freedom of speech? This is probably what the FCC and the TV stations wanted to know. However, the Supreme Court dodged the question by ruling that the FCC violated Fifth Amendment Due Process by failing "to give Fox or ABC fair notice prior to the broadcasts in question that fleeting expletives and momentary nudity could be found actionably indecent." Because due process requires "clarity in regulation," the FCC's effort to levy $1 million sanctions against the stations was unconstitutional. If a *Fox III* reaches the Supreme Court, it is anybody's guess whether the justices' final word will be *bleep*.

Sources: Federal Communications Commission v. Fox Television Stations, 556 U.S. 502 (2009); Federal Communications Commission v. Fox Television Stations, 132 S. Ct. 2307 (2012).

be fairly called a "potato chip." Some of these rules make rather odd reading: Frozen fried fish sticks are defined as "clean, wholesome, rectangular-shaped unglazed masses of cohering pieces not ground of fish flesh coated with breading and partially cooked. . . . Frozen fried fish sticks weigh up to and including 1½ ounces; are at least three-eighths of an inch thick and their largest dimension is at least three times the next largest dimension."[17] Such a rule has its purpose—to prevent misleading the consumer and to serve specific economic interests. In 1987, for instance, the National Milk Producers Federation and the Committee for Fair Pizza Labeling fought a minor political battle over whether pizza made without cheese should be required to carry a prominent label to the effect that it contains "cheese substitute."[18] The rules for labeling products "organic" and canned tuna "dolphin-safe" have also provoked controversy.

There is some rationale behind all the regulatory rules placed in the massive *Federal Register* in any given year. When OSHA decided to drop some 900 rules considered to be "nitpicking," it received some serious objections. Although it is easy to poke fun at some of the regulatory agencies' rules, it must be remembered that they also deal with matters of true gravity, such as auto safety, airline safety, food poisoning, dangerous products, deadly pollution, and radioactive contamination of the environment.

Adjudication

Many regulatory agencies are also engaged in adjudication. Here an agency such as the FTC may charge a business with deceptive advertising practices, or one such as the NLRB may be called on to decide whether an employer or a union has engaged in an unfair labor practice. By and large, *adjudicatory procedure* is regulated by administrative law and constitutional concerns. We will address these topics later in this chapter. However, there is a good deal of administrative flexibility as to how cases should be selected. This is a matter of *adjudicatory policy*.

In general, adjudicatory policy can be considered either reactive or proactive. Reactive strategies depend on complaints being filed with the regulatory agency by private parties or other governmental agencies. Agency employees respond to these complaints in several ways: some are dismissed as frivolous; some are routed to more appropriate agencies; some are acted on in an effort to obtain some form of restitution for the complainant; some lead the agency to take action against the party that allegedly committed a breach of proper conduct. Additional steps may include investigating, bringing formal charges and holding formal hearings within the agency, and litigating in the courts. Complaints tend to concern matters of "conduct"; that is, they involve allegations by an individual or organization that some business enterprise has engaged in an unfair or illegal practice. For example, such complaints may be made by consumers against merchants or repair services, by employees alleging discrimination on the part of their employers, or by unions or employers (including public employers) alleging unfair labor practices. Sometimes such cases are also filed by businesses that believe their competitors are engaging in prohibited practices. By their nature, **conduct cases** pertain to relatively concrete practices and to specific sets of events.

Proactive cases are those developed by a regulatory agency through an investigation or study of some kind. Based on its observations about the practices of a business or another entity, the agency may conclude that some violation of law or its rules has occurred. Proactive cases initiated by field investigations often resemble conduct cases. The inspectors may find violations and issue citations, which can become the subject of adjudication. Housing inspectors, OSHA inspectors, and health service inspectors are examples. Proactive cases may also be structural. **Structural cases** do not arise from specific events, but rather are the result of patterns and broad practices deemed by the agency to be prohibited. Whereas in a conduct case a health inspector in a restaurant will stick a thermometer into the chili to see if it is too cold, a structural case is more likely to consider whether a chain of restaurants is mislabeling its products or engaging in unfair or anticompetitive practices. Rather than ask, "What temperature is the beef?" or even "Where's the beef?" the structural case will tend to ask, "What is the economic relationship of the seller of the beef to its franchisees and to the producers?"

But structural cases are often far more complicated than this. They deal with the structure of competition in whole industries, such as petroleum or information technology products, or patterns and practices of discrimination against members of minority groups or women by a large employer or even within an entire industry. The federal government's litigation against Microsoft in 2000 is an example. The question was whether Microsoft's bundling of its Internet browser into its Windows operating system constituted an illegal anticompetitive practice.

Structural cases are often informed by theory. For example, to learn whether prohibited monopolization has occurred in an industry, a regulatory agency will need to know how firms behave and how pricing operates. Assessing such matters may depend on a theoretical understanding of the differences between the behavior of firms in competitive markets and their behavior in monopoly markets. Similarly, because monopolization is not necessarily against the public interest, it may be necessary to determine whether the concentration of market power has produced inefficiency or will do so in the future.

Although structural cases have the potential to regulate dynamically what the agency considers to be prohibited practices, they also have some important drawbacks. First, they are difficult and time-consuming to adjudicate and litigate. The parties charged with the prohibited behavior often have great opportunity to delay these cases and drag them on for years. Second, they often involve new legal theories or new interpretations of existing theory. Consequently, administrative law judges and judges in the courtroom may require a great deal of convincing that the agency's interpretation is correct. Third, they tend to create a personnel problem because agency lawyers often want experience in adjudication and litigation as opposed to the lengthy preparation of cases. Conduct cases offer a far greater opportunity for this experience. Finally, structural cases can engulf considerable amounts of an agency's resources. For example, the Department of Justice spent $17 million on a 13-year antitrust case against IBM.[19]

Inspection and Compliance

At this point, a word should be said about inspectors, who are functionally agents of rule enforcement that can lead to adjudication. Many regulatory agencies depend on inspectors to implement their policies. Inspectors hold a complex job. They are street-level bureaucrats who have a great deal of discretion, cannot be fully supervised or held accountable by the administrative hierarchy, and are highly visible and even intimidating to the businesses they inspect. They have the ability to make the regulatory process work well or work poorly. When inspectors provoke hostility on the part of the inspected and when they seek to enforce every rule in a highly technical way, regulation is not likely to work well. Private parties may be evasive; they may seek to require that the inspector obtain a warrant before entering the premises; they will try to fool or mislead the inspector. When the inspector wins the confidence of those being inspected, the latter may strike a much more cooperative posture and try to take advantage of the inspector's expertise in eliminating dangerous, unhealthful, or other prohibited practices in the workplace. Because the object of regulatory policy in the first place is to evoke responsible social and economic behavior, cooperation and voluntary compliance by private parties with the spirit of regulation can certainly serve an agency's purposes.

Just as a responsible police officer seeks to promote the safety of persons and property, rather than to write numerous tickets for minor traffic, noise, and other violations, an effective inspector seeks to promote substantial and voluntary compliance with the spirit of agency regulations and the specific letter of those requirements that protect against immediate dangers or seriously antisocial behavior. Consequently, an effective inspector must be technically competent, honest, tough-minded, and willing to exercise authority while also being empathetic and able to get along well with people. This combination of characteristics is not easy to find. Eugene Bardach and Robert Kagan conclude that a "good inspector" listens with respect to the regulated party, avoids the "literal application [or rules] to a particular violation" when it "would be unreasonable or of secondary importance," and provides "*information* to the regulated enterprise that reduces the difficulty or cost of compliance, or at least makes the required compliance measures seem understandable and justifiable."[20] One of the advantages to regulatory agencies of having "good inspectors" is that it may make their missions far more manageable. Voluntary compliance is crucial to the missions of agencies such as OSHA and EEOC, whose jurisdictions cover millions of workplaces.

Regulatory agencies also rely on *testing* to implement their objectives. This is especially pronounced in the areas of health and safety, but it also pertains to some aspects of consumer affairs generally. Testing may be done by the regulatory agency, may be outsourced, or may be required of the private parties that produce and market a product. The FDA, for instance, relies heavily on testing, but largely by evaluating the tests done by drug companies and others. The EPA, by contrast, directly engages in monitoring and testing. Testing can be either premarket or postmarket. Drugs, food additives, and other substances for human consumption are likely to be tested in advance of being marketed because of their potential danger. Additional postmarket tests may be undertaken, especially if a suspicion develops that a product is not safe under certain conditions or if some reevaluation of the premarket tests suggests that they were faulty in some way. Product recalls are often the result of postmarket testing. In either case, the testing may be elaborate and costly to the producer and the agency. For example, a new drug application at the FDA may contain as many as 200 volumes.[21]

◆◆ COMMON CRITICISMS OF REGULATORY ADMINISTRATION

It is plausible that no aspect of public administration has been subject to as much criticism as regulation. It is inherently intrusive and consequently annoying to some, who find its constraints and expense burdensome. In the 1970s and 1980s criticism of regulatory administration reached its modern zenith. The network of regulations on businesses had grown dense and complex and many rules were adopted without cost-benefit analysis or only rudimentary studies. Many rules seemed unnecessary, and some appeared pointless or counterproductive. Compliance costs were high—far too high for the benefits (if any) in the eyes of many. Enforcement was also expensive and often involved litigation. Court decisions added to the fragmentation of control over administration and to the difficulties of coordinating regulatory policy. For much of the period, the nation's economy was in a slump, partly attributed to too much regulation. Deregulation and regulatory reform gained political favor. Advocating further regulation, especially at the federal level, was a nonstarter. The attack on regulatory policy was also part of a growing dissatisfaction with public administration in general. Accordingly, many of the problems critics found in regulatory administration were considered generic to all administration. Calls for less regulation *and* smaller government went together. Eventually the desire for regulatory reform helped fuel NPM efforts to reinvent public administration more fully.

Yet there seems to be something ineluctable about the urge or need to regulate. One of the ironies of federal regulatory administration is that deregulation and reform can require new rules. By the end of the 1990s, some 40,000 additional federal rules had been issued. Many of these rules were no doubt technical amendments to existing rules or otherwise limited in scope. Still, the amount of activity alone is daunting. In 2000 alone, federal agencies were said to be working on 4,538 new rules. About 22 percent of these were in the Department of Transportation (539) and the EPA (456).[22]

9.3   Number of Final Rules and Major Final Rules by Calendar Year: 1997–2010

Calendar Year	Number of Final Rules	Number of Major Final Rules
1997	3,960	61
1998	4,420	76
1999	4,373	51
2000	4,113	77
2001	3,454	70
2002	3,608	51
2003	3,785	50
2004	3,703	66
2005	3,352	56
2006	3,083	56
2007	2,971	61
2008	3,117	95
2009	3,492	84
2010	3,271	100

Sources: Curtis W. Copeland and Maeve P. Carey (Congressional Research Service), *REINS Act: Number and Types of "Major Rules" in Recent Years* (Washington, DC: Congressional Research Service, February 24, 2011), p. 5; GAO rules database, available at http://www.gao.gov/fedrules/, as of February 15, 2011.

The table in Box 9.3 shows the number of final rules and major rules promulgated by federal agencies annually from 1997 through 2010. Major rules are defined by the Congressional Review Act of 1996 as effecting or likely to effect the national economy by $100 million annually, to cause or likely to cause major increases in costs or prices for consumers, individual industries, governments, or regions, or have or are likely to have significant adverse effects on U.S. economic competitiveness. The table leaves no doubt that despite significant deregulation in the 1970s and 1980s and ongoing calls for less regulation, rulemaking continues to be a major federal administrative activity.

From a generic perspective, agency rulemaking is essentially the same as congressional lawmaking. Both rules and statutes have the force of law. However, agency heads and rule makers are not elected and, consequently, their rulemaking tends to draw more negative attention than legislation. There is also more rulemaking than legislating, which may make agencies seem more intrusive in the economy and society than Congress. In any event, rulemaking has been subject to a great deal of criticism over the years. The following are the main concerns voiced about regulatory administration.

Regulation Is Expensive

Much regulation is clearly necessary. It saves lives and promotes economic competition, environmental protection, health, and safety. However, it is also expensive. The aggregate cost of regulation to society is unknown. The Heritage Foundation calculated the *new* costs of regulation in 2009 to be $6.2 billion, $4 billion of which was imposed by the Obama administration.[23]

Adding up the budgets of regulatory agencies at all levels of government would not begin to tell the story. Compliance can be expensive and raise costs. In 1999, compliance costs were estimated at $758 billion, which amounted to 8 percent of the nation's GDP. By one set of calculations, these cost an average of $7,400 per household.[24] A more recent study places the total annual cost of federal regulations at $1 trillion.[25] Much of this regulation clearly affects productivity, innovation, and competitiveness. Compliance burdens can present a significant barrier to new firms seeking to enter some industries (and may be favored by established firms for that reason).

Regulation Dampens Economic Performance

It has long been thought that regulation has serious negative impacts on the productivity, growth, and innovation of the economy. In this context, regulation has been criticized for doing and not doing at once. Where it regulates competition by restricting entrance to an industry or by setting rates or fares, regulatory administration has been attacked for protecting weak companies or industries at the expense of consumers and others who use their products. The ICC and the CAB, as noted earlier, were criticized from this perspective. Public utility commissions are frequently criticized on this basis as well. By contrast, the FTC has been accused of being antibusiness, resulting ultimately in harm to the consumer; the Department of Justice's Antitrust Division has been criticized on the grounds that it vacillates between too vigorous and too lackadaisical enforcement, both of which fail to promote or protect economic competition.[26]

In performance, the FCC has been viewed by some as holding back the nation's progress in communications, and the FDA has kept some useful and safe drugs off the market too long and has inhibited the development of new drugs by the pharmaceutical industry. In 1980, one analyst even claimed that the FDA's regulations would have kept penicillin and aspirin off the market if they had just been developed.[27]

Regulation Produces Delay, Extravagant Red Tape, and Paperwork

Another criticism of regulatory administration is that it is too slow and cumbersome. Some examples are legendary; for instance, it took the FDA nine years and a 7,736-page transcript to determine whether peanut butter should contain 90 percent or only 87.5 percent peanut products.[28] For 33 of its first 40 years, the FCC was trying to resolve a dispute between radio stations DOB in Albuquerque and WABC in New York.[29] The EPA's Worker Protection Standard for farmworkers issued in 1992 took 2,529 days (about 7 years) to finalize and even then it was not fully complete.[30] In some cases major responsibility for the delays can be attributed to the private parties involved rather than to the agency, but nonetheless, delay on the part of regulatory agencies can be frustrating. This is especially likely to be the case when an individual or firm requires a license or permission to perform a service, market a product, or open a place of business.

Red tape is endemic to administrative life, and regulatory administration is certainly no exception. Sometimes the agencies create their own red tape. For instance, they write long inspection manuals in obtuse administrative terminology ("bureaucratese") and require their employees, often inspectors, to fill out lengthy forms pertaining to their official activities.

Regulators not only create red tape for themselves, they also thrust a huge and growing paperwork burden on those they regulate. In 1980, the Office of Management and Budget (OMB) estimated that federal rules and requirements created 1.5 *billion* hours of paperwork annually for Americans and others doing business in the United States.[31] By 1994, this burden had more than quadrupled to 6.5 billion hours and was estimated to cost as much as 9 percent of the nation's gross domestic product.[32] By fiscal year 2011, the paperwork burden had reached 9.14 billion hours, up 355 million burden hours from the previous year.[33] Congress has periodically tried to squelch federal administrators' generation of paperwork, though apparently without much success. The Paperwork Reduction Acts of 1980 and 1995 require agencies to publish in the *Federal Register* for public comment notices of their intent to collect information from individuals and businesses. Their forms and other instruments seeking information from the public must be cleared by OMB's Office of Information and Regulatory Affairs (OIRA), which tries to eliminate duplication among agencies and requests for unnecessary information.

Incompetence and Impropriety

Historically, incompetence and impropriety were common in regulatory administration. The regulatory commissions in particular were frequently staffed at the top with political appointees with less than impressive qualifications. As the *Wall Street Journal* put it in 1974, "the Washington regulatory landscape is strewn with old friends of Presidents, unprepared for their assignments and largely uninterested in the industries they regulate."[34] Regulatory commissions were also criticized for developing cozy relationships with those they were charged with regulating. "Incredible love affairs" were said to be "going on between the regulators and the regulated."[35] By calling greater attention to the problems of incompetence and impropriety, the movements toward deregulation and regulatory reform brought considerable improvement, though certainly not perfection. In 2007, it was revealed that since 2002 the heads of the Consumer Product Safety Commission had taken 30 trips costing $60, 000 fully or partially paid by those subject to the agency's regulation. One was an 11-day trip to Hong Kong and China paid for by the American Fireworks Standards Laboratory; other jaunts were to Spain, San Francisco, New Orleans, and Hilton Head Island, SC.[36] Although the ethics of such arrangements are highly questionable, there is still sometimes a trade-off between competence and coziness, especially in the regulation of single industries such as communications, securities, and nuclear power. To be competent, top-level appointees may have to be drawn from the very industries they are charged with regulating. Whenever these appointees appear soft on regulation, they may also create the appearance of being too close to industry.

Overinclusiveness of Regulation

Another criticism of regulatory administration is that there has been a tendency to write overinclusive rules and then to expand them. The problem of overinclusiveness is that it is difficult to write a set of comprehensive rules in advance that can be applied *strictly and reasonably* in a wide variety of circumstances. For instance, consider New York City's effort to regulate as many as 15,000 restaurants. These establishments serve an amazing variety of foods in an astonishing range of settings. Some are among the fanciest in the world; others are rundown take-out shops. Yet all fall under the same rules: Failure to pass inspection is automatic if cold food is more than 45 degrees Fahrenheit or if hot food is less than 140 degrees.[37] It is implausible that food 1 degree too hot or cold that has just been prepared to order in an otherwise hygienic establishment is dangerous; we have all consumed such food with no ill effects in our own kitchens. Not to be outdone, Bergan County, New Jersey, applied regulations for running concessions on public property to a one-man shoeshine stand that had been operating in the county courthouse for 27 years. The regulations required the shoeshine man to submit a competitive bid for the operation, use a cash register, post charges and fees, wear a smock (dark brown or burgundy, knee-length, front pocket, three-quarter sleeves), and carry a million-dollar liability policy! The county was unimpressed by the shoeshine man's protest that "For 27 years not even a woman has gotten a run in her stocking here" and that "No shoeshine man has a cash register."[38] At the federal level, the Oil Protection Act of 1990 applied equally to spills of toxic oils, such as petroleum, and those of nontoxic edible oils—something that aroused the ire of the American Fats and Oils Association, the Institute of Shortening and Edible Oils, the National Fish Meal and Oil Association, the National Renderers Association, the U.S. Canola Association, and other proponents of the Edible Oil Regulatory Reform Act of 1995.[39] Once rules are written there are strong pressures on inspectors to enforce them rigorously, *even if unreasonably*. Failure to enforce rules can be viewed as corrupt—coziness with the regulated. Moreover, if an inspector mistakenly assumes that a rule violation is inconsequential to the safety of workers or the public and a tragedy occurs, the inspector will face many liabilities—moral, legal, and professional. When one considers not just the restaurants in New York but all the workplaces under OSHA's jurisdiction or all those personnel systems under the EEOC's, for example, the problem of overinclusiveness becomes self-evident.

Overinclusiveness is also a product of the **regulatory ratchet** effect.[40] This is the tendency of regulation to be additive. Agencies are likely to spend more time developing new regulations than deleting those that have become obsolete. Fire codes are an example. As new technologies such as sprinkler systems and fire-retardant construction materials are required, no effort may be made to determine whether older approaches such as fire doors are still necessary. It often takes a special initiative, such as the National Performance Review (NPR), to prod agencies to delete outdated rules. This is understandable because, from the agency's point of view, deleting rules is not directly related to the regulatory mission, it can be viewed as backtracking by critics, there is sometimes a possibility that in a remote instance a deleted regulation would have had a positive effect, and, according to some, deleting rules is just plain boring.[41] Noting the problems of overinclusiveness and the ratchet effect, the NPM is particularly eager to redesign regulation so that it involves fewer specific rules and more cooperation on general principles. In 2012, the Obama administration announced that it had joined the effort to reduce rules and their costs by eliminating five regulations that could save the economy $6 billion.[42]

Determining Success

Finally, there is no agreed on standard for levels of success in regulation. Economists prefer to measure success in benefits and costs, but cost-benefit analysis is not always technically feasible or accepted as appropriate. Determining what would happen in the absence of regulation (of a new technology, for example) is often inherently difficult or impossible, as is assessing the degree of risk involved in doing things one way or another. One may anticipate that a landlord strapped for cash might defer elevator maintenance, but who would expect a major passenger airline to skimp on maintenance to the point of flying unsafe planes? Yet this is apparently what Alaska Airlines did in 2000 before grounding its planes in the wake of a fatal crash.[43] Moreover, the costs of regulation are sometimes economic whereas the benefits are social. For example, how can we determine what it is worth to us collectively to have peace of mind for our safety when we use an elevator, take an airplane, or bite into a hamburger? The FDA may inhibit the development and marketing of new drugs, but it also has done a great deal to assure that the drugs available to us are not dangerous. We may be able to ascertain the costs of the EEOC's enforcement of antidiscrimination regulations, but how can we measure the benefits gained in the form of fairer treatment for minorities, disabled persons, and women? OSHA regulations are expensive, but they do save lives and prevent injuries. At some point we may agree that they are *too* expensive. At some other point the society might favor spending more. But how can we arrive at an acceptable cost-benefit ratio in between?

Regulation, like many other aspects of public administration, confronts the society with some difficult moral problems. If we agree to antipollution regulation that adds $500 per car, perhaps it is because as a population we are asking the government to require us to do what we believe is good for us, society, and future generations. If this is true, we are recognizing that we will not do it as individuals, suggesting that we believe that for any single individual, in the absence of cooperation by others, the costs would be too great for the benefits obtained. This is the basic "collective action" problem. Some benefits to the society require widespread participation or cooperation of individuals whose personal economic incentive is not to join a group effort. (Why be the only one in the country whose car does not contribute to pollution? Why not be the only one whose car does pollute? What tangible difference will it make?) But if the benefits depend on nearly universal cooperation or compliance or relate to some long-term future state of affairs, how will we evaluate the regulatory problem? Clearly, cost-benefit analysis will not be wholly adequate, especially when assessed in per capita terms (e.g., the cost per vehicle equipped with antipollution devices and the benefits to the owner). Even a solid analysis of what the average American voter might be willing to pay for regulations, such as those dealing with conservation and the environment, is unlikely to give adequate weight to the interests of future generations. Nor do the aggregate costs alone tell us much more than that regulation is expensive.

Concern with the level of compliance raises a related problem. The marginal cost of enforcing regulations may often rise as administrators approach obtaining universal (total) compliance. This is true, for example, where regulation involves inspections of a large number of sites, some of which are small (as in restaurant inspection) and possibly remote as well. The marginal benefits, whether calculable or not, of obtaining greater compliance are likely to decline when the few recalcitrant rule evaders are small establishments with a limited capacity to do serious harm. A point might be reached where the marginal costs of more enforcement clearly exceed the marginal benefits. But this would not necessarily be a compelling argument for curtailing enforcement efforts. Legal principles, such as equal application of the law, social concepts of fairness and risk elimination, and the enforcement interest in deterrence, might well lead to the conclusion that an effort should be made to enforce the regulations in *all* the cases to which they apply.

The difficulties involved in calculating benefits and costs require caution in the application of cost-benefit analysis. Underlying assumptions, putative causal connections, price tags, and ignored costs should be considered with care. For example, in 2002 the EPA offered two cost-benefit analyses, based on different assumptions, of a proposed rule to reduce harmful airborne particulate pollution from snowmobiles, all-terrain vehicles, forklifts, and electric generators. The first analysis valued human life at $6.1 million. The second set it at $3.7 million for those 70 years old and younger and at $2.3 million for those over 70. Other differences in the analyses dealt with short-term and long-term effects of inhaling the exhaust particles. Using the first analysis, the projected benefits by 2030 were $77 billion, a figure that came all the way down to $8.8 billion in the second analysis. Former OIRA Administrator John Graham explained why two analyses may be better than one: "Together, the

9.4   ESTIMATES OF THE TOTAL ANNUAL BENEFITS AND COSTS OF MAJOR FEDERAL RULES BY AGENCY, OCTOBER 1, 2002–SEPTEMBER 30, 2012 (BILLIONS OF DOLLARS)

Agency	Number of Rules	Benefits	Costs
Department of Agriculture	5	$0.9–$1.3	$0.8–$1.2
Department of Energy	12	$8.2–$15.3	$3.6–$5.5
Department of Health and Human Services	19	$16.6–$40.2	$2.4–$5.2
Department of Homeland Security	2	$0–$0.5	$0.1–$0.3
Department of Housing and Urban Development	1	$2.3	$0.9
Department of Justice	4	$1.8–$4.0	$0.8–$1.0
Department of Labor	8	$7.3–$21.4	$2.3–$5.1
Department of Transportation (DOT)	29	$16.2–$27.6	$7.9–$14.1
Environmental Protection Agency (EPA)	32	$112.0–$637.6	$30.4–$36.5
Joint EPA & DOT	3	$27.3–$49.6	$7.3–$14.0
Total	**115**	**$192.7–$799.7**	**$56.6–$83.7**

Source: White House: http://www.whitehouse.gov/sites/default/files/omb/inforeg/2013_cb/draft_2013_cost_benefit_report.pdf.

two estimates provide an indication of the scientific uncertainty about these difficult issues. If only one of the two estimates were presented, the regulator and the public would be given *a false sense of precision about the science and economics*" underlying the analyses.[44] Taking a dimmer view of cost-benefit analysis, the executive director of the Clean Air Trust, an environmental organization, noted, "You can change five to six assumptions and you get a radically different number."[45] Note how widely the figures for both benefits and costs range in the table in Box 9.4.

Logically, cost-benefit analysis should often be complemented by **comparative risk analysis,** which considers whether a proposed rule will cause individuals to change their behavior in ways that create greater risks to their welfare. For example, in the 1990s the FAA considered requiring specially designed safety seats for all children under the age of two flying on scheduled U.S. commercial airlines. The point was to prevent death and injury in air crashes and severe air turbulence. Critics of the proposal offered a simple risk analysis that indicated that safety seats would actually lead to more infant deaths and injuries. Why? Because air travel would become more expensive for families flying with under-two-year-olds. No longer able to hold these children on their laps, they would have to purchase a full seat on the airline, to which the safety seat would be strapped. The higher cost of flying would lead many families to drive to their destinations—which statistically is much more dangerous than flying. Some data suggested that young children were *16* times more likely to die in automobile accidents than in plane crashes.[46] In short, regulation can lead to compensatory behavior that is as dangerous as or more dangerous than the activity being regulated.

Because of their imprecision and uncertainty, approaches such as cost-benefit analysis and risk analysis are often augmented by psychological, social, legal, and political perspectives. Government officials, interest groups, and substantial numbers of political activists argue that regulation should reduce individual anxiety and risk concerning the safety of foods, drugs, vehicles, jobs, motels, hotels, office buildings, elevators, new technologies, and so forth. They also believe that it is partly the job of regulatory administration to protect individuals' lives even when those individuals are reluctant to do so themselves, as in the case of mandatory seat belt and motorcycle helmet laws. This is partly because other people are socially dependent on or socially connected to these individuals and therefore, it is argued, serious injuries or deaths will adversely affect the society. For example, if the use of seat belts can save the lives of parents, should they be optional in view of the social costs of orphanhood? From a political angle, many favor regulation for the safety of groups in the population who might otherwise be especially vulnerable. The regulation of child labor and day care and elder care facilities falls into this category. In this sense, regulation is a microcosm of all public administration. The question it addresses concerns the type of society we want government to help establish and maintain.

◆◆ DEREGULATION AND REGULATORY REFORM

Deregulation

The problems involved in regulatory administration prompted a broad movement toward deregulation and regulatory reform that began in the 1970s and continued into the mid-1990s, when it began to sputter and reverse course. Deregulation is usually supported by one or more of four basic arguments (other than that the cost of regulation is too high). One is that free markets can provide more benefits to the society than can regulated ones. This view applies primarily to surrogate-market regulation and some aspects of market-functioning and employment regulation. Deregulation of the airlines and that of trucking industries are leading contemporary examples, though their success is a matter of dispute.[47]

A second argument raised by those in favor of deregulation is that liability law can be used to assure safety in many aspects of life. For example, the potential of suits against automobile manufacturers can provide them with a strong incentive to design safe cars. The same logic would apply to the drugs produced by pharmaceutical companies. Proponents of this approach believe that once the incentive is strong enough, the private sector can be innovative and responsible in designing safe products and in developing safe and healthful work processes. And it can do so without having to deal with the unproductive consequences of overinclusive regulatory rules and red tape. However, even if one accepts this view, there may be a dispute as to whether liability laws need to be rewritten in some areas to provide strong enough incentives to market only safe products.

Another argument advanced in favor of deregulation is that there is great potential for the private sector to engage in self-regulation. For example, many firms and unions do employ safety inspectors and take an active interest in establishing and maintaining healthful and safe conditions in the workplace. In some cases, public law may require enterprises to engage in self-regulation, as in the hazardous waste disposal business, trucking, and the manufacture of intravenous solutions by pharmaceutical firms.[48]

Finally, proponents of deregulation sometimes argue that if business enterprises were required to disclose information relevant to the safety, healthfulness, and security of their products, services, or other offerings, the public could act as its own inspectors. Food labeling for calories, fat, carbohydrates, sodium, protein, vitamins, and minerals is now ubiquitous due to government regulations. Tobacco companies print the tar and nicotine content of their cigarettes. Used-car dealers can be required to reveal known defects in the cars they sell. Credit agreements indicate the yearly interest rate, and stock and banking offerings are subject to a number of mandatory disclosure regulations. In other words, the argument goes, give customers enough information and they will force firms to act responsibly.

Formal and Informal Rule Making

Regardless of the desirability and political feasibility of deregulation, virtually all knowledgeable observers agree that regulatory administration can be improved. Federal regulatory reforms since the 1970s have sought greater coordination, centralized OMB review of agency rule making agendas and proposed rules, more thoroughgoing assessment of the impact of proposed regulations and possible alternatives, deletion of obsolete rules and promulgation of fewer new ones, greater emphasis on cooperative compliance, and consensual rule making. For the most part, reforms were aimed at augmenting the rule making provisions contained in the Administrative Procedure Act of 1946 (APA). As noted earlier and in Chapter 2, the APA provides for two main types of legislative (also known as substantive) rule making: informal and formal. Informal rule making requires that proposed rules be published in the *Federal Register* for public comment. Litigation challenging new rules has made it standard practice for agencies to docket such comments and respond to them in some fashion. All final rules are also published in the *Federal Register,* along with an explanation of the basis for them. Formal rule making is much more procedurally oriented and complicated. It involves quasi-judicial hearings, a showing that the proposed rule is supported by substantial evidence in the record of the proceedings as a whole, cross-examination, and a legal prohibition on one-sided (ex parte) communications with the agency decision maker.

The APA leaves the choice of rule making formats up to the agencies. They are unlikely to engage in formal rule making unless required to do so by another statute. The APA also allows agencies to dispense with informal rule making when they have "good cause." This provision permits them to issue direct and interim final rules. Direct final rules go into effect at a specified future date unless adverse comments are filed. Interim final rules are immediately effective but may be withdrawn or revised after adverse comments are filed.

From the reformers' perspectives, the main shortcomings of the APA's rule making provisions are that they do not require agencies to meet a substantive policy test, such as that the benefits outweigh the costs, or provide a mechanism for coordinating rule making government-wide. Under the APA, it is possible for agencies to work at cross-purposes and issue conflicting rules. Reformers also favored augmenting the APA's informal rule making with hearings, though less elaborate ones than those required by formal rule making, and by encouraging the agencies to negotiate their rules with the entities most affected by them.

Beginning with President Nixon and continuing into the Obama administration, presidents have required executive branch agencies to address specific values in their rule making, such as costs and benefits or impact on families, federalism, and environmental justice and sustainability, and submit proposed regulations to OMB or some other unit for review before initiating APA rule making proceedings.[49] The independent regulatory commissions are largely exempt from such requirements because, as a matter of constitutional law, they are not in the executive branch.[50] However, they may voluntarily comply. Despite this and other limits on presidential power (discussed in Chapter 2), OMB now plays major procedural and substantive roles in structuring the analysis and content of much agency rule making to make it compatible with the president's policy objectives.

President Clinton's Executive Order 12866 (1993), which is still in effect as augmented by Executive Order 13563 issued by President Obama in 2011, encapsulated much of the reformers' thinking with regard to agency regulatory action. It listed the following 12 principles, which can serve as a useful guide to a great deal of administrative activity.

1. Identify the problems addressed.
2. Assess the contributions, if any, of existing regulations to those problems.
3. Identify alternatives to regulations.
4. Consider risks.
5. Assess cost-effectiveness.
6. Weigh costs and benefits.
7. Base decisions on the best obtainable information.
8. Assess alternatives among regulatory possibilities.
9. Seek the views of state, local, and tribal governments.
10. Avoid inconsistency.
11. Impose the least burden on society.
12. Write regulations in simple, understandable language.

Negotiated Rule Making

Like other reforms, the Negotiated Rulemaking Act of 1990 (NRMA) is an effort to improve the quality of rules. The idea is that rules negotiated with interested parties will be timely, better reflect the needs of the regulated as well as those of the regulators, and result in fewer lawsuits. Rule making committees, generally limited to 25 members, negotiate the rules with the aid of a facilitator, mediator, or similar functionary. Unanimity is required. The agency is a participant but ultimately retains control of the outcome because negotiated rules are subject to the notice and comment requirements of informal rule making under the APA. To date, experience has been mixed for speeding up the rule making process and reducing litigation.[51]

The regulatory reforms of the past four decades or so now enjoy broad congressional, judicial, and bipartisan support. Consequently, it appears likely that change in the near term will continue to emphasize coordination, simplification, better analysis, reduction of unnecessary regulation, and cost-consciousness. However, as Box 9.1 strongly suggests, deregulation seems to have run its course—for now. The collapse of much of the savings and loan industry in the 1980s, the massive 6.5 million Bridgestone/Firestone tire recall in 2000, the deceptive accounting involved in the spectacular Enron bankruptcy in 2001, and California's disastrous experiment in deregulating electric power challenge some of the fundamental premises on which deregulation is based. More recently, in the wake of the 2008 economic crisis, the Dodd-Frank Wall Street Reform and Consumer Protection Act of 2010, billed as the most sweeping reform of the financial services industry since the 1930s, created the Financial Stability Oversight Council and Office of Financial Research in the Department of the Treasury and an independent Bureau of Consumer Financial Protection. All three new administrative units play a role in regulating the financial services industry. Within this general framework of regulatory reform and caution regarding deregulation, the various perspectives on public administration offer different visions of what to emphasize in regulatory administration.

◆✦ PERSPECTIVES ON REGULATORY ADMINISTRATION

The Traditional Managerial Perspective

As in other areas, the traditional managerial perspective on regulatory administration emphasizes the values of effectiveness, efficiency, and economy. In regulation, effectiveness has often been considered the avoidance of a major failure viewed by the public as a crisis or scandal. As James Q. Wilson observes, for agencies such as the EPA, OSHA, and the FDA, "a major scandal would be a dramatic loss of life or catastrophic injury among people nominally protected by the decisions of the agency."[52] The Nuclear Regulatory Commission was scandalized by the Three Mile Island catastrophe in 1979. The FAA was severely criticized in 1996 after 110 people were killed in a ValuJet crash in

Florida. For the FDIC, failure would come in the form of a run on insured banks. The SEC's performance was brought into question in the late 1980s and early 1990s in the wake of a number of major scandals involving leading Wall Street firms and figures, again in 2001 with the collapse of Enron and 2008 when its failure to catch the huge Bernard Madoff Ponzi scheme became clear.

But how can regulatory administration be managed to avoid scandals and crises while also remaining efficient and economical?

First, the effort to be effective dictates a conservative approach to rule enforcement and decision making. There is a strong tendency toward strict—even rigid—enforcement of the rules. This is because any exercise of discretion or departure from the rules that results in scandal or crisis will be severely criticized by the legislature, the media, and other political actors. It may trigger legal liabilities. An agency's failure to enforce its own rules that results in tragedy may even bring about a thorough administrative reorganization of its functions. Conversely, even if a crisis develops, when an agency has followed its own rules and when those rules are pursuant to legislation and have been previously tested in the courts, the agency may claim that it has done all it could within its power in the face of an unforeseeable event or future. It may turn the crisis into a request for greater authority so that it can handle such matters in the future. The FDA, for example, was given greater authority over the marketing of drugs as a result of the sulfanilamide scandal in the 1930s and the thalidomide scandal in the early 1960s, even though the latter, which resulted in the birth of children with misshapen limbs (phocomelia, or "seal limbs"), was mostly confined to Europe and Canada. If nothing else, strictly following the rules tends to absolve an agency of any taint of corruption or inconsistency.

Second, as noted earlier, there will be a strong tendency to avoid deleting rules even though it may appear that they are outmoded. Just as rules tend to be overinclusive, rescinding the ones that seem unnecessary may mistakenly overlook a single facility, work process, or economic relationship where the rule would make a difference. Should a scandal or crisis result because of the agency's dropping of the rule, the agency would be subject to massive criticism. When the FDA contemplated redirecting its emphasis in regulating the food industry from poor sanitation to chemical and microbiological health hazards, it was severely criticized by *Consumer Reports* articles on the grounds that it had "casually dismissed" the problem of "filth" (see Box 9.5).[53]

Third, the development of new rules and the application of new policies will be slow. Major departures from past approaches, such as widespread and immediate deregulation, are likely to be avoided because the results may be unpredictable.

The major difficulty with cautious approaches from a managerial standpoint is that they can undercut efficiency and economy. Strict enforcement of additive rules and conservatism in responding to rapidly changing conditions and technologies can lead to the expenditure of an agency's human and economic resources on aspects of regulation that make no real difference in terms of safety, environmental quality, economic competition, and so forth.

Pursuant to Title 21, *Code of Federal Regulations*, Part 110.110, the Food and Drug Administration established maximum levels of natural or unavoidable defects in food for human use that present no health hazard. The significance of the defects is aesthetic, and the levels are set in recognition that it is economically impractical to harvest or process raw products totally free of the defects listed.

The mixing or blending of food with a defect at or above the action level is not permitted. Food at or above the defect level is regarded as adulterated and subject to enforcement action under the Food, Drug, and Cosmetic Act. The list is updated from time to time through notices in the *Federal Register*. The following are among the foods listed. What did you eat today? Will you eat it tomorrow?

Product	Action Level*	Defect Source
Apple butter	4 rodent hairs/100 grams	Postharvest, processing
Asparagus	10% spears or pieces with 6 beetle eggs and/or sacs; 40 thrips/100 grams; insects (whole or equivalent) 3 mm or longer aggregate to 7 mm/100 grams	Preharvest infestation
Berries (frozen raspberries, blackberries, etc.)	4 insect larvae/500 grams; 10 insects/500 grams	Preharvest infestation
Chocolate and chocolate liquor	60 insect fragments/100 grams; 1 rodent hair/ 100 grams	Postharvest, processing
Cocoa beans	10 mg mammalian excreta/pound	Postharvest, processing
Cocoa powder	75 insect fragments/50 grams; 2 rodent hairs/ 50 grams or 4 rodent hairs/any subsample	Postharvest, processing
Coffee beans	10% insect infested or damaged; 1 live insect	Preharvest and postharvest, processing
Condimental seeds (excludes fennel and sesame seeds)	3 mg mammalian excreta/pound	Postharvest, processing
Corn, sweet canned	2 or more 3 mm long corn ear worm or borer larvae	Preharvest infestation
Oregano:		
Ground	1250 insect fragments/10 grams	Preharvest and postharvest, processing
	5 rodent hairs/10 grams	Postharvest, processing
Crushed	300 insect fragments/10 grams; 2 rodent hairs/ 10 grams	Preharvest and postharvest, processing
Peanut butter	30 insect fragments/100 grams;	Preharvest and postharvest, processing
	1 rodent hair/100 grams	Postharvest, processing
Pizza sauce	30 fly eggs/100 grams; 15 fly eggs and 1 maggot/ 100 grams; 2 maggots/100 grams	Preharvest and postharvest, processing
Tomato juice	10 fly eggs/100 grams, or 5 fly eggs and 1 maggot/ 100 grams, 2 maggots/100 grams	Preharvest and postharvest, processing
Tomato puree	20 fly eggs/100 grams, or 10 fly eggs and 1 maggot/ 100 grams; or 2 maggots/100 grams	Preharvest and postharvest, processing
Tomatoes, canned	10 fly eggs/500 grams or 5 fly eggs and 1 maggot/ 500 grams; 2 maggots/500 grams	Preharvest and postharvest, processing

*Numbers are averages and/or averages per subsamples.

Source: Department of Health and Human Services, Food and Drug Administration, Washington, DC 20204 (May 1995).

Enforcement of the rules for their own sake is the essence of a bureaucratic approach, in the worst sense. This is the NPM's major complaint against the traditional managerial approach to regulatory enforcement.

The New Public Management Approach to Regulation

The NPM's general approach toward regulation stands in stark contrast to the traditional managerial model. It rejects the proposition "that a ruthless and efficient investigation and enforcement capability will produce compliance through the mechanism of deterrence."[54] This "classic enforcement mentality" must be replaced by a compliance-oriented culture that:

1. Views segments of the public less as a regulated community than as partners who will engage in collaborative risk assessment and cooperative risk abatement
2. Emphasizes customer service for regulatees, which includes setting up single points of contact and one-stop service for them
3. Focuses on impacts and effectiveness rather than outputs and efficiency by setting targets for compliance
4. Defines the unit of work as problems or risks instead of incidents or violations
5. Casts off the myth of universal enforcement in favor of dealing with what is feasible, is most important, and presents the greatest risks
6. Uses a range of tactics to resolve problems, including education, strengthening regulatees' commitment and sense of responsibility, working with other government agencies at all levels, persuasion, and negotiation
7. Strategically selects enforcement targets to strengthen compliance, prompt the building of partnerships, and obtain judicial backing for enforcement efforts
8. Retains the capacity to deal effectively with the worst offenders so that it never appears possible to get away with serious violations[55]

Perhaps the most striking aspect of NPM regulatory enforcement is its willingness to trust regulatees and become partners with them. The NPR told the following story about a program called "Maine 200":

> Following [traditional OSHA] rules, [Bill] Freeman's inspectors would move into a company, spend three months on-site, another three months preparing reports, and then anywhere from six months to two years in court. And when all was said and done, they'd find themselves telling the company to do the same things they'd told them years before. . . .
>
> Fed up with getting nowhere, Freeman went to the 200 companies that had the highest injury rates in the state [of Maine] and offered them a deal: you and your workers draw up a safety program that meets the law's objectives, and we'll stop playing "Gotcha!" No more months-long "wall-to-wall" inspections, no more "ignorance is no excuse" enforcement, no more by-the-book fines. We'll stop being cops. We'll be partners instead—you, your workers, and OSHA. And any time you need help, we'll be there.

Industry's response was immediate and positive. All but two of the 200 signed up. Employer/worker safety teams in the participating firms are identifying—and fixing—*14 times* more hazards than OSHA's inspectors ever could have found, including hazards for which the agency didn't even have regulations. . . .

The new program is working so well that in two years, the group's injury rates dropped 35 percent.[56]

Nevertheless, when the NPR expanded the award-winning Maine 200 experiment into a nationwide Cooperative Compliance Program, it ran into stiff opposition from the U.S. Chamber of Commerce, the National Association of Manufacturers, and other business groups. These opponents claimed that OSHA's checklist of voluntary standards was "ambush rulemaking" because they had not been subject to normal APA notice and comment procedures. Moreover, they alleged that the program was "more like coercion than cooperation" because it was widely believed that firms that failed to join the program "voluntarily" would be subject to punitive wall-to-wall OSHA inspections. The program was discontinued after the District of Columbia Circuit Court of Appeals agreed that it was illegal. The court's ruling illustrates one of reinvention's pitfalls—even well-intentioned, cost-effective measures must be subordinated to preexisting administrative law that seeks to promote other values, including the protection of individuals and organizations from arbitrary, capricious, discriminatory, or illegal administrative action.[57] Despite OSHA's setback with the Cooperative Compliance Program, cooperation and partnership remain viable strategies in a variety of contexts.

Another key feature of NPM regulatory enforcement is the substitution of discretion for rules. The focus is on results, and compliance with rules is considered of secondary or lesser importance. The NPR happily reported that, under heavy pressure from President Clinton, 35 agencies reversed the regulatory ratchet by eliminating 16,000 *Federal Register* pages of outdated or unnecessary rules and by rewriting about 40 percent of their remaining rules to "conform to a new regulatory spirit of trust and cooperation."[58] Agencies also deleted 640,000 pages of internal regulations.[59]

The NPM raised new questions and bears careful watching over a long term. The results of new initiatives, such as those reported in the Maine 200 experiment, may turn out to be "Hawthorne effects" that reflect the positive impact of communication rather than the new enforcement model's direct impact (see Chapter 4). The partnership model may not be inclusive enough to recognize all aspects of the public interest, as in the case of the Cooperative Compliance Program. Critics have also charged that the Customs Service's focus on partnerships led it to weaken its efforts at interdicting illegal drugs.[60] Viewing discretionary law enforcement as a positive good may weaken commitment to the rule of law in a society already plagued by high crime rates and evasion of regulatory rules. Discretionary enforcement also makes it more difficult to hold public administrators accountable, and it expands the potential for corruption (see Chapter 12). Any enforcement model based on trust must also recognize the possibility that some partners are not trustworthy.

Much regulatory administration is aimed at preventing deception, often a real danger to the public where the safety of food, drugs, products, and technologies is involved. Finally, the NPM model does conflict at some points with values central to the political and legal perspectives on regulation.

Collaborative Governance

Because regulation and service are often mixed together, building on the NPM's overall approach to enforcement, collaborative governance might be appropriate where self-regulation is appropriate. In many respects, the FDA partners with the pharmaceutical industry on which it depends substantially to promote drug safety. Nonprofit agencies collaborating with government in the field of social welfare, such as at risk youth and adoption services, also engage in self-regulation. However, when enforcement goes beyond self-regulation and involves individuals or organizational entities that are the subject of administrative regulations, the utility of collaborative arrangements is limited.

The Political Approach to Regulatory Administration

In the not-so-distant past, it was common for "political hacks" to be appointed to regulatory commissions. Their chief ethos appears to have been to seek reappointment by avoiding enemies rather than by making friends.[61] In practice, this dictated not upsetting the status quo. In consequence, many agencies did seem to be in the last phase of the traditional "life cycle," that of being captured by the industries ostensibly being regulated. Where this was the case, many of the politicos were assured cushy jobs in the industry after they stepped off the regulatory commissions.

Today, however, the situation is different. The movement toward deregulation and regulatory reform, as well as the scrutiny of regulatory activities by public interest groups, legislators, and the media has transformed the political approach toward regulatory administration. Three key values have emerged.

One is greater attention to the full range of constituencies of a regulatory program, or expanded representation. In the past, after the life cycle went through its first phase, the constituency of the regulatory agency was often considered to be the regulatees. Today, however, the public, or segments of it, may often be viewed as an important constituency of the regulatory agency. Sometimes the public is presumed to be represented by public interest groups such as Common Cause and Public Citizen. In other cases, the agencies pay more attention to their mandates to serve the public interest. For example, the FCC, long faulted for promoting anticompetitive practices in the broadcast industry and being oblivious to the quality of radio and TV programming, came under pressure to use its influence to improve "kid-vid" (children's TV programming). In other areas, segments of the public, such as the American Association of Retired Persons, have become politically mobilized to make sure that regulatory administration relevant to their interests, such as care centers, does serve their needs rather than primarily the desires of the regulated industries. Consumers' groups have also mobilized in this way to gain greater protection of their interests. An important corollary of paying greater attention to the public is the establishment of procedural mechanisms for public participation in administrative decision making. In the past this was especially pronounced in the regulation at the state level. Today federal agencies use electronic rule making (e-rule making), which greatly facilitates the dissemination of proposed rules and public comment on them.[62]

William Gormley found the emphasis on public participation and representation so new and far-reaching that he called it a "revolution." In his words,

> The most striking finding to emerge from this review of the literature is that public representation in state regulation can promote substantive representation. Citizens' groups have effectively participated in coastal zone management hearings and water quality planning hearings. Ombudsmen have successfully resolved complaints by nursing home patients for whom the regulatory process has been disappointing. Proxy advocates have effectively championed consumer interests in rate relief and more liberal disconnecting policies.
>
> These successes are all the more remarkable because they have involved different settings, strategies, and goals. In environmental regulation, citizens' groups have converted community support and political pressure into formidable weapons. In nursing home regulation, ombudsmen have used technical expertise and jawboning to secure service responsiveness. In utility regulation, proxy advocates have utilized technical expertise, a knowledge of administrative law, and adversarial strategies to promote policy responsiveness.[63]

A second emergent value in the political approach toward regulatory administration is the importance placed on forward-looking assessments of the probable impact of rules or actions on interests that government seeks to protect. Such impact assessments go beyond benefit-cost analyses and have been used to protect the environment, the American family, federalism, and other concerns as well as to promote environmental justice. Perhaps the best single example is the National Environmental Policy Act of 1969 (NEPA). The act cuts across a wide range of federal administrative activities, including regulation. The purposes are to promote a "productive and enjoyable harmony between man and his environment," to "eliminate damage to the environment and biosphere and stimulate the health and welfare of man," and to "enrich the understanding of the ecological systems and natural resources important to the nation." It requires administrative agencies to develop "environmental impact" statements. These statements must discuss any proposed action having a substantial impact on the environment. They describe possible adverse environmental effects, alternatives, long-term consequences, and irreversible and irretrievable commitments. The impact statements are to be made available to federal, state, and local agencies dealing with environmental matters; to the president; to the federal Council on Environmental Quality; and to the public. Some of these statements can be highly elaborate and expensive, such as the Department of the Interior's report on the trans-Alaska pipeline, which filled nine volumes and cost $25 million to prepare.[64] Although such a vast amount of information can be forbidding, many political actors, such as legislators, their staff, and public interest groups, frequently devote enough attention to environmental impact statements to assure a greater degree of administrative accountability. The judiciary has also been active in reviewing procedures under NEPA. When agencies' procedures include public hearings, the impact statements may become the basis for informed public participation in regulatory administration. In addition, the federal judiciary has been friendly to suits by individuals seeking to compel agencies to fulfill their obligations under the act.

The forward-looking impact assessment model used by NEPA has been adopted in a wide range of federal statutes and executive orders. For instance, the Regulatory Flexibility Act of 1980 requires agencies to assess the impact of regulatory measures on small businesses and other entities and to minimize those that are adverse. In 1996, the Small Business Regulatory Enforcement Fairness Act went further by requiring OSHA and EPA to solicit perspectives from small governments, businesses, and other organizations. The Paperwork Reduction Acts seek to reduce the "burden hours" of regulatory paperwork. Presidents have required agencies to assess the impact of proposed regulations on American families, federalism, and environmental justice and sustainability. The 1998 Assessment of Federal Regulations and Policies on Families Act mandates that agencies develop "family policy assessments" to determine whether their proposed actions will strengthen or erode family stability, safety, marital commitment, parental authority, independence from government, and income.

At the state and local levels, environmental impact statements have fostered a good deal of citizen participation. Much of this takes the form of the NIMBY (not-in-my-backyard) and NOPE (not on planet earth) syndromes, in which participation is aimed at preventing undesirable public activities from being located in one's neighborhood, town, county, state, region, or anywhere. Nevertheless, even NIMBY and NOPE are forms of grassroots participation.

At the federal level, a third value of the contemporary political approach is to subject agency rules to substantive congressional review. The logic behind such review is clear. Because Congress delegates its legislative authority to agencies to make rules, it ought to be able to negate those that are not in keeping with its intent. Proposals for some kind of congressional review go back at least as far as the 1940s. Michigan adopted legislative review in 1944, and many states have followed suit.[65]

Congress set up a process for reviewing agency rules in the Small Business Regulatory Enforcement Fairness Act of 1996,[66] a section of which is called the Congressional Review Act. So far there have been very few serious congressional efforts to block agency rules through the review process. However, the political significance of congressional review may lie less in the formal disapproval of rules than in the likelihood that the review process strengthens the influence of committees and subcommittees in dealing with agencies. Rule writers put a great deal of time and effort into rulemaking. With formal legislative review in place, they are more likely to maintain open communication with the relevant committees and their staffs to avoid "late hits" that nullify their work.

The Legal Approach to Regulatory Administration

Regulatory administration in the United States has been highly legalistic in its approach, processes, and organization. The legalistic quality of regulatory administration is understandable, because regulation affects the rights of individuals, groups such as labor unions, and business enterprises. It also concerns the use and disposition of their property, including intangible property such as trademarks. Additionally, regulatory rules constrain the policies and operations of other administrative agencies and subnational political jurisdictions. Like the managerial and political approaches, the legalistic perspective places a distinct emphasis on certain values.

Adversary Procedure

At the stage of deciding how regulatory rules should be enforced, the legalistic approach tends to favor adjudication, which places the agency or one party against another in an **adversary proceeding.** This follows from the view that regulation involves the definition of rights and obligations pursuant to statutes or agency rules. However, it has two important consequences that distinguish it from other approaches to regulatory administration.

First, the legal approach depends on the *building of cases* for adjudication. This is true even though many conflicts are settled by consent prior to going to formal hearings or court. Building a record entails uncovering violations. This places the agency in an adversarial role in relation to the individuals, groups, or firms it is investigating. Whereas the managerial and political approaches often tend to view regulatory administration as oriented toward solving problems, the adversarial approach of the legal perspective tends to view it as developing, documenting, and winning cases. Moreover, in the adversarial mode, the agency, or part of it, becomes an *advocate* for a perspective. Consequently, it may emphasize the information that supports its case and downplay information or reasoning to the contrary. From the point of view of those being regulated, this can be extremely frustrating. They are usually seeking to run an economic enterprise profitably and within the law rather than seeking to build a record to protect themselves from regulatory adjudication.

Second, the legal approach tends to favor relatively simple conduct cases in which one party or the agency alleges that another has violated the law. It tends to shy away from the complicated structural cases that rest on theory and often depend on novel interpretations of the law. Conduct cases fit the adjudicatory process better; simple conduct cases enable the agency to develop a strong record of winning.

Neutrality and the Administrative Law Judge

At the level of adjudication, the legal approach relies on the adversary proceeding before an impartial administrative law judge, similar functionary, or court. In practice, the neutrality of the administrative law judge stands in stark contrast to the traditional managerial emphasis on control through hierarchy, the NPM's effort to form cooperative partnerships, and the political perspective's stress on accountability.

Due Process Protection

The rights of the private party being charged with a violation or being sued will be protected through a set of formal procedural requirements. Such parties will often have constitutional protections at the stage in which the agency is gathering information and building its case. For instance, searches, wiretaps, bugging, and the surveillance of mail will be controlled by constitutional standards, although with the proper restrictions against abuse, they may be allowable. If the agency decides to press the case, the regulated parties must be given adequate notice of the charges against them and the agency's proposed action. Normally, the parties will be given an opportunity to respond either in writing or orally. If the matter is serious enough, a hearing is likely to be afforded at some point; the regulated party may also have a right to take the case to court for judicial review of the agency's behavior and decision making. At either the administrative hearing stage or in court, the party will have the right to be represented by counsel, though generally not at the agency's expense. Many of these rights are spelled out in the APA, as amended. At the state level, similar provisions apply.

Reasonableness

At the level of determination of the outcome of the case, the legal approach will emphasize fairness not only of procedure but also in the result. This often involves a judicial assessment of the reasonableness of the agency's action. From the late 1930s to the 1970s, the judiciary seemed far more concerned with whether a matter was under an agency's jurisdiction and whether proper procedures were followed than with the quality of the agency's decision in its substantive content. Since the 1970s, however, in an effort to protect the rights and property of individual parties and check abuses of administrative discretion, the judiciary has been more inclined to question the logic and substance of the agency's decision. This is called the "hard look" approach. It applies to the content of rules and decisions to take action. For instance, in *Citizens to Preserve Overton Park v. Volpe* (1971), the Supreme Court authorized federal district courts to conduct a "substantial inquiry" into the facts and logic on which administrative decisions are made.[67] In the benzene case, discussed in Chapter 7, the Court found that the agency involved, OSHA, had failed to provide scientific support for its regulatory rule.

Beginning in the 1980s, property rights have been the focus of cases dealing with "regulatory takings." The Constitution's protection of private property rights in the Fifth and Fourteenth Amendments prohibits depriving individuals of their property without due process or just compensation. In several cases the Supreme Court held that zoning or environmental regulations may so severely limit the use of private property that they effectively take it from the owners.[68] In *Dolan v. City of Tigard* (1994) the Court placed a significant burden of persuasion on governments when they issue building permits containing conditions that interfere with property rights.[69]

Although the overall direction of judicial review of administrative action since the 1960s has been to take a harder look at the reasonableness of agencies' rules and adjudicative decisions, there are also some relatively clear limits on how much judges can require. In *Vermont Yankee Nuclear Power Corporation v. Natural Resources Defense Council* (1978), the Supreme Court held that the courts should not force agencies to engage in rule making procedures more elaborate than the minimum requirements of the Administrative Procedure Act.[70] In *Chevron v. Natural Resources Defense Council* (1984), the Court held that the judiciary should accept reasonable interpretations of statutes by agencies rather than substitute other plausible (and presumably equally reasonable) ways of reading them.[71] The Court limited the "Chevron doctrine" in *United States v. Mead Corporation* (2001) to cases in which Congress has clearly delegated its legislative authority to an agency to make rules having the force of law and the agency has engaged in rule making proceedings.[72] In other circumstances, under *Mead,* the agencies' statutory interpretation is entitled to less judicial deference. In *City of Arlington, Texas v. Federal Communications Commission* (2013), the Court extended the Chevron doctrine to agencies' interpretation of their own statutory jurisdiction.[73] Finally, in *Heckler v. Chaney* (1985), the Court held that, at least under some circumstances, the judiciary should not review agencies' discretionary decisions not to enforce statutes.[74] The *Heckler* case supports the NPM emphasis on broad discretion in enforcement. Taken as a whole, these decisions give the agencies considerable flexibility in choosing rule making procedures and interpreting and enforcing statutes.

In sum, the legal approach to regulation emphasizes adversary relationships, the legal obligations and rights of the parties, procedural fairness, and reasonableness in the substantive content of regulatory administrative decisions. These values and concerns are merely sketched out here; many volumes can be and have been written on the administrative law of regulation.

Conclusion: Synthesizing Approaches toward Regulatory Administration

There are many conflicts and tensions among the managerial, political, and legal approaches toward regulatory administration. The managerial approach's desire for effectiveness, that is, focusing on the impact that regulation has on the regulated entities, is frequently at odds with the political approach's current emphasis on making regulation responsive to organized, broad constituencies and subject to greater legislative review. Economy and impact assessment are certainly at odds, at least in the short run, over the requirement that environmental impact and similar statements be developed and publicized. Cost-benefit analysis can be an expensive deterrent to rule making. Efficiency is frequently at odds with adjudication and procedural due process, which require that agencies "build cases" and adjudicate them fairly (and also at some expense). Adjudication is also in conflict with the traditional managerial perspective's desire to control administrative operations tightly through unity of command; administrative law judges are not subject to direct hierarchical control by an agency's managers. The NPM favors discretionary enforcement and opposes legal procedure and judicial review. The political perspective's effort to protect broad constituencies, such as consumers, can be in tension with the legalistic approach's emphasis on the protection of the private parties' property and business interests.

All these values are in competition in a wide range of aspects of regulatory administration. Can they be synthesized through the development of a perspective that would enable at least some important priorities to be established?

One way of thinking about such a synthesis is first to identify the broad objectives of regulation and then to consider which of the perspectives is most suitable to it. In the past, there has been a tendency to view *all* regulatory administration from the point of governmental penetration of the economy and society. Consequently, some observers thought that *deregulating* surrogate markets while *strengthening* antitrust enforcement was contradictory, even though the objective of each policy initiative is to promote competition. Similarly, deregulation of surrogate markets is not necessarily inconsistent with greater health, safety, employment, or environmental regulation.[75] In the future, finer distinctions should be drawn. For the sake of illustration, the following approach is suggested.

The Public Interest

Where regulatory administration involves a very broad public interest, the political approach seems most suitable. This is often the case with environmental regulation. As NEPA recognizes, what happens to the environment may affect the nation as a whole now or in the future. Air pollution, global warming, unhealthful drinking water, acid rain, the destruction of wetlands, and degradation of ecosystems are national concerns even though their impact may be most directly felt in particular geographic areas. That is the rationale for environmental impact statements even though they are costly, can reduce short-term economic development, and sometimes induce "analysis paralysis." If we are all involved in one way or another, accountability becomes paramount. Otherwise, the public loses control of government decisions affecting the nation's future and democracy is seriously compromised. At times it will be difficult to determine when the public interest is so broad that regulatory administration should stress participation and forward-looking impact assessments over other goals. Yet the place to start is by considering each regulatory program individually on its merits from this perspective, rather than trying to prejudge everything at once on the basis of theory.

Balancing the Interests of Private Parties against Each Other

Where regulation aims to strike a proper balance between two private concerns, such as monopoly producers and consumers or businesses and organized labor, the legal approach is most suitable. For example, the regulation of utility and other rates fits into this area. Rate setting was a standard judicial function even before regulatory and public utility commissions were created. The objective is to allow utilities or other regulated enterprises to earn a fair rate of return on their investments. Although competition is increasing, utilities still tend to have monopoly status and therefore could gouge the public. Conversely, if turned completely over to the political approach's emphasis on representing constituencies, regulatory administration in this area could result in unreasonable harm to the profitability of such enterprises. It could also lead to one group of rate payers absorbing the costs, perhaps unwittingly and unwillingly, of providing service to others. Adjudication of such matters enables a balancing among the competing interests with an acceptable compromise as the result. The adjudication of numerous and repetitive violations of fair trade practices and routine health and safety regulations also seems to protect private parties against intrusive administration while enabling regulation to proceed vigorously. Assessing the fairness of various labor practices has also been largely accomplished through adjudication. In all likelihood, most antitrust activity would fall into the category of balancing rights against one another. However, cases might be so broad as to make the political approach more salient.

Where the legal approach is most appropriate, its efficacy can be enhanced by using alternative dispute resolution (ADR). As noted in Chapter 4, the Administrative Dispute Resolution Act (ADRA) of 1990, which was strengthened in 1996, tries to obtain the benefits of adjudication without having to go through laborious adjudicative processes. The ADRA authorizes agencies to substitute ADR for adjudication under the APA. It requires each agency to appoint a senior official to serve as a dispute resolution specialist. The act authorizes minitrials and arbitration in addition to dispute resolution techniques, such as mediation, that strive for voluntary agreement between the parties involved. The Negotiated Rulemaking Act of 1990 also aims at avoiding tedious and expensive litigation by having representatives of all the interested parties negotiate regulatory rules. ADR is broadly supported by all but the traditional managerial perspective. The NPM favors it because, by substituting negotiation for command and control enforcement, ADR is closer to the partnership model. From the political perspective ADR is beneficial because it is potentially more inclusive of and responsive to a broad variety of interests that may not gain consideration in formal adjudication. The legal approach will support ADR insofar as the procedures used and outcomes are fair and rational. Along with the other perspectives, the traditional managerial approach appreciates the potential efficiency and economy of ADR. However, it tends to oppose any procedure that compromises administrative authority to determine outcomes or that yields administrative decisions on any basis other than administrative expertise. Binding arbitration challenges the traditional approach's commitment to unity of command.

Protection against Disaster

Where regulatory administration is aimed at protecting against disastrous events and accidents, as in the regulation of drugs and air transportation safety, a mix of the managerial perspectives may be most suitable. Here the point is prevention; inspections, voluntary compliance, and cooperation are desirable. Whereas all the legal approach demands is minimal compliance with the law, the managerial orientation seeks cooperation with the purposes of the regulatory administration. For instance, the FDA punishes violations, but it also tries to get drug companies to engage in sound premarket testing. Airlines engage in safety maintenance, but few would suggest they should merely comply with a checklist of FAA required procedures. Rather, they carefully consider any additional safety procedures that appear reasonable to them. In a similar way, as the Maine 200 experiment suggested, OSHA is likely to be far more effective in preventing accidents in the workplace when its inspectors avoid a legalistic approach to violations and seek to help firms eliminate genuine safety risks. Until some measure of deregulation set in with problematic results, banking was another area largely treated from the managerial perspective toward regulatory administration. The purpose was largely to prevent a collapse of a major bank or the banking system as a whole because that would bring economic damage to the nation or a specific group of people. However, "too big to fail" proved costly.

It is necessary to emphasize once again that in the regulatory world, as in public administration in general, cases do not come in such neat packages all the time. Many cases will be mixed and more difficult than those presented here. Knowing how best to respond to them is part of the art of public administration.

Study Questions

1. Regulation remains an important political issue. Do you think the United States is "overregulated" in some areas of economic or social life? "Underregulated" in any? What criteria can you develop to help you decide?

2. Some economists are adamant about regulation being treated from a cost-benefit perspective. Assuming it is technically possible to do a solid cost-benefit analysis, do you think such an approach is appropriate in all areas of policy? Where and where not? Why?

3. To what kinds of regulatory administration is your college or university subject? Assess their costs, benefits, and appropriateness (from your perspective).

4. The chapter illustrates a simple risk analysis with regard to the FAA's interest in requiring child safety seats on scheduled commercial flights in the United States. Do you find the conclusion that such a requirement would pose greater dangers to small children convincing? Why or why not? What might a family impact assessment of such a rule consider?

Notes

1. Paul J. Quirk, "Food and Drug Administration," in James Q. Wilson, Ed., *The Politics of Regulation* (New York: Basic Books, 1980), 191–235, at 194.
2. See Wesley Marx, *The Frail Ocean* (New York: Ballantine, 1967).
3. Lawrence J. White, *Reforming Regulation* (Englewood Cliffs, NJ: Prentice-Hall, 1981), chap. 3; and Barry Friedman, *Regulation in the Reagan-Bush Era* (Pittsburgh, PA: University of Pittsburgh Press, 1995), chap. 1.
4. Wilson, *The Politics of Regulation.*
5. James Q. Wilson, "The Politics of Regulation," in Wilson, *The Politics of Regulation,* 357–394, at 376.
6. Ibid., 368.
7. Ibid., 369.
8. Quoted in ibid., 358; originally, George J. Stigler, "The Theory of Economic Regulation," *Bell Journal of Economics and Management Science* 2 (Spring 1971): 3. The same basic theory was presented earlier by Grant McConnell, *Private Power and American Democracy* (New York: Knopf, 1966).
9. Quoted in McConnell, *Private Power and American Democracy,* 284.
10. Marver Bernstein, *Regulating Business by Independent Regulatory Commission* (Princeton, NJ: Princeton University Press, 1955).
11. See McConnell, *Private Power and American Democracy,* chap. 8.
12. Wilson, "The Politics of Regulation," 370.
13. Ibid., 371–372.
14. Eugene Bardach and Robert A. Kagan, *Going by the Book: The Problems of Regulatory Unreasonableness* (Philadelphia: Temple University Press, 1982), 12.
15. *United States Government Manual,* 1999–2000 (Washington, DC: Government Printing Office, 1999), 524.
16. See David H. Rosenbloom, *Administrative Law for Public Managers* (Boulder, CO: Westview, 2003), chapter 3 for an overview.
17. Quoted in Bardach and Kagan, *Going by the Book,* 260 (50 CFR 261.1).
18. Clyde Farnsworth, "Line-Item Pepperoni? Fiscally Sound Anchovies?" *New York Times,* 29 June 1987.
19. Robert A. Katzmann, "Federal Trade Commission," in Wilson, *The Politics of Regulation,* 152–187, at 157.
20. Bardach and Kagan, *Going by the Book,* 130–131.
21. Quirk, "Food and Drug Administration," 207.
22. Wayne Crews, "Regulations Are Rampant, but Their Costs Go Unchecked," *Federal Times,* 18 September 2000, 23.
23. James Gattuso and Stephen Keen, "Red Tape Rising: Regulation in the Obama Era" (Washington, DC: The Heritage Foundation, March 31, 2010); http://www.heritage.org/research/reports/2010/03/red-tape-rising-regulation-in-the-obama-era.
24. Crews, "Regulations Are Rampant, but Their Costs Go Unchecked," p. 23.
25. Gattuso and Keen, "Red Tape Rising."
26. Suzanne Weaver, "Antitrust Division of the Department of Justice," in Wilson, *The Politics of Regulation,* 123–151, at 125; and Walter Adams and James Brock, "Why Flying Is Unpleasant," *New York Times,* 6 August 1987.
27. Quirk, "Food and Drug Administration," 203. In 1983, an "orphan drug" law was passed by the federal government. It allows drug companies to market

drugs to small numbers of people with unusual medical problems without first requiring that rigorous and expensive premarket tests be undertaken.

28. Kenneth Warren, *Administrative Law in the Political System,* 3d ed. (Upper Saddle River, NJ: Prentice-Hall, 1996), 253. See also Herbert Kaufman, *Red Tape* (Washington, DC: Brookings Institution, 1977), 20.

29. *Wall Street Journal,* 15 October 1974.

30. Cary Coglianese, "Assessing Consensus: The Promise and Performance of Negotiated Rulemaking," *Duke Law Journal,* 46 (No. 6/April 1997), 1255–1349, at p. 1279.

31. Cindy Skrzycki, "Congress: Fewer Forms or Budgets Will Suffer," *Washington Post,* 14 August 1998, G2.

32. Peter Strauss, Todd Rakoff, Roy Schotland, and Cynthia Farina, *Gellhorn and Byse's Administrative Law: Cases and Comments,* 9th ed. (Westbury, NY: Foundation Press, 1995), 872.

33. Office of Management and Budget, Office of Information and Regulatory Affairs, *Information Collection Budget of the United States* (Washington, DC: OMB, 2012), p. IV.

34. *Wall Street Journal,* 25 October 1974.

35. *Wall Street Journal,* 1 November 1974.

36. Elizabeth Williamson, "Industries Paid for Top Regulators' Travel," *Washington Post,* November 2, 2007; http://www.washingtonpost.com/wp-dyn/content/article/2007/11/01/AR2007110102732.html?hpid=topnews.

37. *New York Times,* 15 July 1984.

38. Robert Hanley, "Bergen County Fights Nonregulation Shoeshines," *New York Times,* 17 September 1993, B1, B6.

39. Cindy Skrzycki, "The Regulators: Salad Days on the Hill: Food Processors Give Their Oil for a Rule Distinction," *Washington Post,* 13 October 1995, D1–2.

40. Bardach and Kagan, *Going by the Book,* chap. 7.

41. Ibid., 195–196.

42. David Jackson, "Obama Cuts Five Regulations, Says it Will Save $6 Billion," *USA Today,* May 10, 2012. See http://www.federaltimes.com/article/20120510/AGENCY04/205100303/1001. The regulations dealt with state and local street signs, railroad costs, eliminating two unnecessary sets of regulatory reporting requirements by doctors and hospitals, and eliminating outdated regulatory burdens on gas stations.

43. "Alaska Airlines Returns All Grounded Planes to Service," CNN.com, 4 August 2000; "Alaska Airlines Maintenance Records Raise New Questions," CNN.com, 14 February 2000.

44. Cindy Skrzycki, "The Wrong Price on a Life Lost?" *Washington Post,* 10 December 2002, E4.

45. Ibid.

46. Jane Garvey, "FAA IS Doing the Right Thing," *USA Today,* 20 December 1999, 26A; Editorial, "Requiring Child Safety Seats on Planes Masks Deeper Dangers," *USA Today,* 20 December 1999, 26A.

47. Paul Stephen Dempsey, "Deregulation and Reregulation: Policy, Politics, and Economics," in David H. Rosenbloom and Richard Schwartz, Eds., *Handbook of Regulation and Administrative Law* (New York: Marcel Dekker, 1994), 175–206.

48. Bardach and Kagan, *Going by the Book,* 224–225.

49. See Cornelius Kerwin, *Rulemaking* (Washington, DC: CQ Press), 118–123.

50. Angel Manuel Moreno, "Presidential Coordination of the Independent Regulatory Process," *Administrative Law Journal of the American University* 8 (Fall 1994): 461–516.

51. Cary Coglianese, "Assessing Consensus: The Promise and Performance of Negotiated Rulemaking," *Duke Law Journal* 46, no. 6 (1997): 1255–1349; Juliet Williams, "The Delegation Dilemma: Negotiated Rulemaking in Perspective," *Policy Studies Review* 17 (2000): 125–146.

52. Wilson, "The Politics of Regulation," 375.

53. Bardach and Kagan, *Going by the Book,* 204–205.

54. Malcolm Sparrow, *Imposing Duties* (Westport, CT: Praeger, 1994), ix; see also Christine Parker, "Reinventing Regulation within the Corporation," *Administration & Society* 32 (November 2000): 529–565.

55. Sparrow, *Imposing Duties,* xxiii–xxvi.

56. Al Gore, *Common Sense Government Works Better & Costs Less* (Washington, DC: Government Printing Office, 1995), 25–26.

57. Christy Harris, "Lack of Procedure Kills OSHA Reinvention Program," *Federal Times,* 26 April 1999, 3, 18; *Chamber of Commerce (U.S.) v. OSHA,* No. 98–1036, April 9, 1999 (D.C. Circuit Court of Appeals).

58. National Performance Review, *Reinvention Roundtable* 2 (Summer 1995): 1, 11.

59. Ian Littman, Ed., *The Business of Government* (Arlington, VA: PriceWaterhouseCoopers, 1999), 7.

60. "In Brief," *Washington Post,* 5 February 1996, A19, reported that Senator Dianne Feinstein was highly critical of the Customs Service effort to turn itself from "an enforcement agency into a [trade] facilitation agency." In a 1996 operational plan inspired by the NPR, Commissioner George Weise "listed drug interdiction fourth among seven goals, below 'processing more passengers, cargo and revenues.'"

61. Wilson, "The Politics of Regulation," 378.

62. Cindy Skrzycki, "U.S. Opens Online Portal to Rulemaking: Web Site Invites Wider Participation in the Regulatory Process," *Washington Post,* 23 January 2003, E1, E6. The site is http://www.regulation.gov.

63. William Gormley, "The Representation Revolution," *Administration & Society* 18 (August 1986): 179–196, 190.

64. Kenneth C. Davis, *Administrative Law and Government,* 2d ed. (St. Paul, MN: West, 1975), 336.

65. See David H. Rosenbloom, *Building a Legislative-Centered Public Administration: Congress and the Administrative State, 1946–1999* (Tuscaloosa: University of Alabama Press, 2000), 45–48.

66. See Daniel Cohen and Peter Strauss, "Congressional Review of Agency Regulations," *Administrative Law Review* 49 (1997): 95–110.

67. *Citizens to Preserve Overton Park v. Volpe,* 401 U.S. 402 (1971).

68. *First Evangelical Lutheran Church of Glendale v. County of Los Angeles,* 482 U.S. 304 (1987); *Nollan v. California Coastal Commission,* 483 U.S. 825 (1987); *Lucas v. South Carolina Coastal Council,* 505 U.S. 1003 (1992).

69. *Dolan v. City of Tigard,* 512 U.S. 374 (1994).

70. *Vermont Yankee Nuclear Power Corporation v. Natural Resources Defense Council,* 435 U.S. 519 (1978).

71. *Chevron v. Natural Resources Defense Council,* 467 U.S. 837 (1984).

72. *United States v. Mead Corporation,* 533 U.S. 218 (2001).
73. *City of Arlington, Texas v. Federal Communications Commission,* U.S. Supreme Court No. 11-1545 (May 20, 2013).
74. *Heckler v. Chaney,* 470 U.S. 821 (1985).
75. See Larry Gerston, Cynthia Fraleigh, and Robert Schwab, *The Deregulated Society* (Pacific Grove, CA: Brooks/Cole, 1988), 45, for an opposing point of view.

ADDITIONAL READING

Cato Institute (Washington, DC). *Regulation Magazine.* Periodical.

Fiorino, Daniel. *The New Environmental Regulation.* Cambridge, MA: MIT Press, 2006.

Kerwin, Cornelius M. and Scott R. Furlong. *Rulemaking: How Government Agencies Write Law and Make Policy,* 4th ed. Washington, DC: CQ Press, 2011.

Lubbers, Jeffrey S. *A Guide to Federal Agency Rulemaking,* 5th ed. Chicago: American Bar Association, 2012.

Parker, Christine. "Reinventing Regulation within the Corporation: Compliance-Oriented Regulatory Innovation," *Administration & Society* 32 (November 2000): 529–565.

Sparrow, Malcolm. *The Regulatory Craft.* Washington, DC: Brookings Institution, 2000.

REGULATORY AFFAIRS WEB SITES

Federal regulatory matters can be tracked through the following Web sites:

OMB Watch, which changed its name to Center for Effective Government in 2013, a private organization bringing a good deal of transparency to the U.S. Office of Management and Budget and federal rule making more generally, is at http://www.foreffectivegov.org.

Regulatory information from the Office of Information and Regulatory Affairs can be accessed at http://www.whitehouse.gov/omb/inforeg_default.

Regulations.gov offers a portal for submitting comments on proposed rules and reading others' comments: http://www.regulations.gov/#!home.

Public Administration and the Public

CHAPTER 10

PUBLIC ADMINISTRATION AND THE PUBLIC

Key Learning Objectives

1. Understand the complexity of the public's interaction with and evaluation of public administration.

2. Appreciate the main concerns regarding public administration's effects on individuals in the society, political system, and economy.

3. Understand the managerial, political, and legal public administrative perspectives on the public.

4. Be aware of strategies for improving public administration's relationship with the public.

The public interacts with public administration in several roles: as client, customer, contractor, regulatee, participant, and litigant as well as in street-level encounters. Public administration penetrates the economy and society. The public's evaluation of public administration is complex; it is sometimes accurate, and often not so accurate. As citizens, people harbor opinions of government as wasteful, untrustworthy, and unresponsive. As clients and customers, they find it satisfactory; and when subject to government regulations, they are less favorable. The managerial, political, and legal perspectives offer different views of the public. The political perspective emphasizes participation, which offers some possibilities for strengthening the "public" in public administration. The new public management, by contrast, views the public primarily as customers. These perspectives can be synthesized to a certain extent by applying them to different areas of public administration, such as social services. There is also broad agreement that practical improvements, such as paperwork reduction, plain language, and **e-government**, can improve the relationship between public administration and the public.

The development and growth of the contemporary administrative state have many ramifications for the public. Certainly, the public has benefited greatly from public administration. (Just think of the national highways and public education, for example.) Public administrators are concerned with the provision of public goods and quasi-public goods, such as defense of the political community, roads, and recreational and cultural facilities. They are also actively involved in providing justice, safety, economic security, health, education, and other benefits to the public or segments of it. But the provision of these benefits has not been without important social, political, and economic costs. Too often in the past, the study of public administration has failed to address the place of the "public" in the public administrative state. The purpose of this chapter is to place relationships with the public at the forefront of public administrative theory and practice.

◆→ THE PUBLIC'S INTERACTION WITH PUBLIC ADMINISTRATION

Every person in the United States is affected by some public administrative actions almost all the time. For example, whether we are awake or asleep, in an urban metropolis or on a remote mountain peak, protecting each of our lives is in some sense the responsibility of public administrators in the Departments of Homeland Security and Defense. We are all generally affected by the activities of the Environmental Protection Agency, the Food and Drug Administration, and the U.S. Department of Agriculture's inspection and crop-related programs. If we listen to the radio or watch network TV, the FCC is involved; wherever we are, some police department has formal responsibility for our safety and conduct. The list could go on and on. It would be an interesting exercise to keep track of how many of one's daily activities are in some way affected by a public administrative agency. But such a review of the extent to which public administrators affect our well-being and have an impact on our daily lives does not begin to tell the full story of the relationship between the public and public administrators.

The public interacts directly with public administrators in several contexts. For the sake of analysis, these can be placed into six main overlapping categories.

Clients and Customers

The public interacts with public administrators as *clients* or *customers.** The range of possibilities in this context is extensive. In the 1970s, one study found that more than half (57.5 percent) of a sample of the general population had had at least one direct recent contact with an administrative agency dealing with one of the following areas: employment, job training, worker's compensation, unemployment compensation, public assistance, hospital/medical care, or retirement benefits.[1] If public education, postal service, recreation, and other functions such as contact with agencies dealing with consumer fraud and the like were added to the list, the amount of contact would increase considerably. The essence of the client or customer role is that the individual seeks to obtain a benefit or service from an administrative agency.

The Regulated Public

The public interacts with public administrators as *regulatees*. For instance, four of the more common situations in which members of the public meet public administrators in the role of being regulated are motor vehicle licenses, traffic violations, income taxes, and police matters.[2] The full extent of interactions in these four categories is unknown, but such a figure certainly does not encompass all the possible situations in which the citizen is a regulatee of an administrative agency. As pointed out in the first chapter, often service and constraint are combined. The client or customer may also be a regulatee, as in the case of individuals seeking public housing, public assistance, and even public education. Moreover, at the end of 2011, 6.9 million members of society were under adult correctional supervision in the United States.[3] Such people, amounting to one in every thirty-four adults in the U.S. population, are not merely regulated or constrained; they are controlled and/or restrained. Additionally, many people are subject to legal constraints in the role of employee or employer, especially in terms of regulation of occupational health and safety, equal opportunity, and labor relations.

Participants

The public interacts with public administrators as *participants* in public administration. Many public administrative programs, especially in the realm

---

*The dictionary definition of "client" includes "customer." Clients are usually thought of as receiving professional or craft services, whereas customers are shoppers. The NPM used the term "customer" to emphasize its view that government agencies should operate like market-driven businesses and stores.

of agriculture and education, provide for direct public participation. Public utility commissions, housing agencies, and other public agencies often hold public hearings as well. Members of the public respond to agencies' rule making proposals. Overall, it appears that the level of public use of opportunities to participate is low (as it is in politics usually), but nonetheless the opportunity is there. In some cases groups are so effective in using participation to make public administrators responsive to them that they are considered an agency's "constituency."

Litigants

The public interacts with public administrators as *litigants*. A limited segment of the population seeks to litigate claims or complaints against public administrators. Litigation in this context may mean nothing more than a direct response to an agency's notice that it proposes to do something that will harm the individual, such as cutting off public assistance benefits. It may involve an appeal through administrative hierarchies, a hearing before an administrative law judge, or a suit in a state or federal court. Although the proportion of the public that engages in litigation is small, their cases are often numerous enough to place substantial burdens on agencies' and courts' ability to hear them. For instance, the federal Equal Employment Opportunity Commission has almost always struggled with a substantial backlog of cases. Moreover, the ramifications of a few court decisions on public administration can be extensive. Supreme Court decisions requiring procedural due process in many administrative actions have forced welfare agencies, in particular, to change their processes and modify their structures extensively.[4] The Court's equal protection decisions have had a major impact on public sector human resources management.[5]

Street-Level Encounters

The public interacts with public administrators through *street-level encounters*. Street-level encounters, discussed in Chapter 8, are often a feature of the individual role of regulatee. However, sometimes they do not involve regulation per se, but rather an effort by a street-level bureaucrat to determine whether constraints should be applied or whether assistance should be rendered. Police are perhaps the best example. Their role involves the application of constraints and the provision of assistance. Street-level interaction with them can be touched off in any number of ways, including asking them for directions, injuring oneself in an accident, and engaging in suspicious or prohibited conduct.

Contractors

The number of people employed on contracts by the nation's 89,000 governments is unknown, as is the total dollar value of their contracts. Governments contract for a very broad array of goods and services, ranging from purchasing paper clips, to developing proposed rules, to handling space shuttle launches. Contracting is so pervasive, it is fair to say, "But for a handful of functions dealing with national security and criminal justice, it is not clear that there is a pure and inherently governmental function left today."[6] These contracts are let to both for-profit and nonprofit corporations. By one systematic estimate, the federal government averages three contract workers for each of its civilian, military, and postal employees, for a total of about 14.6 million.[7] State and local governments undoubtedly employ several million more. Overall, contracts involve over five hundred billion dollars.[8] Contractors are involved in voluntary quid pro quo relationships with agencies that may subject them to considerable governmental oversight and require them to meet specific standards for performance, working conditions, and, sometimes, transparency.

In sum, there is little doubt that the public is deeply affected by public administration and is frequently involved in direct interactions with public administrators. These interactions are part and parcel of the evolution of the contemporary administrative state. They help define contemporary American political, economic, and social life.

◆✦ The Individual in the Administrative State

The Individual in Society

Public administration thoroughly permeates American society. Many matters once left to families, communities, and religious organizations are now the subject of administrative activity. Examples are education, child abuse prevention, provision for one's economic security and health in old age, welfare benefits (formerly charity), and housing. Although there is currently a tendency for government to rely on private and nonprofit organizations to carry out its functions, historically, administrative services have replaced many privately provided social services and administrative controls have augmented more traditional social controls exercised by families, communities, and religious organizations.

Equally important, public administration has tended to be bureaucratically organized despite the NPM's successes in changing this to some extent. Bureaucracy, in particular, is often in tension with traditional social values. Consequently, individuals may have to be socialized to interact well with bureaucracy, and in the process their values and those of society may be modified.

Ralph Hummel explains that bureaucracy is at odds with society because it relies on rationally organized "bureaucratic action," rather than "social action."[9] Hummel defines the differences between bureaucratic action and social action in practical terms:

> Social action is normally initiated by a human being who has certain intentions or purposes. The action is intended to convey such goals or purposes and is addressed to a social partner whose understanding of the action is a key part of the purpose. Social action, then, consists of a human initiator, the action itself, and a human recipient, or co-actor.

Bureaucratic action is reduced to the action itself. It does not have a human originator in the sense of expressing the private will or intentions of a human being; it originates—and this is a key characteristic of bureaucracy as a system—in an office whether or not a specific human being fills the role of officeholder. (In automated bureaucracies, the action may originate in a computer.) Next there is the operation or function itself. What makes it an operation or function, however, is not primarily related to the logical end point which was the original purpose of the action. What makes it an operation or function is determined by whether or not the action meets the values and standards of higher offices charged with control.[10]

Hummel's last point about rationally organized action is important. It gets at the "one-directional" aspects of bureaucracy and public administration organized according to traditional managerial principles. Commands flow downward through the hierarchy; information flows upward. The client or regulatee supplies information but cannot give commands. This means the client or regulatee cannot sensibly ask the bureaucrat to modify his or her administrative behavior and routines. These can be modified only by direction from above in the bureaucracy. In essence, rationally organized action at the level of the client or regulatee tends to be a problem-*processing* activity rather than a problem-*solving* activity. This is something the NPM is changing by empowering frontline employees to develop and implement solutions for their customers. Problem solving (and NPM administration) demands two-way communication. The difference is as follows: "Let's discuss it" implies social action; "*We* (the agency) will need the following information from you (the client or regulatee)" suggests rationally organized bureaucratic action.

Hummel carries this line of thought at least two steps further. On the level of the individual who works in a bureaucratic setting, he notes that emotional feelings are transformed. In his view, intended to portray the impact of bureaucratization at its outermost limits, the individual in bureaucratic life is taught (1) not to attach "affect" (positive emotional feelings) directly to persons; (2) to attach affect to their administrative functions; and (3) to attach affect to the exercise of power or authority. This diverges considerably from ordinary social values. Society, in the normal sense of the term, cannot exist where people feel no affect toward one another, where they care primarily about the performance of their functions, and when they exercise their power to the exclusion of empathizing with other people or identifying with groups and individuals outside their workplace. In such a "society," there would be no sympathy, trust, love, or other emotional feelings between people. This may sound far-fetched, but the impersonality that characterizes bureaucracy can reduce to a sterile, empty process lacking sympathy, trust, and emotional engagement.

Hummel also maintains that as bureaucracy permeates public life, it creates a tension between its values and those of society. Inevitably, the values of *both* are modified in the process, but those of bureaucracy tend to become dominant. Ask yourself what you think bureaucracy values most and then what you personally think is of most importance in life. Hummel's list is shown in Box 10.1.[11] In sum, he finds that "the *cultural* conflict between bureaucracy and society is between systems needs and human needs."[12]

10.1   BUREAUCRACY VERSUS SOCIETY

Bureaucracy	Society
Precision	Justice
Stability	Freedom
Discipline	Violence
Reliability	Oppression
Caculability of results	Happiness
Formal rationality	Gratification
Formalistic impersonality	Poverty
Formal equality of treatment	Illness
	Death
	Victory
	Love and hate
	Salvation and damnation

One does not have to agree with Hummel entirely to get the picture: public administration, bureaucratically organized, tends to be in tension or conflict with society in terms of styles of action, emotional feelings, and overriding concerns. The differences between societal and bureaucratic values, in short, are social interaction versus administrative action; feeling versus doing; and belief, randomness, and emotionalism versus specialized expertise, systemization, and impersonality. These ideas are abstract but they have real effects. Perhaps if you think about some of your experiences with bureaucratically organized administrative agencies, they will become more concrete.

The juxtaposition between social action and rationally organized action is often clearest when the individual is considered in the role of client. Clients approach the public administrator with an understanding of the society's culture. But the culture of bureaucracy can require behavior with which they are unfamiliar or ill at ease. As Victor Thompson once pointed out,

> The bureaucratic culture makes certain demands upon the clients as well as
> upon organization employees. There are many people in our society who
> have not been able to adjust to these demands. To them bureaucracy is a
> curse. They see no good in it whatsoever, but view the demands of modern
> organization as "red tape."[13]

Such people do not possess "the aptitudes and attitudes needed to obtain reasoned consideration" of their cases by public administrators.[14] Their "low powers of abstraction" and "need to personalize the world" seem to be the most important barriers to their ability to deal effectively with public administrators.[15] Functional illiteracy is also a problem for some clients. Inability to comprehend bureaucratic language ("bureaucratese") is a problem for many more. The entire client-public administrator interaction may be distasteful and threatening to many. In some cases, "A claim which he [the client] believes legitimate is not taken 'at face value.' He must either supply proof or allow it to be investigated. . . . The individual enters the situation on 'official,' 'technical,' or 'public' business, and feels that he ends up by being investigated as a person."[16]

The National Performance Review (NPR) was highly critical of these aspects of traditional public administration. One of its fundamental purposes was to build trust between administrators and customers.

The client role can be difficult for anyone. However, lower-class populations have been identified as having particular difficulty in dealing with public bureaucracies. In part, this is because the agencies they deal with often provide a mixture of service and constraint, as in welfare and public housing programs. Members of the lower class may typically be heavily dependent on public agencies and consequently feel at their "mercy." It has even been argued that "bureaucratic systems are the key medium through which the middle class maintains its advantaged position vis-à-vis the lower class."[17] Public educational systems and some aspects of social welfare administration are examples (see Boxes 10.2 and 10.3).

10.2   THE CLIENT AT A BUREAUCRATICALLY ORGANIZED WELFARE OFFICE

The following is a description by a welfare advocate of a typical client's meeting with a social worker in a bureaucratized welfare agency. Note how many of Hummel's points apply:

[I]n the interview booth, they have children's little plastic chairs for clients to sit in and an adult chair for the worker. And so the client, like their chin is on the table and the worker is like hovering over them shouting. And you know, you take a seat in one of those children's chairs and all of the sudden you're clearly not on the same level as the person who's interrogating you. . . .

I don't know how many times I went in with somebody and the worker felt that they had to explain to me how the person had screwed up, and then turn around, you know the way people talk to folks about them as if they're deaf say, "Isn't that true. Didn't I talk to

you about this? Didn't I tell you you had to turn your form in and if you didn't this would happen? Isn't that true?" Like they're totally humiliated. . . . [I]t was so effective that very rarely did the client . . . not say, "Yes, it's true." Even if they hadn't, it was better to say "Yes" than to argue that point. They were totally intimidated. And then we had to work on trying to build self-esteem, like trying to model how to respond to this person who is being totally inhumane and degrading and feeling above all as a person receiving the benefits that had no choice; that if you really had a choice, you'd have nothing to do with this place ever again. But guess what folks, you have to come back here tomorrow, and this is how you are treated. You have no choice.

Source: Lucie White, "*Goldberg v. Kelly* on the Paradox of Lawyering for the Poor," *Brooklyn Law Review* 56 (1990): 861–887.

10.3   "Undercover Boss": New York's Human Resources Chief Seeks Welfare

In 1992, Barbara Sabol, the head of New York City's Human Resources Administration, tried an experiment. Armed with an officially created false identity and disguised in a wig or scarf, sweatshirt, jeans, and glasses, Sabol spent about 23 days applying for welfare benefits. She received food stamps, home relief benefits, and a mandatory work assignment. The experience was an eye opener. Her personal documents were lost, she was repeatedly sent to the wrong places and given the wrong forms, she waited in long lines and sat in run-down waiting rooms with broken furniture, defunct telephones, and an abundance of cockroaches. When an interview for which she had waited 45 minutes finally began, she made the mistake of inquiring about the delay—only to be sent back to wait for another 45 minutes!

Using the lingo of public administration, Sabol said she felt "depersonalized." Explaining further, she told reporters, "I ceased to be." "I go to this window. They do not ask me my name. They say, 'What is your Zip Code?'" Upon hearing the Zip, the intake worker told the chief, "Baby, you're in the wrong place." In what place should she be? That basic question could stump the system. One "frustrated worker" condescendingly exclaimed, "Listen to me! Look at me! You can't get this unless you have a number. They wouldn't have sent you to me if you didn't have a number." After giving up the charade, Sabol planned no disciplinary actions, but pledged to make the system more user-friendly.

Source: Based on Alison Mitchell, "Posing as Welfare Recipient, Agency Head Finds Indignity," *New York Times,* 5 February 1993, A1, B2.

The norms of the administrative culture tend to permeate mainstream culture in the United States to a large extent. For example, it has been noted that public school education is typically hierarchically organized and that "the process of obtaining passes, excuses, and permission slips to be granted entrances or exit serves as a useful apprenticeship for dealing with the bureaucracies later in life."[18] Americans generally depersonalize the exercise of authority by distinguishing between an administrative action and the person taking it. For instance, we find no contradiction in the phrase "She's a good person with a bad job."

To the extent that administrative values, especially hierarchy and impersonality, replace traditional social values, they can pose a serious problem for the individual in the society. Not only may using public agencies effectively be difficult, there is also the risk that each individual will deal impersonally with others and will feel isolated and relatively unable to achieve control over his or her environment. Feeling that one has lost control over his or her life and fate is referred to as **anomie.** There are many aspects of American society that have become increasingly impersonal, as the traditional roles of family, community, and religious organizations have been partly superseded by public administration.

For instance, day care, after-school care, and care of the elderly are increasingly an organizational as opposed to a family function, deterring and reporting crime have largely become a police function as opposed to a community one, and charity is largely managed by impersonal nonprofit secular organizations. Contemporary calls for administrative decentralization and devolution to state and local governments—placing some functions closer to the people themselves— reflect the widespread concern that the public is relatively powerless in dealing with large-scale, remote, intrusive federal administration.

The Individual in the Political System

The individual's role in the political system also undergoes major transformations with the rise of the administrative state. First, voters' impact on government is attenuated because they have inadequate mechanisms for controlling administrative agencies and holding them accountable. Frederick Mosher succinctly summarized the problem:

> The accretion of specialization and of technological and social complexity seems to be an irreversible trend, one that leads to increasing dependence upon the protected, appointive public service, thrice removed from direct democracy. Herein lies the central and underlying problem. . . . [H]ow can a public service so constituted be made to operate in a manner compatible with democracy? How can we be assured that a highly differentiated body of public employees will act in the interest of all the people, will be an instrument of all the people?[19]

Today the delivery of so many government services by "third parties," through privatization, collaborative governance arrangements, and devolution, removes the electorate even further from exercising direct control over public administration.

The ideal of popular sovereignty is compromised by the tendency of the public to become subjects of the bureaucratically organized administrative state. In a classic treatise on *Democracy in the Administrative State* (1969), Emmette Redford claimed that "the first characteristic" of citizens in the administrative state is that "they are dormant regarding most of the decisions being made with respect to them. Their participation cannot in any manner equal their subjection."[20] In the early 1990s, the NPR made the same point as follows:

> [The traditional administrative state] . . . put the government's customers— which is to say, all of us—at the bottom of the priority list. The first priority was the rules; the second was those who checked whether the rules were being followed (such as auditors and inspectors general); the third was those who made the rules in the first place (such as Congress and interest groups). Customers came in last, if at all. It was a sort of "iron triangle"—special interests told Congress what "the people" wanted; Congress passed laws, and then told the agencies what to do about them.
>
> Citizens, understandably, do not like being low in the pecking order— or worse, being ignored altogether. And honest people . . . don't like being treated like potential criminals.[21]

Even the growing body of research that shows that Congress, political executives, and the courts can steer administrative agencies does not resolve Mosher's question.[22] The link between the public and the elected is too "loose" to ensure a high degree of political representation or responsiveness on most policy issues. Voter participation in presidential elections has hovered around 50 percent for decades. On average, it is considerably lower in midterm congressional elections. It is in some ways very telling that the NPR looked toward making agencies responsive to customers, rather than elections, as the primary means of overcoming the public's lack of control over public administration.

As the passage from the NPR quoted previously suggests, democracy and bureaucratically organized public administration clash in regard to structure and values. Box 10.4 lists the main requirements of each. It indicates that when one moves from being a *democratic citizen* to being a *bureaucratic subject*, one is crossing into a different culture and system of rule.

It is not possible to link today's limited participation in politics definitively with the development of large-scale public administration. There is some sense that the country is being run by bureaucrats. A long-term decline in the public's faith in government coincided with a period during which the scope and general salience of regulatory administration increased (see Chapter 9). Between 1958 and the early 1990s, the public's perception was that government became more wasteful, more oriented toward a few big interests, less trustworthy to do what was right, and less responsive to the ordinary citizenry.[23]

The public's level of trust in government is considered particularly salient. The NPR assumed that better administrative performance could promote a virtuous circle by increasing the public's trust in government. Trust, in turn, would enhance administrative flexibility and empowerment—and therefore performance—by enabling government to shed some of its more heavy-handed accountability procedures (red tape) and oversight mechanisms

---

10.4   DEMOCRACY VERSUS BUREAUCRATICALLY ORGANIZED ADMINISTRATION

Democracy Requires:	*Bureaucracy Favors:*
Equality	Hierarchy
Rotation in office	Seniority
Freedom	Command
Pluralism	Unity
Citizen participation	Participation based on expertise
Openness	Secrecy
Community	Impersonality
Legitimacy based on election	Legitimacy based on expertise

(particularly nitpicking by inspectors general). In fact, there is a statistically significant positive association between government performance and trust.[24] However, it is far too weak to explain much about the rather dramatic fluctuations in the proportion of Americans who trust the government in Washington to do what is right just about always or most of the time. In 1964, 76 percent of the public had such levels of trust in government. This declined fairly steadily until the early 1980s, falling below 30 percent. It then climbed into the 40 percent range, only to fall to a low point of 20 percent in 1994. Trust spiked at 64 percent after September 11, 2001, but then sank back to 40 percent by May 2002.[25] The rising dissatisfaction with the Iraq War and disapproval of President George W. Bush may have been reflected in these figures. Additionally, throughout much of this period, a majority agreed with the statement that "sometimes politics and government seem so complicated that a person like me can't really understand what is going on." Public ignorance about government may be due partly to lack of interest. In the mid-1990s, the average American was more likely to be able to name the Three Stooges than three justices on the Supreme Court (59 percent to 17 percent)![26] Only 6 percent could correctly name the chief justice. About a quarter of those polled knew the term of office to which senators are elected.[27]

Some of the public's disaffection is focused on the federal government in particular. One of the NPR's justifications for trying to reinvent federal administration was that in 1992 the public thought Uncle Sam wasted 48 cents out of every tax dollar collected.[28] This proportion has not improved in the years since then.

In 2002, 61 percent of the public thought that the federal government was doing only a fair or poor job running its programs. Fifty-six percent pointed to inefficiency. Sixty-two percent strongly or somewhat agreed that "the federal government controls too much of our daily lives."[29] Not surprisingly, there has been a trend toward favoring giving more power to the states. In 1981, 56 percent of the public wanted to do so; by 1995, the figure was up to 64 percent.[30] In 1997, when only 22 percent of the public expressed a lot of confidence in the federal government, 32 percent and 38 percent did so with regard to state and local governments, respectively.[31] In 2002, 60 percent thought the federal government was too powerful.[32] In a January 2013 poll, 53 percent, a majority for the first time, reported believing that the federal government actually threatened their personal rights and freedoms.[33]

In sum, the public is relatively disaffected with government on several dimensions. "The burst of support for the federal government that followed September [11] is over . . . some measures have fallen close to their pre-9/11 levels."[34] Since the attacks of 9/11, public confidence in government has deteriorated: most people hold unfavorable views of members of Congress (68 percent), and many view the U.S. political system as "broken" (32 percent).[35] Perhaps most troubling, in 2013, 73 percent of Americans trusted the federal government only some of the time or never.[36]

The Individual in the Economy

The contemporary administrative state also changes the character of the individual's place in the economic system. As public administration penetrates the society and economy to a greater extent, government inevitably gains greater control over the nation's economic resources. (In Chapter 6 we noted that government spending constitutes about one-third of GDP.) Charles Reich explains this development in straightforward terms:

> One of the most important developments in the United States during the past decade [1950s] has been the emergence of government as a major source of wealth. Government is a gigantic syphon. It draws revenue and power, and pours forth wealth: money, benefits, services, contracts, franchises, and licenses. Government has always had this function. But while in early times it was minor, today's distribution of largess is on a vast, imperial scale.
>
> The valuables dispensed by government take many forms, but they all share one characteristic. They are steadily taking the place of traditional forms of wealth—forms which are held as private property. Social insurance substitutes for savings; a government contract replaces a businessman's customers and goodwill. The wealth of more and more Americans depends upon a relationship to government. Increasingly, Americans live on government largess.[37]

Public administrative control or direction of a large share of the nation's economic resources has important consequences for the individual. First, it makes the individual dependent on government for his or her economic well-being. If government controls access to resources, occupations, markets, franchises, technologies, and the right to operate such enterprises as utilities, broadcasting, and transportation, individuals cannot function in a wide variety of economic areas except on the conditions established by government. Public employees and the increasing number of those doing outsourced public administrative work on contracts are especially dependent on government.

It is inevitable that government becomes the focus of efforts to enhance one's economic status and well-being. Much political effort is directed toward obtaining economic benefits or advancement through the adoption of specific public policies. "Loopholes" in the tax code (also called *tax expenditures* or *tax preferences*) are prime examples. As Reich points out, this development is new not in kind but rather in scope—and its scope is far larger today than it was when he first called our attention to it.

A second consequence of the accumulation of wealth in the hands of the administrative state is that the government gains greater leverage and control over the individual's life. This is a feature of the contemporary role of government to which political and economic conservatives have long been vehemently opposed. In Reich's words, "When government—national, state, or local—hands out something of value, whether a relief check or a television license, government's power grows forthwith; it automatically gains such power as is necessary and proper to supervise its largess. It obtains new rights to investigate, to regulate, and to punish."[38] This development tends to erode the protections private property once afforded the individual against the exercise of governmental power. The late Nobel Prize winner Milton Friedman was among those economists who contend that "Economic freedom is also an indispensable means toward the achievement of political freedom." Friedman explained,

> The citizen of the United States who is compelled by law to devote something like 10 percent of his income to the purchase of a particular kind of retirement contract, administered by the government, is being deprived of a corresponding part of his personal freedom. How strongly this deprivation may be felt and its closeness to the deprivation of religious freedom, which all would regard as "civil" or "political" rather than "economic," were dramatized by an episode involving a group of farmers of the Amish sect. On grounds of principle, this group regarded compulsory federal old age programs as an infringement of their personal individual freedom and refused to pay taxes or accept benefits. As a result, some of their livestock were sold by auction in order to satisfy claims for social security levies. . . .
>
> A citizen of the United States who under the laws of various states is not free to follow the occupation of his own choosing unless he can get a license for it, is likewise being deprived of an essential part of his freedom. . . . So is the Californian man who was thrown into jail for selling Alka Seltzer at a price below that set by the manufacturer under so-called "fair-trade" laws. So also is the farmer who cannot grow the amount of wheat he wants.[39]

As Friedman suggests, not all of the freedom lost in conjunction with the government's larger role in the economy can be categorized as "economic freedom." People have been denied public sector jobs, contracts, permits, licenses, and welfare and other benefits because of their political views, "lack of good character," and lawful sexual activity.[40]

Economist Friedrich Hayek, also a Nobel Prize recipient, viewed government participation in the economy as creating leverage over both the economy and society that constituted a drive down "the road to serfdom."[41] If this is unchecked, he argued, nearly all important individual preferences will be replaced by governmental preferences and important economic and social questions will be transformed into public policy ones. According to this view, economic dependence on the administrative state produces a very powerful government that subsumes the roles traditionally played by families, religious organizations, private groups, communities, and private economic firms.

This argument is an extreme formulation of the transformation that has been taking place in conjunction with the rise of the administrative state in the United States. However extreme, it does pinpoint certain tendencies we can clearly recognize and which are sometimes characterized as "cradle to grave" government: members of the public whose prenatal welfare was subsidized by government, who were born in a public hospital at public expense, who were raised in public housing with the assistance of public welfare funds, whose diets were subsidized through the food stamp program, whose education took place in a public school, whose incomes were earned in the public sector or augmented by public benefits, whose health care has been subsidized by the government, and who receive governmental benefits in old age, and who will, perhaps, even be buried in a public cemetery at government expense.

Although some oppose the contemporary governmental role in the economy on the grounds that it makes the public too dependent on government, much support for the modern "womb-to-tomb" welfare state is based on the belief that increased governmental power can be exercised humanely with proper regard for individual freedoms, value preferences, and liberties. In this view, government penetration of the economy is a suitable means of protecting individuals from abuse by the economic power of other individuals and private firms. Governmental encroachment on traditional economic freedoms may be considered less troublesome than the lack of protection individuals had from boom-and-bust business cycles prior to governmental efforts to mitigate them. As in so many aspects of public administration, the overall picture is hardly as simple as the partisans of one or another particular viewpoint would have us believe.

➧ The Public's Evaluation of Public Administration

The public's evaluation of public administration is complex and, in some respects, puzzling. The public opinion surveys discussed previously clearly indicate that the public has had negative attitudes toward government and administration. But the overall negativity tells only part of the story. Surveys frequently find that substantial majorities would choose government social programs over tax cuts. For instance, in early 1996, 69.5 percent of the public favored smaller tax cuts and more government spending on health, education, and other social programs.[42] During the 2000 election campaign, the public was more favorable toward using the surplus to pay down the national debt than to finance tax cuts. In 2002, the public expressed a relatively strong preference for maintaining federal programs.[43] Within this overall framework, African Americans and Hispanics are more likely to support government programs than are non-Hispanic whites.[44] Women as a whole may tend to trust government less than men do.[45] In 2013, these relationships also held, but a majority of each group did not trust government: African-Americans (59%); Hispanics (54%), and non-Hispanic whites (79%).[46]

Client and Customer Satisfaction

A large number of surveys of clients' evaluations of interactions with public administrators yield the general conclusions that most citizens actually react positively to their own encounters with bureaucrats. For instance,

> Citizens perceive their concrete experiences with bureaucracy in a generally favorable light. Usually the preponderant majority of persons asked describes their recollections or immediate experiences in highly approving terms.
> Most positive evaluation response rates are at least at the two-thirds level,

and many reach beyond 75 percent. Disapproval levels are almost always in the distinct minority, and most fall well below one-third. The vast majority of clients of bureaucracy reports itself as satisfied with the encounter and transaction therein. In most instances bureaucratic personnel are described as helpful, efficient, fair, considerate, and courteous. They are, furthermore, usually perceived as trying to assist, ready to listen, and even willing to adapt the rules and look out for client interest. Also, the actual performance output of bureaucracy is usually praised. The picture presented by citizens in their assessments of bureaucracy appears, in sum, as an almost complete contradiction of the hate image depicted in popular media and academic writing.[47]

Just what accounts for this disparity between abstract views of bureaucracy and concrete interaction remains something of a puzzle.

One can point to three common explanations, though no doubt others could be developed as well:

Flawed Surveys

First, some have argued that the surveys of client/customer evaluations of public administrative encounters are inherently unreliable. Among the pitfalls such surveys allegedly face are that (1) public expectations of bureaucracy are so low that any positive treatment is viewed favorably, (2) respondents to the surveys feel under social (or even political) pressure to answer favorably (the so-called "spiral of silence" effect[48]), and (3) the questions tend to be worded so as to evoke positive responses.[49] These defects are important, but to what extent is a matter of dispute in the literature of public administration.[50]

Unrealistic Public Expectations

Second, there is a commonsense approach to understanding why concrete interactions with public bureaucracy as clients tend to be viewed favorably at the same time that bureaucracy in general is viewed negatively. As Charles Goodsell explains in *The Case for Bureaucracy,*

> Perhaps bureaucracy should be thought of as not so much a terrible beast as a fairly good used car, quite old but well maintained and functioning not all but most of the time. It is those mornings when the car does not start—perhaps once or twice every winter?—that we recognize the machine's fallibility and then malign it furiously. For a fundamental feature of bureaucracy is that it continually performs millions of tiny acts of individual service, such as approving applications, delivering the mail, and answering complaints. Because this ongoing mass of routine achievement is not in itself noteworthy or even capable of intellectual grasp, it operates silently, almost out of sight. The occasional breakdowns, the unusual scandals, the individual instances where a true injustice is done, are what come to our attention and color our overall judgment.[51]

This explanation of the discrepancy between the public's general evaluation of bureaucracy and its specific evaluations of individual encounters in the role of client or customer is supported by some comprehensive empirical analysis. In what remains the most complete research on the matter, Daniel Katz and associates propose in *Bureaucratic Encounters* that "closer examination . . . reveals that general evaluation is related to specific experience if the experience was negative, but not if it was positive. A negative experience with an agency lowers one's general evaluation of government, but a positive experience does not raise it."[52] In Goodsell's terms, those who experience the car's failure to start curse it forever; those for whom it does start seem to feel lucky and to consider themselves exceptions to a pervasive rule. In other words, despite their good fortune with bureaucracy, a large share of the public may nevertheless expect that it usually will not work so well.

Immediacy Bias

A third possible explanation is that "general evaluations of bureaucracy may tap the ideological level, and specific evaluations of experiences may tap the pragmatic level" of an individual's thinking about public administration.[53] It is easy to see how this effect works. We may be satisfied with the courteous, prompt, and fair treatment we receive at the motor vehicle department or the post office and still think, as a matter of public policy, public bureaucracies generally are too expensive for the society to support and too distracting for elected officials to control while also performing their policy making and representational functions well. We could believe that the services that are immediately present to us—the ones that we use personally—are worthwhile, but that those which other people may use—and which we never experience, and perhaps have no personal need for—are undesirable. Those who benefit directly from the Security and Exchange Commission's regulation of securities markets and those who benefit from public welfare programs may be two largely separate groups of people. In other words, in pragmatic terms we may like what *we* get from public administration, whereas we begrudge what it gives to others. We like our subsidies but hate our taxes. As a result, legislators find that it is politically easier to spend than to cut back on expenditures or raise more revenues.

Such attitudes may also be an outgrowth of the deficit spending that prevailed in the 1970s and 1980s. But rather than attack the deficit head-on through reducing popular spending or raising taxes, politicians were prone to suggest that budgets could be balanced by means of tough management that eliminated administrative waste and fraud. Hence, the "bash-a-bureaucrat" syndrome was used with some success by Jimmy Carter and Ronald Reagan, among others. This dynamic abated considerably in the wake of the 1990s surpluses, the Clinton-Gore administration's reinvention effort, and public reversion after so many federal employees were killed and injured in the 1995 Oklahoma City bombing. Without bashing bureaucrats (though with no love for their unions), President George W. Bush placed a heavy emphasis on improving internal administrative management and contracting out as means of promoting cost-effectiveness in response to the huge deficits caused partly by the war on terrorism, especially the military actions in Afghanistan and Iraq. The record high federal deficits that have returned under President Barack Obama have been accompanied by a return of bureaucrat and government bashing.

Each of these explanations for the disparity between the public's general and specific evaluations of public bureaucracy is plausible. Presumably each explains *something* about the disparity, and consequently, each provides a basis for trying to improve the public's understanding of and interaction with public administration and improve public administrators' thinking and dealing with the public.

A Look at Typical Government Services

The public's evaluation of local government services has been studied extensively. Using a method called Percent to Maximum (PTM), Thomas Miller and Michelle Miller analyzed 261 citizen surveys administered in 40 states during the 1980s.[54] The results covered a total population of more than 200,000 Americans and included more than 3,000 questions. PTM converts ratings using different categories and numbers of options into a common scale. For example, it can be used to array three-point scales (good, fair, poor), as well as five-point scales (very good, good, fair, poor, very poor) on a single scale ranging from 0 to 100. A 100 on the scale indicates very good, 75 is good, 50 is neither good nor bad, 25 is bad, and 0 is very bad. Miller and Miller found that overall, local government services are rated positively. The public thinks well of the 21 services studied. Fire protection, library, and trash services were rated above 75. Planning/zoning and street repair were rated lowest, but still somewhat positively. Miller and Miller found that the ratings were stable from one community to another. Consequently, a PTM score of 70 would be unusually positive for street repair, poor for a library, and slightly below average for police.

Theodore Poister and Gary Henry used the PTM scale to report the public's evaluation of the quality of public and private services in Georgia.[55] Overall, they reinforce Miller and Miller's main findings but also offer some surprises. The private sector stacks up less well than the conventional view would suggest. For instance, fast-food restaurants rank lower than the U.S. Postal Service and there is no difference between private doctors' offices and public health clinics. Poister and Henry found that respondents who had used a service during the past six months tended to rate it 10 points higher, on average, than the general public did. However, the overall pattern of responses was not substantially altered: public and private sector ratings were interspersed along the PTM.

Summing up the research on the public's evaluations of public administration is difficult. Not all functions have been studied carefully. As Katz and associates' research suggests, people may evaluate constraint functions much differently than they evaluate fire protection and libraries. Nevertheless, it is clear that the public thinks more highly of many government services than popular rhetoric would suggest. But as Miller and Miller ask, "Is a 'Good' evaluation for police good enough? Can more be expected from a street repair service that gets only 'Fair' evaluations?"[56] All else being equal, almost everyone would want public administration to enjoy even higher ratings. But all else is rarely equal in the public sector. There are competing values, competing visions, and different strategies for dealing with the public.

◆→ PUBLIC ADMINISTRATIVE PERSPECTIVES ON THE PUBLIC

The Traditional Managerial Approach to the Public

From a traditional managerial perspective, interaction with the public should maximize the values of efficiency, economy, and effectiveness. The overwhelming tendency of this perspective is to depersonalize the client or regulatee by turning him or her into a "case." Traditional management puts less reliance on outsourcing than does the NPM. However, when contracting out, it favors selecting the lowest priced competent bidder, and seeks to avoid the appearance of favoritism that can be caused by personal relationships or partnerships with contractors.

Agencies engage in a number of activities to overcome this depersonalization. One strategy is to engage in public relations not only to generate greater political support for their activities but also to help clients, regulatees, and others understand what they do. Educational efforts can be important, as it has been thought that one reason for the public's negative view of public administration is that "the policy makers are remote and their basic goals are not understood."[57]

Another managerial approach for dealing with the public is to institute **ombudsman** arrangements of some sort. In a traditional sense, ombudsmen are independent agents of the legislature who are empowered to investigate specific complaints by individuals alleging maladministration. Such agents can criticize, publicize, and make recommendations, but they cannot reverse the administrative action at issue. The classic ombudsmen originated in Sweden in 1808 and can be found in other Scandinavian countries and several other nations. In the United States, ombudsmen do not fit the traditional concept completely because they are often attached to the administrative agency or executive branch rather than the legislature. Moreover, in the United States, individual members of state legislatures and Congress sometimes effectively function as ombudsmen for their constituents, although here the function is referred to as constituency service or casework. The ombudsman concept is useful from a managerial perspective because it acts as a genuine check on the poor administrative and public relations practices by subordinate public administrators.

Finally, those pursuing the traditional managerial approach should be wary of its tendency to shift the burdens of cost and time to individual members of the public. For example, public administration can be improved from the clients' perspective through **human services integration.** This approach enables individuals seeking or requiring several services, such as food stamps, public health care, and public housing, to apply to one office only. Such "one-stop shopping" for benefits is easier for clients, enables them to gain a better understanding of what programs are available and how they are related to one another, and may also efficiently reduce paperwork.

Dealing with the public is an area where the managerial values of economy and effectiveness may frequently be at odds with one another. Although it is often cheapest to follow the impersonal approach by treating individuals as cases, this approach may be inappropriate to the function being served. This is particularly true in therapeutic functions, such as mental health care and social work. It is more expensive to treat each individual on a personal basis in these areas. Yet by now the record is clear that failure to do so makes it nearly impossible for the administrative function to be performed effectively. In the area of mental health, the courts have sometimes required that each patient or resident of a state facility be provided with some amount of individual treatment.[58]

In view of the tension between social values and those embodied in the traditional managerial approach to public administration, there is no doubt that public administrators should be concerned with the public in all facets of their work. Historically, public administrative theory and practice paid inadequate attention to some aspects of dealing with the public. One result has been marked *underutilization* of services provided by public administrative agencies.[59] This, in itself, would tend to make the administrative state less effective in intervening in the society and economy to promote the public interest.

The New Public Management Approach to the Public

The Public as Customers

The NPM views the public primarily as customers. The term "customer" is used to denote almost all encounters with public agencies. It includes service and regulatory relationships as well as public employment. Welfare recipients are customers of social service agencies; taxpayers are customers of the IRS; applicants for federal jobs are customers of the Office of Personnel Management and/or other agencies. As customers, the public is to be served in a businesslike manner. The emphasis is on effectiveness, efficiency, and cost reduction.

The NPR noted that the term "customer" raises some concern:

> The National Performance Review has received letters and phone calls
> from a few taxpayers who objected to being referred to as the government's
> customers. These people correctly pointed out that they are the government's
> owners or, at the very least, stockholders. But it is possible to be an owner
> and a customer too. For example, if you own stock in Ford Motors,
> your relationship to the company is something like a taxpayer's to the
> government: you own a piece of it. A Ford stockholder can enter another

relationship with the company by buying a Taurus and becoming a valued customer. When taxpayers call the Social Security Administration or stop by the post office, they are customers too. . . .

Applying the customer service concept to government has clear management advantages. . . . It focuses attention on the results the customers want. It highlights the expenditures that yield those results and, by contrast, eliminates the expenditures that don't contribute to good service.[60]

The NPM's devotion to customer service and satisfaction raises some unsettled issues. Because members of the public are not truly the customers of a wide range of agencies, what they want cannot necessarily be determined by what they purchase. To find out *how* the public wants government to serve them when it is not market-driven, the NPM relies on surveys to gain feedback from customers. It also imputes preferences to its customers by emulating the best practices in the private sector through benchmarking. According to the NPR, based on surveys, at the broadest level Americans "want a more efficient government, but they are desperate for a more *effective* government."[61] Consequently, they want government to stop doing things that it cannot do well or that are unnecessary. They do not want to cut costs at the price of effectiveness. At the level of individual agencies, surveys indicate that the public wants faster and more convenient treatment, as well as specific channels for voicing complaints. The NPM strongly supports human services integration, or "one-stop shopping," for its combination of convenience and reduction of redundancy. Benchmarking led to some clear improvements, including the Social Security Administration's "800" telephone service having been considered the best in the business.

These approaches to ascertaining customer preferences downplay the utility of traditional political channels for determining what the public wants. In consequence, at least two problems potentially arise. First, the customers of specific agencies are often a limited segment of the population. Responding to them may be at odds with what a majority of the voters would prefer. For instance, the customers of social welfare agencies or public schools may have preferences for eligibility or educational requirements that differ from those of the electorate at large. Similarly, those subject to regulation may want less red tape, more flexibility, and greater responsiveness to their needs. The NPM is willing to give it to them as long as the results are satisfactory. But when it comes to safety and some environmental matters, the public may not be satisfied with holding regulatees accountable after the fact.

Second, political systems like that of the United States have built-in barriers to making public policy by simple majority preference. For example, providing each state with two senators gives an equal voice to Wyoming and California, even though the latter is more than 76 times larger in population. (In 2012, Wyoming had the smallest population of any U.S. state, according to the U.S. Census Bureau: 576,412). Requirements for supermajorities for treaties and other matters also strengthen the voice of those in the minority on political issues.

Another set of issues that arises when the public is viewed as customers is which customers to satisfy when not all customers have identical or harmonious interests. In the free market, firms would presumably seek to satisfy customers based on long- and/or short-term profitability. For most public agencies, this option does not exist. Even if they were to substitute survey responses for profits, they are likely to operate under a norm or legal requirement of providing service equally to all customers. The U.S. Postal Service is not free to charge its customers the true cost of delivering first-class mail—the price for sending it across the street or across the continent is the same. Consequently, those who primarily send local mail are subsidizing those whose mail goes mostly long distance. Working under a norm of universal service, public school systems cannot write off the customers they find it most costly to serve. The National Labor Relations Board would lose its legitimacy if it were not perceived as reasonably neutral in dealing with the conflicts between its major customers, business and labor. Politics and law, not customer preferences, are usually used to resolve conflicts among the users of government services.

Finally, though not an insuperable problem, identifying customers can be a thorny one. Who are the customers of the criminal justice system? Lawyers, jurors, the victims, or perpetrators of crimes? Who are the customers of prisons, the inmates or the taxpayers who buy space to confine them? Are the Federal Aviation Administration's customers the flying public, people in neighborhoods near airports, the airlines, pilots, air traffic controllers, companies that build passenger airplanes, or airline maintenance firms? As noted previously, because different groups served by agencies have disparate interests, answering "all of the above" is not always useful.

These problems are real, but they do not mean that considering the public to be customers is inappropriate or unfeasible. Treating the public as customers can reinvigorate and strengthen agencies' commitment to service. During the 1990s, more than 100 federal agencies set standards for serving customers.

Contractors as Partners

The NPM treats contractors as partners in delivering public goods and services and in obtaining results. The idea of partnering with contractors flows from the NPM's tenet that government should steer, not row. The private for-profit and nonprofit sectors are viewed as a valuable resource for accomplishing governmental ends.

The NPR sought to "simplify the procurement process by rewriting federal regulations—shifting from rigid rules to guiding principles."[62] These principles were aimed at eliminating a great deal of red tape and restoring common sense and trust to dealings with contractors. Agencies were encouraged to establish more effective processes for "listening" to "vendors who do business with the government."[63]

As noted in Chapter 2, Congress took a far greater step toward partnering with contractors by enacting the Federal Activities Inventory Reform Act of 1998, generally known by its acronym, FAIR. The act requires executive agencies annually to provide the Office of Management and Budget (OMB) with inventories of activities that are not inherently governmental and therefore could potentially be outsourced. For example, the General Services Administration identified about 4,000 jobs as "commercial competitive," including positions dealing with maintenance, repair, supply, and personnel management.[64]

FAIR gave new impetus to the A-76 competitive sourcing process mentioned in Chapter 2. However, OMB efforts notwithstanding, A-76 remained a cumbersome impediment to more substantial partnering with contractors. Both labor and business have criticized its rules as biased against them. As one Senate staffer said, "It doesn't matter what side you are on, no one is happy with the A-76 process,"[65] and as noted earlier, there has been a congressionally imposed moratorium on its use since 2009.

The fate of A-76 notwithstanding, partnering with contractors is already widespread in the Department of Energy and in many local governments. In many situations, government employees and their contractor counterparts work side-by-side in the same workplace. It is an area in which reinvention brings about fundamental change in public administrative practices and one that will continue to merit a great deal of study in the coming years.

The Political Approach to the Public

The political approach to public administration emphasizes the values of representation, responsiveness, and accountability to the public. This often dictates that the public be afforded means for *participating* in public administration. Public participation of some kind is viewed as contributing to the ability of public administrators to understand and respond to the public's concerns. It also requires that the administrators explain their actions, policies, and so forth to the public and is seen as a means of more completely incorporating the citizenry into the governing of the administrative state. Specifically, it is argued that:

1. A lack of public participation in modern governance reduces the capacity of the political system to be representative and responsive.
2. Nonparticipation also erodes the quality of citizenship in democratic nations by reducing the citizen's sense of moral and political obligation to take part in governance.
3. Nonparticipation promotes ignorance about the way government functions; participation, in contrast, promotes understanding.
4. The absence of meaningful channels for citizen participation in government leads to alienation on the part of the public. Without participation, the public feels no sense of "ownership" of or responsibility for governmental actions. On the contrary, the citizenry believes that it is acted upon (that is, subject) rather than being an actor in government. Participation also reduces alienation by providing the public with a greater sense of control over its environment.

5. Participation promotes a sense of political community and political integration. It helps individuals see the relationship between what they want from government and what others, with conflicting viewpoints, are seeking. Ideally, participation enables people to understand and respect each other's political perspectives. Rather than promoting conflict and competition, participation is viewed as promoting cooperation.

6. Participation promotes the sense that government is legitimate and fosters compliance with its decisions. Bureaucratic expertise, specialization, and impersonality have been considered particularly important in this regard.[66] However, as noted previously, impersonality may not be well suited to some administrative functions involving service and therapy. In these areas, individuals are thought to be more apt to comply with administrative decisions, procedures, and directives if they are allowed to participate in their formulation and implementation. Negotiated rule making, discussed in Chapter 9, is based on a similar theory.

There is a large body of literature and thought behind each of these propositions concerning the desirability of public participation in public administration.[67] Each proposition remains debatable, but for the most part, the political approach to public administration is committed to finding means of expanding public participation to improve civic-mindedness and administration.

Direct Participation

There are some outstanding examples of long-term citizen participation in public administration. Public school governance is one example. Historically, it strongly emphasized the need for local control, and accordingly, there has been great diversity in teacher qualifications, curriculum, extracurricular activities, class size, school calendar, extent of collective bargaining, and grouping of pupils in schools by age and ability. The growing federal role in public education is reducing the efficacy of such grassroots public participation. The participation of farmers and ranchers is a long-standing feature of agricultural administration. New York State's citizen-participation specialists have been effective in facilitating public participation in dealing with environmental problems such as toxic waste sites and water pollution.[68] Participation through organized interest groups is also prevalent, as noted in Chapter 2, and has been institutionalized at the federal level by the Federal Advisory Committee Act of 1972.

These examples of workable citizen participation in public administration notwithstanding, there have also been some remarkable failures. Both the Economic Opportunity Act of 1964 and the Model Cities Act of 1966 sought to incorporate citizen participation in federal programs dealing with the needs of the poor, especially the urban poor. The Economic Opportunity Act was the basis for the poverty program. It sought to incorporate citizen participation through representation on the governing boards of community action programs. These boards also included public officials and representatives of private social service agencies. The representatives of the poor were to be elected by the poor. Participatory community action agencies (CAAs) were also relied on by the Model Cities Program. In both cases, the drive for citizen participation was frustrated. For one reason or another, the poor did not participate. As Daniel Patrick Moynihan observed, "The turnouts [in elections to CAAs] in effect declared that the poor weren't interested: in Philadelphia 2.7 percent; Los Angeles 0.7 percent; Boston 2.4 percent; Cleveland 4.2 percent; Kansas City, Mo. 5.0 percent. Smaller communities sometimes got larger turnouts, but never anything nearly approaching that of a listless off-year election."[69]

Moynihan claimed that these low turnouts indicated that participation is a middle-class value of little interest to the lower class. The poor, in his view, needed money, jobs, housing, and many other things much more than they needed "identity," "a sense of community," and "control over their destiny." Others have argued that representation of the poor was further compromised by the tendency of their elected representatives to be co-opted and to have sometimes docilely allowed the middle-class representatives on community action agencies to direct funds toward the real clientele—not the poor but the city's businesses.[70]

Client-Centered Administration

On balance it is reasonable to conclude that participation can work in some programs and among some groups of the population, as in the case of public school governance, farmers, and a considerable range of advisory committees representing economic and social interests. However, it clearly does not work among all programs and groups, as experience with poverty and model cities programs indicates. Advocates of greater public participation in public administration have argued that, consequently, administrative agencies dealing with clients who for one reason or another are unable to represent themselves effectively should be **client-centered**.[71] Being client-centered is like being customer-oriented except that the "customers" are unable to play their role well. Prime candidates for becoming client-centered include agencies dealing with children; the mentally ill or disabled; illiterates; and, in some cases, the chronically poor.

Client-centered agencies are advocates for their clientele. They promote human services integration where specialization frustrates the ability of clients, such as the poor, to receive all the assistance they need. Combining housing benefits, health programs, and nutritional programs provides an illustration. When programs dealing with these areas are placed in different agencies and not integrated even though they are directed toward many of the same clients, the client is apt to face redundancies in filling out forms, to encounter public administrators in three agencies rather than just one, and possibly to face different eligibility standards that frustrate gaining assistance.

Equally important, because no single agency has full responsibility for the client, each is likely to be responsive to other interests that may be in conflict with what the client is seeking. Housing agencies may be more responsive to construction, banking, building maintenance, and business interests; health agencies may be more responsive to medical and pharmaceutical interests; and nutritional programs may be placed in agricultural agencies, as is true of the federal food stamp program. Yet it would be hard to argue that health and nutrition are not related or that housing is not relevant to programs seeking to promote clients' health and nutrition. If all these programs were placed in the same agency, the argument goes, it could not help but see the client as the center of things and the other interests as peripheral. The case of "Bad Blood," discussed in Chapter 8, in which the Public Health Service sought to advance medical knowledge at the expense of the health of the "patients," is a dramatic example of what can go wrong when agencies are not client-centered. A more mundane benefit of client-centered organization is that it may make service delivery easier.

Coproduction

In some ways, **coproduction** is the opposite of client-centered public administration. Client-centered administration seeks to create organizational structures and programmatic arrangements that focus on clients' interests, because the clients are believed to be unable to assert these interests adequately. Coproduction assumes that the public can understand its interests and cooperate with public administrators in performing functions. Coproduction is "the joint provision of public services by public agencies and service consumers."[72] Everyday examples are residents carrying trash out to the curb for collection, sorting it for recycling, and participating voluntarily in organizing recreation programs that use public facilities. Other possibilities include community-based crime prevention groups; a statewide "green-up" (that is, clean up litter) day, as has long existed in Vermont; and groups such as "friends" of the library, parks, or symphony.

The simplicity of some aspects of coproduction should not obscure the political importance of this approach to public administration. It puts forward a different model of administrative service delivery. In this type of joint venture, the citizen is a participant, not merely a consumer, customer, or subject. Citizens are jointly responsible for productivity and the quality of services. Consequently, they may learn about how a public administrative function is organized and operated. A citizen-based crime prevention organization cannot fail to learn more about the problems faced by the police and how they cope with them. Moreover, some believe that coproduction can help "to build in citizens a *loyalty* to place, neighbors, and their community."[73] This loyalty results from "face-to-face contact and an investment of energy in the improvement of neighborhoods and communities."[74]

Public Interest Groups

Public interest groups are another vehicle for increasing the public's voice in public administration, albeit somewhat amorphously.[75] In Chapter 2, we noted that public interest groups seek collective goods that do not selectively and materially benefit their membership. While the distinction between this type of group and a traditional interest group may at times be blurred, there is a difference in emphasis. Public interest groups seem concerned with "representing the people against the special interests."[76] Common Cause, Public Citizen, the Natural Resources Defense Council, the Center for Effective Government (formerly OMB Watch), and Consumers Union are examples. These groups often interact with public administrators in an effort to promote the groups' views of the public's interest. They make considerable use of the opportunity, afforded by the Administrative Procedure Act of 1946, to participate in administrative rule making by submitting information, presenting their views, and/or testifying before agencies. They also use the National Environmental Policy Act of 1969 in this regard.

Public interest groups provide an important counterbalance to traditional interest groups in the realm of bureaucratic politics. The average citizen has neither time nor inclination to monitor what agencies are doing, challenge their proposed rules, or present his or her perspective to agencies. But the public interest group does, and through various means of monitoring and constant attention to agency proposals in the *Federal Register* and equivalent volumes in the states, these groups can have an important cumulative impact. The main issue is less whether they have an impact than whether they represent their members in any meaningful sense. There is no way of ascertaining this, but to the extent that such groups represent the public, it is broad middle-class interests on which they focus.

The Legal Approach to the Public

The legal approach to the interaction of the public with public administration seeks to assure that individuals' constitutional and statutory rights are protected. This concern has been reflected in a number of changes in constitutional doctrine and administrative law practices over the years, especially since 1946. Together, these changes led to the judicialization of many public administrative practices and greater judicial review of public administrators by the courts. Administrative hearings before administrative law judges or similar functionaries are now a standard feature of public administration in the United States. In most instances, the individual member of the public is entitled to be represented by counsel, provided at his or her expense, at such a hearing. A considerable body of constitutional rights for customers, clients, regulatees, and litigants now exists. Street-level encounters are also regulated by constitutional law as are some aspects of government relations with contractors (see Chapter 11). The opportunities and rights of individuals to participate in public administrative activities are defined by statute, but once established by law they cannot usually be denied to a specific individual without due process of law. The individual's ability to initiate litigation has been enhanced by a number of developments, including the enactment of the National Environmental Policy Act and the development of judicial doctrines that allow for relatively broad "standing" * to litigate an injury to an interest caused by some aspect of public administration.[77]

---

* Standing is the ability to show sufficient stake (e.g., personal injury) to bring suit in a justiciable controversy.

Overall, the legal approach creates a network of rights to protect the public against arbitrary, capricious, invidious, illegal, or unconstitutional administrative action. It provides individuals with avenues to contest administrative actions before judges or other neutral decision makers. As discussed in the next chapter, it establishes an important check on administrative values, such as efficiency and economy, which can adversely affect individual rights.

Conclusion: Putting the Public Back in Public Administration

The growing concern with "the public" is one of the most important recent developments in American public administrative theory and practice. In the past, public administration paid lip service to the concept of the "public" and the existence of a public. The notion that somehow the public must be the focus of public administration seemed too threatening and too irrelevant to expert, politically neutral public administration. One expert's rendition of the top 10 reasons why public administrators have been reluctant to involve the public is presented in Box 10.5. Many dismissed the concept of a public as too ambiguous, too romanticized a notion, too politically oriented, and too much an aggregation to be of serious use.[78] In an effort to make the concept of the public more concrete, the traditional managerial approach tended to focus on the public as clients or regulatees, processed as cases. Today the NPM views the public more as customers.

The political approach tends to aggregate individuals into social and economic interest groups. This is an effort to promote the values of representativeness, responsiveness, and administrative accountability through greater opportunities for public participation in public administration. The citizenry is considered in such categories as "farmers," "the poor," and so forth.

10.5 The Top 10 Reasons Not to Involve the Public in Administrative Decisions

10. We didn't have to in the good old days.
9. We are the experts, and our way is the right way.
8. This issue is too technical for the public to understand.
7. They all hate us.
6. The public can't understand why this project is needed.
5. There are too many of "them" and "they" are too organized.
4. We won't be able to do everything they want.
3. No one cares.
2. We don't have time—our schedule and budget are too tight.
1. It didn't work the last time we tried.

Source: Martha Rozelle, "The Top 10 Reasons Not to Involve the Public in Your Decisions," *The New Public Innovator,* No. 95 (Spring–Summer 1999): 22 ff.

The Federal Advisory Committee Act of 1972 affords the opportunity for participation to a wide range of interests with which federal agencies are involved.

The legal approach views the public as a collection of individuals who possess certain constitutional and statutory rights that must be protected against administrative encroachment. It regards the protection of these rights as obviously in the public interest.

For the most part, these perspectives are so broad that a synthesis may be possible. However, the conflicts among their values and approaches for achieving these values should not be underestimated. In the past, the traditional managerial perspective considered public participation inefficient and ineffective because it brought amateurs into public administration. Public participation was also viewed as too expensive. Those imbued with the traditional managerial perspective would admit, though, that the citizenry could legitimately act as an "authoritative critic" of administrative actions, to use Woodrow Wilson's term.[79] Certainly, the "citizen-subject" or "citizen-consumer" of administrative action could develop a legitimate and informed opinion about it. The trouble was that the public seemed unclear in its evaluation of public administration. In the abstract the public was critical, in the area of services it was generally positive, and in the area of constraint it was negative.

Neither the traditional managerial approach nor the NPM is as rights-oriented as the legal perspectives. Both are at odds with the legal approach's promotion of "judicialization" of public administration, which has a tendency to fragment authority and to be time-consuming. No doubt, those committed to the traditional managerial view that administrative legitimacy flows from technical expertise are also opposed to the increasing scope of judicial review and oversight of administrative action as well as to the NPM's focus on satisfying customers. Finally, there is plenty of potential for the political and legal approaches to clash over the basic question "Who is eligible to participate?" Many categorizations of people for participation in public administration run the risk of violating the constitutional requirements of equal protection (discussed in the following chapter).

Despite these conflicts among the perspectives, matters pertaining to the public and public administration have tended to sort themselves out by *function*. While recognizing that the categories are broad and imperfect, the following patterns have emerged.

Service

The traditional managerial perspective toward the public prevails where the function is service of a nontherapeutic nature, such as retirement benefits, unemployment compensation, and workers' compensation. For the most part, these services involve routine handling of numerous individuals who fall into similar categories (e.g., reach the age of retirement). Treating them as "cases" is efficient and apparently does not seriously offend the clients, as is suggested by the public's evaluation of such activities. Nevertheless, the NPM would change the focus from cases to customers and emphasize better service.

Therapy

Therapeutic service and regulation for the purpose of providing therapy, as in public mental health facilities and prisons, tend to require a more client-centered and/or participatory approach. Prisons and residential mental health facilities come close to being totally client-centered in the sense that all the ostensible needs of the client (or regulatee, in this context) are met there. Welfare and some health programs also tend to be client-centered to a considerable extent. Therapy requires individualized attention. This is true in medical and psychological terms, but it is also pertinent in a social sense. It is not an accident that social workers deal with their clients on an individual basis and in a face-to-face context. Social work may involve visits by a public administrator to the home of the client, and a plan of therapeutic action may be developed for each client, based on his or her needs. A basic notion here, though perhaps a somewhat paternalistic one, is that those subject to therapy are unable to assert their interest adequately. Regarding the poor as customers may overlook the possibility that some people are poor because, for one reason or another and quite possibly beyond their control, they are unable to function well in markets. Where sociotherapy is organized bureaucratically, as Ms. Sabol found (Box 10.3), it may become an impediment to meeting the client's needs.

Regulation

Regulation not involving therapy tends to be organized along the lines of the traditional managerial perspective but is also strongly influenced by considerations of legal rights and procedures. Examples would be regulation by tax agencies and motor vehicle departments. Agencies engaged in these functions treat individuals as cases and seek to process them as efficiently and economically as possible. However, because some fundamental rights are involved, the legal perspective is incorporated to a considerable degree, or even overarching as a means of protecting individuals. Customer service standards also help assure fair, prompt, and less burdensome encounters.

Litigation and Street-Level Encounters

These kinds of interaction between the public and public administrators are largely informed by the values of the legal approach. The rights of the individual are specified in some detail, and certain procedures are required to assure that these rights are respected. This has gone so far that it may be considered unconstitutional for the police to approach an individual walking on the street and ask who he or she is and what he or she is doing—unless there is a reasonable suspicion that the person has done or is about to do something illegal.[80]* The courts have been particularly active in defining the constitutional limits on "stop and frisk" operations by police. Litigation is the full realization of

---

* By contrast, motor vehicle stops at checkpoints to question motorists about criminal activity they may have witnessed are constitutional, if reasonable. See *Illinois v. Lidster*, 540 U.S. 419 (2004) and *Michigan Department of State Police v. Sitz*, 496 U.S. 444 (1990).

the legal perspective. As in the case of regulation, in general, customer service standards can play a significant role in improving these encounters.

Participation

Individuals also participate in public administration. This role is dictated almost entirely by the political perspective, and the values associated with it overlay some of the practices found in the realm of service delivery and therapy. Participation is prevalent in federal agricultural policy. It is important in some environmental and public works policies. The regulation of economic concerns and activities, though not of individuals, also tends to emphasize participation by organized interest groups, as we saw in the previous chapter. But participation is so fundamental a political process for obtaining representativeness, responsiveness, and accountability that it has worked its way into many aspects of public administration. For instance, coproduction is a means of participation in service delivery. Client-centered administrative operations are viewed as a means of representing and responding to the interests of individuals who otherwise might not be able to assert them well. Mental health patients are a clear example.

At a broader level of economic regulation and subsidization, client-centered agencies become "clientele" agencies, such as the U.S. Departments of Agriculture, Commerce, and Labor. Here the political approach is followed in imputing the same sets of interests to all the members of a categorical group, such as organized labor, seen as the political constituency of the agency. Public school governance is another manifestation of society's overriding concern with the values of the political approach to public administration.

The association of these approaches and values with different administrative functions in different degrees does create tensions for day-to-day public administration. Yet as long as the society seeks conflicting goals— greater administrative efficiency, customer satisfaction, public participation, strict protection of an individual's constitutional and legal rights—the balance already reached in the public's interaction with public administration seems reasonably sound. No doubt adjustments can be made, but once again, no fundamental changes are likely unless conflicts among the values and goals of public administration can be fully resolved. There are, however, at least two aspects of the public and public administration that all analysts agree on.

First, the public would benefit from a better understanding of public administration, and public administration would benefit from a public that knew more about its functions, concepts, values, and processes. As Woodrow Wilson, who is credited with beginning the self-conscious study of public administration in the United States, noted, "The problem is to make public opinion efficient without suffering it to be meddlesome. . . . [A]s superintending the greater forces of formative policy alike in politics and administration, public criticism is altogether safe and beneficent, altogether indispensable."[81]

Second, the public's interaction with public administration can be vastly improved through paperwork reduction, the use of plain language, and the expansion of e-government.

- *Paperwork reduction.* Public administration requires paperwork—lots of it. The Paperwork Reduction Acts of 1980 and 1995, mentioned in Chapter 9, are premised on the belief that less is more. Regardless, the annual paperwork burden thrust on the public rose to 8.2 billion hours in 2002.[82] The vast majority of paperwork is produced by the Internal Revenue Service (6.5 billion hours, constituting 81 percent of the total in 2002). The Environmental Protection Agency, the Securities and Exchange Commission, and the Departments of Health and Human Services, Transportation, and Labor are also large generators at more than 100 million hours annually.[83] The managerial, political, and legal approaches to public administration agree that the less paperwork, the better. The question is not whether but how to achieve reductions. At the federal level, the Office of Management and Budget's Office of Information and Regulatory Affairs is charged with blocking agencies' unnecessary and duplicative efforts to collect information. However, its efforts have been inconsistent and, in any case, may be the equivalent of trying to bail out a sinking supertanker with a leaky bucket.[84]
- *Plain language.* The NPR emphasized the desirability of using plain, understandable language in federal administration. "Bureaucratese" is thought to alienate and confuse the public, create mistakes, cause complaints, and waste time and resources. Somehow, administrative language turns ordinary desks into "student classroom modules" and employee dismissals into "involuntary career events."[85] Experts urge periodic or continuing reviews of all documents, forms, regulations, and directives, especially those used by the public. When writing, administrators should use short sentences and simple tenses. They should avoid abbreviations and acronyms as well as "strings of nouns" as in "surface water quality protection procedures."[86]
- *E-government.* E-gov holds great potential for facilitating the public's interaction with public administration. Agencies can use the Internet to disseminate reports, studies, rules, information about their operations, procedures, and eligibility requirements for benefits. They can create electronic reading rooms to reduce the number of freedom of information requests they receive and process. E-gov initiatives can increase public participation in agency rule making and other decision making. E-gov can enable individuals to pay taxes and fees as well as apply for benefits and licenses electronically. In some cases, adjudication—especially appeals—can also be handled electronically. Because e-gov ordinarily reduces agency expenses, its use is limited primarily by imagination and technology.[87]

Together, paperwork reduction, plain language, and e-gov can create synergies that may substantially transform the relationship between public administration and the public. Twenty-five years ago, few, if any, would have thought that someone renewing a vehicle registration would be considered a customer who could be served online at home or at an electronic kiosk in a shopping mall. Twenty years from now, it is quite possible that the public will know much more about what agencies do and how they do it, and find it far easier to deal with them.

STUDY QUESTIONS

1. Consider a recent interaction you had with some aspect of public administration. How would you describe your role? What approach did the agency or official take toward you in that role? How satisfactory or unsatisfactory was the experience? Why?

2. Do you find yourself to be like the public generally in expressing both criticism and praise of public administration? If so, how would you explain your evaluations of it? If not, what is your personal evaluation of public administration? How did you come by that evaluation?

3. It would appear that the public can love and hate bureaucracy at the same time. How would you account for these seemingly contradictory attitudes? In your judgment, are public attitudes towards bureaucracy "rational"?

4. How realistic do you think greater citizen participation in public administration is? Do you favor or oppose it? Why?

5. The National Performance Review indicated that many people are uneasy with the idea that the American people are customers of government. How appropriate do you find the term "customers"? Why?

6. E-gov can facilitate the public's interaction with public administration in many contexts, especially as clients and customers. Do you think it also has the potential to strengthen democratic citizenship in the contemporary administrative state? Why or why not?

NOTES

1. Daniel Katz et al., *Bureaucratic Encounters* (Ann Arbor: University of Michigan, Institute for Social Research, 1975), table 2.1.

2. Ibid., 101–116.

3. U.S. Bureau of Justice Statistics, "One in 34 U.S. Adults Under Correctional Supervision in 2011, Lowest Rate Since 2000," (November 29, 2012); http://www.bjs.gov/content/pub/press/cpus11ppus11pr.cfm. Of the total, about 2,239,800 were in prisons or jails and the remainder were either on probation or parole.

4. See Cesar Parales, "The Fair Hearing Process," *Brooklyn Law Review* 56 (1990): 889–898.

5. David H. Rosenbloom, Rosemary O'Leary, and Joshua Chanin, *Public Administration and Law,* 3rd ed. (Boca Raton, FL: CRC/Taylor & Francis, 2010), chap. 6.

6. Paul Light, *The True Size of Government* (Washington, DC: Brookings Institution, 1999), 9–10.

7. Christopher Lee, "Big Government Gets Bigger," *Washington Post,* October 6, 2006. Online at http://www.washingtonpost.com/wp-dyn/content/article/2006/10/05/AR2006100501782.html. The federal government does not collect comprehensive data on federal contract workers. The 14.6 million figure cited in the text is larger than the 2 million reported by the Bureau of Labor Statistics because the General Services Administration's Federal Procurement Data System and the Employment Requirements Matrix from the Bureau of Labor Statistics undercounts contract employees whose jobs derive from federal contract work. See Kathryn Anne Edwards, "Outsourced Federal Jobs Likely to be Low Wage," *Economic Snapshot,* Economic Policy Institute, February 11, 2009. Online at: http://www.epi.org/publication/snapshots_20090210/.

8. Light, *The True Size of Government,* 154. For recent federal data, see: Barack Obama, "Memorandum for the Heads of Executive Departments and Agencies, Subject: Government Contracting," Washington, DC: The White House Press Office, March 4, 2009. Online at: http://www.whitehouse.gov/the_press_office/Memorandum-for-the-Heads-of-Executive-Departments-and-Agencies-Subject-Government.

9. Ralph P. Hummel, *The Bureaucratic Experience* (New York: St. Martin's, 1977), 20.

10. Ibid., 29.

11. Ibid., 57.

12. Ibid., 56.

13. Victor Thompson, *Modern Organization* (New York: Knopf, 1961), 170.

14. Reinhard Bendix, *Nation Building and Citizenship* (New York: John Wiley, 1964), 129.

15. Thompson, *Modern Organization,* 172–173.

16. Alvin Gouldner, "Red Tape as a Social Problem," in R. K. Merton et al., Eds., *Reader in Bureaucracy* (Glencoe, IL: Free Press, 1952), 413.

17. Gideon Sjoberg et al., "Bureaucracy and the Lower Class," in F. Rourke, Ed., *Bureaucratic Power in National Politics,* 3d ed. (Boston: Little, Brown, 1978), 40.

18. Katz et al., *Bureaucratic Encounters,* 193.

19. Frederick Mosher, *Democracy and the Public Service* (New York: Oxford University Press, 1968), 3–4.

20. Emmette S. Redford, *Democracy in the Administrative State* (New York: Oxford University Press, 1969), 66.

21. Al Gore, *Common Sense Government Works Better & Costs Less* (Washington, DC: Government Printing Office, 1995), 19.

22. See B. Dan Wood and Richard W. Waterman, *Bureaucratic Dynamics* (Boulder, CO: Westview Press, 1994); Rosenbloom, O'Leary, and Chanin, *Public Administration and Law,* 3d ed., chap. 9; and Robert Katzmann, "Explaining Agency Decision-Making," in David H. Rosenbloom and Richard Schwartz, Eds., *Handbook of Regulation and Administrative Law* (New York: Marcel Dekker, 1994), chap. 12.

23. Seymour Martin Lipset and William Schneider, *The Confidence Gap: Business, Labor, and Government in the Public Mind* (New York: Free Press, 1983), 1–2; Dan Balz and Richard Morin, "A Tide of Pessimism and Political Powerlessness Rises," *Washington Post,* 3 November 1991.

24. G. Calvin Mackenzie and Judith Labiner, *Opportunity Lost: The Rise and Fall of Trust and Confidence in Government after September 11* (Washington, DC: Center for Public Service, Brookings Institution, 2002), 6.

25. Ibid., 3; Richard Morin and Claudia Deane, "Poll: Americans' Trust in Government Grows," *Washingtonpost.com,* 28 September 2001.

26. Richard Morin, "Unconventional Wisdom," *Washington Post,* 8 October 1995, C5.

27. Richard Morin, "Reality Check: The Politics of Mistrust," *Washington Post,* 29 January 1996, A1, A6.

28. Al Gore, *From Red Tape to Results: Creating a Government That Works Better & Costs Less* (Washington, DC: Government Printing Office, 1993), 1. In 1991, the figure was 49 cents on the dollar; Balz and Morin, "A Tide of Pessimism and Political Powerlessness Rises."

29. Mackenzie and Labiner, *Opportunity Lost,* 11, 12.

30. Alliance for Redesigning Government/National Academy of Public Administration, *The Public Innovator,* no. 28, 11 May 1995, 2.

31. Stephen Barr, "Americans Gain a Small Measure of Confidence in Government," *Washington Post,* 24 March 1997, A17.

32. Mackenzie and Labiner, *Opportunity Lost,* 13.

33. Pew Research Center for the People & the Press, *Majority Says the Federal Government Threatens Their Personal Rights,* January 31, 2013. Online at: http://www.people-press.org/2013/01/31/majority-says-the-federal-government-threatens-their-personal-rights/.

34. Mackenzie and Labiner, *Opportunity Lost,* 2.

35. Pew Research Center, *Majority Says the Federal Government Threatening.*

36. Ibid.

37. Charles Reich, "The New Property," *Yale Law Journal* 73 (1964): 733–787.

38. Ibid., 746.

39. Milton Friedman, *Capitalism and Freedom* (Chicago: University of Chicago Press, 1962), 8–9.

40. Reich, "The New Property," 747; David H. Rosenbloom, *Federal Service and the Constitution* (Ithaca, NY: Cornell University Press, 1971), chap. 6; Ralph S. Brown, Jr., *Loyalty and Security* (New Haven, CT: Yale University Press, 1958), vii, 18, 377; *Board of County Commissioners, Wabaunsee County v. Umbehr,* 518 U.S. 669 (1996); *O'Hare Truck v. City of Northlake,* 518 U.S. 712 (1996).

41. Friedrich A. Hayek, *The Road to Serfdom* (Chicago: University of Chicago Press, 1944).

42. Michael Fletcher, "Blacks Value Government, Poll Shows," *Washington Post,* 4 March 1996, A13.

43. Mackenzie and Labiner, *Opportunity Lost,* 10. The mean was 3.96 on a scale from 1 (cut back greatly) to 6 (maintain).

44. Ibid., 5.

45. Steven Pearlstein, "Reality Check: The Politics of Mistrust," *Washington Post,* 30 January 1996, A1, A5.

46. Pew Research Center, *Majority Says the Federal Government Threatening.*

47. Charles T. Goodsell, *The Case for Bureaucracy* (Chatham, NJ: Chatham House, 1983), 29.

48. Elisabeth Noelle-Neumann, *The Spiral of Silence: Public Opinion—Our Social Skin.* (Chicago: The University of Chicago Press, 1984).

49. Ibid., 31.

50. Ibid., chap. 2.

51. Goodsell, *The Case for Bureaucracy,* 37.

52. Katz et al., *Bureaucratic Encounters,* 186.

53. Ibid., 187.

54. Thomas Miller and Michelle Miller, "Standards of Excellence: U.S. Residents' Evaluations of Local Government Services," *Public Administration Review* 51 (November/December 1991): 503–513.

55. Theodore Poister and Gary Henry, "Citizen Ratings of Public and Private Service Quality," *Public Administration Review* 54 (March/April 1994): 155–160.

56. Miller and Miller, "Standards of Excellence," 504.

57. Katz et al., *Bureaucratic Encounters,* 188.

58. *Wyatt v. Stickney,* 325 F. Supp. 781; 334 F. Supp. 1341 (1971); 344 F. Supp. 373; 344 F. Supp. 387 (1972); *Youngberg v. Romeo,* 451 U.S. 982 (1982).

59. Katz et al., *Bureaucratic Encounters,* chap. 2.

60. Bill Clinton and Al Gore, *Putting Customers First: Standards for Serving the American People* (Washington, DC: Government Printing Office, 1994), 5–7.

61. Gore, *Common Sense Government,* 14.

62. Gore, *From Red Tape to Results,* 28.

63. Ibid., 29.

64. U.S. General Accounting Office, *Competitive Contracting: The Understandability of FAIR Act Inventories Was Limited* (Washington, DC: General Accounting Office, 2000), 26.

65. George Cahlink, "Privatization Rules May Get Overhaul," *Federal Times,* 3 July 2000, 18.

66. Max Weber, *From Max Weber: Essays in Sociology,* Trans. and Ed. H. H. Gerth and C. W. Mills (New York: Oxford University Press, 1958), chap. 8.

67. See Samuel Krislov and David H. Rosenbloom, *Representative Bureaucracy and the American Political System* (New York: Praeger, 1981), chap. 5, for a brief review.

68. Richard Schwartz, "Public Participation and Democratic Decisionmaking: Clean Water for the Empire State?" Paper delivered at the Annual Meeting of the Society for the Study of Social Problems, Chicago, 14 August 1987.

69. Daniel P. Moynihan, *Maximum Feasible Misunderstanding* (New York: Free Press, 1970), 137.

70. William Morrow, *Public Administration* (New York: Random House, 1975), 198.

71. This term gained currency in the movement for a "new public administration." See Frank Marini, Ed., *Toward a New Public Administration: The Minnowbrook Perspective* (Scranton, PA: Chandler, 1971).

72. Charles Levine, "Citizenship and Service Delivery: The Promise of Coproduction," *Public Administration Review* 44 (Special Issue, March 1984): 181.

73. Ibid., 185.

74. Ibid.

75. See Krislov and Rosenbloom, *Representative Bureaucracy,* 170–175.

76. Ibid., 172.

77. Rosenbloom, O'Leary, and Chanin, *Public Administration and Law,* 3rd ed., chaps. 2, 3, and 8.

78. David Mathews, "The Public in Practice and Theory," *Public Administration Review* 44 (Special Issue, March 1984): 120–125.

79. Woodrow Wilson, "The Study of Administration," *Political Science Quarterly* 56 (December 1941): 498 (originally published in 1887).
80. *Kolender v. Lawson*, 461 U.S. 352 (1983). See also *Hiibel v. Sixth Judicial District Court of Nevada*, 542 U.S. 177 (2004).
81. Wilson, "The Study of Administration," 499.
82. Mollie Ziegler, "Agencies Fail to Rein in Paperwork Burden on Public," *Federal Times*, 21 April 2003, 6.
83. Ibid.
84. Ibid.
85. Robert Beck, "Drop the Jargon," *Federal Times*, 16 December 2002, 18.
86. Ibid.
87. Jane Fountain, *Building the Virtual State* (Washington, DC: Brookings Institution, 2001); Kelly Edmiston, "State and Local E-Government," *American Review of Public Administration* 33 (March 2003): 20–45.

ADDITIONAL READING

Frederickson, H. George, and Ralph Clark Chandler, Eds. "Citizenship and Public Administration." *Public Administration Review* 44 (Special Issue, March 1984): 97–204.

Goodsell, Charles. *The Case for Bureaucracy,* 4th ed. Washington, DC: CQ Press, 2003.

Hummel, Ralph P. *The Bureaucratic Experience,* 5th ed. Armonk, NY: M.E. Sharpe, 2007.

Schacter, Hindy Lauer. *Reinventing Government or Reinventing Ourselves.* Albany: State University Press of New York, 1997.

PUBLIC ADMINISTRATION AND THE PUBLIC WEB SITES

The National Academy of Public Administration and the Brookings Institution publish studies of public administration and the public from time to time at http://www.napawash.org and http://www.brookings.edu.

CHAPTER 11

PUBLIC ADMINISTRATION AND DEMOCRATIC CONSTITUTIONALISM

Key Learning Objectives

1. Understand constitutional values and how they can be in tension with the three sets of public administrative values.

2. Know the structure of constitutional substantive rights, property rights under the "takings" clause, procedural due process, equal protection, and Fourth Amendment privacy rights.

3. Gain a general understanding of "state action" doctrine and why it is important in contemporary public administration.

This chapter explains why public administrators must understand constitutional values and discusses the nature of those values. Among the constitutional values considered are the separation of powers, legitimacy, diversity, liberty and freedom, property rights, procedural due process, equal protection, individuality and privacy, and equity. This chapter does not attempt to teach constitutional law but rather to explain the nature of these fundamental values in the context of public administration. It sets forth the general structure of several constitutional rights. The concept of state action, which has important implications for privatization, collaborative governance, and governmental efforts to operate corporate-style agencies, is also analyzed.

There are times when the values of managerially and politically oriented public administration may be in pronounced conflict with the values and principles of democratic constitutionalism. There have been many instances in which public administrative action, taken in good faith and seeking to maximize values inherent in the traditional managerial and political approaches, has been declared unconstitutional by the courts. The new public management (NPM) has not resolved the tension between management and democratic constitutionalism and has had a few significant setbacks in court.[1] The concept of state action, discussed later in the chapter, is particularly relevant to NPM's interest in outsourcing, public-private partnerships, collaborative governance, and corporate-like performance-based organizations. So deep does the tension between constitutional arrangements and contemporary public administration run that on one occasion the chief justice of the United States observed that, from the perspectives of the modern administrative state, "The choices we discern as having been made in the Constitutional Convention impose burdens on governmental processes that often seem clumsy, inefficient, even unworkable."[2] Looking at the same problem of the tension between public administration and democratic constitutionalism from the perspective of public administration, Dwight Waldo, one of the 20th century's leading administrative theorists, contended, "It *cannot be solved*—acceptably, workably—given our constitutional system, our constitutional history, and our democratic ideology. All we can hope for is piecemeal solutions, temporary agreements."[3]

The objective of this chapter is to impart an understanding of the nature of the conflicts and tensions between public administration and democratic constitutionalism. A comprehensive appreciation of these conflicts and tensions is an absolute prerequisite to determining how to take public administrative action that is constitutional and maximizes appropriate managerial and political values. Our approach to this subject will emphasize the fundamental principles and values of the Constitution rather than immediate interpretations of its specific clauses or the historical development of its doctrines.

◆→ WHY PUBLIC ADMINISTRATORS MUST UNDERSTAND THE CONSTITUTION

Historically, few if any texts on U.S. public administration devoted a chapter to a discussion of "democratic constitutionalism." It was frequently taken as a given that Woodrow Wilson was correct when he observed that for the most part the concerns of public administration were far removed from those of framing and amending the Constitution.[4] Today, however, judicial involvement in public administration is so pronounced and the legal approach is so encompassing that the need for public administrators to understand the Constitution is almost self-evident. There are four aspects of the relationship between public administration and the Constitution that should be emphasized in this regard.

First, as Wilson indicated, the principles on which to base a sound public administration in the United States "must be principles which have democratic policy very much at heart."[5] Public administration cannot be based on these principles unless it understands them and appreciates their worth. It is difficult to contest seriously the view that the ultimate object for public administration in the United States is a combination of the values of the managerial and political approaches that is fully compatible with constitutional principles and values. This is something that all public administrators should be working toward.

Second, public administrators take an oath to support the Constitution. Cynics may dismiss this as a pro forma requirement, utterly devoid of any significant meaning. However, the oath speaks to the overarching importance of upholding the nation's fundamental rule of law even in the face of seemingly legitimate orders from a direct superior (see Box 11.1). The oath is also a reminder that public office is public trust.

Third, as discussed earlier in Chapters 1 and 5, many public administrators can be held personally liable in civil suits for compensatory and punitive damages when they violate the constitutional rights of individuals or groups. These damages may be assessed at the amount a jury considers adequate to compensate the injured party and punish the public administrator and deter others from taking similar action.[6] The Supreme Court established the general standard that a public administrator can be personally sued for damages if he or she reasonably should have known that his or her action would be in violation of others' clearly established constitutional rights. In the eyes of the judiciary, public administrators' basic job competence requires reasonable knowledge of the constitutional rights of the people upon whom they act. If for no other reason, public administrators need to understand the Constitution to protect their pocketbooks from civil suits for damages.

Fourth, and more generally, there has been a renewed interest in "constitutional literacy" in the public service. Constance Horner, former director of the Office of Personnel Management, promoted the idea as follows:

> We may often disagree about what our shared commitment to constitutional
> values requires—what liberty or equality or justice demands in any given
> instance. But discourse about those principles should be the unique, common
> language of the Federal executive. Literacy in these concepts and ideas—
> constitutional literacy—can help unify and vivify the Federal executive corps.
> From many professions, it can make one vocation.[7]

In keeping with Horner's concept, the Consolidated Appropriations Act of 2005 requires federal agencies annually to "provide educational training materials concerning the United States Constitution to each employee of the

11.1   PUTTING CONSTITUTIONAL VALUES IN PUBLIC ADMINISTRATION: A RIGHT TO DISOBEY?

57 Cal. Rptr. 623
Benny Max PARRISH, Plaintiff
and Appellant,
v.
The CIVIL SERVICE COMMISSION OF the
COUNTY OF ALAMEDA, etc., et al.,
Defendants and Respondents.
S.F. 22429.
Supreme Court of California,
En Banc
March 27, 1967.

The Supreme Court . . . held that where county failed to secure legally effective consent to search homes of welfare recipients, through early morning mass raids to determine welfare eligibility, and, even if effective consent had been obtained, county could not constitutionally condition continued receipt of welfare benefits upon giving such consent, such raids, in which county directed social worker to take part, transgressed constitutional limitations, and thus social worker, in light of his knowledge as to scope and methods of projected raids, possessed adequate grounds for declining to participate and could not properly be found guilty of insubordination warranting his discharge.

476 F. Supp. 191
John R. HARLEY
v.
SCHUYLKILL COUNTY et al.
Civ. A. No. 78-861
United States District Court,
E. D. Pennsylvania.
Aug. 23, 1979.

Discharged prison guard filed civil rights suit against county and warden, alleging that his discharge was wrongful in that it was a deprivation of his liberty interest without according him due process, constituted a violation of his First Amendment rights, was based on his refusal to perform an unconstitutional act, and constituted a violation of rights secured under the Pennsylvania Constitution. On a defense motion to dismiss, the District Court . . . held that: (1) the right to refuse to perform an unconstitutional act is a right "secured by the Constitution" within the meaning of the Civil Rights Act of 1871; accordingly, . . . [the] . . . prison guard had the right to refrain from performing an act, ordered by the warden, which would have deprived prisoner of his constitutional rights, and (2) a county is liable for acts of its employees which violate Article 1, section 1 of the Pennsylvania Constitution, where those employees are acting within the scope of their official duties.

agency on September 17," which is known as Constitution Day and Citizenship Day.[8] This requirement recognizes that public administrators are charged with promoting the public interest, and in our system, that requires a commitment to doing so within the framework of the Constitution, the supreme law of the land.

Unfortunately, understanding the Constitution is easier said than done. We alluded to this problem in Chapter 1. As far as the public administrator is concerned, the Constitution must be considered a set of values and principles that far exceeds the wording of its clauses and holdings in past judicial decisions. The Constitution's language and the case law expounding it provide only part of the necessary understanding. The Constitution's current requirements are derived from legal, philosophical, moral, and political considerations as to how the Constitution should be applied in a variety of contemporary circumstances unforeseen by the Founders and unanticipated by earlier legal decisions. For example, some of the principles we will consider in this chapter are the notions of "chilling effect," "least restrictive alternative," and the "three-tier structure" of equal protection. Each of these principles is absolutely critical to an understanding of the Constitution, but none can be found in the words of that document. In addition, some fundamental constitutional rights, such as the right to personal privacy and the right to travel among the states, may flow from the principles and values of the Constitution, as well as from specifically enumerated clauses within it.

The broad and unspecific quality of the Constitution can be frustrating to those who seek to understand it and model their administrative conduct accordingly. Sometimes it is best to think of the Constitution as a body of values and principles inherent in the nation's political culture, social ethos, and history. These values and principles are not articulated all at once. Rather, the courts declare what they are when the proper occasions arise in individual cases. In most instances where there is a real and protracted dispute over what the Constitution requires, the Supreme Court will be the final judicial arbiter. Its members will follow their consciences and philosophical and political views in interpreting what the words, principles, values, and previous constitutional decisions require in any set of circumstances.[9]

At the same time, the justices and judges are not free to "rewrite" or reinterpret the Constitution at will. There are checks on the courts, and the questions they address are framed by the litigation before them, just as the answers they provide are partly framed by past precedents and previous considerations of the nature of constitutional values and principles. Few judges and constitutional scholars truly believe that the Constitution should (or could) be interpreted *solely* from the perspectives of the framers' "original intent" in all cases—especially because the Fourteenth Amendment (1868) radically extended the Constitution's constraints to state and local governments. But, by the same token, few believe that the "original intent" is irrelevant to present interpretations.

Constitutional law derived in this way has certainly had its oddities over the years. Sometimes one decision is overturned by another within a period of but a few years.[10] At other times adherence to precedent seems almost an "imprisonment of reason."[11] For instance, in 1922 the Supreme Court ruled that professional baseball was beyond the scope of the commerce clause because it was a matter of personal effort rather than commercial production. The Court reiterated this view in 1953, though certainly by then judicial interpretation had broadened the commerce clause enough to reach professional sports. Subsequently, the Court held that the federal government could regulate boxing (1955) and football (1957). However, in 1972, it adhered to its earlier rulings regarding baseball, saying that if Congress wanted federal antitrust laws to apply to the national pastime, it would have to say so specifically![12]

Despite its abstract qualities and quirks, the great virtue of the United States' system of constitutional law is that it enables the polity to adapt the fundamental values and principles of an 18th-century document to continually changing political, economic, social, international, technological, and environmental circumstances. Moreover, it helps the society maintain a good deal of political consensus on those fundamental principles and values. As a result, rather than trying to govern itself through the "dead hand of the past," the United States has a written, but also a "living," constitution. And without a doubt, public administration is now a part of it.

❖❖ ADMINISTRATIVE STRUCTURE AND CONSTITUTIONAL STRUCTURE

Administrative Separation of Functions

Public administrative and constitutional doctrines advocate the separation of functions among different structural units, such as agencies, bureaus, and branches of government. However, there are crucial differences. When following the managerial approaches, public administrative agencies place different functions in different units for the sake of specialization and the efficiency, economy, effectiveness, and customer service derived from the division of labor. When the political approach dictates the organization of agencies, it is likely that the separation of functions goes by policy areas, regions, or clientele groups and is intended to enhance administrative representativeness and political responsiveness.

Constitutional Separation of Powers

The Constitution, however, seeks to separate powers—legislative, executive, and judicial—for the sake of creating checks and balances that safeguard against authoritarian or tyrannical government. As James Madison explained in the *Federalist Papers,* the combination of legislative, executive, and judicial power in the same hands could be considered the essence of tyranny. He also explained that the system of checks and balances was intended to provide "great security against a gradual concentration of the several powers in the same department [i.e., branch of government] . . . [by] giving to those who administer each department the necessary constitutional means and personal motives to resist encroachment of the others."[13] Hence, the Constitution provides for different terms of office and modes of election or appointment of members of each house of Congress, the president, and the judiciary. But, as Chief Justice Burger pointed out, it is precisely this system that sometimes makes the federal government seem cumbersome and even unworkable in the contemporary administrative age.

Collapse of the Separation of Powers

In an effort to overcome the slow and cumbersome quality of government according to the separation of powers and checks and balances, since the 1930s the United States has increasingly vested combinations of legislative, executive, and judicial functions in individual administrative agencies. In other words, there has been a tendency to *collapse* the functions of the three constitutional branches into federal agencies. Regulatory commissions are the clearest example of agencies that engage in legislative functions (rule making), executive activities (implementation and enforcement), and judicial roles (adjudication). Although many criticize bureaucratic organization for its slow and lumbering qualities, historically, public administration has been viewed as more flexible than government strictly according to the constitutional separation of powers as originally designed. For instance, agency rule making and rescission of rules can be far simpler, and generally much quicker, than congressional legislating. Unlike the House and Senate, individual agencies are unified and coordinated by hierarchy to a large extent. Agency adjudication is usually faster and more flexible than litigation before the judiciary is.

The "collapsing" of the separation of powers into the administrative branch has both administrative and constitutional consequences. Among the most important is that public administrators can be held responsible to each of the three constitutional branches. Aside from serving the public, many federal administrators serve three masters, not one: Congress, the president, and the federal judiciary. Because public administrators exercise functions originally assigned to each of the three constitutional branches, it is to be expected that each of those branches will be concerned about the way those functions are performed. As Madison noted, each of these sets of actors has a different term of office, a different constitutional role, and different interests. Sometimes this has the effect of complicating public administration to the point of exasperation.

The *Phillips* Case

One concrete example of this problem was presented in the case of *Local 2677, American Federation of Government Employees v. Phillips* (1973).[14] Phillips was acting director of the Office of Economic Opportunity (OEO). Upon hearing the president's budgetary message indicating his intent to eliminate the OEO and not seek any additional funding for it, Phillips began to cut back on spending the appropriations previously granted for the then current fiscal year. (Remember, the budgetary message is for the next fiscal year and does not directly affect the current one.) In Phillips's view, it seemed wasteful and administratively inappropriate to spend money for a program that was likely to come to a screeching halt at the end of the fiscal year. Some of the funds had been earmarked for projects and perhaps equipment intended to be of long-run utility. Sinking more funds into projects with no future would be pointless and wasteful. However, Phillips's cutbacks were opposed by the American Federation of Government Employees, a labor union, because they would eliminate the jobs of some of its members. The intended beneficiaries of some of the previously planned projects also opposed the cutbacks. But Phillips considered himself to be responsible to the president and to be engaging in sound, economizing public administration.

Phillips's view was deemed inappropriate by a circuit court of appeals. It reasoned that Phillips should not have defined his responsibilities so narrowly. First, he had a legal obligation to spend funds already allotted by Congress. His responsibility was to the law and legislature in this regard. Second, because the president's budgetary message was only a *message,* having no binding effect on Congress, Phillips was wrong to take direction from it. After all, Congress could allocate funds to the OEO despite the president's opposition. The separation of powers and checks and balances give the legislature a critical role in budgeting—that of passing bills authorizing the spending and appropriation of federal funds. Congress has constituencies that differ from those of the president, and it might have a different political outlook on the desirability of the OEO. The constitutional world of public administration was far more complicated than Phillips maintained.

On the one hand, it is easy to see Phillips's mistake. On the other, was he wrong in not wanting to spend money for projects likely to be abandoned and unlikely to do much good unless continued for a long time? One lesson is that "democracy is not cheap."[15] The costs of the separation of powers may seem irrational in managerially oriented public administration, while from a constitutional perspective they may be considered fully justified.

Administrative Discretion and "Guerrilla Government"

There is a tension in American administrative thought between giving administrators the discretion to employ their expertise on behalf of the public, and the requirements of democratic governance that agencies be closely monitored and tightly controlled. Simply put, it concerns how much leeway administrators ought to have in making and implementing decisions. This controversy extends back many decades, and it basically pits the managerial values of efficiency, economy, and effectiveness against the political values of representation, responsiveness, and accountability. If asked, the public would likely respond that it would like to maximize both sets of values. Insofar as they are in conflict, there may be no easy way out of this dilemma.

A complicating factor is that administrators may be the only ones in a position to know what truly is best. They are, after all, the experts, as Max Weber pointed out almost a century ago. Many are in positions where they can ignore, resist, or subvert the wishes of their superiors. In a recent book on the subject, Rosemary O'Leary explores what she calls "guerrilla government," which she defines as a form of dissent carried out by administrators who are dissatisfied with their agency's performance, but who—for a variety of reasons—choose not to take their complaints public.[16] Essentially, administrative guerrillas envision themselves as fighting lethargy, inertia, cowardice, and unlawful acts. They see themselves as silent guardians of the public good. But in order to be effective, they may be secretive, be disloyal to their superiors, and lie to their peers. Yet there is a dilemma: the organization may not be able to function effectively without them.

According to O'Leary, guerrillas may employ a wide assortment of tactics in order to achieve their ends: going over a superior's head, leaking information to the press, forging clandestine links to key legislators, delaying actions, and documenting for a future lawsuit the extent of the illegal acts that they may witness, among others.[17] Certainly, the public would condone neither the intentions nor the tactics of guerrillas. O'Leary observes that these dissidents generally resort to guerrilla tactics because the formal organization provides few channels for expressing genuine concern about the activities that they are involved in. Consequently, O'Leary recommends creating an organizational climate that encourages candid dialogue and debate, one that truly listens to its internal voices of dissent before they resort to guerrilla tactics.[18]

As to the public's concerns about administrative discretion in general, the Office of Personnel Management 2006 Human Capital Survey of 150,000 federal employees found that an overwhelming majority of civil servants believe that they perform important, satisfying work, and that they believe themselves to be accountable for results in meaningful ways.[19]

The Three "Masters" of Public Administration

The separation of powers complicates public administration by frequently making it responsible to more than one branch of government and by pulling it in different directions at once, as in *Phillips*. These tendencies often make it difficult for agencies to maximize the values of the managerial or political approaches to public administration. The unity of structure and control sought by the traditional managerial approach is easily frustrated by the effects of the separation of powers. The representativeness and responsiveness sought by the political approach become muddled when more than one constitutional actor, each having different motives and interests, becomes involved in public administration. The effect may be frustrating from all perspectives.

An irony of constitutional structure is that by placing several masters over public administration, in practice it may sometimes provide public administrators with none. (Recall *Morrison v. Olson*, Box 1.1, in which a Department of Justice employee with prosecutorial functions was appointed by a court and, by statute, could not be fired by the president or the attorney general except for specific—and limited—causes.) The efforts of the constitutional branches of government to control the administrative branch are sometimes frustrated by the Constitution. But the same Constitution and system of separation of powers and checks and balances can also frustrate administrative action informed by sound administrative values and theories.

There are different conclusions to draw from this irony. One is that public administrators should try to play one constitutional branch off against another in a quest for independence and autonomy. Another is that a fundamental task of agency leadership is to coordinate the separation of powers by mediating conflicts between the president and Congress. Yet another is that because the Constitution does not establish a fully adequate system of practical control by the constitutional branches over public administrators, administrators' obligations to the Constitution must be augmented by a more direct responsibility to uphold its fundamental values and principles. This is precisely what Article VI of the Constitution requires: "The Senators and Representatives before mentioned, and the Members of the several State Legislatures, and all executive and judicial Officers, both of the United States and several States, shall be bound by Oath or Affirmation, to support this Constitution." The need to understand constitutional principles and values is evident.

✦✦   CONSTITUTIONAL VALUES

Legitimacy

There is a stark contrast between the bases of legitimacy on which democratic constitutionalism rests and those values in the managerial and political approaches believed to legitimize public administrative activity. Legitimacy in this context can be thought of as the population's belief that public administrators have a right to help make and implement public policy and to exercise political authority and discretion. Legitimacy is extremely important because it strongly fosters voluntary compliance with administrative directives and decisions.

According to the traditional managerial approach, the legitimacy of public administrators' authority is derived from their politically neutral technical competence, their specialized expertise, and the rationality and law-bound quality of their processes. Following Max Weber, sometimes this is referred to as legitimacy based on the rational/legal quality of administrative operations.[20] The NPM holds that performance—especially customer satisfaction—will legitimize public administrative action. The political approach seeks to base administrative legitimacy on the representativeness, responsiveness, and accountability of public administrators and agencies. The Constitution has a somewhat different emphasis. It promotes the principle that governmental legitimacy, including that involving the exercise of administrative authority, rests on the consent of the governed. The framers provided that the Constitution would have to be ratified by special conventions in the states, rather than by the state legislatures. Within the existing sociopolitical framework limiting participation to white males, this would assure that the Constitution would rest on popular consent rather than on the consent of state governments. The Constitution also guarantees that each state will have a republican form of government. But consent, in this context, is not merely the agreement of a majority. An extraordinary majority may be required, as in the case of amending the Constitution or the approval of treaties by the Senate. Moreover, constitutional principles and values seek to protect the fundamental rights of minorities from encroachment by majorities. The consent of those who may be at odds with the majority of citizens is not to be compelled, but rather won through the protection of their rights.

In this context, the differences between constitutional theory, on the one hand, and the managerial and political perspectives, on the other, are profound and reach to the core of the concepts on which the political system is based. Constitutional theory views the government as an outgrowth of a *contract* formed by "We the People." That contract, the Constitution, fixes limits on governmental power, as in the First Amendment's prohibition on "an establishment of religion." The managerial and political perspectives are less contractarian than utilitarian in their fundamental premises. They tend to favor the legitimization of governmental action on the basis of the greatest good for the greatest number or, more broadly, on pursuit of the public interest. In practice, they tend to view legitimacy as based on performance rather than on adherence to the contractual terms of the Constitution alone. This is one reason why there has been only limited concern for constitutional values, such as transparency, that are lost or weakened when government outsources its work to private entities to which the Constitution, other than the Thirteenth Amendment, ordinarily does not apply (see the section on "State Action" further on in this chapter). For both the traditional and NPM managerial perspectives, performance that is efficient, economical, and effective contributes to the legitimization of government. The NPM adds responsiveness to customers. For the political approach, performance is viewed in terms of the representativeness, political responsiveness, and accountability of government to organized constituencies and/or to a majority of the people.

West Virginia State Board of Education v. Barnette (1943)[21] serves as an example of these fundamental differences regarding legitimacy. The case involved a public school system's requirement that all students salute and pledge allegiance to the flag. The political and administrative rationale for the regulation was that it would promote feelings of loyalty toward the United States and a sense of political community among students. The regulation was enforced with a two-pronged strategy. Students who refused to salute and say the pledge were expelled. If they were not placed in suitable private schools, their parents could face criminal charges for the truancy of their school-age children. This was a heavy-handed strategy, but it could be considered cost-effective and efficient. Given the potential penalties, it was likely that the pupils would at least say the pledge and possibly develop the proper feelings of patriotism. Politically, the measure was probably popular. It was wartime, patriotism and loyalty were considered desirable if not essential sentiments, and a majority of the state's population no doubt strongly supported the promotion of such feelings in the schools. Moreover, refusal to salute the flag and say the pledge could be taken as a sign of disrespect for the nation, the majority of citizens who supported it, and the armed forces members who were risking their lives and sustaining heavy casualties to protect its liberty and national interests. However, one group of citizens was opposed to the salute and pledge. These were the Jehovah's Witnesses, who believed that engaging in the salute and pledge showed disrespect for their God and therefore violated their religion. Despite a decision just three years earlier to the contrary, the

Supreme Court held that the compulsory flag salute and pledge violated the rights of a minority not only because it limited their religious freedom, but also because it tended to compel their support (consent) for the political system. In Justice Jackson's eloquent words, "If there is any fixed star in our constitutional constellation, it is that no official, high or petty, can prescribe what shall be orthodox in politics, nationalism, religion, or other matters of opinion, or force citizens to confess by word or act their faith therein. If there are any circumstances which permit an exception, they do not now occur to us." The compulsory salute and pledge were unconstitutional because they compelled consent, something wholly antithetical to the Constitution's approach to governmental legitimacy.

Diversity among the Citizenry

One of the most outstanding conflicts between traditional managerially oriented public administration and constitutional values concerns the desirability of uniformity as opposed to diversity. The traditional managerial perspective strongly supports uniformity in a broad range of administrative contexts. It relies on impersonality among public employees to assure that individual diversity in interpreting regulations and implementing programs is eliminated to the extent practicable. Max Weber saw this as the special virtue of bureaucracy and, accordingly, viewed bureaucrats as "cogs."[22] In related fashion, clients are turned into "cases," which can often be treated impersonally and, therefore, with relative uniformity. These aspects of the traditional managerial approach were discussed in greater detail in Chapter 1.

By contrast, the Constitution values diversity to a great extent. In some ways, the entire design of the constitutional scheme rests on the desire to maintain and promote diversity. In *Federalist Paper No. 10*, James Madison argued that a large, extended republican form of government would necessarily include so much social and economic diversity that it would preclude the development of a majority faction, that is, a majority political group that was united by a common interest that was adverse to the good of the nation as a whole. He considered fostering diversity to be the first object of government. Additionally, the Constitution incorporates diversity in the sense of federalism, bicameralism, separation of powers, different modes of election and appointment for the constitutional branches, and different terms of office. This is partly intended to assure that the government will not be subject to complete overturn at the hands of a majority united only for a brief time by a common interest or passion. It can take at least four and possibly six years to elect enough Senators to constitute the two-thirds majority necessary to approve treaties and propose constitutional amendments.

The political approach to public administration tends to fall between those two poles on the continuum from uniformity to diversity. It favors diversity to a considerable extent but has a tendency to try to exclude groups thought to be politically marginal because of their deviation from the nation's political, economic, and social mainstream and limited power. Sometimes it also attempts to silence individuals whose opinions are considered dangerous to the political system. For example, the Communist Party and its members have been subjected to a number of regulations and restrictions in public employment, labor union affairs, and other aspects of life, the application of which has never been considered with regard to the Democratic and Republican Parties or their members. At other times the political approach seeks diversity in public administration as a means of providing representation and responsiveness to politically "acceptable" groups, such as farmers, union members, social groups, and trade associations. Like the political approach, the NPM rejects the traditional managerial perspective's tendency to favor "one-size-fits-all" administration. It values individualized customer service but does not appear to have a strong commitment to diversity, especially if it might raise costs and lower efficiency.

Many Supreme Court decisions emphasize the constitutional value of diversity. For instance, in *Barnette,* discussed earlier, the Supreme Court pointed out that although the promotion of national unity is permissible, "individual freedom of mind" should be given preference to "officially disciplined uniformity" because history shows that "[t]hose who begin coercive elimination of dissent soon find themselves exterminating dissenters. Compulsory unification of opinion achieves only the unanimity of the graveyard." *Keyishian v. Board of Regents* (1967) presents another example.[23] There a complicated New York State scheme for excluding persons with subversive ideas from its educational system was under challenge. The U.S. Supreme Court held that the regulations were too imprecise to withstand constitutional scrutiny because they excluded individuals who were not subversive as well as those who were. In the course of its ruling, the Court pointed out that

> our Nation is deeply committed to safeguarding academic freedom, which is of transcendent value to all of us and not merely to the teachers concerned. That freedom is therefore a special concern of the First Amendment, which does not tolerate laws that cast a pall of orthodoxy over the classroom. . . . The classroom is peculiarly the "marketplace of ideas." The Nation's future depends upon leaders trained through wide exposure to that robust exchange of ideas which discovers truth "out of a multitude of tongues, [rather] than through any kind of authoritative selection."

In *Grutter v. Bollinger* (2003), the Court held that diversity was a sufficiently compelling governmental interest to justify the use of race and ethnicity as factors in admissions to state law schools: "Effective participation by members of all racial and ethnic groups in the civic life of our Nation is essential if the dream of one Nation, indivisible, is to be realized."[24] (See Box 11.2 for another example of putting the constitutional value of diversity into practice.)

Freedom and Liberty

Constitutional values place great emphasis on individual freedom and liberty. According to one view of constitutional theory, perhaps the dominant view, individual freedom and liberty are antecedent to the Constitution. Because

11.2   PUTTING CONSTITUTIONAL VALUES IN PUBLIC ADMINISTRATION: PUBLIC SCHOOL AND THE SANTERÍA FAITH AND "CONSTITUTIONAL POLICING"

The Santería faith is a centuries-old African religion that originated with the Yoruba tribe of Nigeria and was brought to the Caribbean by slaves. About 50,000 people in southern Florida practice the religion, which involves initiation rights lasting three to four weeks. Initiation as a priestess takes place when the high priest determines it is time; it does not depend on age. A schoolgirl, whose age was given as eight or nine, missed a month of public school to undergo initiation rites. The Dade County (Florida) School Board has a policy that five or more unexcused absences in a semester precludes granting a student credit for classes. The school board first questioned whether the Santería faith could be considered a religion and then whether the pupil could be given initiation during the summer when classes were not in session. It received a legal opinion from an attorney to the effect that, "in this instance, the compulsory attendance laws must give way to the freedom of religion laws. We have concluded that an absence of up to a month is a religious necessity when a person is being initiated into the priesthood of the Santería." The board decided to excuse the absence and allow the girl to make up the schoolwork she missed. As another school board attorney put it, "You can't change Christmas to the weekend just because it doesn't fall on Sunday."

About a thousand miles north of Dade County, Prince George's County, Maryland, had a problem with police canine units featuring "snarly, excessively ferocious dogs" that bit about 800 people over a period of seven years. Under prodding from the U.S. Department of Justice, the County police chief substituted a policy of "bark and hold" for bark and bite. The chief explained he wanted his department to be all about "constitutional policing" and that meant not violating the Fourth Amendment's guarantee against "unreasonable seizures." It took some effort to train the dogs, but complaints about the unit's use of excessive force declined significantly.

Sources: "School Case Backs an Ancient Ritual," *New York Times,* 9 December 1984. "Bark and Hold," *Washington Post,* 23 February 2007.

freedom and liberty existed before the creation of the constitutional government in 1789, they are given both specific and general protections against governmental encroachment in the Bill of Rights. The Ninth Amendment in particular makes this point: "The enumeration in the Constitution, of certain rights, shall not be construed to deny or disparage others retained by the people." Rights to freedom and liberty therefore do not come from the Constitution; they are merely recognized by it as aspects of life that lie outside the legitimate realm of the exercise of governmental power. Such fundamental rights, following the Declaration of Independence, are often considered **natural rights:** "We hold these truths to be self-evident, that all men are created equal, that they are endowed by their Creator with certain unalienable Rights,

that among these are Life, Liberty and the pursuit of Happiness." This is not
to say that rights are "absolute"; they can be abridged or infringed when the
government has an overriding, compelling need to do so. But the burden will
fall on the government to show that it does have such a need and that the
means chosen are the least damaging to the exercise of protected rights or are
narrowly tailored to limit infringements on them.

Values Conflicts

This approach is frequently at odds with public administration in either the
traditional managerial or the political perspective. Public administration, as
we have seen, provides both services and constraints. It is often involved in
direct or indirect regulation and consequently enforces limits on the freedom
and liberty of individuals. Such constraints are considered in the public interest
as they are generally intended to promote the public's security, safety, health,
and welfare and/or the political and economic viability of the nation. The conflict between constitutional values and principles on the one side and public
administration on the other, therefore, is typically over means, not ends. This
is likely to be true of NPM administration as well because it is not oriented
toward individual rights or due process, which it views as overly encumbering.

There are many dramatic examples of this conflict over appropriate
means. The *Keyishian* decision, reviewed previously, is one. The Supreme
Court had little quarrel with the state's overall objective of barring subversive teachers from the public educational system. The issue was over the
means, which the Court found inappropriate because they compromised individual freedoms and liberty too much. An intriguing additional example can
be found in *Shelton v. Tucker* (1960).[25] There the Supreme Court declared
unconstitutional an Arkansas statute requiring every teacher, as a condition of
employment in a state-supported school or college, to file "annually an affidavit listing without limitation every organization to which he has belonged
or regularly contributed within the preceding five years." The state's purpose
in seeking this information was somewhat unclear. The act was based on the
desire "to provide assistance in the administration and financing of the public
schools" and to help resolve problems involved in responding to the Supreme
Court's school desegregation decisions. There was no stated desire to discipline teachers based on their organizational affiliations, and it appears that
only refusal to submit the affidavit would be clear cause for action against the
employee. In other words, on the face of it at least, all the state wanted was to
know to which organizations its teachers belonged. However, there was some
reason to believe that teachers belonging to the NAACP might be victimized as
a result of the regulation.

Although it recognized that the state had a legitimate interest in promoting the fitness and competence of its teachers, the Court found that the act
placed too much of a strain on the right to freedom of association, which, in
the Court's words, "lies at the foundation of a free society." This was because
the "breadth" of abridgment of constitutional rights "must be viewed in the

light of less drastic means for achieving the same basic purpose." Less drastic and more appropriate means, in this case, for promoting competence and fitness could have been to ask certain teachers or even all teachers about *certain* organizational affiliations or about the number of organizations to which they belonged. But to ask *every* teacher about *every* organization was too great an impairment of teachers' freedom of association.

Means were also the issue in *Gratz v. Bollinger* (2003), an affirmative action case decided the same day as *Grutter,* mentioned above. Although race and ethnicity can be taken into account in admitting students to state universities, the Court found that a "policy, which automatically distributes 20 points, or one-fifth of the points needed to guarantee admission, to every single 'underrepresented minority' solely because of race" is too race-based to satisfy the Fourteenth Amendment's equal protection clause. If race is taken into account, it should be in the context of an "individualized consideration" of each applicant. Important for public administrators, the Court responded to the University of Michigan's claim that the volume of applications made such consideration impracticable by pointing out that "the fact that the implementation of a program capable of providing individualized consideration might present administrative challenges does not render constitutional an otherwise problematic system."[26] In other words, constitutional means trump the exigencies of administrative means.

Legal Constraints on Administrative Action

The *Shelton* case is pertinent because it illustrates three constitutional principles relating to freedom and liberty that serve as constraints on public administrative action:

1. *Chilling effect.* Although the regulation involved did not prohibit or punish association, it had the tendency to deter the free exercise of the right to association. This was particularly true because the statute did not prohibit public disclosure and placed heavy "pressure upon a teacher to avoid any ties which might displease those who control his professional destiny." In other words, a teacher's ardor for freedom of association would be "chilled."

2. *Overbreadth.* As noted, a regulation that abridges or chills one's exercise of constitutional rights must be narrowly drawn so that it does not unnecessarily infringe on legitimate activity. A regulation is overly broad if, in the process of legitimately constraining some activities, it gratuitously infringes on others protected by the Constitution. In *Shelton,* for example, if the state were concerned that some of its teachers belonged to so many organizations that they did not have enough time left to devote to the proper performance of their professional duties, it could have inquired about the number of associations with which the teachers were affiliated. If the state were concerned about membership in certain organizations, it could have asked directly about those organizations, although it would need a

strong governmental interest for doing so. Its scheme, however, had the tendency to deter membership in legitimate organizations for fear of public disclosure or reprisal by the state's educational system.

3. *The least restrictive alternative.* Overbreadth deters the exercise of legitimate rights on which the government has no compelling need or reason to place restrictions. The least restrictive alternative principle accepts the state's legitimate need to deal with an area of behavior but requires that the government do so in the fashion that constitutes the least practicable infringement on protected rights. In other words, in *Shelton,* could the state have found a means of promoting competence and fitness that was less of an invasion of constitutionally protected freedom of association? From the traditional managerial perspective, the answer is "yes, but"—it could prove to be expensive, inefficient, and time-consuming. For instance, one alternative that would be much less restrictive would have been to identify teachers whose competence and fitness were marginal and then inquire of those teachers only whether they had extensive organizational affiliations that were diverting their attention from their professional performance. To do so, however, would require elaborate administrative means of measuring fitness and competence and hearings or investigations to ascertain the amount of time and nature of commitment a teacher devoted to his or her organizational memberships. From a managerial perspective, it was more satisfactory to achieve this in reverse: find the organizations to which every teacher belonged and then identify teachers whose performance might be improved if they abandoned some of their affiliations.

Two additional constitutional principles that restrict the means public administrators may use in pursuing legitimate ends should be mentioned as well. *Narrow tailoring* is similar to the least restrictive alternative, but it affords greater leeway. Rather than requiring that the means be the absolutely least invasive of protected constitutional rights, it looks for an approach that closely fits achieving the government's compelling objectives while doing limited damage to those rights. Narrow tailoring has a more specific meaning in the context of equal protection, as is explained later in the chapter.

Underinclusiveness refers to means that restrict constitutionally protected activity in a putative effort to achieve a legitimate governmental purpose, but fail to deal with other practices that would necessarily have to be included in the regulatory scheme to achieve the desired policy outcome. For example, the City of Hialeah, Florida, passed a number of ordinances allegedly intended to protect animals from cruelty and slaughter and to promote public health by regulating the disposal of animal remains. However, the ordinances were drawn in such a way that they prohibited animal sacrifices in Santería religious rituals, but not other activity involving the killing and disposal of animals. For instance, other small-scale slaughtering was permitted, as was fishing and hunting. Restaurants, which process a lot of animal remains, were outside the scope of the regulations. Consequently, the Supreme Court had little trouble finding that the ordinances were underinclusive and unconstitutional because they targeted religious practices without serving a compelling governmental purpose.[27]

The principles of "chilling effect," "overbreadth," and "least-restrictive alternative" or narrow tailoring have emerged in a great number of cases involving the constitutionality of public administrative action. The public administrator who seeks to adhere to constitutional values should treat them as guides rather than barriers to effective action. They do not prohibit the attainment of legitimate ends through public administrative action. Rather, they stand for the general view that freedom and liberty are so valuable that they should not be compromised more than is necessary to accomplish such an end (see Box 11.3).

Structure of Substantive Rights

Beyond the principles that restrict the means available to administrators, there are also major limitations on the ends that government may legitimately seek. These are found in the applied structure of basic constitutional rights. Saying that rights have a structure is intended to convey the idea that there are a series of "if-then" statements one ordinarily asks about government practices challenged on constitutional grounds. Further, although judges and justices come and go and disagree with one another as to whether specific practices are constitutional, they all tend to apply the same structure when analyzing the cases before them.

The typical structure of substantive constitutional rights, such as freedom of speech, association, and exercise of religion, is presented in Box 11.4. The initial question is whether a governmental practice infringes on an individual's constitutional rights, even indirectly, as in the case of chilling effects. If not, there is no violation of the Constitution. If so, however, the next question is whether the practice tightly serves any government interest. Overbreadth is of concern because it prohibits more than is necessary to serve the government's interests in a rational way. Underinclusiveness is also relevant. If the practice does not serve a governmental interest, the infringement on rights is gratuitous and therefore unconstitutional. If it does serve such interests, it may still be unconstitutional unless it serves one that is compelling, that is, of great importance to the political system (such as national security or combating a deadly epidemic). Even then, the practice will be considered unconstitutional if it is not the least restrictive way of achieving the government's compelling interest or, depending on the specifics, is not narrowly tailored. For public administrators in most circumstances, efficiency, economy, and administrative convenience, as important as they are managerially, are not considered compelling interests by the courts. When analyzing substantive rights, the courts apply strict scrutiny: the government will carry a heavy burden of persuasion, and the judges will extend little deference to its claims.

11.3   Putting Constitutional Values to Work at the U.S. Customs Service

In 1999, Customs Commissioner Raymond W. Kelly found himself engulfed in "a public relations nightmare." In fiscal 1998, 3,017 airline passengers entering the country were required by Customs' inspectors to take off some of their clothing as part of the agency's contribution to the nation's war on drugs. Sometimes the inspectors took passengers to clinics and hospitals for full body searches. Abuses were so substantial that Representative John Lewis, a Georgia Democrat on the House Ways and Means Committee, held congressional hearings. Lewis wanted to know if Customs was engaging in racial profiling. He and his colleagues got an earful. A Hispanic woman said she had been strip searched, denied access to a telephone, forced to take laxatives, and detained for 25 hours in 1994. An African American woman received worse treatment in 1997. Seven months pregnant, she was held for two days, handcuffed to a hospital bed, and given laxatives. Like 82 percent of those searched, neither woman was carrying drugs.

In 1998, another woman was awarded $450,000 in federal court for having received the detainment-strip search-laxative treatment in 1994. But Kelly, a Marine Vietnam combat veteran and New York City police commissioner in 1992–1994, who served again after appointment in 2002, wasn't so much concerned about the money as about the breaches of liberty and decency involved. He exclaimed, "We're taking people's liberty away!" "Just imagine if your wife or your daughter was subjected to this!" He also noted that basing searches on race "is certainly not part of our policy. We have strongly prohibited that in our handbook, but we want to make certain that it is not part of our practices."

Kelly's solution was a mix of old-fashioned constitutional law, traditional public management, and newer technologies. Agents were forbidden to take anyone off airport grounds without the permission of the top Customs officer present. That official was required to consult with local Department of Justice lawyers before making his or her decision as to whether the agents had a sufficiently "reasonable suspicion" to detain someone for more than eight hours. A supervisor's approval was required for most personal searches. Kelly also put a number of accountability measures in place to prevent racial discrimination and other abuses. Additionally, he planned to rely much more on x-rays and body scanners than on strip searches.

Kelly's strategy quickly paid off. In fiscal year 2000, there were 14,100 fewer searches than in the previous year, but 242 *more* seizures of heroin, cocaine, ecstasy, and other drugs. Reflecting that Customs' new sensitivity to individual rights yielded better results, Kelly observed, "We have this very powerful authority. But we did not think about it enough."

Sources: Stephen Barr, "Customs Tightens Detention Rules: Magistrate's Approval to Be Sought for Extended Searches," *Washington Post,* 12 August 1999, A25; Stephen Barr, "Aiming to Enforce Change at Customs," *Washington Post,* 17 February 1999, A15; and Michael Fletcher, "Fewer People Searched by Customs in Past Year," *Washington Post,* 19 October 2000, A29.

Property Rights

Property, like liberty, is highly valued by the Constitution. The due process clauses of the Fifth and Fourteenth Amendments rank life, liberty, and property alongside one another and afford them all protection from arbitrary, invidious, or capricious governmental encroachment. Like liberty, property has frequently been considered anterior to the formation of the constitutional government. Property and property rights existed prior to 1789, and the adoption of the Constitution is not typically seen as infringing on them. On the contrary, the Constitution is viewed as affording them governmental protection. In the past,

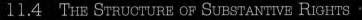

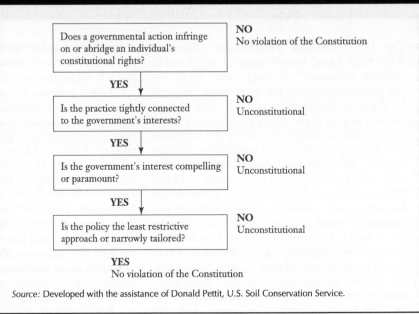

11.4   THE STRUCTURE OF SUBSTANTIVE RIGHTS

Does a governmental action infringe on or abridge an individual's constitutional rights? → **NO** No violation of the Constitution

YES ↓

Is the practice tightly connected to the government's interests? → **NO** Unconstitutional

YES ↓

Is the government's interest compelling or paramount? → **NO** Unconstitutional

YES ↓

Is the policy the least restrictive approach or narrowly tailored? → **NO** Unconstitutional

YES
No violation of the Constitution

Source: Developed with the assistance of Donald Pettit, U.S. Soil Conservation Service.

political theorists sometimes considered "liberty" and "property" as almost interchangeable or codeterminate. For example, James Madison once wrote that property exists not only in land and possessions but also in opinions, religious principles, and general liberty.[28] Moreover, he viewed property as an important factor in the development of individual personality and political preferences. As in the case of liberty, though, property rights are not absolute: The U.S. legal tradition has established the authority of the government to "take" private property by eminent domain as part of its sovereign power.[29] Private property can be taken for a legitimate public use, although under the Fifth Amendment, just compensation must be provided. In takings accomplished by zoning regulations ("regulatory takings"), the denial of a use of the owner's property does not have to be compensated but it must be roughly proportional to the putative public purpose sought. Blighted, hazardous, and other property posing a danger to the public interest may be taken without compensation if the owner does not remedy the situation. Similarly, searches and seizures of personal property can be undertaken by government, but only after a warrant is issued or the circumstances are such that there is constitutionally sufficient reason for them.

A Brief History of Eminent Domain
The U.S. Supreme Court has explicitly recognized the power of the federal government to acquire private property for legitimate public use.[30] The government's power to take private property has traditionally been restrained by two limits, however: (1) eminent domain must be "necessary and proper" to carry

out the powers enumerated in Article 1, section 8 of the Constitution; and (2) "just compensation" must be given in the case of property taken under the Fifth Amendment's "public use" clause. The Supreme Court has applied the Fifth Amendment takings doctrine to the states via the "due process clause" of the Fourteenth Amendment, which was ratified after the Civil War. Ever since then, the states may impose on themselves more restrictive requirements than the federal ones, but they cannot be less restrictive.

During most of the nation's history, the Court developed a more or less literal "public use" doctrine, whereby the taking of private property was legitimate only if it were put to an explicit public use. This generally meant that the property that was seized actually had to be used by the public, or occupied in some way by the general public. The public use doctrine has been widely used in taking land to build highways and other infrastructure projects, for example. In these circumstances, there is a clear public benefit that is widely shared. But later the literal public use doctrine began a slow process of erosion, for instance, in the case of quasi-public goods (e.g., common carriers, such as railroads) whose benefits are not necessarily shared widely. Gradually, the doctrine of public use evolved into a more open-ended doctrine of "public purpose," even if, for example, the seized property is to be sold to private developers for urban renewal purposes.[31] The Court has thus come to recognize as legitimate the taking of private property under eminent domain that is "rationally related to a conceivable public purpose"—apparently even where there is no direct or even clear public use.[32]

In June 2005, in the landmark decision *Kelo v. City of New London,* the Court ruled that the power of eminent domain could be used to take property from one private landowner, to be given to another for economic development purposes.[33] What makes *Kelo* so important is that the Court relied upon earlier precedents to dramatically extend the "public purpose" doctrine, permitting the taking of property even when that purpose was expressed quite vaguely. In this case, the mere assertion of a "public benefit" was sufficient to satisfy a majority of the Court, even in the absence of a clear plan of what to do with the acquired property. The word of public officials that a public benefit was intended was sufficient. The decision is therefore highly deferential to government officials. Under the ruling, such public benefits may now be very broad in scope, affecting virtually any aspect of the public welfare, including "spiritual as well as physical, aesthetic as well as monetary" benefits.[34] The Court left it to the discretion of the government to determine what constitutes a public benefit, qualitatively and on an individualized case-by-case basis.

In a strong dissent, Justice Sandra Day O'Connor lamented that the decision would permit the taking of private property for virtually any reason, using economic development as a mere pretext.[35] Indeed, soon after the opinion was rendered, there were fears that a flood of takings would ensue. But the public backlash that *Kelo* produced quickly prompted 34 states to enact legislation in 2005 and 2006 effectively preventing a recurrence of the situation. By 2011, they were joined by at least another eight states.[36] The lesson here is that often the strongest defenders of democratic values are the people themselves. Box 11.5 presents the general structure of the takings clause after *Kelo.*

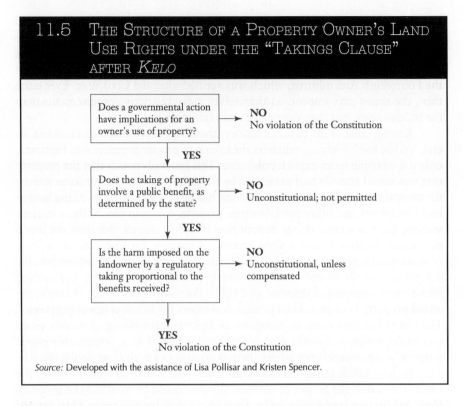

11.5   THE STRUCTURE OF A PROPERTY OWNER'S LAND
        USE RIGHTS UNDER THE "TAKINGS CLAUSE"
        AFTER *KELO*

Does a governmental action have implications for an owner's use of property? → **NO** No violation of the Constitution

YES

Does the taking of property involve a public benefit, as determined by the state? → **NO** Unconstitutional; not permitted

YES

Is the harm imposed on the landowner by a regulatory taking proportional to the benefits received? → **NO** Unconstitutional, unless compensated

YES
No violation of the Constitution

Source: Developed with the assistance of Lisa Pollisar and Kristen Spencer.

"New Property" Rights

During the 1960s and 1970s, the idea took hold that governmental benefits (or largess or entitlements), such as welfare payments, occupational licenses, and public housing, should be considered a form of "new property" and afforded constitutional protection.[37] This was a revolutionary development with major ramifications for public administration. Perhaps no case made this clearer than *Goldberg v. Kelly* (1970).[38] The issue was whether New York City could terminate welfare benefits to an individual without first affording him or her a full evidentiary hearing. The city did provide seven days' prior notice and an opportunity to respond in writing. For a majority on the Supreme Court, however, more procedural due process was required. In the course of its opinion, the Court observed that "it may be realistic today to regard welfare entitlements as more like 'property' than a 'gratuity.' Much of the existing wealth in this country takes the form of rights that do not fall within the traditional common-law concepts of property." The emergence of this "new property" interpretation is made clear by Justice Black's vigorous dissent:

> The Court . . . in effect says that the failure of the government to pay a promised charitable installment to an individual deprives that individual of *his own property,* in violation of the Due Process Clause of the Fourteenth Amendment. It somewhat strains credulity to say that the government's promise of charity to an individual is property belonging to that individual when the government denies that the individual is honestly entitled to receive such a payment.

Black went on to observe that "the procedure required today as a matter of constitutional law finds no precedent in our legal system."

The current constitutional concept that governmental benefits or largess, including much of public employment, are a form of "new property" to be afforded constitutional protection is an example of how the Constitution can be adapted to changing circumstances. The more dependent individuals became on the largess of the administrative or welfare state, the more they needed protection from arbitrary, invidious, or capricious treatment by it. By considering largess to be a form of property, the individual who receives or is entitled to it has a constitutional right to procedural due process if the government seeks to withhold it. From any managerial perspective, due process is an expensive, ineffective, and inefficient means of organizing and implementing public administration. Nevertheless, due process is now required in a wide range of administrative actions dealing with the distribution of benefits or largess.

Procedural Due Process

As noted many times throughout this text, procedural due process is fundamental to the legal approach to public administration. It is also a constitutional value of great importance. Procedural due process seeks to assure fundamental fairness when the government is taking action that will injure the life, liberty, or property interests of one or a few specific individuals.

The Supreme Court has said that due process is "an elusive concept. Its exact boundaries are undefinable, and its content varies according to specific factual contexts."[39] But, like substantive rights and the takings clause, procedural due process has a structure (see Box 11.6). It requires a balance of three concerns: the individual interests at stake, such as traditional property or new property; the likelihood, relative to other possible procedures, that the procedure used will result in errors; and the government's financial and administrative interests in using the current procedure. An underlying presumption of this structure is that more elaborate procedures will be both more accurate and more costly. As the individual interests at stake become more substantial, due process is less tolerant of error and less sensitive to costs. To take the extreme example, the procedures used in capital punishment cases should leave no room for error, regardless of cost. In cases involving a short disciplinary suspension from a civil service job, by contrast, far less exacting procedures can be used because the harm to the individual is limited and reversible (through back pay, for instance).

Despite its flexibility, several constitutional principles of due process are reasonably well settled in the context of ordinary public administration:

1.   The individual whose interests are likely to be injured by the governmental denial or cutoff of benefits during the term for which they were offered, such as welfare, Social Security, public school attendance, or public employment, is entitled to advance *notice* of the proposed action.

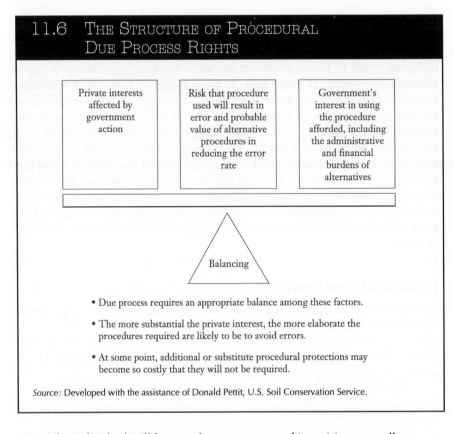

11.6   THE STRUCTURE OF PROCEDURAL DUE PROCESS RIGHTS

| Private interests affected by government action | Risk that procedure used will result in error and probable value of alternative procedures in reducing the error rate | Government's interest in using the procedure afforded, including the administrative and financial burdens of alternatives |

Balancing

• Due process requires an appropriate balance among these factors.

• The more substantial the private interest, the more elaborate the procedures required are likely to be to avoid errors.

• At some point, additional or substitute procedural protections may become so costly that they will not be required.

Source: Developed with the assistance of Donald Pettit, U.S. Soil Conservation Service.

2. The individual will have a chance to *respond* in writing or orally.

3. Depending on the nature of the action, the individual may have a right to a full-fledged *administrative hearing* prior to governmental implementation of the proposed action, as in the termination of welfare benefits.

4. The individual usually has a right to a posttermination hearing if no prior hearing is afforded.

5. Depending on the interests at stake, the individual may have the right to *confrontation and cross-examination,* to be represented by an *attorney* (at least, at one's own expense), and to present *witnesses* on one's behalf before an *impartial governmental decision maker,* such as an administrative law judge or hearing examiner. In some instances, due process may require that the hearing be open to the press and public. Remember that the purpose of a hearing is to reduce the likelihood of an erroneous decision harming an individual's protected liberty or property interests. If all the pertinent information is agreed on and/or there is no controversy, a hearing may not be required.[40]

The constitutional principle that procedural due process of some degree applies to deprivations of the "new property" has been a major factor in the "judicialization" of much public administration. Welfare and public housing agencies, the Social Security Administration, occupational licensing boards, and many other types of agencies have had to revamp their administrative procedures to accommodate this constitutional value. Public personnel administration has also been deeply affected by it (see Chapter 5). Moreover, accommodating due process has been expensive and sometimes inefficient and ineffective as a means of reducing fraud, preventing the distribution of benefits to individuals legally ineligible to receive them, and removing unfit public employees. This is one of the policy concerns with entitlements. However, procedural due process is not required when a benefit expires because it has been offered for a fixed period. The Supreme Court has not been oblivious to the administrative costs of procedural due process but, on the whole, has sought to protect individuals from harm through arbitrary, capricious, invidious, or patently unfair administrative actions.

Equal Protection

The Fourteenth Amendment provides that no state shall "deny to any person within its jurisdiction the equal protection of the laws." Equal protection is within the meaning of the "liberty" protected in the Fifth Amendment and therefore applies to the federal government as well. The original purpose of the Fourteenth Amendment's equal protection clause was, at least, to protect freed slaves and African Americans generally in the South. Whether those who drafted it expected more is a moot point. Today constitutional values and principles dictate broad application of the clause. An elaborate structure for determining what is required has been developed (see Box 11.7).

Classifications

It is often desirable or necessary in matters of public policy to classify people according to economic, social, demographic, or other characteristics. For instance, taxpayers may be classified by the amount of income they earn; individuals may be classified by age, veteran status, education, and geographic residence, citizenship, or alienage. They can also be classified by race, color, religion, gender, or national origin (ethnicity). Over the years, the Supreme Court has developed a "three-tier" approach to dealing with classifications of individuals. Some classifications are called "suspect" because they may potentially violate the core guarantee of equal protection by discriminating against "certain racial and ethnic groups [that] have frequently been recognized as 'discrete and insular minorities' who are relatively powerless to protect their interests in the political process."[41] When a classification is suspect, the burden of proof is on the government to demonstrate that the categorization serves a compelling governmental interest in a narrowly tailored fashion. This is difficult though possible to do, as in *Grutter* and cases in which the suspect classification was used to remedy past, proven unconstitutional discrimination.[42] The courts apply strict scrutiny to governmental efforts to justify suspect classifications in order to assure that there is no breach of equal protection.

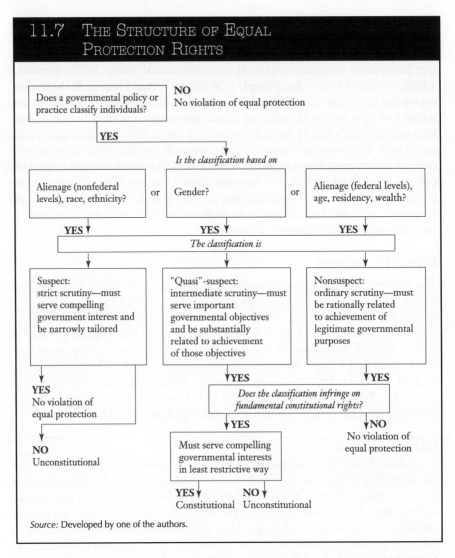

11.7   THE STRUCTURE OF EQUAL PROTECTION RIGHTS

Source: Developed by one of the authors.

Narrow tailoring requires that the classification closely fit the problem the government is trying to remedy and that the remedy be efficacious relative to means available that do not classify people by race or ethnicity. "Narrow tailoring does not require exhaustion of every conceivable race-neutral alternative," but it makes it necessary to consider obvious options.[43] It also requires that there be a fixed, logical termination point to the use of the classification, such as a future date or a successful policy outcome. Means that leave third parties not involved in the case seriously worse off, such as firing members of one race to create openings for members of another, are not narrowly tailored. Depending on the circumstances, narrow tailoring may require that the government involved be allowed to waive the classification where its use would result in unintended and undesirable consequences. For example, if the classification is intended to remedy past, proven racial discrimination in public employment, a waiver provision will protect the government from having to hire or promote individuals clearly not qualified to do the work at hand.[44] When evaluating narrow tailoring, the courts apply strict scrutiny to the government's choice of means.[45] At present, classifications based on race and ethnicity are suspect. This is true even if they are intended to help a group, as in the case of affirmative action. State and local governmental classifications based on citizenship are also usually suspect.

By contrast, some classifications, such as those based on age, wealth, or residency, are "nonsuspect" (or "ordinary"). There is no reason to believe they violate the purpose of the equal protection clause. Such classifications are found in a wide array of public policies, including laws prohibiting the sale of alcoholic beverages to those who have not reached the age of 21 or providing reduced tuition at state universities for bona fide state residents. These classifications are subject to routine judicial scrutiny and are valid if they serve a legitimate governmental purpose in a rational way. The burden of persuasion typically falls on those challenging such classifications. Federal classifications based on citizenship are not treated as suspect because the Constitution specifically provides Congress with broad powers regarding naturalization (Article I, section 8).

Gender-based classifications fall in between the suspect and nonsuspect categories. They trigger intermediate scrutiny and must be substantially related to the achievement of important governmental objectives. At an earlier time, legislation treating women and men differently was common. Often the purpose was allegedly to protect women, but the result was to place barriers in the path of their employment, property rights, full citizenship, and educational and other opportunities. Society is now far more cognizant of unequal treatment of women, and the courts have taken a deeper look at gender-based classifications. In particular, the courts have "invalidated statutes employing gender as an inaccurate proxy for other, more germane bases of classification."[46] Eventually, such classifications may be considered as suspect as those based on race, require a compelling state interest, and be subject to strict scrutiny and narrow tailoring. In *United States v. Virginia* (1996), a case dealing with the constitutionality of Virginia Military Institute's refusal to admit women, the Supreme Court emphasized that the government's justification for gender classifications must be "exceedingly persuasive."[47]

Discriminatory Purpose

Many governmental regulations do not establish explicit classifications but tend to have a harsher impact on one social group than another. For example, the Supreme Court speculated that this may be true of "a whole range of tax, welfare, public service, regulatory, and licensing statutes that may be more burdensome to the poor and to the average black than to the more affluent white."[48] Such regulations are not considered in violation of equal protection unless a discriminatory purpose can be shown. In the Court's words, "Our cases have not embraced the proposition that a law or other official act, without regard to whether it reflects a racially discriminatory purpose, is unconstitutional *solely* because it has a racially disproportionate impact."[49] Rather, a purpose to discriminate must be present if the regulation is to be found in violation of equal protection. Such a purpose does not have to be "express or appear on the face of the statute," and it "may often be inferred from the totality of the relevant facts, including the fact . . . that the law bears more heavily on one race than another."[50] In short, the disproportionately harsh impact of a regulation on members of one racial or other social group is not enough to demonstrate a violation of equal protection. This was made evident in *Personnel Administrator of Massachusetts v. Feeney* (1979), in which the Supreme Court found that a veteran preference system in state employment strongly favored males over females but did not establish a gender-based classification either overtly or covertly, and was not intended to discriminate against women.[51] Consequently, the preference was held to be constitutional.

Classifications and Fundamental Rights

When a nonsuspect classification is used in a way that treads on fundamental constitutional rights, it will be subject to strict scrutiny and to the compelling governmental interest and least restrictive alternative or narrow tailoring tests. For instance, in *Shapiro v. Thompson* (1969), the Supreme Court concluded that state (and District of Columbia) regulations requiring new residents to wait at least a year before applying for welfare benefits infringed on indigents' constitutional right to "travel interstate."[52] Because the governments involved could not meet the requirement of demonstrating a compelling interest for using the residency classifications, the Court held that they were unconstitutional. The Court confronted a similar issue and reached the same conclusion in *Saenz v. Roe* (1999), which challenged a California statute limiting the welfare benefits of those who had not lived in the state for 12 months to the amount available to them in the state from which they migrated.[53]

Equal Protection's Normative Philosophy

In public administration, there is more to the equal protection clause than may be immediately apparent. The constitutional values and principles of equal protection tend to establish a type of "rationality" different from that inherent in the traditional managerial or political approaches to public administration. This was perhaps best illustrated by the case of *Craig v. Boren* (1976).[54] In an effort to promote traffic safety, Oklahoma enacted a statute that prohibited the sale of "3.2 percent" beer to males under the age of 21. Females could purchase it at the age of 18 and over. The state's rationale was that statistical evidence indicated that males in the 18–20 age bracket were more prone than females of the same age to be involved in alcohol-related driving offenses. These statistics were not overwhelmingly convincing—one survey found that among those arrested in Oklahoma for driving while intoxicated, 0.18 percent of the group were females age 18 to 20, whereas 2 percent of the group were males in the same age range. Nevertheless, this finding seemed to support what was taken to be common knowledge: that males of this age were more of a threat on the road than their female cohorts were. From a traditional managerial perspective, therefore, the regulation appeared sensible. It would be more expensive and less efficient and effective to arrest intoxicated 18- to 20-year-old males for driving offenses than to seek to reduce the likelihood that they would be driving while drunk at all by making it more difficult for them to obtain the 3.2 percent beer. Similarly, the political perspective supported the notion of aggregating all the males of this age into a group and then addressing the circumstances of the group as a whole through legislation. From both perspectives the regulation was considered in the public interest because it promoted the public safety, especially that of the 18- to 20-year-old males.

In assessing the regulation from the perspectives of constitutional values and principles, the Supreme Court reached a startlingly different conclusion. In a key paragraph, the Court's majority opinion attacked both the traditional managerial and political approaches:

> Proving broad sociological propositions by statistics is dubious business, and one that inevitably is in tension with the normative philosophy that underlies the Equal Protection Clause. Suffice to say that the showing offered by the [state] does not satisfy us that sex represents a legitimate, accurate proxy for the regulation of drinking and driving.

We see two important constitutional principles at work here. First, "sociological propositions" that create or are derived from social classifications, such as male/female and black/white, are disfavored by the equal protection clause because they inherently tend to suggest that public policy should treat different social groups differently. In other words, they suggest that different opportunities should be afforded to or different restrictions imposed on distinct social groups. Ideally, a principle of the equal protection clause is that no such classifications should be made in the public sector because the classifications are too broad to apply reasonably to each individual within them. Justice Stevens made this point in a concurring opinion in *Craig* when he protested against the unfairness of treating all 18- to 20-year-old males "as inferior to their female counterparts." Certainly, there must be some males in that age group who could handle 3.2 percent beer and driving. Moreover, some males of that age do not have drivers' licenses and do not drive. Why should 18-year-old female drivers be afforded the right to buy 3.2 percent beer while it is denied to 20-year-old male nondrivers? The latter are clearly less threatening to traffic safety than the former.

The second constitutional principle evident in the Court's opinion is that legislative or administrative classifications based on social groups must at least be accurate proxies for the regulation of the behavior with which the state is concerned. In particular, relying on stereotypes as the basis for such regulations is unacceptable under the equal protection clause. For example, it is not enough to assume that everybody knows that teenage males in Oklahoma are wild "cowboys." If the state wants to treat them differently than it treats teenage females, it has to demonstrate that the quality of being male is substantially related to the achievement of important public policy objectives. Here, then, is a place where solid policy analysis and constitutional law demand the same thing—an accurate understanding of the behavior of the target group. The Supreme Court suggested that such social classifications would have to rest on "predictive empirical relationships." Even then, the classification would be unconstitutional if it authorized disparate treatment of individuals based on race or ethnicity and failed to serve a compelling state interest in a narrowly tailored way.

Clearly, the constitutional values and principles associated with equal protection provide public administrators with a difficult challenge. In a nation with a heterogeneous population, such as the United States, the classification of social groups has long been deeply ingrained in the culture. Private individuals and public policy traditionally used such classifications as proxies for knowing how to act and what to do. For instance, in *Baker v. City of St. Petersburg* (1968), a police chief unconstitutionally used the race of police officers as a proxy for being able to get along with citizens of the same race and to engage in efficient and effective police work.[55] In *U.S. v. Brignoni-Ponce,* "looking Mexican" was taken as a proxy for the likelihood of being an undocumented alien.[56] Consequently, what the Supreme Court is saying in *Craig v. Boren* is nothing less than that the equal protection clause demands that we change a traditional way of thinking. Classification by social group is viewed by the Constitution as inherently undesirable. What is the alternative?

Individuality

Constitutional values and principles favor looking at individuals as individuals rather than as members of public policy classifications or categorical statistical groups. Class-action suits are entertained by the courts, but judges sometimes go to considerable pains to assure that such a class exists and that the individual or organization litigating the suit is truly a representative of it. Perhaps public sector mandatory maternity leave cases best illustrate the constitutional emphasis on individuality in the public administrative context.[57] School systems, acting on the basis of managerial values, sought to establish a systematic procedure for replacing pregnant school teachers. In particular, the schools wanted ample notice of when the teachers would no longer be able to fulfill their professional responsibilities. This would enable principals to plan ahead for the hiring of permanent substitutes or other replacements. Allowing a pregnant teacher to determine when she was no longer able to teach classes might provide too short notice to make adequate arrangements for the continuation of her classes. The regulations at issue in the cases reaching the Supreme Court required pregnancy leaves to begin in the fourth and fifth months of pregnancy. The Court found that these regulations infringed on the constitutionally protected Fourteenth Amendment liberty to make personal choices regarding matters of marriage and family. It also found the regulations to be irrational: if the fourth or fifth months of a teacher's pregnancy occurred toward the end of the school year, mandatory maternity leaves would disrupt the continuity of teaching because many teachers would be medically able to continue well beyond that time. The infringement on liberty and the irrationality of the regulations, when coupled, violated constitutional values and principles in the Court's view. It suggested that either mandatory leaves should commence very late in the term of a normal pregnancy (during the eighth month) or that leaves should be based on an *individualized* medical determination of a pregnant teacher's ability to perform her professional responsibilities. In either event, the school systems might not receive adequate notice of when the teacher's leave would begin, but the Court stressed the importance of treating the individual as an individual, rather than part of a group, in these circumstances. In short, in many cases, the constitutional value of individuality is likely to outweigh the administrative burdens it imposes.

Fourth Amendment Privacy Rights

The constitutional rights to privacy are related to the value of individuality. Constitutional law protects two types of privacy, informational and decisional. Informational privacy falls under the Fourth Amendment, which partially states that "The right of the people to be secure in their persons, houses, papers, and effects, against unreasonable searches and seizures, shall not be violated. . . ." The amendment enables individuals to have spheres into which the government cannot easily intrude. Decisional privacy is derived from the word "liberty" in the due process clauses of the Fifth and Fourteenth Amendments. The full scope of its application is a point of contention among Supreme Court justices and other jurists. At a minimum, however, it protects the "right 'to be free from unwarranted governmental intrusion into matters so fundamentally affecting a person as the decision whether to bear or beget a child.'"[58] Jurisprudence regarding liberty rights that are not specifically enumerated in the Constitution is called **"substantive due process."**

Like other constitutional rights, Fourth Amendment rights are not absolute. The protection is only against "unreasonable" searches and seizures, and what is reasonable has been subject to interpretations that vary with the circumstances. For instance, the constitutional privacy protections public employees can claim in the workplace are more limited than those held by private citizens.[59] The broad structure of Fourth Amendment rights is diagrammed in Box 11.8.

Basic Structure of Privacy Rights

Once it is determined that a governmental action has some implications for an individual's privacy, the key question is whether the individual had a reasonable expectation of privacy in the circumstances. Reasonable in this context means an expectation that society is prepared to support (according to the judiciary).

11.8   STRUCTURE OF FOURTH AMENDMENT PRIVACY RIGHTS

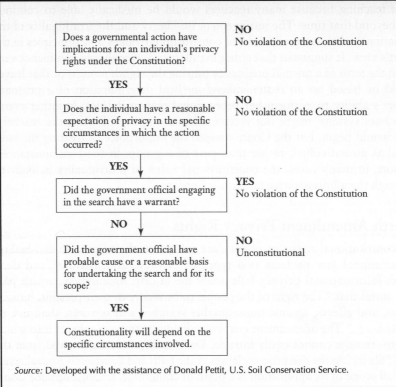

Does a governmental action have implications for an individual's privacy rights under the Constitution?

NO No violation of the Constitution

YES ↓

Does the individual have a reasonable expectation of privacy in the specific circumstances in which the action occurred?

NO No violation of the Constitution

YES ↓

Did the government official engaging in the search have a warrant?

YES No violation of the Constitution

NO ↓

Did the government official have probable cause or a reasonable basis for undertaking the search and for its scope?

NO Unconstitutional

YES ↓

Constitutionality will depend on the specific circumstances involved.

Source: Developed with the assistance of Donald Pettit, U.S. Soil Conservation Service.

If there is no such expectation, the individual's Fourth Amendment rights cannot be violated. For example, an individual cannot claim a reasonable expectation of privacy in the contents of a carry-on bag being brought onto a commercial airplane. Similarly, depending on a public employee's workplace practices, he or she may not be able to claim a reasonable expectation of privacy regarding the content of filing cabinets or desk drawers. By contrast, many public employees not subject to security screening would probably be able to claim successfully a reasonable expectation of privacy in a handbag or small backpack.

Assuming the individual has a reasonable expectation of privacy, the government needs either a warrant or probable cause for undertaking a law enforcement search. In either case, the scope and objectives of the search must be clearly established. Snooping around someone's home or papers to see what turns up is unconstitutional. Warrants may also be required for administrative inspections, including those by the Occupational Health and Safety Administration,[60] but non-law-enforcement searches are often subject to weaker requirements. For example, the Supreme Court has held that public employers and public schools have special needs that make warrants and probable cause impracticable. Searches in these contexts are usually governed by a standard of reasonableness in inception and scope. However, the Supreme Court has also upheld suspicionless urinalysis drug testing of some categories of public employees and public school students.[61] The constitutionality of such tests depends on the degree to which those tested have a reasonable expectation of privacy, the rationale for testing them, and the overall reasonableness of the procedures. The constitutional limits on physical and electronic searches in the interests of national security under the Foreign Intelligence Surveillance Act of 1978, as reauthorized in 2013, are uncertain.

Equity

Equity is a final constitutional value that should be mentioned. It is thought of as "the power to dispense with the harsh rigor of general laws in particular cases."[62] In other words, when following the law to the letter would result in an unfair or unreasonable resolution of a case, equity allows a principled exception to be made. Equity also enables the judiciary to develop *remedies* for breaches of constitutional rights even though such remedies are not specifically provided for in any statutes. For example, the federal judiciary has ordered "forced busing" and funding as means of desegregating school systems that have unconstitutionally separated students by race.[63] It has also fashioned "quota" hiring and promotional systems to remedy racial discrimination in public personnel administration.[64] It has mandated far-reaching prison and public mental health reforms.[65] Although the Constitution provides that the judicial power shall "extend to all cases, in law and equity," it is sometimes contended that the judiciary has used its powers in equity to transform the Constitution into "an omnibus piece of legislation."[66] Such criticism notwithstanding, public administrators should recognize that contemporary constitutional values are unlikely to tolerate harsh and unfair results in particular cases dictated by rigidly strict adherence to rules and precedents. Traditional, although not NPM, administrators may prefer to "go by the book" and avoid making exceptions even when they seem appropriate to protect individual rights. The Constitution, however, is less willing to do so. When combined, equity and the value and principles of procedural due process dictate procedures and substantive results of public administrative action that are considered fundamentally fair. This is true even if these procedures and results cause inefficiency and added expense, hamper effectiveness in some sense, or are politically unpopular.

State Action

With the exception of the Thirteenth Amendment, which prohibits slavery, the Constitution does not ordinarily apply to relationships among private parties. For instance, in the absence of civil rights legislation, private firms were free to (and did) discriminate on the basis of race, sex, national origin, and religion. Constitutional equal protection, due process, free speech, privacy, and other rights are irrelevant to private relationships. However, when private parties engage in "state action," the Constitution may directly constrain their activity. Consequently, state action doctrine is of great importance to privatization, public-private partnerships, hybrid arrangements such as quasi-governmental corporations, and collaborative governance.

State action refers to governmental action, whether at the federal, state, or local level. Historically, the courts have sought to draw a dichotomy between governmental action and private conduct. But they have also recognized that public administration is not always so neatly packaged that one can find a bright line between governmental and nongovernmental activity. In the Supreme Court's words, the "actions of private entities can sometimes be regarded as governmental action for constitutional purposes."[67] This occurs when the action of a private entity can be fairly attributable to a government. Unfortunately for public administrators who like clarity, the Supreme Court has noted that "What is fairly attributable is a matter of normative judgment, and the criteria lack rigid simplicity."[68]

In general, state action will be present when (1) a private party engages in a public function; (2) the government is so deeply involved or entwined in the activity that it is not feasible to separate the private party's actions from those of the government; and/or (3) the government has empowered the private party to exercise governmental authority (e.g., seizing disputed property in a **replevin** action).[69] The main problem of state action doctrine is applying these imprecise and subjective standards to real-world administrative arrangements. The Supreme Court has admitted, "It is fair to say that 'our cases deciding when private action might be deemed that of the state have not been a model of consistency.'"[70] Nevertheless, some matters are clear.

First, the judiciary takes responsibility for determining what constitutes state action. In a case involving Amtrak (see Box 11.9), a hybrid federal corporation, the Supreme Court noted with emphasis that

> it is not for Congress to make the final determination of Amtrak's status as
> a government entity for purposes of determining the constitutional rights
> of citizens affected by its actions. If Amtrak is, by its very nature, what the
> Constitution regards as the Government, congressional pronouncement that
> it is not such can no more relieve it of its First Amendment restrictions than
> a similar pronouncement could exempt the Federal Bureau of Investigation
> from the Fourth Amendment. The Constitution constrains governmental
> action "by whatever instruments or in whatever modes that action may be
> taken."[71]

Second, governmental corporations, performance-based organizations, and many public-private arrangements will be subject to constitutional constraints no matter how much adherents to the NPM or other approaches would

11.9   WHEN IS A NONGOVERNMENTAL ENTITY A GOVERNMENTAL ENTITY?

Michael Lebron contracted to rent the "Spectacular" billboard in Amtrak's Pennsylvania Station in New York City. The Spectacular is approximately 10 feet high and 103 feet long. It is curved and illuminated. Lebron wanted to create the following display:

> The work is a photomontage, accompanied by considerable text. Taking off on a widely circulated Coors beer advertisement which proclaims Coors to be the "Right Beer," Lebron's piece is captioned "Is it the Right's Beer Now?" It includes photographic images of convivial drinkers of Coors beer, juxtaposed with a Nicaraguan village scene in which peasants are menaced by a can of Coors that hurtles toward them, leaving behind a trail of fire, as if it were a missile. The accompanying text, appearing on either end of the montage, criticizes the Coors family for its support of right-wing causes, particularly the contras in Nicaragua. Again taking off on Coors' advertising which uses the slogan of "Silver Bullet" for its beer cans, the text proclaims that Coors is "The Silver Bullet that aims The Far Right's political agenda at the heart of America."

Amtrak refused the display because its policy was not to allow "political advertising" on the Spectacular. Lebron sued.

When the case reached the Supreme Court, the main question was whether Amtrak was a governmental actor. If it was, its refusal to display Lebron's photomontage would be governed by the First Amendment's guarantee of freedom of speech. If it was a private actor, the First Amendment would not apply. Amtrak argued that it is not a government entity. It pointed out that its authorizing act, the federal Rail Passenger Service Act of 1970, declares that Amtrak "will not be an agency or establishment of the United States Government." Amtrak also noted that two previous Supreme Court decisions dealing with commercial matters characterized it as a "nongovernmental entity."

The Court of Appeals agreed that Amtrak was not part of the government.

Nevertheless, the Supreme Court had no trouble concluding that Amtrak was indeed "an agency or instrumentality of the United States for the purpose of individual rights guaranteed against the Government by the Constitution." In a paragraph that would remind modern reformers that performance-based organizations are nothing new, the Court noted:

> A remarkable feature of the heyday of . . . [federal] corporations, in the 1930's and 1940's, was that, even while they were praised for their status as "agencies separate and distinct, administratively and financially and legally, from the government itself, [which] has facilitated their adoption of commercial methods of accounting and financing, avoidance of political controls, and utilization of regular procedures of business management," it was fully acknowledged that they were a "device" of "government," and constituted "federal corporate agencies" apart from "regular government departments."

If this history were not enough, the Court noted that (1) "Amtrak was created by special statute, explicitly for the furtherance of federal government goals"; (2) "six of the corporation's eight externally named directors . . . are appointed directly by the President of the United States—four of them (including the Secretary of Transportation) with the advice and consent of the Senate"; and (3) "the Government exerts its control [over Amtrak] . . . as a policymaker."

Having determined that Amtrak is governmental and therefore subject to constitutional constraints, the Court remanded the case to the lower court to determine whether the railroad had violated Lebron's First Amendment rights to show his distaste for Coors.

Source: Lebron v. National Railroad Passenger Corporation, 513 U.S. 374 (1995).

like them to operate like private sector businesses. As the Supreme Court put it: "It surely cannot be that government, state or federal, is able to evade the most solemn obligations imposed by the Constitution by simply resorting to the corporate form."[72] For example, in one case the Court held that a college "which had been built and maintained pursuant to a privately erected trust, was nevertheless a governmental actor for constitutional purposes because it was operated and controlled by a board of state appointees, which was itself a state agency."[73]

Third, private contractors performing governmental functions can become state actors subject to constitutional constraints.[74] For instance, physicians under contract to provide medical care to prisoners are state actors, regardless of the fact that they are neither state employees nor at the prisons on a full-time basis. They are bound by constitutional interpretation of the Eighth Amendment, which gives prisoners a right to adequate medical treatment. What might be ordinary malpractice in private practice may constitute a constitutional infringement when prisoners are involved. The difference is significant, because violations of constitutional rights can trigger additional liabilities.

Fourth, when private parties engaged in state action violate individuals' constitutional rights they are potentially liable in civil suits for money damages.[75] For example, a physician under contract to a prison who is "deliberately indifferent" to a prisoner's medical needs can be sued for violating the prisoner's Eighth Amendment rights. So can a private prison guard who uses excessive force on an inmate. A private individual involved in such a suit could be held liable even though he or she was acting in accordance with established laws, agency procedures, or corporate directives that later turned out to be unconstitutional. Depending on the circumstances, a private individual sued in such a constitutional tort case may or may not be entitled to the qualified immunity available to public employees.[76]

Unlike public employees, private individuals may not be able to defend themselves in such suits on the basis that they could not reasonably have known their actions were unconstitutional.

Contemporary state action doctrine has broad implications for public administration organized according to NPM principles. Deregulating agencies by turning them into performance-based, corporate-style organizations outside of normal civil service regulations will not relieve them of their constitutional obligations. Their employment and customer relationships will still be governed by constitutional due process, equal protection, privacy, and First Amendment rights. Similarly, public-private partnerships and privatization can carry constitutional responsibilities with them. As experience with NPM arrangements grows, there will certainly be an increasing number of lawsuits involving questions of state action. Their outcome could be of particular importance to privatization and public-private partnerships. Subjecting such arrangements to constitutional constraints and attendant liabilities would complicate them significantly.

CONCLUSION: AN ONGOING PARTNERSHIP

Constitutional values and principles have often stood at odds with those of public administration. Today, however, both the judiciary and public managers are more frequently realizing that there is a need to develop an ongoing partnership.[77] More searching judicial review of administrative action and the development of far greater personal and local governmental liabilities for public administration that violates individuals' constitutional or legal rights have forced public administrators to be aware of and responsive to constitutional values and principles. As judges have become more involved in administrative activity through overseeing the management of public institutions, such as schools, mental health facilities, and prisons, they have recognized the worth of some public administrative values and the practical constraints of administrative action. It was once taken for granted by judges that they could bring these institutions up to constitutional standards by issuing decrees or directly involving the court in their day-to-day management. In retrospect, most would probably recognize that this assumption was too optimistic.[78] Their decrees and redesigns of public school systems have sometimes been frustrated by "white and middle class flight," or the withdrawal of white and middle class minority students from the school systems. Their orders for reforms of prison and mental health facilities have likewise foundered upon the unmanageability of those institutions. After three decades or so of a relatively high degree of confrontation between public administrators and judges, both sides gained a greater appreciation of the values and perspectives of the other.

A remarkable feature of the American constitutional law is its adaptive quality. The Constitution is a living document. Drafted in the horse-and-buggy age, it has survived through the Industrial Revolution, the rise of the contemporary administrative state, and the consequent transformation of governmental structure and role. It continues with us into the digital age. There is little doubt that its values and principles will be more completely synthesized with those of public administration in the future. Public administrators and judges have no choice but to make their partnership work, and they have the means to do so—for it depends primarily on both exercising their powers of reason.

STUDY QUESTIONS

1. Should federal judges become involved in the management of (a) prisons, (b) public mental health facilities, (c) public schools? If the answer is yes, what forms should their involvement take? In addressing these questions, what political and administrative aspects of such judicial involvement seem most troublesome to you?
2. Classifications based on gender are currently "quasi-suspect" and are subject to intermediate scrutiny under equal protection analysis. Do you think they should be fully "suspect"? Why or why not? What differences would such a change make in terms of public administration?

3. In several states, including Florida, Georgia, and Texas, many public employees do not have "new property" rights in their jobs because civil service law does not convey tenure. How might this affect these employees' efforts to do their jobs? In general, do you think public employees and clients or customers of public agencies should have new property rights? Why or why not?

4. Students engaged in extracurricular activities may be subject to suspicionless drug testing as part of a reasonable program to reduce drug abuse in public schools. Pottawatomie County, Oklahoma, authorized drug tests for athletes, Future Farmers of America, Future Homemakers of America, and members of the Academic Team, band, choir, and pom-pom and cheerleading squads. Assess the desirability of Pottawatomie's policy from the perspective of public administration.

5. The duty of government to protect its citizens would appear to require it to expand its surveillance of Americans' communications with foreigners, who are potentially enemies of the United States. Under what conditions, if any, does this objective justify intruding on citizens' constitutional rights to privacy?

Notes

1. The demise of the Occupational Safety and Health Administration's Cooperative Compliance Program (CCP) has already been mentioned (Chapter 9). The National Performance Review considered the Maine 200 program, on which the CCP was based, to be a major success and a model for regulation generally. See Al Gore, *Common Sense Government Works Better & Costs Less* (Washington, DC: Government Printing Office, 1995), 25–27. Supreme Court decisions regarding state action (discussed later in this chapter) and contractors' constitutional rights and liabilities also undercut some of the premises of new public management reforms. See David H. Rosenbloom, "Constitutional Problems for the New Public Management in the United States," in Khi Thai and Rosalynn Carter, Eds., *Current Public Policy Issues* (Philadelphia: PrAcademics Press, 1999), 143–174.

2. *Immigration and Naturalization Service v. Chadha,* 462 U.S. 919 (1983). See also Rosenbloom, "Constitutional Problems."

3. Dwight Waldo, *The Administrative State,* 2d ed. (New York: Holmes and Meier, 1984), xviii.

4. Woodrow Wilson, "The Study of Administration," *Political Science Quarterly* 56 (December 1941): 481–506, at 484 (originally published in 1887).

5. Ibid., 504.

6. *Smith v. Wade,* 461 U.S. 31 (1983). See also *BMW v. Gore,* 517 U.S. 559 (1996).

7. Constance Horner, "Remarks on FEI's [Federal Executive Institute's] 20th Anniversary Dinner," Charlottesville, VA, 14 October 1988, 14.

8. Public Law 108-447; 118 Statutes at Large 3344, section 111. (December 8, 2004). The Constitution was signed on September 17, 1787.

9. Jeffrey Segal and Harold Spaeth, *The Supreme Court and the Attitudinal Model* (New York: Cambridge University Press, 1993).

10. *Minersville School District v. Gobitis,* 310 U.S. 586 (1940); *West Virginia State Board of Education v. Barnette,* 319 U.S. 624 (1943).

11. The term is Justice Felix Frankfurter's, used while noting that adherence to precedent should not be mindless. *U.S. v. International Boxing Club,* 348 U.S. 236, 249 (1955).

12. *Federal Baseball Club v. National League,* 259 U.S. 200 (1922); *Toolson v. New York Yankees,* 346 U.S. 356 (1953); *U.S. v. International Boxing Club* (1955); *Radovich v. National Football League,* 352 U.S. 445 (1957); *Flood v. Kuhn,* 407 U.S. 258 (1972).

13. *Federalist Paper No. 51,* in Clinton Rossiter, Ed., *The Federalist Papers* (New York: Mentor, 1961), 321–322.

14. *Local 2677, American Federation of Government Employees v. Phillips,* 358 F. Supp. 60 (1973).

15. Governor Richard Snelling of Vermont, quoted in the *Burlington Free Press,* 24 July 1983.

16. Rosemary O'Leary, *The Ethics of Dissent: Managing Guerrilla Government* (Washington, DC: CQ Press, 2005).

17. Ibid.

18. Ibid.

19. For the 2006 Human Capital Survey Report, see http://www.fhcs2006.opm.gov.

20. Max Weber, *From Max Weber: Essays in Sociology,* Trans. and Ed. H. H. Gerth and C. W. Mills (New York: Oxford University Press, 1958), chaps. 4 and 8.

21. *West Virginia State Board of Education v. Barnette,* 319 U.S. 624 (1943).

22. Weber, *From Max Weber,* 228.

23. *Keyishian v. Board of Regents,* 385 U.S. 589 (1967).

24. *Grutter v. Bollinger,* 539 U.S. 306, 332 (2003).

25. *Shelton v. Tucker,* 364 U.S. 479 (1960).

26. *Gratz v. Bollinger,* 539 U.S. 244, 271, 275 (2003).

27. *Church of Lukumi Babalu Aye, Inc. v. City of Hialeah,* 508 U.S. 520 (1993).

28. See John Rohr, *Ethics for Bureaucrats* (New York: Marcel Dekker, 1978), 213.

29. *U.S. v. 7.92 Acres of Land, More or Less, situated in the Towns of Provincetown and Travo, County of Barnstable, Commonwealth of Massachusetts,* 769 F. 2d 4 (1st Cir. 1985).

30. See *Kohl v. United States,* 91 U.S. 367, 372–373 (1876), wherein the Court wrote, "The Constitution itself contains an implied recognition of it [here referring to eminent domain] beyond what may justly be implied from the express grants. The Fifth Amendment contains a provision that private property shall not be taken for public use without just compensation. What is that but an implied assertion, that, on making just compensation, it [here referring to private property] may be taken?"

31. See *Berman v. Parker,* 348 U.S. 26 (1954). In this case, the Court ruled that taking private property to reduce or eliminate urban blight is a legitimate public purpose under the requirements of the Fifth Amendment.

32. *Hawaii Housing Authority v. Midkiff,* 467 U.S. 229 (1984). The State of Hawaii was concerned that the concentration of vast amounts of private property in the hands of a few landowners limited competition in the market for real estate. The Court upheld Hawaii's taking land for the explicit purpose of selling it to other private individuals.

33. *Susette Kelo et al. v. City of New London,* 545 U.S. 469 (2005).

34. Ibid.

35. Ibid.

36. Data are from the National Conference of State Legislatures, Eminent Domain Project, available online at http://www.ncsl.org/programs/natres/EMINDOMAIN.htm. See also, R. Benjamin Lingle, "Post-*Kelo* Eminent Domain Reform: A Double-Edged Sword for Historic Preservation," *Florida Law Review* 63 (2011): 985–1012 at p. 933.

37. Charles Reich, "The New Property," *Yale Law Journal* 73 (1964): 733–787.

38. *Goldberg v. Kelly,* 397 U.S. 254 (1970).

39. *Hannah v. Larche,* 363 U.S. 420, 442 (1960).

40. *Codd v. Velger,* 429 U.S. 624 (1977).

41. *San Antonio Independent School District v. Rodriguez,* 411 U.S. 1, 105 (dissent by Justice Thurgood Marshall).

42. *United States v. Paradise,* 480 U.S. 149 (1987).

43. *Grutter v. Bollinger,* 539 U.S. 306, 340 (2003).

44. Ibid.

45. *Fisher v. University of Texas at Austin,* U.S. Supreme Court No. 11-345 (June 24, 2013).

46. See *Craig v. Boren,* 429 U.S. 190, 198 (1976).

47. *United States v. Virginia,* 518 U.S. 515 (1996).

48. *Washington v. Davis,* 426 U.S. 229, 248 (1976).

49. Ibid., 239.

50. Ibid., 241–242.

51. *Personnel Administrator of Massachusetts v. Feeney,* 442 U.S. 256 (1979).

52. *Shapiro v. Thompson,* 384 U.S. 618 (1969).

53. *Saenz v. Roe,* 526 U.S. 489 (1999).

54. *Craig v. Boren,* 429 U.S. 190 (1976).

55. *Baker v. City of St. Petersburg,* 400 F.2d 294 (1968).

56. *United States v. Brignoni-Ponce,* 422 U.S. 873 (1975).

57. *Cleveland Board of Education v. LaFleur; Cohen v. Chesterfield Co. School Board,* 414 U.S. 632 (1974), argued and decided together.

58. Ibid., at 640.

59. *O'Connor v. Ortega,* 480 U.S. 709 (1987). See also *City of Ontario v. Quon,* 130 S. Ct. 2619 (2010).

60. *Marshall v. Barlows, Inc.,* 436 U.S. 307 (1978).

61. *National Treasury Employees Union v. Von Raab,* 489 U.S. 656 (1989); *Vernonia School District v. Acton,* 515 U.S. 646 (1995); *Board of Education of Independent School District No. 92 of Pottawatomie County v. Earls,* 536 U.S. 822 (2002). This last decision upheld drug testing of students involved in the Future Homemakers of America, Future Farmers of America, and choir, among other extracurricular activities.

62. Gary L. McDowell, *Equity and the Constitution* (Chicago: University of Chicago Press, 1982), 5.

63. *Swann v. Charlotte-Mecklenburg Board of Education,* 402 U.S. 1 (1971); *Missouri v. Jenkins,* 495 U.S. 33 (1990); 515 U.S. 70 (1995).

64. *U.S. v. Paradise,* 480 U.S. 150 (1987).

65. See David H. Rosenbloom, Rosemary O'Leary, and Joshua Chanin, *Public Administration and Law,* 3rd ed. (Boca Raton, FL: CRC/Taylor & Francis, 2010).

66. Henry Abraham, foreword, in McDowell, *Equity and the Constitution,* xi.

67. *Lebron v. National Railroad Passenger Corporation,* 513 U.S. 374 (1995).

68. *Brentwood Academy v. Tennessee Secondary School Athletic Association,* 531
U.S. 288, 295 (2001).

69. Jerome Barron and C. Thomas Dienes, *Constitutional Law in a Nutshell,*
4th ed. (St. Paul, MN: West, 1999), chap. 9; *Brentwood Academy v. Tennessee
Association,* 531 U.S. 288 (2001).

70. *Lebron v. National Railroad Passenger Corporation,* 513 U.S. 374, 378 (1995).

71. Ibid., 392.

72. Ibid., 397.

73. Ibid.

74. See *West v. Atkins,* 487 U.S. 46 (1988).

75. Ibid.; *Wyatt v. Cole and Robbins,* 504 U.S. 158 (1992); and *Richardson v.
McKnight,* 521 U.S. 399 (1997).

76. See *Filarsky v. Delia,* 132 S. Ct. 1657 (2012) for an explanation. As it stands now
a private individual hired by a municipality to do investigative work is entitled to
qualified immunity but a prison guard working for a private corporation is not.

77. David L. Bazelon, "The Impact of the Courts on Public Administration,"
Indiana Law Journal 52 (1976): 101–110, and David H. Rosenbloom, "Public
Administrators and the Judiciary: The 'New Partnership,'" *Public Administration
Review* 47 (January/February 1987): 75–83.

78. See Rosenbloom, O'Leary, and Chanin, *Public Administration and Law,* chap. 9.

ADDITIONAL READING

Barron, Jerome A., and C. Thomas Dienes. *Constitutional Law in a Nutshell,* 7th ed.
St. Paul, MN: Thomson Reuters, 2010.

O'Leary, Rosemary. *The Ethics of Dissent: Managing Guerrilla Government*
(Washington, DC: CQ Press, 2005).

Rosenbloom, David H. *Administrative Law for Public Managers.* Boulder, CO:
Westview Press, 2003.

Rosenbloom, David H., Rosemary O'Leary, and Joshua Chanin. *Public
Administration and Law,* 3rd ed. Boca Raton, FL: CRC/Taylor & Francis,
2010.

Warren, Kenneth. *Administrative Law in the American Political System,* 5th ed.
Boulder, CO: Westview, 2010.

CONSTITUTIONAL LAW WEB SITES

The text of many federal court decisions and related legal information can be found on FindLaw's
Web site at http://www.findlaw.com and at Justia.com: http://www.justia.com/.

Supreme Court decisions can be accessed at http://www.supremecourt.gov/opinions/opinions.aspx

The Web site for the American Constitution Society for Law and Policy has a wealth of reports
and materials on constitutional law at http://www.americanconstitutionsociety.org.

The Legal Information Institute at Cornell provides a wealth of information on court decisions
and related matters: http://www.law.cornell.edu/

OYEZ.Org at Chicago-Kent College of Law is an excellent site for accessing cases and keeping
up with the Supreme Court on a weekly basis: http://www.oyez.org/

CHAPTER 12

ACCOUNTABILITY AND ETHICS

Key Learning Objectives

1. Learn the important lesson that the nature of public service imposes higher standards of conduct on civil servants than are placed on private sector employees.

2. Understand the critical connection between ethics and accountability and the challenges of ensuring that administrative behavior is accountable.

3. Be able to explain the sources of a possible disconnect between citizen preferences and administrative decisions and the ways in which citizens may interpret such differences.

4. Understand three different approaches to ethical decision making and the attempts to synthesize these approaches.

5. Understand the managerial, political, and legal perspectives on ensuring accountability.

6. Learn the general features of codes of ethics in professional conduct to which modern public administrators are expected to adhere.

Public administrators may be seen as the "guardians" of the contemporary administrative state. This raises a fundamental issue in political thought: "Who guards the guardians?" Public administrators must be held accountable because there are aspects of their jobs that can lead to misconception of the public interest, corruption, and subversion. In general, public servants are held to higher standards of conduct than are private or nonprofit sector employees. This is the modern reality. But there are many aspects of public administration that make it difficult to attain a satisfactory level of accountability. This chapter will consider managerial, political, and legal perspectives on accountability and ethics. Ethics can be considered a form of self-accountability, or an "inner check" on public administrators' conduct. However, the inner check may be enforced by requirements that administrators' behavior comport with a variety of external standards. The various approaches are in many ways complementary: The legal approach tends to favor the inner check; the traditional managerial approach, a check external to the individual but internal to the agency; and the political and new public management (NPM) approaches, a check external to the agency and exercised through outside oversight. Many consider a new sense of professionalism, including perhaps a "code of ethics," to be a sensible means of helping the "guardians" guard themselves.

Public administrators have become an important locus of political power and influence in the United States. Sometimes individually, but generally collectively, they play an active role in the formulation of public policies. They also have a great deal to do with the style, pace, and tone of the execution of those policies. Out of this set of conditions arises a fundamental problem; as Frederick Mosher put it, "How does one square a permanent civil service—which neither the people by their vote nor their representatives by their appointments can replace—with the principle of government 'by the people'?"[1] To many concerned citizens and political authorities in nations throughout the world, this is the fundamental *political* issue presented by the development of the contemporary administrative state.

It is also a central issue of modern management. As Victor Thompson noted, the increasing specialization and technical expertise of subordinate employees have created a severe imbalance between the formal hierarchical authority and responsibility of high-level administrators, on the one hand, and their intellectual capacity to manage their staff, on the other.[2] That is one reason why the new public management (NPM) opposes hierarchy and favors employee empowerment. Accountability is also a legal matter. It concerns such questions as "Who is liable for what?" and "What kinds of conduct are illegal?"

This chapter tackles the issue of ensuring that public administrators do not violate their public trust. It discusses traditional managerial, new public management, political, and legal perspectives on accountability and ethics. Ethics is considered an internal, personal check—a sense of personal responsibility; accountability is the process of applying external checks on public administrators. Because the ethics and accountability of public administrators are truly a worldwide concern, it is worth taking some time to consider precisely why public administrators may abuse their public trust and act in ways not considered by the citizenry and/or political authorities to be in the public interest.

❖❖ WHY THE GUARDIANS NEED GUARDING

Although American public administration is considered exceptionally honest and able by world standards, it still needs guarding. No matter how well trained, like everyone else, administrators sometimes use poor judgment, make mistakes, blunder, or otherwise fail to do their jobs properly. Poor performance is a potential problem, but three other types of violations of public administrators' public trust have been of greater concern in ethics and accountability. These are misconception of the public interest, corruption, and subversion.

Misconception of the Public Interest

There are several forces frequently at work in public administration that could lead civil servants to misconceive or misconstrue the public interest. First are the social forces. Public administrators, especially in the higher-level, more complex, and typically more politically influential jobs, may not constitute a social group representative of the nation's population. At the least, they are likely to be disproportionately drawn from the ranks of the middle class.[3] They may come heavily from the upper class, as was true during the early years of the federal government. The social class basis of the civil service is important because it colors perceptions of how people live, what their problems are, and what they want and need. It also is an important element in the creation of individual and group values and norms of proper behavior. To a considerable extent, one's worldview is likely to be influenced by one's social attributes. As Seymour Lipset found, "The behavior of government bureaucrats varies with the nongovernmental social background and interest of those controlling the bureaucratic structure."[4] In this regard categories are generally clear cut: one is born female or male, to one race or ethnicity or another, to a social class. Overall, in comparison to the nation's general population, public administrators in the United States are thought to be disproportionately middle class, and in the upper levels of public services, they are still disproportionately white and male.[5] While there may be signs of increasing female and minority representation in the federal bureaucracy, there is still a gap to be overcome. For example, while women hold 50 percent of advanced degrees in the United States, they still comprise only 39 percent of top leadership in U.S. federal regulatory agencies, and these tend to be in agencies focused on feminine issues. However, this is still better representation than on private corporate boards (15 percent) or in Congress (19 percent).[6]

A second factor that can lead public administrators to misconceive the public interest is an artifact of their specialization. Public administrators—like others who perform highly specialized functions—may eventually develop a narrow outlook concerning the public interest. They may tend to exaggerate the importance of what they do and downgrade the importance of what others do. They may also develop ways of thinking that make it difficult to understand alternative approaches or recognize the dominance or even the legitimacy of competing values. There are many well-known instances of this in American life. Lawyers, for example, sometimes successfully defend individuals they know are guilty of horrible crimes. Their rationale is that everyone is entitled to the best defense possible and that our system of justice cannot properly function otherwise. For the layperson, however, it may be somewhat more difficult to find a moral distinction between one who, for example, helps a child rapist escape from the scene of the crime and a lawyer who uses the technical rules of evidence to get the rapist off after an arrest has been made. Similarly, public health administrators, imbued with professional values emphasizing economy, have been known to authorize the routine nighttime drugging of patients to reduce staffing costs.[7] Although that practice is medically undesirable and potentially dangerous, it can be seen as desirable from a narrow administrative perspective concerned with cutting costs. Public administrators who deal with a particular type of client or population may eventually come to view their clients as truly representative of the population as a whole or of "human nature." Police in urban settings are so accustomed to dealing with hardcore criminals, prostitutes, and deviants that they may develop a distorted sense of the public. Boxes 12.1 and 12.2 present startling examples of agencies' misconceptions of the public interest and failure to act ethically.

These are familiar patterns that affect the thinking of individuals in some specialized job settings, including those in the civil service. They are augmented by various kinds of socialization that occur in the workplace. In bureaucracies, socialization is often thought to be an important mechanism for inculcating values in employees and consequently influencing their on-the-job behavior. For instance, Anthony Downs notes that any administrative agency is apt to develop a **bureau ideology** that

1. emphasizes the positive benefits of the bureau's activities and deemphasizes their costs;
2. indicates that further expansion of the bureau's services would be desirable and any curtailment thereof would be undesirable;
3. emphasizes the benefits that the bureau provides for the society, rather than its services to particular "special interests";
4. stresses the high present level of the bureau's efficiency;
5. emphasizes its achievements and future capabilities and ignores or minimizes its failures and inabilities.[8]

Moreover, in his view, these ideologies are imparted to the bureaucracy's key employees because "officials exhibit relatively strong loyalty to the organization controlling their job security and promotion."[9] When taken together, administrative specialization and socialization can be important in coloring

12.1 MISCONSTRUING THE PUBLIC INTEREST AT THE ATOMIC ENERGY COMMISSION

During the 1950s, the Atomic Energy Commission (AEC) conducted a number of nuclear tests in Nevada. The agency was aware of the dangers that radioactive fallout posed to those downwind from the test sites, mostly in Nevada and Utah. In some of the tests, the explosive devices were known to be "dirty" in the sense that the fallout would be especially heavy. Dirty weapons might have strategic military benefits, but they also had administrative ones. In 1957, the director of the AEC's division of biology and medicine explained that "if we continue to reduce the fraction [of radiation] we are willing to release, we eventually reach a cost of control [that] makes the operation prohibitive." In other words, there was a trade-off between administrative economy and known danger to the public.

There was also a sense that the public was expendable. By 1955, the downwinders were becoming concerned about their exposure to radiation. But their apprehension was outweighed by the AEC's apprehension of the Soviet Union's nuclear threat. One commissioner said that "people have got to learn to live with the facts of life, and part of the facts of life are fallout." In another's view, "We must not let anything interfere with this series of tests—nothing."

Political scientist Howard Ball explains what followed:

The next day, Feb. 24 [1955], another pinkish cloud appeared over Cedar City, Utah, and remained there for several hours. The sky was hazy, and fallout dusted the ground. Local children, recounted a resident, "ate it, walked in it, breathed it. . . . You know how little kids love snow. They went out and would eat the 'snow.'"

Years later, large numbers of leukemia cases developed among the downwinders, many of whom had no history of cancer in their families. In one family never previously affected by the disease, four teenagers died; in another, a man recounted the losses of a wife, niece, sister, sister-in-law, mother-in-law, uncle, grandmother, and two great-uncles to cancer.

Litigation was brought against the U.S. government, which denied responsibility for the sickness and death. Eventually, in 1984, a federal court found the government liable for $2.7 million in damages. In so doing, the judge announced the following ethical principle:

At the core of this case is a fundamental principle, a time-honored rule of law, an ethical rule, a moral tenet: The law imposes a duty on everyone to avoid acts in their nature dangerous to the lives of others.

It may seem obvious to almost everyone that at the least the public interest required federal authorities to warn the downwinders not to let children eat the radioactive "snow." Nonetheless, the government appealed the verdict.

Source: Based on Howard Ball, "Downwind from the Bomb," *New York Times Magazine,* 9 February 1986, 33 ff.

the public administrator's worldview. We are accustomed to educators, military officials, and urban development, health, and other public administrators considering their functions to be the most crucial to the future welfare of society.

A close relationship with a particular clientele group or constituency is another factor that can lead public administrators to misconstrue the public interest. As noted in Chapter 2, the development of the American administrative state was partly an outgrowth of clientelism. Different economic interest and social groups sought the establishment of government agencies to promote

12.2   MISCONSTRUING THE PUBLIC INTEREST AT THE FBI

Martin Luther King, Jr., received the uncommon honor of having a public holiday created in his name. From that fact, it is wholly evident that he is to be publicly regarded as a national hero. Under the leadership of J. Edgar Hoover, however, the FBI reached a different conclusion. The agency viewed King's quest for racial justice not as something in the public interest to which the nation should aspire but rather as a subversive threat to it. The following text, from the "Report of the U.S. Senate Select Committee to Study Governmental Operations with Respect to Intelligence Activities (1975–1976)," shows how far off course an administrative agency can go.

> From "late 1963" until his death in 1968, Martin Luther King, Jr. was the target of an intensive campaign by the Federal Bureau of Investigation to "neutralize" him as an effective civil rights leader. In the words of the man in charge of the FBI's "war" against Dr. King, "No holds were barred."
>
> The FBI gathered information about Dr. King's plans and activities through an extensive surveillance program, employing nearly every intelligence-gathering technique at the Bureau's disposal to obtain information about the "private activities of Dr. King and his advisors" to use to "completely discredit" them.
>
> The program to destroy Dr. King as the leader of the civil rights movement included efforts to discredit him with executive branch officials, congressional leaders, foreign heads of state, American ambassadors, churches, universities, and the press.
>
> The FBI mailed Dr. King a tape recording made from microphones hidden in his hotel rooms that one agent testified was an attempt to destroy Dr. King's marriage.
>
> The tape recording was accompanied by a note Dr. King and his advisors interpreted as

threatening to release the tape recording unless Dr. King committed suicide.

The extraordinary nature of the campaign to discredit Dr. King is evident from two documents:

—At the August 1963 March on Washington, Dr. King told the country of his "dream" that:

> all of God's children, black men and white men, Jews and Gentiles, Protestants and Catholics, will be able to join hands and sing in the words of the old Negro spiritual, "Free at last, free at last, thank God Almighty, I'm free at last."

The Bureau's Domestic Intelligence Division concluded that this "demagogic speech" established Dr. King as the "most dangerous and effective Negro leader in the country." Shortly afterwards, and within days after Dr. King was named "Man of the Year" by *Time* magazine, the FBI decided to "take him off his pedestal," "reduce him completely in influence," and select and promote its candidate "to assume the leadership of the Negro people."

—In early 1968, Bureau headquarters explained to the field that Dr. King must be destroyed because he was seen as a potential "messiah" who could "unify and electrify" the "black nationalist movement." Indeed, to the FBI he was a potential threat because he might "abandon his supposed 'obedience' to white liberal doctrines (non-violence)." In short, a nonviolent man was to be secretly attacked and destroyed as insurance against his abandoning nonviolence.

Source: See Eugene Lewis, *Public Entrepreneurship* (Bloomington: Indiana University Press, 1980), chap. 5, for a general discussion of this episode.

their interests. Sometimes, however, this process has led an agency to confuse the interests of the clientele or constituency with the public interest and to act as an advocate for those interests. Public administrators in such agencies may mistakenly consider the interest groups with which they deal to be wholly representative of all individuals in the economic sectors or social groups involved. Joseph LaPalombara referred to this condition as a "clientela"[10] relationship in which

> an interest group, for whatever reasons, succeeds in becoming in the eyes of a given administrative agency, the natural expression and representative of a given social sector which, in turn, constitutes the natural target or reference point for the activity of the administrative agency.[11]

Such relationships between financial regulators and the financial industry may have contributed to the 2008 financial crisis. As the report, "Wall Street and the Financial Crisis: Anatomy of a Financial Collapse," released by the Senate Permanent Subcommittee on Investigations in April 13, 2011[12] (also known as the Levin-Coburn Report) argues, agencies such as the Office of Thrift Supervision in the U.S. Department of Treasury viewed the institutions it regulated as constituents. In an interview, Senator Levin stated, "The overwhelming evidence is that those institutions deceived their clients and deceived the public, and they were aided and abetted by deferential regulators and credit ratings agencies who had conflicts of interest."[13]

In the United States, clientela relationships form the basis of mutually supportive alliances among interest groups, administrative bureaus, and legislative committees that may view the public interest with acute tunnel vision.

Corruption

Corruption can be defined as a betrayal of the public trust for reasons of private interest. By many accounts, corruption in public administration is a worldwide phenomenon and a serious limitation on the ability of governments to accomplish some of their objectives. To mention only a few examples, during the Cold War, the "bash the bureaucrat" syndrome prevailed in both the Soviet Union and the United States, and examples of administrative corruption were ferreted out by the press and publicly denounced by officials; in many countries throughout the world, corruption in the form of bribery and the use of personal contacts has become institutionalized, and "baksheesh," "la mordida," "shtraff," "la bustarella," "speed money," "dash," "protekzia," and "guanxi" are considered as common a way of dealing with bureaucrats as is filling out forms.* In the United States, the suffix "gate" has become part of the political lexicon, as in Watergate, Iran-Contragate, Whitewatergate, Filegate, Plamegate, Memogate, and NAFTAgate.

The main reason for the worldwide presence of public administrative corruption is that public administrators have something to allocate that other people want. As Michael Johnston explains:

> The demand for government's rewards frequently exceeds the supply, and routine decision-making processes are lengthy, costly, and uncertain in their outcome.

---

* "Baksheesh," a "tip" or bribe in the Middle East; "la mordida," "the bite" in Latin America; "shtraff," a small bribe in Russia; "la bustarella," "the little envelope" in Italy; "speed money," used in India to expedite the processing of forms and requests; "dash," a tip or bribe in West Africa; "protekzia" and "guanxi" exploitation of personal contacts to achieve favorable treatment in Israel and China respectively.

For these reasons, legally sanctioned decision-making processes constitute a "bottleneck" between what people want and what they get. The temptation to get around the bottleneck—to speed things up and make favorable decisions more probable—is built into this relationship between government and society. To get around the bottleneck, one must use political influence—and corruption, which by definition cuts across established and legitimate processes, is a most effective form of influence.[14]

Although the source of corruption is similar in all public administrative settings, precisely what is considered a betrayal of public trust and corrupt activity on the part of administrators varies among (and sometimes within) political cultures.[15]

Every country has norms and values that define the legitimacy of different kinds of **political exchanges.** Political exchanges can be thought of as quid pro quo relationships involving government and politics. For example, if a candidate for Congress says, "You vote for me and I'll reduce your taxes," that constitutes a political exchange. So does the plea to a traffic officer, "Let me go with a warning this time and I won't speed again." Trading votes and support for one another's positions in legislatures, in the drafting of political party platforms, and in the recruitment of party candidates for public office is an example of political exchange.

No political system could operate without political exchanges. But not all types of political exchanges are considered legitimate in all societies. For example, in the United States a candidate for Congress may say, "Vote for me and I'll reduce your taxes," but if he or she says, "Vote for me and I'll give you $20," it becomes a crime. A public administrator may be requested to expedite a case involving congressional casework, but if the same case were speeded up because the private individual concerned paid the administrator to do so, it would be a criminal offense. One of the difficulties in understanding administrative corruption, therefore, lies in determining precisely which kinds of political exchanges are widely considered acceptable parts of political life even though they may be illegal.

In the United States, defining administrative corruption has largely involved a contest between the norms and values of two types of political cultures. One is the **boss-follower,** or **political-machine-based, culture.** The other is referred to as the modern **civic culture.** These cultures were represented in the epic contest over political ethics presented by the 19th-century civil service reform and the early-20th-century Progressive movements, on the one hand, and political machines, on the other. In the machine-based political culture, political exchanges were generally between citizens and the boss or his agents and between the machine and businesses. Votes were traded for jobs and favors; money, for licenses, franchises, and public works contracts. For the most part, these exchanges were not considered unacceptable, though sometimes they were termed "honest graft." Similarly, it was commonplace and acceptable for administrative officials to deviate from administrative rules or laws in minor ways to benefit supporters of the machine or friends.

12.3 "Honest Graft"

Everybody is talkin' these days about Tammany men growin' rich on graft, but nobody thinks of drawin' the distinction between honest graft and dishonest graft. There's all the difference in the world between the two. Yes, many of our men have grown rich in politics. I have myself. I've made a big fortune out of the game, and I'm gettin' richer every day, but I've not gone in for dishonest graft—blackmailin' gamblers, saloon-keepers, disorderly people, etc.—and neither has any of the men who have made big fortunes in politics.

There's an honest graft, and I'm an example of how it works. I might sum up the whole thing by sayin': "I seen my opportunities and I took 'em."

Just let me explain by examples. My party's in power in the city, and it's goin' to undertake a lot of public improvements. Well, I'm tipped off, say, that they're goin' to lay out a new park at a certain place.

I see my opportunity and I take it. I go to that place and I buy up all the land I can in the neighborhood. Then the board of this or that makes its plan public, and there is a rush to get my land, which nobody cared particular for before.

Ain't it perfectly honest to charge a good price and make a profit on my investment and foresight? Of course, it is. Well, that's honest graft.

Source: From William L. Riordan, *Plunkitt of Tammany Hall* (New York: Knopf, 1948), 3–8.

Historically, public officials might also accept gifts from clients and others for the purpose of generating generalized goodwill. Public employees were expected to take part in electioneering and to contribute money to the political party in power. On election day, they would be expected to help "get out the vote" (among party loyalists), while being paid from the public treasury. Public officials might also legitimately profit from "insider" knowledge, as in the case of knowing in advance where a new road or building was to be located. In general, the purpose of politics in this system was not to accomplish any ideological or policy goals but rather to make personal gain by trading political support and money for the granting of governmental benefits and advantages.[16] (See Plunkitt's description of "honest graft" in Box 12.3.)

Modern civic culture has a radically different outlook. When this culture is violated, there are both political and legal ramifications. For example, links to corrupt lobbyist Jack Abramoff played a role in former Republican House Majority Leader Tom DeLay's decision to resign from office[17] and Ohio Republican Congressman Bob Ney's guilty plea on charges of conspiracy and making false statements in regard to gifts from Abramoff.[18] At its essence, modern civic culture is "community-regarding" in the sense of promoting public, rather than merely private, interests. It is also impersonal. Government is not looked on as a means of dispensing largess and favors, but as an organization charged with advancing the general welfare of the community. Rather than considering the "boss" as the protector of individuals' interests, the civic culture holds that this is the role of the state, as embodied in a written or unwritten constitution. In such a system, trading votes for jobs is considered illegitimate. Offering money for licenses, franchises, and contracts is also considered corrupt. These benefits are to be allocated according to impersonal and community-regarding rules, such as contracts to the lowest competent bidder.

Public administrators are forbidden to use their "inside" information for private gain, and conflict-of-interest laws are adopted to prevent them from so doing. They may also be prohibited from taking part in a wide range of partisan and electioneering activities. Rules are applied impersonally, without regard to partisanship, and bribery is strictly forbidden.[19] Even offering a bribe may be illegal.

Part of the problem of identifying administrative corruption in the United States is a result of the coexistence of the norms of each of these two political cultures. Political machines have dwindled, have become fragmented, and are much weaker than they were in the early part of the 20th century. This has been an intended consequence of the civil service reform and Progressive movements. However, the norms, the values, and some of the practices common to machines in the past still play a role in partisan politics. Some positions, those denoted "political executive," are still allocated on a partisan basis. Government largess is still used to manipulate votes, though its distribution in the form of "pork-barrel" projects is aimed at winning support from whole communities or states rather than from specific individual beneficiaries. Contracts for governmental supplies, ranging from pencils to expensive military hardware, may be allocated, under political pressure, on a regional basis. Access to major decision makers may be an implied quid pro quo for substantial campaign contributions; so may tax loopholes. But contemporary public administration is nonetheless imbued with the norms and values of the civic culture. It looks down on the intrusion of partisan politics in administration as an unhealthy perversion of the need to be community-regarding and to operate in accordance with impersonal rules. Some important legislation has been aimed at minimizing the extent to which such intrusions can occur. Political neutrality statutes and merit systems are leading examples.

Because public administrators are engaged in the allocation of governmental benefits, they are sometimes pulled or pushed in opposing directions by the machine-based and civic-culture-based approaches to government. This is part of the tension sometimes found between political executives seeking to implement an electoral "mandate" of some kind and career public administrators who seemingly are intransigent in clinging to what they regard as established procedures for promoting community-regarding, impersonal administrative activity. The divergence between the machine-based and civic-culture-based approaches is sometimes reflected in legislation. For instance, conflict-of-interest statutes may prohibit public administrators from quitting the public sector to work for private corporations with which they have had official dealings. Yet, the campaigns of candidates for public office, including incumbents, may benefit from media spots by political action committees (PACs) and office seekers may hold economic interests in firms with which the government deals. But public administrators are often under a strict standard, requiring them to eliminate even an *appearance* of impropriety or wrongdoing.[20]

Definitions of "corruption" vary with political cultures, but within any political or administrative system there will be several types of corruption.

One useful way to organize thinking about corruption is to consider the mode of execution and the purpose of the corrupt activity.[21] Corruption may involve a single individual or agency and be **unilateral** in the sense that it does not involve a direct exchange with another individual or corporate entity. For instance, an individual administrator may cover up his or her mistakes; so may a unit of an agency or even the agency as a whole. That is one reason why there was so much congressional interest in the Obama White House's experience with disappearing e-mails and files and the State Department's knowledge about the deadly attack on its diplomatic mission in Benghazi, Libya in 2012. Individuals and agencies may also falsify data and records to make it look as though they are doing a better job. In these examples, the purpose of the individual or agency is to retain, augment, or attain authority of some kind. But unilateral corruption can also be aimed at obtaining material benefits. Theft, embezzlement, and use of official resources for private gain are leading examples.

Corruption can also be **transactional,** involving a direct exchange. Where exchange enhances administrative authority, such behavior might take the form of extremely strong clientela relationships. In return for support from the clientele group, the individual administrator or agency grants it benefits that are not even arguably in the public interest. It was precisely because of the potential for such perversions of the public interest that President Eisenhower once warned the nation about the possibility of the "military-industrial complex" extracting too much wealth from the society. Transactional corruption can also be for the purpose of obtaining material benefits. Bribery, extortion, kickbacks, and so forth, are examples.

Subversion

Public administrators may also betray their public trust by engaging in subversion. This has been a serious fear many times in United States history, particularly in wartime. The clearest and most recent example occurred in the late 1940s and early 1950s, during the McCarthy era, in which there was pandemic fear of communism. The fear of subversion declined dramatically with the ebbing of the Cold War and its demise in 1991. However, it flared up again in 2000 with respect to the possibility that one or more government scientists at the Department of Energy's Los Alamos, New Mexico, lab had passed top-secret nuclear weapons information to China and Robert Hanssen's 2001 arrest for selling state secrets to the former Soviet Union and Russia. Chinese espionage is currently a growing concern. In 2008, Gregg Bergersen, a weapons system analyst with the Defense Department, pled guilty to conspiracy to disclose national defense secrets. As of 2013, President Barack Obama's administration had relied on the Espionage Act of 1917 to prosecute six individuals having military, civilian, or contractual relationships with the federal government for leaking secret information.[22] Responses to the threat of subversion are sometimes clouded by reactions bordering on hysteria, as occurred when the 1952 Republican Party platform charged that the Democrats had "permitted communists and fellow travelers to serve in many key agencies and to infiltrate our American life."[23]

Nonetheless, a few points seem clear. First, subversion is a genuine concern, and the federal government makes a substantial effort to reduce its likelihood. For instance, federal personnel in sensitive positions are subject to background investigations, and there are a variety of systems for limiting access to information that could compromise national security. Second, the potential for damage to the public interest from subversive civil servants is considerable. Third, in today's global competition, economic subversion is a growing concern.[24] Fourth, although it is common to think of subversion in terms of efforts instigated by foreign governments to weaken or destroy the government, conscious subversion of administrative programs can occur for several reasons. For example, it can be the result of unilateral or transactional corruption for private gain. It can also be due to extreme discontent with one's position in the public service. Finally, it should be noted that the line between whistle blowing and leaking is sometimes in the eye of the beholder.

◆◆   WHY IT IS DIFFICULT TO GUARD THE GUARDIANS

Public administrators must be held accountable for their actions, especially as there are many opportunities for them to abuse their trust. However, finding satisfactory means of establishing accountability has been difficult in the United States and other countries. Indeed, in reaction to the September 11th terrorist attacks, there has been a greatly reduced role for some of the "guards." From the National Security Agency (NSA) conducting domestic warrantless surveillance and wiretapping of U.S. citizens to the Federal Bureau of Investigation's (FBI's) greatly expanded use of "national security letters" (a type of administrative subpoena), the judiciary's role in monitoring administrative action has been greatly reduced. Several reasons for this and other difficulties in holding public officials accountable for their actions are discussed in this section.

The Accretion of Special Expertise and Information

Public administrators are often expert at what they do. Outsiders are unable to match their knowledge or properly second-guess their decisions and activities. Public administrators also have information available to them that others have difficulty obtaining; it may be information that the administrators decided to generate. This information is often the basis of decision making. Other information could lead one to make different decisions, but the initial decision about what information to gather is frequently left up to the administrators (see Chapter 8). Because public administrators have such special expertise and access to information, at times it may be beyond the ability of those charged with oversight to hold the administrators accountable. There are also costs to obtaining information. The reporting requirements Congress imposes on agencies can impinge on administrators' ability to do other parts of their jobs.

The Advantage of Full-Time Status

For the most part, public administrators do their jobs on a full-time basis. Outsiders who would hold them accountable typically are engaged in other activities and cannot devote sufficient time to watching the public administrators. For instance, this is true of congressional oversight of administrative activities. Members of Congress and their staffs have a great deal more to do than look over the shoulders of public administrators. Moreover, the incentives to engage in forceful oversight on a routine basis are often weak. Short of the scent of scandal, for Congress the result is that most oversight activity is left up to the congressional staff. While oversight activity by the staff is useful, it cannot possibly be panoptic or even digest all the administrative information and reports Congress requests from the agencies.

The Protective Nature of Personnel Systems

Public personnel systems in the United States and elsewhere tend to afford public administrators a great deal of job security. Discipline and dismissal are possible but are cumbersome and difficult to accomplish. Consequently, petty infractions, such as using public resources of limited value for private purposes, are likely to go unpunished. However, the cumulative impact of such infractions can be quite significant. If each federal employee used a dollar's worth of public property for private purposes, the total cost would be more than $2 million. Similarly, deviation from administrative rules or their misapplication may not be deemed worthy of discipline unless the consequences are severe and, possibly, public. Dealing with poor performers has also been a challenge.

The "Law of Counter Control"

It takes bureaucracy to control bureaucracy. Anthony Downs has maintained that there is a "law of counter control": "The greater the effort made by a sovereign or top-level official to control the behavior of subordinate officials, the greater the efforts made by those subordinates to evade or counteract such control."[25] But the greater the efforts in either direction, the more staff likely to be needed to try to secure accountability. The greater the number of staff is, the more likely it is that the effort to control one bureaucracy will result in the creation of another. For instance, one could characterize the creation of the Congressional Budget Office in 1974 as a counterforce to the executive's Office of Management and Budget in these terms.[26]

The Problem of Coordination

In the United States, the separation of powers complicates the quest for accountability. The president is charged with the faithful execution of the laws, but congressional involvement is necessary to create, fund, staff, and empower administrative agencies. Without coordination between the president and Congress, accountability is difficult to obtain. But because both branches of government have different constituencies, roles, incentives, and interests, coordination is not a simple matter. There are times when one branch impedes the efforts of the other to hold public administrators accountable. In more recent times, the balance has slipped. In the name of national security, Congress has removed controls on the executive branch. The lack of transparent judicial oversight of NSA Internet, email, and telephone monitoring and FBI national security letters has raised serious concerns about the executive branch's unchecked ability to violate individual civil rights.

The Lack of Political Direction

The United States political process does not provide comprehensive direction to public administrators. Political parties are fragmented, and elections do not convey clear mandates. Undoubtedly, most public administrators would follow clear mandates if they existed, but in their absence, political direction of public agencies is uncertain. This is exacerbated by the relatively short tenure of appointed political executives, in the range of two to three years. Coupled with the protective nature of personnel systems, the absence of clear mandates and the short tenure of political executives provide career public administrators with little incentive to depart substantially from their views of the public interest and the interests of their agencies. Many political executives have complained bitterly about the difficulty of changing the career service.

The Fragmentation of Agency Structures and Functions

The structure of public agencies in the United States can be quite fragmented, and missions are often overlapping. Fragmentation and overlapping responsibilities, addressed in Chapter 4, have their sources and benefits. However, they may make it difficult to pinpoint responsibility for any given administrative action. Agencies can be dexterous in obscuring and shifting the blame for even the clearest of their failures.

The Large Size and Scope of Public Administration

On average, the federal government spends more than $120,000 per second every second of the year. Some administrative departments and agencies have more than 100,000 employees. The Department of Defense has at times employed more than a million civilians. The U.S. Postal Service employs more than 630,000 and maintains a fleet of over 200,000 vehicles. The *Federal Register* frequently tops 50,000 pages in length annually. In 1940, when the federal service was only about half its current size in personnel, there were almost 19 million vouchers covering government expenditures.[27] Even with advances in computer technology, who can keep track of all these dollars, people, regulations, forms, and so forth? Unless there is some reason to suspect that public administrators or agencies have deviated from the public interest in some way, there is little possibility of using routine audits to find serious infractions. Rather, as in the case of the 2010 General Service Administration's (GSA) $823,000 conference in Las Vegas for 300 people,[28] the scandal must break first—and by then it is often too late to prevent whatever damage the infractions have caused.

"Third-Party" Government

The contracting out or other outsourcing of governmental functions can make it difficult to determine who is responsible for what. To take a tragic private sector example, the crash of a ValuJet plane in the Everglades on May 11, 1996, resulted in 110 deaths. The Federal Aviation Administration (FAA) admitted it had difficulty inspecting the airline's operations because so much of its maintenance was contracted out to "geographically diverse low bidders" throughout its flying region.[29] One expert noted, "There is no question that outsourcing maintenance increases the risk of miscommunication and greatly complicates the FAA's inspection task."[30] But what is true for the FAA and the airlines is also true for oversight and accountability within the government. Outsourcing requires careful monitoring, and in government, the monitoring will also have to be monitored. It also requires continual upgrading of the contract negotiation and management skills public administrators need as they move from providers of service to contractors of service.

These barriers to holding the "permanent" civil service accountable in a systematic fashion are so formidable that the formal theory of accountability in democracies is clearly at odds with the reality. In the formal theory,

> power emanates from the people and is to be exercised in trust for the people. Within the government each level of executive authority is accountable to the next, running on up to the President or the Cabinet. The executive authority as a whole is accountable to the Congress or Parliament, which is assisted in its surveillance of expenditures by an independent audit agency. Officials are required to submit themselves to periodic elections as a retrospective evaluation of their performances and to receive a new mandate from the people.[31]

However, as the authors of the passage point out, perhaps inevitably, "accountability gets lost in the shuffle somewhere in the middle ranges of the bureaucracy."[32] How can we find and retrieve it?

◆◆   ETHICS AND PUBLIC ADMINISTRATORS: THREE
       BROAD APPROACHES TO ETHICAL DECISION MAKING

The study of administrative ethics concerns "efforts to identify and formulate rules for the wise and proper use of administrative discretion."[33] Three broad philosophical approaches to ethical decision making guide public administrators: virtue/intuition, deontological, and teleological approaches.[34]

The *virtue/intuition* approach relies on a person's understanding of what it means to be a "good person" and to display the traits necessary to enact that understanding. Those characteristics include honesty, integrity, trustworthiness, loyalty, fairness, caring for others, respect for others, responsible citizenship, pursuit of excellence, accountability, rationality, prudence, respect for law, self-discipline, civility, and independence. The *deontological,* or principles-based, approach relies on a set of agreed upon principles that guide an administrator's decisions. In this approach the means cannot be divorced from ends. The decision maker must appropriately apply these principles in order to act ethically. The *teleological* approach, sometimes referred to as the utilitarian or consequences approach, argues that there are no overriding moral principles to guide all actions, so the consequences of the actions becomes the determining factor in evaluating the ethics of a decision. Under this approach, the decision that provides the greatest net good to society is the appropriate decision to make.

As Carol Lewis and others have noted,[35] there is not one approach to ethical decision making that is superior to others. Each approach has strengths and weaknesses. For example, the virtue/intuition approach is relatively easy for individuals to grasp. It assumes that people want to do good and relies on commonly accepted social values to drive the decision. However, notions of good are culturally bound and, when there are multiple ways to do good, there is no criterion to help the administrator choose the appropriate alternative. In the deontological approach, the required actions of an ethical administrator are clearly stated and based on universal ethical principles. Should multiple principles come into conflict, however, there is no necessary guide to the ordering of which principle should dominate. Finally, in the utilitarian approach, tools such as cost-benefit analysis have been developed to help administrators decide among competing choices to provide the greatest good for the greatest number. However, while this approach may be intuitively appealing, it can also be used to justify benefiting the majority of citizens at the expense of a minority through unacceptable means.

Rather than trying to pick which approach is appropriate in all cases, theorists in administrative ethics are developing tools to help public administrators balance these three approaches to avoid the problems of ethical extremism resulting from following the dictates of only one ethical tradition. Lewis offers a decision making model based on balancing legal obligations with individual responsibility and ways to consider competing viewpoints.[36] James Svara argues that public administrators must utilize all three philosophical traditions and create an "ethical triangle."[37] By operating within the triangle, where each decision is influenced by the demands of justice/fairness from the deontological tradition, *and* the greatest good from the utilitarian tradition, *and* the personal integrity from the virtue/intuition tradition, public administrators avoid the problems of ethical extremism.

Regardless of which model public administrators use to help guide their decision making, the underlying commonality of these approaches is that no one ethical lens is complete enough to understand the implications of a particular decision. Using multiple perspectives forces public administrators to understand and confront the ethical trade-offs they make in their service to the public.

❖   PERSPECTIVES ON ACCOUNTABILITY AND ETHICS

The Traditional Managerial Perspective

The basic tenets of the traditional managerial approach to accountability and ethics are probably fairly well known to those who have had dealings with public administrative organizations. As mentioned in Chapter 10, there has been a tendency for some managerially oriented norms to work their way into the cultural values of the American middle class. Specifically, however, in keeping with its emphasis on efficiency, economy, and effectiveness, the traditional managerial approach emphasizes the need for organizational unity as a means of establishing accountability and as a deontological and virtue-based guide to ethics.

First, the traditional managerial approach emphasizes that authority and responsibility must be clearly assigned. Overlapping functions, which tend to obscure responsibility and consequently to frustrate accountability, should be reduced to a minimum. The lines of hierarchical authority should be clear and comprehensive. Ideally, they should culminate in a single position, rather than a commission of some kind. Plural agency heads are frowned on because they can muddle the lines of authority and cloud issues of responsibility. They can also divide the loyalties of subordinates.

Second, this approach emphasizes the need for strict subordination, the other side of the coin of hierarchy. Underlings must strictly obey the directives and commands of superordinates. This is necessary for organizational effectiveness and accountability. An act of disobedience, termed insubordination, is a substantial offense against the organization, according to this view. It is often punishable by dismissal. Logically, this is necessary, for otherwise superordinates would be officially responsible for behavior beyond their control. Accordingly, under the traditional managerial approach, a public administrator who is unwilling to follow orders is expected to leave his or her organization through either transfer or resignation. In the traditional approach, loyalty (going along) and exit (quitting) are appropriate, but voicing one's opposition to hierarchical authorities is not.

As noted earlier, the traditional managerial approach finds street-level administration problematic because it is so difficult to supervise and control. Indeed, traditional management may go to considerable lengths to monitor street-level employees. In the summer of 1996, the U.S. Postal Service initiated a test to use Department of Defense reconnaissance satellites to keep track of postal trucks. The system has the potential to track 128 factors, including truck location, speed, and whether the driver has run a stop sign.[38]

Third, concern with strict subordination dictates a limited span of control. The span of control, it will be recalled, is the number of subordinates directly responsible to a superordinate. Orthodox public administrative theory paid a great deal of attention to determining the optimal span of control. This was oriented toward effective management, but concern with accountability was built into the concept.

Fourth, subordinates are encouraged to be loyal to the organization and to their superiors. Loyalty is generated in several ways. One is through organizational socialization that attempts to inculcate the importance of the agency's mission and the need to work toward it with a high degree of unity. Another is through occupational specialization that makes it difficult for employees to find equivalent work elsewhere; firefighters are a good example of this, but so are employees with deep expertise in an agency's processes for budgeting, personnel administration, adjudication, and so forth.

Yet another way is to make the employees materially dependent on the organization to a great extent. Aside from pay, pensions and conflict-of-interest regulations have an important role here. Sometimes pension plans create a strong incentive to remain with an organization. Conflict-of-interest regulations may seek to make the employee economically dependent on the organization. The employee may be required to divest himself or herself of economic assets that could create conflicting interests or loyalties. Attempting to "close the revolving door"—preventing public employees from taking private employment with firms they previously dealt with in their official capacities—is a related effort to make them dependent on and loyal to their public employers. At the federal level in the United States, both traditional conflict-of-interest statutes and anti-revolving-door regulations are comprehensive.[39]

Fifth, the traditional managerial approach relies on formal disciplinary systems to enforce accountability and subordination. These systems seek to identify breaches of proper conduct. As already noted, insubordination typically ranks high on the scale of misbehavior. Other matters may range from broad prohibitions on "immoral and notoriously disgraceful" conduct to specific considerations of misuse of agency authority or property. For example, using stationery with the agency's letterhead for personal purposes is sometimes considered a serious breach of ethics. It violates the concept of unity of authority within the agency, because it is unauthorized, and also suggests that government property is being misused for private purposes.

John A. Rohr points out in *Ethics for Bureaucrats* that some agencies develop elaborate codes of conduct intended to impart a sense of what is to be considered ethical or unethical behavior.[40] These codes can concern the use of office equipment (including telephones) for personal business, the use of government automobiles for personal purposes, and whether the agency can take action against employees who fail to pay personal debts. Rohr evaluates this approach as reducing ethical behavior to "staying out of trouble" and emphasizing "meticulous attention to trivial questions."[41] In his view, "These exercises provide a clear example of the worst aspects of the mentality that continues to dichotomize politics and administration."[42] In 1989, President

George H.W. Bush issued Executive Order 12674, which directed the Office of Government Ethics (OGE) to develop a single comprehensive set of standards of conduct for the entire executive branch. The Standards of Conduct,[43] which took effect in 1993, cover issues such as gifts, conflicting financial interests, impartiality, seeking employment, misuse of position, and outside activities. These standards are designed to address actual conflicts of interest as well as activities that give rise to the appearance of such conflicts. However, this code is still more concerned with a personal phone call than with whether an administrator engages in behavior that abridges someone's constitutional rights to due process.

The type of disciplinary system the traditional managerial approach prefers in enforcing these codes of conduct and organization norms is one that is simple and always under the control of the agency's hierarchy. Otherwise unity and hierarchy are weakened—and these are the goals of the codes of conduct. However, pressures for the fair treatment of employees have often led to collective bargaining agreements that seriously reduce managerial authority to discipline employees. In addition, the legal perspective's concern with protection of the constitutional rights of public employees has promoted more elaborate adverse action hearing systems and judicial review of managerial disciplinary decisions and procedures.

Sixth, the traditional managerial perspective's concern with fiscal regularity and employee performance places emphasis on the use of internal audits. Audits can be a strong deterrent to corruption or other abuse of the public trust. Preaudits are effective in blocking the misuse of funds; postaudits create a deterrent to abuses and sometimes are performed by a unit within an organization, as the traditional managerial approach prefers. Other times, however, it is thought that an outside auditing body is more desirable, such as the Government Accountability Office, an agency of Congress. At times a compromise is adopted: the audit bureau is within the agency but independent of its hierarchy. Audits can be concerned with general fiscal matters of performance and management or matters of reporting, such as the number of cases closed.

Several federal agencies use "inspectors general" (IGs) as a kind of internal policing mechanism with authority to engage in investigations and audits in a broad range of circumstances. The IGs report directly to Congress and the heads of their departments and agencies. Their ability to investigate financial matters was strengthened by the Chief Financial Officers Act of 1990. The act requires federal agencies to appoint chief financial officers (CFOs) to centralize financial management and adopt more standardized accounting practices. The CFOs prepare financial statements for administrative and legislative use.

These approaches are important in promoting accountability and ethics. They are found in a vast array of contemporary public and private organizations in one form or another. Their main limitation, as Rohr points out, is their narrow focus. They are concerned with protecting managerial values more than with protecting the public from a breach of trust in a more political sense.

The New Public Management

The NPM has a radically different view of accountability and ethics. It takes a teleological approach and focuses almost exclusively on performance and results. It views the type of procedural safeguards on which the traditional managerial approach relies as obstacles to cost-effective government. It favors external oversight by legislatures that assesses performance but opposes that which focuses on internal managerial matters, including spending, personnel administration, and organization. It advocates allowing employees to use agency credit cards for travel and the purchase of routine office supplies. It opposes controls and oversights imposed by central budget, procurement, and personnel agencies, such as the Office of Management and Budget, the General Services Administration, and the Office of Personnel Management. Accountability for results can also be enforced through market mechanisms and customers' judgments. However, viewing the public as customers, the NPM does not put much stock in traditional avenues for political participation, including elections and rule making proceedings (not to mention legislative casework).

In the National Performance Review's (NPR's) version of the NPM, ethics amounted to achieving results with a high degree of customer satisfaction. The NPR discounted concern with corruption for two reasons. First, it assumed that the overwhelming number of public employees are good people. According to the NPR,

> people—in government or out—are, for the most part, neither crooked nor stupid. Most people want to do the right thing, so long as the right thing makes sense. Perhaps the most important thing about the reinvention initiative, and its regulatory reform work in particular, is that it is based on a new assumption: that people are honest and that if you tell people what needs to be done, and let them get on with doing it, the chances are it will be done better—and more cheaply—than if you tell them how. Moreover, it values them as human beings.[44]

Treating honest and smart people as though they were crooked and stupid binds them in pointless and harmful red tape. As the NPR put it,

> This lack of trust in its own employees is one reason why doing almost anything in the government has always required a couple of dozen signatures: to be sure no one was cheating the taxpayer. Of course the process sometimes cost more than what was protected, but at least no one could be blamed if something went wrong.[45]

Second, given that most people are good, the cost of ferreting out and deterring corruption is too high in terms of the red tape such efforts create. In the NPR's words,

> innovation, by its nature, requires deviation. Unfortunately, faced with so many controls, many employees have simply given up. They do everything by the book—whether it makes sense or not. They fill out forms that should never have been created, follow rules that should never have been imposed,

and prepare reports that serve no purpose—and are often never even read. In the name of controlling waste, we have created paralyzing inefficiency.[46]

In short, the NPR sought to replace many of the accountability and ethics controls imposed on public employees with a culture of trust:

> The essential ingredient in bringing about so great a people-led change—indeed, the essential ingredient of self-government—is trusting the people involved. In this case, that means government employees and the people they serve. . . .
>   When we are not trusted, when nothing we say or do seems to make a difference, we feel powerless. Elections alone do not restore that power. The power that matters in a self-governing democracy is the power we can exercise "over-the-counter," on a daily basis, whenever we interact with our government, whenever we seek to make our needs known. Someone must be listening. Someone must act.[47]

This approach stands in remarkable contrast to the checks and balances so carefully crafted by the Constitution's framers—as the NPR freely admitted.[48] It not only views the potential for corruption as largely insignificant, it also asserts that agency and individual self-interest are inconsequential (although, somewhat ironically, it embraces markets, in which all activity is assumed to be motivated by self-interest). Aside from the difficulties posed by accurately measuring performance, discussed in Chapter 8, the NPM's results orientation does not deal with the fundamental ethical problem of when ends may justify means. However, as the previous chapter explains, a great deal of American constitutional law centers on ends-means issues; that is precisely what procedural due process and the compelling governmental interest and least restrictive alternative tests are about. Not surprisingly, the political approach to public administrative accountability and ethics takes a different view.

The Political Perspective

In contrast to the traditional managerial perspective but in agreement with the NPM, the political approach emphasizes the need for developing mechanisms for accountability *external* to public administrative agencies. In the past, this was done primarily through political control of public personnel through patronage appointments. Now, however, the political approach must rely on other means. Among some of the more familiar are the following.

General Legislative Oversight

Legislative oversight is exercised by members of the legislature, their staffs, and legislative agencies, such as the federal Government Accountability Office and the Congressional Budget Office. Depending on the incentives facing the legislature, oversight can be a forceful means of promoting the accountability of public administrators. Legislatures are more likely to exercise careful oversight when crises develop than they are when operations seem to be running on a routine basis. This may change if legislatures begin to focus more systematically

12.4   THE U.S. OFFICE OF GOVERNMENT ETHICS

The Ethics in Government Act of 1978 created an Office of Government Ethics (OGE) in the Office of Personnel Management. The Ethics Reform Act of 1989 strengthened the OGE, now an independent agency within the executive branch. The OGE is headed by a director, who holds a five-year term and is removable for cause only. There are designated agency ethics officials within each agency. The OGE is the federal government's central agency for ethics policy. Its mission includes

- Regulatory authority to establish rules regarding conflicts of interest, standards of conduct, postemployment, and financial disclosure
- Review of financial disclosure statements
- Education and training
- Guidance and interpretation of rules and laws
- Enforcement
- Evaluation

As of 2013, the OGE had 80 full-time-equivalent employees and a budget of $14 million. According to its former director, Stephen Potts, ethics education is a key priority.

Potts noted that one of the major difficulties in developing standards for ethical behavior is that whereas ideally rules should be intuitive, in practice there are so many facets to ethics that regulations are inevitably complicated and legalistic. More information can be found on its Web site, www .oge.gov.

Sources: See Stuart Gilman, "The U.S. Office of Government Ethics," *The Bureaucrat* (Spring 1991): 13–16. Potts discussed his priorities at a meeting of the Standing Panel of the Public Service, National Academy of Public Administration, Washington, DC, 28 May 1991. Telephone interview with Stuart Gilman held on 7 June 1996.

on program results. Under the federal Government Performance and Results Act of 1993 and Government Performance and Results Act Modernization Act of 2010, agencies must regularly submit meaningful results-oriented reports to Congress. The Office of Government Ethics, an independent agency within the executive branch, assists the Senate in the process of confirming or rejecting presidential appointees to federal positions, especially in regard to financial disclosure. (See Box 12.4 for a brief review of the Office of Government Ethics.)

Budgetary Control

Historically, the "power of the purse" was considered an extremely important legislative check on the executive's "power of the sword." Although legislatures in the United States retain a great deal of the power of the purse, they now tend to share the budgeting function with the executive. Nonetheless, they are apt to monitor agency spending in a variety of ways, including using overhead agencies such as the Government Accountability Office, relying on CFO reports, and holding hearings. They also can become directly involved in agency decision making, sometimes denounced as "micromanagement." Despite the pejorative term, micromanagement does not always involve pork-barrel forays. It can also concern major policy disputes.[49]

Rotation in Office

The political approach has long emphasized the need to rotate public administrators from office to office or in and out of the public service. This is a matter of preventing misperception of the public interest because of too much specialization in one agency or function. In the 1840s and 1850s rotation took place through the spoils system, whereas today it is accomplished in a number of ways in modern public personnel systems. For instance, the creation of the Senior Executive Service (SES) in the federal civil service reform of 1978 was intended, in part, to enable top-level career civil servants to move from agency to agency in the hope that they would consequently develop a broader perspective of the public interest. In practice, almost all of the mobility has been among bureaus within individual agencies, but this, too, may help SESers avoid acute tunnel vision. The federal Intergovernmental Personnel Act authorized public administrators to move temporarily from positions in the federal government to the states and vice versa. Political executives are routinely rotated out of office when a new president or governor takes office, especially when there is a change in parties.

Representation and Public Participation

As rotation is aimed at reducing misconception of the public interest, encouraging pluralism within public administration can subject public administrators to a greater diversity of perspectives and interests. A socially representative public service is likely to be more diversified, in values and political perspectives, than is a homogeneous one. Allowing public participation and interest group representation in administrative processes further brings public administrators into contact with the views of the public, or at least segments of it. The Administrative Procedure Act of 1946, the Federal Advisory Committee Act of 1972, and the Civil Service Reform Act of 1978 all contain provisions, mentioned earlier in this book, that encourage representation or participation.

"Going Public"

The political perspective holds that it is proper and ethical for public employees to inform the public or its representatives, such as legislators, of misconduct by public administrators and violations of the public trust or interest by agencies. In other words, they are expected to use their voices to protest administrative activities they consider illegal and/or immoral. Public resignations and whistle-blowing are viewed as appropriate, and often highly moral, acts. Whistle-blowing is statutorily protected at the federal level. In addition, the federal government has institutionalized a fraud, waste, and abuse hotline, called FraudNet (http://www.gao.gov/fraudnet/fraudnet.htm), whereby employees or others can anonymously report instances of misconduct to the Government Accountability Office for further investigation.[50] Some of these tips have resulted in the removal of public administrators from the federal service. More important, though, is their deterrent effect. Where whistle-blowing and reporting maladministration are regarded as virtuous activities, loyalty to the agency and superiors, in the managerial sense, is inevitably weakened.

Agencies have sometimes issued "gag" orders to prevent employees from going public. But cover-ups are more difficult, and individual acts of corruption are riskier. Today federal employees who engage in whistle-blowing are afforded considerable statutory protection. These protections reach beyond reporting mismanagement and fiscal abuse to speaking out on specific and substantial dangers to the public health or safety. Public employees at all levels of government also have some constitutional protections in speaking out on matters of public concern. One of the thornier issues in this area is when anonymous or secretive "leaks" to the press are appropriate. Sometimes the unauthorized disclosure of information can prematurely foreclose an agency's policy options or adversely affect the behavior of the public, as would be the case if someone in the Federal Deposit Insurance Corporation announced that a certain large bank was nearly insolvent.

"Sunshine"

As mentioned earlier, Supreme Court Justice Louis Brandeis famously remarked that "sunlight is said to be the best of disinfectants; electric light the most efficient policeman."[51] The political perspective embraces the belief that open, public dealings are an important means of securing the accountability and proper conduct of public officials. Consequently, it has promoted a number of approaches to fostering "sunshine" in public administration. These approaches range from the requirement that some hearings and meetings be open to the public to the Freedom of Information Act's creation of a right for members of the public to obtain many categories of federal administrative documents. At the federal level, freedom of information and open hearings provisions have been incorporated into the basic administrative law, the Administrative Procedure Act (originally enacted in 1946).

Conflict of Interest

The political approach agrees with the traditional managerial approach that conflicts of interest ought to be eliminated. It also holds that the "revolving door" should be watched carefully, though not sealed, because it does make agencies more responsive to the economic interests with which they deal. The rationale is less to bolster hierarchical authority within agencies than to eliminate the temptation to misuse positions of public trust for private gain.

The political approach to accountability emphasizes the need for external checks on public administrative conduct. Unlike the traditional managerial perspective, it is not content to allow the maintenance of accountability to be largely the purview of the administrative hierarchy. There has long been debate over how efficacious this approach can be. Max Weber maintained that outside (extra-agency) checks on public administration are inherently inadequate. Even if they functioned well, they would militate against the maximization of the values of the traditional managerial perspective for efficiency, economy, and effectiveness. But relying exclusively on checks within agencies has obvious limits. The world is too familiar with self-serving administrative action and corruption to expect the guardians alone to guard themselves. Moreover, both the political and traditional managerial approaches rely primarily on enforcement mechanisms that are *external to the individual*. This may seem inappropriate because "responsible conduct of administrative functions is not so much enforced as it is elicited."[52] In other words, the desire to engage in ethical behavior must spring, to a large extent, from within the individual public administrator. Similarly, the strongest system of accountability would be self-imposed.

From the perspective of ethics as an inner, personal check on public administrators' conduct, the traditional managerial approach's emphasis on loyalty is regarded as being sound but too narrow. John Rohr observes that it must be enlarged to encompass a broader sense of professionalism and to include dedication to **regime values**.[53] Combining these two concerns and adding some of the externally oriented approaches of the political perspective can provide the beginnings of a synthesis in ethics and accountability in contemporary public administration. We will return to this prospect after mapping out the legal perspective, which stresses the concept of "regime values."

The Legal Perspective

We have noted at many points throughout this book how constitutional values and requirements can be at odds with the perspectives of the traditional managerial and political approaches to public administration. In response to this disjuncture, the federal judiciary has articulated a number of constitutional rights viewed as protections of individuals against certain administrative actions. Moreover, the judiciary has adjusted the standards of public administrators' liabilities for causing unconstitutional infringements of these rights. In the process, the courts have intentionally provided public administrators with a strong and *personally internalized incentive* to protect, or at least avoid abridging, the constitutional rights of the individuals on whom they act in their official capacities. John Rohr notes that what the courts have done is tantamount to articulating a set of regime values to which public administrators should be accountable. Moreover, these regime values provide ethical guidance to public administrators.

More specifically, Rohr notes that the regime-values approach rests on three considerations: "(1) That ethical norms should be derived from the salient values of the regime; (2) That these values are normative *for bureaucrats* because they have taken an oath to uphold the regime; (3) That these values can be discovered in the public law of the regime."[54] To a considerable extent, the regime values of the United States can be found in its constitutional law, and adherence to the values it articulates can be the internalized guide for public administrators' ethical behavior and broad accountability. As noted in Chapter 11, the courts have even embraced the concept that public administrators have a right to *disobey* unconstitutional orders, and many have a clear statutory right to engage in whistle-blowing.

Because the nation's regime values are ultimately situated in a broader morality, they go beyond the latest legal precedents and rest on the principles and premises that underlie government and the public order. For instance, Kathryn Denhardt proposes that the moral foundations of American public administration do and should include the values of honor, benevolence, and justice. Honor requires "adherence to the highest standards of responsibility, integrity, and principle." Benevolence is the "disposition to do good and to promote the welfare of others."[55] Justice is treating others fairly and respecting their rights.

The legal approach to public administrative ethics can also emphasize the need for clear rules of conduct and enforcement mechanisms to assure compliance. Law is viewed as providing a minimal threshold for ethical administration. Behavior that fails to meet the threshold should be punished. An agency such as the federal Office of Government Ethics may be used to clarify and publicize standards. For matters potentially involving aggravated breaches of law, the legal approach may favor using independent counsels or special prosecutors to investigate and bring cases against government officials. In theory, independent counsels and special prosecutors are politically and administratively independent (as noted in the discussion of *Morrison v. Olson* in Chapter 1). Their responsibility is to the rule of law. In practice, these functionaries sometimes appear to be partisan in their zeal to uncover embarrassing wrongdoing associated with a political party's leaders or appointees.

The focus of a great deal of ethics legislation and rules is on economic relationships. For instance, not only are blatant conflicts of interest outlawed, the acceptance of hospitality, however harmless it may appear, is sometimes prohibited. Sometimes the effort to avoid appearances of impropriety can bump up against public administrators' constitutional rights. For instance, in *U.S. v. National Treasury Employees Union* (1995), the Supreme Court found a First Amendment violation in regulations that prohibited federal employees below the GS-16 level from accepting honoraria for appearances, speeches, or the writing of articles.[56] In the Court's view, the nexus between the ban and the government's interest in avoiding the appearance of improper conduct was too tenuous because "federal employees below Grade GS-16, [are] an immense class of workers with negligible power to confer favors on those who might pay to hear them speak or to read their articles."

The legal approach also has a process that can deter fraud in contracting and collaborative governance relationships. Known as *qui tam* ("kwee tam"), it authorizes whistleblowers to try to recover public funds by suing a person or organization that has allegedly defrauded a government. *Qui tam* is short for "*qui tam pro rege quam pro sic ipso in hoc parte sequitur*," which means "who as well as for the king as for himself sues in this matter." When successful, *qui tam* suits enable a private individual and a government to recover funds while advancing the public interest in ethical collaborative governance and contractor behavior as well as conserving tax dollars. Depending on the particulars, the government may join in the prosecution of the civil suit.

At the federal level, *qui tam* suits were first authorized by the False Claims Act of 1863. Today, successful *qui tam* plaintiffs (called relators) can receive 25–30 percent of the recovery in the absence of Department of Justice participation in the suit and 15–25 percent with it. The current law prohibits contractors from taking adverse actions against *qui tam* whistle-blowing employees. Penalties for retaliation against employees include reinstatement with double back pay and other compensation. To prevail, a plaintiff has to show by a preponderance of the evidence (i.e., more than a 50–50 likelihood) that the fraud occurred. There are roughly 300–400 federal *qui tam* suits filed annually and total recovery has reached well into billions of dollars for both whistleblowers and the government.[57]

The efficacy of ethics laws depends largely on their clarity and certainty of enforcement—two conditions often absent. In any event, mere compliance with the law, a prerequisite for ethical behavior, does not fully encompass ethics. For example, the law may contain loopholes that could be exploited by public administrators for their personal gain. Although legal, the ensuing behavior would be considered unethical.

CONCLUSION: PERSONAL RESPONSIBILITY

Much of the American public administrative community has expressed considerable interest in questions of accountability and ethics. This is partly due to the emphasis the NPM places on deregulating government, empowering employees, and focusing on accountability for results (rather than procedure). Perhaps the most influential contemporary framework for analyzing accountability is that developed by Barbara Romzek and Melvin Dubnick.[58] Their discussion of accountability relationships closely tracks our own but uses the term "hierarchical" for what we call traditional managerial and adds a fourth category, "professional." The latter is the "individual responsibility of the administrator . . . to exercise . . . discretion in a manner that is consistent with the best professional practices." More broadly, personal responsibility has emerged as a common thread in the managerial, political, and legal perspectives toward public administrative accountability and ethics. As noted as long ago as 1936 in a classic book called *The Frontiers of Public Administration* by John Gaus, public employees, whether professionals or not, are expected to exercise an "inner check,"[59] derived from professional standards of administration and ideals.

Today, that inner check is sometimes constitutionally required to avoid personal liability. Moreover, constitutional requirements have been augmented by a widely accepted, comprehensive code of ethics that can fruitfully inform an inner check. The American Society for Public Administration

12.5   AMERICAN SOCIETY FOR PUBLIC ADMINISTRATION CODE OF ETHICS

The American Society for Public Administration (ASPA) advances the science, art, and practice of public administration. The Society affirms its responsibility to develop the spirit of responsible professionalism within its membership and to increase awareness and commitment to ethical principles and standards among all those who work in public service in all sectors. To this end, we, the members of the Society, commit ourselves to uphold the following principles:

1. **Advance the Public Interest.** Promote the interests of the public and put service to the public above service to oneself.

2. **Uphold the Constitution and the Law.** Respect and support government constitutions and laws, while seeking to improve laws and policies to promote the public good.

3. **Promote Democratic Participation.** Inform the public and encourage active engagement in governance. Be open, transparent and responsive, and respect and assist all persons in their dealings with public organizations.

4. **Strengthen Social Equity.** Treat all persons with fairness, justice, and equality and respect individual differences, rights, and freedoms. Promote affirmative action and other initiatives to reduce unfairness, injustice, and inequality in society.

5. **Fully Inform and Advise.** Provide accurate, honest, comprehensive, and timely information and advice to elected and appointed officials and governing board members, and to staff members in your organization.

6. **Demonstrate Personal Integrity.** Adhere to the highest standards of conduct to inspire public confidence and trust in public service.

7. **Promote Ethical Organizations.** Strive to attain the highest standards of ethics, stewardship, and public service in organizations that serve the public.

8. **Advance Professional Excellence.** Strengthen personal capabilities to act competently and ethically and encourage the professional development of others.

Source: American Society for Public Administration, 1120 G Street NW, Suite 700, Washington, DC 20005-3885.

(ASPA), a leading organization of concerned public administrators at all levels of government, recently revised its Code of Ethics in 2013 to focus on the principles that public administrators ought to aspire to the highest levels of ethical conduct and social responsibility. It is printed in Box 12.5.

ASPA's ethical code is broad enough to encompass each of the perspectives toward public administration discussed throughout this book. It requires attention to NPM and constitutional concerns, as well as to those of the traditional managerial and political approaches. Understanding the different perspectives toward public administration, along with appreciating their breadth, is a prerequisite to recognizing the complexity of the demands public administrators face. But the hard work lies less in identifying their diverse ethical requirements than in integrating them in real-world, on-the-job situations. As discussed earlier, Svara's "ethical triangle" and Lewis's tools are attempts to systematize an ethical decision making process. Knowing what to emphasize when, how to combine or prioritize disparate requirements, how to bridge and negotiate the separation of powers, and much more are part of the art and craft of contemporary public administration. As the NPR contended, improving accountability and advancing ethics ultimately depends on the individual actions of public servants:

> If the American people and our government—which, after all, is simply more American people—are to build trust in one another, it can only happen through thousands, even millions, of personal interactions. . . . We have to do it ourselves, individually and through association with one another.[60]

To the contention that such change can take a long time, former Vice President Gore would reply, "Then there's no time to lose," we had better start now![61]

Study Questions

1. Can you identify a case of public administration with which you are familiar where the official violated his or her public trust, in your view? If so, what seems to have been the cause? How was the breach of trust discovered, and how was the issue resolved? Do you believe the resolution was the best one possible?

2. How realistic do you think the notion of an "inner check" on administrators' conduct is?

3. Do you think public administrative corruption is a serious problem in the United States relative to corruption among elected officials? If you see a disparity, what might account for it? What can it teach us about accountability?

4. Because most public employees are good and competent people, comprehensive efforts to regulate conflicts of interest and other unethical behavior are not cost-effective. Do you agree or disagree with the assumptions underlying these points? Why?

5. Identify an ethical dilemma that a public administrator has faced. Apply the "ethical triangle" to this dilemma. What are the trade-offs made between each point in the triangle? How practical is it for public administrators to undertake this exercise as part of their decision making process? What is gained in the decision? What is lost?

Notes

1. Frederick Mosher, *Democracy and the Public Service* (New York: Oxford University Press, 1968), 5.

2. Victor Thompson, *Modern Organization* (New York: Knopf, 1961).

3. Samuel Krislov and David H. Rosenbloom, *Representative Bureaucracy and the American Political System* (New York: Praeger, 1981), esp. chap. 2.

4. Seymour M. Lipset, "Bureaucracy and Social Change," in R. K. Merton et al., Eds., *Reader in Bureaucracy* (Glencoe, IL: Free Press, 1952), 221–232, at 230.

5. Kenneth Meier, "Representative Bureaucracy: An Empirical Analysis," *American Political Science Review* 69 (June 1975): 526–542; David H. Rosenbloom, *Federal Equal Employment Opportunity* (New York: Praeger, 1977); V. Subramaniam, "Representative Bureaucracy: A Reassessment," *American Political Science Review* 61 (December 1967): 1010–1019; Katherine Naff, *To Look Like America* (Boulder, CO: Westview Press, 2000).

6. Amy E. Smith and Karen R. Monaghan, "Some Ceilings Have More Cracks: Representative Bureaucracy in Federal Regulatory Agencies," *The American Review of Public Administration* 43 (No. 1, 2013): 50–71.

7. *Heller v. Doe by Doe,* 509 U.S. 312 (1993).

8. Anthony Downs, *Inside Bureaucracy* (Boston: Little, Brown, 1967), 279.

9. Ibid., 276.

10. Joseph LaPalombara, *Interest Groups in Italian Politics* (Princeton, NJ: Princeton University Press, 1963).

11. Ibid., 262.

12. *Wall Street And The Financial Crisis: Anatomy Of A Financial Collapse: Report And Appendix Before The Permanent Subcommittee On Investigations Of The Committee On Homeland Security And Governmental Affairs, United States Senate, One Hundred Twelfth Congress, First Session, April 13, 2011.* Washington: U.S. Government Printing Office: 2011. Print.

13. Gretchen Morgenson and Louise Story, "Senate Report Names Culprits in Financial Crisis," *The New York Times,* 14 April 2011, B1.

14. Michael Johnston, *Political Corruption and Public Policy in America* (Monterey, CA: Brooks/Cole, 1982), 3.

15. Arnold J. Heidenheimer, Ed., *Political Corruption: Readings in Comparative Analysis* (New York: Holt, Rinehart and Winston, 1970).

16. For a concise discussion, see Edward Banfield and James Q. Wilson, *City Politics* (Cambridge, MA: Harvard University Press and the M.I.T. Press, 1963), chap. 9.

17. Philip Shenon, "Ohio Congressman Is Said to Agree to Plead Guilty," *New York Times,* 15 September 2006.

18. Philip Shenon, "Bound for Prison, Ohio House Member Keeps Hold on Office," *New York Times,* 19 October 2006.

19. Heidenheimer, *Political Corruption,* Introduction.

20. Robert N. Roberts, "Lord, Protect Me from the Appearance of Wrongdoing," in David H. Rosenbloom, Ed., *Public Personnel Policy: The Politics of Civil Service,* (Port Washington, NY: Associated Faculty Press, 1985), chap. 11.

21. See Johnston, *Political Corruption,* 11–12.

22. See Thomas Stackpole, "The Obama Administration Has a Long Record of Prosecuting Leakers," *Mother Jones,* May 15, 2013: http://www.motherjones .com/mojo/2013/05/obama-admins-record-prosecuting-leaks.

23. *New York Times,* 11 July 1952.

24. For a general discussion, see Martin Tolchin and Susan Tolchin, *Selling Our Security—The Erosion of America's Assets* (New York: Knopf, 1992).

25. Downs, *Inside Bureaucracy,* 262.

26. See David Nachmias and David H. Rosenbloom, *Bureaucratic Government, USA* (New York: St. Martin's Press, 1980), chap. 4.

27. Bruce Smith and James Carroll, Eds., *Improving the Accountability and Performance of Government* (Washington, DC: Brookings Institution, 1982), 21.

28. Jonathan Weisman, "Agency Administrator Fires Deputies, Then Resigns, Amid Spending Inquiry," *New York Times,* 4 April 2012, A11.

29. Adam Bryant, "F.A.A. Struggles as Airlines Turn to Subcontracts," *New York Times,* 2 June 1996, 1, 26.

30. Ibid., 26.

31. Bruce Smith and D. Hague, *The Dilemma of Accountability in Modern Government* (New York: St. Martin's Press, 1971), 26–27.

32. Ibid.

33. Lloyd G. Nigro and William D. Richardson, "Between Citizen and Administrator: Administrative Ethics and PAR," *Public Administration Review* 50 (No. 6, 1990): 623–635.

34. This following discussion draws from James H. Svara, "The Ethical Triangle: Synthesizing the Bases of Administrative Ethics," *Public Integrity Annual 1997*: 33–41.

35. Carol W. Lewis, *The Ethics Challenge in Public Service* (San Francisco: Jossey-Bass, 1991). For example, see Kathryn G. Denhardt, *The Ethics of Public Administration: Resolving Moral Dilemmas in Public Organizations* (New York: Greenwood, 1988).

36. Lewis, *The Ethics Challenge in Public Service*, esp. chap. 6.

37. Svara, "The Ethical Triangle," 38–41.

38. Chet Bridger, "Carriers Plan More Protests," *Federal Times*, 3 June 1996, 10.

39. Carolyn Ban, "The Revolving Door: Have We Shut It Too Tightly?" Paper delivered at the Annual Meeting of the American Political Science Association, Washington, DC, 30 August–2 September 1984. See also Robert N. Roberts, "Conflict-of-Interest Regulation and the Federal Service: The Legacy of Civil Service Reform," in David H. Rosenbloom, Ed., *Centenary Issues of the Pendleton Act of 1883* (New York: Marcel Dekker, 1982), chap. 7; and Robert Roberts and Marion Doss, Jr., "Public Service and Private Hospitality: A Case Study in Federal Conflict-of-Interest Reform," *Public Administration Review* 52 (No. 3, 1992): 260–270.

40. John A. Rohr, *Ethics for Bureaucrats* (New York: Marcel Dekker, 1978), 51–55.

41. Ibid., 54.

42. Ibid.

43. The code can be found at: http://www.oge.gov/Laws-and-Regulations/Employee-Standards-of-Conduct/Standards-of-Ethical-Conduct-for-Employees-of-the-Executive-Branch-(PDF)/.

44. Al Gore, *Common Sense Government Works Better & Costs Less* (Washington, DC: Government Printing Office, 1995), 33.

45. Ibid.

46. Al Gore, *From Red Tape to Results: Creating a Government That Works Better & Costs Less* (Washington, DC: Government Printing Office, 1993), 3.

47. Gore, *Common Sense Government*, 93.

48. Ibid., 92.

49. Kenneth Mayer, "Policy Disputes as a Source of Congressional Controls: Congressional Micromanagement of the Department of Defense," *Public Administration Review* 53 (No. 4, 1993): 293–302.

50. See http://www.gao.gov/fraudnet.htm and "U.S. Hot Line on Fraud Shows Handsome Returns," *New York Times*, 30 September 1984, p. 21.

51. Quoted in *Buckley v. American Law Foundation*, 525 U.S. 182, 223 (1999).

52. Carl J. Friedrich, "Public Policy and the Nature of Administrative Responsibility," in Alan Altshuler and Norman Thomas, Eds., *The Politics of the Federal Bureaucracy*, 2d ed. (New York: Harper & Row, 1977), 333–343, at 340.

53. Rohr, *Ethics for Bureaucrats*, esp. chap. 2.

54. Ibid., 59.

55. Kathryn Denhardt, "Unearthing the Moral Foundations of Public Administration," in James Bowman, Ed., *Ethical Frontiers in Public Management* (San Francisco: Jossey-Bass, 1991), 91–114.

56. *United States v. National Treasury Employees Union,* 513 U.S. 454 (1995).

57. See Yongjin Chang, *The Importance of the False Claims Act in the Middle Age of NPM and Reinventing Government Stream* (Saarbrucken, Germany: VDM Verlag Dr. Muller, 2009).

58. See Barbara Romzek and Melvin Dubnick, "Accountability," in Jay Shafritz, Ed., *The International Encyclopedia of Public Policy and Administration* (Boulder, CO: Westview Press, 1998), 6–11, which builds on their well-known article "Accountability in the Public Service: Lessons from the Challenger Tragedy," *Public Administration Review* 47 (No. 3, 1987): 227–239.

59. Quoted in Friedrich, "Public Policy," 339.

60. Gore, *Common Sense Government,* 93.

61. Gore, *From Red Tape to Results,* iv.

ADDITIONAL READING

Cooper, Terry. *The Responsible Administrator: An Approach to Ethics for the Administrative Role,* 6th ed. San Francisco: Jossey-Bass, 2012.

Cooper, Terry, Ed. *Handbook of Administrative Ethics,* 2d ed. New York: Marcel Dekker, 2001.

Heidenheimer, Arnold, Michael Johnston, and Victor LeVine. *Political Corruption,* 3rd ed. New Brunswick, NJ: Transaction, 2001.

Menzel, Donald. *Ethics Management for Public Administrators,* 2d ed. Armonk, NY: M.D. Sharpe, 2012.

Pasquerella, Lynn, Alfred Killilea, and Michael Vocino, Eds. *Ethical Dilemmas in Public Administration.* Westport, CT: Praeger, 1996.

Rohr, John. *Ethics for Bureaucrats,* 2d ed. New York: Marcel Dekker, 1989.

GOVERNMENT ETHICS WEB SITES

The U.S. Office of Government Ethics provides a comprehensive Web site that is complete with links to the relevant statutes and regulations, including the 82-page *Standards of Ethical Conduct for Employees of the Executive Branch.* A little searching will also lead the interested Web surfer to the 2000 ethics survey of federal employees, available at http://www.oge.gov.

The Department of the Navy has an instructive site on U.S. Government Ethics Standards at http://www.nbvc.navy.mil/fprotect/SecGuide/Ethics/Intro.htm. There is also a user-friendly "Ethics Compass" at http://www.ethics.navy.mil.

The U.S. Senate Select Committee on Ethics maintains a Web site with an ethics handbook for its members and employees (it is 542 pages long!) at http://ethics.senate.gov.

The U.S. House of Representatives Committee on Standards of Official Conduct Web site may be found at http://www.house.gov/ethics.

A useful and interesting state-level ethics Web site is maintained by the Idaho Office of the Attorney General. Its *Ethics in Government Manual* is available at http://www2.state.id.us/ag/manuals/ethicsingovernment.pdf.

CHAPTER 13

THE FUTURE

Key Learning Objectives

1. Identify trends and concerns that are likely to affect the future of public administration in the United States.

2. Understand what the effects of these trends and concerns may be by considering alternative futures.

In the foreseeable future, public administration in the United States will be characterized by: 1) greater complexity, 2) be subject to redefinition through politics regarding policies, programs, and the national debt, 3) place increasing importance on law, 4) emphasize performance and achievement of results, 5) undergo disaggregation as an overall field of study and practice, 6) witness further fragmentation of the federal civil service, 7) redefine management, 8) emphasize personal responsibility, and 9) move toward a different administrative culture. Some of these trends already are discernible.

In the wake of the September 11, 2001, terrorist strikes, many commentators on government and public affairs remarked that "everything had changed." Certainly everything *did* change for the immediate victims, those who suffered their unbearable loss or became their caregivers, and many others. A great deal, but far from everything, has also changed in public administration. The federal government gained a sprawling conglomerated Department of Homeland Security (DHS) with legacy agencies such as the Coast Guard and Secret Service having distinctive personnel systems, organizational designs, and cultures that set them apart from other units in that department. Several of the agencies that were transferred into the DHS have been restructured, reconfigured, and reoriented. While this conglomeration was intended to remove organizational barriers to interagency communication, the anemic response to Hurricane Katrina in 2005 points to the challenges to coordination and communication in large, poorly integrated administrative organizations. Compounding these structural problems, the placement of political cronies in positions that require technical knowledge and management skills in large federal departments and agencies further hampers the government's ability to respond in this time of recurring natural and human abetted disasters, national security threats, and economic problems.

The challenge of coordinating intergovernmental relations has become a top priority, especially in terms of responding to the newly understood threats of mass destruction and potential pandemics. Public health services have turned their attention to identifying and dealing with bioterrorist threats. Concerted efforts were undertaken to make the cultures of the CIA and FBI more functional in preventing new strikes. The USA Patriot Act and related measures have substantially altered the federal criminal justice system as it relates to national security. This list could continue almost indefinitely. Public libraries, schools, local police forces, and the overwhelming number of the more than 89,000 U.S. governments have responded to 9/11 in some fashion.

But have the fundamentals of U.S. public administration really changed very much? The responses to 9/11 reinforced and escalated some trends that were already under way. By contrast, the sharp economic downturn of 2008 triggered a federal response that belied President Bill Clinton's 1996 State of the Union statement that the "era of big government is over." In making predictions about public administration in today's volatile globalized world, one cannot discount the unpredictability and significance of events. Nevertheless, to a large extent public administration is everywhere organized bureaucratically and bureaucracy is perhaps the most stable complex organizational form known to humankind. Persistence amid change is a common phenomenon.

One way of thinking about U.S. public administration is to view it as standing at a crossroads where it has stood for a long time. More than six decades have elapsed since the traditional managerial approach was convincingly attacked for being too limited in its vision of government. Ironically, the crossroads has become more complicated as new avenues have been brought to it. Today, it may be more like a multi-ringed traffic circle with many points of ingress and egress than a crossroads. We have moved from a time when the traditional managerial approach dominated, to a present in which the political and legal perspectives analyzed throughout this book broadly inform almost all public administrative activity. Twenty years ago, the new public management (NPM) joined the intersection of these earlier multifaceted approaches. The immediate problem of American public administrative practice and theory is to integrate or sort out the values, structural and procedural arrangements, and techniques associated with each of the perspectives. There is no map, which is one reason why we have remained at the crossroads and now go round and round in the traffic circle. Much of the task of moving ahead will fall on public administrators in the day-to-day performance of their jobs. Nevertheless, some cautious generalizations about the future seem apt.

❖❖ COMPLEXITY IS HERE TO STAY

Contemporary public administration is amazingly complex and is becoming more complicated all the time. Public administrative activities range from trash collection to the exploration of outer space, from regulating the most developed postindustrial economies to helping some people move beyond the most rudimentary subsistence farming, from developing and using the most advanced biomedical technologies to the grinding task of going door to door at census time—and much more. The essence of public administration is dealing with relationships among political, economic, social, ethical, organizational, managerial, legal, scientific, technological, and national security values and systems at both microlevels and macrolevels. Public administrators bridge and coordinate the separation of powers, federalism, and inter-agency programs as well as the relationships between government, on the one side, and the economy and society, on the other. Many work in an international arena as well. Boundaries are often blurred, and bright lines are likely to fade even more as governments increasingly outsource their work or coordinate it with transnational organizations, and seek to accomplish their missions through collaborative governance arrangements.

At the least, public administrators need to be cognizant of the various approaches discussed throughout this book as they bear on their jobs. Each perspective brings much to the traffic circle. Although none is adequate on its own, each has a degree of internal coherence and enjoys substantial political, cultural, and intellectual support. Where they agree with one another, the path is clear. But their disagreements are also instructive because they raise the main issues facing today's public administration.

◆→   ## PUBLIC ADMINISTRATION WILL BE DEFINED BY POLITICS

Historically, American public administration has always been defined by dominant political groups, parties, and/or coalitions.[1] From 1789 to 1828, federal administration was an extension of the elite who dominated national politics. The Jacksonian revolution turned the federal service into the arm of the political parties. Building on the efforts of the 19th-century civil service reformers, the Progressives were able to institutionalize the politics-administration dichotomy and to base public administration on politically neutral, scientific, and technical expertise. Later, the New Deal placed federal administration under greater presidential control and made it more representative of and responsive to the clientele groups with which agencies dealt.

Beginning with the enactment of the Administrative Procedure Act (APA) in 1946, Congress has imposed a wide variety of processes and requirements on federal administration to promote the democratic-constitutional values of representation, participation, transparency, and fairness.[2] The federal courts, too, have made public administration more cognizant of the need to protect individuals' constitutional rights.[3] The National Performance Review (NPR) was an effort by "New Democrats" to show that government can be a cost-effective and responsive tool for intervening in the society and the economy. Given public concern with the cost of government, deficits, and the national debt, the alternative to making public administration "cost less and work better" is to eliminate many of its programs. In his inaugural address in 1981, President Ronald Reagan advocated for that approach: "In this present crisis, government is not the solution to our problem; government is the problem." President George W. Bush's administration extended the NPR and NPM "steering, not rowing" approach to providing public services, constraints, and national security through outsourcing. Bush also emphasized being results and performance oriented and customer centered. However, his administration differed from the NPR's vision by focusing on national security functions and reemphasizing executive control, managerial authority, performance, and e-government. President Barack Obama has not articulated a distinctive approach to managing federal administration. Unlike his predecessors, he has not put forward major reforms or putative "silver bullet" solutions to federal administrative problems like MBO (management by objective; Nixon), ZBB or major civil service reform (zero base budgeting and the Civil Service Reform Act of 1978; Carter), downsizing (Reagan), "reinvention" (Clinton-Gore), or a President's Management Agenda (Bush II). His administration has much in common with NPR and NPM approaches, though with some desire to limit outsourcing, as well as with Bush II's lack of enthusiasm for transparency.[4]

During his second term, discord with the Republican Party majority in the House of Representatives forestalled agreement on debt and deficit reduction as well as enactment of a budget. In response to his inability to win congressional approval for several initiatives, Obama has achieved some of his objectives through executive orders and other tools of presidential power.[5] Like Bush before him, he has continued the long-term trend to attempt to increase executive control through the appointment of politically loyal, but potentially technically unqualified, individuals into key positions in the agencies.[6] Such appointees may well decrease the efficiency and effectiveness of government.[7]

The reality that politics has always defined dominant administrative practice in the United States is only thinly veiled by reformers' typical claims that their programs for change are apolitical. Like the civil service reformers more than a century earlier, the NPR claimed that its reforms were intended to make the government more businesslike. And, like them, it ultimately admitted that the big picture is political. For the nineteenth century reformers, it was a matter of changing the nation's political leadership; for the NPR, it was restoring the public's trust in government.[8] Administrative theory and practice are political theory and practice as well.[9] The successful advocacy of major administrative change in the United States has always been part of the overall program or vision of those in or gaining political power. Administrative ideas and techniques may be developed and implemented independently of politics— and they may be of great value—but the overall definition of what public administration should be is likely to continue to be politically determined.

Consequently, administrative doctrine and practice are not immutable. They have changed dramatically in the past, and they will probably change again in the future. But how, if at all, will politics redefine public administration in the near future?

Building on the NPM offers one strong prospect for continuing change, as has been discussed throughout this book. The NPM transformed administrative theory, language, organization, and practice—and may continue to do so. However, by the end of Obama's second term, it will be 24 years old and hardly "new." Whether it will have established its legacy yet run its course by then is uncertain.

Another possibility for politically inspired change should be mentioned as well. American government goes through periods when the strength of one institution grows relative to that of others. The New Deal presidency, institutionalized under the rubric of administrative reform, is an example. Since the 1990s, Congress has taken several steps toward reasserting the powerful role in federal administration that the Constitutional Convention designed for it. The Government Performance and Results Act Modernization Act of 2010 has the potential to subordinate agencies more clearly to legislative committees and subcommittees. The Congressional Review Act of 1996 is another tool Congress can use to gain greater influence over agency rulemaking. Both statutes are in keeping with the model for directing public administration that Congress sought to establish in 1946 when it enacted the Administrative Procedure

Act to regulate the agencies' exercise of delegated authority and the Legislative Reorganization Act to strengthen Congress's oversight capacity. Other tools include the inspectors general, chief financial officers, chief operating officers, Congressional Budget Office, Government Accountability Office, Congressional Research Service, and the committee/subcommittee system.

Prior to 9/11, Congress looked resurgent vis-à-vis federal administration. Historically, however, executive power tends to increase—sometimes dramatically—when national security is threatened. After 9/11 this tendency was fully evident. Under Bush II, presidential power expanded, especially in international relations, budgetary matters, and the wielding of managerial authority within the executive branch. Obama has used many of the same tools of presidential power as Bush, but has also been stymied by a divided Congress on several major matters, including budgets and moving enemy combatants detained at the U.S. Guantanamo military base elsewhere. The immediate outcome of interbranch competition for influence over federal agencies and administration is uncertain. Much will depend on the outcome of the midterm elections in 2014 and the presidential election of 2016. If the next president is a Republican, "reinvention" may be reinvented in a concerted effort to initiate another round of deregulation and debt reduction.

◆→ LAW WILL CONTINUE TO BE CENTRAL TO PUBLIC ADMINISTRATION

In 1926, when Leonard White wrote the first American textbook on public administration, *Introduction to the Study of Public Administration,* he was correct in asserting that "the study of administration should start from the base of management rather than the foundation of law, and is therefore more absorbed in the affairs of the American Management Association than in the decisions of the courts."[10] Today the relative importance of law is much greater, and it is likely to expand in the future. Judicial decisions beginning in the 1950s, crystalizing in the mid-1970s, and continuing into the present have added a powerful legal perspective to American public administration.[11] A great number of administrative practices and activities must now be based on and responsive to constitutional rights and doctrines. Public administration is infused with concerns for procedural due process and equal protection. Public administrators who violate individuals' constitutional rights may be personally subject to civil suits for compensatory and punitive damages. The courts have been deeply involved in the operation of some administrative institutions and systems. Until sometime in the 1970s, it would not have been possible to point to a distinct legal perspective on a core administrative matter such as personnel or decision making. Since then, as Chapter 11 suggests, the application of constitutional constraints to public administration has expanded incrementally. At present, the feasibility of privatization and public-private partnerships depends partly on how the courts apply state action doctrine. The Supreme Court has made it clear that government will not be able to avoid its constitutional responsibilities by outsourcing its work.[12] In addition, the judiciary has done a great deal to define the APA, which, as amended and augmented, remains the generic law regulating federal administrative processes. Many state courts have actively affected state and local governmental administration in parallel ways.

The importance of law in public administration is likely to continue to expand. Although it is possible for the courts to reverse constitutional doctrines, the "rights revolution" of the 1950s to the 1970s has become part of the political culture. In the 1990s, the Supreme Court strengthened the First Amendment rights of contractors and private entities engaged in collaborative governance relationships.[13] The Court has also done much to strengthen the power of the states in the federal equation at the expense of the national government's power under the Constitution's commerce clause.[14] Moreover, to the extent that public administrators are increasingly called on to reconcile competing claims, law will remain central to their decision making, along with other tools for resolving conflicts.

◆→ PERFORMANCE

The NPM's emphasis on performance is probably a permanent addition to the mix of public administrative concerns. It was very strongly supported by the George W. Bush administration and it is unlikely that any president can ignore poor administrative performance, especially if it is wasteful or abusive.[15] The performance orientation stems from at least two developments that seem irreversible. First, since the tax revolts of the 1970s, the public has continued to demand greater value for its tax dollars. Politicians, appointed political executives, and the public service are under great pressure to deliver what the public wants at a low cost. Tax and expenditure limitations at the state and local levels have institutionalized the need for cost-effectiveness. In the 1990s, the federal government's focus on eliminating the deficit had similar consequences. Today's huge deficits and growing national debt also place an emphasis on performance. Second, globalization makes poor government performance a greater liability than it was in earlier times. To be competitive, national economies cannot be burdened with excessive governmental costs. In the past the main problem in this regard was corruption, but today it is advisable to be lean as well as clean. At the federal level, GPRA Modernization Act seeks to institutionalize a performance orientation through strategic planning, and agency performance reports, placing responsibilities for performance in chief operating officers and performance improvement officers.

The need for performance is clear, but prescriptions for it may be inadequate. The Government Performance and Results Act of 1993 promised to enhance legislative direction, program definition, and oversight. But it was not well implemented and Congress paid limited attention to agency strategic planning and performance reporting. The NPR promised to do more with less, but it may have stretched the federal government's administrative capacity to the limit. The Bush II administration had a strong management focus but nevertheless contributed substantially to deficit spending. Still, the days when the society was willing to invest in the traditional managerial structures of overhead control seem long gone. Experimentation may well replace doctrine in the future quest for performance.

◆✦ DISAGGREGATION OF PUBLIC ADMINISTRATION

Leonard White assumed that public "administration is a single process, substantially uniform in its essential characteristics wherever observed," whether at the state, federal, or local level of government.[16] Today most people would probably disagree with White's assumption. Certainly, the federal government's highly developed separation of powers distinguishes its administration in important respects from that of local government under city managers. The vast array of activities in which administrators engage also detracts from the idea of a single process. Some administrators are generalists in program management; others specialize in functions such as personnel or budgeting; still others work in fields, including economics and engineering, that span both the public and private sectors. Intellectually, public administration has no single paradigm or conceptual framework. It has been suggested in several places throughout this book that one or more of the perspectives analyzed may be more applicable to different policy or program areas. There does not seem to be any compelling reason to treat, for example, overhead functions, sociotherapy, service, and public utility, safety, and environmental regulation as a single process.

◆✦ FRAGMENTATION OF THE CIVIL SERVICE

Disaggregation promotes fragmentation of the civil service. The NPR sought to reduce "one size fits all" regulations and systems in the federal service. Instead, it advocated tailoring personnel and other systems to agencies' individual missions. As sensible as that may be, it contributed to the weakening of two concepts that were central to traditional management. One is that any particular government, whether federal, state, or local, should act as a single, unified employer. The other is the concomitant idea of a unified civil service. The single employer concept was vital to the development of centralized public personnel systems with comprehensive position classification and pay schedules. A government, rather than its individual agencies, was the employer. Accordingly, the employee was a career civil servant rather than a worker for one agency or another. These concepts were stronger in the federal government than in most of the states, which traditionally had less well-developed administrative components, weaker central personnel agencies, and more limited merit systems. They have been seriously compromised to the point that one could question whether they are still operable.

First, the radical decentralization implemented by the U.S. Office of Personnel Management (OPM) in conjunction with the NPR places agencies largely in charge of their own personnel systems. They hire, train, and promote with little central oversight. For the most part, the famously comprehensive regulations of the *Federal Personnel Manual* are gone. Second, and relatedly, many agencies have gained exemption from the uniform body of law that regulates federal employment (that is, Title 5 of the U.S. Code). Whereas once perhaps 80 to 90 percent of federal executive branch employees were subject to the same statutes and regulations, today the number is less than 50 percent and is declining. A large chunk of those who are exempt work for the corporatized Postal Service, but others are in regular executive agencies such as the Federal Aviation Administration and the Department of Veterans Affairs. As mentioned earlier, the DHS has multiple personnel systems. The huge Department of Defense gained authorization to opt out of Title 5 restrictions in late 2003.

When the federal government was viewed as a single employer, the House Post Office and Civil Service Committee and the Senate Governmental Affairs Committee had subject matter jurisdiction for most civil service matters. They were part of a policy network that supported a strong, career-oriented civil service. In the future, as agency personnel practices are based on individual statutes tailored to their circumstances, jurisdiction will be dispersed among the various committees with oversight for those agencies and their programs.

Information technology (IT) also promotes fragmentation. The "workplace" of the future may be no "place" at all. Telecommuting and IT may redefine work sites as arenas "through which information circulates—information to which intellective effort is applied."[17] Coupled with a customer orientation, IT should make it possible for individuals to transact a great deal of their business with government online. For example, the proportion of individual federal tax returns filed electronically reached 80 percent in 2012.[18] Finally, government will lose its distinctiveness as outsourcing blurs the boundaries between it and the private sector.

These changes may be highly beneficial. After all, the problems of the old government-wide personnel and other regulations and systems are well documented and real. However, they will also fundamentally alter the concept of civil service and further fragment government.

✦ THE CHANGING FACE OF MANAGEMENT

As its label suggests, the NPM is premised on the belief that, as a function, management must drastically change. From its perspective, the traditional view of management as voiced by Henry Mintzberg, a leading theorist, is quaintly archaic: "No job is more vital to our society than that of the manager. It is the manager who determines whether our social institutions serve us well or whether they squander our talents and resources."[19] To the contrary, the NPM claims that the empowered employees, entrepreneurs, and public-private partnerships are vital to government performance. Traditional managers create bottlenecks, protect turf, and hoard information.

Whatever one's view of traditional management, IT is already modifying the need for managers and their functions. Twenty-five years ago Shoshana Zuboff studied the "informated" workplace ("informated" is as dramatic a change as was "automated," but it refers to electronic communication and computerization rather than mechanization).[20] She left no doubt that management was being reconceived. Traditional management changes or becomes obsolete when computers and electronic information technology give employees access to a vast array of information; the capacity to communicate almost instantaneously with each other, clients, and customers; and the tools with which to redesign work processes. IT can also replace the traditional role managers played in assuring that employees were doing the work assigned to them. Furthermore, as a whole, today's public employees are much better educated in problem solving than was the case in the past. They are less dependent on management to show them how to do their jobs well. That is precisely why the NPM believes they should be empowered. The unanswered question is how decentralized agencies with empowered employees and multiple contractors can be coordinated.

◆◆   PERSONAL RESPONSIBILITY

There is broad agreement that public administrators should be held personally responsible for their actions. The NPM is explicit in emphasizing that empowered employees must be held accountable for results. Contemporary constitutional law is equally explicit in making public employees potentially personally liable for violating individuals' constitutional rights. Ethics law and rules demand that public employees avoid giving even the appearance of impropriety. Some aspects of environmental law impose criminal liability on public administrators, regardless of their hierarchical level, for illegal pollution.[21] External approaches to oversight and accountability are clearly being augmented by a sense that public employees must individually have a strong sense of personal responsibility. The potential for administrators to do harm to other individuals, taxpayers, communities, national security, and to the environment is so great that "going by the book" is inadequate. After 9/11, the culture in which "CYA" (cover your a[natomy]) would get one off the hook is no longer acceptable. Administration should not be "rule by nobody."[22] President Harry S. Truman famously kept a sign on his desk that read, "*The BUCK STOPS here.*" His point was that if the top of the hierarchy evades personal responsibility, how can citizens expect other federal employees to accept responsibility for their actions? Today's concepts of responsible and accountable public administration require that the buck stop everywhere, high and low, wherever career civil servants or political appointees engage in maladministration.

Personal responsibility sometimes requires behavior that traditionally was unacceptable and that remains uncomfortable. Statutes protecting whistle-blowers create a moral obligation to expose various kinds of waste, fraud, abuse, and especially specific and immediate dangers to public health or safety. From a traditional perspective, whistle-blowing is insubordination, and whistle-blowers are still frequently treated harshly. Yet their responsibility is clear.[23] Had the FBI listened to Colleen Rowley, an agent who tried unsuccessfully to call attention to the threat of a terrorist strike using airliners before 9/11, we might be living in a very different world. In terms of personal responsibility, it is noteworthy that along with the constitutional right to whistle-blow there is a clear right and obligation to disobey unconstitutional directives.[24]

If reliance on contractors and those engaged in collaborative government arrangements continue to play a large part in public administration, as seems likely, the demands for personal responsibility are likely to increase and reach private individuals engaged in government work. The more attenuated the formal chains of accountability become as work is outsourced, the more the public may demand that specific individuals—not complex, inanimate systems—take responsibility for things gone wrong.

CONCLUSION: A NEW ADMINISTRATIVE CULTURE

Whether public administration finds an avenue out of its current crossroads or traffic circle, it is likely that a new **administrative culture** will emerge. Public administrators of the future will have to be at ease with complexity, law, technological advances, and flexibility. They will be performance-oriented, have a strong service ethic, span boundaries, and be adroit at conflict avoidance and resolution. Public administrators will be personally responsible for their actions. They will have to be comfortable with change, often rapid change.

But some things will remain constant. First, the Constitution will remain central to public administration at all levels of U.S. government. Public administrators will need constitutional competence to guard against breaches of individuals' rights and avoid potential liability for committing constitutional torts. As in the past, they will have to be responsive to three "masters" with different perspectives on public administration: legislators, elected and appointed executives, and the judiciary. Administrators' responses will directly involve them in coordinating the separation of powers so that policies can be formulated and implemented. Likewise, administrators will continue to have a major role in coordinating federalism and intergovernmental relations.

Second, public administration will remain interesting, challenging, and a key to a better society and world. In 1926, Leonard White wrote that "administration has become, and will continue to be the heart of the problem of modern government."[25] More than half a century later, Dwight Waldo reiterated White's point in words that instruct and remind us of public administration's overarching importance:

> Whatever the future, excepting only oblivion—*no* future—public administration will have an important role in it. Public administration joins

two major forces, government and administrative technology. Together they have been an integral part of the enterprise of civilization. They will not disappear unless and until civilization disappears, through decay or destruction, or through transformation into a new human condition.[26]

To improve public administration is to improve civilization. The NPR invited everybody to participate.

There are people in America who think that any individual who attempts to take responsibility for the common good is hopelessly naive. There are others who think such actions are dangerously radical. But we are a nation of hopelessly naive radicals—of people who will not give up the dream of a nation run by its own people.[27]

This book provides the knowledge, information, and understanding necessary to join fruitfully in the effort to build a public administration appropriate for the 21st century. You can help create a better future by using it as a citizen, member of the general public, customer, coproducer of public goods and services, or public servant.

STUDY QUESTIONS

1. Do you agree or disagree that the predictions made in this chapter describe public administration's likely near-term future? Why? What additional ones would you add?
2. Based on your values, what kind of public administrative future would you like to see, and what could you do to bring it about?

NOTES

1. David H. Rosenbloom, *Federal Service and the Constitution* (Ithaca, NY: Cornell University Press, 1971).
2. David H. Rosenbloom, *Building a Legislative-Centered Public Administration: Congress and the Administrative State, 1946–1999* (Tuscaloosa: University of Alabama Press, 2000).
3. David H. Rosenbloom, Rosemary O'Leary, and Joshua Chanin, *Public Administration and Law,* 3rd ed. (Boca Raton, FL: CRC/Taylor & Francis 2010). See also David H. Rosenbloom, "Retrofitting the Administrative State to the Constitution: Congress and the Judiciary's Twentieth Century Progress," *Public Administration Review* 60 (January/February 2000): 39–46.
4. J.B. Wogan, "Obama's Transparency Record: Lots of Data, Not as much Sunlight," *Tampa Bay Times* "Politifact.com", July 16, 2012; http://www .politifact.com/truth-o-meter/article/2012/jul/16/obama-report-card-transparency-sunlight/.
5. Charlie Savage, "Shift on Executive Power Lets Obama Bypass Rivals," *New York Times,* 22 April 2012; http://www.nytimes.com/2012/04/23/us/politics/shift-on-executive-powers-let-obama-bypass-congress.html?pagewanted=all.
6. According to a poll by Government Executive, career employees give Obama's appointees a "C" or 2.0 grade compared with a 2.3 for those of Bush II.

Moreover, 30 percent gave them a "D" or an "F" for overall performance. See David Jackson, "Obama's Political Appointees Get Low Marks," *USA Today,* 31 May 2011; http://content.usatoday.com/communities/theoval/post/2011/05/ obama-appointees-get-low-marks/1#.Ua0cml3D-Uk.

7. Paul Light, *Thickening Government* (Washington, DC: Brookings Institution, 1995).

8. Al Gore, *Common Sense Government Works Better & Costs Less* (Washington, DC: Government Printing Office, 1995), 92–93.

9. This is an old lesson that is too often neglected. See the classic statement by Dwight Waldo in *The Administrative State* (New York: Ronald Press, 1948); 2d ed. (New York: Holmes and Meier, 1984).

10. Leonard D. White, *Introduction to the Study of Public Administration* (New York: Macmillan, 1926), Preface. Excerpts are published in Jay Shafritz and Albert Hyde, Eds., *Classics of Public Administration,* 2d ed. (Chicago: Dorsey Press, 1987), 55–64.

11. Rosenbloom, O'Leary, and Chanin, *Public Administration and Law.*

12. *Board of County Commissioners v. Umbehr,* 518 U.S. 668 (1996); *O'Hare Truck Service v. City of Northlake,* 518 U.S. 712 (1996).

13. Ibid.

14. David H. Rosenbloom and Bernard H. Ross, "Toward a New Jurisprudence of Constitutional Federalism: The Supreme Court in the 1990s and Public Administration," *American Review of Public Administration* 28 (June 1998): 107–125.

15. As this is being written, the Obama administration is dealing with congressional and public outrage over the Internal Revenue Service's unfavorable handling of requests by conservative organizations for special tax status under section 501c of the federal tax code as well as the IRS' spending on conferences that included $3,000 a night hotel suites. Earlier, in August 2012, the Obama administration had to deal with the General Services Administration's lavish spending on conferences for its employees, particularly one that cost $800,000 in Las Vegas.

16. White, *Introduction to the Study of Public Administration,* Preface.

17. Shoshana Zuboff, *In the Age of the Smart Machine* (New York: Basic Books, 1988), 395.

18. Jay Starkman, "E-Filing and the Explosion of Tax-Return Fraud," *Wall Street Journal,* January 13, 2013; http://online.wsj.com/article/SB10001424127887323 374504578222130665022160.html.

19. Quoted in Shan Martin, *Managing without Managers* (Beverly Hills, CA: Sage, 1983), 19.

20. Zuboff, *In the Age of the Smart Machine.*

21. Rosenbloom, O'Leary, and Chanin, *Public Administration and Law,* chap. 3.

22. The phrase is Hannah Arendt's. See Owen Fiss, "The Bureaucratization of the Judiciary," *Yale Law Journal* 92 (1983): 1442–1468, for a discussion of its implications in the American context.

23. Marcia Miceli and Janet Near, *Blowing the Whistle* (New York: Lexington Books, 1992); and Deborah D. Goldman and David H. Rosenbloom, "Whistleblower," in Jay Shafritz, Ed., *International Encyclopedia of Public Policy and Administration* (Boulder, CO: Westview Press, 1998), 2397–2400.

24. Robert Vaughn, "Public Employees and the Right to Disobey," *Hastings Law Journal* 29 (1977): 261–295.

25. White, *Introduction to the Study of Administration,* Preface.
26. Dwight Waldo, *The Enterprise of Public Administration* (Novato, CA: Chandler & Sharp, 1980), 189.
27. Gore, *Common Sense Government,* 93.

ADDITIONAL READINGS

Denhardt, Janet, and Robert Denhardt. *The New Public Service: Serving Not Steering, expanded edition.* Armonk, NY: M.E. Sharpe, 2007.

Kettl, Donald. *The Transformation of Governance: Public Administration for Twenty-First Century America.* Baltimore: Johns Hopkins University Press, 2002.

Light, Paul. *The New Public Service.* Washington, DC: Brookings Institution, 1999.

Glossary*

Administrative culture (572)   The set of shared values underlying administrative performance and the general structures and processes for achieving them.

Administrative decentralization (107)   The delegation of administrative responsibility, authority, and discretion to administrative units that have jurisdiction over at least one program or function in a subnational geographic territory.

Administrative law (5)   The regulatory law of public administration, consisting of statutes, constitutional requirements, executive orders, and other regulations that control administrative matters such as rule making, adjudication, enforcement, and handling of information.

Adversary proceeding (440)   The enforcement of statutes or regulatory rules by placing an agency or a party against another.

Advocacy administration (197)   An approach to administration in which those with authority act on behalf of the less powerful members of a community.

Affirmative action (245)   The use of goals and timetables for hiring and promotion of women and members of minority groups as part of an equal employment opportunity program.

Alternative dispute resolution (33)   Settling disputes by means other than courtroom procedure, including mediation, arbitration, and fact-finding.

Anomie (460)   A feeling of isolation and loss of control over one's life and environment.

Arbitration (255)   A means of resolving disputes, including impasses reached in collective bargaining.

Balanced budget amendment (280)   A proposed constitutional amendment requiring a balanced annual federal budget (except in emergency situations).

Bargaining units (253)   Groups of employees, often according to occupation, who have a legal right to select a bargaining agent (union) to negotiate working conditions on their behalf.

Boss-centered (leadership style) (162)   A leadership style characterized by managerial control of the decision making process.

Boss-follower culture (537)   A type of political culture that involves political exchanges between citizens and the political "boss" or the boss's agents and between the machine and businesses. Also referred to as political-machine-based culture.

Bureau ideologies (533)   Beliefs developed in bureaucracies that tout their virtues.

Bureaucratic politics (61)   The study of how administrative agencies' power, authority, enforcement, policy making, and decision making are affected by their interaction with interest groups, legislators, legislative committees, chief executives and their appointees, courts, the public, and other political actors.

Career reserved (SES position) (222)   A type of SES position limited to career appointees.

Career SES appointments (221)   A type of SES appointment made in the federal bureaucracy.

Case law (342)   The legal principles that can be derived by analyzing decisions in previous legal cases.

Casework (71)   Services rendered by members of Congress to constituents, generally aimed at resolving constituent difficulties with administrative agencies. Also referred to as constituency service.

Categorical ranking (229)   Grouping applicants into categories based on a competitive assessment of their qualifications. Allows hiring officials to select any applicant within the group from which hires are being made regardless of where the applicant ranks within the group.

*A separate glossary of budget terms appears in Chapter 6.

Civic culture (537) A type of political culture that emphasizes the community and promotion of the public interest over private interests.

Client-centered (476) An approach to administration that seeks to create organizational structures and programmatic arrangements focusing on clients' interests.

Client politics (412) A type of politics that occurs when the benefits of a governmental policy or activity are concentrated but the costs are widely distributed.

Clientele departments (48) Departments that deal largely with, and often supply services to, a well-defined group of people with common economic interests, such as tobacco growers.

Codetermination (252) A model of public personnel administration that involves joint policy making through collective bargaining.

Commerce clause (109) Article I, section 8, clause 3, of the Constitution, giving Congress the power "To regulate Commerce with foreign Nations, and among the several States, and with the Indian tribes." The source of the federal government's authority to develop and enforce nationwide economic regulatory policies.

Commission plan (118) A form of municipal government in which a number of elected commissioners perform both legislative and executive functions. Each commissioner generally has executive responsibility for the operations of a specific department, such as transportation.

Common law (50) Law made by judges in deciding cases as opposed to statutory law enacted by legislatures. Pertains primarily to government and the security of persons and property.

Comparability (236) In pay, the degree to which jobs in the public sector are compensated comparably to those in the private sector.

Comparable worth (236) A concept that addresses the pay rates for different occupations by the same employer, especially where some occupations are staffed predominantly by women and others predominantly by men. The concept promotes equal pay for dissimilar jobs considered to be of equal value to the employer.

Comparative risk analysis (428) A consideration of whether a policy will cause individuals to change their behavior in ways that create risks to their welfare, such as the impact of regulations raising airfares on the likelihood that individuals will incur statistically greater risks by driving to their destinations.

Concurrent validation (231) A merit examination validation technique that administers an exam to those already employed and then seeks to determine the statistical relationship between their scores and their performance appraisals.

Conduct cases (419) Regulatory or law enforcement actions taken in the belief that an individual's or firm's conduct has been in violation of regulations.

Constitutional torts (77) Violations of individuals' constitutional rights that are redressable through civil suits.

Cooperative federalism (112) Interdependency, overlapping power, and shared responsibility between the states and the national government in formulating and implementing public policies.

Coproduction (477) An approach to providing governmental services that involves service provision by both a governmental agency and a user.

Council-manager (118) A form of municipal government composed of an elected council with legislative authority and a manager, hired by the council, who serves as the chief executive officer of the jurisdiction.

Creative federalism (114) The allocation of federal grants directly to local governments (i.e., bypassing the states) to promote specific policy objectives such as the reduction of poverty or crime.

Criterion-related (231) An approach to merit examination validation that attempts to relate exam scores to on-the-job performance.

Cross subsidies (409) A type of price regulation that results in one set of customers paying prices intended to subsidize another set of customers.

Deferral (294) An executive technique to control spending that delays the spending of appropriated funds.

Democratic organization (195) An organization that integrates citizen and employee participation into its policy making and decision making processes.

Dillon's rule (132) Court interpretation that local governments possess only the powers expressly allocated to them by the states.

Direct hiring (229) Noncompetitive hiring of any qualified applicant.

Dual federalism (112) A division of governmental authority in which states are supreme in some policy areas and the national government is supreme in others, with very limited overlapping jurisdiction.

E-government (453) Using the Internet to facilitate administrative interactions with the public, such as submitting applications and commenting on proposed rules.

Eligibles register (229) A tool used in selection decisions; a list of those who passed an examination, ranked in order of their scores.

Entitlements (131) Government benefits required by law to be paid to eligible individuals, groups, or other governments.

Entrepreneurial politics (413) A type of politics that occurs when the benefits of a governmental policy or activity are widely distributed but the costs are concentrated.

Entrepreneurs (policy) (413) Individuals who effectively represent groups and are not directly involved in legislative policy making.

Equal protection clause (134) Clause in the Fourteenth Amendment to the Constitution requiring the states to afford equal protection of the laws to everyone within their jurisdiction.

Equity (32) In law, justice based on fairness. The power of judges to fashion remedies for violations of an individual's rights or other injuries.

Ex parte (192) One-sided contacts with agency decision makers when they are engaged in adjudication.

Exclusive recognition (of a union) (253) The designation by a collective bargaining unit of a single union to bargain on behalf of all the employees in the unit.

Executive Office of the President (EOP) (65) A federal organization created in 1939 to enable the president to exercise greater control over federal agencies. The EOP currently includes such important units as the White House Office, the Office of Management and Budget, and the National Security Council.

Executive privilege (69) Based on the separation of powers, allows the president and other top-level executive branch officials to withhold information and documents from Congress and the courts in appropriate circumstances. Executive privilege is intended to protect the free flow of ideas and information as well as confidentiality in the highest levels of the executive branch.

Expectancy theory (167) Job motivation will depend on the extent to which individuals expect that a certain activity will lead to some degree of satisfaction of their goals.

Federalism (101) A form of governmental organization that divides political authority between a central government and state or provincial governments.

Final offer arbitration (255) The arbitrator or panel must choose the last offer of one side or the other either in its entirety (whole package) or on each item (item by item).

Full faith and credit clause (133) The clause in Article IV of the Constitution requiring states to recognize the legal acts of other states even though their policies and laws may differ.

General SES position (222) A type of SES position open to any type of SES appointee.

Hiring freeze (294) A technique used to control spending that prohibits the filling of vacant positions.

Human relations approach (156) An approach to management that attempts to develop ways of making work in organizations more socially and psychologically acceptable to employees while enhancing or at least maintaining efficiency.

Human services integration (471) An approach to administration that enables individuals seeking or requiring several services to apply to one office only.

Hygienes (166) Environmental and contextual factors that have the capacity to make workers dissatisfied if they are inadequately met; however, they do not lead to job satisfaction in and of themselves.

Impact analysis (367) A technique concerned with examining the extent to which a policy causes change in the intended direction.

Implementation evaluation (372) A determination of whether the implementation or effect of a policy is appropriate.

Impoundment (294) A technique used by governors and the president to control spending; disallows an executive agency to spend the funds that have been allotted to it.

Income taxes (271) Taxes levied on the earnings of individuals and corporations.

Incremental model (335) An approach to decision making emphasizing small steps toward a general objective.

Incrementalism (29) An approach to budgeting or decision making that focuses on limited changes in funding, programs, or policies.

Interest group politics (412) A type of politics that occurs when both the costs and the benefits of a governmental policy or activity are narrowly concentrated.

Job performance (230) The reality of how much work gets done.

Job proficiency (230) The ability to perform the functions of a job.

Judicial activism (74) The involvement of judges in public administrative and policy matters.

Judicialization (30) The tendency for administrative processes increasingly to resemble courtroom procedures. Increases the role of legal values in agency decision making.

Keynesian approach (276) An approach to fiscal policy that holds that governmental spending can be used to counteract the normal boom-and-bust tendencies of the business cycle.

Leadership (158) The ability to influence people, motivate them to serve a common purpose, and fulfill the functions necessary for successful group action.

Limited emergency SES appointments (222) A type of noncompetitive SES appointment that can last up to 18 months.

Limited-term SES appointments (221) A type of noncompetitive SES appointment that is nonrenewable and can last up to three years.

Line-item budget (302) A type of budget that requires that appropriations be linked to objects of expenditure.

Majoritarian politics (412) A type of politics that occurs when the costs and benefits of a governmental policy or activity are widely distributed.

Management by objectives (MBO) (181) A management technique that requires active participation by subordinates in goal setting.

Marginal costs (375) The additional cost of providing an additional unit of a good, service, or constraint.

Mayor-council (118) A form of government in which an elected mayor performs primarily executive functions while a council performs both executive and legislative functions.

Median voter (89) Conceptualizing political preferences on policy or electoral choices as arrayed on an continuum from totally opposed to totally supportive, the median voter is the hypothetical voter whose preference lies precisely at the the mid-point where equal numbers of other voters would lie toward the opposed and supportive sides of him or her.

Mixed-scanning approach (351) An approach to decision making that attempts to combine incrementalism with the rational-comprehensive approach.

Moral approach to leadership (162) The ability to lead based on shared moral beliefs and goals on the part of the leader and the followers.

Motivators (167) Factors that can produce greater job satisfaction.

Natural rights (502) Fundamental rights to freedom and liberty that exist independently of government; for instance, natural rights theory holds that all individuals have a right to reasonable self-defense.

New federalism (114) Initially associated with President Richard Nixon, the use of block grants and general revenue sharing to provide the states with greater flexibility in developing and implementing public policy.

Noncareer SES appointments (211) A type of SES appointment held by political appointees who assist top-level political executives of departments and agencies.

Non-distribution constraint (89) A prohibition preventing nonprofit organizations from distributing excess revenues (i.e., profits in the for profit context) to stakeholders.

Nonexperimental design (367) A research design that does not use a control group; assumes a connection between policy outputs and changes in the condition of the target group or target phenomenon.

Ombudsman (470) Independent governmental agent empowered to investigate specific complaints by individuals alleging maladministration of some kind.

Operations management (181) A management approach that seeks to identify the specific operational responsibilities of government agencies and design their organizations and work flows to maximize productivity.

Opportunity costs (377)　The cost one choice imposes by foreclosing other possible choices, such as when the decision to protect an endangered species prevents logging in a forest.

Organization development (185)　An approach for improving organization that assumes that organizations will be more effective at problem solving and coping with their environments when there is more trust, support, and cooperation among their members.

Outcome analysis (367)　(see **Impact analysis**) A technique concerned with examining the extent to which a policy causes change in the intended direction.

Overhead agencies (54)　Administrative units, such as personnel agencies, that perform services for other agencies or are engaged in overseeing aspects of their operations.

Performance budget (302)　A budget that relates performance levels to appropriations.

Picket-fence federalism (114)　A metaphor in which federalism is visualized as a picket fence with the pickets being specific policy areas, such as health or environmental protection, and the rails being the three levels of government with federal at the top, state in the middle, and local at the bottom.

Pluralism (28)　A distribution of political power characterized by dispersal among many groups, none of which can dominate others in all policy areas.

Police power (106)　Governmental authority to regulate matters such as social behaviors, morals, health, public safety, and zoning.

Policy design (371)　The choice of means to achieve a public policy's objectives.

Policy impact (364)　The effects of policy outputs.

Policy outcome (364)　The end result or impact of a policy.

Policy output (364)　The activities intended to achieve a policy objective.

Political exchanges (537)　Quid pro quo relationships involving government and politics, for instance, receiving an administrative position in return for political campaign activity.

Political executives (67)　Top executives appointed to positions in the Executive Office of the President and other units as a means of bringing presidential policy direction to the bureaucracy.

Political-machine-based culture (537)　A type of political culture that involves political exchanges between citizens and the political "boss" or the boss's agents and between the machine and businesses. Also referred to as boss-follower culture.

Political neutrality (210)　Restrictions on the right of public employees to take an active part in the management of partisan political activities or engage in partisan political campaigns.

Pork-barrel legislation (72)　The spending of federal funds for public works in the home district of a member of Congress.

Position classification (18)　The personnel management process of designing jobs, organizing them into useful managerial and career categories, and establishing their rates of pay.

Predictive validation (231)　A method for assessing merit examination validation; it takes scores of examinees and associates them statistically with on-the-job performance at a later time.

Preprogram-postprogram analysis (368)　A method of determining policy impact by comparing the condition of the target population before and after program implementation.

Procedural due process (31)　The value of fundamental fairness requiring procedures designed to protect individuals from malicious, arbitrary, erroneous, capricious, or unconstitutional deprivation of life, liberty, or property by the government.

Procedural rules (51)　Administrative rules that govern an agency's internal organization and operations, such as communication channels among its units and how it will process applications and hold hearings.

Process analysis (370)　A technique for assessing the ways in which a policy is being implemented.

Program budget (303)　A budget that links funding to the achievement of agency purposes.

Property taxes (274)　Taxes levied on the value of real estate.

Prospective adjudication (340)　Future-oriented adjudication requesting a modification or change in a party's operations.

Public goods (9)　Goods or services characterized by nonexcludability and nondivisibility. One person's consumption does not exclude another's and does not exhaust or significantly diminish the good. Also referred to as collective goods.

Pure experimental design (367)   A research design that assesses the effect of an intervention by comparing the behavior of the group that receives it (treatment group) with a similar one that does not (control group).

Quasi-experimental design (367)   A method of determining policy impact that attempts to determine the impact of policies by contrasting performance among groups exposed to the policy and those not exposed while statistically controlling for confounding conditions.

Recruitment (228)   The process of encouraging individuals to apply for positions.

Regime values (554)   The core values of a political system, such as those embodied in a constitution.

Regulatory ratchet (426)   The tendency of regulatory agencies to add more regulations without deleting those that have become obsolete.

Remedial law (31)   A term used to denote judicial imposition of far-reaching reforms on administrative institutions or processes, such as public school systems, prisons, public mental health facilities, and public personnel systems.

Repackaging (299)   A strategy that seeks increased funding of existing programs by explaining them in terms that seem to fit new presidential priorities.

Replevin (522)   A legal action enabling one to recover property that is rightfully his or hers from another who has possession of it.

Representative bureaucracy (187)   A concept holding that the social backgrounds and statuses of public administrators can affect their job performance and that the social composition of government agencies will affect their legitimacy.

Reprogramming (296)   A device used to shift funds within agencies; funds are transferred between programs with permission of relevant congressional committees.

Rescission (294)   An executive technique to control spending that terminates funds for an agency or a program.

Retrospective adjudication (340)   Adjudication that involves alleged past wrongdoing by a party.

Sales taxes and use taxes (272)   Taxes levied on the sale or use of goods or services.

Schedule C (67)   Federal civil service positions that are exempt from competitive merit system hiring

and promotion because they involve policy making or a close confidential relationship with a high-level political appointee.

Scientific management (154)   A systematic management approach that aims to determine scientifically the most efficient way to design jobs and pay systems. Also referred to as Taylorism.

Scope of bargaining (253)   The conditions of employment subject to negotiation between unions and employers.

Selection (228)   The process of choosing among applicants.

Situational factors (230)   Aspects of the work environment that can affect performance, such as noise levels.

Sovereignty (11)   Supreme political authority within a particular jurisdiction.

Span of control (107)   The extent of an administrator's responsibility, typically expressed in the number of subordinates an administrator supervises.

Spoils system (85)   A system of rewarding political supporters with government positions.

Strategic plans (309)   Used in decision making to respond to foreseeable environmental shifts through organizational and policy changes.

Street-level administrator (30)   An administrator who interacts directly with the public in a visually unsupervised manner, such as police and social workers.

Structural cases (419)   Adjudicatory cases that are the result of patterns and broad practices deemed by an agency to be prohibited.

Subordinate-centered (leadership style) (162)   A leadership style that emphasizes subordinate participation in the decision making process.

Substantive due process (519)   Constitutional rights encompassed by the guarantee of "liberty" in the Fifth and Fourteenth Amendment.

Substantive rights (31)   Rights such as freedom of speech, press, exercise of religion, and association. Contrast with procedural rights (see **Procedural due process**).

Substantive rules (51)   Also known as legislative rules, they are like statutes. For example, they regulate private parties' conduct, impose performance standards, and establish eligibility for benefits.

Sunset provisions (315)   A type of legislation that provides for the automatic termination of a program at some future date unless the program is reauthorized by statute at that time.

Sunshine laws (390)   Laws requiring that government agencies allow access by the public and the press to certain types of meetings and hearings.

Total quality management (TQM) (182)   A management philosophy that aims to build quality into an organization's products, rather than weed out defects through inspections and the like.

Transactional corruption (540)   A type of corruption that involves a direct exchange with another individual or entity.

Transfers (budgetary) (296)   A device used to shift funds within agencies; funds are transferred from one purpose to another.

Unilateral corruption (540)   A type of corruption that does not involve a direct exchange with another individual or entity.

Voluntary sector failures (92)   Failure of nonprofit organizations due to insufficient financial and human resources, particular missions, and other factors.

Zero-base budgeting (ZBB) (306)   An approach to budgeting that requires annual justification of existing programs and activities.

CREDITS

Text Credits

Box 3.4, Bureaucratic Size and Growth in the States, 1954–2005: Data from *The Book of the States, 1954–56*, 2010 Edition. Reprinted with permission from the Council of State Governments.

Box 4.4, Continuum from Boss- to Subordinate-Centered Leadership Styles: From "How to Choose a Leadership Pattern" by Robert Tannenbaum and Warren H. Schmidt in *Harvard Business Review*, May–June 1973, Exhibit 1 "Continuum of Leadership Behavior," p. 4. Copyright © 1973 Harvard Business School Publishing Corporation. Reprinted with permission. All rights reserved.

Box 4.6, Organizational Personalities: A Sampling: (1) From *Inside Bureaucracy* by Anthony Downs, published by Little Brown, 1967. Copyright © RAND Corporation, Santa Monica, CA. (2) From *The Organizational Society* by Robert Presthus. Copyright © 1962 by Robert Presthus. Used by permission of Alfred A. Knopf, an imprint of the Knopf Doubleday Publishing Group, a division of Random House LLC. All rights reserved. (3) From "A Study of Role Conceptions in Bureaucracy," by Leonard Reissman, in *Social Forces* (March 1949): 305–310. (4) Reprinted with the permission of Simon & Schuster Publishing Group from *The Gamesman: The New Corporate Leaders* by Michael Maccoby. Copyright © 1977 by Michael Maccoby. All rights reserved.

Box 4.7, Contents: Previously unpublished research by Mary Maureen Brown, Robert S. Kravchuk and Robert Flowe on the financial interdependencies among major defense acquisition programs (MDAPs). For more information on this ongoing project, contact author Kravchuk at Indiana University.

Box 5.6, General Schedule Pay by Grade and Step, 2012: 2012 Annual Rates by Grade and Step.

www.federaljobs.net Copyright Brookhaven Press, LLC. Reprinted with permission.

Box 6.4, State Taxes and Expenditures: Data for 1980–2008 are from Council of State Governments, *The Book of the States, 2010 Edition* (Lexington, KY, 2010), Table 7.21. Data for 2008 are from United States Bureau of the Census, *Statistical Abstract of the United States, 2011* (Washington, DC: 2012), Table 436.

Box 8.2, Experimental Research Design: Reprinted with the permission of Simon & Schuster Publishing Group from the Free Press edition of *Bad Blood: The Tuskegee Syphilis Experiment*, by James H. Jones. Copyright © 1981, 1993 by The Free Press. All rights reserved.

Box 10.3, "Undercover Boss": New York City's Chief of Human Resources Seeks Welfare: From "Posing as Welfare Recipient, Agency Head Finds Indignity," by Alison Mitchell, in *The New York Times*, February 5, 1993, A1, B2. Copyright © 1993 The New York Times Co.

Box 10.5, The Top 10 Reasons Not to Involve the Public in Administrative Decisions: From "The Top 10 Reasons Not to Involve the Public in Your Decisions," by Martha Rozelle in *The New Public Innovator*, No. 95 (Spring–Summer 1999). Reprinted with permission of The Alliance for Redesigning Government, National Academy of Public Administration.

Box 11.2, Putting Constitutional Values in Public Administration: From "School Case Backs an Ancient Ritual," as it appeared in *The New York Times*, December 9, 1984; "Bark and Hold," *Washington Post*, 23 February 2007.

Box 12.5, American Society for Public Administration Code of Ethics: Copyright © by the American Society of Public Administration (ASPA), 1301 Pennsylvania Ave. NW, Suite 840, Washington, DC 20004. All rights reserved. Reprinted with permission.

Photo Credits

INDEX